Developing Java Applications with Spring and Spring Boot

Practical Spring and Spring Boot solutions for building effective applications

A learning path in 3 sections

Packt>

BIRMINGHAM - MUMBAI

I0051427

Developing Java Applications with Spring and Spring Boot

Copyright © 2018 Packt Publishing

All rights reserved. No part of this learning path may be reproduced, stored in a retrieval system, or transmitted in any form or by any means, without the prior written permission of the publisher, except in the case of brief quotations embedded in critical articles or reviews.

Every effort has been made in the preparation of this learning path to ensure the accuracy of the information presented. However, the information contained in this learning path is sold without warranty, either express or implied. Neither the authors, nor Packt Publishing or its dealers and distributors, will be held liable for any damages caused or alleged to have been caused directly or indirectly by this learning path.

Packt Publishing has endeavored to provide trademark information about all of the companies and products mentioned in this learning path by the appropriate use of capitals. However, Packt Publishing cannot guarantee the accuracy of this information.

Authors: Claudio Eduardo de Oliveira, Greg L. Turnquist, Alex Antonov
Reviewers: Paulo Zanco, Zoltan Altfatter, Ricky Yim, Tejaswini Mandar Jog
Content Development Editor: Manjusha Mantri
Graphics: Jisha Chirayil
Production Coordinator: Aparna Bhagat

Published on: August 2018

Production reference: 1020818

Published by Packt Publishing Ltd.
Livery Place
35 Livery Street
Birmingham
B3 2PB, UK.

ISBN 978-1-78953-475-7

www.packtpub.com

Mapt

`mapt.io`

Mapt is an online digital library that gives you full access to over 5,000 books and videos, as well as industry leading tools to help you plan your personal development and advance your career. For more information, please visit our website.

Why subscribe?

- Spend less time learning and more time coding with practical eBooks and Videos from over 4,000 industry professionals

- Improve your learning with Skill Plans built especially for you

- Get a free eBook or video every month

- Mapt is fully searchable

- Copy and paste, print, and bookmark content

PacktPub.com

Did you know that Packt offers eBook versions of every book published, with PDF and ePub files available? You can upgrade to the eBook version at `www.PacktPub.com` and as a print book customer, you are entitled to a discount on the eBook copy. Get in touch with us at `service@packtpub.com` for more details.

At `www.PacktPub.com`, you can also read a collection of free technical articles, sign up for a range of free newsletters, and receive exclusive discounts and offers on Packt books and eBooks.

Table of Contents

Preface

With growing demands, organizations are looking for systems that are robust and scalable. Therefore, the Spring Framework has become the most popular framework for Java development. It not only simplifies software development but also improves developer productivity. Besides being flexible for Java development it also results in tedious configuration work. Spring Boot addresses the configuration difficulties of Spring and makes it easy to create standalone, production-grade Spring-based applications. It not only simplifies software development but also improves developer productivity.

By focusing on developers, community, and customers, Spring Boot has alleviated untold hours of time normally spent plumbing infrastructure. It has also upset that apple cart and shown that we can, in fact, focus on building features our customers want on day one.

Today almost one of every two Java developers, is using some part of the Spring portfolio. Spring Boot is solving problems for legions of customers, and this learning path can help you close the gap in your understanding.

Who this learning path is for

Java developers wanting to build production grade application using the newest and popular Spring tools for a rich end to end application development experience.

What this learning path covers

Section 1, Spring 5.0 By Example, will not only simplify software development but will also improve developers productivity. This section will cover effective ways to develop robust applications in Java using Spring.

Section 2, Learning Spring Boot 2.0-Second edition, provides a variety of features that address today's business needs with a powerful database and state of the art MVC framework. This section will help you get up and running with all the latest features of Spring Boot.

Section 3, Spring Boot 2.0 Cookbook-Second edition, provides great flexibility for Java development, which also results in tedious configuration work. Spring Boot addresses the configuration difficulties of Spring and makes it easy to create stand-alone, production-grade Spring-based applications.

This practical guide makes the existing development process more efficient. As developers, you will gain the skills and expertise to efficiently develop, test, deploy, and monitor applications using Spring Boot on premise and in the cloud.

To get the most out of this learning path

1. The readers are expected to have a basic knowledge of Java including the latest features added by JDK 1.8 and Java Developer Kit (JDK) 8 or higher
2. To execute code files in this learning path, you would need to have the following software/dependencies:

- IntelliJ IDEA Community Edition
- Docker CE and Docker Compose
- RabbitMQ 3.6 or higher
- MongoDB 3.0 or higher
- Gradle build tool

The rest of the software, such as Java libraries, like Spring Boot, Spring Framework, and its dependencies, as well as Docker, Consul, Graphite, Grafana, and Dashing will be all installed throughout the recipes. You will be assisted with installation processes,etc through this learning path.

Download the example code files

You can download the example code files for this learning path from your account at www.packtpub.com. If you purchased this learning path elsewhere, you can visit www.packtpub.com/support and register to have the files emailed directly to you.

You can download the code files by following these steps:

1. Log in or register at www.packtpub.com.
2. Select the **SUPPORT** tab.

3. Click on **Code Downloads & Errata**.
4. Enter the name of the learning path in the **Search** box and follow the onscreen instructions.

Once the file is downloaded, please make sure that you unzip or extract the folder using the latest version of:

- WinRAR/7-Zip for Windows
- Zipeg/iZip/UnRarX for Mac
- 7-Zip/PeaZip for Linux

The code bundle for this learning path is also hosted on GitHub at https://github.com/PacktPublishing/Developing-Java-Applications-with-Spring-and-Spring-Boot. In case there's an update to the code, it will be updated on the existing GitHub repository.

We also have other code bundles from our rich catalog of books and videos available at https://github.com/PacktPublishing/. Check them out!

Conventions used

There are a number of text conventions used throughout this learning path.

CodeInText: Indicates code words in text, database table names, folder names, filenames, file extensions, pathnames, dummy URLs, user input, and Twitter handles. Here is an example: "Mount the downloaded WebStorm-10*.dmg disk image file as another disk in your system."

A block of code is set as follows:

```
html, body, #map {
 height: 100%;
 margin: 0;
 padding: 0
}
```

When we wish to draw your attention to a particular part of a code block, the relevant lines or items are set in bold:

```
[default]
exten => s,1,Dial(Zap/1|30)
exten => s,2,Voicemail(u100)
exten => s,102,Voicemail(b100)
exten => i,1,Voicemail(s0)
```

Any command-line input or output is written as follows:

```
$ mkdir css
$ cd css
```

Bold: Indicates a new term, an important word, or words that you see onscreen. For example, words in menus or dialog boxes appear in the text like this. Here is an example: "Select **System info** from the **Administration** panel."

Warnings or important notes appear like this.

Tips and tricks appear like this.

Get in touch

Feedback from our readers is always welcome.

General feedback: Email feedback@packtpub.com and mention the learning path title in the subject of your message. If you have questions about any aspect of this learning path, please email us at questions@packtpub.com.

Errata: Although we have taken every care to ensure the accuracy of our content, mistakes do happen. If you have found a mistake in this learning path, we would be grateful if you would report this to us. Please visit www.packtpub.com/submit-errata, selecting your learning path, clicking on the Errata Submission Form link, and entering the details.

Piracy: If you come across any illegal copies of our works in any form on the Internet, we would be grateful if you would provide us with the location address or website name. Please contact us at copyright@packtpub.com with a link to the material.

If you are interested in becoming an author: If there is a topic that you have expertise in and you are interested in either writing or contributing to a book, please visit authors.packtpub.com.

Reviews

Please leave a review. Once you have read and used this learning path, why not leave a review on the site that you purchased it from? Potential readers can then see and use your unbiased opinion to make purchase decisions, we at Packt can understand what you think about our products, and our authors can see your feedback on their book. Thank you!

For more information about Packt, please visit `packtpub.com`.

Spring 5.0 By Example 1

Grasp the fundamentals of Spring 5.0 to build modern, robust, and scalable Java applications

Journey to the Spring World 1

Spring is an open source modular framework for the JVM platform. A framework is a collection of libraries whose primary goal is to address common software development problems. The framework should solve these problems in a generic form.

Rod Johnson created the Spring Framework in 2002 together with his book publication, which was called *Expert One-on-One J2EE Design and Development*. The idea behind the creation of the framework was to tackle the complexities of Java Enterprise Edition.

At that time, this kind of solution-focused a lot on the details of the infrastructure, and a developer using the solution would spend a lot of time writing code to solve infrastructural problems. Since its creation, one of Rod Johnson's primary concerns has been to increase developer productivity.

The framework was first seen as a lightweight container for Java Runtime Environment, and it became popular in the community, especially because of the dependency injection feature. The framework made dependency injection incredibly easy. Developers hadn't seen such a feature before, and as a consequence, people the world over adopted the project. Year by year, its popularity within the software development world has been increasing.

In the earliest versions, the framework had to work with the XML file to configure the container. At the time, this was so much better than J2EE applications, where it was necessary to create many `Ant` files to create the boilerplate classes and interfaces.

The framework was always seen as an advanced technology for the Java platform, but in 2014, the Spring team launched the Spring Boot platform. This platform was incredibly successful in the Java Enterprise ecosystem, and it changed the way in which developers built Java Enterprise applications.

Today, Spring is the *de facto* framework for Java development, and companies around the world use it in their systems. The community is vibrant and contributes to development in different ways, such as opening issues, adding the code, and discussing the framework in the most important Java conferences around the world. Let's look at and play with the famous framework for Java developers.

We will cover the following topics in this chapter:

- Main modules of the Spring Framework
- Spring annotations for each module
- Setting up the development environment
- Docker and Docker commands

Spring modularity

Since its foundation, the framework has had a particular focus on modularity. It is an important framework characteristic because it makes the framework an excellent option for different architectural styles and different parts of applications.

It means the framework is not an opinionated, full-stack framework that dictates the rules to make everything work. We can use the framework as we need and integrate it with a wide range of specification and third-party libraries.

For example, for portal web applications, the Spring MVC supports features such as template engines and REST endpoints and integrates them with the popular JavaScript framework, AngularJS.

Also, if the application needs support for a distributed system, the framework can supply an amazing module called Spring Cloud, which has some essential features for distributed environments, such as service registration and discovery, a circuit breaker, intelligent routing, and client-side load balancing.

Spring makes the development applications for Java Runtime easy with different languages, such as Java, Kotlin, and Groovy (with which you can choose the flavor and make the development task fun).

It is divided into various modules. The main modules are as follows:

- Spring Core
- Spring Data

- Spring Security
- Spring Cloud
- Spring Web-MVC

In this book, we will cover the most common solutions involved in Java Enterprise applications, including the awesome Spring Cloud project. Also, we can find some interesting projects such as Spring Batch and Spring Integration, but these projects are for specific needs.

Spring Core Framework

This module is the base of the framework and contains the essential support for dependency injection, web features supported by Spring **MVC (model-view-controller)** and the pretty new WebFlux frameworks, and aspect-oriented programming. Also, this module supports the foundation for JDBC, JMS, JPA and a declarative way to manage transactions. We will explore it and understand the main projects of this module. So let's do it!

Core container

The core container is the basis of the whole Spring ecosystem and comprehends four components—core, beans, context, and expression language.

Core and beans are responsible for providing the fundamentals of the framework and dependency injection. These modules are responsible for managing the IoC container, and the principal functions are the instantiation, configuration, and destruction of the object residents in the Spring container.

> Spring contexts are also called Spring IoC containers, which are responsible for instantiating, configuring, and assembling beans by reading configuration metadata from XML, Java annotations, and/or Java code in the configuration files.

There are two critical interfaces inside these modules—`BeanFactory` and `ApplicationContext`. The `BeanFactory` takes care of the bean lifecycle, instantiating, configuring, managing, and destroying, and the `ApplicationContext` helps developers to work with files resources in a generic way, enable to publish events to registered listeners. Also, the `ApplicationContext` supports internationalization and has the ability to work with messages in different Locales.

These modules help the context component to provide a way to access the objects inside the container. The context component has the `ApplicationContext` interface with the essential class for the container.

> Some common annotations are `@Service`, `@Component`, `@Bean`, and `@Configuration`.

Spring Messaging

Spring Framework supports a wide range of messaging systems. The Java platform is recognized as providing excellent support for messaging applications, and Spring Framework follows this approach and offers a variety of projects to help developers to write powerful applications with more productivity and fewer lines of infrastructure code. The basic idea of these projects is to provide some template classes that have the convenience methods to interact with the messaging systems.

Also, the project supplies some listener annotations to provide support for listening to messages from the brokers. The framework maintains the standard for different projects. In general, the prefix of the annotations is the name of the messaging system, for example, `@KafkaListener`.

The framework supplies many abstractions to create messaging applications in a generic way. This is interesting stuff because the application requirements change during the application lifecycle and the message broker solution may change as well. Then, with small changes, the application built with the Spring message module can work in different brokers. This is the goal.

Spring AMQP

This subproject supports the AMQP protocol in Spring Framework. It provides a template to interact with the message broker. A template is like a super high-level API that supports the `send` and `receive` operations.

There are two projects in this set: `spring-amqp`, which can be used for ActiveMQ for instance, and `spring-rabbit`, which adds support for the RabbitMQ broker. This project enables broker administration through the APIs to declare queues, bindings, and exchanges.

These projects encourage the extensive use of dependency injection provided by the core container, because they make the configuration more declarative and easy to understand.

Nowadays, the RabbitMQ broker is the popular choice for the messaging applications, and Spring provides full support for client interactions up to the level of administration tasks.

> Some common annotations are `@Exchange` and `@QeueueBinding`.

Spring for Apache Kafka

Spring for Apache Kafka supports the broker-based Apache Kafka applications. It provides a high-level API to interact with Apache Kafka. Internally, the projects use the Kafka Java APIs.

This module supports the annotation programming model. The basic idea is that with a couple of annotations and some POJO models, we can bootstrap the application and start listening to and producing messages.

`KafkaTemplate` is a central class of this project. It enables us to send messages to Apache Kafka with a high-level API. Asynchronous programming is supported as well.

This module offers support for transactions via annotations. This feature is enabled via standard transactional annotations used in Spring-based applications, such as `@Transactional`.

We also learned about Spring AMQP. This project adds the Spring concept of creating applications based on this broker. The dependency injection features are supported as well.

> Some common annotations are `@EnableKafka` and `@KafkaListener`.

Spring JMS

The idea of this project provides a JMS integration with ideas of Spring Framework projects and supplies a high-level API to interact with brokers. The worst part of a JMS specification is that it has a lot of boilerplate code to manage and close connections.

The `JmsTemplate` is a central class for this module, and it enables us to send messages to the broker. The JMS specification has a lot of intrinsic behaviors to handle the creation and releases resources, for instance, the `JmsTemplate` class do this tasks automatically for developers.

The module also supports transactional requirements. The `JmsTransactionManager` is the class that handles the transactional behavior of the Spring JMS module.

Spring removes the boilerplate code with a couple of annotations. The framework increases the readability of the code and makes the code more intuitive as well.

Some common annotations are `@JmsListener` and `@EnableJms`.

Spring Web MVC

This module is the first one built by the Spring Team to support the web applications in Spring Framework. This module uses the Servlet API as its foundation, and then these web applications must follow the Servlet Specification and be deployed into servlet containers. In version 5.0, the Spring Team created a Reactive web framework, which will be covered later in this book.

The Spring Web MVC module was developed using the front controller pattern. When the framework was created, this pattern was a common choice for many frameworks, such as Struts and JSF, among others. Under the hood, there is the main servlet in Spring called `DispatcherServlet`. This servlet will redirect through an algorithm to do the desired work.

It enables developers to create amazing web applications on the Java platform. This portion of the framework provides full support to develop this kind of application. There are some interesting features for this purpose, such as support for internationalization and support for handling cookies. Also, multipart requests are an exciting feature for when the application needs to handle upload files and support routing requests.

These characteristics are common for most web applications, and the framework has excellent support for these features. This support makes the framework a good choice for this kind of application. In `Chapter 2`, *Starting in the Spring World - The CMS Application,* we will create an application using this module and the main features will be explored in depth.

The module has full support for annotation programming since to declare HTTP endpoints until to wrap the request attribute in an HTTP request. It makes the application extremely readable without the boilerplate code to get the request parameter, for example.

Web application-wise, it enables developers to work with robust template engines such as Thymeleaf and Freemarker. It is entirely integrated with routing features and bean validation.

Also, the framework allows developers to build REST APIs with this module. Given all of this support, the module has become a favorite in the Spring ecosystem. Developers have started to create APIs with this stack, and some important companies have started to use it, especially given that the framework provides an easy way to navigate through the annotations. Because of this, the Spring Team added the new annotation `@RestController` in version 4.0.

We will work a lot with this module. Chapter by chapter, we will learn interesting things about this part of the framework.

> Some common annotations are `@RequestMapping`, `@Controller`, `@Model`, `@RestController`, and `@RequestBody`.

Spring WebFlux

A new module introduced in Spring 5.0, Spring WebFlux, can be used to implement web applications built with Reactive Streams. These systems have nonblocking characteristics and are deployed in servers built on top of Netty, such as Undertown and servlet containers that support + 3.1.

Netty is an open source framework that helps developers to create network applications—that is, servers and clients using the asynchronous, event-driven pattern. Netty provides some interesting advantages, such as lower latency, high throughput, and less resource consumption. You can find more information at `https://netty.io`.

This module supports annotations based on Spring MVC modules, such as `@GetMapping`, `@PostMapping`, and others. This is an important feature that enables us to migrate to this new version. Of course, some adjustments are necessary, such as adding Reactor classes (Mono or Flux).

This module meets the modern web requirements to handle a lot of concurrent channels where the thread-per-request model is not an option.

We will learn about this module in `Chapter 3`, *Adding Persistence with Spring Data and Putting it into Reactive Fashion* and implement a fully Reactive application based on Reactive Streams.

Some common annotations are `@RequestMapping`, `@RestController`, and `@RequestBody`.

Spring Data

Spring Data is an interesting module that provides the easiest way to manage application data with Spring-based programming. The project is an umbrella project, with subprojects to support different databases technologies, even relational and nonrelational databases. The Spring Team supports some databases technologies, such as Apache Cassandra, Apache Solr, Redis, and JPA Specification, and the community maintains the other exciting projects, such as ElasticSearch, Aerospike, DynamoDb, and Couchbase. The full list of projects can be found at `http://projects.spring.io/spring-data`.

The goal is to remove the boilerplate code from the persistence code. In general, the data access layer is quite similar, even in different projects, differing only in the project model, and Spring Data provides a powerful way to map the domain model and repository abstraction.

There are some central interfaces; they're a kind of marker to instruct the framework to choose the correct implementation. Under the hood, Spring will create a proxy and delegate the correct implementation. The amazing thing here is that developers don't have to write any persistence code and then take care of this code; they simply choose the required technology and Spring takes care of the rest.

The central interfaces are `CrudRepository` and `PagingAndSortingRepository`, and their names are self-explanatory. `CrudRepository` implements the CRUD behaviors, such as `create`, `retrieval`, `update`, and `delete`. `PagingAndSortingRepository` is an extension of `CrudRepository` and adds some features such as paging and sorting. Usually, we will find derivations of these interfaces such as `MongoRepository`, which interacts with MongoDB database technology.

> Some common annotations are `@Query`, `@Id`, and `@EnableJpaRepositories`.

Spring Security

Security for Java applications was always a pain for developers, especially in Java Enterprise Edition. There was a lot of boilerplate code to look up objects in the application servers, and the security layer was often heavily customized for the application.

In that chaotic scenario, the Spring Team decided to create a Spring Security project to help developers handle the security layer on the Java application.

In the beginning, the project had extensive support for Java Enterprise Edition and integration with EJB 3 security annotations. Nowadays, the project supports many different ways to handle authorization and authentication for Java applications.

Spring Security provides a comprehensive model to add authorization and authentication for Java applications. The framework can be configured with a couple of annotations, which makes the task of adding a security layer extremely easy. The other important characteristics concern how the framework can be extended. There are some interfaces that enable developers to customize the default framework behaviors, and it makes the framework customized for different application requirements.

It is an umbrella project, and it is subdivided into these modules:

- `spring-security-core`
- `spring-security-remoting`
- `spring-security-web`
- `spring-security-config`
- `spring-security-ldap`
- `spring-security-acl`
- `spring-security-cas`
- `spring-security-openid`
- `spring-security-test`

These are the main modules, and there are many other projects to support a wide range of types of authentication. The module covers the following authentication and authorization types:

- LDAP
- HTTP Basic
- OAuth
- OAuth2
- OpenID
- CAAS
- JAAS

The module also offers a **domain-specific language** (**DSL**) to provide an easy configuration. Let's see a simple example:

```
http
  .formLogin()
    .loginPage("/login")
    .failureUrl("/login?error")
      .and()
    .authorizeRequests()
      .antMatchers("/signup","/about").permitAll()
      .antMatchers("/admin/**").hasRole("ADMIN")
      .anyRequest().authenticated();
```

> The example was extracted from the spring.io blog. For more details, go to https://spring.io/blog/2013/07/11/spring-security-java-config-preview-readability/.

As we can see, the DSL makes the configuration task extremely easy and very understandable.

Spring Security's main features are as follows:

- Session management
- Protection against attacks (CSRF, session fixation, and others)
- Servlet API integration
- Authentication and authorization

We will learn more about Spring Security in `Chapter 8`, *Circuit Breakers and Security*. We will also put it into practice.

> `@EnableWebSecurity` is a common annotation.

Spring Cloud

Spring Cloud is another umbrella project. The primary goal of this project is to help developers create distributed systems. Distributed systems have some common problems to solve and, of course, a set of patterns to help us, such as service discovery, circuit breakers, configuration management, intelligent route systems, and distributed sessions. Spring Cloud tools have all these implementations and well-documented projects.

The main projects are as follows:

- Spring Cloud Netflix
- Spring Cloud Config
- Spring Cloud Consul
- Spring Cloud Security
- Spring Cloud Bus
- Spring Cloud Stream

Spring Cloud Netflix

Spring Cloud Netflix is perhaps the most popular Spring module nowadays. This fantastic project allows us to integrate the Spring ecosystem with the Netflix OSS via Spring Boot AutoConfiguration features. The supported Netflix OSS libraries are Eureka for service discovery, Ribbon to enable client-side load balancing, circuit breaker via Hystrix to protect our application from external outages and make the system resilient, the Zuul component provides an intelligent routing and can act as an edge service. Finally, the Feign component can help developers to create HTTP clients for REST APIs with a couple of annotations.

Let's look at each of these:

- **Spring Cloud Netflix Eureka**: The focus of this project is to provide service discovery for applications while conforming to Netflix standards. Service discovery is an important feature and enables us to remove hardcoded configurations to supply a hostname and ports; it is more important in cloud environments because the machine is ephemeral, and thus it is hard to maintain names and IPs. The functionality is quite simple, the Eureka server provides a service registry, and Eureka clients will contact its registers themselves.

  Some common annotations are `@EnableEurekaServer` and `@EnableEurekaClient`.

- **Spring Cloud Feign**: The Netflix team created the Feign project. It's a great project that makes the configuration of HTTP clients for REST applications significantly easier than before. These implementations are based on annotations. The project supplies a couple of annotations for HTTP paths, HTTP headers, and much more, and of course, Spring Cloud Feign integrates it with the Spring Cloud ecosystem through the annotations and autoconfiguration. Also, Spring Cloud Feign can be combined with the Eureka server.

  Some common annotations are `@EnableFeignClients` and `@FeignClient`.

- **Spring Cloud Ribbon**: Ribbon is a client-side load balancer. The configuration should mainly provide a list of servers for the specific client. It must be named. In Ribbon terms, it is called the **named client**. The project also provides a range of load-balancing rules, such as Round Robin and Availability Filtering, among others. Of course, the framework allows developers to create custom rules. Ribbon has an API that works, integrated with the Eureka server, to enable service discovery, which is included in the framework. Also, essential features such as fault tolerance are supported because the API can recognize the running servers at runtime.

> Some common annotations are
> `@RibbonClient` and `@LoadBalanced`.

- **Spring Cloud Hystrix**: An acclaimed Netflix project, this project provides a circuit breaker pattern implementation. The concept is similar to an electrical circuit breaker. The framework will watch the method marked with `@HystrixCommand` and watch for failing calls. If the failed calls number more than a figure permitted in configuration, the circuit breaker will open. While the circuit is open, the fallback method will be called until the circuit is closed and operates normally. It will provide resilience and fault-tolerant characteristics for our systems. The Spring ecosystem is fully integrated with Hystrix, but it works only on the `@Component` and `@Service` beans.

> Some common annotations are `@EnableCircuitBreaker` and
> `@HystrixCommand`.

Spring Cloud Config

This exciting project provides an easy way to manage system configurations for distributed systems, and this is a critical issue in cloud environments because the file system is ephemeral. It also helps us to maintain different stages of the deployment pipeline. Spring profiles are fully integrated with this module.

We will need an application that will provide the configuration for other applications. We can understand its workings by thinking of the concepts of the **server** and the **client**, the server will provide some configurations through HTTP and the client will look up the configuration on the server. Also, it is possible to encrypt and decrypt property values.

There are some storage implementations to provide these property files, and the default implementation is Git. It enables us to store our property files in Git, or we can use the file system as well. The important thing here is that the source does not matter.

> **Git** is a distributed version control. The tool is commonly used for development purposes, especially in the open-source community. The main advantage, when you compare it to some market players, such as SVN, is the *distributed architecture*.

There is an interesting integration between **Spring Cloud Bus** and this module. If they are integrated, it is possible to broadcast the configuration changes on the cluster. This is an important feature if the application configuration changes with frequency. There are two annotations that tell Spring to apply changes at runtime: @RefreshScope and @ConfigurationProperties.

In Chapter 7, *Airline Ticket System*, we will implement an exciting service to provide external configurations for our microservices using this module. Server concepts will be explained in more detail. The client details will be presented as well.

> @EnableConfigServer is a common annotation.

Spring Cloud Consul

Spring Cloud Consul provides integrations with Hashicorp's Consul. This tool addresses problems in the same way as service discovery, a distributed configuration, and control bus. This module allows us to configure Spring applications and Consul with a few annotations in a Spring-based programming model. Autoconfiguration is supported as well. The amazing thing here is that this module can be integrated with some Netflix OSS libraries, such as Zuul and Ribbon, via Spring Cloud Zuul and Spring Cloud Ribbon respectively (for example).

> `@EnableDiscoveryClient` is a common annotation.

Spring Cloud Security

This module is like an extension from Spring Security. However, distributed systems have different requirements for security. Normally, they have central identity management, or the authentication lies with the clients in the case of REST APIs. Normally, in distributed systems, we have microservices, and these services might have more than one instance in the runtime environment whose characteristics make the authentication module slightly different from monolithic applications. The module can be used together with Spring Boot applications and makes the OAuth2 implementation very easy with a couple of annotations and a few configurations. Also, some common patterns are supported, such as single sign-on, token relay, and token exchange.

For the microservice applications based on the Spring Cloud Netflix, it is particularly interesting because it enables downstream authentication to work with a Zuul proxy and offers support from Feign clients. An interceptor is used to fetch tokens.

> Some commons annotations are `@EnableOAuth2Sso` and `@EnableResourceServer`.

Spring Cloud Bus

The main goal of this project is to provide an easy way to broadcast changes spread throughout the cluster. The applications can connect the distributed system nodes through the message broker.

It provides an easy way for developers to create a publish and subscribe mechanism using the `ApplicationContext` provided by Spring Container. It enables the possibility to create applications using the event-driven architecture style with the Spring Ecosystem.

To create custom events, we need to create a child class from `RemoteApplicationEvent` and mark the class to be scanned via `@RemoteApplicationEventScan`.

The projects support three message brokers as the transport layer:

- AMQP
- Apache Kafka
- Redis

> `@RemoteApplicationEventScan` is a common annotation.

Spring Cloud Stream

The idea behind this module is to provide an easy way to build message-driven microservices. The module has an opinionated way of configuration. It means we need to follow some rules to create these configurations. In general, the application is configured by the `yaml|properties` file.

The module supports annotations as well. This means that a couple of annotations are enough to create consumers, producers, and bindings; it decouples the application and makes it easy to understand. It supplies some abstractions around the message brokers and channels, and it makes the developer's life more comfortable and productive as well.

Spring Cloud Stream has Binder implementations for RabbitMQ and Kafka.

> Some common annotations are `@EnableBinding`, `@Input`, and `@Output`.

Spring Integration

This module supports a lot of Enterprise Application patterns and brings the Spring programming model to this topic. The Spring programming model enables extensive dependence injection support and is annotations programming-centric. The annotations instruct us as to how the framework needs to be configured and defines framework behaviors.

The POJO model is suggested because it is simple and widely known in the Java development world.

This project has some intersections with the other modules. Some other projects use these module concepts to do their work. There is a project called Spring Cloud Stream, for instance.

The Enterprise Integration patterns are based on a wide range of communication channels, protocols, and patterns. This project supports some of these.

The modules support a variety of features and channels, such as the following:

- Aggregators
- Filters
- Transformers
- JMS
- RabbitMQ
- TCP/UDP
- Web services
- Twitter
- Email
- And much more

There are three main concepts of Enterprise application integration:

- Messages
- Message channel
- Message endpoint

Finally, the Spring Integration module offers a comprehensive way to create application integration and enables developers to do it using amazing support.

> Some common annotations are `@EnableIntegration`, `@IntegrationComponentScan`, and `@EnablePublisher`.

Spring Boot

Spring Boot was released in 2014. The idea behind this project was to present a way to deploy the web application outside of any container, such as Apache Tomcat, Jetty, and so on. The benefit of this kind of deployment is the independence from any external service. It allows us to run the web applications with one JAR file. Nowadays, this is an excellent approach because this forms the most natural way to adopt DevOps culture.

Spring Boot provides embedded servlet containers, such as Apache Tomcat, Jetty, and Undertow. It makes the development process more productive and comfortable when testing our web applications. Also, customizations during configuration are allowed via a configuration file, or by providing some beans.

There are some advantages when adopting the Spring Boot framework. The framework does not require any XML for configuration. This is a fantastic thing because we will find all the dependencies in the Java files. This helps the IDEs to assist developers, and it improves the traceability of the code. Another important advantage is that the project tries to keep the configuration as automatic as possible. Some annotations make the magic happen. The interesting thing here is that Spring will inject the implementation of any code that is generated at runtime.

The Spring Boot framework also provides interesting features to help developers and operations, such as health checks, metrics, security, and configuration. This is indispensable for modern applications where the modules are decomposed in a microservices architecture.

There are some other interesting features that can help the developers DevOps-wise. We can use the `application-{profile}.properties` or `application.yaml` files to configure different runtime profiles, such as development, testing, and production. It is a really useful Spring Boot feature.

Also, the project has full support for the tests, since the web layer up to the repository layer.

The framework provides a high-level API to work with unit and integration tests. Also, the framework supplies many annotations and helpers classes for developers.

The Spring Boot project is a production-ready framework with default optimized configurations for the web servers, metrics, and monitoring features to help the development team deliver high-quality software.

We can develop applications by coding in the Groovy and Java languages. Both are JVM languages. In version 5.0, the Spring Team announced the full support for Kotlin, the new language for JVM. It enables us to develop consistent and readable codes. We will look at this feature in depth in Chapter 7, *Airline Ticket System*.

Setting up our development environment

Before we start, we need to set up our development environment. Our development environment consists of the following four tools:

- JDK
- Build tool
- IDE
- Docker

We will install JDK version 8.0. This version is fully supported in Spring Framework 5. We will present the steps to install Maven 3.3.9, the most famous build tool for Java development, and in the last part, we will show you some detailed instructions on how to install IntelliJ IDEA Community Edition. We will use Ubuntu 16.04, but you can use your favorite OS. The installation steps are easy.

Installing OpenJDK

OpenJDK is a stable, free, and open source Java development kit. This package will be required for everything related to code compilation and runtime environments.

Also, it is possible to use an Oracle JDK, but you should pay attention to the **License and Agreements**.

To install OpenJDK, we will open a terminal and run the following command:

```
sudo apt-get install openjdk-8-jdk -y
```

> **TIP**
> We can find more information on how to install Java 8 JDK in the
> installation section (`http://openjdk.java.net/install/`) of the
> OpenJDK page.

Check the installation using the following command:

```
java -version
```

You should see the OpenJDK version and its relevant details displayed as follows:

```
ubuntu@ubuntu-xenial:~$ java -version
openjdk version "1.8.0_131"
OpenJDK Runtime Environment (build 1.8.0_131-8u131-b11-2ubuntu1.16.04.3-b11)
OpenJDK 64-Bit Server VM (build 25.131-b11, mixed mode)
ubuntu@ubuntu-xenial:~$
```

Now that we have installed the Java development kit, we are ready for the next step. In the real world, we must have a build tool to help developers to compile, package, and test the Java applications.

Let's install Maven in the next section.

Installing Maven

Maven is a popular build tool for Java development. Some important open source projects were built using this tool. There are features that facilitate the build process, standardize the project structure, and provide some guidelines for best practices development.

We will install Maven, but the installation step should be executed after the OpenJDK installation.

Open a terminal and execute the following:

```
sudo apt-get install maven -y
```

Check the installation using this command:

```
mvn -version
```

You should see the following output, although the version may be different for you:

```
ubuntu@ubuntu-xenial:~$ mvn -version
Apache Maven 3.3.9
Maven home: /usr/share/maven
Java version: 1.8.0_131, vendor: Oracle Corporation
Java home: /usr/lib/jvm/java-8-openjdk-amd64/jre
Default locale: en_US, platform encoding: ANSI_X3.4-1968
OS name: "linux", version: "4.4.0-97-generic", arch: "amd64", family: "unix"
ubuntu@ubuntu-xenial:~$
```

Well done. Now we have Maven installed. Maven has a vibrant community that produces many plugins to help developers with important tasks. There are plugins to execute a unit test and plugins to prepare the project for the release event that can be integrated with SCM software.

We will use the `spring boot maven` plugin and `docker maven` plugin. The first converts our application to a JAR file and the second enables us to integrate with Docker Engine to create images, run containers, and much more. In the next few chapters, we will learn how to configure and interact with these plugins.

Installing IDE

The IDE is an important tool to help developers. In this book, we will use the IntelliJ IDEA as an *official* tool for developing our projects. There are no restrictions for other IDEs because the project will be developed using Maven as a build tool.

The IDE is a personal choice for developers, and in general, it involves passion; what some people love, other developers hate. Please feel free to use your favorite.

IntelliJ IDEA

IntelliJ IDEA is a JetBrains product. We will use the Community Edition, which is open source and a fantastic tool with which to code Java and Kotlin. The tool offers a fantastic autocomplete feature, and also fully supports Java 8 features.

Go to `https://www.jetbrains.com/idea/download/#section=linux` and download the Community Edition. We can extract the `tar.gz` and execute it.

Spring Tools Suite

The Spring Tools Suite is based on Eclipse IDE, provided by the Eclipse Foundation, of course. The goal is to provide support for the Spring ecosystem and make the developer's life easier. Interesting features such as Beans Explorer are supported in this tool.

Download the tool at the following link:
```
http://download.springsource.com/release/STS/3.6.4.RELEASE/dist/e4.4/
groovy-grails-tool-suite-3.6.4.RELEASE-e4.4.2-linux-gtk-x86_64.tar.gz
```

Installing Docker

Docker is an open source project that helps people to run and manage containers. For developers, Docker helps in different stages of the development lifecycle.

During the development phase, Docker enables developers to spin up different infrastructure services such as databases and service discoveries like Consul without installation in the current system operational. It helps the developers because developers do not need to install these kinds of systems in the operating system layer. Usually, this task can cause conflicts with the libraries during the installation process and consumes a lot of time.

Sometimes, developers need to install the exact version. In this case, it is necessary to reinstall the whole application on the expected version. It is not a good thing because the developer machine during this time becomes slow. The reason is quite simple, there are many applications that are used during software development.

Docker helps developers at this stage. It is quite simple to run a container with MongoDB. There is no installation and it enables developers to start the database with one line. Docker supports the image tag. This feature helps to work with different versions of the software; this is awesome for developers who need to change the software version every time.

Another advantage is that when the developers need to deliver the artifacts for test or production purposes, Docker enables these tasks via Docker images.

Docker helps people to adopt the DevOps culture and delivers amazing features to improve the performance of the whole process.

Let's install Docker.

The easiest way to install Docker is to download the script found at `https://get.docker.com`:

```
curl -fsSL get.docker.com -o get-docker.sh
```

After the download is completed, we will execute the script as follows:

```
sh get-docker.sh
```

Wait for the script execution and then check the Docker installation using the following command:

```
docker -v
```

The output needs to look like the following:

```
ubuntu@ubuntu-xenial:~$ docker -v
Docker version 17.10.0-ce, build f4ffd25
ubuntu@ubuntu-xenial:~$
```

Sometimes, the version of Docker can be increased, and the version should be at least **17.10.0-ce**.

Finally, we will add the current user to the Docker group, and this enables us to use the Docker command line without the `sudo` keyword. Type the following command:

```
sudo usermod -aG docker $USER
```

We need to log out to effect these changes. Confirm whether the command works as expected by typing the following. Make sure that the `sudo` keyword is not present:

```
docker ps
```

The output should be as follows:

```
ubuntu@ubuntu-xenial:~$ docker ps
CONTAINER ID        IMAGE        COMMAND        CREATED        STATUS        PORTS        NAMES
ubuntu@ubuntu-xenial:~$
```

Introducing Docker concepts

Now, we will introduce some Docker concepts. This book is not about Docker, but some basic instructions on how to use Docker are necessary to interact with our containers during the next few chapters. Docker is a de facto tool that is used to manage containers.

Docker images

The Docker image is like a template for a Docker container. It contains a set of folders and files that are necessary to start the Docker container. We will never have an image in execution mode. The image provides a template for Docker Engine to start up the container. We can create an analogy with object orientation to understand the process better. The image is like a class that provides an *infrastructure* to instantiate some objects, and instances are like a container.

Also, we have a Docker registry to store our images. These registries can be public or private. Some cloud vendors provide these private registries. The most famous is Docker Hub. It can be free, but if you choose this option, the image should be public. Of course, Docker Hub supports private images, but in this case, you have to pay for the service.

Containers

Docker containers are a *lightweight* virtualization. The term lightweight means that Docker uses the SO functionalities to cage the system process and manager memory, processors, and folders. This is different from virtualization with VMs because, in this mode, the technology needs to simulate the whole SO, drivers, and storage. This task consumes a lot of computational power and can sometimes be inefficient.

Docker networks

A Docker network is a layer that provides runtime isolation for containers. It is a kind of sandbox in which to run containers that are isolated from other containers. When the Docker is installed, by default it creates three networks that should not be removed. These three networks are as follows:

- `bridge`
- `none`
- `host`

Also, Docker provides the user with an easy way to create your network. For this purpose, Docker offers two drivers—**bridge** and **overlay**.

Bridge can be used for the local environment, and it means this kind of network is allowed on a single host. It will be useful for our applications because it promotes isolation between containers regarding security. This is a good practice. The name of the container attached to this kind of network can be used as a **DNS** for the container. Internally, Docker will associate the container name with the container IP.

The overlay network provides the ability to connect containers to different machines. This kind of network is used by Docker Swarm to manage the container in a clustered environment. In the newest version, the Docker Compose tool natively supports Docker Swarm.

Docker volumes

Docker volumes are the suggested way to persist data outside of a container. These volumes are fully managed by Docker Engine, and these volumes can be writable and readable depending on the configuration when they are used with a Docker command line. The data of these volumes is persisted on a directory path on a host machine.

There is a command-line tool to interact with volumes. The base of this tool is the `docker volume` command; the `--help` argument on the end shows the help instructions.

Docker commands

Now we will take a look at Docker commands. These commands are used mainly in the development life cycle, commands such as `spin up container`, `stop containers`, `remove`, and `inspect`.

Docker run

`docker run` is the most common Docker command. This command should be used to start the containers. The basic structure of a command is as follows:

```
docker run [OPTIONS] IMAGE[:TAG|@DIGEST] [COMMAND] [ARG...]
```

The options arguments enable some configurations for the container, for instance, the `--name` argument permits you to configure a name for a container. It is important for DNS when the container is running in a bridge network.

The network settings can be configured on the `run` command as well, and the parameter is `-- net`. This enables us to configure the network to which the container will be attached.

Another important option is `detached`. It indicates whether the container will run in the background. The `-d` parameter instructs Docker to run a container in the background.

Docker container

The `docker container` command permits you to manage the containers. There are many commands, as shown in the following list:

- `docker container attach`
- `docker container commit`
- `docker container cp`
- `docker container create`
- `docker container diff`
- `docker container exec`
- `docker container export`
- `docker container inspect`
- `docker container kill`
- `docker container logs`
- `docker container ls`
- `docker container pause`
- `docker container port`
- `docker container prune`
- `docker container rename`
- `docker container restart`
- `docker container rm`
- `docker container run`
- `docker container start`
- `docker container stats`

- docker container stop
- docker container top
- docker container unpause
- docker container update
- docker container wait

There are some important commands here. The docker container exec permits you to run commands on a running container. This is an important task to debug or look inside the container files. The docker container prune removes the stopped containers. It is helpful in the development cycle. There are some known commands, such as docker container rm, docker container start, docker container stop, and docker container restart. These commands are self-explanatory and have similar behaviors.

Docker network

The docker network commands enable you to manage the Docker network stuff via the command line. There are six basic commands, and the commands are self-explanatory:

- docker network create
- docker network connect
- docker network ls
- docker network rm
- docker network disconnect
- docker network inspect

docker network create, docker network ls, and docker network rm are the main commands. It is possible to compare them with the Linux commands, where the rm command is used to remove things and the ls command is usually used to list things such as folders. The create command should be used to create networks.

The docker network connect and docker network disconnect commands allow you to connect the running container to the desired network. They may be useful in some scenarios.

Finally, the docker network inspect command provides detailed information on the requested network.

Docker volume

The `docker volume` command permits you to manage the Docker volumes via the command-line interface. There are five commands:

- `docker volume create`
- `docker volume inspect`
- `docker volume ls`
- `docker volume prune`
- `docker volume rm`

The `docker volume create`, `docker volume rm` and `docker volume ls` commands are effectively used to manage the `docker volume` by Docker Engine. The behaviors are quite similar to those of the networks, but for volumes. The `create` command will create a new volume with some options allowed. The `ls` command lists all volumes and the `rm` command will remove the requested volume.

Summary

In this chapter, we looked at the main concepts of Spring Framework. We understood the main modules of the framework and how these modules can help developers to build applications in different kinds of architecture, such as messaging applications, REST APIs, and web portals.

We also spent some time preparing our development environment by installing essential tools, such as Java JDK, Maven, and IDE. This was a critical step to take before we continue to the next chapters.

We used Docker to help us to set up a development environment, such as containers for databases and delivery for our application in Docker images. We installed Docker and looked at the main commands for managing containers, networks, and volumes.

In the next chapter, we will create our first Spring application and put it into practice!

Starting in the Spring World – the CMS Application

2

Now, we'll create our first application; at this point, we have learned the Spring concepts, and we are ready to put them into practice. At the beginning of this chapter, we'll introduce the Spring dependencies to create a web application, also we know that Spring Initializr is a fantastic project that enables developers to create Spring skeleton projects, with as many dependencies as they want. In this chapter, we will learn how to put up our first Spring application on IDE and command line, expose our first endpoint, understand how this works under the hood, and get to know the main annotations of Spring REST support. We will figure out how to create a service layer for the **CMS (Content Management System)** application and understand how Dependency Injection works in a Spring container. We will meet the Spring stereotypes and implement our first Spring bean. At the end of this chapter, we will explain how to create a view layer and integrate that with AngularJS.

In this chapter, the following topics will be covered:

- Creating the project structure
- Running the first Spring application
- Introducing the REST support
- Understanding the Dependency Injection in Spring

Creating the CMS application structure

Now we will create our first application with the Spring Framework; we will create a basic structure for the CMS application with Spring Initializr. This page helps to bootstrap our application, it's a kind of guide which allows us to configure the dependencies on Maven or Gradle. We can also choose the language and version of Spring Boot.

The page looks like this:

In the **Project Metadata** section, we can put the coordinates for Maven projects; there is a group field which refers to the `groupId` tag, and we have artifacts which refer to the `artifactId`. This is all for the Maven coordinates.

The dependencies section enables the configuration of the Spring dependencies, the field has the autocomplete feature and helps developers to put in the correct dependency.

The CMS project

Before we start to code and learn amazing things, let's understand a little bit about the CMS project, the main purpose of this project is to help companies manage the CMS content for different topics. There are three main entities in this project:

- The `News` class is the most important, it will store the content of the news.
- It has a *category* which makes the search easier, and we can also group news by category, and of course, we can group by the user who has created the news. The news should be approved by other users to make sure it follows the company rules.
- The news has some *tags* as well, as we can see the application is pretty standard, the business rules are easy as well; this is intentional because we keep the focus on the new things we will learn.

Now we know how Spring Initializr (`https://start.spring.io`) works and the business rules we need to follow, we are ready to create the project. Let's do it right now.

Project metadata section

Insert `spring-five` in the **Group** field and `cms` in the **Artifact** field. If you want to customize it, no problem, this is a kind of informative project configuration:

Project Metadata

Artifact coordinates

Group

    spring-five

Artifact

    cms

The dependencies section

Type the MVC word in the **Search for Dependencies** field. The Web module will appear as an option, the Web module contains the full-stack web development with Embedded Tomcat and Spring MVC, select it. Also, we need to put Thymeleaf dependencies in this module. It is a template engine and will be useful for the view features at the end of this chapter. Type Thymeleaf, it includes the Thymeleaf templating engine, and includes integration with Spring. The module will appear, and then select it as well. Now we can see **Web** and **Thymeleaf** in the **Selected Dependencies** pane:

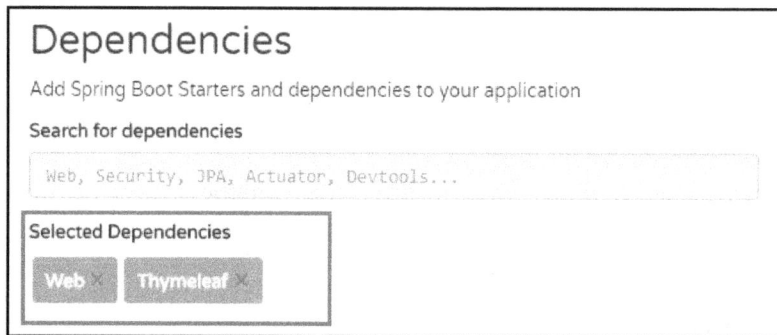

Dependencies

Add Spring Boot Starters and dependencies to your application

Search for dependencies

Web, Security, JPA, Actuator, Devtools...

Selected Dependencies

Web ✕ Thymeleaf ✕

Generating the project

After we have finished the project definition and chosen the project dependencies, we are ready to download the project. It can be done using the **Generate Project** button, click on it. The project will be downloaded. At this stage, the project is ready to start our work:

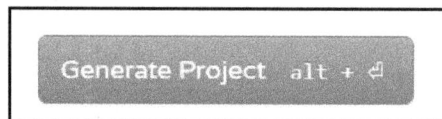

Generate Project alt + ↵

> **TIP**
>
> The zip file will be generated with the name cms.zip (the **Artifact** field input information) and the location of the downloaded file depends on the browser configuration.

>Before opening the project, we must uncompress the artifact generated by **Spring Initializr** to the desired location. The command should be: `unzip -d <target_destination> /<path_to_file>/cms.zip`. Follow the example: `unzip -d /home/john /home/john/Downloads/cms.zip`.

Now, we can open the project in our IDE. Let's open it and take a look at the basic structure of the project.

Running the application

Before we run the application, let's have a walk through our project structure.

Open the project on IntelliJ IDEA using the **Import Project** or **Open** options (both are similar), the following page will be displayed:

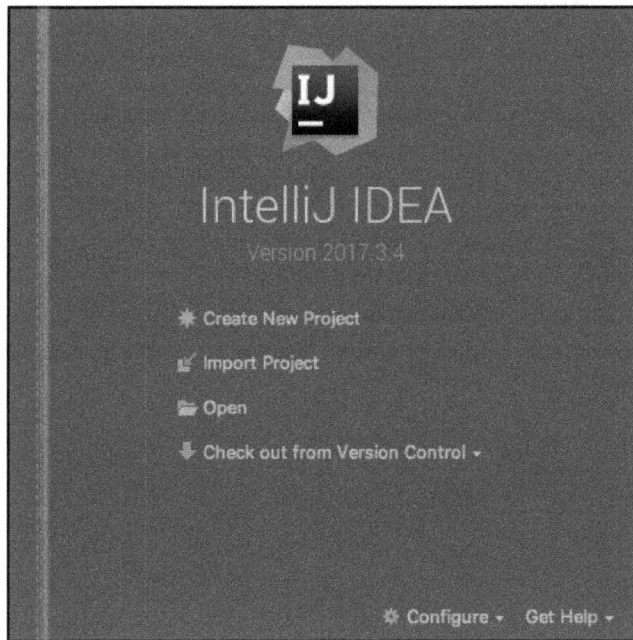

Then we can open or import the `pom.xml` file.

The following project structure should be displayed:

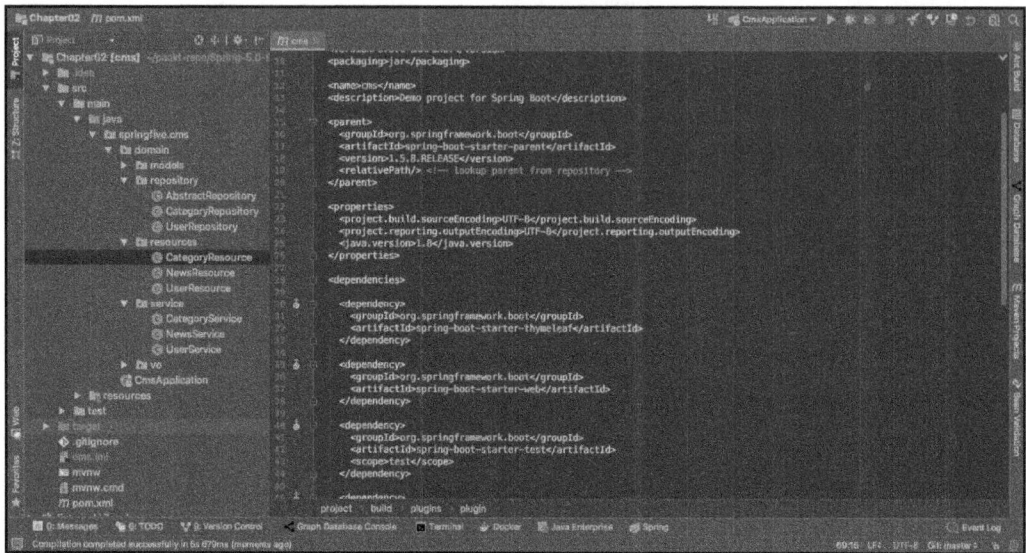

Open the `pom.xml,` we have three dependencies, `spring-boot-starter-thymeleaf`, `spring-boot-starter-web`, `spring-boot-starter-test`, and an interesting plugin, `spring-boot-maven-plugin`.

These `starter` dependencies are a shortcut for developers because they provide full dependencies for the module. For instance, on the `spring-boot-starter-web`, there is `web-mvc`, `jackson-databind`, `hibernate-validator-web`, and some others; these dependencies must be on the classpath to run the web applications, and starters make this task considerably easier.

Let's analyze our `pom.xml`, the file should look like this:

```
<?xml version="1.0" encoding="UTF-8"?>
<project xmlns="http://maven.apache.org/POM/4.0.0"
  xmlns:xsi="http://www.w3.org/2001/XMLSchema-instance"
  xsi:schemaLocation="http://maven.apache.org/POM/4.0.0
http://maven.apache.org/xsd/maven-4.0.0.xsd">
  <modelVersion>4.0.0</modelVersion>

  <groupId>spring-five</groupId>
  <artifactId>cms</artifactId>
  <version>0.0.1-SNAPSHOT</version>
  <packaging>jar</packaging>
```

```xml
<name>cms</name>
<description>Demo project for Spring Boot</description>

<parent>
  <groupId>org.springframework.boot</groupId>
  <artifactId>spring-boot-starter-parent</artifactId>
  <version>1.5.8.RELEASE</version>
  <relativePath/> <!-- lookup parent from repository -->
</parent>

<properties>
  <project.build.sourceEncoding>UTF-8</project.build.sourceEncoding>
<project.reporting.outputEncoding>UTF-8</project.reporting.outputEncod
ing>
  <java.version>1.8</java.version>
</properties>

<dependencies>

  <dependency>
    <groupId>org.springframework.boot</groupId>
    <artifactId>spring-boot-starter-thymeleaf</artifactId>
  </dependency>

  <dependency>
    <groupId>org.springframework.boot</groupId>
    <artifactId>spring-boot-starter-web</artifactId>
  </dependency>

  <dependency>
    <groupId>org.springframework.boot</groupId>
    <artifactId>spring-boot-starter-test</artifactId>
    <scope>test</scope>
  </dependency>

  <dependency>
    <groupId>org.projectlombok</groupId>
    <artifactId>lombok</artifactId>
    <version>1.16.16</version>
    <scope>provided</scope>
  </dependency>

  <dependency>
    <groupId>io.springfox</groupId>
    <artifactId>springfox-swagger2</artifactId>
    <version>2.7.0</version>
  </dependency>
```

```
    <dependency>
      <groupId>io.springfox</groupId>
      <artifactId>springfox-swagger-ui</artifactId>
      <version>2.7.0</version>
    </dependency>

  </dependencies>

  <build>
    <plugins>
      <plugin>
        <groupId>org.springframework.boot</groupId>
        <artifactId>spring-boot-maven-plugin</artifactId>
      </plugin>
    </plugins>
  </build>

</project>
```

Also, we have a `spring-boot-maven-plugin`, this awesome plugin provides Spring Boot support for Maven. It enables you to package the application in a Fat-JAR, and the plugin supports the run, start, and stop goals, as well interacting with our applications.

> **Fat-JAR**: a JAR which contains all project class files and resources packed together with all its dependencies.

For now, that is enough on Maven configurations; let's take a look at the Java files.

The Spring Initializr created one class for us, in general, the name of this class is artifact name plus `Application`, in our case `CmsApplication`, this class should look like this:

```java
package springfive.cms;

import org.springframework.boot.SpringApplication;
import org.springframework.boot.autoconfigure.SpringBootApplication;

@SpringBootApplication
public class CmsApplication {

  public static void main(String[] args) {
    SpringApplication.run(CmsApplication.class, args);
  }
}
```

Looking under the hood

We have some interesting things here, let's understand them. The
@SpringBootApplication is the essential annotation for the Spring Boot
application; it's a kind of alias for @Configuration, @EnableAutoConfiguration,
and @Component annotations. Let's dig in:

- The first annotation, @Configuration indicates that the class can produce
  a beans definitions for the Spring container. This is an interesting
  annotation to work with external dependencies such as DataSources; this
  is the most common use case for this annotation.
- The second annotation, @EnableAutoConfiguration means that with the
  Spring ApplicationContext container, it will try to help us configure the
  default beans for the specific context. For instance, when we create the web
  MVC application with Spring Boot, we will probably need a web server
  container to run it. In a default configuration, the Spring container, together
  with @EnableAutoConfiguration, will configure a bean Tomcat-
  embedded container for us. This annotation is very helpful for developers.
- The @Component is a stereotype, the container understands which class is
  considered for auto-detection and needs to instantiate it.

The SpringApplication class is responsible for bootstrapping the Spring
application from the main method, it will create an ApplicationContext instance,
take care of configurations provided by the configuration files, and finally, it will load
the singleton beans that are defined by annotations.

> **Stereotype Annotations** denote a conceptual division in an
> architecture layer. They help the developers understand the purpose
> of the class and the layer which the beans represent, for example,
> @Repository means the data access layer.

Running the application

We will run the application in IntelliJ IDEA and command line. It is an important task
to learn because we are working in different development environments; sometimes
the configurations of the application are a little bit complicated, and we are not able to
run it with IDEs, or sometimes the companies have different IDEs as standard, so we
will learn about two different ways.

IntelliJ IDEA

In general, the IntelliJ IDEA recognizes the main class annotated with
@SpringBootApplication and creates a run configuration for us, but it depends on
the version of the tool, let's do it.

Command line

The command line is a more generic tool to run the project. Also, this task is easy,
thanks to the Spring Boot Maven plugin. There are two ways to run, and we will
cover both.

Command line via the Maven goal

The first one is a goal of the Spring Boot Maven plugin, and it is straightforward;
open the terminal then go to the root project folder, pay attention as this is the same
folder where we have the pom.xml, and execute the following command:

```
mvn clean install spring-boot:run
```

The Maven will now compile the project and run the main class, the class
CmsApplication, and we should see this output:

Command line via the JAR file

To run it through the Java file, we need to compile and package it, and then we can run the project with the Java command line. To compile and package it, we can use the pretty standard Maven command like this:

```
mvn clean install
```

After the project is compiled and packaged as a Fat-JAR, we can execute the JAR file, go to the target folder and check the files from this folder, probably the result will look like this:

```
classes/            generated-sources/      generated-test-sources/ maven-archiver/      maven-status/       surefire-reports/       test-classes/
ubuntu@ubuntu-xenial:/vagrant/cms$ cd target/
ubuntu@ubuntu-xenial:/vagrant/cms/target$ ls -l
total 20808
drwxr-xr-x 1 ubuntu ubuntu      128 Oct 28 16:44 classes
-rw-r--r-- 1 ubuntu ubuntu 21301788 Oct 28 16:44 cms-0.0.1-SNAPSHOT.jar
-rw-r--r-- 1 ubuntu ubuntu     2745 Oct 28 16:44 cms-0.0.1-SNAPSHOT.jar.original
drwxr-xr-x 1 ubuntu ubuntu       96 Oct 28 16:44 generated-sources
drwxr-xr-x 1 ubuntu ubuntu       96 Oct 28 16:44 generated-test-sources
drwxr-xr-x 1 ubuntu ubuntu       96 Oct 28 16:44 maven-archiver
drwxr-xr-x 1 ubuntu ubuntu       96 Oct 28 16:44 maven-status
drwxr-xr-x 1 ubuntu ubuntu      128 Oct 28 16:44 surefire-reports
drwxr-xr-x 1 ubuntu ubuntu       96 Oct 28 16:44 test-classes
ubuntu@ubuntu-xenial:/vagrant/cms/target$
```

We have two main files in our target folder, the cms-0.0.1-SNAPSHOT.jar and the cms-0.0.1-SNAPSHOT.jar.original, the file with the .original extension is not executable. It is the original artifact resulting from the compilation, and the other is our executable file. It is what we are looking for, let's execute it, type the following command:

```
java -jar cms-0.0.1-SNAPSHOT.jar
```

The result should be as displayed. The application is up and running:

That is it for this part, in the next section, we will create the first **REST** (**Representational State Transfer**) resources and understand how the REST endpoints work.

Creating the REST resources

Now, we have an application up and running in this section, and we will add some REST endpoints and model some initial classes for the CMS application, the REST endpoints will be useful for the AngularJS integration.

One of the required characteristics for the APIs is the documentation, and a popular tool to help us with these tasks is Swagger. The Spring Framework supports Swagger, and we can do it with a couple of annotations. The project's Spring Fox is the correct tool to do this, and we will take a look at the tool in this chapter.

Let's do this.

Models

Before we start to create our class, we will add the `Lombok` dependency in our project. It is a fantastic library which provides some interesting things such as `GET`/`SET` at compilation time, the `Val` keyword to make variables final, `@Data` to make a class with some default methods like getters/setters, `equals`, and `hashCode`.

Adding Lombok dependency

Put the following dependency in a `pom.xml` file:

```xml
<dependency>
  <groupId>org.projectlombok</groupId>
  <artifactId>lombok</artifactId>
  <version>1.16.16</version>
  <scope>provided</scope>
</dependency>
```

The `provided` scope instructs Maven not to include this dependency in the JAR file because we need it at compile time. We do not need it at runtime. Wait for Maven to download the dependency, that is all for now.

Also, we can use the **Reimport All Maven Projects** provided by IntelliJ IDEA, located in the Maven Projects tab, as shown here:

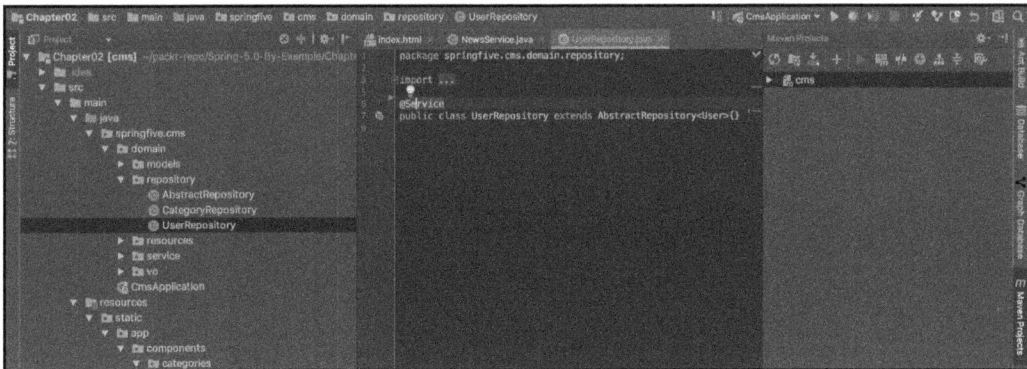

Creating the models

Now, we will create our models, which are Java classes annotated with `@Data`.

Tag

This class represents a tag in our system. There isn't necessarily any repository for it because it will be persisted together with our `News` entity:

```
package springfive.cms.domain.models;

import lombok.Data;

@Data
public class Tag {

  String value;

}
```

Category

A category model for our CMS application can be used to group the news. Also, the other important thing is that this makes our news categorized to make the search task easy. Take a look at the following code:

```
package springfive.cms.domain.models;

import lombok.Data;

@Data
public class Category {

  String id;

  String name;

}
```

User

It represents a user in our domain model. We have two different profiles, the author who acts as a news writer, and another one is a reviewer who must review the news registered at the portal. Take a look at the following example:

```
package springfive.cms.domain.models;

import lombok.Data;

@Data
public class User {

    String id;

    String identity;

    String name;

    Role role;

}
```

News

This class represents news in our domain, for now, it does not have any behaviors. Only properties and getters/setters are exposed; in the future, we will add some behaviors:

```
package springfive.cms.domain.models;

import java.util.Set;
import lombok.Data;

@Data
public class News {

    String id;

    String title;

    String content;

    User author;

    Set<User> mandatoryReviewers;
    Set<Review> reviewers;
```

```
    Set<Category> categories;

    Set<Tag> tags;

}
```

The `Review` class can be found at GitHub: (`https://github.com/PacktPublishing/`
`Spring-5.0-By-Example/tree/master/Chapter02/src/main/java/springfive/cms/`
`domain/models`).

As we can see, they are simple Java classes which represent our CMS application domain. It is the heart of our application, and all the domain logic will reside in these classes. It is an important characteristic.

Hello REST resources

We have created the models, and we can start to think about our REST resources. We will create three main resources:

- `CategoryResource` which will be responsible for the `Category` class.
- The second one is `UserResource`. It will manage the interactions between the `User` class and the REST APIs.
- The last one, and more important as well, will be the `NewsResource` which will be responsible for managing news entities, such as reviews.

Creating the CategoryResource class

We will create our first REST resource, let's get started with the `CategoryResource` class which is responsible for managing our `Category` class. The implementation of this entity will be simple, and we will create CRUD endpoints such as create, retrieve, update, and delete. We have two important things we must keep in mind when we create the APIs. The first one is the correct HTTP verb such as `POST`, `GET`, `PUT` and `DELETE`. It is essential for the REST APIs to have the correct HTTP verb as it provides us with intrinsic knowledge about the API. It is a pattern for anything that interacts with our APIs. Another thing is the status codes, and it is the same as the first one we must follow, this is the pattern the developers will easily recognize. The *Richardson Maturity Model* can help us create amazing REST APIs, and this model introduces some levels to measure the REST APIs, it's a kind of thermometer.

Firstly, we will create the skeleton for our APIs. Think about what features you need in your application. In the next section, we will explain how to add a service layer in our REST APIs. For now, let's build a `CategoryResource` class, our implementation could look like this:

```java
package springfive.cms.domain.resources;

import java.util.Arrays;
import java.util.List;
import org.springframework.http.HttpStatus;
import org.springframework.http.ResponseEntity;
import org.springframework.web.bind.annotation.DeleteMapping;
import org.springframework.web.bind.annotation.GetMapping;
import org.springframework.web.bind.annotation.PathVariable;
import org.springframework.web.bind.annotation.PostMapping;
import org.springframework.web.bind.annotation.PutMapping;
import org.springframework.web.bind.annotation.RequestMapping;
import org.springframework.web.bind.annotation.ResponseStatus;
import org.springframework.web.bind.annotation.RestController;
import springfive.cms.domain.models.Category;
import springfive.cms.domain.vo.CategoryRequest;

@RestController
@RequestMapping("/api/category")
public class CategoryResource {

  @GetMapping(value = "/{id}")
  public ResponseEntity<Category> findOne(@PathVariable("id") String
id){
     return ResponseEntity.ok(new Category());
  }

  @GetMapping
  public ResponseEntity<List<Category>> findAll(){
    return ResponseEntity.ok(Arrays.asList(new Category(),new
Category()));
  }

  @PostMapping
  public ResponseEntity<Category> newCategory(CategoryRequest
category){
     return new ResponseEntity<>(new Category(), HttpStatus.CREATED);
  }

  @DeleteMapping("/{id}")
  @ResponseStatus(HttpStatus.NO_CONTENT)
  public void removeCategory(@PathVariable("id") String id){
```

```
    }

    @PutMapping("/{id}")
    public ResponseEntity<Category> updateCategory(@PathVariable("id")
String id,CategoryRequest category){
        return new ResponseEntity<>(new Category(), HttpStatus.OK);
    }

}
```

The `CategoryRequest` can be found at GitHub (`https://github.com/PacktPublishing/Spring-5.0-By-Example/tree/master/Chapter02/src/main/java/springfive/cms/domain/vo`).

We have some important concepts here. The first one is `@RestController`. It instructs the Spring Framework that the `CategoryResource` class will expose REST endpoints over the Web-MVC module. This annotation will configure some things in a framework, such as `HttpMessageConverters` to handle HTTP requests and responses such as XML or JSON. Of course, we need the correct libraries on the classpath, to handle JSON and XML. Also, add some headers to the request such as `Accept` and `Content-Type`. This annotation was introduced in version 4.0. It is a kind of syntactic sugar annotation because it's annotated with `@Controller` and `@ResponseBody`.

The second is the `@RequestMapping` annotation, and this important annotation is responsible for the HTTP request and response in our class. The usage is quite simple in this code when we use it on the class level, it will propagate for all methods, and the methods use it as a relative. The `@RequestMapping` annotation has different use cases. It allows us to configure the HTTP verb, params, and headers.

Finally, we have `@GetMapping`, `@PostMapping`, `@DeleteMapping`, and `@PutMapping`, these annotations are a kind of shortcut to configure the `@RequestMapping` with the correct HTTP verbs; an advantage is that these annotations make the code more readable.

Except for the `removeCategory`, all the methods return the `ResponseEntity` class which enables us to handle the correct HTTP status codes in the next section.

UserResource

The `UserResource` class is the same as `CategoryResource`, except that it uses the `User` class. We can find the whole code on the GitHub (`https://github.com/PacktPublishing/Spring-5.0-By-Example/tree/master/Chapter02`).

NewsResource

The NewsResource class is essential, this endpoint enables users to review news previously registered, and it also provides an endpoint to return the updated news. This is an important feature because we are interested only in the relevant news. Irrelevant news cannot be shown on the portal. The resource class should look like this:

```
package springfive.cms.domain.resources;

import java.util.Arrays;
import java.util.List;
import org.springframework.http.HttpStatus;
import org.springframework.http.ResponseEntity;
import org.springframework.web.bind.annotation.DeleteMapping;
import org.springframework.web.bind.annotation.GetMapping;
import org.springframework.web.bind.annotation.PathVariable;
import org.springframework.web.bind.annotation.PostMapping;
import org.springframework.web.bind.annotation.PutMapping;
import org.springframework.web.bind.annotation.RequestMapping;
import org.springframework.web.bind.annotation.ResponseStatus;
import org.springframework.web.bind.annotation.RestController;
import springfive.cms.domain.models.News;
import springfive.cms.domain.models.Review;
import springfive.cms.domain.vo.NewsRequest;

@RestController
@RequestMapping("/api/news")
public class NewsResource {

  @GetMapping(value = "/{id}")
  public ResponseEntity<News> findOne(@PathVariable("id") String id){
    return ResponseEntity.ok(new News());
  }

  @GetMapping
  public ResponseEntity<List<News>> findAll(){
    return ResponseEntity.ok(Arrays.asList(new News(),new News()));
  }

  @PostMapping
  public ResponseEntity<News> newNews(NewsRequest news){
    return new ResponseEntity<>(new News(), HttpStatus.CREATED);
  }

  @DeleteMapping("/{id}")
  @ResponseStatus(HttpStatus.NO_CONTENT)
```

```
   public void removeNews(@PathVariable("id") String id){
   }

   @PutMapping("/{id}")
   public ResponseEntity<News> updateNews(@PathVariable("id") String
id,NewsRequest news){
      return new ResponseEntity<>(new News(), HttpStatus.OK);
   }

   @GetMapping(value = "/{id}/review/{userId}")
   public ResponseEntity<Review> review(@PathVariable("id") String
id,@PathVariable("userId") String userId){
      return ResponseEntity.ok(new Review());
   }

   @GetMapping(value = "/revised")
   public ResponseEntity<List<News>> revisedNews(){
      return ResponseEntity.ok(Arrays.asList(new News(),new News()));
   }

}
```

The NewsRequest class can be found at GitHub.

Pay attention to the HTTP verbs and the HTTP status code, as we need to follow the correct semantics.

Adding service layer

Now, we have the skeleton for the REST layer ready, and in this section, we will start to create a service layer for our application. We will show how the Dependency Injection works under the hood, learn the stereotype annotations on Spring Framework and also start to think about our persistence storage, which will be presented in the next section.

Changes in the model

We need to make some changes to our model, specifically in the News class. In our business rules, we need to keep our information safe, then we need to review all the news. We will add some methods to add a new review done by a user, and also we will add a method to check if the news was reviewed by all mandatory reviewers.

Adding a new review

For this feature, we need to create a method in our `News` class, the method will return a `Review` and should look like this:

```
public Review review(String userId,String status){
    final Review review = new Review(userId, status);
    this.reviewers.add(review);
    return review;
}
```

We do not need to check if the user, who performs the review action, is a mandatory reviewer at all.

Keeping the news safely

Also, we need to check if the news is fully revised by all mandatory reviewers. It is quite simple, we are using Java 8, and it provides the amazing `Stream` interface, which makes the collections interactions easier than before. Let's do this:

```
public Boolean revised() {
    return this.mandatoryReviewers.stream().allMatch(reviewer ->
this.reviewers.stream()
        .anyMatch(review -> reviewer.id.equals(review.userId) &&
"approved".equals(review.status)));
}
```

Thanks, Java 8, we appreciate it.

Before starting the service layer

Our application needs to have a persistence storage where our records can be loaded, even if the application goes down. We will create the fake implementation for our repositories. In chapter 3, *Persistence with Spring Data and Reactive Fashion*, we will introduce the Spring Data projects which help developers create amazing repositories with a fantastic DSL. For now, we will create some Spring beans to store our elements in memory, let's do that.

CategoryService

Let's start with our simplest service, the `CategoryService` class, the behaviors expected of this class are CRUD operations. Then, we need a representation of our persistence storage or repository implementation, for now, we are using the ephemeral storage and `ArrayList` with our categories. In the next chapter, we will add the real persistence for our CMS application.

Let's create our first Spring service. The implementation is in the following snippet:

```
package springfive.cms.domain.service;

import java.util.List;
import org.springframework.stereotype.Service;
import springfive.cms.domain.models.Category;
import springfive.cms.domain.repository.CategoryRepository;

@Service
public class CategoryService {

  private final CategoryRepository categoryRepository;

  public CategoryService(CategoryRepository categoryRepository) {
    this.categoryRepository = categoryRepository;
  }

  public Category update(Category category){
    return this.categoryRepository.save(category);
  }

  public Category create(Category category){
    return this.categoryRepository.save(category);
  }

  public void delete(String id){
    final Category category = this.categoryRepository.findOne(id);
    this.categoryRepository.delete(category);
  }

  public List<Category> findAll(){
    return this.categoryRepository.findAll();
  }

  public Category findOne(String id){
    return this.categoryRepository.findOne(id);
  }
```

```
}
```

There is some new stuff here. This class will be detected and instantiated by the Spring container because it has a @Service annotation. As we can see, there is nothing special in that class. It does not necessarily extend any class or implement an interface. We received the CategoryRepository on a constructor, this class will be provided by the Spring container because we instruct the container to produce this, but in Spring 5 it is not necessary to use @Autowired anymore in the constructor. It works because we had the only one constructor in that class and Spring will detect it. Also, we have a couple of methods which represent the CRUD behaviors, and it is simple to understand.

UserService

The UserService class is quite similar to the CategoryService, but the rules are about the User entity, for this entity we do not have anything special. We have the @Service annotation, and we received the UserRepository constructor as well. It is quite simple and easy to understand. We will show the UserService implementation, and it must be like this:

```java
package springfive.cms.domain.service;

import java.util.List;
import java.util.UUID;
import org.springframework.stereotype.Service;
import springfive.cms.domain.models.User;
import springfive.cms.domain.repository.UserRepository;
import springfive.cms.domain.vo.UserRequest;

@Service
public class UserService {

  private final UserRepository userRepository;

  public UserService(UserRepository userRepository) {
    this.userRepository = userRepository;
  }

  public User update(String id,UserRequest userRequest){
    final User user = this.userRepository.findOne(id);
    user.setIdentity(userRequest.getIdentity());
    user.setName(userRequest.getName());
    user.setRole(userRequest.getRole());
    return this.userRepository.save(user);
```

```
  }

  public User create(UserRequest userRequest){
    User user = new User();
    user.setId(UUID.randomUUID().toString());
    user.setIdentity(userRequest.getIdentity());
    user.setName(userRequest.getName());
    user.setRole(userRequest.getRole());
    return this.userRepository.save(user);
  }

  public void delete(String id){
    final User user = this.userRepository.findOne(id);
    this.userRepository.delete(user);
  }

  public List<User> findAll(){
    return this.userRepository.findAll();
  }

  public User findOne(String id){
    return this.userRepository.findOne(id);
  }

}
```

Pay attention to the class declaration with `@Service` annotation. This is a very common implementation in the Spring ecosystem. Also, we can find `@Component`, `@Repository` annotations. `@Service` and `@Component` are common for the service layer, and there is no difference in behaviors. The `@Repository` changes the behaviors a little bit because the frameworks will translate some exceptions on the data access layer.

NewsService

This is an interesting service which will be responsible for managing the state of our news. It will interact like a *glue* to call the domain models, in this case, the `News` entity. The service is pretty similar to the others. We received the `NewsRepository` class, a dependency and kept the repository to maintain the states, let's do that.

The `@Service` annotation is present again. This is pretty much standard for Spring applications. Also, we can change to the `@Component` annotation, but it does not make any difference to our application.

Configuring Swagger for our APIs

Swagger is the de facto tool for document web APIs, and the tool allows developers to model APIs, create an interactive way to play with the APIs, and also provides an easy way to generate the client implementation in a wide range of languages.

The API documentation is an excellent way to engage developers to use our APIs.

Adding dependencies to pom.xml

Before we start the configuration, we need to add the required dependencies. These dependencies included Spring Fox in our project and offered many annotations to configure Swagger properly. Let's add these dependencies.

The new dependencies are in the pom.xml file:

```
<dependency>
  <groupId>io.springfox</groupId>
  <artifactId>springfox-swagger2</artifactId>
  <version>2.7.0</version>
</dependency>

<dependency>
  <groupId>io.springfox</groupId>
  <artifactId>springfox-swagger-ui</artifactId>
  <version>2.7.0</version>
</dependency>
```

The first dependency is the core of Swagger with annotations and related kinds of stuff. Spring Fox Swagger UI dependency provides a rich interface in HTML which permits developers to interact with the APIs.

Configuring Swagger

The dependencies are added, now we can configure the infrastructure for Swagger. The configuration is pretty simple. We will create a class with @Configuration to produce the Swagger configuration for the Spring container. Let's do it.

Take a look at the following Swagger configuration:

```
package springfive.cms.infra.swagger;

import org.springframework.context.annotation.Bean;
import org.springframework.context.annotation.Configuration;
```

```
import org.springframework.web.bind.annotation.RestController;
import springfox.documentation.builders.ParameterBuilder;
import springfox.documentation.builders.PathSelectors;
import springfox.documentation.builders.RequestHandlerSelectors;
import springfox.documentation.spi.DocumentationType;
import springfox.documentation.spring.web.plugins.Docket;
import springfox.documentation.swagger2.annotations.EnableSwagger2;

@Configuration
@EnableSwagger2
public class SwaggerConfiguration {

  @Bean
  public Docket documentation() {
    return new Docket(DocumentationType.SWAGGER_2)
        .select()
.apis(RequestHandlerSelectors.withClassAnnotation(RestController.class
))
        .paths(PathSelectors.any())
        .build();
  }

}
```

The `@Configuration` instructs the Spring to generate a bean definition for Swagger. The annotation, `@EnableSwagger2` adds support for Swagger. `@EnableSwagger2` should be accompanied by `@Configuration`, it is mandatory.

The `Docket` class is a builder to create an API definition, and it provides sensible defaults and convenience methods for configuration of the Spring Swagger MVC Framework.

The invocation of method `.apis(RequestHandlerSelectors.withClassAnnotation(RestController.c lass))` instructs the framework to handle classes annotated with `@RestController`.

There are many methods to customize the API documentation, for example, there is a method to add authentication headers.

That is the Swagger configuration, in the next section, we will create a first documented API.

First documented API

We will start with the `CategoryResource` class, because it is simple to understand, and we need to keep the focus on the technology stuff. We will add a couple of annotations, and the magic will happen, let's do magic.

The `CategoryResource` class should look like this:

```
package springfive.cms.domain.resources;

import io.swagger.annotations.Api;
import io.swagger.annotations.ApiOperation;
import io.swagger.annotations.ApiResponse;
import io.swagger.annotations.ApiResponses;
import java.util.List;
import org.springframework.http.HttpStatus;
import org.springframework.http.ResponseEntity;
import org.springframework.web.bind.annotation.DeleteMapping;
import org.springframework.web.bind.annotation.GetMapping;
import org.springframework.web.bind.annotation.PathVariable;
import org.springframework.web.bind.annotation.PostMapping;
import org.springframework.web.bind.annotation.PutMapping;
import org.springframework.web.bind.annotation.RequestBody;
import org.springframework.web.bind.annotation.RequestMapping;
import org.springframework.web.bind.annotation.ResponseStatus;
import org.springframework.web.bind.annotation.RestController;
import springfive.cms.domain.models.Category;
import springfive.cms.domain.service.CategoryService;
import springfive.cms.domain.vo.CategoryRequest;

@RestController
@RequestMapping("/api/category")
@Api(tags = "category", description = "Category API")
public class CategoryResource {

  private final CategoryService categoryService;

  public CategoryResource(CategoryService categoryService) {
    this.categoryService = categoryService;
  }

  @GetMapping(value = "/{id}")
  @ApiOperation(value = "Find category",notes = "Find the Category by
ID")
  @ApiResponses(value = {
      @ApiResponse(code = 200,message = "Category found"),
      @ApiResponse(code = 404,message = "Category not found"),
  })
```

```java
public ResponseEntity<Category> findOne(@PathVariable("id") String
id){
    return ResponseEntity.ok(new Category());
}

@GetMapping
@ApiOperation(value = "List categories",notes = "List all
categories")
@ApiResponses(value = {
    @ApiResponse(code = 200,message = "Categories found"),
    @ApiResponse(code = 404,message = "Category not found")
})
public ResponseEntity<List<Category>> findAll(){
    return ResponseEntity.ok(this.categoryService.findAll());
}

@PostMapping
@ApiOperation(value = "Create category",notes = "It permits to
create a new category")
@ApiResponses(value = {
    @ApiResponse(code = 201,message = "Category created
successfully"),
    @ApiResponse(code = 400,message = "Invalid request")
})
public ResponseEntity<Category> newCategory(@RequestBody
CategoryRequest category){
    return new ResponseEntity<>(this.categoryService.create(category),
HttpStatus.CREATED);
}

@DeleteMapping("/{id}")
@ResponseStatus(HttpStatus.NO_CONTENT)
@ApiOperation(value = "Remove category",notes = "It permits to
remove a category")
@ApiResponses(value = {
    @ApiResponse(code = 200,message = "Category removed
successfully"),
    @ApiResponse(code = 404,message = "Category not found")
})
public void removeCategory(@PathVariable("id") String id){
}

@PutMapping("/{id}")
@ResponseStatus(HttpStatus.NO_CONTENT)
@ApiOperation(value = "Update category",notes = "It permits to
update a category")
@ApiResponses(value = {
    @ApiResponse(code = 200,message = "Category update
```

```
successfully"),
    @ApiResponse(code = 404,message = "Category not found"),
    @ApiResponse(code = 400,message = "Invalid request")
})
public ResponseEntity<Category> updateCategory(@PathVariable("id")
String id,CategoryRequest category){
    return new ResponseEntity<>(new Category(), HttpStatus.OK);
}

}
```

There are a lot of new annotations to understand. The @Api is the root annotation which configures this class as a Swagger resource. There are many configurations, but we will use the tags and description, as they are enough.

The @ApiOperation describes an operation in our API, in general against the requested path. The value attribute is regarding as the summary field on Swagger, it is a brief of the operation, and notes is a description of an operation (more detailed content).

The last one is the @ApiResponse which enables developers to describe the responses of an operation. Usually, they want to configure the status codes and message to describe the result of an operation.

> **TIP**
>
> Before you run the application, we should compile the source code. It can be done using the Maven command line using the mvn clean install, or via IDE using the **Run Application**.

Now, we have configured the Swagger integration, we can check the API documentation on the web browser. To do it, we need to navigate to http://localhost:8080/swagger-ui.html and this page should be displayed:

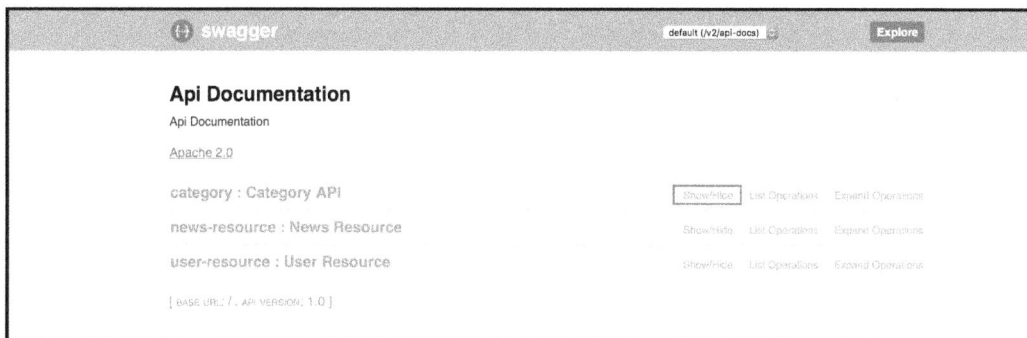

We can see APIs endpoints configured in our CMS application. Now, we will take a look at **category** which we have configured previously, click on the **Show/Hide** link. The output should be:

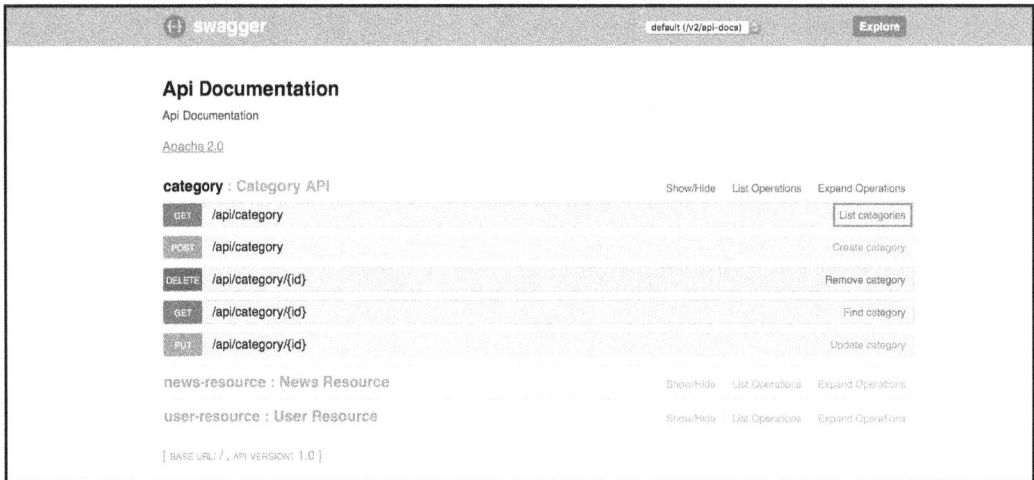

As we can see, there are five operations in our **Category API**, the operation has a path and a summary to help understand the purpose. We can click on the requested operation and see detailed information about the operation. Let's do it, click on **List categories** to see detailed documentation. The page looks like this:

Apache 2.0

category : Category API   Show/Hide   List Operations   Expand Operations

GET /api/category   List categories

Implementation Notes
List all categories

Response Class (Status 200)
Categories found

Model **Example Value**

```
[
  {
    "id": "string",
    "name": "string"
  }
]
```

Response Content Type */*

Response Messages

HTTP Status Code	Reason	Response Model	Headers
401	Unauthorized		
403	Forbidden		
404	Category not found		

Try it out!

Outstanding job. Now we have an amazing API with excellent documentation. Well done.

Let's continue creating our CMS application.

Integrate with AngularJS

The AngularJS Framework has been becoming a trend for a few years, the community is super active, the project was created by Google.

The main idea of the framework is to help developers handle the complexities of the frontend layer, especially in the HTML part. The HTML markup language is static. It is a great tool to create static documents, but today it is not a requirement for modern web applications. These applications need to be dynamic. The UX teams around the world, work hard to create amazing applications, with different effects, these guys try to keep the applications more comfortable for the users.

AngularJS adds the possibility of extending the HTML with some additional attributes and tags. In this section, we will add some interesting behaviors on the frontend application. Let's do it.

AngularJS concepts

In our CMS application, we will work with some Angular components. We will use `Controllers` which will interact with our HTML and handle the behavior of some pages, such as those that show error messages. The `Services` is responsible for handling the infrastructure code such as interacting with our CMS API. This book is not intended to be an AngularJS guide. However, we will take a look at some interesting concepts to develop our application.

The AngularJS common tags are:

- `ng-app`
- `ng-controller`
- `ng-click`
- `ng-hide`
- `ng-show`

These tags are included in the AngularJS Framework. There are many more tags created and maintained by the community. There is, for example, a library to work with HTML forms, we will use it to add dynamic behaviors in our CMS Portal.

Controllers

Controllers are part of the framework to handle the business logic of the application. They should be used to control the flow of data in an application. The controller is attached to the DOM via the `ng-controller` directive.

To add some actions to our view, we need to create functions on controllers, the way to do this is by creating functions and adding them to the `$scope` object.

The controllers cannot be used to carry out DOM manipulations, format data and filter data, it is considered best practice in the AngularJS world.

Usually, the controllers inject the service objects to delegate handling the business logic. We will understand services in the next section.

Services

Services are the objects to handle business logic in our application. In some cases, they can be used to handle state. The services objects are a singleton which means we have only one instance in our entire application.

In our application, the services are responsible for interacting with our CMS APIs built on Spring Boot. Let's do that.

Creating the application entry point

The Spring Boot Framework allows us to serve static files. These files should be in the classpath in one of these folders, `/static`, `/public`, `/resources`, or `/META-INF/resources`.

We will use the `/static` folder, in this folder, we will put our AngularJS application. There are some standards to modularize the AngularJS application folder structure which depends on the application size and requirements. We will use the most simple style to keep the attention on Spring integration. Look at the project structure:

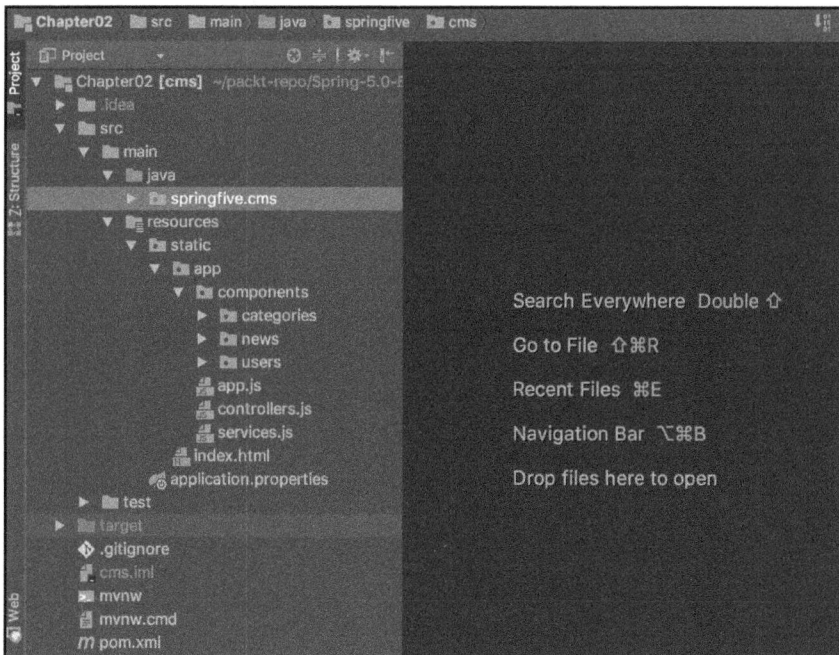

There are some assets to start and run an AngularJS application. We will use the Content Delivery Network (CDN) to load the AngularJS Framework, the Angular UI-Router which helps to handle routing on our web application, and the Bootstrap Framework which helps to develop our pages.

> Content Delivery Network is distributed proxy servers around the world. It makes the content more high availability and improves performance because it will be hosted nearer the end user. The detailed explanation can be found at CloudFare Page (`https://www.cloudflare.com/learning/cdn/what-is-a-cdn/`).

Then we can start to configure our AngularJS application. Let's start with our entry point, `index.html`:

```html
<!DOCTYPE html>
<html lang="en">
<head>
  <meta charset="utf-8">
  <meta http-equiv="X-UA-Compatible" content="IE=edge">
  <meta name="viewport" content="width=device-width, initial-scale=1">
  <title>Spring Boot Security</title>
  <link rel="stylesheet"
href="https://maxcdn.bootstrapcdn.com/bootstrap/3.3.7/css/bootstrap.min.css">
</head>
<body ng-app="cms">

<!-- Header -->
<nav class="navbar navbar-default navbar-fixed-top">
  <div class="container">
    <div class="navbar-header">
      <button type="button" class="navbar-toggle collapsed" data-
toggle="collapse" data-target="#navbar"
              aria-expanded="false" aria-controls="navbar">
        <span class="sr-only">Toggle navigation</span>
        <span class="icon-bar"></span>
        <span class="icon-bar"></span>
        <span class="icon-bar"></span>
      </button>
      <a class="navbar-brand" href="#">CMS</a>
    </div>
    <div id="navbar" class="collapse navbar-collapse">
      <ul class="nav navbar-nav">
        <li class="active"><a href="#">Home</a></li>
        <li><a href="#users">Users</a></li>
        <li><a href="#categories">Categories</a></li>
        <li><a href="#news">News</a></li>
```

```
        </ul>
      </div>
    </div>
  </nav>

  <!-- Body -->
  <div class="container">
    <div ui-view></div>
  </div>

  <script
  src="https://ajax.googleapis.com/ajax/libs/angularjs/1.4.8/angular.min
  .js"></script>
  <script
  src="https://cdnjs.cloudflare.com/ajax/libs/angular-ui-router/1.0.3/an
  gular-ui-router.js"></script>

  <script type="text/javascript" src="app/app.js"></script>

  <script type="text/javascript" src="app/controllers.js"></script>
  <script type="text/javascript" src="app/services.js"></script>

  <script type="text/javascript"
  src="app/components/categories/category-controller.js"></script>
  <script type="text/javascript"
  src="app/components/categories/category-service.js"></script>

  <script type="text/javascript" src="app/components/news/news-
  controller.js"></script>
  <script type="text/javascript" src="app/components/news/news-
  service.js"></script>

  <script type="text/javascript" src="app/components/users/user-
  controller.js"></script>
  <script type="text/javascript" src="app/components/users/user-
  service.js"></script>

  </body>
  </html>
```

There are some important things here. Let's understand them.

The ng-app tag is a directive which is used to bootstrap the AngularJS application. This tag is the root element of the application and is usually placed on the <body> or <html> tags.

The `ui-view` tag instructs the Angular UI-Router about which portion of the HTML document will be handled by the application states, in other words, the designated part has the dynamic behaviors and change depends on the routing system. Look at the following code snippet:

```
<!-- Body -->
<div class="container">
  <div ui-view></div>
</div>
```

This part of the code can be found at `index.hml` file.

Following the `ui-view`, we have our JavaScript files, the first one is the AngularJS Framework, in this version the file is minified. Look at our JavaScript files, the files were created in the `/static/app/components` folder. Take a look at the image here:

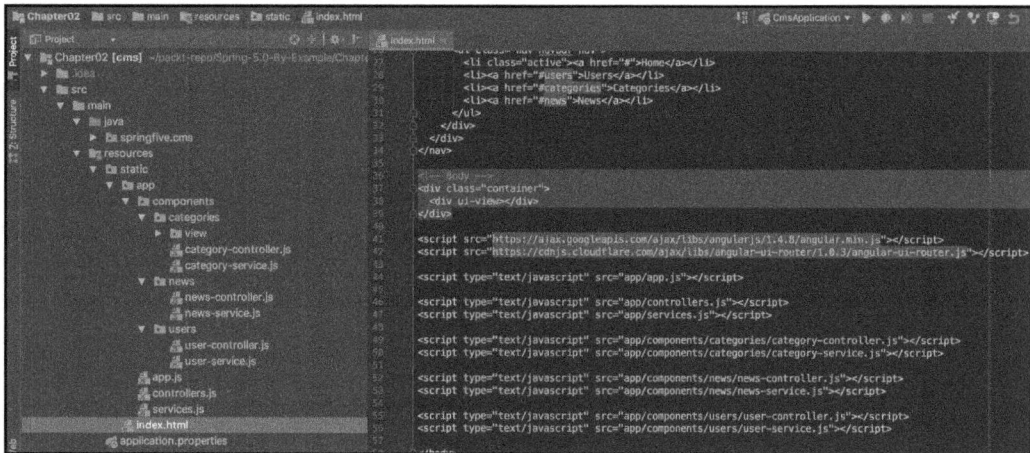

The second one is the UI-Router which helps us to manage our routes. Finally, we have our JavaScript files which configure the AngularJS application, our controllers, and the services to interact with our CMS APIs.

Also, we have some Bootstrap classes to align fields and make design easier.

Creating the Category Controller

Now, we need to create our controllers. We will start with the simplest to make the example more easy to understand. The `CategoryController` has the responsibility of controlling the data of the `Category` entity. There are two controllers, one enables us to create a category, and another lists all categories stored in the database.

The `category-controller.js` should be like this:

```
(function (angular) {
  'use strict';

  // Controllers
  angular.module('cms.modules.category.controllers', []).

  controller('CategoryCreateController',
      ['$scope', 'CategoryService','$state',
        function ($scope, CategoryService,$state) {

          $scope.resetForm = function () {
            $scope.category = null;
          };

          $scope.create = function (category) {
            CategoryService.create(category).then(
                function (data) {
                  console.log("Success on create Category!!!")
                  $state.go('categories')
                }, function (err) {
                  console.log("Error on create Category!!!")
                });
          };
        }]).

  controller('CategoryListController',
      ['$scope', 'CategoryService',
        function ($scope, CategoryService) {
          CategoryService.find().then(function (data) {
            $scope.categories = data.data;
          }, function (err) {
            console.log(err);
          });
        }]);
}) (angular);
```

We have created an AngularJS module. It helps us to keep the functions organized. It acts as a kind of namespace for us. The `.controller` function is a constructor to create our controller's instances. We received some parameters, the AngularJS framework will inject these objects for us.

Creating the Category Service

The `CategoryService` objects is a singleton object because it is an AngularJS service. The service will interact with our CMS APIs powered by the Spring Boot application.

We will use the `$http` service. It makes the HTTP communications easier.

Let's write the `CategoryService`:

```
(function (angular) {
  'use strict';

  /* Services */
</span>  angular.module('cms.modules.category.services', []).
    service('CategoryService', ['$http',
      function ($http) {

        var serviceAddress = 'http://localhost:8080';
        var urlCollections = serviceAddress + '/api/category';
        var urlBase = serviceAddress + '/api/category/';

        this.find = function () {
          return $http.get(urlCollections);
        };

        this.findOne = function (id) {
          return $http.get(urlBase + id);
        };

        this.create = function (data) {
          return $http.post(urlBase, data);
        };

        this.update = function (data) {
          return $http.put(urlBase + '/id/' + data._id, data);
        };

        this.remove = function (data) {
          return $http.delete(urlBase + '/id/' + data._id, data);
        };
      }
```

```
    ]);
}) (angular);
```

Well done, now we have implemented the `CategoryService`.

The `.service` function is a constructor to create a service instance, the `angular` acts under the hood. There is an injection on a constructor, for the service we need an `$http` service to make HTTP calls against our APIs. There are a couple of HTTP methods here. Pay attention to the correct method to keep the HTTP semantics.

Summary

In this chapter, we created our first Spring application. We saw Spring Initializr, the amazing tool that helps developers create the application skeleton.

We looked at how Spring works under the hood and how the framework got configured with a couple of annotations. Now, we have a basic knowledge of the Spring Bootstrap functions, and we can understand the Dependency Injection and component scan features present in the framework.

This knowledge is the basis for the next chapters, and now we are ready to start to work with more advanced features, such as persistence. Here we go. See you in the next chapter.

3
Persistence with Spring Data and Reactive Fashion

In the previous chapter, we created our **Content Management System** (**CMS**) application. We also introduced **REST** (**Representational State Transfer**) support in Spring, which enabled us to develop a simple web application. Also, we learned how dependency injection works in the Spring Framework, which is probably the most famous feature of the framework.

In this chapter, we will add more features to our application. Systems in the real world need to persist their data on a real database; this is an essential characteristic for a production-ready application. Also, based on our model, we need to choose the correct data structure to achieve performance and avoid the impedance mismatch.

In the first part of this chapter, we will use the traditional SQL database as a store for our application. We will deep dive on the Spring Data **JPA** (**Java Persistence API**) to achieve the persistence for our CMS application. We will understand how to enable transactions with this amazing Spring module.

After that, we will change to a more modern type of database called **NoSQL technologies**. In this field, we will use the famous database document model called **MongoDB** and then we will create the final solution for our CMS application.

MongoDB offers a fantastic solution for our application because it has support for a document storage model and enables us to store our objects in the form of JSON, which makes our data more readable. Also, MongoDB is schema-less, which is a fantastic feature because one collection can store different documents. It means records can have different fields, content, and sizes. The other important characteristic from MongoDB is the query model. It offers a document-based query that is easy to understand, and, based on JSON notations, our queries will be more readable than any other database can be.

Finally, we will add the most important feature present in Spring 5.0: support for Reactive Streams. Our application will be transformed into a modern web application which has some important requirements.

Here's an overview of what you will learn in this chapter:

- Implementing the Spring Data JPA
- Creating repositories with Spring Data Reactive MongoDB
- Learning the Reactive Spring
- Understand the Project Reactor

Learning the basics of Docker

We learned about Docker concepts in `Chapter 1`, *Journey to the Spring World*. Now, it is time to test our knowledge and put it into practice. In the first part of this chapter, we will start MongoDB and Postgres instances to serve as a database for our application. We will configure connection settings in the application.

In the last part of this chapter, we will introduce the Maven plugin which provides an easy way to create Docker images via `pom.xml` with a couple of configurations on file. Finally, we will run our application in a Docker container.

Preparing MongoDB

Let's create our MongoDB container. We will use the official image provided by the Docker Hub.

First, we need to pull the image:

```
docker pull mongo:3.4.10
```

Then, we will see the Docker Engine downloading the image contents.

To create an isolation from our containers, we will create a separated network for our application and database. The network should use the bridge driver to allow the container communications.

Let's create a `docker network`:

```
docker network create cms-application
```

The command output should be an ID of a created network. Your ID will probably be different compared to mine:

```
2 updates are security updates.

Last login: Wed Nov  1 00:13:53 2017 from 10.0.2.2
ubuntu@ubuntu-xenial:~$ docker network create cms-application
5a8485d8da42a4680347635e57041b35d2d09642ac9f5e1194c7334a5e4bfe92
ubuntu@ubuntu-xenial:~$
```

To check if the network was created successfully, the `docker network ls` command can help us.

We will start our MongoDB. The network should be `cms-application`, but we will map the database port to a host port. For debugging purposes, we will connect a client to a running database, but please don't do this in a non-development environment.

> Exposing a port over host is not a best practice. Hence, we use a Docker container, which is one of the main advantages is process isolation. In this case, we will have no control over the network. Otherwise, we may cause some port conflicts.

To start, type the following command:

```
docker run -d --name mongodb --net cms-application -p 27017:27017
mongo:3.4.10
```

> Also, we can stop the Docker MongoDB container using `docker stop mongodb` and start our container again by using the following command: `docker start mongodb`.

The output will be a hash which represents the ID of the container.

The parameter instructions are:

- `-d`: This instructs Docker to run the container in a background mode
- `--name`: The container name; it will be a kind of hostname in our network

- `--net`: The network where the container will be attached
- `-p`: The host port and container port, which will be mapped to a container on a host interface

Now, we have a pretty standard MongoDB instance running on our machines, and we can start to add a persistence in our CMS application. We will do that soon.

Preparing a PostgreSQL database

Like MongoDB, we will prepare a PostgreSQL instance for our CMS application. We will change our persistence layer to demonstrate how Spring Data abstracts it for developers. Then, we need to prepare a Docker Postgres instance for that.

We will use the version 9.6.6 of Postgres and use the `alpine` tag because it is smaller than other Postgres images. Let's pull our image. The command should be like this:

```
docker pull postgres:9.6.6-alpine
```

Then, wait until the download ends.

In the previous section, we created our Docker network called `cms-application`. Now, we will start our Postgres instance on that network as we did for MongoDB. The command to start the Postgres should be the following:

```
docker run -d --name postgres --net cms-application -p 5432:5432 -e
POSTGRES_PASSWORD=cms@springfive
postgres:9.6.6-alpine
```

The list of parameters is the same as we passed for MongoDB. We want to run it in background mode and attach it to our custom network. As we can see, there is one more new parameter in the `docker run` command. Let's understand it:

- `-e`: This enables us to pass environment variables for a container. In this case, we want to change the password value.

Good job. We have done our infrastructure requirements. Let's understand the persistence details right now.

Spring Data project

The Spring Data project is an umbrella project that offers a familiar way to create our data access layer on a wide range of database technologies. It means there are high-level abstractions to interact with different kinds of data structures, such as the document model, column family, key-value, and graphs. Also, the JPA specification is fully supported by the Spring Data JPA project.

These modules offer powerful object-mapping abstractions for our domain model.

There is support for different types of data structures and databases. There is a set of sub-modules to keep the framework modularity. Also, there are two categories of these sub-modules: the first one is a subset of projects supported by the Spring Framework Team and the second one is a subset of sub-modules provided by the community.

Projects supported by the Spring Team include:

- Spring Data Commons
- Spring Data JPA
- Spring Data MongoDB
- Spring Data Redis
- Spring Data for Apache Cassandra

Projects supported by the community include:

- Spring Data Aerospike
- Spring Data ElasticSearch
- Spring Data DynamoDB
- Spring Data Neo4J

The base of the repositories interfaces chain is the `Repository` interface. It is a marker interface, and the general purpose is to store the type information. The type will be used for other interfaces that extend it.

There is also a `CrudRepository` interface. It is the most important, and the name is self-explanatory; it provides a couple of methods to perform CRUD operations, and it provides some utility methods, such as `count()`, `exists()`, and `deleteAll()`. Those are the most important base interfaces for the repository implementations.

Spring Data JPA

The Spring Data JPA provides an easy way to implement a data access layer using the JPA specification from Java EE. Usually, these implementations had a lot of boilerplate and repetitive code and it was hard to maintain the changes in the database code. The Spring Data JPA is trying to resolve these issues and provides a comprehensible way to do that without boilerplate and repetitive code.

The JPA specification provides an abstraction layer to interact with different database vendors that have been implemented. Spring adds one more layer to the abstraction in a high-level mode. It means the Spring Data JPA will create a repositories implementation and encapsulate the whole JPA implementation details. We can build our persistence layer with a little knowledge of the JPA spec.

> The *JPA Specification* was created by the **JCP** (**Java Community Process**) to help developers to persist, access, and manage data between Java classes and relational databases. There are some vendors that implement this specification. The most famous implementation is Hibernate (`http://hibernate.org/orm/`), and by default, Spring Data JPA uses Hibernate as the JPA implementation.

Say goodbye to the **DAO** (**Data Access Object**) pattern and implementations. The Spring Data JPA aims to solve this problem with a well-tested framework and with some production-ready features.

Now, we have an idea of what the Spring Data JPA is. Let's put it into practice.

Configuring pom.xml for Spring Data JPA

Now, we need to put the correct dependencies to work with Spring Data JPA. There are a couple of dependencies to configure in our `pom.xml` file.

The first one is the Spring Data JPA Starter, which provides a lot of auto-configuration classes which permits us to bootstrap the application quickly. The last one is the PostgreSQL JDBC driver, and it is necessary because it contains the JDBC implementation classes to connect with the PostgreSQL database.

The new dependencies are:

```
<dependency>
  <groupId>org.springframework.boot</groupId>
  <artifactId>spring-boot-starter-data-jpa</artifactId>
</dependency>
```

```
<dependency>
  <groupId>org.postgresql</groupId>
  <artifactId>postgresql</artifactId>
  <version>42.1.4</version>
</dependency>
```

Simple and pretty easy.

Configuring the Postgres connections

To connect our application with our recently created database, we need to configure a couple of lines in the `application.yaml` file. Once again, thanks to Spring Data Starter, our connection will be configured automatically.

We can produce the connection objects using the `@Bean` annotations as well, but there are many objects to configure. We will go forward with the configuration file. It is more simple and straightforward to understand as well.

To configure the database connections, we need to provide the Spring Framework a couple of attributes, such as the database URL, database username, password, and also a driver class name to instruct the JPA framework about the full path of the JDBC class.

The `application.yaml` file should be like this:

```
spring:
  datasource:
    url: jdbc:postgresql://localhost:5432/postgres
    username: postgres
    password: cms@springfive
    driver-class-name: org.postgresql.Driver
  jpa:
    show-sql: true
    generate-ddl: true
```

In the `datasource` section, we have configured the database credentials connections and database host as well.

The JPA section in `application.yaml` can be used to configure the JPA framework. In this part, we configured to log SQL instructions in the console. This is helpful to debug and perform troubleshooting. Also, we have configured the JPA framework to create our tables in a database when the application gets the startup process.

Awesome, the JPA infrastructure is configured. Well done! Now, we can map our models in the JPA style. Let's do that in the following section.

Mapping the models

We have configured the database connections successfully. Now, we are ready to map our models using the JPA annotations. Let's start with our `Category` model. It is a pretty simple class, which is good because we are interested in Spring Data JPA stuff.

Our first version of the `Category` model should be like this:

```
package springfive.cms.domain.models;

import javax.persistence.Entity;
import javax.persistence.GeneratedValue;
import javax.persistence.Id;
import javax.persistence.Table;
import lombok.Data;
import org.hibernate.annotations.GenericGenerator;

@Data
@Entity
@Table(name = "category")
public class Category {

    @Id
    @GeneratedValue(generator = "system-uuid")
    @GenericGenerator(name = "system-uuid", strategy = "uuid2")
    String id;

    String name;

}
```

> We need to change some model classes to adapt to the JPA specification. We can find the model classes on GitHub at: `https://github.com/PacktPublishing/Spring-5.0-By-Example/tree/master/Chapter03/cms-postgres/src/main/java/springfive/cms/domain/models`.

There is some new stuff here. The `@Entity` annotation instructs the JPA framework that the annotated class is an entity, in our case, the `Category` class, and then the framework will correlate it with a database table. The `@Table` annotation is used to name the table in the database. These annotations are inserted on the class level, which means on top of the class declaration.

The @Id annotation instructs the JPA as to which annotated field is the primary key of the database table. It is not a good practice to generate IDs sequentially for entities, especially if you are creating the APIs. It helps hackers to understand the logic about the IDs and makes the attacks easier. So, we will generate UUIDs (Universally Unique IDentifiers) instead of simple sequentially IDs. The @GenericGenerator annotation instructs Hibernate, which is a JPA specification implementation vendor, to generate random UUIDs.

Adding the JPA repositories in the CMS application

Once the whole infrastructure and JPA mappings are done, we can add our repositories to our projects. In the Spring Data project, there are some abstractions, such as Repository, CrudRepository, and JpaRepository. We will use the JpaRepository because it supports the paging and sorting features.

Our repository will be pretty simple. There are a couple of standard methods, such as save(), update(), and delete(), and we will take a look at some DSL query methods which allow developers to create custom queries based on attribute names. We created an AbstractRepository to help us to store the objects in memory. It is not necessary anymore. We can remove it.

Let's create our first JPA repository:

```
package springfive.cms.domain.repository;

import java.util.List;
import org.springframework.data.jpa.repository.JpaRepository;
import springfive.cms.domain.models.Category;

public interface CategoryRepository extends JpaRepository<Category,
String> {

  List<Category> findByName(String name);

  List<Category> findByNameIgnoreCaseStartingWith(String name);

}
```

As we can see, the JpaRepository interface is typed with the desired entity and the type of ID of the entity as well. There is no secret to this part. This amazing thing happens to support the custom queries based on attribute names. In the Category model, there is an attribute called name. We can create custom methods in our CategoryRepository using the Category model attributes using the By instruction.

As we can see, above `findByName(String name)`, Spring Data Framework will create the correct query to look up categories by name. It is fantastic.

There are many keywords supported by the custom query methods:

Logical Keyword	Logical Expressions
AND	And
OR	Or
AFTER	After, IsAfter
BEFORE	Before, IsBefore
CONTAINING	Containing, IsContaining, Contains
BETWEEN	Between, IsBetween
ENDING_WITH	EndingWith, IsEndingWith, EndsWith
EXISTS	Exists
FALSE	False, IsFalse
GREATER_THAN	GreaterThan, IsGreaterThan
GREATHER_THAN_EQUALS	GreaterThanEqual, IsGreaterThanEqual
IN	In, IsIn
IS	Is, Equals, (or no keyword)
IS_EMPTY	IsEmpty, Empty
IS_NOT_EMPTY	IsNotEmpty, NotEmpty
IS_NOT_NULL	NotNull, IsNotNull
IS_NULL	Null, IsNull
LESS_THAN	LessThan, IsLessThan
LESS_THAN_EQUAL	LessThanEqual, IsLessThanEqual
LIKE	Like, IsLike
NEAR	Near, IsNear
NOT	Not, IsNot
NOT_IN	NotIn, IsNotIn
NOT_LIKE	NotLike, IsNotLike
REGEX	Regex, MatchesRegex, Matches
STARTING_WITH	StartingWith, IsStartingWith, StartsWith
TRUE	True, IsTrue
WITHIN	Within, IsWithin

There are many ways to create a query based on attributes names. We can combine the keywords using keywords as well, such as `findByNameAndId`, for instance. The Spring Data JPA provides a consistent way to create queries.

Configuring transactions

When we use the JPA specification, most of the applications need to have support for transactions as well. Spring has excellent support for transactions even in other modules. This support is integrated with Spring Data JPA, and we can take advantage of it. Configuring transactions in Spring is a piece of cake; we need to insert the `@Transactional` annotation whenever needed. There are some different use cases to use it. We will use the `@Transactional` in our services layer and then we will put the annotation in our service classes. Let's see our `CategoryService` class:

```
package springfive.cms.domain.service;

import java.util.List;
import java.util.Optional;
import org.springframework.stereotype.Service;
import org.springframework.transaction.annotation.Transactional;
import springfive.cms.domain.exceptions.CategoryNotFoundException;
import springfive.cms.domain.models.Category;
import springfive.cms.domain.repository.CategoryRepository;
import springfive.cms.domain.vo.CategoryRequest;

@Service
@Transactional(readOnly = true)
public class CategoryService {

  private final CategoryRepository categoryRepository;

  public CategoryService(CategoryRepository categoryRepository) {
    this.categoryRepository = categoryRepository;
  }

  @Transactional
  public Category update(Category category) {
    return this.categoryRepository.save(category);
  }

  @Transactional
  public Category create(CategoryRequest request) {
    Category category = new Category();
    category.setName(request.getName());
    return this.categoryRepository.save(category);
```

```java
  }

  @Transactional
  public void delete(String id) {
     final Optional<Category> category =
this.categoryRepository.findById(id);
     category.ifPresent(this.categoryRepository::delete);
  }

  public List<Category> findAll() {
     return this.categoryRepository.findAll();
  }

  public List<Category> findByName(String name) {
     return this.categoryRepository.findByName(name);
  }

  public List<Category> findByNameStartingWith(String name) {
     return
this.categoryRepository.findByNameIgnoreCaseStartingWith(name);
  }

  public Category findOne(String id) {
     final Optional<Category> category =
this.categoryRepository.findById(id);
     if (category.isPresent()) {
       return category.get();
     } else {
       throw new CategoryNotFoundException(id);
     }
  }
}
```

There are many `@Transactional` annotations in the `CategoryService` class. The first annotation at class level instructs the framework to configure the `readOnly` for all methods present in those classes, except the methods configured with `@Transactional`. In this case, the class-level annotation will be overridden with `readOnly=false`. This is the default configuration when the value is omitted.

Installing and configuring pgAdmin3

To connect on our PostgreSQL instance, we will use pgAdmin 3, which is the free tool provided by the Postgres team.

To install pgAdmin 3, we can use the following command:

```
sudo apt-get install pgadmin3 -y
```

This will install pgAdmin 3 on our machine.

After installation, open pgAdmin 3 and then click on **Add a connection to a server**. The button looks like this:

Then, fill in the information, as shown in the following screenshot:

The password should be: cms@springfive.

Awesome, our pgAdmin 3 tool is configured.

Checking the data on the database structure

The whole application structure is ready. Now, we can check the database to get our persisted data. There are many open source Postgres clients. We will use pgAdmin 3, as previously configured.

The first time you open the application, you will be asked about the credentials and host. We must put the same information as we configured on the `application.yaml` file. Then, we are able to make instructions in the database.

Before checking the database, we can use Swagger to create some categories in our CMS system. We can use the instructions provided in `Chapter 2`, *Starting in the Spring World – The CMS Application,* to create some data.

After that, we can execute the following SQL instruction in the database:

```
select * from category;
```

And the result should be the categories created on Swagger calls. In my case, I have created two categories, `sports`, and `movies`. The result will be like the ones shown in the following screenshot:

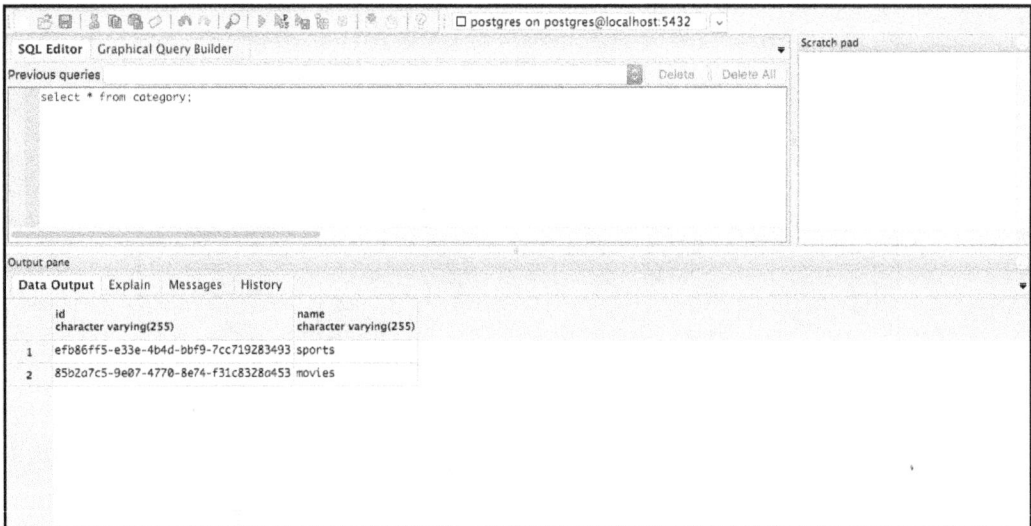

Awesome work, guys. The application is fully operational.

Now, we will create our final solution for the repositories. We have learned the basics of the Spring Data project and in the next section, we will change the persistence layer to a modern database.

Creating the final data access layer

We have played with the Spring Data JPA project, and we have seen how easy it can be. We learned how to configure the database connections to persist the real data on the Postgres database. Now, we will create the final solution for the data access layer for our application. The final solution will use MongoDB as a database and will use the Spring Data MongoDB project, which provides support for MongoDB repositories.

We will see some similarities with the Spring Data JPA projects. It is amazing because we can prove the power of Spring Data abstractions in practice. With a couple of changes, we can move to another database model.

Let's understand the new project and put it into practice in the following sections.

Spring Data MongoDB

The Spring Data MongoDB provides integration with our domain objects and the MongoDB document. With a couple of annotations, our entity class is ready to be persisted in the database. The mapping is based on a **POJO** (**Plain Old Java Object**) pattern, which is known by all Java developers.

There are two levels of abstraction supplied by the module. The first one is a high-level abstraction. It increases the developer productivity. This level provides a couple of annotations to instruct the framework to convert the domain objects in MongoDB documents and vice versa. The developer does not need to write any code about the persistence; it will be managed by the Spring Data MongoDB framework. There are more exciting things at this level, such as the rich mapping configurations provided by the Spring Conversion Service. The Spring Data projects provide a rich DSL to enable developers to create queries based on the attribute names.

The second level of abstraction is the low-level abstraction. At this level, behaviors are not automatically managed by the framework. The developers need to understand a little bit more about the Spring and MongoDB document model. The framework provides a couple of interfaces to enable developers to take control of the read and write instructions. This can be useful for scenarios where the high-level abstraction does not fit well. In this case, the control should be more granular in the entities mapping.

Again, Spring provides the power of choice for developers. The high-level abstraction improves the developer performance and the low-level permits developers to take more control.

Now, we will add mapping annotation to our model. Let's do it.

Removing the PostgreSQL and Spring Data JPA dependencies

We will convert our project to use the brand new Spring Data Reactive MongoDB repositories. After that, we will not use the Spring Data JPA and PostgreSQL drivers anymore. Let's remove these dependencies from our `pom.xml`:

```
<dependency>
  <groupId>org.springframework.boot</groupId>
  <artifactId>spring-boot-starter-data-jpa</artifactId>
</dependency>

<dependency>
  <groupId>org.postgresql</groupId>
  <artifactId>postgresql</artifactId>
  <version>42.1.4</version>
</dependency>
```

And then, we can add the following dependency:

```
<dependency>
  <groupId>org.springframework.boot</groupId>
  <artifactId>spring-boot-starter-data-mongodb-reactive</artifactId>
</dependency>
```

> The final version of `pom.xml` can be found on GitHub at https://github.com/PacktPublishing/Spring-5.0-By-Example/blob/master/Chapter03/cms-mongo-non-reactive/pom.xml.

Mapping the domain model

We will add mapping annotations on our domain model. The Spring Data MongoDB will use these annotations to persist our objects in the MongoDB collections. We will start with the Category entity, which should be like this:

```
package springfive.cms.domain.models;

import lombok.Data;
import org.springframework.data.annotation.Id;
import org.springframework.data.mongodb.core.mapping.Document;

@Data
@Document(collection = "category")
public class Category {

  @Id
  String id;

  String name;

}
```

We added two new annotations in the Category class. The @Document from Spring Data MongoDB enables us to configure the collection name. Collections in MongoDB are similar to tables in SQL databases.

The @Id annotation is from the Spring Data Commons project. It is interesting because, as we can see, it is not specific for MongoDB mappings. The field annotation with this will be converted in the _id field on MongoDB collection.

With these few annotations, the Category class is configured to be persisted on MongoDB. In the following section, we will create our repository classes.

We need to do the same task for our other entities. The User and News need to be configured in the same way as we did for the Category class. The full source code can be found on GitHub at: https://github.com/PacktPublishing/Spring-5.0-By-Example/tree/master/Chapter03/cms-mongo-non-reactive/src/main/java/springfive/cms/domain/models.

Configuring the database connection

Before we create our repositories, we will configure the MongoDB connection. The repository layer abstracts the driver implementation, but is necessary to configure the driver correctly.

On the resources directory, we will change the `application.yaml` file, previously configured for the Spring Data JPA. The Spring Framework supports the configuration through the YAML file. This kind of file is more readable for humans and has a kind of hierarchy. These features are the reason to choose this extension.

The `application.yaml` file should be like the following example:

```
spring:
  data:
    mongodb:
      database: cms
      host: localhost
      port: 27017
```

> The `application.yaml` file for MongoDB can be found on GitHub (https://github.com/PacktPublishing/Spring-5.0-By-Example/blob/master/Chapter03/cms-mongo-non-reactive/src/main/resources/application.yaml).

The file is quite simple for now. There is a `database` tag for configuring the database name. The `host` and `port` tags are about the address that the MongoDB instance is running.

We also can configure the connections programmatically with a couple of objects, but it requires us to code a lot of boilerplate code. Spring Boot offers it out of the box for us. Let's enjoy it.

Excellent, the connection was configured successfully. The infrastructure requirements are solved. Let's go on to implement our repositories.

> Spring Boot Framework supports profiles in `application.properties`or`application.yaml`. This means that if the application was configured in a properties file style, we could use `application-<profile>.properties`. Then, these properties will be applied to the required profile. In YAML style, we can use only one file with multiples profiles.

Adding the repository layer

Once the entities have been mapped, and the connections are done, it's time to create our repositories. The Spring Data Framework provides some interfaces that can be used in different use cases. We will use the specialization for the MongoDB database, which is `MongoRepository`. It extends the `PagingAndSortingRepository` and `QueryByExampleExecutor`. The first is about pagination and sorting features, and the other is about queries by example.

> In some cases, the database query result set can be very large. This can cause some application performance issues because we will fetch a lot of database records. We can limit the number of records fetched from the database and configure limits for that. This technique is called **Pagination**. We can find the full documentation at *Spring Data Commons Documentation* (`https://docs.spring.io/spring-data/commons/docs/current/reference/html/`).

This interface offers a lot of built-in methods for convenience. There are a couple of methods to insert one or more instances, methods for listing all instances of requested entities, methods to remove one or more instances, and many more features, such as ordering and paging.

It enables developers to create repositories without code or even without a deep knowledge of MongoDB. However, some knowledge of MongoDB is necessary to troubleshoot various errors.

We will start by creating the `CategoryRepository`. Change the type of `CategoryRepository` to an interface instead of a class. The code in this interface is not necessary. The Spring container will inject the correct implementation when the application starts.

Let's create our first concrete repository, which means the repository will persist the data on the MongoDB we previously configured. The `CategoryRepository` needs to be like this:

```
package springfive.cms.domain.repository;

import org.springframework.data.mongodb.repository.MongoRepository;
import springfive.cms.domain.models.Category;

public interface CategoryRepository extends
MongoRepository<Category,String> {}
```

The type is an `interface`. Repositories do not have any stereotypes anymore. The Spring container can identify the implementation because it extends the `MongoRepository` interface.

The `MongoRepository` interface should be parameterized. The first argument is the type of model that it represents. In our case, it represents a repository for the `Category` class. The second parameter is about the type of ID of the model. We will use the string type for that.

Now, we need to do the same for the other entities, `User`, and `News`. The code is quite similar to the preceding code. You can find the full source code on GitHub at: `https:/ /github.com/PacktPublishing/Spring-5.0-By-Example/tree/master/Chapter03/ cms-mongo-non-reactive/src/main/java/springfive/cms/domain/repository`.

In the next section, we will check the database to assert that the rows are persisted correctly.

Checking the persistence

Now, we can test the persistence and all layers of the application. We will provide the API documentation for that. Let's open the Swagger documentation and create some records in our CMS application.

Creating sample categories on Swagger:

Fill in the category JSON, as shown in the preceding screenshot, and then click on **Try it out!**. It will invoke the Category API and persist the category on the database. Now, we can check it.

To connect to the MongoDB instance and check the collection, we will use the `mongo-express` tool. It is a web-based tool written in NodeJS to interact with our database instance.

The tool can be installed, but we will run the tool on a Docker container. The Docker tool will help us in this part. Let's start the container:

```
docker run -d --link mongodb:mongo--net cms-application -p 8081:8081
mongo-express
```

It instructs Docker to spin up a container with the `mongo-express` tool and connect to the desired instance. The `--link` argument instructs Docker to create a kind of *hostname* for our MongoDB instance. Remember the name of our instance is `mongodb`; we did it on the run command previously.

Good job. Go to `http://localhost:8081` and we will see this page:

There are a couple of databases. We are interested in the CMS database. Click on the **View** button next to **cms**. Then, the tool will present the collections of the selected database; in our case, the CMS database. The view should be like this:

The category is presented as a collection. We can **View**, **Export**, and export as JSON, but for now, we are interested in checking if our CMS application persisted the data properly. So, click on the **View** button. We will use the MongoDB collection data like this:

As we can see, the data was stored in MongoDB as expected. There are two categories in the database—**sports** and **travel**. There is a `_class` field that helps Spring Data to convert domain classes.

Awesome job, the CMS application is up and running, and also persisting the data in MongoDB. Now, our application is almost production ready, and the data is persisted outside in the amazing document datastore.

In the following section, we will create our Docker image, and then we will run the CMS application with Docker commands. It will be interesting.

Creating the Docker image for CMS

We are doing an awesome job. We created an application with the Spring Boot Framework. The application has been using the Spring REST, Spring Data, and Spring DI.

Now we will go a step forward and create our Docker image. It will be useful to help us to deliver our application for production. There are some advantages, and we can run the application on-premise or on any cloud providers because Docker abstracts the operating system layer. We do not need Java to be installed on the application host, and it also allows us to use different Java versions on the hosts. There are so many advantages involved in adopting Docker for delivery.

We are using Maven as a build tool. Maven has an excellent plugin to helps us to create Docker images. In the following section, we will learn how Maven can help us.

Configuring the docker-maven-plugin

There is an excellent Maven plugin provided by fabric8 (`https://github.com/fabric8io/docker-maven-plugin`). It is licensed under the Apache-2.0 license, which means we can use it without any worries.

We will configure our project to use it, and after image creation, we will push this image on Docker Hub. It is a public Docker registry.

The steps are:

1. Configure the plugin
2. Push the Docker image
3. Configure the Docker Spring profile

Then, it is show time. Let's go.

Adding the plugin on pom.xml

Let's configure the Maven plugin. It is necessary to add a plugin to the plugin section on our `pom.xml` and add some configurations. The plugin should be configured as follows:

```
<plugin>
    <groupId>io.fabric8</groupId>
    <artifactId>docker-maven-plugin</artifactId>
    <version>0.21.0</version>
    <configuration>
        <images>
            <image>
<name>springfivebyexample/${project.build.finalName}</name>
                <build>
                    <from>openjdk:latest</from>
                    <entryPoint>java -Dspring.profiles.active=container -
jar /application/${project.build.finalName}.jar</entryPoint>
                    <assembly>
                        <basedir>/application</basedir>
                        <descriptorRef>artifact</descriptorRef>
                        <inline>
                            <id>assembly</id>
```

```
                        <files>
                            <file>
<source>target/${project.build.finalName}.jar</source>
                            </file>
                        </files>
                    </inline>
                </assembly>
                <tags>
                    <tag>latest</tag>
                </tags>
                <ports>
                    <port>8080</port>
                </ports>
            </build>
            <run>
                <namingStrategy>alias</namingStrategy>
            </run>
            <alias>${project.build.finalName}</alias>
        </image>
    </images>
  </configuration>
</plugin>
```

There are a couple of new configurations here. Let's start with the `<name>` tag—it configures the repository and Docker image name to push to Docker Hub. For this book, we will use `springfivebyexample` as a Docker ID. We can see there is a *slash* as a separator for the repository and image name. The image name for us will be the final project name. Then, we need to configure it.

> The Docker ID is free to use, which can be used to access some Docker services, such as Docker Store, Docker Cloud, and Docker Hub. We can find more information at Docker Page (`https://docs.docker.com/docker-id/`).

This configuration should be the same as shown in the following code snippet:

```
<build>
  <finalName>cms</finalName>
  ....
</build>
```

Another important tag is `<entrypoint>`. This is an exec system call instruction when we use the `docker run` command. In our case, we expected the application to run when the container bootstraps. We will execute `java -jar` passing the container as an active profile for Spring.

We need to pass the full path of the Java artifact. This path will be configured on the <assembly> tag with the <basedir> parameter. It can be any folder name. Also, there is a configuration to the Java artifact path. Usually, this is the target folder which is the result of the compilation. It can be configured in the <source> tag.

Finally, we have the <port> configuration. The port of the application will be exposed using this tag.

Now, we will create a Docker image by using the following instruction:

```
mvn clean install docker:build
```

It should be executed in the root folder of the project. The goal of the docker:build command is to build a Docker image for our project. After the build ends, we can check if the Docker image has been created successfully.

Then, type the following command:

```
docker images
```

The springfivebyexample/cms image should be present, as shown in the following screenshot:

REPOSITORY	TAG	IMAGE ID	CREATED	SIZE
springfivebyexample/cms	latest	94f297e9082f	29 minutes ago	773MB
mongo-express	latest	3fe03c9f9d40	2 weeks ago	246MB
mongo	latest	d22888af0ce0	3 weeks ago	361MB

Good. The image is ready. Let's push to the Docker Hub.

Pushing the image to Docker Hub

The Docker Hub is a public repository to store Docker images. It is free, and we will use it for this book. Now, we will push our image to the Docker Hub registry.

The command for that is pretty simple. Type:

```
docker push springfivebyexample/cms:latest
```

> I have used the springfivebyexample user that I have created. You can test the docker push command creating by your own user on Docker Hub and changing the user on the docker push command. You can create your Docker ID at Docker Hub (https://cloud.docker.com/).

Then, the image will be sent to the registry. That is it.

> We can find the image at Docker Hub (`https://store.docker.com/community/images/springfivebyexample/cms`). If you have used your own user, the link will probably change.

Configuring the Docker Spring profile

Before we run our application in a Docker container, we need to create a YAML file to configure a container profile. The new YAML file should be named as `application-container.yaml` because we will use the container profile to run it. Remember, we configured the `entrypoint` on `pom.xml` in the previous section.

Let's create our new file. The file should be the same content as described in the following snippet:

```
spring:
  data:
    mongodb:
      database: cms
      host: mongodb
      port: 27017
```

The host must be changed for MongoDB. We have been running the MongoDB container with this name in the *Preparing a MongoDB* section. It is an important configuration, and we need to pay attention at this point. We cannot use localhost anymore because the application is running in the Docker container now. The localhost in that context means it is in the same container, and we do not have MongoDB in the CMS application container. We need to have one application per container and avoid multiple responsibilities for one container.

Done. In the following section, we will run our first application in the Docker container. It will be amazing. Let's do it.

Running the Dockerized CMS

In the previous section, we have created our file to configure the container profile properly. Now, it is time to run our container. The command is quite simple, but we need to pay attention to the arguments.

The instruction we run should be the same as the following code:

```
docker run -d --name cms --link mongodb:mongodb --net cms-application
-p 8080:8080 springfivebyexample/cms:latest
```

We have been setting the link for the MongoDB container. Remember, we made this configuration in the YAML file, in the `host` property. During the bootstrapping phase, the application will look for MongoDB instance named `mongodb`. We solved this by using the link command. It will work perfectly.

We can check if our application is healthy by using the `docker ps` command. The output should be like this:

CONTAINER ID	IMAGE	COMMAND	CREATED	STATUS	PORTS	NAMES
4855a23b3ac1	springfivebyexample/cms:latest	"/bin/sh -c 'java ..."	22 minutes ago	Up 22 minutes	0.0.0.0:8080->8080/tcp	cms
e7ff58bc1a4b	mongo-express	"tini -- node app"	19 hours ago	Up 19 hours	0.0.0.0:8081->8081/tcp	friendly_goodall
dd71620d4f76	mongo	"docker-entrypoint..."	20 hours ago	Up 20 hours	0.0.0.0:27017->27017/tcp	mongo

In the first line, we have our application container. It is up and running.

Awesome work. Our application is fully containerized and ready to deploy anywhere we want.

Putting in Reactive fashion

We have been creating an amazing application with Spring Boot. The application was built on the traditional web stack present on Spring Framework. It means the application uses the web servers based on Servlet APIs.

The servlet specification was built with the blocking semantics or one-request-per-thread model. Sometimes, we need to change the application architecture because of non-functional requirements. For example, if the application was bought by a huge company, and that company wanted to create a plan to launch the application for the entire world, the volume of requests would probably increase a lot. So, we need to change the architecture to adapt the application structure for cloud environments.

Usually, in a cloud environment, the machines are smaller than traditional data centers. Instead of a big machine, it is popular to use many small machines and try to scale applications horizontally. In this scenario, the servlet spec can be switched to an architecture created upon Reactive Streams. This kind of architecture fits better than servlet for the cloud environments.

Spring Framework has been creating the Spring WebFlux to helps developers to create Reactive Web Applications. Let's change our application architecture to reactive and learn the pretty new Spring WebFlux component.

Reactive Spring

The Reactive Stream Spec is the specification that provides a standard for asynchronous programming for stream processing. It is becoming popular in the programming world nowadays, and Spring introduces it on the framework.

This style of programming is more efficient regarding resources usage and fits amazingly with the new generation of machines with multiple cores.

Spring reactive uses the Project Reactor as the implementation for the Reactive Streams. The Project Reactor is powered by Pivotal and has the very good implementation of the Reactive Streams Spec.

Now, we will deep dive in the reactive module for Spring Boot and create an amazing reactive API and try the new style of the Spring Framework.

Project Reactor

The Project Reactor was created by the Spring and Pivotal teams. This project is an implementation of Reactive Streams for JVM. It is a fully non-blocking foundation and helps developers to create a non-blocking application in the JVM ecosystem.

There is a restriction to using Reactor in our application. The project runs on Java 8 and above. It is important because we will use many lambda expressions in our examples and projects.

The Spring Framework internally uses the Project Reactor as an implementation of Reactive Streams.

Components

Let's look at the different components of the Project Reactor:

- **Publishers**: The publishers are responsible for pushing data elements to the stream. It notifies the subscribers that a new piece of data is coming to the stream.

- The publisher interface is defined in the following code snippet:

```
/*****************************************************************
***********
 * Licensed under Public Domain (CC0)
 *
  *
 *
 * To the extent possible under law, the person who associated
CC0 with   *
 * this code has waived all copyright and related or
neighboring         *
 * rights to this code.
 *
  *
 *
 * You should have received a copy of the CC0 legalcode along
with this  *
 * work. If not, see
<http://creativecommons.org/publicdomain/zero/1.0/>.*
 *****************************************************************
**********/

package org.reactivestreams;

/**
 * A {@link Publisher} is a provider of a potentially
unbounded number of sequenced elements, publishing them
according to
 * the demand received from its {@link Subscriber}(s).
 * <p>
 * A {@link Publisher} can serve multiple {@link Subscriber}s
subscribed {@link #subscribe(Subscriber)} dynamically
 * at various points in time.
 *
 * @param <T> the type of element signaled.
 */
public interface Publisher<T> {

    public void subscribe(Subscriber<? super T> s);

}
```

- **Subscribers**: The subscribers are responsible for making the data flow in the stream. When the publisher starts to send the piece of data on the data flow, the piece of data will be collected by the `onNext(T instance)` method, which is the parametrized interface.

The subscriber interface is defined in the following code snippet:

```
/****************************************************************
***********
 * Licensed under Public Domain (CC0)
 *
  *
 *
 * To the extent possible under law, the person who associated
CC0 with   *
 * this code has waived all copyright and related or
neighboring        *
 * rights to this code.
 *
  *
 *
 * You should have received a copy of the CC0 legalcode along
with this   *
 * work. If not, see
<http://creativecommons.org/publicdomain/zero/1.0/>.*
 ****************************************************************
**********/

package org.reactivestreams;

/**
 * Will receive call to {@link #onSubscribe(Subscription)}
once after passing an instance of {@link Subscriber} to {@link
Publisher#subscribe(Subscriber)}.
 * <p>
 * No further notifications will be received until {@link
Subscription#request(long)} is called.
 * <p>
 * After signaling demand:
 * <ul>
 * <li>One or more invocations of {@link #onNext(Object)} up
to the maximum number defined by {@link
Subscription#request(long)}</li>
 * <li>Single invocation of {@link #onError(Throwable)} or
{@link Subscriber#onComplete()} which signals a terminal state
after which no further events will be sent.
 * </ul>
 * <p>
```

```
     * Demand can be signaled via {@link
   Subscription#request(long)} whenever the {@link Subscriber}
   instance is capable of handling more.
     *
     * @param <T> the type of element signaled.
     */
   public interface Subscriber<T> {
       public void onSubscribe(Subscription s);

       public void onNext(T t);

       public void onComplete();
   }
```

Hot and cold

There are two categories of reactive sequences—hot and cold. These functions affect the usage of the implementation directly. Hence, we need to understand them:

- **Cold**: The cold publishers start to generate data only if it receives a new subscription. If there are no subscriptions, the data never comes to the flow.
- **Hot**: The hot publishers do not need any subscribers to generate the data flow. When the new subscriber is registered, the subscriber will only get the new data elements emitted.

Reactive types

There are two reactive types which represent the reactive sequences. The Mono objects represent a single value or empty 0|1. The Flux objects represent a sequence of 0|N items.

We will find many references in our code. The Spring Data reactive repository uses these abstractions in their methods. The findOne() method returns the Mono<T> object and the findAll() returns a Flux<T>. The same behavior we will be found in our REST resources.

Let's play with the Reactor

To understand it better, let's play with the Reactor. We will implement and understand the difference between hot and cold publishers in practice.

Cold publishers do not produce any data until a new subscription arrives. In the following code, we will create a cold publisher and the `System.out:println` will never be executed because it does not have any subscribers. Let's test the behavior:

```
@Test
public void coldBehavior(){
    Category sports = new Category();
    sports.setName("sports");
    Category music = new Category();
    sports.setName("music");
    Flux.just(sports,music)
        .doOnNext(System.out::println);
}
```

As we can see, the method `subscribe()` is not present in this snippet. When we execute the code, we will not see any data on the standard print output.

We can execute the method on the IDE. We will able to see the output of this test. The output should be like this:

The process has finished, the test passed, and we will not be able to see the print. That is the cold publisher's behavior.

Now, we will subscribe the publisher and the data will be sent on the data flow. Let's try this.

We will insert the subscribe instruction after `doOnNext()`. Let's change our code:

```
@Test
 public void coldBehaviorWithSubscribe(){
    Category sports = new Category();
    sports.setId(UUID.randomUUID().toString());
    sports.setName("sports");
    Category music = new Category();
    music.setId(UUID.randomUUID().toString());
    music.setName("music");
    Flux.just(sports,music)
        .doOnNext(System.out::println)
        .subscribe();
 }
```

The output should be like this:

```
objc[4922]: Class JavaLaunchHelper is implemented in both /Library/Java/JavaVirtualMachines/jdk1.8
22:45:42.537 [main] DEBUG reactor.util.Loggers$LoggerFactory - Using Slf4j logging framework
Category(id=ce49b83b-2aee-47dd-8f68-e601eb1454da, name=sports)
Category(id=8fb25e99-a25b-4542-94be-ab35a1854104, name=music)

Process finished with exit code 0
```

In the preceding screenshot, we can see that the publisher pushes the data on the stream after the stream got subscribed. That is the cold publisher behavior after the subscription.

Hot publishers do not depend on any subscribers. The hot publisher will publish data, even if there is no subscriber to receive the data. Let's see an example:

```
@Test
public void testHotPublisher(){
   UnicastProcessor<String> hotSource = UnicastProcessor.create();
   Flux<Category> hotPublisher = hotSource.publish()
       .autoConnect().map((String t) ->
Category.builder().name(t).build());
   hotPublisher.subscribe(category -> System.out.println("Subscriber 1:
"+ category.getName()));
   hotSource.onNext("sports");
   hotSource.onNext("cars");
   hotPublisher.subscribe(category -> System.out.println("Subscriber 2:
"+category.getName()));
   hotSource.onNext("games");
   hotSource.onNext("electronics");
   hotSource.onComplete();
}
```

Let's understand what happens here. The `UnicastProcessor` is a processor that allows only one `Subscriber`.The processor replays notifications when the subscriber requests. It will emit some data on a stream. The first subscription will capture all the categories, as we will see, because it was registered before the event emissions. The second subscription will capture only the last events because it was registered before the last two emissions.

The output of the preceding code should be:

Awesome. This is the hot publisher's behavior.

Spring WebFlux

The traditional Java enterprise web applications are based on the servlet specification. The servlet specification before 3.1 is synchronous, which means it was created with blocking semantics. This model was good at the time because computers were big with a powerful CPU and hundreds of gigabytes of memory. Usually, the applications at the time were configured with a big thread pool with hundreds of threads because the computer was designed for this. The primary deployment model at that time was the replica. There are some machines with the same configuration and application deployments.

The developers have been creating applications like this for many years.

Nowadays, most of the applications are deployed in cloud vendors. There are no big machines anymore because the price is much higher. Instead of big machines, there are a number of small machines. It is much cheaper and these machines have a reasonable CPU power and memory.

In this new scenario, the application with the huge thread pools is not effective anymore, because the machine is small and it does not have the power to handle all these threads.

The Spring Team added the support for the Reactive Streams in the framework. This model of programming changes the application deployment and the way to build applications.

Instead of a thread-per-request model, the applications are created with the event-loop model. This model requires a small number of threads and is more efficient regarding resource usage.

Event-loop model

Popularized by the NodeJS language, this model is based on event-driven programming. There are two central concepts: the events which will be enqueued on a queue, and the handlers which keep track of and process these events.

There are some advantages of adopting this model. The first one is the ordering. The events are enqueued and dispatched in the same order in which the events are coming. In some uses cases, this is an important requirement.

The other one is the synchronization. The event-loop must be executed on only one thread. This makes the states easy to handle and avoids the shared state problems.

There is an important piece of advice here. The handlers must not be synchronous. Otherwise, the application will be blocked until the handlers end their workload.

Spring Data for Reactive Extensions

The Spring Data projects have some extensions to work with a reactive foundation. The project provides a couple of implementations based on asynchronous programming. It means the whole stack is asynchronous since database drivers are as well.

The Spring reactive repository supports Cassandra, MongoDB, and Redis as database stores. The repository implementations offer the same behaviors as the non-reactive implementation. There is a **DSL** (**Domain-Specific Language**) to create domain-specific query methods.

The module uses the Project Reactor as a reactive foundation implementation, but is possible to change the implementation to RxJava as well. Both libraries are production-ready and are adopted by the community. One point to be aware of is that if we change to RxJava, we need to ensure our method returns to `Observable` and `Single`.

Spring Data Reactive

The Spring Data Project has support for the reactive data access. Until now, Spring has support for MongoDB, Apache Cassandra, and Redis, all of which have reactive drivers.

In our CMS application, we will use the MongoDB reactive drivers to give the reactive characteristics for our repositories. We will use the new reactive interface provided by the Spring Data reactive. Also, we need to change the code a little bit. In this chapter, we will do that step by step. Let's start.

Reactive repositories in practice

Before we start, we can check out the full source code at GitHub, or we can perform the following steps.

Now, we are ready to build our new reactive repositories. The first thing that we need to do is add the Maven dependencies to our project. This can be done using pom.xml.

Let's configure our new dependency:

```
<dependency>
  <groupId>org.springframework.boot</groupId>
  <artifactId>spring-boot-starter-data-mongodb-reactive</artifactId>
</dependency>
```

Our project is ready to use reactive MongoDB repositories.

Creating the first Reactive repository

We have a couple of repositories in our CMS project. Now, we need to convert these repositories to reactive ones. The first thing we will do is remove the extension from CrudRepository, which is not necessary anymore. Now, we want the reactive version of that.

We will update the ReactiveMongoRepository interface. The parameters of the interface are the same as the ones we inserted before. The interface should be like this:

```
package springfive.cms.domain.repository;

import
org.springframework.data.mongodb.repository.ReactiveMongoRepository;
import springfive.cms.domain.models.Category;

public interface CategoryRepository extends
ReactiveMongoRepository<Category,String> {
}
```

This is quite similar to the one we created before. We need to extend the new `ReactiveMongoRepository` interface, which contains methods for the CRUD operations and much more. The interface returns `Mono<Category>` or `Flux<Category>`. The methods do not return the entities anymore. It is a common way of programming when the Reactive Stream is adopted.

We need to change the other repositories as well. You can find the full source code on GitHub at: `https://github.com/PacktPublishing/Spring-5.0-By-Example/tree/master/Chapter03/cms-mongodb/src/main/java/springfive/cms/domain/repository`.

Now, we need to change the service layer. Let's do that.

Fixing the service layer

We need to change the service layer to adopt the new reactive programming style. We changed the repository layer, so now we need to fix the compilation problem result because of this change. The application needs to be reactive. Any point of the application can be blocked because we are using the event-loop model. If we do not do this, the application will be getting blocked.

Changing the CategoryService

Now, we will fix the `CategoryService` class. We will change the return type of a couple of methods. Before, we could return the model class, but now we need to change to return `Mono` or `Flux`, similar to what we did in the repository layer.

The new `CategoryService` should be like the implementation shown in the following code snippet:

```
package springfive.cms.domain.service;

import org.springframework.stereotype.Service;
import reactor.core.publisher.Flux;
import reactor.core.publisher.Mono;
import springfive.cms.domain.models.Category;
import springfive.cms.domain.repository.CategoryRepository;
import springfive.cms.domain.vo.CategoryRequest;

@Service
public class CategoryService {
```

```
    private final CategoryRepository categoryRepository;

    public CategoryService(CategoryRepository categoryRepository) {
      this.categoryRepository = categoryRepository;
    }

    public Mono<Category> update(String id,CategoryRequest category){
      return
this.categoryRepository.findById(id).flatMap(categoryDatabase -> {
        categoryDatabase.setName(category.getName());
        return this.categoryRepository.save(categoryDatabase);
      });
    }

    public Mono<Category> create(CategoryRequest request){
      Category category = new Category();
      category.setName(request.getName());
      return this.categoryRepository.save(category);
    }

    public void delete(String id){
      this.categoryRepository.deleteById(id);
    }

    public Flux<Category> findAll(){
      return this.categoryRepository.findAll();
    }

    public Mono<Category> findOne(String id){
      return this.categoryRepository.findById(id);
    }

}
```

As we can see, the return types changed in the methods.

The important thing here is that we need to follow the reactive principles. When the method returns only one instance, we need to use `Mono<Category>`. When the method returns one or more instances, we should use `Flux<Category>`. This is essential to follow because developers and Spring containers can then interpret the code correctly.

The `update()` method has an interesting call: `flatMap()`. The project reactor allows us to use a kind of DSL to compose calls. It is very interesting and very useful as well. It helps developers to create code that is easier to understand than before. The `flatMap()` method is usually used to convert the data emitted by `Mono` or `Flux`. In this context, we need to set the new name of the category on the category retrieved from the database.

Changing the REST layer

We will make some fixes on the REST layer as well. We changed the service layer, and it caused some compilation problems in our resources classes.

We need to add the new dependency, `spring-web-reactive`. This supports the `@Controller` or `@RestController` annotations for the reactive non-blocking engine. The Spring MVC does not support the reactive extensions, and this module enables developers to use reactive paradigms, as they did before.

`spring-web-reactive` will change many contracts on the Spring MVC foundations, such as `HandlerMapping`, and `HandlerAdapter`, to enable reactive foundations on these components.

The following image can help us to better understand the Spring HTTP layers:

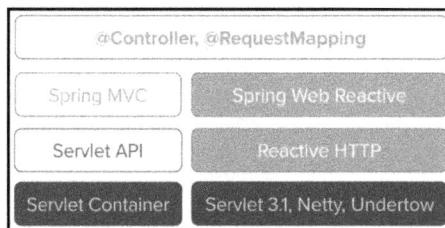

As we can see, `@Controller` and `@RequestMapping` can be used for different approaches in the Spring MVC traditional applications, or by using the Spring web reactive module.

Before we start to change our REST layer, we need to remove the Spring Fox dependencies and annotations in our project. At present, the Spring Fox has no support for reactive applications yet.

The dependencies to remove are:

```
<dependency>
  <groupId>io.springfox</groupId>
  <artifactId>springfox-swagger2</artifactId>
  <version>2.7.0</version>
</dependency>

<dependency>
  <groupId>io.springfox</groupId>
  <artifactId>springfox-swagger-ui</artifactId>
  <version>2.7.0</version>
</dependency>
```

After that, we need to remove the annotations from the Swagger packages, such as `@Api` and `@ApiOperation`.

Now, let's adjust our REST layer.

Adding the Spring WebFlux dependency

Before we start to change our REST layer, we need to add the new dependency to our `pom.xml`.

First, we will remove the Spring MVC traditional dependencies. To do this, we need to remove the following dependency:

```
<dependency>
  <groupId>org.springframework.boot</groupId>
  <artifactId>spring-boot-starter-web</artifactId>
</dependency>
```

We do not need this dependency anymore. Our application will be reactive now. Then, we need to add the new dependencies described in the following code snippet:

```
<dependency>
  <groupId>io.netty</groupId>
  <artifactId>netty-transport-native-epoll</artifactId>
</dependency>

<dependency>
  <groupId>org.springframework.boot</groupId>
  <artifactId>spring-boot-starter-webflux</artifactId>
</dependency>
```

`spring-boot-starter-webflux` is a kind of syntax sugar for dependencies. It has the `spring-boot-starter-reactor-netty` dependency, which is the Reactor Netty, as embedded in the reactive HTTP server.

Awesome, our project is ready to convert the REST layer. Let's transform our application into a fully reactive application.

Changing the CategoryResource

We will change the `CategoryResource` class. The idea is pretty simple. We will convert our `ResponseEntity`, which is parametrized with the models class to `ResponseEntity` using `Mono` or `Flux`.

The new version of the `CategoryResource` should be like this:

```
package springfive.cms.domain.resources;

import org.springframework.http.HttpStatus;
import org.springframework.http.ResponseEntity;
import org.springframework.web.bind.annotation.DeleteMapping;
import org.springframework.web.bind.annotation.GetMapping;
import org.springframework.web.bind.annotation.PathVariable;
import org.springframework.web.bind.annotation.PostMapping;
import org.springframework.web.bind.annotation.PutMapping;
import org.springframework.web.bind.annotation.RequestBody;
import org.springframework.web.bind.annotation.RequestMapping;
import org.springframework.web.bind.annotation.ResponseStatus;
import org.springframework.web.bind.annotation.RestController;
import reactor.core.publisher.Flux;
import reactor.core.publisher.Mono;
import springfive.cms.domain.models.Category;
import springfive.cms.domain.service.CategoryService;
import springfive.cms.domain.vo.CategoryRequest;

@RestController
@RequestMapping("/api/category")
public class CategoryResource {

  private final CategoryService categoryService;

  public CategoryResource(CategoryService categoryService) {
    this.categoryService = categoryService;
  }

  @GetMapping(value = "/{id}")
  public ResponseEntity<Mono<Category>> findOne(@PathVariable("id")
```

```
String id){
    return ResponseEntity.ok(this.categoryService.findOne(id));
  }

  @GetMapping
  public ResponseEntity<Flux<Category>> findAll(){
    return ResponseEntity.ok(this.categoryService.findAll());
  }

  @PostMapping
  public ResponseEntity<Mono<Category>> newCategory(@RequestBody
CategoryRequest category){
    return new ResponseEntity<>(this.categoryService.create(category),
HttpStatus.CREATED);
  }

  @DeleteMapping("/{id}")
  @ResponseStatus(HttpStatus.NO_CONTENT)
  public void removeCategory(@PathVariable("id") String id){
    this.categoryService.delete(id);
  }

  @PutMapping("/{id}")
  public ResponseEntity<Mono<Category>>
updateCategory(@PathVariable("id") String id,CategoryRequest
category){
    return new
ResponseEntity<>(this.categoryService.update(id,category),
HttpStatus.OK);
  }


}
```

The code is quite similar to what we did before. We have used the `@RequestBody` annotation in the method argument; otherwise, the JSON converter will not work.

The other important characteristic here is the `return` method. It returns `Mono` or `Flux`, which are parameterized types for `ResponseEntity`.

We can test the reactive implementation by using the command line. It will persist the `Category` object on MongoDB. Type the following command on the Terminal:

```
curl -H "Content-Type: application/json" -X POST -d
'{"name":"reactive"}' http://localhost:8080/api/category
```

And then, we can use the following command to check the database. Using the browser, go to `http://localhost:8080/api/category`. The following result should be presented:

```
←    C    ⓘ localhost:8080/api/category

[
    {
        "id": "5a86084b6e34490ec986468e",
        "name": "reactive"
    }
]
```

Awesome, our reactive implementation is working as expected. Well done!!!

Summary

In this chapter, we have learned a lot of Spring concepts. We have introduced you to Spring Data projects, which help developers to create data access layers as we have never seen before. We saw how easy it is to create repositories with this project.

Also, we presented some relatively new projects, such as Spring WebFlux, which permits developers to create modern web applications, applying the Reactive Streams foundations and reactive programming style in projects.

We have finished our CMS application. The application has the characteristics of a production-ready application, such as database connections, and services which have been well-designed with single responsibilities. Also, we introduced the `docker-maven-plugin`, which provides a reasonable way to create images using the `pom.xml` configurations.

In the next chapter, we will create a new application using the *Reactive Manifesto* based on message-driven applications. See you there.

4
Kotlin Basics and Spring Data Redis

Spring Boot allows developers to create different styles of application. In `Chapter 2`, *Starting in the Spring World – the CMS Application*, and `Chapter 3`, *Persistence with Spring Data and Reactive Fashion*, we have created a portal application, and now we will create an application based on message-driven architecture. It demonstrates how the Spring Framework fits well in a wide range of application architectures.

In this chapter, we will start to create an application which keeps the tracked hashtags on the Redis database. The application will get hashtags and put them in a couple of queues to our other projects, and consume and handle them appropriately.

As we have been doing in our previous projects, we will continue to use the Reactive Foundation to provide scalable characteristics in the application.

At the end of this chapter, we will have:

- Learned Kotlin basics
- Created the project structure
- Created the Reactive Redis repositories
- Applied some techniques in reactive programming, using the Reactive Redis Client

Let's start right now.

Learning Kotlin basics

The Kotlin language was released officially in February 2016. JetBrains created it and has been developing the language ever since. The company is the owner of the IntelliJ IDEA IDE.

In February 2012, JetBrains made the language open source under the Apache v2 license; the license allows developers to create applications.

The language is one option for **JVM** (**Java Virtual Machine**) languages such as Clojure and Scala, which means that the language can compile bytecode for JVM. As we will see, Kotlin has many similarities with Scala. Kotlin has the Scala language as a reference, but the JetBrains teams believe that Scala has problems with the compilation time.

Kotlin was becoming an adopted language in the Android world and because of this, in the Google I/O, 2017, the Google Team announced official support for the Android ecosystem. Since then, the language has been growing year by year and increasing in popularity.

Main characteristics of Kotlin

The Kotlin language was designed to maintain the interoperability with Java code. It means we can start to code with Java idioms in the Kotlin file.

The language is statically-typed, and it is an excellent attribute because it can help us find some problems at compilation time. Also, statically-typed languages are much faster than dynamic languages. The IDEs can help developers much better than dynamic languages, as well.

Syntax

The syntax is different from Java syntax. At first glance, it can be a problem but after some hours of playing with Kotlin, it is not a problem at all.

There are two interesting reserved words to understand the usage and concepts:

- `var`: This is a variable declaration. It indicates the variable is mutable and can be reassigned, as developers need.

- `val`: This is a variable declaration which indicates the variable is immutable and cannot be reassigned anymore. This definition is like a final declaration in the Java language.

The variable declarations have a name, and after the desired data type, the colon is necessary in the middle as a separator. If the variable is initialized, the type is not necessary because the compiler can infer the correct data type. Let's try it out to understand it better.

Here is a variable with the data type specified:

```
var bookName: String
```

In this case, we need to keep the data type because the variable is not initialized, then the compiler cannot infer the type. The variable, `bookName`, can be reassigned because of the modifier `var`.

Here is a variable without the data type:

```
val book = "Spring 5.0 by Example"
```

It is not a necessity to declare the data type because we have initialized the variable with the value, `Spring 5.0 by Example`. The compiler can infer the type is a kind of *syntactic sugar*. The variable cannot be reassigned because of the modifier `val`. If we try to reassign the instruction, we will get a compilation error.

The semicolons are optional in Kotlin, the compiler can detect the statement terminator. This is another point where Kotlin diverges from the Java programming language:

```
val book = "Spring 5.0 by Example"
var bookName: String
println("Hello, world!")
```

The semicolons were not provided, and the instructions were compiled.

> Immutable programming in the Kotlin language is recommended. It performs better on the multi-core environments. Also, it makes the developer's life easier to debug and troubleshoot scenarios.

Semantics

In Kotlin, there are classes and functions. However, there is no method anymore. The `fun` keyword should be used to declare a function.

Kotlin gets some concepts of the Scala language and brings some special classes such as Data classes and Object classes (which we will learn soon). Before that, we will understand how to declare a function in Kotlin. Let's do that!

Declaring functions in Kotlin

There are many variations in function declarations. We will create some declarations to understand the slight difference from Java methods.

Simple function with parameters and return type

This simple function has two parameters and a String as a return type. Take a look at a parameter declaration and observe the order, name and data type.

```
fun greetings(name:String,greeting:String):String{
   return greeting + name
}
```

As we can see, the type of argument which comes after the variable name is the same as on the variable declarations. The return type comes after the arguments list is separated with semicolons. The same function can be declared in the following way in Java:

```
public String greetings(String name,String greeting){
   return greeting + name;
}
```

There are some differences here. Firstly, there are semicolons in the Java code, and we can see the order of the methods and functions declarations.

Simple function without return

Let's understand how we can construct functions without a return value, the following function will not return any value:

```
fun printGreetings(name:String,greeting:String):Unit{
   println(greeting + name)
}
```

There is one difference, in this case, the `Unit` was introduced; this type of object corresponds to `void` in Java language. Then, in the preceding code, we have a function without a return. The `Unit` object can be removed if you want the compiler to understand the function has no return value.

Single expressions functions

When the function has a single expression we can remove the curly braces, the same as in Scala, and the function body should be specified after the = symbol. Let's refactor our first function, as follows:

```
fun greetings(name:String,greeting:String) = greeting + name
```

We can remove the `return` keyword, as well. Our function is pretty concise now. We removed `return` and the type of return as well. As we can see, the code is more readable now. If you want, the return type can be declared too.

Overriding a function

To override a function on Kotlin, it is necessary to put an `override` keyword on the function declaration, and the base function needs to have the `open` keyword as well.

Let's look at an example:

```
open class Greetings {
  open fun greeting() {}
}

class SuperGreeting() : Greetings() {
  override fun greeting() {
  // my super greeting
  }
}
```

This way is more explicit than Java, it increases the legibility of the code as well.

Data classes

Data classes are the right solution when we want to hold and transfer data between system layers. Like in Scala, these classes offer some built-in functionalities such as `getters`/`setters`, `equals` and `hashCode`, `toString` method and the `copy` function.

Let's create an example for that:

```
data class Book(val author:String,val name:String,val
description:String,val new:Boolean = false)
```

We have some interesting things in the code. The first thing we notice is that all of the attributes are immutable. It means there are no setters for all of them. The second is that in the class declaration, we can see a list of attributes. In this case, Kotlin will create a constructor with all attributes present in this class and because they are `val` it means final attributes.

In this case, there is no default constructor anymore.

Another interesting feature in Kotlin is that it enables developers to have default values on constructors, in our case the `new` attribute, if omitted, will assume the `false` value. We can get the same behavior in the parameters list in functions as well.

Finally, there is a fantastic way to copy objects. The `copy` method allows developers to copy objects with named parameters. This means we can change only attributes as we need. Let's take a look at an example:

```
fun main(args : Array<String>) {
   val springFiveOld = Book("Claudio E. de Oliveira","Spring 5.0 by
Example","Amazing example of Spring Boot Apps",false)
   val springFiveNew = springFiveOld.copy(new = true)
   println(springFiveOld)
   println(springFiveNew)
}
```

In the first object, we have created a book instance with `false` for the `new` attribute, then we copied a new object with `true` for the `new` attribute, and the other attributes are not changed. Goodbye to the complex clone logic and nice to meet the new way to copy objects.

The output of this code should look like the following:

```
Book(author=Claudio E. de Oliveira, name=Spring 5.0 by Example, description=Amazing example of Spring Boot Apps, new=false)
Book(author=Claudio E. de Oliveira, name=Spring 5.0 by Example, description=Amazing example of Spring Boot Apps, new=true)

Process finished with exit code 0
```

As we can see, only the `new` attribute is changed and the `toString` function was generated in good shape as well.

There are some restrictions on Data classes. They cannot be abstract, open, sealed, or inner.

Objects

The singleton pattern is commonly used in applications, and Kotlin provides an easy way to do that without much boilerplate code.

We can instruct Kotlin to create a singleton object using the `object` keyword. Once again, Kotlin used Scala as a reference because there are the same functionalities in the Scala language.

Let's try it:

```
object BookNameFormatter{
   fun format(book: Book):String = "The book name is" + book.name
}
```

We have created a formatter to return a message with the book name. Then, we try to use this function:

```
val springFiveOld = Book("Claudio E. de Oliveira","Spring 5.0 by
Example","Amazing example of Spring Boot Apps",false)
BookNameFormatter.format(springFiveOld)
```

The function format can be called in a static context. There is no instance to call the function because it is a singleton object.

Companion objects

A **companion object** is an object which is common for all instances of that class. It means there are many instances of a book, for example, but there is a single instance of their companion object. Usually, the developers use companion objects as a factory method. Let's create our first `companion object`:

```
data class Book(val author:String,val name:String,val
description:String,val new:Boolean = false{

   companion object {
      fun create(name:String,description: String,author: String):Book{
         return Book(author,name,description)
      }
   }

}
```

If the name of the `companion object` was omitted, the function could be called in a singleton way, without an instance, like this:

```
val myBookWithFactory = Book.create("Claudio E. de Oliveira","Spring
5.0 by Example","Amazing example of Spring Boot Apps")
```

It is like an `object` behavior. We can call it in a static context.

Kotlin idioms

Koltin idioms are a kind of syntax sugar for Java programmers. It is a collection of pieces of code which help developers to create a concise code in Kotlin languages. Let's take a look at common Kotlin idioms.

String interpolation

Kotlin supports string interpolation, it is a little bit complex to do it in the Java language but it is not a problem for Kotlin. We do not require a lot of code to do this task as Kotlin supports it natively. It makes the code easier to read and understand. Let's create an example:

```
val bookName = "Spring 5.0"
val phrase = "The name of the book is $bookName"
```

As we can see, it is a piece of cake to interpolate strings in Kotlin. Goodbye `String.format()` with a lot of arguments. We can use `$bookName` to replace the `bookName` variable value. Also, we can access the functions present in objects, but for that, we need to put curly braces. Check the following code:

```
val springFiveOld = Book("Claudio E. de Oliveira","Spring 5.0 by
Example","Amazing example of Spring Boot Apps",false)
val phrase = "The name of the book is ${springFiveOld.name}"
```

Thanks, Kotlin we appreciate this feature.

Smart Casts

Kotlin supports the feature called Smart Casts which enables developers to use the cast operators automatically. After checking the variable type, in Java, the cast operator must be explicit. Let's check it out:

```
fun returnValue(instance: Any): String {
```

```
    if (instance is String) {
      return instance
    }
    throw IllegalArgumentException("Instance is not String")
}
```

As we can see, the cast operator is not present anymore. After checking the type, Kotlin can infer the expected type. Let's check the Java version for the same piece of code:

```
public String returnValue(Object instance) {
    if (instance instanceof String) {
      String value = (String) instance;
        return value;
      }
      throw IllegalArgumentException("Instance is not String");
}
```

It makes the cast safer because we do not need to check and apply the cast operator.

Range expressions

Range expressions permit developers to work with ranges in `for` loops and `if` comparison. There are a lot of ways to work with ranges in Kotlin. We will take a look at most of the common ones here.

Simple case

Let's look at one simple case:

```
for ( i in 1..5){
    println(i)
}
```

It will iterate from 1 to 5 inclusive because we have used them in the `in` keyword.

The until case

We also can use the `until` keyword in `for` loops, in this case, the end element will be excluded from the interaction. Let's see an example:

```
for (i in 1 until 5) {
    println(i)
}
```

In this case, the 5 value will not be printed on the console, because the end element is not included in the interaction.

The downTo case

The downTo keyword enables developers to interact with the numbers in reverse order. The instruction is self-explanatory, as well. Let's see it in practice:

```
for (i in 5 downTo 1) {
    println(i)
}
```

It is pretty easy as well. The interaction will occur in the reverse order, in this case, the value 1 will be included. As we can see, the code is pretty easy to understand.

Step case

Sometimes we need to interact over values but with the arbitrary steps, not one by one, for example. Then we can use the step instruction. Let's practice:

```
for (i in 1..6 step 2) {
    print(i)
}
```

Here, we will see the following output: 135, because the interaction will start on the 1 value and will be increased by two points.

Awesome. The Kotlin ranges can add more readability to our source code and help to increase the quality of code as well.

Null safety

Kotlin has amazing stuff to work with null references. The null reference is a nightmare for Java developers. The Java 8 has an Optional object, which helps developers work with nullable objects, but is not concise like in Kotlin.

Now, we will explore how Kotlin can help developers to avoid the NullPointerException. Let's understand.

The Kotlin type system makes a distinction between references which can hold null and those which cannot hold null. Due to this, the code is more concise and readable because it is a kind of advice for developers.

When the reference does not allow null, the declaration should be:

```
var myNonNullString:String = "my non null string"
```

The preceding variable cannot be assigned to a null reference, if we do this, we will get a compilation error. Look how easy the code is to understand.

Sometimes, we need to allow for a variable to have null references, in these cases, we can use the ? as an operator, such as follows:

```
var allowNull:String? = "permits null references"
```

Easy. Pay attention to a variable declaration on the ? operator, it makes the variable accept null references.

There are two different ways to avoid the `NullPointerReference` in Kotlin. The first one can be called **safe calls**, and the other can be called the **Elvis Operator**. Let's take a look at those.

Safe calls

The safe call can be written using the . ?. It can be called when the reference holds a non-null value when the value holds a null reference then the null value will be returned:

```
val hash:TrackedHashTag? = TrackedHashTag(hashTag="java",queue="java")
val queueString = hash?.queue
```

When the `hash?` holds null, the null value will be assigned to a `queueString` attribute. If the `hash?` has a valid reference, the queue attribute will be assigned to a `queueString` attribute.

Elvis operator

It can be used when developers expect to return a default value when the reference is null:

```
val hash:TrackedHashTag? = TrackedHashTag(hashTag="java",queue="java")
val queueString = hash?.queue ?: "unrecognized-queue"
```

When the value holds null, the default value will be returned.

Time to use Kotlin in the real world. Let's begin.

Wrapping it up

Now, we can use the basics of the Kotlin language. We saw some examples and practiced a little bit.

We looked at the main concepts of Kotlin. We have learned how data classes can help developers to transfer data between application layers. Also, we learned about singleton and companion objects. Now we can try to create a real project with the pretty new support from Spring Framework.

In the next sections, we will create a project using the Kotlin language, for now, we can forget about the Java language.

Creating the project

Now, we have a good idea about how we can use programming in Kotlin language. In this section, we will create the basic structure for our new project in which the main feature is consuming the Twitter stream. Let's do that.

Project use case

Before we start to code, we need to track the application requirements. The application is message-driven, we will use a broker to provide the messaging infrastructure. We choose the RabbitMQ broker because it provides reliability, high availability, and clustering options. Also, the RabbitMQ is a popular choice for the modern message-driven applications.

The software is powered by the Pivotal company, the same company which maintains Spring Framework. There is a huge community which supports the project.

We will have three projects. These three projects will collect the Twitter stream and send it to a recipient to show Tweets in a formatted way to the end user.

The first one, which will be created in this chapter, will be responsible for keeping the tracked hashtags on the Redis cache.

When the new hashtags are registered, it will send a message to the second project which will start to consume the Twitter stream and redirect it to the desired queue. This queue will be consumed by the other project which will format the Tweet, and finally, show them to the end user.

We will have three microservices. Let's create these things.

Creating the project with Spring Initializr

We have learned how to use the Spring Initializr page. We will go to the page and then select the following modules:

- `Reactive Web`

- `Reactive Redis`

The page content should look like this:

We can choose the group and artifact. There is no problem with using the different name. Then, we can click on **Generate Project** and wait until the download ends.

Adding Jackson for Kotlin

We need to add Jackson for Kotlin dependencies for Maven projects. In fact, we need a Kotlin standard library on our `pom.xml`. Also, we need to put `jackson-module-kotlin`, it allows us to work with JSON on Kotlin, there are some differences from Java in these parts.

This part is pretty simple, and we will add these following dependencies in the dependencies sections in `pom.xml`. The dependencies are as follows:

```xml
<dependency>
 <groupId>com.fasterxml.jackson.module</groupId>
 <artifactId>jackson-module-kotlin</artifactId>
 <version>${jackson.version}</version>
</dependency>
```

Now, we have the dependencies configured, and we can set the plugins to compile the Kotlin source code. In the next section, we will do that.

Looking for the Maven plugins for Kotlin

The project was created with Kotlin configured successfully. Now, we will take a look at the Maven plugin in our `pom.xml`. The configuration is necessary to instruct Maven on how to compile the Kotlin source code and add in the artifacts.

We will add the following plugins in the plugins section:

```xml
<plugin>
  <artifactId>kotlin-maven-plugin</artifactId>
  <groupId>org.jetbrains.kotlin</groupId>
  <version>${kotlin.version}</version>
  <configuration>
    <jvmTarget>1.8</jvmTarget>
  </configuration>
  <executions>
    <execution>
      <id>compile</id>
      <phase>process-sources</phase>
      <goals>
        <goal>compile</goal>
      </goals>
    </execution>
    <execution>
      <id>test-compile</id>
```

```
            <phase>process-test-sources</phase>
            <goals>
              <goal>test-compile</goal>
            </goals>
          </execution>
        </executions>
      </plugin>
```

There is one more thing to do. Take a look how Maven configures the path for our Kotlin code. It is easy peasy. Look at the following:

```
<build>

<sourceDirectory>${project.basedir}/src/main/kotlin<
/sourceDirectory<testSourceDirectory>${project.basedir}/src/
test/kotlin</testSourceDirectory>

.....

</build>
```

We added our Kotlin folders in the source paths.

Awesome, the project structure is ready, and we can start coding!

Creating a Docker network for our application

To create isolation for our application, we will create a custom Docker network. This network was created using the bridge driver. Let's do that using the following command:

```
docker network create twitter
```

Good, now we can check the network list by typing the following command:

```
docker network list
```

The Twitter network should be on the list, like the following:

```
ubuntu@ubuntu-xenial:~$ docker network list
NETWORK ID      NAME              DRIVER      SCOPE
d2bb065f5d06    bridge            bridge      local
5a8485d8da42    cms-application   bridge      local
1d4b5dc3ec8b    host              host        local
46b59abc89c2    none              null        local
fb27a7381539    twitter           bridge      local
```

The last one is our Twitter network. Let's pull the Redis image from the Docker Hub. Take a look at the next section.

Pulling the Redis image from the Docker Hub

The first thing we need to do is download the Redis image from the Docker Hub. To do that, it is necessary to execute the following command:

```
docker pull redis:4.0.6-alpine
```

We have used the alpine version from Redis because it is smaller than the others and has a reasonable security. While the image is downloaded, we can see the downloading status progress.

We can check the result using the following command:

```
docker images
```

The result should look like the following:

```
ubuntu@ubuntu-xenial:~$ docker images
REPOSITORY          TAG             IMAGE ID        CREATED         SIZE
redis               4.0.6-alpine    ed8544cc83de    5 days ago      26.9MB
postgres            9.6.6-alpine    e20de7998161    3 weeks ago     37.8MB
mongo               3.4.10          d22888af0ce0    5 weeks ago     361MB
```

Take a look at the images downloaded. The Redis must be on the list.

Awesome, now we will start the Redis instance.

Running the Redis instance

The image was downloaded, then we will start the Redis instance for our application. The command can be:

```
docker run -d --name redis --net twitter -p 6379:6379 redis:4.0.6-
alpine
```

We have interesting attributes here. We named our Redis instance with redis, it will be useful for running our application in containers in the next chapters. Also, we exposed the Redis container ports to the host machine, the command argument used for that is -p. Finally, we attached the container to our Twitter network.

Good, the Redis instance is ready to use. Let's check out the Spring Data Reactive Redis stuff.

Configuring the redis-cli tool

There is an excellent tool to connect with the Redis instance which is called `redis-cli`. There are some Docker images for that, but we will install it on our Linux machine.

To install it, we can execute the following command:

```
sudo apt-get install redis-tools -y
```

Excellent, now we can connect and interact with our Redis container. The tool can perform the read and write instructions, then we need to be careful to avoid instructions unintentionally.

Let's connect. The default configuration is enough for us because we have exported the port `6379` on the `run` instruction. Type the following command in the Terminal:

```
redis-cli
```

Then we will connect with our running instance. The command line should display the Redis host and port, like the following screenshot:

```
ubuntu@ubuntu-xenial:~$ redis-cli
127.0.0.1:6379>
```

Excellent, the client is configured and tested.

Now, we will execute some Redis commands on our container.

Understanding Redis

Redis is an open source in-memory data structure. Redis fits well for a database cache and is not common, but it can be used as a message broker using the publish-subscribe feature, it can be useful to decouple applications.

There are some interesting features supported by Redis such as transactions, atomic operations, and support for time-to-live keys. Time-to-live is useful for giving a time for the key, the eviction strategy is always hard to implement, and Redis has a built-in solution for us.

Data types

There are a lot of supported data types by Redis. The most common ones are strings, hashes, lists, and sorted sets. We will understand each of these a little bit because it is important to help us to choose the correct data type for our use case.

Strings

Strings are the more basic data type of Redis. The string value can be at max 512 MB in length. We can store it as a JSON in the value of the key, or maybe as an image as well because the Redis is binary safe.

Main commands

Let's look at some important commands we would need:

- SET: It sets the key and holds the value. It is a simple and basic command of Redis. Here's an example:

```
SET "user:id:10" "joe"
```

  The return of the command should be OK. It indicates the instruction has been executed with success.

- GET: This command gets the value of the requested key. Remember GET can only be used with a string data type:

```
GET "user:id:10"
```

  As we can see, the return of that command should be joe.

- INCR: The INCR command increments the key by one. It can be useful to handle sequential numbers atomically in distributed systems. The number increment will be returned as a command output:

```
SET "users" "0"
INCR "users"
GET "users"
```

  As we can see, the INCR command returned 1 as a command output and then we can check this using the GET and obtain the value.

- DECR: The DECR command is opposite of INCR, it will decrement the value atomically as well:

```
GET "users"
DECR "users"
GET "users"
```

The value of the users key was decremented by one and then transformed to 0.

- INCRBY: It will increment the value of the key by the argument. The new incremented value will be returned:

```
GET "users"
INCRBY "users" 2
GET "users"
```

The new value was returned as a command output.

Lists

Lists are simple lists of strings. They are ordered by the insertion order. Redis also offers instructions to add new elements at the head or tail of the list.

Lists can be useful for storing groups of things, groups of categories, for example, grouped by the categories key.

Main commands

LPUSH: Insert the new element at the head of the key. The command also supports multiple arguments, in this case, the values will be stored in the reverse order as we passed on the arguments.

Here are some command examples:

```
LPUSH "categories" "sports"
LPUSH "categories" "movies"
LRANGE "categories" 0 -1
```

Take a look at the LRANGE output, as we can see the value of the movie is the first one on the list because the LPUSH inserted the new element on the head.

RPUSH: Insert the new element at the tail of the key. The command supports multiple arguments as well, in this case, the values will respect the respective order.

Here are some command examples:

```
RPUSH "categories" "kitchen"
RPUSH "categories" "room"
LRANGE "categories" 0 -1
```

As we can see, in the LRANGE output, the new values are inserted at the tail of the values. It is the behavior of the RPUSH command.

LSET: It sets the element on the requested index.

Here are some command examples:

```
LSET "categories" 0 "series""
LRANGE "categories" 0 -1
```

The new value of the zero index is series. The LSET command does that for us.

LRANGE: It returns the specified elements of the key. The command arguments are the key, the start index, and finally the stop element. The -1 on the stop argument will return the whole list:

```
LRANGE "categories" 0 2
LRANGE "categories" 0 -1
```

As we can see, the first command will return three elements because the zero index will be grouped.

Sets

A **set** is a collection of strings. They have a property which does not allow repeated values. It means that if we add the pre-existing value on the sets, it will result in the same element, in this case, the advantage is not necessary to verify if the element exists on the set. Another important characteristic is that the sets are unordered. This behavior is different from the Redis lists. It can be useful in different use cases such as count the unique visitor, track the unique IPs, and much more.

Main commands

The following are the main commands listed with their usages:

- SADD: It adds the element in a requested key. Also, the return of this command is the number of the element added to the set:

```
SADD "unique-visitors" "joe"
SADD "unique-visitors" "mary"
```

As we can see, the command returned one because we added one user each time.

- SMEMBERS: It returns all the members of a requested key:

```
SMEMBERS "unique-visitors"
```

The command will return joe and mary because those are the values stored in the unique-visitors key.

- SCARD: It returns the numbers of elements of a requested key:

```
SCARD "unique-visitors"
```

The command will return the number of elements stored in the requested keys, in this case, the output will be 2.

Spring Data Reactive Redis

Spring Data Redis provides an easy way to interact with the Redis Server from Spring Boot Apps. The project is part of the Spring Data family and provides high-level and low-level abstractions for the developers.

The Jedis and Lettuce connectors are supported as a driver for this project.

The project offers a lot of features and facilities to interact with Redis. The Repository interfaces are supported as well. There is a CrudRepository for Redis like in other implementations, Spring Data JPA, for example.

The central class for this project is the `RedisTemplate` which provides a high-level API to perform Redis operations and serialization support. We will use this class to interact with set data structures on Redis.

The Reactive implementation is supported by this project, these are important characteristics for us because we are looking for Reactive implementations.

Configuring the ReactiveRedisConnectionFactory

To configure the `ReactiveRedisConnectionFactory`, we can use the `application.yaml file`, because it is easier to maintain and centralize our configuration.

The principle is the same as other Spring Data Projects, we should provide the host and port configurations in the `application.yaml` file, as follows:

```
spring:
  redis:
    host: localhost
    port: 6379
```

In the preceding configuration file, we point the Redis configuration to the `localhost`, as we can see. The configuration is pretty simple and easy to understand as well.

Done. The connection factory is configured. The next step is to provide a `RedisTemplate` to interact with our Redis instance. Take a look at the next section.

Providing a ReactiveRedisTemplate

The main class from Spring Data Redis is the `ReactiveRedisTemplate`, then we need to configure and provide an instance for the Spring container.

We need to provide an instance and configure the correct serializer for the desired `ReactiveRedisTemplate`. `Serializers` is the way Spring Data Redis uses to serialize and deserialize objects from raw bytes stored in Redis in the `Key` and `Value` fields.

We will use only the `StringRedisSerializer` because our `Key` and `Value` are simple strings and the Spring Data Redis has this serializer ready for us.

Let's produce our `ReactiveRedisTemplate`. The implementation should look like the following:

```
package springfive.twittertracked.infra.redis

import org.springframework.context.annotation.Bean
import org.springframework.context.annotation.Configuration
import
org.springframework.data.redis.connection.ReactiveRedisConnectionFacto
ry
import org.springframework.data.redis.core.ReactiveRedisTemplate
import
org.springframework.data.redis.serializer.RedisSerializationContext

@Configuration
open class RedisConfiguration {

  @Bean
  open fun
reactiveRedisTemplate(connectionFactory:ReactiveRedisConnectionFactory
):
                                 ReactiveRedisTemplate<String, String>
{
      return ReactiveRedisTemplate(connectionFactory,
RedisSerializationContext.string())
  }

}
```

Awesome. That is our first code using Kotlin in the Spring Framework. The keyword `open` is the opposite of Java's `final` keyword. It means this function can be inherited from this class. By default, all classes in Kotlin are final. Spring Framework requires non-final functions on `@Bean` on the `@Configuration` class and then we need to insert `open`.

We received `ReactiveRedisConnectionFactory` as a parameter. Spring knows which we produced in the `application.yaml` file using the configurations for Redis. Then the container can inject the factory.

Finally, we declare `ReactiveRedisTemplate<String, String>` as a return value for our function.

Interesting work, we are ready to work with our Redis template. Now, we will implement our first repository for Redis. See you in the next section.

Creating Tracked Hashtag repository

We have created the `ReactiveRedisTemplate`, then we can use this object in our repository implementation. We will create a simple repository to interact with Redis, remember the repository should be reactive, it is an important characteristic of our application. Then we need to return `Mono` or `Flux` to make the repository Reactive. Let's look at our repository implementation:

```
package springfive.twittertracked.domain.repository

import org.springframework.data.redis.core.ReactiveRedisTemplate
import org.springframework.stereotype.Service
import reactor.core.publisher.Flux
import reactor.core.publisher.Mono
import springfive.twitterconsumer.domain.TrackedHashTag

@Service
class TrackedHashTagRepository(private val redisTemplate:
ReactiveRedisTemplate<String, String>){

  fun save(trackedHashTag: TrackedHashTag): Mono<TrackedHashTag>?
{
    return this.redisTemplate
            .opsForSet().add("hash-tags",
"${trackedHashTag.hashTag}:${trackedHashTag.queue}")
            .flatMap { Mono.just(trackedHashTag) }
  }

  fun findAll(): Flux<TrackedHashTag> {
    return this.redisTemplate.opsForSet().members("hash-
tags").flatMap { el ->
      val data = el.split(":")
      Flux.just(TrackedHashTag(hashTag = data[0],queue = data[1]))
    }
  }
}
```

We received the `ReactiveRedisTemplate<String, String>` as an injection on our class, the Spring Framework can detect the constructor and inject the correct implementation.

For now, we need these two functions. The first one is responsible for inserting our entity, `TrackedHashTag` on the set structure from Redis. We add the value of the `hash-tags` key on Redis. This function returns a `Mono` with the `TrackedHashTag` value. Pay attention to the `save` function. We have created a pattern for our value, the pattern follows the `hashtag, queue` where the hashtag is the value to gather Tweets and the queue we will use in the next sections to send to a RabbitMQ queue.

The second function returns all values from the `hash-tags` key, it means all tracked hashtags from our system. Moreover, we need to do some logic to create our model, `TrackedHashTag`, as well.

The repository is finished, now we can create our service layer to encapsulate the repository. Let's do that in the next section.

Creating the service layer

Our repository is ready to use, now we can create our service layer. This layer is responsible for orchestrating our repository calls. In our case, it is pretty simple but in some complex scenarios, it can help us to encapsulate the repository calls.

Our service will be called `TrackedHashTagService`, which will be responsible for interacting with our repository created previously. The implementation should look like the following:

```
package springfive.twittertracked.domain.service

import org.springframework.stereotype.Service
import springfive.twitterconsumer.domain.TrackedHashTag
import springfive.twitterconsumer.domain.repository.TrackedHashTagRepository

@Service
class TrackedHashTagService(private val repository:
TrackedHashTagRepository) {

  fun save(hashTag:TrackedHashTag) = this.repository.save(hashTag)

  fun all() = this.repository.findAll()

}
```

Well done. Here, there is basic stuff. We have the construct which injects our repository to interact with Redis. The interesting point here is the function declarations. There is not a body and return type because the Kotlin compiler can infer the return type, it helps the developer to avoid writing boilerplate code.

Exposing the REST resources

Now, we have created the repository and service layer, and we are ready to expose our service through HTTP endpoints:

```
package springfive.twittertracked.domain.resource

import org.springframework.web.bind.annotation.*
import springfive.twitterconsumer.domain.TrackedHashTag
import
springfive.twitterconsumer.domain.service.TrackedHashTagService


@RestController
@RequestMapping("/api/tracked-hash-tag")
class TrackedHashTagResource(private val
service:TrackedHashTagService) {

  @GetMapping
  fun all() = this.service.all()

  @PostMapping
  fun save(@RequestBody hashTag:TrackedHashTag) =
this.service.save(hashTag)

}
```

The code is pretty concise and simple. Take a look at how concise this piece of code is. The preceding code is an example of how Kotlin helps developers to create readable codes. Thanks, Kotlin.

Creating a Twitter application

For this project, we will need to configure an application on the Twitter platform. It is necessary, because we will use Twitter's API to search Tweets, for example, and the Twitter account is the requirement for that. We will not explain how to create a Twitter account. There are plenty of articles about that on the internet.

After the Twitter account is created, we need to go to `https://apps.twitter.com/` and create a new app. The page is quite similar to the following screenshot:

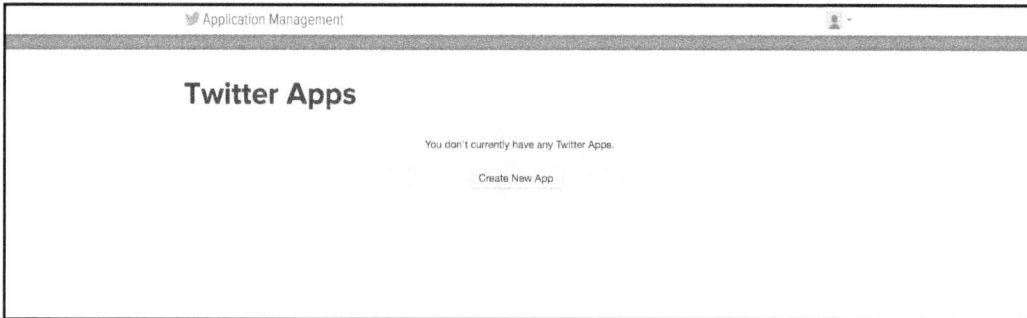

We will click on the **Create New App** button to start the creation process. When we click on that button, the following page will be displayed. We need to fill the required fields and accept the Twitter agreements:

We can choose the application name, fill in the description, and website. These details are up to you.

Then, we need to accept the agreements and click on **Create your Twitter application**:

Developer Agreement

☑ Yes, I have read and agree to the Twitter Developer Agreement.

Create your Twitter application

Awesome job. Our Twitter application is almost ready to use.

Now, we just need to configure the application for usage.

We need to check if our Keys and Access Tokens are correctly configured. Let's click on the **Keys and Access Tokens** tab and check the values, shown as follows:

springfivebyexample

Test OAuth

Details   Settings   Keys and Access Tokens   Permissions

Application Settings

Keep the "Consumer Secret" a secret. This key should never be human-readable in your application.

Consumer Key (API Key)	gupfxwn43NBTdxCD3Tsf1JgMu
Consumer Secret (API Secret)	pH4uM5LIYxKzfJ7huYRwFbaFXn7ooK01LmqCP69QV9a9kZrHw5
Access Level	Read-only (modify app permissions)
Owner	springfivebyexa
Owner ID	940015005860290560

As we can see, there are some important configurations in the preceding screenshot. The **Consumer Key** and **Consumer Secret** are mandatory to authenticate with Twitter APIs. Another important point here is the **Access Level**; be sure it is configured as read-only, as in the preceding screenshot, we will not do write actions on Twitter.

Let's Dockerize it.

Awesome. We have the system which keeps the tracked hashtags on the Redis instance. The application is fully Reactive and has no blocking threads.

Now, we will configure the Maven plugin to generate the Docker images. The configuration is quite similar to what we did in Chapter 3, *Persistence with Spring Data and Reactive Fashion*. However, now we will create a first container which we will run with the Kotlin language. Let's do that.

Configuring pom.xml

Now, we will configure our pom.xml to be able to generate our Docker image. The first thing we need to change is our final name artifact because Docker images do not allow the - character, then we need to configure properly.

The configuration is pretty simple, put the <finalName> tag on the <build> node. Let's do that:

```
<build>

  <finalName>tracked_hashtag</finalName>

  . . . .

</build>
```

Good. We have configured the final name properly to generate the Docker image correctly. Now, we will configure the Maven Docker plugin to generate the Docker image by the Maven goal.

In the plugins section inside the build node, we should put in the following plugin configuration:

```
<plugin>
  <groupId>io.fabric8</groupId>
  <artifactId>docker-maven-plugin</artifactId>
  <version>0.21.0</version>
  <configuration>
    <images>
      <image>
<name>springfivebyexample/${project.build.finalName}</name>
        <build>
          <from>openjdk:latest</from>
          <entryPoint>java -Dspring.profiles.active=container -jar
        /application/${project.build.finalName}.jar</entryPoint>
          <assembly>
```

```
                    <basedir>/application</basedir>
                    <descriptorRef>artifact</descriptorRef>
                    <inline>
                      <id>assembly</id>
                      <files>
                        <file>
  <source>target/${project.build.finalName}.jar</source>
                        </file>
                      </files>
                    </inline>
                  </assembly>
                  <tags>
                    <tag>latest</tag>
                  </tags>
                  <ports>
                    <port>9090</port>
                  </ports>
                </build>
                <run>
                  <namingStrategy>alias</namingStrategy>
                </run>
                <alias>${project.build.finalName}</alias>
              </image>
            </images>
          </configuration>
        </plugin>
```

The configuration is pretty simple. We did this before. In the configuration section, we configured from the image, in our case the `openjdk:latest`, Docker entry point and exposed ports as well.

Let's create our Docker image in the next section.

Creating the image

Our project was previously configured with the Maven Docker plugin. We can generate the Docker image with the Maven Docker plugin using the `docker:build` goal. Then, it is time to generate our Docker image.

To generate the Docker image, type the following command:

```
mvn clean install docker:build
```

Now, we must wait for the Maven build and check if the Docker image was generated with success.

Check the Docker images and we should see the new image generated. To do this, we can use the `docker images` command:

```
docker images
```

Right, we should see the `springfivebyexample/tracked_hashtag:latest` on the image list, like the following screenshot:

Awesome, our Docker image is ready to run with our first Spring Boot Application in the Kotlin language. Let's run it right now.

Running the container

Let's run our container. Before that, we need to keep in mind some things. The container should be run on the Twitter network to be able to connect to our Redis instance which is running on the Twitter network as well. Remember the `localhost` address for Redis does not work anymore when running in the containers infrastructure.

To run our container, we can execute the following command:

```
docker run -d --name hashtag-tracker --net twitter -p 9090:9090
springfivebyexample/tracked_hashtag
```

Congratulations, our application is running in the Docker container and connected to our Redis instance. Let's create and test our APIs to check the desired behaviors.

Testing APIs

Our container is running. Now, we can try to call the APIs to check the behaviors. In this part, we will use the `curl` command line. The `curl` allows us to call APIs by the command line on Linux. Also, we will use `jq` to make the JSON readable on the command line, if you do not have these, look at the Tip Box to install these tools.

Let's call our create API, remember to create we can use the POST method in the base path of API. Then type the following command:

```
curl -H "Content-Type: application/json" -X POST -d
'{"hashTag":"java","queue":"java"}'
 http://localhost:9090/api/tracked-hash-tag
```

There are interesting things here. The `-H` argument instructs `curl` to put it in the request headers and `-d` indicates the request body. Moreover, finally, we have the server address.

We have created the new `tracked-hash-tag`. Let's check our GET API to obtain this data:

```
curl 'http://localhost:9090/api/tracked-hash-tag' | jq '.'
```

Awesome, we called the `curl` tool and printed the JSON value with the `jq` tool. The command output should look like the following screenshot:

> To install `curl` on Ubuntu, we can use `sudo apt-get install curl -y`. Moreover, to install `jq`, we can use `sudo apt-get install jq -y`.

Summary

In this chapter, we have been introduced to the Kotlin language, which is the most prominent language for the JVM, because it has a super-fast compiler, if we compare it to Scala, for example. It also brings the simplicity of code and helps developers to create more concise and readable code.

We have also created our first application in the Spring Framework using Kotlin as the basic concepts of the language, and we saw how Kotlin helps the developers in a practical way.

We have introduced Redis as a cache and Spring Data Reactive Redis, which supports Redis in a Reactive paradigm.

In the last part of the chapter, we learned how to create a Twitter application which required us to create our next application, and start to consume the Twitter API in reactive programming with a Reactive Rest Client.

Let's jump to the next chapter and learn more about Spring Reactive.

5
Reactive Web Clients

Until now, we have created the whole project infrastructure to consume the Twitter stream. We have created an application which stores the tracked hashtags.

In this chapter, we will learn how to use the Spring Reactive Web Client and make HTTP calls using the reactive paradigm, which is one of the most anticipated features of Spring 5.0. We will call the Twitter REST APIs asynchronously and use the Project Reactor to provide an elegant way to work with streams.

We will be introduced to Spring Messaging for the RabbitMQ. We will interact with the RabbitMQ broker using the Spring Messaging API and see how Spring helps developers use the high-level abstractions for that.

At the end of this chapter, we will wrap up the application and create a docker image.

In this chapter, we will learn about:

- Reactive web clients
- Spring Messaging for RabbitMQ
- RabbitMQ Docker usage
- Spring Actuator

Creating the Twitter Gathering project

We learned how to create Spring Boot projects with the amazing Spring Initializr. In this chapter, we will create a project in a different way, to show you an alternative way of creating a Spring Boot project.

Create the `tweet-gathering` folder, in any directory. We can use the following command:

```
mkdir tweet-gathering
```

Then, we can access the folder created previously and copy the `pom.xml` file located at GitHub: `https://github.com/PacktPublishing/Spring-5.0-By-Example/blob/master/Chapter05/tweet-gathering/pom.xml`.

Open the `pom.xml` on IDE.

There are some interesting dependencies here. The `jackson-module-kotlin` helps to work with JSON in Kotlin language. Another interesting dependency is `kotlin-stdlib`, which provides the Kotlin standard libraries in our classpath.

In the plugin sections, the most important plugin is the `kotlin-maven-plugin`, which permits and configures the build for our Kotlin code.

In the next section, we will create a folder structure to start the code.

Let's do it.

Project structure

The project structure follows the maven suggested pattern. We will code the project in the Kotlin language, then we will create a `kotlin` folder to store our code.

We made that configuration on the `pom.xml` created before, so it will work fine. Let's take a look at the correct folder structure for the project:

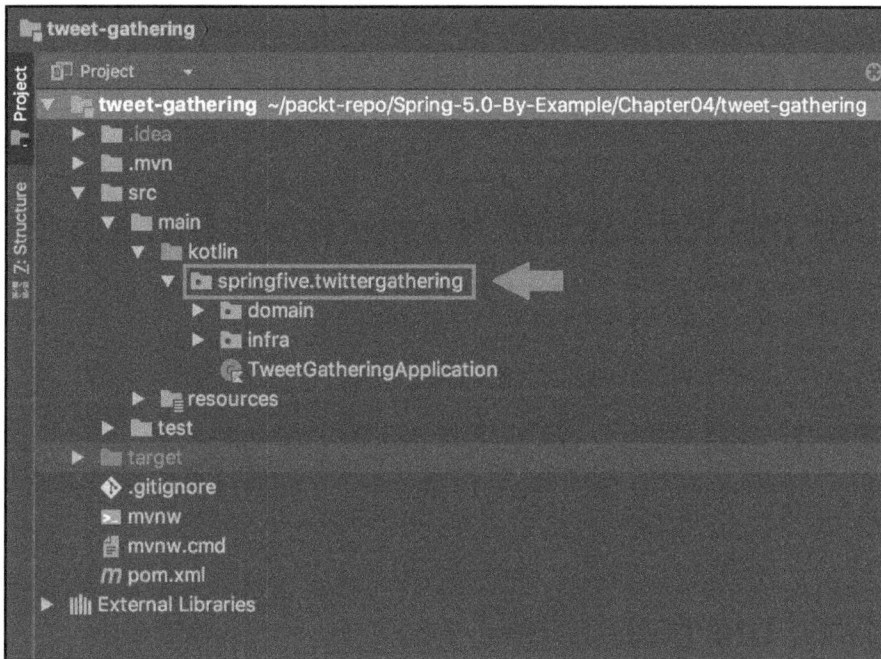

As we can see, the base package is the `springfive.twittergathering` package. Then, we will start to create sub-packages in this package as soon.

Let's create our infrastructure for the microservice.

> The full source code can be found at GitHub: `https://github.com/ PacktPublishing/Spring-5.0-By-Example/tree/master/ Chapter05/tweet-gathering`.

Starting the RabbitMQ server with Docker

We can use Docker to spin up the RabbitMQ server. We do not want to install the server on our developer machines as it can create library conflicts and a lot of files. Let's understand how to start RabbitMQ in a Docker container.

Let's do that in the next couple of sections.

Pulling the RabbitMQ image from Docker Hub

We need to pull the RabbitMQ image from Docker Hub. We will use the image from the official repository as it is more safe and reliable.

To get the image, we need to use the following command:

```
docker pull rabbitmq:3.7.0-management-alpine
```

Wait for the download to end and then we can move forward to the next section. In the next section, we will learn how to set up the RabbitMQ server.

Starting the RabbitMQ server

To start the RabbitMQ server, we will run the Docker command. There are some considerations which we need to pay attention to; we will run this container on the Twitter Docker network created previously, but we will expose some ports on the host, as it makes it easier to interact with the broker.

Also, we will use the management image because it provides a page which enables us to manage and see the RabbitMQ information on something similar to a control panel.

Let's run:

```
docker run -d --name rabbitmq --net twitter -p 5672:5672 -p
15672:15672 rabbitmq:3.7.0-management-alpine
```

Wait for a few seconds so that RabbitMQ establishes the connections and then we can connect to the management page. To do that, go to http://localhost:15672 and log on to the system. The default user is **guest**, and the password is guest as well. The control panel looks like this:

There is a lot of interesting information on the panel, but for now, we are going to explore the channels and some interesting parts.

Awesome. Our RabbitMQ server is up and running. We will use the infrastructure soon.

Spring Messaging AMQP

This project supports the AMQP-based messaging solutions. There is a high-level API to interact with desired brokers. These interactions can send and receive messages from a broker.

Like in the other Spring projects, these facilities are provided by the *template* classes, which expose the core features provided by the broker and implemented by the Spring Module.

This project has two parts: `spring-amqp` is the base abstraction, and `spring-rabbit` is the RabbitMQ implementation for RabbitMQ. We will use `spring-rabbit` because we are using the RabbitMQ broker.

Adding Spring AMQP in our pom.xml

Let's add the `spring-amqp` jars to our project. `spring-amqp` has a starter
dependency which configures some common things for us, such
as `ConnectionFactory` and `RabbitTemplate`, so we will use that. To add this
dependency, we will configure our `pom.xml` follows:

```
<dependency>
  <groupId>org.springframework.boot</groupId>
  <artifactId>spring-boot-starter-amqp</artifactId>
</dependency>
```

The next step is to configure the connections; we will use the `application.yaml` file
because we are using the starter. In the next section, we will do the configuration.

Integrating Spring Application and RabbitMQ

We have configured the `spring-amqp` dependencies in our project. Now, it is time to
configure the RabbitMQ connections properly. We will use the `RabbitMQTemplate`
to send messages to the broker; this has some converters which help us convert our
domain models into JSON and vice versa.

Let's configure our RabbitMQ connections. The configurations should be in
the `application.yaml` file and should look like this:

```
spring:
  rabbitmq:
    host: localhost
    username: guest
    password: guest
    port: 5672
```

As we can see, some Spring configurations are quite similar to others, the same style,
and the node in `yaml` is the name of the technology followed by a couple of attributes.

We are using the default credentials for the RabbitMQ. The host and port are related
to the RabbitMQ Broker address. The configuration is quite simple but does a lot of
things for us such as `ConnectionFactory`.

Understanding RabbitMQ exchanges, queues, and bindings

We are doing some interesting things with RabbitMQ. We configured connections successfully. There are some other things that we have not done yet, such as configuring the exchanges, queue, and bindings, but before we do that, let's understand a little bit more about these terms.

Exchanges

Exchanges are RabbitMQ entities where the messages are sent. We can make an analogy with a river where the water is flowing; the river is the course of the messages. There are four different kinds of exchanges which we will understand in the following sections.

Direct exchanges

The direct exchanges allow for route messages based on the routing key. The name is self-explanatory, it permits to send the messages directly to the specified customer, who is the one listening to the exchange. Remember, it uses the routing key as the argument to route the message to the customers.

Fanout exchanges

The fanout exchanges route the messages for all the queues bound independently of the routing key. All the bound queues will receive the message sent to fanout exchanges. They can be used to have the topic behavior or distributed listings.

Topic exchanges

The topic exchanges are similar to direct exchanges, but topic exchanges enable us to use pattern matching as compared to the direct exchanges, which permit only the exact routing key. We will use this exchange in our project.

Header exchanges

Header exchanges are self-explanatory, the behavior is like the topic exchange, but instead of using the routing key, it uses the header attributes to match the correct queue.

Queues

Queues are the buffer where the exchanges will write the messages respecting the routing key. Queues are the place where consumers get the messages which are published to exchanges. Messages are routed to queues depending on the exchange type.

Bindings

Binding can be thought of as a link between exchanges and queues. We can say that it is a kind of traffic cop which instructs the messages where they should be redirected based on the configuration, in this case, links.

Configuring exchanges, queues, and bindings on Spring AMQP

The Spring AMQP project has abstractions for all the RabbitMQ entities listed previously, and we need to configure it to interact with the broker. As we did in other projects, we need a `@Configuration` class, which will declare the beans for the Spring container.

Declaring exchanges, queues, and bindings in yaml

We need to configure the entity names to instruct the framework to connect with the broker entities. We will use the `application.yaml` file to store these names, since it is easier to maintain and is the correct way to store application infrastructure data.

The section with the entity names should look like this snippet:

```
queue:
  twitter: twitter-stream
exchange:
  twitter: twitter-exchange
routing_key:
  track: track.*
```

The properties are self-explanatory, the `exchange` node has the name of the exchange, the `queue` node has the queue name, and finally, the `routing_key` node has the routing argument.

Awesome. The properties are configured, and now we will create our
@Configuration class. Let's do that in the next section. We are almost ready to
interact with the RabbitMQ broker.

Declaring Spring beans for RabbitMQ

Now, let's create our configuration class. The class is pretty simple and as we will see
with the Spring abstraction, they are easy to understand too, especially because the
class names allude to the RabbitMQ entities.

Let's create our class:

```
package springfive.twittergathering.infra.rabbitmq

import com.fasterxml.jackson.databind.ObjectMapper
import com.fasterxml.jackson.module.kotlin.KotlinModule
import org.springframework.amqp.core.Binding
import org.springframework.amqp.core.BindingBuilder
import org.springframework.amqp.core.Queue
import org.springframework.amqp.core.TopicExchange
import
org.springframework.amqp.support.converter.Jackson2JsonMessageConverte
r
import org.springframework.beans.factory.annotation.Value
import org.springframework.context.annotation.Bean
import org.springframework.context.annotation.Configuration

@Configuration
open class RabbitMQConfiguration(@Value("${queue.twitter}") private
val queue:String,
                                 @Value("${exchange.twitter}") private
val
exchange:String,
                                 @Value("${routing_key.track}")
private val routingKey:String){

    @Bean
    open fun queue():Queue{
        return Queue(this.queue,false)
    }

    @Bean
    open fun exchange():TopicExchange{
        return TopicExchange(this.exchange)
    }
```

```
    @Bean
    open fun binding(queue: Queue, exchange: TopicExchange): Binding {
        return
BindingBuilder.bind(queue).to(exchange).with(this.routingKey)
    }

    @Bean
    open fun converter(): Jackson2JsonMessageConverter {
        return
Jackson2JsonMessageConverter(ObjectMapper().registerModule(KotlinModul
e()))
    }

}
```

There are interesting things to pay attention to here. In the RabbitMQConfiguration constructor, we injected the values configured in the application.yaml file to name the entities. After that, we started to configure the Spring beans for the container to allow it to inject them into the Spring-managed classes. The key point here is that if they do not exist in the RabbitMQ broker, Spring will create them. Thanks, Spring, we appreciate that and love how helpful that is.

We can see the DSL to declare Binding, it makes the developer's life easier and prevents errors in the code.

On the last part of the class, we declared the Jackson2JsonMessageConverter. These converters are used to convert the domain models in JSON and vice versa. It enables us to receive the domain object on Listener instead of an array of bytes or strings. The same behavior can be used in the Producers, we are able to send the domain object instead of JSON.

We need to supply the ObjectMapper to Jackson2JsonMessageConverter, and we have used the Kotlin module because of the way Kotlin handles data classes, which do not have no-args constructors.

Excellent job! Our infrastructure is fully configured. Let's code the producers and consumers right now!

Consuming messages with Spring Messaging

Spring AMQP provides the `@RabbitListener` annotation; it will configure the subscriber for the desired queue, it removes a lot of infrastructure code, such as connect to `RabbitListenerConnectionFactory`, and creates a consumer programmatically. It makes the creation of queue consumers really easy.

The `spring-boot-starter-amqp` provides some automatic configurations for us. When we use this module, Spring will automatically create a `RabbitListenerConnectionFactory` for us and configure the Spring converters to convert JSON to domain classes automatically.

Pretty simple. Spring AMQP really provides a super high-level abstraction for developers.

Let's see an example which will be used in our application soon:

```
@RabbitListener(queues = ["twitter-track-hashtag"])
fun receive(hashTag:TrackedHashTag) {
...
}
```

The full source code can be found at GitHub: `https://github.com/PacktPublishing/Spring-5.0-By-Example/blob/master/Chapter05/tweet-gathering/src/main/kotlin/springfive/twittergathering/domain/service/TwitterGatherRunner.kt`.

A piece of cake. The code is really easy to understand and it makes it possible to pay attention only to the business rules. The infrastructure is not a good thing to maintain because this does not bring real value to the business, as it is only a piece of technology. Spring tries to abstract the whole infrastructure code to help developers write business code. It is a real asset provided by the Spring Framework.

Thanks, Spring Team.

Producing messages with Spring Messaging

The `spring-amqp` module provides a `RabbitTemplate` class, which abstracts high-level RabbitMQ driver classes. It improves the developer performance and makes the application void of bugs because the Spring modules are a very well-tested set of codes. We will use the `convertAndSend()` function which permits to pass exchange, the routing key, and the message object as parameters. Remember this function uses Spring converters to convert our model class into a JSON string.

There are a lot of overloaded functions for `convertAndSend()`, and depending on the use case, others could be more appropriate. We will use the simple one as we saw before.

Let's see the piece of code which sends the message to the broker:

```
this.rabbitTemplate.convertAndSend("twitter-
exchange","track.${hashTag.queue}",it)
```

Good. The first parameter is the `Exchange` name, and the second is the `RoutingKey`. Finally, we have the message object, which will be converted into a JSON string.

We will see the code in action soon.

Enabling Twitter in our application

In this section, we will enable the use of Twitter APIs on our Twitter Gathering application. This application should get Tweets based on the query specified by the user. This query was registered on the previous microservice that we created in the previous chapter.

When the user calls the API to register `TrackedHashTag`, the microservice will store the `TrackedHashTag` on the Redis database and send the message through the RabbitMQ. Then, this project will start to gather Tweets based on that. This is the data flow. In the next chapter, we will do a reactive stream and dispatch Tweets through our Reactive API. It will be amazing.

However, for now, we need to configure the Twitter credentials; we will do that using Spring beans – let's implement it.

Producing Twitter credentials

We will use the `@Configuration` class to provide our Twitter configuration objects. The `@Configuration` class is really good to provide infrastructure beans, if we do not have starter projects for the required module.

Also, we will use the `application.yaml` file to store the Twitter credentials. This kind of configuration should not be kept in the source code repository because it is sensitive data and should not be shared with others. Then, the Spring Framework enables us to declare properties in the `yaml` file and configures the environment variables to fill these properties at runtime. It is an excellent way to keep sensitive data out of the source code repository.

Configuring Twitter credentials in application.yaml

To start configuring the Twitter API in our application, we must provide the credentials. We will use the `yaml` file for this. Let's add credentials in our `application.yaml`:

```
twitter:
  consumer-key: ${consumer-key}
  consumer-secret: ${consumer-secret}
  access-token: ${access-token}
  access-token-secret: ${access-token-secret}
```

Easy peasy. The properties have been declared and then we used the `$` to instruct the Spring Framework that this value will be received as an environment variable. Remember, we configured the Twitter account in the previous chapter.

Modelling objects to represent Twitter settings

We must create abstractions and an amazing data model for our applications. This will create some models which make the developer's life easier to understand and code. Let's create our Twitter settings models.

Twittertoken

This class represents the application token previously configured in Twitter. The token can be used for the application authentication only. Our model should look like this:

```
data class TwitterToken(val accessToken: String,val
accessTokenSecret: String)
```

I love the Kotlin way to declare data classes—totally immutable and without boilerplate.

TwitterAppSettings

`TwitterAppSettings` represents the consumer key and consumer secret. It is a kind of identity for our application, from Twitter's perspective. Our model is pretty simple and must look like this:

```
data class TwitterAppSettings(val consumerKey: String,val
consumerSecret: String)
```

Good job, our models are ready. It is time to produce the objects for the Spring Container. We will do that in the next section.

Declaring Twitter credentials for the Spring container

Let's produce our Twitter configuration objects. As a pattern we have been using, we will use the `@Configuration` class for that. The class should be as follows:

```
package springfive.twittergathering.infra.twitter

import org.springframework.beans.factory.annotation.Value
import org.springframework.context.annotation.Bean
import org.springframework.context.annotation.Configuration


@Configuration
open class TwitterConfiguration(@Value("${twitter.consumer-key}")
private val consumerKey: String,
                                @Value("${twitter.consumer-secret}")
private val consumerSecret: String,
                                @Value("${twitter.access-token}")
private val accessToken: String,
                                @Value("${twitter.access-token-
```

```
secret}") private val accessTokenSecret: String) {

    @Bean
    open fun twitterAppSettings(): TwitterAppSettings {
        return TwitterAppSettings(consumerKey, consumerSecret)
    }

    @Bean
    open fun twitterToken(): TwitterToken {
        return TwitterToken(accessToken, accessTokenSecret)
    }

}
```

Pretty simple and a Spring way to declare beans. We are improving how we use Spring step by step. Well done!

Now, we are done with Twitter configurations. We will consume the Twitter API using the WebClient from the Spring WebFlux, which supports the reactive programming paradigm. Let's understand something before we run the code.

Spring reactive web clients

This is a pretty new feature which was added in Spring Framework 5. It enables us to interact with HTTP services, using the reactive paradigm.

It is not a replacement for a RestTemplate provided by Spring, however, it is an addition to working with reactive applications. Do not worry, the RestTemplate is an excellent and tested implementation for interaction with HTTP services in traditional applications.

Also, the WebClient implementation supports the text/event-stream mime type which can enable us to consume server events.

Producing WebClient in a Spring Way

Before we start to call the Twitter APIs, we want to create an instance of WebClient in a Spring way. It means we are looking for a way to inject the instance, using the Dependency Injection Pattern.

To achieve this, we can use the `@Configuration` annotation and create a `WebClient` instance, using the `@Bean` annotation to declare the bean for the Spring container. Let's do that:

```
package springfive.twittergathering.infra.web

import org.springframework.context.annotation.Bean
import org.springframework.context.annotation.Configuration
import org.springframework.web.reactive.function.client.WebClient

@Configuration
open class WebClientProducer {

    @Bean
    open fun webClient(): WebClient? {
        return WebClient.create()
    }

}
```

There are a couple of known annotations in this class; this is a pretty standard way to declare bean instances in a Spring way. It makes it possible to inject an instance of `WebClient` in other Spring-managed classes.

Creating the models to gather Tweets

If we want to consume the Twitter APIs asynchronously and reactively, then we should create the API client. Before we code the client, we need to create our classes for modeling, according to our requirements.

We do not need all Tweets' attributes. We expect the following attributes:

- `id`
- `text`
- `createdAt`
- `user`

Then, we will model our class based on the attributes listed.

Let's start with the user attribute. This attribute is a JSON attribute, and we will create a separated class for that. The class should look like this:

```
@JsonIgnoreProperties(ignoreUnknown = true)
data class TwitterUser(val id:String,val name:String)
```

We have used the Kotlin `data class`, it fits our use case well, and we want to use that as a data container. Also, we need to put in `@JsonIgnoreProperties(ignoreUnknown = true)` because this annotation instructs the Spring converters to ignore the attribute when it is missing in the JSON response. That is the important part of this portion of code.

We have created the `TwitterUser` class, which represents the user who created the Tweet. Now, we will create the `Tweet` class which represents the Tweet. Let's create our class:

```
@JsonIgnoreProperties(ignoreUnknown = true)
data class Tweet(val id:String, val text:String,
@JsonProperty("created_at")val createdAt:String, val
user:TwitterUser)
```

There are some common things for us and one that's new. The `@JsonProperty` permits developers to customize the attribute name on the class which has a different attribute name in JSON; this is common for Java developers because they usually use *CamelCase* as a way to name attributes, and in JSON notation, people usually use *SnakeCase*. This annotation can help us to solve this mismatch between the programming language and JSON.

> We can find a more detailed explanation of snake case here: `https://en.wikipedia.org/wiki/Snake_case`. Also, we can find a full explanation of camel case here: `https://en.wikipedia.org/wiki/Camel_case`.

Good. Our API objects are ready. With these objects, we are enabled to interact with the APIs. We will create a service to collect the Tweets. We will do that in the next section.

Authentication with Twitter APIs

With our objects ready, we need to create a class to help us handle the Twitter authentication. We will use the Twitter Application Only Auth authentication model. This kind of authentication should be used for backend applications.

The application using this kind of authentication can:

- Pull user timelines
- Access friends and followers of any account
- Access lists and resources
- Search in Tweets
- Retrieve any user information

As we can see, the application is a read-only Twitter API consumer.

We can use the Twitter documentation to understand this kind of authentication in detail. The documentation can be found here: `https://developer.twitter.com/en/docs/basics/authentication/guides/authorizing-a-request`.

We will follow the Twitter documentation to authorize our request, which is a kind of cooking recipe, so we must follow all the steps. The final class should look like this:

```
package springfive.twittergathering.infra.twitter

import org.springframework.util.StringUtils
import
springfive.twittergathering.infra.twitter.EncodeUtils.computeSignature
import springfive.twittergathering.infra.twitter.EncodeUtils.encode
import java.util.*

object Twitter {

    private val SIGNATURE_METHOD = "HMAC-SHA1"

    private val AUTHORIZATION_VERIFY_CREDENTIALS = "OAuth " +
            "oauth_consumer_key="{key}", " +
            "oauth_signature_method="" + SIGNATURE_METHOD + "", " +
            "oauth_timestamp="{ts}", " +
            "oauth_nonce="{nonce}", " +
            "oauth_version="1.0", " +
            "oauth_signature="{signature}", " +
            "oauth_token="{token}""

    fun buildAuthHeader(appSettings: TwitterAppSettings, twitterToken:
TwitterToken, method: String, url: String, query: String):String{
        val ts = "" + Date().time / 1000
        val nounce = UUID.randomUUID().toString().replace("-
".toRegex(), "")
        val parameters =
"oauth_consumer_key=${appSettings.consumerKey}&oauth_nonce=$nounce&oau
```

```
th_signature_method=$SIGNATURE_METHOD&oauth_timestamp=$ts&oauth_token=
${encode(twitterToken.accessToken)}&oauth_version=1.0&track=${encode(q
uery)}"
        val signature = "$method&" + encode(url) + "&" +
encode(parameters)
        var result = AUTHORIZATION_VERIFY_CREDENTIALS
        result = StringUtils.replace(result, "{nonce}", nounce)
        result = StringUtils.replace(result, "{ts}", "" + ts)
        result = StringUtils.replace(result, "{key}",
appSettings.consumerKey)
        result = StringUtils.replace(result, "{signature}",
encode(computeSignature(signature,
"${appSettings.consumerSecret}&${encode(twitterToken.accessTokenSecret
)}")))
        result = StringUtils.replace(result, "{token}",
encode(twitterToken.accessToken))
        return result
    }

}

data class TwitterToken(val accessToken: String,val accessTokenSecret:
String)

data class TwitterAppSettings(val consumerKey: String,val
consumerSecret: String)
```

It is a recipe. The function, `buildAuthHeader`, will create the authorization header using the rules to authorize the request. We have signed some request headers combined with a request body. Moreover, replace the template values with our Twitter credentials objects.

Some words about server-sent events (SSE)

Server-sent events (SSE) is a technology where the server sends events to the client, instead of the client polling the server to check the information availability. The message flow will not get interrupted until the client or server closes the stream.

The most important thing to understand here is the direction of the information flow. The server decides when to send data to a client.

It is very important to handle resource load and bandwidth usage. The client will receive the chunk of data instead to apply load on the server through the polling techniques.

Twitter has a stream API and the Spring Framework WebClient supports SSE. It is time to consume the Twitter stream.

Creating the gather service

The `TweetGatherService` will be responsible for interacting with Twitter APIs and collecting the request tweets according to the requested hashtag. The service will be a Spring bean with some inject attributes. The class should look like this:

```
package springfive.twittergathering.domain.service

import com.fasterxml.jackson.annotation.JsonIgnoreProperties
import com.fasterxml.jackson.annotation.JsonProperty
import org.springframework.http.MediaType
import org.springframework.stereotype.Service
import org.springframework.web.reactive.function.BodyInserters
import org.springframework.web.reactive.function.client.WebClient
import reactor.core.publisher.Flux
import springfive.twittergathering.infra.twitter.Twitter
import springfive.twittergathering.infra.twitter.TwitterAppSettings
import springfive.twittergathering.infra.twitter.TwitterToken


@Service
class TweetGatherService(private val twitterAppSettings:
TwitterAppSettings,
                         private val twitterToken: TwitterToken,
                         private val webClient: WebClient) {

    fun streamFrom(query: String): Flux<Tweet> {
        val url =
"https://stream.twitter.com/1.1/statuses/filter.json"
        return this.webClient.mutate().baseUrl(url).build()
                .post()
                .body(BodyInserters.fromFormData("track", query))
                .header("Authorization",
Twitter.buildAuthHeader(twitterAppSettings, twitterToken, "POST", url,
query))
                .accept(MediaType.TEXT_EVENT_STREAM)
                .retrieve().bodyToFlux(Tweet::class.java)
    }

}

@JsonIgnoreProperties(ignoreUnknown = true)
data class Tweet(val id: String = "", val text: String = "",
```

```
@JsonProperty("created_at") val createdAt: String = "", val user:
TwitterUser = TwitterUser("", ""))

@JsonIgnoreProperties(ignoreUnknown = true)
data class TwitterUser(val id: String, val name: String)
```

There are some important points here. The first is the function declaration; take a look at `Flux<Tweet>`, it means the data can never get interrupted because it represents the N values. In our case, we will consume the Twitter stream until the client or server interrupts the data flow.

After that, we configured the HTTP request body with our desired track to get events. After that, we configured the Accept HTTP header; it is essential to instruct the WebClient what kind of mime type it needs to consume.

Finally, we have used our `Twitter.buildAuthHeader` function to configure the Twitter authentication.

Awesome, we are ready to start to consume the Twitter API, and we only need to code the trigger to use that function. We will do that in the next section.

Listening to the Rabbit Queue and consuming the Twitter API

We will consume the Twitter API, but when?

We need to start to get Tweets when the request for tracking the hashtags comes to our application. To reach that goal, we will implement the RabbitMQ Listener when the `TrackedHashTag` gets registered on our microservice. The application will send the message to the broker to start consuming the Twitter stream.

Let's take a look at the code and step by step understand the behaviors; the final code should look like this:

```
package springfive.twittergathering.domain.service

import org.springframework.amqp.rabbit.annotation.RabbitListener
import org.springframework.amqp.rabbit.core.RabbitTemplate
import org.springframework.stereotype.Service
import reactor.core.publisher.Mono
import reactor.core.scheduler.Schedulers
import springfive.twittergathering.domain.TrackedHashTag
import java.util.concurrent.CompletableFuture
```

```
import java.util.concurrent.TimeUnit

@Service
class TwitterGatherRunner(private val twitterGatherService:
TweetGatherService,private val rabbitTemplate: RabbitTemplate) {

    @RabbitListener(queues = ["twitter-track-hashtag"])
    fun receive(hashTag:TrackedHashTag) {
        val streamFrom =
this.twitterGatherService.streamFrom(hashTag.hashTag).filter({
            return@filter it.id.isNotEmpty() && it.text.isNotEmpty()
&&
            it.createdAt.isNotEmpty()
        })
        val subscribe = streamFrom.subscribe({
            println(it.text)
            Mono.fromFuture(CompletableFuture.runAsync {
                this.rabbitTemplate.convertAndSend("twitter-
                exchange", "track.${hashTag.queue}",it)
            })
        })
        Schedulers.elastic().schedule({ subscribe.dispose()
}, 10L, TimeUnit.SECONDS)
    }


}
```

Keep calm. We will cover the whole code. In the `@RabbitListener,` we configured
the name of the queue we want to consume. The Spring AMQP module will configure
our listener automatically for us and start to consume the desired queue. As we can
see, we received the `TrackedHashTag` object; remember the converters on the
previous sections.

The first instruction will start to consume the Twitter stream. The stream returns
a flux and can have a lot of data events there. After the consumer, we want to filter
the data on the flow. We want `Tweet` in which the `id`, `text`, and `createdAt` are not
null.

Then, we subscribe this stream and start to receive the data in the flow. Also,
the `subscribes` function returns the disposable object which will be helpful in the
next steps. We have created an anonymous function which will print the `Tweet` on
the console and send the Tweet to the RabbitMQ queue, to be consumed in another
microservice.

Finally, we use the schedulers to stop the data flow and consume the data for 10 seconds.

Before you test the Twitter stream, we need to change the Tracked Hashtag Service to send the messages through the RabbitMQ. We will do that in the next sections. The changes are small ones and we will do them quickly.

Changing the Tracked Hashtag Service

To run the whole solution, we need to make some changes to the Tracked Hashtag Service project. The changes are simple and basic; configure the RabbitMQ connection and change the service to send the messages to the broker.

Let's do that.

Adding the Spring Starter RabbitMQ dependency

As we did before in the Twitter Gathering project, we need to add `spring-boot-starter-amqp` to provide some auto-configuration for us. To do that, we need to add the following snippet to our `pom.xml`:

```
<dependency>
  <groupId>org.springframework.boot</groupId>
  <artifactId>spring-boot-starter-amqp</artifactId>
</dependency>
```

Right. Now, it is time to configure the RabbitMQ connections. We will do this in the next section.

Configuring the RabbitMQ connections

We will use the `application.yaml` to configure the RabbitMQ connections. Then, we need to create a couple of properties in it and the Spring AMQP module will use that provided configuration to start the connection factory.

It is pretty simple to configure it. The final `yaml` file for Tracked Hashtag should look like this:

```yaml
spring:
  rabbitmq:
    host: localhost
    username: guest
    password: guest
    port: 5672
  redis:
    host: 127.0.0.1
    port: 6379

server:
  port: 9090

queue:
  twitter: twitter-track-hashtag
exchange:
  twitter: twitter-track-exchange
routing_key:
  track: "*"
---
spring:
  profiles: docker
  rabbitmq:
    host: rabbitmq
    username: guest
    password: guest
    port: 5672
  redis:
    host: redis
    port: 6379

server:
  port: 9090

queue:
  twitter: twitter-track-hashtag
exchange:
  twitter: twitter-track-exchange
routing_key:
  track: "*"
```

There are two profiles in this yaml. Take a look at the different host for the RabbitMQ. In the default profile, we are able to connect the localhost because we exposed the RabbitMQ ports on the host. But on the Docker profile, we are not able to connect the localhost, we need to connect to the `rabbitmq` host, which is the host for the Twitter network.

Our RabbitMQ connection is ready to use. Let's try it in the next section. Let's go.

Creating exchanges, queues, and bindings for the Twitter Hashtag Service

Let's declare our RabbitMQ entities for the Tracked Hashtag usage. We will do that using the `@Configuration` class.

The RabbitMQ connection should look like this:

```
package springfive.twittertracked.infra.rabbitmq

import com.fasterxml.jackson.databind.ObjectMapper
import com.fasterxml.jackson.module.kotlin.KotlinModule
import org.springframework.amqp.core.Binding
import org.springframework.amqp.core.BindingBuilder
import org.springframework.amqp.core.Queue
import org.springframework.amqp.core.TopicExchange
import org.springframework.amqp.support.converter.Jackson2JsonMessageConverter
import org.springframework.beans.factory.annotation.Value
import org.springframework.context.annotation.Bean
import org.springframework.context.annotation.Configuration

@Configuration
open class RabbitMQConfiguration(@Value("${queue.twitter}") private
val queue:String,
                                 @Value("${exchange.twitter}") private
val exchange:String,
                                 @Value("${routing_key.track}")
private val routingKey:String){

    @Bean
    open fun queue():Queue{
        return Queue(this.queue,false)
    }
```

```kotlin
    @Bean
    open fun exchange():TopicExchange{
        return TopicExchange(this.exchange)
    }

    @Bean
    open fun binding(queue: Queue, exchange: TopicExchange): Binding {
        return
BindingBuilder.bind(queue).to(exchange).with(this.routingKey)
    }

    @Bean
    open fun converter(): Jackson2JsonMessageConverter {
        return
Jackson2JsonMessageConverter(ObjectMapper().registerModule(KotlinModul
e()))
    }

}
```

Pretty straightforward. We declared one exchange, queue, and binding, as we did before.

Sending the messages to the broker

This is the most interesting part now. When we want to save the `TrackedHashTag`, we must send the pretty new entity to the RabbitMQ. This process will send the message, and then the Twitter Gathering microservice will start to consume the stream in ten seconds.

We need to change the `TrackedHashTagService` a little bit; the final version should look like this:

```kotlin
package springfive.twittertracked.domain.service

import org.springframework.amqp.rabbit.core.RabbitTemplate
import org.springframework.beans.factory.annotation.Value
import org.springframework.stereotype.Service
import reactor.core.publisher.Mono
import springfive.twittertracked.domain.TrackedHashTag
import
springfive.twittertracked.domain.repository.TrackedHashTagRepository
import java.util.concurrent.CompletableFuture

@Service
class TrackedHashTagService(private val repository:
```

```
TrackedHashTagRepository,
                              private val rabbitTemplate:
RabbitTemplate,
                              @Value("${exchange.twitter}") private val
exchange: String,
                              @Value("${routing_key.track}") private val
routingKey: String) {

    fun save(hashTag: TrackedHashTag) {
        this.repository.save(hashTag).subscribe { data ->
            Mono.fromFuture(CompletableFuture.runAsync {
                this.rabbitTemplate.convertAndSend(this.exchange,
this.routingKey,
                    hashTag)
            })
        }
    }

    fun all() = this.repository.findAll()

}
```

Awesome job. When the new entity comes, it will be sent to the broker. We have finished our changes on the Tracked Hashtag Service.

Finally, we are able to test the whole flow. Let's start to play and perceive the real power of our built application.

It's showtime!!!

Testing the microservice's integrations

Now, we are ready to test the whole solution. Before you start, we need to check the following infrastructure items:

- Redis
- RabbitMQ

If the items are up and running, we can jump to the next section.

> We can use the `docker ps` command, and the command should list the Redis and RabbitMQ containers in running mode.

Running Tracked Hashtag Service

There is no special thing to run this application. It includes the infrastructure connections which are configured in the default profile in `application.yaml`.

Run the main function present on the `TrackedHashTagApplication`. We can use the IDE or command line to do that.

Check the console output; the output will be presented on the IDE or command line. We want to find the following line:

```
[            main] o.s.c.support.DefaultLifecycleProcessor  : Starting beans in phase 2147483647
[ctor-http-nio-1] r.ipc.netty.tcp.BlockingNettyContext      : Started HttpServer on /0:0:0:0:0:0:0:0:9090
[            main] o.s.b.web.embedded.netty.NettyWebServer   : Netty started on port(s): 9090
[            main] s.t.TrackedHashTagApplication$Companion   : Started TrackedHashTagApplication.Companion in 4.179 seconds (JVM running for 5.059)
```

It means the first application is fully operational and we are able to run Twitter Gathering. Please keep the application running as it is required.

Let's run Twitter Gathering!!!

Running the Twitter Gathering

This application is a little bit more complicated to run. We need to configure some environment variables for that. It is required because we do not want the Twitter application credentials in our repository.

It is pretty simple to do in the IDE. To do that, we can configure the run configuration. Let's do it:

1. Click on the **Edit Configurations...** like in the following image:

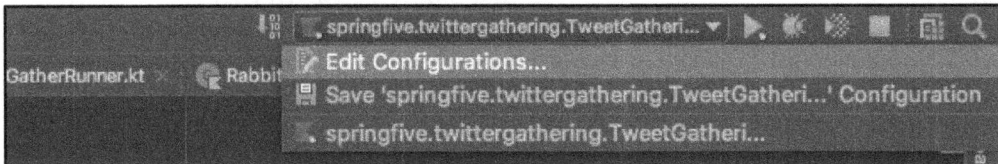

Then, we are able to see the **Environment variables** like this:

2. We need to click on **...**, as highlighted in the proceeding image.
3. The next screen will be shown and we can configure the **Environment Variable**:

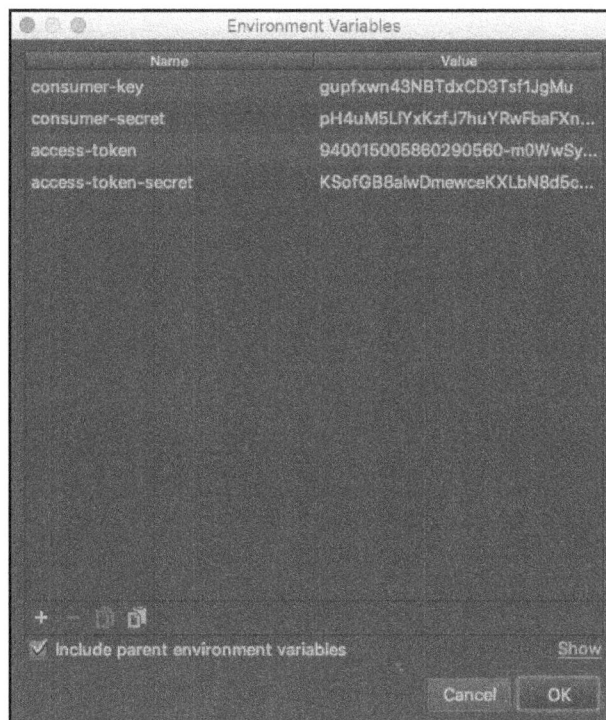

4. We need to configure the following environment variables:
     - **consumer-key**
     - **consumer-secret**
     - **access-token**
     - **access-token-secret**

   These values should be filled with the **Twitter Application Management** values.

Then, we can run the application. Run it!!

Now, we should see the following lines in the console, which means the application is running:

```
2017-12-23 15:58:46.362  INFO 1635 --- [ctor-http-nio-1] r.ipc.netty.tcp.BlockingNettyContext    : Started HttpServer on /0:0:0:0:0:0:0:0:8081
2017-12-23 15:58:46.363  INFO 1635 --- [          main] o.s.b.web.embedded.netty.NettyWebServer : Netty started on port(s): 8081
2017-12-23 15:58:46.369  INFO 1635 --- [          main] s.t.TweetGatheringApplication$Companion : Started TweetGatheringApplication.Companion in 7.012 seconds (JVM running for 7.645)
```

Awesome, our two microservices are running. Let's trigger the Twitter stream. We will do that in the next section.

> There are other ways to run the application, for example, with the maven Spring Boot goals or Java command line. If you prefer to run in the Java command line, keep in mind the -D argument to pass environment variables.

Testing stuff

We are excited to test the full integration. We can use the `curl` tool to send request data to the Tracked Hashtag Service. We want to track the `"bitcoin"` from Twitter.

We can execute the following command line:

```
curl -H "Content-Type: application/json" -X POST -d
'{"hashTag":"bitcoin","queue":"bitcoin"}'
http://localhost:9090/api/tracked-hash-tag
```

Check the HTTP status code; it should be HTTP status 200. After that, we can check the console from the Twitter Gathering project, and there should be a lot of Tweets logged.

Take a look at the log, the log must have Tweets like this:

```
RT @PayperExnet: Bitcoin is going down? GOOD! buy PAX and join the last days of the sale! buy PAX TOKEN NOW!!! @PayperExnet  @Bitcoin https...
RT @AttWorldNews: Bitcoin Goes on Wild Journey and it Could Solely Get Crazier #Bitcoin #Blockchain #LengthyIslandIcedTeaCorp https://t.co/...
@BKBrianKelly #Listen to #Bitcoin #audio #voxpop  #BitcoinMadness #LetMeAsk @AmaroufmediaAsk #YouTube... https://t.co/InqCM9QwOW
The blockchain that wouldn't die #crypto https://t.co/oYXFmg06fL
RT @rajneeshchhabra: No Place Like Home: The Internet Of Things And Its Promise For Consumers https://t.co/vAwghGoECa #IoT #InternetOfThing...
RT @ItsHooverr: *gets one dollar profit with bitcoin* https://t.co/PBdDvP7ydc
3 Cryptocurrencies to Consider Buying Over Bitcoin @themotleyfool #stocks $SAN, $IBM, $AXP, $BP https://t.co/gf1AVE87wo.
So in order to buy 1 bit you'll need to pay 3500 bits in fees. That sounds like fun! That's what the Core developer... https://t.co/un5QHfvNec
RT @lifeinvestasset: #CryptocurrencyLifeInvest (Change 24h):
—#Bitcoin $15.584,80 (-7,82%).
—#BitcoinCash $3.212,84 (-16,70%).
—#Ether $809...
RT @HealthRanger: What do you think: Do #China and #Russia really have this much control over #Bitcoin ? https://t.co/yjKPzOGQsW
RT @ToshiDesk: Guys — Next #ICO to watch out for!

https://t.co/Vfol0rWYce

They already have 10+ courses up on their Educational Site...
RT @AlexanderHaxton: One of my favorite ICOs right now: Trade.io is revolutionising the banking industry. Many #ICO's will be launched on T...
RT @VahapErenTR: Dear @Poloniex !
My friend's account @gurselkaraaslan has been frozen for 10 days.Please respond the #580589 ticket which...
@krios_io Bitcoin Diamond ($BCD) successfully launch mainnet and 28 global exchanges start trades! If you have bala... https://t.co/06uRmCVDY1
Zum ständigen auf und ab der #Bitcoin ein sehr lesenswerter Artikel von @SPIEGELONLINE – danke für das Interview,... https://t.co/iYJzhRibcB
RT @JamesGRickards: OK, let's make this simple. Bitcoin is a multiplayer game dressed up as a real world experience. Enjoy! https://t.co/Lx...
RT @rajneeshchhabra: No Place Like Home: The Internet Of Things And Its Promise For Consumers https://t.co/vAwghGoECa #IoT #InternetOfThing...
Bitcoin value tumbles by 30 per cent as investors face 'reality check' https://t.co/tg8kaTEZrw
Uh what? ?'◡  guess he forgot to show where the Nasdaq is today 😂😂😂 https://t.co/mChT4uMugM
```

Awesome!

Great work guys, we have the full application integrated with RabbitMQ and the Twitter stream.

Spring Actuator

The Spring Boot Actuator is a kind of helper when the application is running in production. The project provides built-in information of a deployed application.

In the microservices world, monitoring instances of applications are the key point to getting success. In these environments, there are usually many applications calling the other applications over the network protocols such as HTTP. The network is an unstable environment and sometimes it will fail; we need to track these incidents to make sure the application is up and fully operational.

The Spring Boot Actuator helps developers in these situations. The project exposes a couple of HTTP APIs with application information, such as the memory usage, CPU usage, application health check, and the infrastructure components of the application, such as a connection with databases and message brokers, as well.

One of the most important points is that the information is exposed over HTTP. It helps integrations with external monitor applications such as Nagios and Zabbix, for instance. There is no specific protocol for exposing this information.

Let's add it to our project and try a couple of endpoints.

Adding Spring Boot Actuator in our pom.xml

Spring Boot Actuator is pretty simple to configure in our `pom.xml`. We extended the parent pom of Spring Boot, so it is not necessary to specify the version of the dependency.

Let's configure our new dependency:

```
<dependencies>
  <dependency>
    <groupId>org.springframework.boot</groupId>
    <artifactId>spring-boot-starter-actuator</artifactId>
  </dependency>
</dependencies>
```

Awesome, really easy. Let's understand a little bit more before we test.

Actuator Endpoints

The projects have a lot of built-in endpoints and they will be up when the application started. Remember, we have used the starter project, which is the one that configures it automatically for us.

There are several endpoints for different requirements, and we will take a look at the most used in production microservices.

- `/health`: The most known actuator endpoint; it shows the application's health, and usually, there is a `status` attribute
- `/configprops`: Displays a collapse `@ConfigurationProperties`
- `/env`: Exposes properties from the Spring `ConfigurableEnvironment`
- `/dump`: Shows the thread dump
- `/info`: We can put some arbitrary information at this endpoint
- `/metrics`: Metrics from the running application
- `/mappings`: `@RequestMappings` endpoints from the current application

There is another important endpoint to show the application logs over the HTTP interface. The `/logfile` endpoint can help us visualize logfiles.

> The list of endpoints created by the Spring Boot Actuator can be found at: `https://docs.spring.io/spring-boot/docs/current/reference/html/production-ready-endpoints.html`.

Application custom information

There is one particular endpoint which we can use to expose custom information from our application. This information will be exposed to `/info` endpoint.

To configure that, we can use the `application.yaml` file and put the desired information respecting the pattern, as follows:

```
info:
    project: "twitter-gathering"
    kotlin: @kotlin.version@
```

Thr desired properties must be preceded by the `info.*`. Then, we can test our first actuator endpoint and check our `/info` resource.

Let's try to access the `http://localhost:8081/info`. The information filled on `application.yaml` should be displayed, as shown here:

```
←    C    ⓘ localhost:8081/actuator/info

{
    "project": "twitter-gathering",
    "kotlin": "1.2.0"
}
```

As we can see, the properties are exposed from the HTTP endpoint. We can use that to put the application version, for instance.

Testing endpoints

In version 2 of Spring Boot, the Spring Actuator management endpoints are disabled by default, because these endpoints can have sensitive data of a running application. Then, we need to configure to enable these endpoints properly.

There is a special point to pay attention to. If the application is exposed publicly, you should protect these endpoints.

Let's enable our management endpoints:

```
management:
  endpoints:
    web:
      expose: "*"
```

In the preceding configuration, we enabled all the management endpoints, and then we can start to test some endpoints.

Let's test some endpoints. First, we will test the metrics endpoints. This endpoint shows the metrics available for the running application. Go to `http://localhost:8081/actuator/metrics` and check the result:

```
← → C | ⓘ localhost:8081/actuator/metrics
▾ {
  ▾ "names": [
      "jvm.buffer.memory.used",
      "jvm.memory.used",
      "jvm.buffer.count",
      "logback.events",
      "process.uptime",
      "jvm.memory.committed",
      "system.load.average.1m",
      "http.server.requests",
      "jvm.buffer.total.capacity",
      "jvm.memory.max",
      "system.cpu.count",
      "process.start.time"
    ]
}
```

> We are using port 8081 because we configured the property
> server.port in application.yaml. The port can be changed as
> you desire.

There are a lot of metrics configured automatically for us. That endpoint exposes only the available metrics. To check the metric value, we need to use another endpoint. Let's check the value of the http.server.request.

The base endpoint to check the value is: http://localhost:8081/actuator/metrics/{metricName}. Then, we need to go to: http://localhost:8081/actuator/metrics/http.server.requests. The result should be:

```
←    C    ⓘ localhost:8081/actuator/metrics/http.server.requests

{
    "name": "http.server.requests",
    "measurements": [
        {
            "statistic": "Count",
            "value": 8
        },
        {
            "statistic": "TotalTime",
            "value": 281213374
        },
        {
            "statistic": "Max",
            "value": 281213374
        }
    ],
    "availableTags": [ … ]  // 4 items
}
```

As you can see, the server received eight calls. Try to hit a few more times to see the metrics changing.

Awesome job. Our microservice is ready for production. We have the docker image and endpoints for monitoring our services.

Summary

In this chapter, we learned and put into practice a lot of Spring Advanced concepts, such as RabbitMQ integration.

We have created a fully reactive WebClient and took advantage of the reactive paradigm; it enables resource computational optimization and increases performance for the application.

Also, we have integrated two microservices through the RabbitMQ broker. This is an excellent solution to integrating applications because it decouples the applications and also permits you to scale the application horizontally really easily. Message-driven is one of the required characteristics to build a reactive application; it can be found at Reactive Manifesto (`https://www.reactivemanifesto.org/en`).

In the next chapter, we will improve our solution and create a new microservice to stream the filtered Tweets for our clients. We will use RabbitMQ one more time.

6
Playing with Server-Sent Events

In Chapter 4, Kotlin Basics and Spring Data Redis and Chapter 5, *Reactive Web Clients*, we created two microservices. The first one is responsible for keeping tracked data on Redis and triggering the second microservice which one will consume the Twitter stream. This process happens asynchronously.

In this chapter, we will create another microservice which will consume the data produced by Twitter Gathering and expose it via a REST API. It will be possible to filter Tweets by text content.

We have consumed the Twitter stream using the **Server-Sent Events** (**SSE**); we created a reactive REST client to consume that. Now, it is time to create our implementation for SSE. We will consume the RabbitMQ queue and push the data to our connected clients.

We will take a look at the SSE and understand why this solution fits well for our couple of microservices.

At the end of the chapter, we will be confident about using SSE in the Spring ecosystem.

In this chapter, we will learn the following:

- Implementation of SSE endpoints with the Spring Framework
- Consuming RabbitMQ using the Reactor Rabbit client

Creating the Tweet Dispatcher project

Now, we will create our last microservice. It will push the Tweets filtered by Twitter Gathering for our connected clients, in this case, consumers.

In this chapter, we will use the Spring Initializr page to help us create our pretty new project. Let's create.

Using Spring Initializr once again

As you can see, the Spring Initializr page is a kind of partner for creating Spring projects. Let's use it one more time and create a project:

Go to `https://start.spring.io` and fill in the data using the following screenshot:

We have selected the **Reactive Web** dependencies; we will also keep using Kotlin as a programming language. Finally, click on the **Generate Project** button. Good, it is enough for us.

There are some missing dependencies which are not displayed in the Spring Initializr. We need to set these dependencies manually. We will do that task in the next section. Let's go there.

Additional dependencies

We need to use the Jackson Kotlin Module as a dependency to handle JSON properly in our new microservice. Also, we will use the Reactor RabbitMQ dependency, which allows us to interact in the reactive paradigm with the RabbitMQ Broker.

To add these dependencies, we need to add the following snippet to `pom.xml`:

```xml
<dependency>
  <groupId>com.fasterxml.jackson.module</groupId>
  <artifactId>jackson-module-kotlin</artifactId>
  <version>${jackson.version}</version>
</dependency>

<dependency>
  <groupId>io.projectreactor</groupId>
  <artifactId>reactor-test</artifactId>
  <scope>test</scope>
</dependency>

<dependency>
  <groupId>io.projectreactor.rabbitmq</groupId>
  <artifactId>reactor-rabbitmq</artifactId>
  <version>1.0.0.M1</version>
</dependency>
```

Awesome. Our dependencies are configured. Our project is ready to start.

Before we start, we need to understand, in depth, the concept of SSE. We will learn this in the next section.

Server-Sent Events

Server-Sent Events (SSE) is a standard way to send data streams from a server to clients. In this next section, we will learn how to implement it using the Spring Framework.

Also, we will understand the main differences between SSE and WebSockets.

A few words about the HTTP protocol

HTTP is an application layer protocol in the OSI model. The application layer is the last layer represented in the OSI model. It means this layer is closer to the user interface. The main purpose of this layer is to send and receive the data input by the user. In general, it happens by the user interface, also known as applications, such as file transfer and sending an email.

There are several protocols on the application layer such as Domain Name Service (DNS), which translates the domain names to IP address, or SMTP, whose main purpose is to deliver an email to a mail manager application.

The application layer interacts directly with software such as email clients, for instance; there are no interactions with the hardware parts. It is the last layer of the OSI model and the closest to the end user as well.

All these layers deal with software, which means there are no concerns about the physical parts represented in the OSI model.

> **TIP**
>
> A more detailed explanation of the OSI model can be found at: `https://support.microsoft.com/en-us/help/103884/the-osi-model-s-seven-layers-defined-and-functions-explained`.

The following is an OSI model representation:

7	Application Layer	HTTP, DNS, FTP, SMTP, etc...
6	Presentation Layer	SSL, SSH, JPEG, GIF, etc..
5	Session Layer	Sockets, RTP, PPTP, etc..
4	Transport Layer	TCP, UDP, etc...
3	Network Layer	IP, ICMP, etc...
2	Data Link Layer	PPP, Ethernet, etc...
1	Physical Layer	Ethernet, USB, etc...

The HTTP protocol uses the TCP protocol as a transportation channel. Then, it will establish a connection and start to flow the data on the channel.

The TCP protocol is a stream protocol and a full duplex channel. This means the server and clients can send data across the connection.

HTTP and persistent connections

The HTTP protocol is a request-response model, where the client submits the message (HTTP Request) and the server processes this message and sends the response (HTTP Response) to the client. The connection will be closed after the response is sent.

Look at the following diagram:

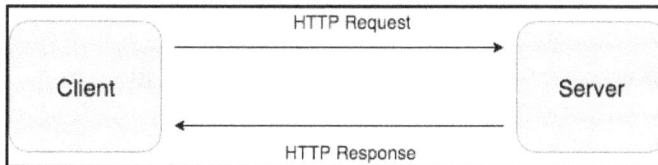

It's pretty simple to understand. The client will send the request, and in this case, the connection will be opened. After that, the server will receive the request to process something and it will send the answer to the client. The connection will be closed after the whole process. If the client needs to send a new request, the connection should be opened again and the flow happens in the same order.

There is a perceived drawback here, the clients need to open the new connection per-request. From the server's eyes, the server needs to process a lot of new connections simultaneously. This consumes a lot of CPU and memory.

On HTTP's 1.0 version, the connections are not persistent. To enable it, the `keep-alive` header should be included on the request. The header should look like this:

```
Connection: keep-alive
```

This is the only way to make an HTTP connection persistent on the 1.0 version, as described previously; when it happens, the connection will not be dropped by the server and the client is able to reuse the opened connection.

On HTTP 1.1, the connections are persistent by default; in this case, as opposed to the first version, the connection is kept opened and the client can use it normally.

There is a perceived improvement here and it can bring some advantages. The server needs to manage fewer connections, and it reduces a lot of CPU time. The HTTP Requests and Responses can be pipelined in the same connection.

As we know, *there is no such thing as a free lunch*. There are some disadvantages to this as well; the server needs to keep the connection opened and the server will reserve the required connection for the client. This may cause server unavailability in some scenarios.

Persistent connections can be useful to maintain a stream between the server and clients.

WebSockets

In the HTTP protocol, the communication supports full-duplex, which means the client and server can send data through the channel. The standard way to support this kind of communication is WebSockets. In this specification, both client and server can send data to each other in the persistent connection. Look at the following diagram:

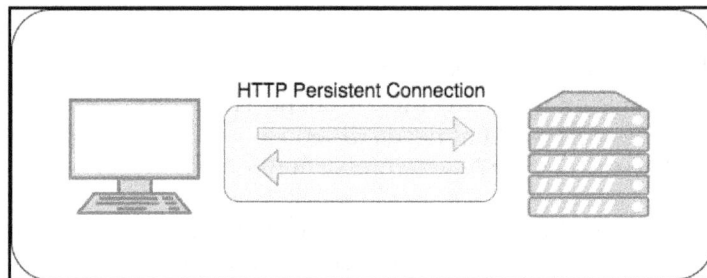

As we can see, the data can be sent and received by the two actors, client, and server—this is how WebSockets works.

In our case, we do not need to send any data to the server during the connection. Because of this characteristic, we will choose SSE. We will learn about them in the following section.

Server-Sent Events

As opposed to the full-duplex communication implemented by WebSockets, the SSE uses a half-duplex communication.

The client sends a request to the server, and when necessary, the server will push the data to the client. Remember the active actor here is the server; the data can be sent only by the server. This is a half-duplex behavior. Look at the following diagram:

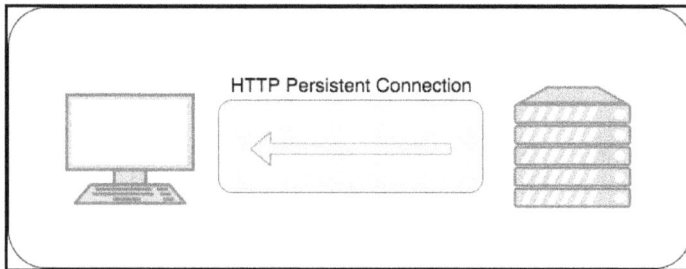

A piece of cake. It is the base of the SSE technology. SSE is self-explanatory. We will use it with the Spring Framework. However, before we do that, let's look at a Reactor RabbitMQ project.

Reactor RabbitMQ

Our solution is fully reactive, so we need to use Reactor RabbitMQ, which allows us to interact with the RabbitMQ broker using the reactive paradigm.

On this new microservice, we do not need to send messages through the message broker. Our solution will listen to the RabbitMQ queues and push the received Tweets for the connected clients.

Understanding the Reactor RabbitMQ

The Reactor RabbitMQ tries to provide a reactive library to interact with the RabbitMQ rboker. It enables developers to create non-blocking applications based on the reactive stream, using RabbitMQ as a message-broker solution.

As we learned before, this kind of solution, in general, does not use a lot of memory. The project was based on the RabbitMQ Java client and has similar functionalities, if we compare it to the blocking solution.

We are not using the `spring-amqp-starter`, so the magic will not happen. We will need to code the beans declarations for the Spring context and we will do that in the following section.

Configuring RabbitMQ Reactor beans

In this section, we will configure the RabbitMQ infrastructure classes in the Spring context. We will use a @Configuration class to declare it.

The configuration class should look like the following:

```
package springfive.twitterdispatcher.infra.rabbitmq

import com.fasterxml.jackson.databind.ObjectMapper
import com.fasterxml.jackson.module.kotlin.KotlinModule
import com.rabbitmq.client.ConnectionFactory
import org.springframework.beans.factory.annotation.Value
import org.springframework.context.annotation.Bean
import org.springframework.context.annotation.Configuration
import reactor.rabbitmq.ReactorRabbitMq
import reactor.rabbitmq.Receiver
import reactor.rabbitmq.ReceiverOptions

@Configuration
class RabbitMQConfiguration(private
@Value("${spring.rabbitmq.host}")  val host:String,
                               private
@Value("${spring.rabbitmq.port}")  val port:Int,
                               private
@Value("${spring.rabbitmq.username}")  val username:String,
                               private
@Value("${spring.rabbitmq.password}")  val password:String){

  @Bean
  fun mapper(): ObjectMapper =
ObjectMapper().registerModule(KotlinModule())

  @Bean
  fun connectionFactory():ConnectionFactory{
    val connectionFactory = ConnectionFactory()
    connectionFactory.username = this.username
    connectionFactory.password = this.password
    connectionFactory.host = this.host
    connectionFactory.port = this.port
    connectionFactory.useNio()
    return connectionFactory
  }

  @Bean
  fun receiver(connectionFactory: ConnectionFactory):Receiver{
      val options = ReceiverOptions()
      options.connectionFactory(connectionFactory)
```

```
return ReactorRabbitMq.createReceiver(options)
    }

}
```

There are two important things here. The first one is that we configured the Jackson support for Kotlin. It allows us to inject the `ObjectMapper` into our Spring beans. The next important thing is related to the RabbitMQ connections' configuration.

We have declared a `ConnectionFactory` bean for the Spring Context. We injected the configurations with `@Value` annotations and received the values on the constructor. We can set the value directly in the attributes, in the Kotlin language; look at the `ConnectionFactory` attributes assignments.

After the `ConnectionFactory` configuration, we are able to declare a receiver, which is a `Reactive` abstraction to consume the queues, using reactive programming. We receive the `ConnectionFactory` previously created and set it as the `ReceiverOptions`.

That is all for the Reactor RabbitMQ configuration.

Consuming the RabbitMQ queues reactively

Now, we will consume the RabbitMQ queues. The implementation is quite similar to what we have seen in the blocking implementation, and the names of the functions are similar as well.

We have consumed some RabbitMQ messages in the previous chapters, but this solution is quite different. Now, we will use the Reactive RabbitMQ implementation. The main idea here is to consume the stream of events; these events represent the messages that have arrived in the broker. These messages arrive and the Reactor RabbitMQ converts these messages to Flux, to enable us to consume in the reactive paradigm.

In the reactive paradigm, the representation of a stream of events (we can think of messages in the queue), is the `Flux`.

Then our function, which is listening to the RabbitMQ, should return `Flux`, an infinite representation of events. The Receiver implementation returns the `Flux` of messages, which is enough for us and fits well with our needs.

Our implementation should look like the following:

```
package springfive.twitterdispatcher.domain.service

import com.fasterxml.jackson.annotation.JsonIgnoreProperties
import com.fasterxml.jackson.annotation.JsonProperty
import com.fasterxml.jackson.databind.ObjectMapper
import com.fasterxml.jackson.module.kotlin.readValue
import org.springframework.beans.factory.annotation.Value
import org.springframework.stereotype.Service
import reactor.core.publisher.Flux
import reactor.core.publisher.Mono
import reactor.rabbitmq.Receiver

@Service
class TwitterDispatcher(private @Value("${queue.twitter}") val
queue: String,
        private val receiver: Receiver,
        private val mapper: ObjectMapper) {

    fun dispatch(): Flux<Tweet> {
        return this.receiver.consumeAutoAck(this.queue).flatMap {
message ->
Mono.just(mapper.readValue<Tweet>(String(message.body)))
        }
    }

}

@JsonIgnoreProperties(ignoreUnknown = true)
data class Tweet(val id: String = "",
    val text: String = "", @JsonProperty("created_at")
    val createdAt: String = "", val user: TwitterUser =
TwitterUser("", ""))

@JsonIgnoreProperties(ignoreUnknown = true)
data class TwitterUser(val id: String, val name: String)
```

Let's understand a little bit more. We received the `Receiver` as an injection in our constructor. When someone invokes the `dispatch()` function, the `Receiver` will start to consume the queue, which was injected in the constructor as well.

The `Receiver` produces `Flux<Delivery>`. Now, we need to convert the instance of `Flux<Delivery>`, which represents a message abstraction, to our domain model Tweet. The `flatMap()` function can do it for us, but first, we will convert the `message.body` to string and then we have used Jackson to read JSON and convert to our Tweet domain model.

Take a look at how simple the code is to read; the API is fluent and really readable.

The consumer will not terminate until the connected client disconnects. We will be able to see this behavior soon.

Filtering streams

We are receiving the messages from RabbitMQ. Now, we need to return the messages to the connected customer.

For that, we will use SSE with Spring WebFlux. The solution is a good fit for us because we will produce a `Flux<Tweet>` and start to push the Tweets for our clients. The clients will send a query to filter the desired Tweets.

The application will be fully reactive. Let's take a look at our code:

```
package springfive.twitterdispatcher.domain.controller

import org.springframework.http.MediaType
import org.springframework.web.bind.annotation.GetMapping
import org.springframework.web.bind.annotation.RequestMapping
import org.springframework.web.bind.annotation.RequestParam
import org.springframework.web.bind.annotation.RestController
import reactor.core.publisher.Flux
import springfive.twitterdispatcher.domain.service.Tweet
import springfive.twitterdispatcher.domain.service.TwitterDispatcher

@RestController
@RequestMapping("/tweets")
class TweetResource(private val dispatcher: TwitterDispatcher) {

  @GetMapping(produces = [MediaType.TEXT_EVENT_STREAM_VALUE])
  fun tweets(@RequestParam("q")query:String):Flux<Tweet>{
    return dispatcher.dispatch()
        .filter({ tweet: Tweet? ->
tweet!!.text.contains(query,ignoreCase = true) })
    }
}
```

Pretty easy and simple to understand. We have declared the `tweets()` function; this function is mapped to a GET HTTP Request and produces a `MediaType.TEXT_EVENT_STREAM_VALUE`. When the client connects to the endpoint, the server will start to send Tweets accordingly with the desired argument.

When the client disconnects, the Reactor RabbitMQ will close the requested RabbitMQ connection.

Dockerizing the whole solution

Now, it is time to wrap the whole solution and create a Docker image for all projects. It is useful to run the projects anywhere we want.

We will configure all the projects step by step and then run the solution in Docker containers. As a challenge, we can use `docker-compose` to orchestrate the whole solution in a single `yaml` file.

For the Tracked Hashtag Service, we have created the docker image. Then, we will start to configure the Tweet Gathering, and the last one is Tweet Dispatcher. Let's do that right now.

> You can find more `docker-compose` project details at: `https://docs.docker.com/compose/`. Also, in the new versions, `docker-compose` supports Docker Swarm to orchestrate the stack between cluster nodes. It can be really useful to deploy Docker containers in production.

Tweet Gathering

Let's configure our `pom.xml` for the Tweet Gathering project.

The build node should look like the following:

```
<plugin>
  <groupId>io.fabric8</groupId>
  <artifactId>docker-maven-plugin</artifactId>
  <version>0.21.0</version>
  <configuration>
    <images>
      <image>
<name>springfivebyexample/${project.build.finalName}</name>
```

```
        <build>
          <from>openjdk:latest</from>
          <entryPoint>java -Dspring.profiles.active=container -jar
/application/${project.build.finalName}.jar</entryPoint>
          <assembly>
            <basedir>/application</basedir>
            <descriptorRef>artifact</descriptorRef>
            <inline>
              <id>assembly</id>
              <files>
                <file>
<source>target/${project.build.finalName}.jar</source>
                </file>
              </files>
            </inline>
          </assembly>
          <tags>
            <tag>latest</tag>
          </tags>
          <ports>
            <port>8081</port>
          </ports>
        </build>
        <run>
          <namingStrategy>alias</namingStrategy>
        </run>
        <alias>${project.build.finalName}</alias>
      </image>
    </images>
  </configuration>
</plugin>
```

Take a look at the port configuration; it should be the same as what we have configured in the `application.yaml`. The configuration is done, so let's create our Docker image:

```
mvn clean install docker:build
```

The command output should look like the following screenshot:

```
[INFO] DOCKER> [springfivebyexample/tweet_gathering:latest] "tweet_gathering": Created docker-build.tar in 196 milliseconds
[INFO] DOCKER> [springfivebyexample/tweet_gathering:latest] "tweet_gathering": Built image sha256:e1973
[INFO] DOCKER> [springfivebyexample/tweet_gathering:latest] "tweet_gathering": Tag with latest
[INFO]
[INFO] BUILD SUCCESS
[INFO]
[INFO] Total time: 13.714 s
[INFO] Finished at: 2018-01-04T22:51:58-02:00
[INFO] Final Memory: 65M/524M
```

There is an image recently created and tagged as a latest; the image is ready to run. Let's do the same thing for our Tweet Dispatcher project.

Tweet Dispatcher

Our new plugin entry should look like this:

```
<plugin>
  <groupId>io.fabric8</groupId>
  <artifactId>docker-maven-plugin</artifactId>
  <version>0.21.0</version>
  <configuration>
    <images>
      <image>
<name>springfivebyexample/${project.build.finalName}</name>
        <build>
          <from>openjdk:latest</from>
          <entryPoint>java -Dspring.profiles.active=container -jar
          /application/${project.build.finalName}.jar</entryPoint>
          <assembly>
            <basedir>/application</basedir>
            <descriptorRef>artifact</descriptorRef>
            <inline>
              <id>assembly</id>
              <files>
                <file>
          <source>target/${project.build.finalName}.jar</source>
                </file>
              </files>
            </inline>
          </assembly>
          <tags>
            <tag>latest</tag>
          </tags>
          <ports>
            <port>9099</port>
          </ports>
        </build>
        <run>
          <namingStrategy>alias</namingStrategy>
        </run>
        <alias>${project.build.finalName}</alias>
      </image>
    </images>
  </configuration>
</plugin>
```

Take a look at the port configuration, one more time. It will be used by Docker to expose the correct port. Now, we can run the image creation command:

```
mvn clean install docker:build
```

Then, we can see the command's output, as shown in the following screenshot:

```
[INFO] DOCKER> [springfivebyexample/tweet_dispatcher:latest] "tweet_dispatcher": Created docker-build.tar in 164 milliseconds
[INFO] DOCKER> [springfivebyexample/tweet_dispatcher:latest] "tweet_dispatcher": Built image sha256:19317
[INFO] DOCKER> [springfivebyexample/tweet_dispatcher:latest] "tweet_dispatcher": Tag with latest
[INFO] ------------------------------------------------------------------------
[INFO] BUILD SUCCESS
[INFO] ------------------------------------------------------------------------
[INFO] Total time: 14.020 s
[INFO] Finished at: 2018-01-04T23:07:29-02:00
[INFO] Final Memory: 61M/528M
[INFO] ------------------------------------------------------------------------
```

Awesome, all images are ready. Let's run it.

> We need to create Docker images for all the projects. The process is the same; configure the maven Docker plugin and then use `mvn clean install docker:build` on the project. The full source code can be found at GitHub. The Tracked Hashtag Service can be found here (`https://github.com/PacktPublishing/Spring-5.0-By-Example/tree/master/Chapter04`), the Tweet Gathering can be found here (`https://github.com/PacktPublishing/Spring-5.0-By-Example/tree/master/Chapter05`) and finally, the Tweet Dispatcher can be found here (`https://github.com/PacktPublishing/Spring-5.0-By-Example/tree/master/Chapter06`).

Running the containerized solution

We are ready to run the solution in Docker containers. We have been running the solution with the IDE or command line, but now we will spin up some container and test the solution and Spring profiles as well.

Before that, let's do a quick recap of the solution:

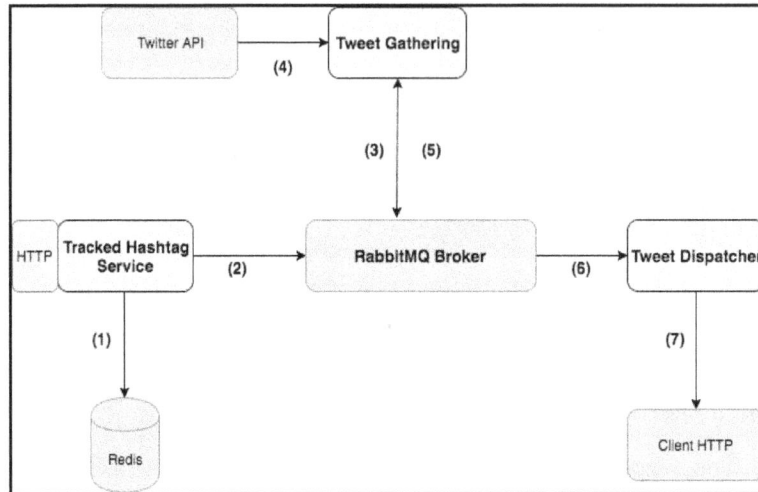

1. The first operation, the **Tracked Hashtag Service**, will persist the hashtag in the **Redis** database.
2. After that, the **Tracked Hashtag Service** will send the newly tracked hashtag to a queue in the **RabbitMQ** Broker.
3. **Tweet Gathering** is listening to the queue to track Tweets and trigger the event and starts by listening to the **Twitter stream**.
4. **Tweet Gathering** starts to get Tweets from the **Twitter stream.**
5. **Tweet Gathering** publishes Tweets to a queue in the **RabbitMQ broker**.
6. **Tweet Dispatcher** consumes the message.
7. **Tweet Dispatcher** sends the message to the **Client** using SSE.

Now that we have understood the solution, let's starts the containers.

Running the Tracked Hashtag Service container

The image has been created in the previous section, so now we are able to spin up the container. The command to start the container should look like this:

```
docker run -d --name tracked --net twitter -p 9090:9090
springfivebyexample/tracked_hashtag
```

Let's explain the instruction. `-d` tells the Docker engine to run the container in background mode or detached. The other important parameter is `--net`, which attaches the container to the desired network.

We can use the following command to tail the container logs at runtime:

```
docker logs tracked -f
```

This command is like the `tail -f` command on Linux, which looks at the last part of the log stream. We can remove the flag `-f` to see the last lines of the log.

The output of docker logs should look like this:

Look at the profile selected, in the logs:

```
INFO 7 --- [            main] s.t.TrackedHashTagApplication$Companion
: The following profiles are active: docker
```

Remember, we have parameterized it in the `pom.xml` file from the Tracked Hash Tag Service. Let's look at the following snippet:

```
<entryPoint>java -Dspring.profiles.active=docker -jar
/application/${project.build.finalName}.jar</entryPoint>
```

Awesome job. Our first service is running properly. Let's run Tweet Gathering; there is some interesting configuration here.

> We have created the Twitter network in `chapter 4`, *Kotlin Basics and Spring Data Redis*, and we need to use this network to enable the containers to see each other by container name in our custom network.

Running the Tweet Gathering container

To run the **Tweet Gathering** application is slightly different. This container needs environment variables which are used to interact with the Twitter API. We can use the `-e` argument on the `docker run` command. Let's do that:

```
docker run -d --name gathering --net twitter -e
CONSUMER_KEY=gupfxwn43NBTdxCD3Tsf1JgMu
-e CONSUMER_SECRET=pH4uM5LlYxKzfJ7huYRwFbaFXn7ooK01LmqCP69QV9a9kZrHw5
-e ACCESS_TOKEN=940015005860290560-m0WwSyxGvp5ufff9KW2zm5LGXLaFLov
-e ACCESS_TOKEN_SECRET=KSofGB8aIwDmewceKXLbN8d5chvZkZyB31VZa09pNBhLo
-p 8081:8081 springfivebyexample/tweet_gathering
```

Take a look at the environment variables we have configured in the `application.yaml` file. The Docker run command will inject these variables into the system and then we can use them in our Java application.

Let's inspect our container logs. We can do that using the following command:

```
2018-01-15 23:54:29.084  INFO 6 --- [cTaskExecutor-1] o.s.a.r.c.CachingConnectionFactory       : Created new connection: rabbitConnectionFactory#57d
7f8ca:0/SimpleConnection@50ecfb4a [delegate=amqp://guest@172.19.0.6:5672/, localPort= 48016]
2018-01-15 23:54:29.088  INFO 6 --- [cTaskExecutor-1] o.s.amqp.rabbit.core.RabbitAdmin          : Auto-declaring a non-durable, auto-delete, or exclu
sive Queue (twitter-stream) durable:false, auto-delete:false, exclusive:false. It will be redeclared if the broker stops and is restarted while the
connection factory is alive, but all messages will be lost.
2018-01-15 23:54:29.088  INFO 6 --- [cTaskExecutor-1] o.s.amqp.rabbit.core.RabbitAdmin          : Auto-declaring a non-durable, auto-delete, or exclu
sive Queue (twitter-track-hashtag) durable:false, auto-delete:false, exclusive:false. It will be redeclared if the broker stops and is restarted whi
le the connection factory is alive, but all messages will be lost.
2018-01-15 23:54:29.235  INFO 6 --- [          main] r.ipc.netty.tcp.BlockingNettyContext      : Started HttpServer on /0.0.0.0:8081
2018-01-15 23:54:29.242  INFO 6 --- [          main] o.s.b.web.embedded.netty.NettyWebServer   : Netty started on port(s): 8081
2018-01-15 23:54:29.246  INFO 6 --- [          main] s.t.TweetGatheringApplication$Companion   : Started TweetGatheringApplication.Companion in 20.5
99 seconds (JVM running for 21.708)
```

Awesome, our application is up and running. As you can see, the application is connected to the RabbitMQ Broker.

> **RabbitMQ** and **Redis** should be running to enable you to run Tweet Gathering. We can check it using the `docker ps` command; it will list the running containers, RabbitMQ and Redis need to be on this list.

Now, we can run the Dispatcher application to complete the whole solution. Let's do that.

Running the Tweet Dispatcher container

There is no secret to running the Tweet Dispatcher container. We can use the following command to run it:

```
docker run -d --name dispatcher --net twitter -p 9099:9099
springfivebyexample/tweet_dispatcher
```

It will spin up the container, it is a good idea to name the container during the run. It can help us manage the container with command-line tools, such as `docker container ls` or `docker ps`, because it shows the container name in the last column. Then, let's check if our container is running, so type the following command:

```
docker container ls
```

Or, you can run the following command:

```
docker ps
```

We should be able to see the Gathering container running, like in the following output:

There are five containers, three applications, and two infrastructure services, **RabbitMQ** and **Redis**.

At any time, we can stop the desired container using the following command:

```
docker stop gathering
```

The `docker stop` will only stop the container; the information will be kept in the container volume. We can use the container name or container ID as well, we named it before. It is easy for us. If we use the `docker ps` command, the image recently stopped will never appear on the list. To show all the containers, we can use `docker ps -a` or `docker container ls -a`.

Now, we will start the container again; the command is self-explanatory:

```
docker start gathering
```

The container is running again. We have practiced more with Docker.

Awesome job, guys. The whole application is containerized. Well done.

> We can use the Linux instruction and execute some batch instructions. For instance, we can use `docker stop $(docker ps -q)` — it will stop all containers running. The `docker ps -q` command will bring only the container's IDs.

The docker-compose tool

In the microservices architectural style, the whole solution is decoupled in small and well-defined services. Usually, when we adopt these styles, we have more than one artifact to deploy.

Let's analyze our solution; we have three components to deploy. We have used the Docker containers and we have run these containers using the `docker run` command. One by one, we have used `docker run` three times. It is quite complex and very hard to do in the development routine.

`docker-compose` can help us in this scenario. It is a tool which helps to orchestrate Docker containers in complex scenarios like ours.

Let's imagine our application is growing fast and we need to build four more microservices to achieve the desired business case, it will implicate on four more `docker run` commands and will probably be painful to maintain, especially during the development life cycle. Sometimes, we need to promote the artifacts to test the environment and we probably need to modify our command line to achieve this.

`docker-compose` enables us to deploy multiple containers with a single `yaml` file. This `yaml` file has a defined structure which allows us to define and configure several containers in the same file. Moreover, we can run the solution configured in this `yaml` file with a single command, it makes development life easy.

The tool can work on the local machine or we can integrate it with the Docker Swarm tool which can manage clusters of Docker hosts.

Docker Swarm is a native tool to manage docker clusters. It makes it easy to deploy a container on the Docker cluster. In the new version, `docker-compose` is fully integrated with Docker Swarm. We can define it from Docker Swarm properties in `docker-compose.yaml`. The Docker Swarm documentation can be found at: `https://docs.docker.com/engine/swarm/`.

The `docker-compose yaml` has a defined structure to follow; the documentation can be found here: `https://docs.docker.com/compose/compose-file/#compose-and-docker-compatibility-matrix`. We will create a simple file to understand the `docker-compose` behaviors. Let's create our simple `yaml`— the `yaml` should look like this:

```
version: '3'
services:
  rabbitmq:
    image: rabbitmq:3.7.0-management-alpine
    ports:
      - "5672:5672"
      - "15672:15672"
  redis:
    image: "redis:alpine"
    ports:
      - "6379:6379"
```

The `yaml` in the preceding code will create the structure detailed in the following diagram:

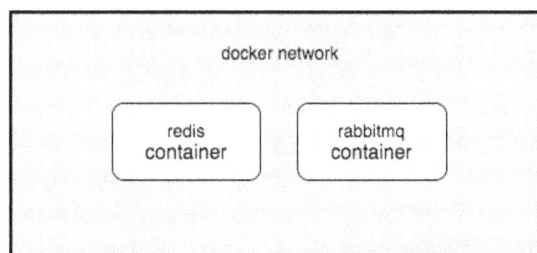

It simplifies the development time. Now, we will learn how to install `docker-compose`.

Installing docker-compose

The `docker-compose` installation is pretty simple and well-documented. We are using Linux, so we will use the Linux instructions.

Open the terminal and use the following command:

```
sudo curl -L
https://github.com/docker/compose/releases/download/1.18.0/docker-comp
ose-`uname -s`-`uname -m` -o /usr/local/bin/docker-compose
```

Wait for the download and then we can execute the following instructions to give executable permissions for the program. Let's do this by executing the following command:

```
sudo chmod +x /usr/local/bin/docker-compose
```

As you may know, you may be asked for the administrator password. Our `docker-compose` is now installed. Let's check it:

```
docker-compose --version
```

The prompt will display the installed version, like the following screenshot:

```
docker-compose version 1.18.0, build 8dd22a9
```

`docker-compose` is up and running, so let's jump to the next section and start to create our `yaml` file and deploy the whole stack with one single command.

> For different operating systems, the instructions can be found here: `https://docs.docker.com/compose/install/#install-compose`. Then, you can navigate around the instructions and click on the desired operating system.

Creating a docker-compose file

Now, we have `docker-compose` installed and we can try to work with the tool. We want to run the whole stack with a single command. We will create the `yaml` file to represent the stack. Our `yaml` file should have the Redis container, the RabbitMQ container, the Tracked Hashtag application, the Gathering application, and finally, the Dispatcher application.

We can create a `docker-compose.yaml` file wherever we want, there is no restriction for that.

Our `docker-compose.yaml` file should look like the following:

```yaml
version: '3'
services:
  rabbitmq:
    image: rabbitmq:3.7.0-management-alpine
    hostname: rabbitmq
    ports:
      - "5672:5672"
      - "15672:15672"
    networks:
      - solution
  redis:
    image: "redis:4.0.6-alpine"
    hostname: redis
    ports:
      - "6379:6379"
    networks:
      - solution
  tracked:
    image: springfivebyexample/tracked_hashtag
    ports:
      - "9090:9090"
    networks:
      - solution
  gathering:
    image: springfivebyexample/tweet_gathering
    ports:
      - "8081:8081"
    networks:
      - solution
    environment:
      - CONSUMER_KEY=gupfxwn43NBTdxCD3Tsf1JgMu
      -
CONSUMER_SECRET=pH4uM5LlYxKzfJ7huYRwFbaFXn7ooK01LmqCP69QV9a9kZrHw5
      - ACCESS_TOKEN=940015005860290560-
m0WwSyxGvp5ufff9KW2zm5LGXLaFLov
      -
ACCESS_TOKEN_SECRET=KSofGB8aIwDmewceKXLbN8d5chvZkZyB31VZa09pNBhLo
  dispatcher:
    image: springfivebyexample/tweet_dispatcher
    ports:
      - "9099:9099"
    networks:
      - solution
```

```
networks:
    solution:
        driver: bridge
```

As you can see, we have defined the whole stack in the `yaml`. Something to note is that we can find some similarities with the `docker run` command, in fact, it will use the Docker engine to run. The `environment` node in yaml has the same behavior as – e in the Docker run command.

We have defined the application ports, docker images, and have also connected the containers to the same network. This is really important because when we use the `docker-compose` file name on the network, it can find that the container name has a kind of DNS behavior.

For instance, inside the defined network `solution`, the container can find the Redis container instance by the name `redis`.

Running the solution

`docker-compose` simplifies the process to run the whole stack. Our `yaml` file was configured and defined properly.

Let's start the solution. Run the following command:

```
docker-compose up -d
```

The command is pretty simple, the -d parameter instructs Docker to run the command in the background. As we did on the Docker run command.

The output of this command should be the following:

```
Creating network "compose_solution" with driver "bridge"
Creating compose_gathering_1  ... done
Creating compose_redis_1      ... done
Creating compose_tracked_1    ... done
Creating compose_rabbitmq_1   ... done
Creating compose_dispatcher_1 ... done
```

Take a look, `docker-compose` has created a network for our stack. In our case, the network driver is a bridge, after the network creation, the containers are started.

Testing the network

Let's test it, find the Gathering container – the container name in `docker-compose` is prefixed by the folder name, where `docker-compose` was started.

For instance, I have started my `docker-compose` stack in the compose folder. My container name will be `compose_gathering_1` because of the folder name.

Then, we will connect the Gathering container. It can be achieved using the following command:

```
docker exec -it compose_gathering_1  /bin/bash
```

The `docker exec` command allows us to execute something inside the container. In our case, we will execute the `/bin/bash` program.

The command structure is like this:

```
docker exec -it <container name or container id> <program or
instruction>
```

Awesome, pay attention to the command line. It should be changed because now we are in the container command line:

```
root@cc6520b2bdc5:/# ls -l
total 68
drwxr-xr-x    2 root root 4096 Jan 11 00:11 application
drwxr-xr-x    1 root root 4096 Sep 14 04:18 bin
```

We are not connected as a root on our host, but now we are a root on the container. This container is on the same network as the Redis container instance, which is called `redis`.

Let's test with the `ping` command; we should be able to find the `redis` container by the name `redis`, let's do it. Type the following:

```
ping redis
```

The command output should be the following:

```
root@cc6520b2bdc5:/# ping redis
PING redis (172.19.0.2): 56 data bytes
64 bytes from 172.19.0.2: icmp_seq=0 ttl=64 time=0.280 ms
64 bytes from 172.19.0.2: icmp_seq=1 ttl=64 time=0.368 ms
64 bytes from 172.19.0.2: icmp_seq=2 ttl=64 time=0.221 ms
64 bytes from 172.19.0.2: icmp_seq=3 ttl=64 time=0.255 ms
64 bytes from 172.19.0.2: icmp_seq=4 ttl=64 time=0.310 ms
^C--- redis ping statistics ---
5 packets transmitted, 5 packets received, 0% packet loss
round-trip min/avg/max/stddev = 0.221/0.287/0.368/0.050 ms
```

Awesome, our container can find the Redis container by the name. The `yaml` file is fully working.

Summary

In this chapter, we completed our second solution. We were introduced to the RabbitMQ Reactor library, which enables us to connect to RabbitMQ, using the reactive paradigm.

We have prepared the whole solution in Docker containers and connected it to the same network to enable the applications to talk to each other.

We also learned the important pattern for pushing data from server to client through the HTTP persistent connection, and we learned the difference between WebSockets and Server-Sent Events, as well.

Finally, we learned how `docker-compose` helps us to create the stack and run the whole solution with a couple of commands.

In the following chapters, we will build a fully microservice solution, using some important patterns such as Service Discovery, API Gateway, Circuit Breakers, and much more.

Airline Ticket System

7

Our last projects—Twitter Consumers, Twitter Gathering, and Twitter Dispatcher—were excellent. We learned several exciting features, and they were implemented using the new features present in Spring 5.0. All of them are implemented in Reactive Streams and use Kotlin as the programming language. They are the hottest features in Spring 5.0; it was an impressive progression.

However, there are notably missing parts on these projects; we have microservice needs in mind. There are no infrastructure services such as service discovery, distributed configurations, API Gateway, distributed tracing, and monitoring. These kinds of services are mandatory in distributed systems such as microservice architectures.

There are several reasons for that. Firstly, we can think of the configuration management. Let's imagine the following scenario – in the development cycle, we have three environments: DEV, TST, and PROD. This is a pretty simple standard found in companies. Also, we have an application decoupled in 4 microservices, then with the minimum infrastructure, we have 12 instances of services; remember, this is a good scenario because in a real situation, we will probably have several instances of microservice applications.

In the earlier scenario, we will maintain at least three configuration files per microservice, remember there are three environments for which we need to keep the configurations. Then, we will have 12 *versions* of settings. It is a hard task to maintain the configurations, to keep the files synchronized and updated. These files probably contain sensitive information, such as database passwords and message brokers' configurations, and it is not recommended that you put these files on the host machines.

In this case, the distributed configuration can solve our problems easily. We will learn about configuration servers in this chapter, and other infrastructure services as well.

Let's summarize what we will learn in this chapter:

- How to create a Config Server
- Implementing a service discovery with Eureka
- Monitoring applications with Spring Cloud Zipkin
- Exposing the applications with the Spring Cloud Gateway

The Airline Ticket System

In these last few chapters, we will work on the Airline Ticket System. The solution is quite complex and involves a lot of HTTP integrations and message-based solutions. We will explore what we have learned from the book journey.

We will use Spring Messaging, Spring WebFlux, and Spring Data components to create the solution. The application will split up into several microservices to guarantee the scalability, elasticity, and fault tolerance for the system.

Also, we will have some infrastructure services to help us deliver an efficient system. Some new patterns will be introduced, such as circuit breakers and OAuth. In the infrastructure layer, we will use the Netflix OSS components integrated with the Spring Framework ecosystem.

The main purpose of our application is to sell airline tickets, but to achieve this task, we need to build an entire ecosystem. We will build a microservice which will manage the seats and planes' characteristics. There will also be a microservice to manage available company flights; the basic idea is to manage flight dates and routes. Of course, we will have a microservice to manage passengers, fares, bookings, and payments. Finally, we will have an `e-commerce` API with which end users will buy airline tickets.

Airline functionalities

We will create some microservices to compose the solution and then we will decompose the solution into small pieces, that is, microservices. For that, we will use the Bounded Context pattern which is an essential part of the **Domain-Driven Design (DDD)**.

Let's look at the following diagram to have an idea about what we will build:

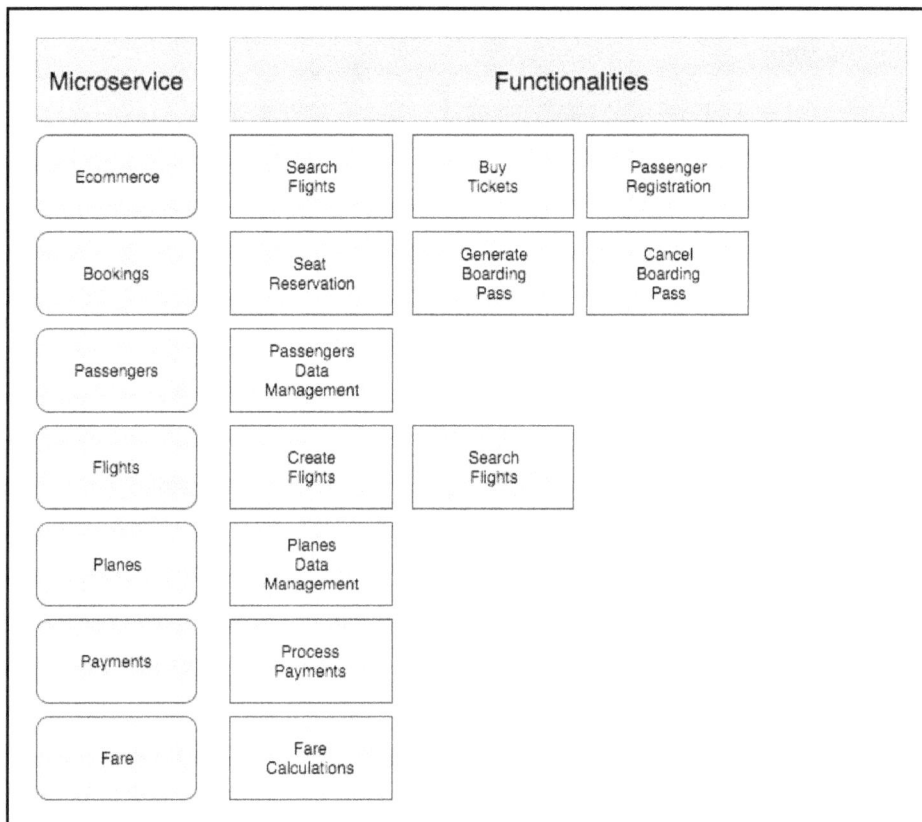

It is a summary of what we will do in these few chapters; we have defined the basic functionalities for each microservice.

Now, we will take a look at components; let's go to the next section.

Solution diagram

The following diagram illustrates the whole solution, which we will implement in the following chapters:

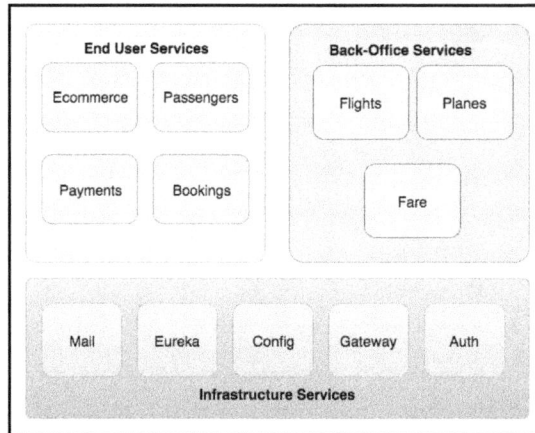

As we can see, there are different kinds of components. Some components will be exposed through the **Gateway** for end users, in our case, our customers. There is a category which the company users will use to register flights, for instance, where these microservices will be exposed on **Gateway** as well.

The infrastructure category will not be exposed over the internet, except the **Gateway** service. These services help the solution infrastructure and should be not exposed because there is sensitive data in there.

There a lot of things to do; let's get on with the show.

> DDD enables us to deal easily with microservices. Some DDD patterns fit well for the microservices architectural style. There are many interesting books in the Packt catalog.

Spring Cloud Config Server

When we adopt the microservices architectural style, there are some challenges to solve. One of the first problems to solve is how to manage the microservices configurations in the cluster, and how to make them easy and distributed, as well?

Spring Cloud Config provides a Spring way, based on annotations and Spring beans. It is an easy way to solve this problem in a production-ready module. There are three main components in this module, the Configuration Repository, that is, version control system, the Config Server, which will provide the configurations, and finally, the Configuration Client, which will consume the configuration from the Config Server.

This module supplies the configuration files over an HTTP interface. It is the main feature provided by this project and it acts as a central repository for configuration in our architecture.

We want to remove the `application.yaml` file from our classpath; we do not need this file in classpath anymore, and so we will use the Config Server to serve this file for our application.

Now, our microservices will not have the configuration file, that is, `application.yaml`. During the application bootstrap, the application will look at the Config Server to get the correct configuration, and after that, the application will finish the bootstrap to get them up and into running status.

The following diagram explains the **Config Server** and Config Client:

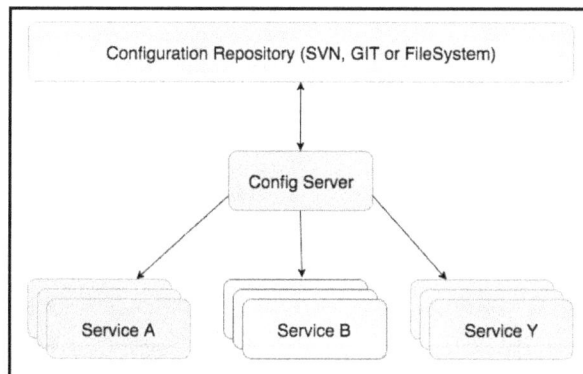

As we can see, the basic idea here is to try to distribute the configuration through the **Config Server**. There are some advantages to using this approach. The first one keeps the configuration in the central repository. It makes the configuration easy to maintain. The second one is that the configurations are served with a standard protocol, such as HTTP. Most of the developers know the protocol and make the interaction easy to understand. Finally, and most importantly, when the properties change, it can reflect immediately in other microservices.

Time to implement it. Let's go there.

> The Config Server is usually maintained on private networks, if we are deploying in cloud environments, although the Spring Cloud Config supports encrypt and decrypt based on symmetric or asymmetric keys. Keep in the mind that the microservices configurations should not be published on public networks.

Creating the Config Server project

Let's create our project with Spring Initializr. Go to Spring Initializr (`https://start.spring.io/`) and follow the image instructions:

Click on **Generate Project** and then we can open the project on the IDE.

Enabling Spring Cloud Config Server

We will use the Git repository as a property source, and then we need to create a repository to keep these files. However, before that, let's navigate to the `pom.xml` file and see some interesting stuff. We can find the following dependency:

```
<dependency>
  <groupId>org.springframework.cloud</groupId>
  <artifactId>spring-cloud-config-server</artifactId>
</dependency>
```

It is a Config Server dependency. It enables us to use the Config Server in our application. Remember, we need to put this into the `pom.xml` file to achieve the required Config Server.

Using GitHub as a repository

The Spring Cloud Config Server enables us to use different datastore technologies to work as a properties repository. There are some options such as Git repository, filesystem, or SVN and others, provided by the community.

We will choose the Git repository, and use GitHub as a host.

> We will use the Git repository that has the source code of the book. The repository is located at: `https://GitHub.com/PacktPublishing/Spring-5.0-By-Example/tree/master/config-files`.
> The Spring Cloud Config Server also supports private repositories. For that purpose, we need to supply the private/public keys.

Configuring the Spring Boot application

It's a piece of cake to enable and run the Config Server and provide our configuration HTTP protocol. To achieve it, we need to put the following annotation in our Spring Boot starter class. The implementation is as follows:

```
package springfive.airline.configserver;

import org.springframework.boot.SpringApplication;
import org.springframework.boot.autoconfigure.SpringBootApplication;
import org.springframework.cloud.config.server.EnableConfigServer;
```

```
@EnableConfigServer
@SpringBootApplication
public class ConfigServerApplication {

  public static void main(String[] args) {
     SpringApplication.run(ConfigServerApplication.class,
args);
  }

}
```

Awesome. @EnableConfigServer does the magic for us. It will stand up the Config Server and make the application ready to connect.

Configuring the Git repository as a properties source

Our Config Server needs to be configured. For that purpose, we will use the application.yaml file. This file should be simple and with minimal configurations as well. The configuration file should look like this:

```
server:
  port: 5000

spring:
  cloud:
    config:
      name: configserver
      server:
        git:
          uri:
https://github.com/PacktPublishing/Spring-5.0-By-Example
          search-paths: config-files*
```

We have configured the application port, which is a common task. We named our Config Server, and the most important part is the server.git.uri configuration property which instructs the Spring Framework to get the configurations files.

Another configuration is search-paths; it allows us to search the configuration in git repository folders, instead of a root address in the repository.

Running the Config Server

Awesome job; our configuration server is ready to use. Then let's run it. We can use the JAR file, or through IDE as well, it is up to you to choose the desired way.

We can use the Java command line or IDE to run it. I prefer to use IDE because it enables us to debug and make some code changes.

Run it.

The output should look like this:

Tomcat started successfully; our Config Server is up and running. We can find some different endpoints in our Config Server. These endpoints are exposed to serve the configuration file.

The Spring Cloud Config Server supports profiles as well, providing different configurations for different environments is important.

The pattern supported by the Config Server is as follows:

```
<application-name>-<profile>.<properties|yaml>
```

It is really important to keep this in mind. Also, it makes it mandatory to declare the `application.name` property in our microservices, to identify the application.

We can find the endpoints provided by the Spring Cloud Config Server on the application bootstrap. Take a look at the log:

Remember the Config Server supports environments; because of this, there is a kind of regex on endpoints. Look at the "`/{name}-{profiles}.yml`" endpoint.

Testing our Config Server

We are able to test our Config Server over the REST API.

Let's create a simple `yaml` file to create the test; the file should be called `dummy.yaml`:

```yaml
info:
  message: "Testing my Config Server"
  status: "It worked"
```

Push it to GitHub – if you are using the GitHub book, this step is unnecessary. Then, we can call the Config Server API using the following command:

```
curl http://localhost:5000/dummy/default | jq
```

The command looks for the `dummy` configuration in the profile `default`; the URL is self-explanatory. The following output should be displayed:

```
  % Total    % Received % Xferd  Average Speed   Time    Time     Time  Current
                                 Dload  Upload   Total   Spent    Left  Speed
100   309    0   309    0     0    261      0 --:--:--  0:00:01 --:--:--   261
{
  "name": "dummy",
  "profiles": [
    "default"
  ],
  "label": null,
  "version": "bca0b9ad5fdd1f853744d7dc2abf92411423e2b1",
  "state": null,
  "propertySources": [
    {
      "name": "https://github.com/PacktPublishing/Spring-5.0-By-Example/config-files/dummy.yaml",
      "source": {
        "info.message": "Testing my Config Server",
        "info.status": "It worked"
      }
    }
  ]
}
```

Our Config Server is fully operational. Now, we will configure our service discovery using Netflix Eureka.

Spring Cloud service discovery

The service discovery is one of the key points of the microservices architecture. The basis of the microservices architecture is to decouple the monolithic application into smaller pieces of software which have well-defined boundaries.

This impacts our system design in the monolithic application. In general, the application logic stays in a single place with regards to the code. It means the procedure or methods calls are invoked in the same context when the application is running.

When we adopt the microservices architectural style, these invocations are typically external, in other words, they will invoke the service through HTTP calls, for example, in another application context or web server.

Then, the services need to call other services through HTTP, for instance, but how do the services call the others if the instances of these services change with a considerable frequency? Remember, we are creating distributed and scalable systems, where the instances of services can be increased according to the system usage.

The services need to know where the other services are running to be able to call them. Let's imagine that we are considering putting the services IPs in the configuration; it will be hard to manage and impossible to track the machine changes during that time.

The service discovery pattern addresses this challenge. In general, the solution involves a Service Registry, which knows the locations of all the running services. The client then needs to have a kind of Service Registry Client to be able to query this Service Registry to obtain the valid address for the desired service; the Service Registry will then return a healthy address, and finally, the client can invoke the desired service.

Let's look at the following diagram:

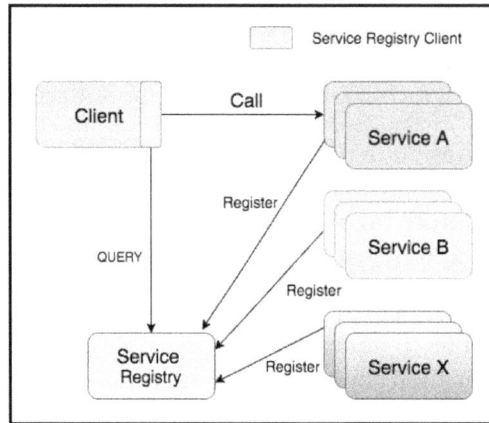

> The full documentation of this pattern can be found at `http://microservices.io/patterns/client-side-discovery.html` and `https://www.nginx.com/blog/service-discovery-in-a-microservices-architecture/`. There are so many implementations for that pattern.

The Spring Cloud service discovery supports some service discovery implementations, such as Hashicorp Consul provided by the Spring Cloud Consul, and Apache Zookeeper provided by the Spring Cloud Zookeeper.

We are using the Netflix OSS stack where we will use the Eureka server, which was provided by the Spring Netflix OSS. It enables us to use the Eureka server as a managed Spring bean.

The Spring Eureka Client provides a client aware of the Service Registry, and it can be done with a couple of annotations and some configurations – we will do that soon.

We will start to create and configure the Eureka server in the following sections. Let's do that.

> The full documentation for the Spring Cloud Consul can be found at: `https://cloud.spring.io/spring-cloud-consul`, and the Spring Cloud Zookeeper can be found at: `https://cloud.spring.io/spring-cloud-zookeeper`.

Creating Spring Cloud Eureka

To enable service discovery in our infrastructure, we need to create an instance of a service which will act as a service discovery. The Spring Cloud Eureka server enables us to achieve this task. Let's create our project. Go to Spring Initializr and fill in the information, as shown in the following screenshot:

Take a look at the required dependencies. The Eureka server is the dependency which allows us to spin up a service discovery server.

Let's open the project on IDE and start to configure it. We will do this in the following section.

Creating the Eureka server main class

Before we start the configuration, we will create the `main` class. This class will start the Spring Boot application. The Eureka server is embedded in the application. It is a pretty standard Spring Boot application with a single annotation.

The `main` application class should look like this:

```
package springfive.airline.eureka;

import org.springframework.boot.SpringApplication;
import
org.springframework.boot.autoconfigure.SpringBootApplication;
import
org.springframework.cloud.netflix.eureka.server.EnableEurekaSe
rver;

@EnableEurekaServer
@SpringBootApplication
public class EurekaApplication {

  public static void main(String[] args) {
    SpringApplication.run(EurekaApplication.class, args);
  }

}
```

The `@EnableEurekaServer` annotation will start the embedded Eureka server in our application and make it ready to use. It will enable the service registry in our application as well.

Configuring the Spring Cloud Eureka server

Our Eureka server needs to be configured using the Spring Cloud Server configured in the previous sections. Then, we need to keep the `application.yaml` off our project, to use the Config Server properly. Instead of the `application.yaml`, we need to put the `bootstrap.yaml` and put the Config Server address on it.

Then, we need to:

- Create `discovery.yaml` on GitHub
- Create `bootstrap.yaml` file in the classpath project

Let's start with the `discovery.yaml` file. The file should look like this:

```
server:
  port: 8761

eureka:
  instance:
    hostname: localhost
```

```
        health-check-url-path: /actuator/health
        status-page-url-path: /actuator/info
      client:
        registerWithEureka: false
        fetchRegistry: false
    logging:
      level:
        com.netflix.discovery: 'ON'
        org.springframework.cloud: 'DEBUG'
```

There are some interesting things to explore. We are using the localhost as `hostname` because we are running on the developer machine. There are a couple of configurations about the URLs health check and status page – pay attention to the configurations that are related to the server. They are placed below the `eureka.instance` YAML node. The configurations are `health-check-url-path` and `status-page-url-path`. We can use the default values as well, but the new Spring Boot Actuator changes the URL for those two features, so we need to configure them properly.

The `eureka.client` YAML node is about the client configuration; in our case, we set `registerWithEureka` to false. We do not want the Eureka server to act as a client as well. The same is true for the `fetchRegistry` configuration, it is a client configuration and it will cache the Eureka registry's information.

The `logging` node is about logging configuration.

Awesome – our `gateway.yaml` is ready.

Let's create our `bootstrap.yaml` file in the Eureka server project classpath. The file should look like this:

```
spring:
  application:
    name: discovery
  cloud:
    config:
      uri: http://localhost:5000
      label: master
```

Easy peasy – we have configured `spring.cloud.config`. It instructs Spring of the Config Server address. Also, we have configured the `label`, which is the branch when we are using the **version control system** (**VCS**) as a repository.

Well done. The configuration is ready. Time to run it. Let's do it in the following section.

Running the Spring Cloud Eureka server

The Eureka server is ready to use. We will start the Spring Boot application and put our Eureka server online. We can use the Java command line or IDE to run it. I prefer to use IDE because it enables us to debug and make some code changes.

> **TIP**
>
> The Config Server needs to be running because the discovery will find the configuration file to bootstrap the server properly.

Run it!

We should see the following lines in the application bootstrap logs:

Awesome. Look at the following line of the log:

```
2018-01-07 14:42:42.636  INFO 11191 --- [       Thread-32]
e.s.EurekaServerInitializerConfiguration : Started Eureka
Server
```

It means our Eureka server is ready to use. To check the solution, we can go to the Eureka server home page. Go to http://localhost:8761/ and the following page will be displayed:

As we can see, there is no instance of service available yet. We can find some relevant information such as the server **Uptime**, the current **Data center**, and the **Current time**. There is some information in the **General Info** section, information regarding the server where the Eureka server is running.

Good job. Our service discovery service is running. We will use this infrastructure soon.

Spring Cloud Zipkin server and Sleuth

Our solution involves some microservices; it makes our solution easy to deploy and easy to write code. Each solution has a particular repository and codebase.

In the monolith solution, the whole problem is solved in the same artifact to be deployed. Usually, in Java, these artifacts are `.jar`, `.war`, or `.ear`, if the application was written in the Java EE 5/6 specifications.

The logging strategies for these kinds of applications is quite easy to work with (hence problems can be solved easily) because everything happens in the same context; the requests are received from the same application server or web server, which have the business components. Now, if we go to the logs, we will probably find the log entries we want. It makes the trace application easier to find errors and debug.

In the microservices solution, the application behaviors are split in the distributed systems; it increases the trace tasks substantially because the request probably arrives in the API Gateway and comes into microservices. They log the information in different sources. In this scenario, we need a kind of log aggregator and a way to identify the whole transaction between services.

For this purpose, the Spring Cloud Sleuth and Spring Cloud Zipkin can help us and make the trace features more comfortable for developers.

In this section, we will look at and understand how it works under the hood.

Infrastructure for the Zipkin server

Before we start to work, we need to configure a service which the Zipkin server needs. By default, the Zipkin server uses in-memory databases, but it is not recommended for production; usually, developers use this feature to demonstrate Zipkin features.

We will use MySQL as a data store. The Zipkin server also supports different sources, such as Cassandra and Elasticsearch.

Spring Cloud Sleuth supports synchronous and asynchronous operations. The synchronous operations are over the HTTP protocol and asynchronous can be done by RabbitMQ or Apache Kafka.

To use the HTTP, that is, REST API, we should use `@EnableZipkinServer`, it will delegate the persistence for REST tier through the `SpanStore` interface.

We will choose the asynchronous solution, since it fits well for our project, and we do not want the trace collector to cause some performance issues. The asynchronous solution uses the Spring Cloud Stream binder to store the `Spans`. We choose the RabbitMQ message broker to do that. It can be achieved using the `@EnableZipkinStreamServer` annotations which configure Spring Sleuth to use streams for store `Spans`.

Let's create our `docker-compose-min.yaml` to bootstrap our RabbitMQ and MySQL containers. The file should look like this:

```
version: '3'
services:

  rabbitmq:
    hostname: rabbitmq
```

```
      image: rabbitmq:3.7.0-management-alpine
      ports:
        - "5672:5672"
        - "15672:15672"
      networks:
        - airline

    mysql:
      hostname: mysql
      image: mysql:5.7.21
      ports:
        - "3306:3306"
      environment:
        - MYSQL_ROOT_PASSWORD=root
        - MYSQL_DATABASE=zipkin
      networks:
        - airline

    mongo:
      hostname: mongo
      image: mongo
      ports:
        - "27017:27017"
      networks:
        - airline

    redis:
      hostname: redis
      image: redis:3.2-alpine
      ports:
        - "6379:6379"
      networks:
        - airline

  networks:
    airline:
      driver: bridge
```

> The `docker-compose-min.yaml` file can be found at `GitHub`, there is a MongoDB and Redis – they will be used in the next chapter.

There is nothing special here. We have declared two containers—RabbitMQ and MySQL— and exposed the ports on the host machine. Also, we have created the `airline` network; we will use this network to attach our infrastructure microservices.

Now, we can create our Zipkin server, which we will do in the next section.

Creating the Spring Cloud Zipkin server

We will create our Zipkin panel structure in Spring Initializr, and then we need to follow the instructions:

Awesome – take a look at the **Selected Dependencies** section, all of them are required. Pay attention to the Spring Boot version. We choose 1.5.9, because there is no support for Zipkin server in Spring Boot 2. It is not a problem because we do not need specific features from Spring Boot 2.

Click on the **Generate Project** button and wait for the download to finish. Afterwards, open the project in IDE.

In order to enable service discovery and store Spans on a database, we need to put the following dependencies in our pom.xml:

```
<dependency>
 <groupId>org.springframework.cloud</groupId>
 <artifactId>spring-cloud-starter-netflix-eureka-
client</artifactId>
</dependency>

<dependency>
```

```
   <groupId>org.springframework.boot</groupId>
   <artifactId>spring-boot-starter-jdbc</artifactId>
 </dependency>

 <dependency>
  <groupId>mysql</groupId>
  <artifactId>mysql-connector-java</artifactId>
  <version>6.0.6</version>
 </dependency>
```

The first dependency is for the service discovery client and the others are to JDBC connections to MySQL. It makes our project dependencies fully configured.

Let's create our `main` class to start our Zipkin server. The class is pretty standard but with some new annotations:

```
package springfive.airline;

import org.springframework.boot.SpringApplication;
import
org.springframework.boot.autoconfigure.SpringBootApplication;
import
org.springframework.cloud.netflix.eureka.EnableEurekaClient;
import
org.springframework.cloud.sleuth.zipkin.stream.EnableZipkinStr
eamServer;

@SpringBootApplication
@EnableZipkinStreamServer
@EnableEurekaClient
public class ZipkinServerApplication {

  public static void main(String[] args) {
   SpringApplication.run(ZipkinServerApplication.class, args);
  }

 }
```

The `@EnableEurekaClient` annotation enables the application to connect to the Eureka server. The new annotation, `@EnableZipkinStreamServer`, instructs the framework to connect with the configured broker to receive the `Spans`. Remember, it can be done using the Spring Cloud Stream Binder.

Configuring boostrap.yaml and application.yaml

In the section, we created our `main` class. Before we run it, we should create our two configuration files. The `bootstrap.yaml` inside the `src/main/resources` directory and the `application.yaml` on our GitHub repository. They will be downloaded via Config Server and provided by the Zipkin server project.

Let's start with `bootstrap.yaml`:

```
spring:
  application:
    name: zipkin
  cloud:
    config:
      uri: http://localhost:5000
      label: master
```

Nothing special, we have configured our Config Server address.

Let's jump to our `application.yaml`:

```
server:
  port: 9999

spring:
  rabbitmq:
    port: 5672
    host: localhost
  datasource:
    schema: classpath:/mysql.sql
    url:
jdbc:mysql://${MYSQL_HOST:localhost}/zipkin?autoReconnect=true
    driver-class-name: com.mysql.cj.jdbc.Driver
    username: root
    password: root
    initialize: true
    continue-on-error: true
  sleuth:
    enabled: false

zipkin:
  storage:
    type: mysql

logging:
```

```
level:
  ROOT: INFO

eureka:
  client:
    serviceUrl:
      defaultZone: http://localhost:8761/eureka/
```

There are some interesting things here. In the `spring.rabbitmq` node, we have configured our RabbitMQ broker connection. It will be used to receive `Spans`. In the `spring.datasource`, we have configured the MySQL connection. The Zipkin server will use it to store data. Also, we have configured how to execute the DDL script to create the `zipkin` database.

The `spring.sleuth` node was configured to not produce any `Span` because it is a server, not a client application, and we will not perform a trace on the Zipkin server.

The `zipkin` node had been used to configure the Zipkin server storage type, MySQL, in our case.

Let's run it!!!

Running the Zipkin server

We have configured the Zipkin server properly, so now we will be able to run it properly.

We can run the main class `ZipkinServerApplication`. We can use the IDE or Java command line, after running the following output:

```
2018-01-16 14:37:47.396 INFO [zipkin,,,] 3715 --- [main] o.s.i.endpoint.EventDrivenConsumer       : Adding {message-handler:inbound.sleuth.sleuth} as a subscriber to the 'bridge.sleuth
2018-01-16 14:37:47.396 INFO [zipkin,,,] 3715 --- [main] o.s.i.endpoint.EventDrivenConsumer       : started inbound.sleuth.sleuth
2018-01-16 14:37:47.397 INFO [zipkin,,,] 3715 --- [main] o.s.c.support.DefaultLifecycleProcessor  : Starting beans in phase 2147483647
2018-01-16 14:37:47.474 INFO [zipkin,,,] 3715 --- [main] s.b.c.e.t.TomcatEmbeddedServletContainer : Tomcat started on port(s): 9999 (http)
2018-01-16 14:37:47.475 INFO [zipkin,,,] 3715 --- [main] .s.c.n.e.s.EurekaAutoServiceRegistration  : Updating port to 9999
2018-01-16 14:37:47.479 INFO [zipkin,,,] 3715 --- [main] s.airline.ZipkinServerApplication         : Started ZipkinServerApplication in 13.782 seconds (JVM running for 14.868)
```

Good job – the Zipkin server is running now. We can take a look at the index page to see what it looks like.

Go to Zipkin page; the page should look like the following screenshot:

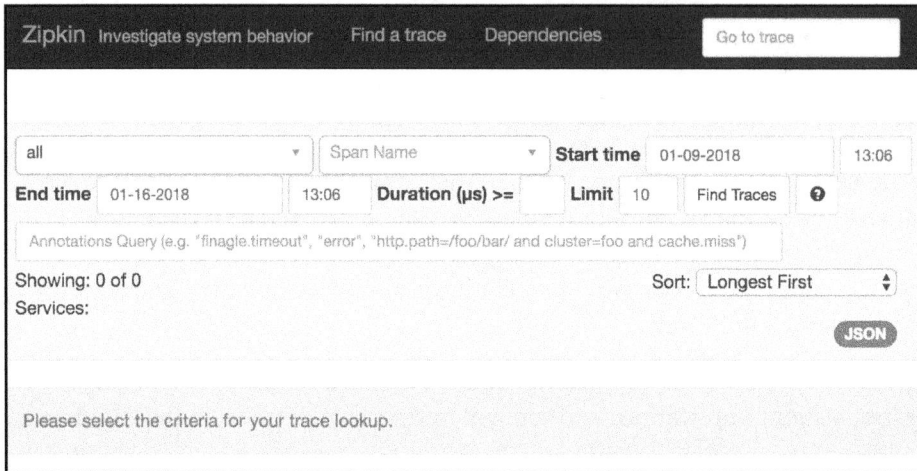

Also, we can check the RabbitMQ panel to find the queue created by the Zipkin server. Go to the RabbitMQ Queues (`http://localhost:15672/#/queues`) section, the page should look like this:

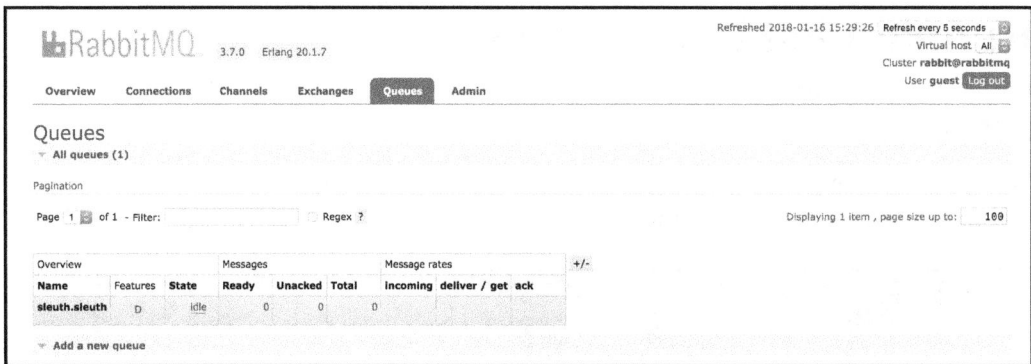

Looking at the queues, the project has created the `sleuth.sleuth` queue, well done.

The Zipkin server is ready. For now, we will not have any `Span`, because there is no application sending data to Zipkin. We will do that in the next chapter.

Spring Cloud Gateway

The API Gateway pattern helps us to expose our microservices through a single known entrypoint. Usually, it acts as an entrypoint to external access and redirects the call to internal microservices.

There are many benefits when we adopt the API Gateway in our application. The first one can be recognized easily, it makes the API consumption easy for the clients, which means the clients do not need to know the different microservices endpoints.

Other benefits are a consequence of the first one. When we have a unique entrypoint, we can address some cross-application concerns such as filtering, authentication, throttling, and rate limit, as well.

It is an essential part when we adopt the microservices architecture.

The Spring Cloud Gateway enables us to have these features in a Spring-managed bean, in a Spring way using Dependency Injection and other features provided by the Spring Framework.

The project was built on the Spring Framework 5, which uses the Project Reactor as a basis. There are some interesting features provided, such as Hystrix Circuit Breaker integration and with the Spring Cloud Discovery client, as well.

Look at the diagram to understand the benefits of the API Gateway:

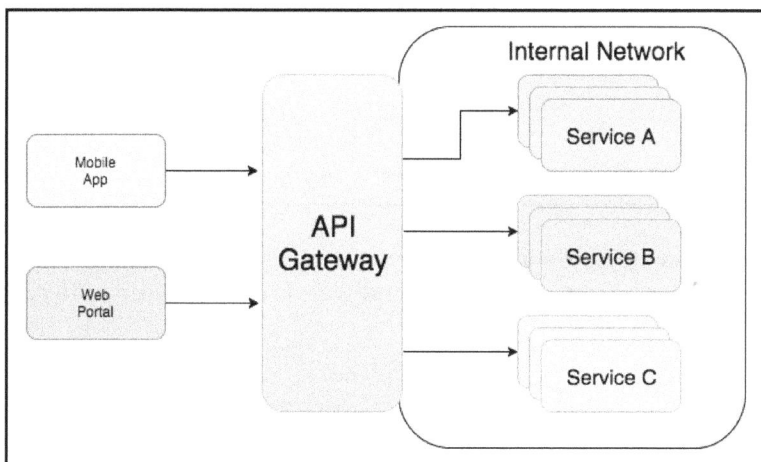

> The full documentation of the API Gateway Pattern can be found at: `http://microservices.io/patterns/apigateway.html`.

Creating the Spring Cloud Gateway project

We will use the Spring Initializr to create our Spring Cloud Gateway project; we will need to add some dependencies manually. Let's go to the **Spring Initializr** page and create our project:

There is a brand new dependency Gateway, it enables us to work with Spring Cloud Gateway. Then click on **Generate Project** and wait for the download to complete.

After that, we need to add a missing dependency. The missing dependency is required by the Gateway to interact with the Eureka server; the name of the dependency is `spring-cloud-starter-netflix-eureka-client`. Then, let's add the dependency on our `pom.xml`, we will need to add the following snippet:

```
<dependency>
 <groupId>org.springframework.cloud</groupId>
 <artifactId>spring-cloud-starter-netflix-eureka-client</artifactId>
</dependency>
```

Excellent, our project is configured correctly to work with the Eureka server. In the following section, we will configure the project to work with the Config Server as well.

Creating the Spring Cloud Gateway main class

There is no secret to this part. The Spring Cloud Gateway works in the same way as the common Spring Boot applications. There is a `main` class which will start the embedded server and starts the whole application.

Our `main` class should look like this:

```
package springfive.airline.gateway;

import org.springframework.boot.SpringApplication;
import org.springframework.boot.autoconfigure.SpringBootApplication;
import org.springframework.cloud.netflix.eureka.EnableEurekaClient;

@EnableEurekaClient
@SpringBootApplication
public class GatewayApplication {

  public static void main(String[] args) {
    SpringApplication.run(GatewayApplication.class, args);
  }

}
```

As we can see, it is a pretty standard Spring Boot application, configured with `@EnableEurekaClient` to work with the Eureka server as a service discovery implementation.

Configuring the Spring Cloud Gateway project

The primary project structure is ready. We will create the project configurations in this section. To achieve this, we need to carry out the following steps:

- Add a `gateway.yaml` file to GitHub
- Create the `bootstrap.yaml` in the Gateway project

We are using the Spring Cloud Config Server, so it is necessary to create the new file in GitHub because the Config Server will try to find the file on the repository. In our case, we are using GitHub as a repository.

The second task is necessary because the `bootstrap.yaml` file is processed before the application is fully ready to run. Then, during this phase, the application needs to look up the configuration file and to achieve this, the application needs to know the `repository`, in our case, the Config Server. Remember the address of the Config Server always needs to be placed on the `bootstrap.yaml`.

Let's create our `gateway.yaml` file – the file should look like this:

```
server:
  port: 8888
eureka:
  client:
    serviceUrl:
      defaultZone: http://localhost:8761/eureka/
logging:
  level: debug
```

The `eureka.client` node in the YAML file is responsible for configuring the Eureka Client configurations. We need to configure our Eureka server address instance. It should be pointed to the correct address.

> There are more options for the Eureka Configuration Client properties. The full documentation can be found in `https://github.com/Netflix/eureka/wiki/Configuring-Eureka`; the Netflix team maintains Eureka.

Then, we need to create our `bootstrap.yaml` file on the Gateway project. This file will instruct the Spring Framework to look up the configuration file on the Config Server and then download the required file to finish the application bootstrap. Our file should look like this:

```
spring:
  application:
      name: gateway
  cloud:
    config:
      uri: http://localhost:5000
      label: master
```

Pretty simple. The `application.name` is required to instruct the framework to look up the correct file. Usually, there are many configuration files for different applications and environments as well.

On the `cloud.config` node, we need to put in the Spring Cloud Config Server address, which we configured in the previous sections.

The project final structure should look like this:

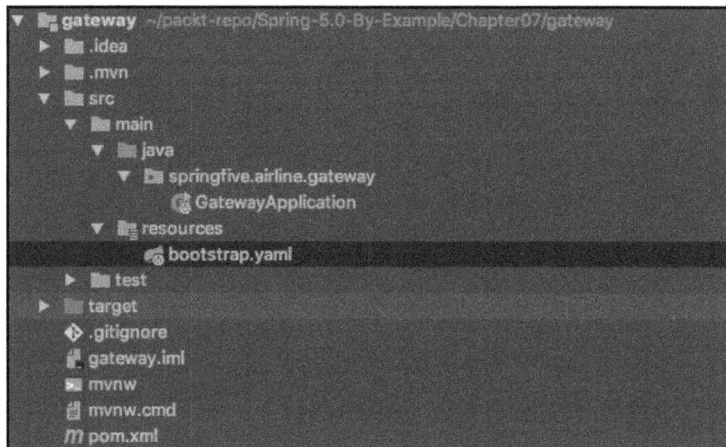

Look at the screenshot. There is no `application.yaml` in the classpath. This gives us several advantages; there is no configuration file in classpath projects, which helps us a great deal in managing the microservices configurations.

In the next section, we will run it and explain the whole application bootstrap process. Let's do it.

Running the Spring Cloud Gateway

The project is well-configured, so now it is time to run it. We can use the Java command line or IDE. There is no difference either way.

The Config Server and Eureka server need to stay up; it is mandatory that the Gateway project works correctly. Then, we can run the project.

Run the project and look at the logs. We can see some interesting stuff, such as the project connecting to the Config Server and download the configuration and after this, it connects to the Eureka server and self-registers. The following diagram explains the application bootstrap flow:

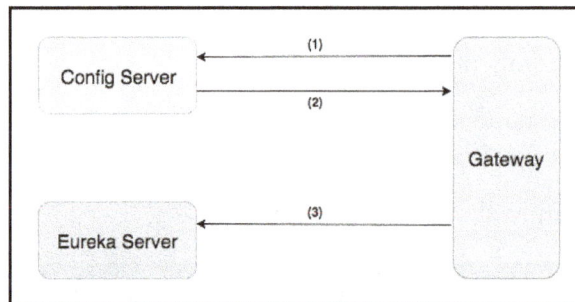

Let's look at what the different flows are and understand them:

1. The Gateway application requests the configuration file
2. The Config Server serves the config file
3. The Gateway application registers to the Eureka server

Awesome, our Gateway application is connected to our infrastructure services.

Checking the Eureka server

Our Gateway is running. Now, we can check the Eureka server page to confirm this information.

Go to `http://localhost:8761/`, and check the **Instances currently registered with Eureka** section. We should see the Gateway application, as shown in the following screenshot:

Excellent. It worked well. The Gateway application is successfully registered, and it can be looked up via the service discovery. Our Gateway will connect to the Eureka server to get the service available and distribute the requested calls to the correct services.

Well done. Now, we can create our routes in the Gateway. We will do this in the next chapter when we create our airline microservices.

Creating our first route with Spring Cloud Gateway

Our Gateway is running. Before we start the real routes for our Airline application, let's try to use some fake routes to test the Spring Cloud Gateway behaviors. We will use the `https://httpbin.org/` site, which helps us to test some routes.

Let's create a class with the @Configuration annotation to provide the routes for the Spring Container. Let's create a package called springfive.airline.gateway.infra.route, then create the following class:

```
package springfive.airline.gateway.infra.route;


import java.util.function.Function;
import org.springframework.cloud.gateway.route.RouteLocator;
import org.springframework.cloud.gateway.route.builder.PredicateSpec;
import
org.springframework.cloud.gateway.route.builder.RouteLocatorBuilder;
import
org.springframework.cloud.gateway.route.builder.RouteLocatorBuilder.Bu
ilder;
import org.springframework.context.annotation.Bean;
import org.springframework.context.annotation.Configuration;

@Configuration
public class SampleRoute {

   private Function<PredicateSpec, Builder> addCustomHeader =
predicateSpec -> predicateSpec
       .path("/headers")
       .addRequestHeader("Book", "Spring 5.0 By Example")
       .uri("http://httpbin.org:80");

   @Bean
   public RouteLocator sample(RouteLocatorBuilder builder) {
     return builder.routes()
        .route("custom-request-header", addCustomHeader)
        .route("add-query-param", r ->
r.path("/get").addRequestParameter("book", "spring5.0")
           .uri("http://httpbin.org:80"))
        .route("response-headers", (r) -> r.path("/response-headers")
           .addResponseHeader("book","spring5.0")
           .uri("http://httpbin.org:80"))
        .route("combine-and-change", (r) ->
r.path("/anything").and().header("access-key","AAA")
           .addResponseHeader("access-key","BBB")
           .uri("http://httpbin.org:80"))
        .build();
   }

}
```

There are some different types to configure routes; the first one we extracted is the function to a private attribute called `addCustomHeader`, which will be used in the `custom-request-header` route. We will use **curl** to test some routes created previously.

The first one we will test is the `custom-request-header`, the route was configured to route to: `http://httpbin.org:80` and the path will be `/headers`. This service will return the Request Headers sent to the server. Take a look at `addCustomHeader`, we have configured it to add a custom header to the Request. It will be **Book** as the key and **Spring 5.0 By Example,** as the value. Let's call the gateway URL, using curl:

```
curl http://localhost:8888/headers
```

The output should look like this:

```
{
    "headers": {
      "Accept": "*/*",
      "Book": "Spring 5.0 By Example",
      "Connection": "close",
      "Host": "httpbin.org",
      "User-Agent": "curl/7.54.0"
    }
}
```

Let's analyze the output. The first thing to look at is we have called the localhost address. The `Host` key in the Request shows `httpbin.org`, it means the Spring Cloud Gateway has changed the address. Awesome, but we expected it. The second one is where we have added the `Book` key, and bingo, there it is in the Request Headers. The Gateway worked as expected, and with a few lines of code, we did some interesting stuff.

Let's do one more test. We will test the `combine-and-change`, this route is configured to answer the `/anything` with the Request `Header access-key: AAA`, so the command line should be:

```
curl -v -H "access-key: AAA" http://localhost:8888/anything
```

As we can see, the -v argument makes the call in verbose mode, it is useful for debugging purposes and the -H indicates the Request Headers. Let's look at the output:

```
*   Trying ::1...
* TCP_NODELAY set
* Connected to localhost (::1) port 8888 (#0)
> GET /anything HTTP/1.1
> Host: localhost:8888
> User-Agent: curl/7.54.0
> Accept: */*
> access-key: AAA
>
< HTTP/1.1 200 OK
< access-key: BBB
< Connection: keep-alive
< Server: meinheld/0.6.1
< Date: Wed, 10 Jan 2018 00:49:29 GMT
< Content-Type: application/json
< Access-Control-Allow-Origin: *
< Access-Control-Allow-Credentials: true
< X-Powered-By: Flask
< X-Processed-Time: 0.00110197067261
< Content-Length: 329
< Via: 1.1 vegur
<
{
  "args": {},
  "data": "",
  "files": {},
  "form": {},
  "headers": {
    "Accept": "*/*",
    "Access-Key": "AAA",
    "Connection": "close",
    "Host": "httpbin.org",
    "User-Agent": "curl/7.54.0"
  },
```

Awesome. If you look at the access-key value, the Gateway changed to a requested value BBB. Good job guys. There are some endpoints to test, feel free to test as you want.

> You can find the httpbin documentation at: https://httpbin.org/.
> There are some interesting other methods to test HTTP.

Putting the infrastructure on Docker

Our infrastructure is ready and it enables us to develop the application. We can create a Docker compose file to spin up the infrastructure services; during the development life cycle, components such as Eureka, Config Server, Trace Server, and API Gateway do not suffer changes because they interact as an infrastructure.

Then, it enables us to create component images and use them in the `docker-compose.yaml` file. Let's list our components:

- Config Server
- Eureka
- Zipkin
- RabbitMQ
- Redis

We know how to create Docker images using the Fabric8 Maven plugin, we have done this several times in the previous chapters – let's do it.

Let's configure one as an example, keep in mind we need do the same configuration for all projects, Eureka, Gateway, Config Server, and Gateway. The following snippet configures the `docker-maven-plugin` to generate a Docker image:

```
<plugin>
  <groupId>io.fabric8</groupId>
  <artifactId>docker-maven-plugin</artifactId>
  <version>0.21.0</version>
  <configuration>
    <images>
      <image>
        <name>springfivebyexample/${project.build.finalName}</name>
        <build>
          <from>openjdk:latest</from>
          <entryPoint>java -Dspring.profiles.active=docker -jar
/application/${project.build.finalName}.jar</entryPoint>
          <assembly>
            <basedir>/application</basedir>
            <descriptorRef>artifact</descriptorRef>
            <inline>
              <id>assembly</id>
              <files>
                <file>
<source>target/${project.build.finalName}.jar</source>
                </file>
              </files>
```

```
            </inline>
          </assembly>
          <tags>
            <tag>latest</tag>
          </tags>
          <ports>
            <port>8761</port>
          </ports>
        </build>
        <run>
          <namingStrategy>alias</namingStrategy>
        </run>
        <alias>${project.build.finalName}</alias>
      </image>
    </images>
  </configuration>
</plugin>
```

It is a pretty simple configuration. A simple Maven plugin with a couple of configurations. Then, after the plugin configuration, we are able to generate the Docker image. The command to generate Docker images is:

```
mvn clean install docker:build
```

It will generate a Docker image for us.

The projects configured can be found on GitHub; there are so many configurations to do as in the previous chapters. We need to configure the docker-maven-plugin and generate the Docker images.

> **TIP**
>
> Fully configured projects can be found in the chapter seven folder. The GitHub repository is: https://github.com/PacktPublishing/ Spring-5.0-By-Example/tree/master/Chapter07.

After the images have been created, we are able to create a Docker compose file defining the whole thing. The docker-compose-infra-full.yaml file should look like this:

```
version: '3'
services:

  config:
    hostname: config
    image: springfivebyexample/config
    ports:
      - "5000:5000"
```

```
    networks:
      - airline
  rabbitmq:
    hostname: rabbitmq
    image: rabbitmq:3.7.0-management-alpine
    ports:
      - "5672:5672"
      - "15672:15672"
    networks:
      - airline
  mysql:
    hostname: mysql
    image: mysql:5.7.21
    ports:
      - "3306:3306"
    environment:
      - MYSQL_ROOT_PASSWORD=root
      - MYSQL_DATABASE=zipkin
    networks:
      - airline
  redis:
    hostname: redis
    image: redis:3.2-alpine
    ports:
      - "6379:6379"
    networks:
      - airline

  zipkin:
    hostname: zipkin
    image: springfivebyexample/zipkin
    ports:
      - "9999:9999"
    networks:
      - airline
networks:
  airline:
    driver: bridge
```

There are some interesting things to pay attention to here. It is very important that all container instances are attached to the same Docker network called `airline`. Pay attention to the ports exposed by the containers, it is important to enable service discovery features in Docker.

Then, we can execute the instruction to spin up the whole infrastructure; it can be done using the following command:

```
docker-compose -f docker-compose-infra-full.yaml up -d
```

The following output should appear:

```
Creating network "docker_airline" with driver "bridge"
Creating docker_zipkin_1     ... done
Creating docker_rabbitmq_1   ... done
Creating docker_mysql_1      ... done
Creating docker_config_1     ... done
Creating docker_gateway_1    ... done
Creating docker_discovery_1 ... done
```

Also, we can execute the following instruction to check the container's execution:

```
docker-compose -f docker-compose-infra-full.yaml ps
```

It will list the running containers, as shown in the following screenshot:

```
      Name                Command              State                                 Ports
---------------------------------------------------------------------------------------------------------------------------
docker_config_1      /bin/sh -c java -Dspring.p ...  Up      0.0.0.0:5000->5000/tcp
docker_discovery_1   /bin/sh -c java -Dspring.p ...  Up      0.0.0.0:8761->8761/tcp
docker_mysql_1       docker-entrypoint.sh mysqld      Up      0.0.0.0:3306->3306/tcp
docker_rabbitmq_1    docker-entrypoint.sh rabbi ...  Up      15671/tcp, 0.0.0.0:15672->15672/tcp, 25672/tcp, 4369/tcp, 5671/tcp, 0.0.0.0:5672->5672/tcp
docker_redis_1       docker-entrypoint.sh redis ...  Up      0.0.0.0:6379->6379/tcp
docker_zipkin_1      /bin/sh -c java -Dspring.p ...  Up      0.0.0.0:9999->9999/tcp
```

All applications are up and running. Well done.

To remove the containers, we can use:

```
docker-compose -f docker-compose-infra-full.yaml down
```

It will remove the containers from the stack.

Excellent job, our infrastructure is fully operational in Docker containers. It is a base for starting to create our microservices.

Summary

In this chapter, we have built the essential infrastructures services adopting the microservices architectural style.

We have learned how Spring Framework eliminates the infrastructure code from our microservices and enables us to create these services, using a couple of annotations.

We understand how it works under the hood; it is extremely important to debug and troubleshoot when the application gets some errors in the production stage.

Now, we are ready to create scalable, fault tolerant, and responsive systems. We have built the foundations of our system.

In the next chapter, we will start to build our Airline Ticket System, understand how to connect the new microservices with the whole infrastructure, and enable service discovery and other amazing features.

See you there.

Circuit Breakers and Security

8

In the previous chapter, we configured the microservices that will act in our infrastructure, and we created a Eureka server to work as a service discovery for our solution. Also, we have created a Config Server application that will serve as the configurations for our microservices.

In this chapter, we will create microservices to interact with our previous infrastructure. We will discover how to apply service discovery features for our business microservices and understand how the Circuit Breaker pattern can help us to bring resilience to our applications.

During the chapter, we will understand how the microservices can communicate with other services through the HTTP asynchronous call powered by the Spring WebFlux client.

By the end of this chapter, we will have learned how to:

- Connect microservices with service discovery
- Pull the configuration from the configuration server
- Understand how `Hystrix` brings resilience to microservices
- Show the Edge API strategy
- Present the Spring Boot Admin

Understanding the service discovery power

We will create our first microservice with business requirements. We will create a `planes` microservice, which will maintain data about company planes, such as characteristics, model, and some other attributes.

The `planes` microservice will be used to serve plane characteristics for our second microservice, the `flights` microservice. It needs to get some plane information to be able to create a flight, such as the number of seats.

The `planes` microservice is an excellent candidate to start with because there is no business-related dependency to be created.

Our `planes` microservice will be useful soon. Time to create it. Let's go.

Creating the planes microservice

As we have been doing in the previous chapters, we will use the Spring Initializr for that purpose. The following dependencies should be selected, as shown in the following screenshot:

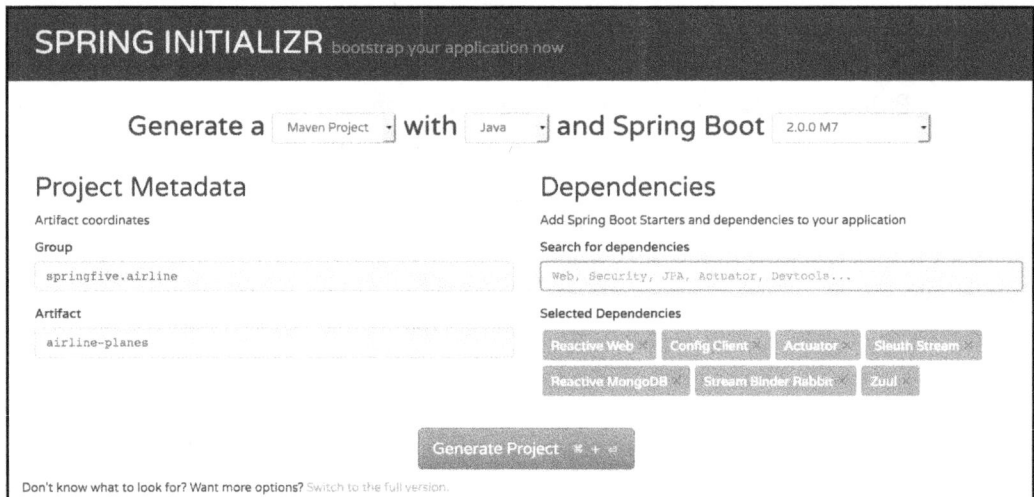

There are some necessary dependencies. The **Stream Binder Rabbit** and **Sleuth Stream** dependencies are necessary to enable us to the send data spans, and to enable application trace, across to the RabbitMQ message broker. We will use MongoDB to act as a database for this specific application, so we need **Reactive MongoDB** for that. **Config Client** is mandatory for all microservices present in the solution. We will not have any application configuration on the classpath. The **Actuator** provides production-ready metrics and information about the running application; it's an essential characteristic of the microservice's architectural style. Moreover, **Zuul** will be essential to enable us to connect the application with our Edge API. We will learn more about it during the course of the chapter.

We can now press the **Generate Project** button to download the project. Open the project on the IDE.

The `planes` microservice will be created using the Spring Boot 2 framework because we are interested in implementing the reactive foundation for our plane service.

Also, we need to include one more dependency, and it can be done using the following snippet on our `pom.xml`:

```
<dependency>
  <groupId>org.springframework.cloud</groupId>
  <artifactId>spring-cloud-starter-netflix-eureka-client</artifactId>
</dependency>
```

The `spring-cloud-starter-netflix-eureka-client` enables the service discovery, powered by the Eureka server in our application.

Coding the planes microservice

We will add some features on the application. For this specific application, we will create CRUD functionalities with Spring Reactive WebFlux.

The `Plane` class represents the plane model in our microservices and the class should be like this:

```
package springfive.airline.airlineplanes.domain;

import com.fasterxml.jackson.annotation.JsonInclude;
import com.fasterxml.jackson.annotation.JsonInclude.Include;
import java.util.Set;
import lombok.Builder;
import lombok.Data;
import lombok.NonNull;
```

```java
import org.springframework.data.annotation.Id;
import org.springframework.data.mongodb.core.mapping.Document;
import springfive.airline.airlineplanes.resource.data.PlaneRequest;

@Data
@Document(collection = "planes")
@JsonInclude(Include.NON_NULL)
public class Plane {

  @Id
  String id;

  String owner;

  PlaneModel model;

  Set<Seat> seats;

  String notes;

  @Builder
  public static Plane newPlane(String owner,PlaneModel
planeModel,Set<Seat> seats,String notes){
    Plane plane = new Plane();
    plane.owner = owner;
    plane.model = planeModel;
    plane.seats = seats;
    plane.notes = notes;
    return plane;
  }

  public Plane fromPlaneRequest(@NonNull PlaneRequest planeRequest){
    this.owner = planeRequest.getOwner();
    this.model = planeRequest.getModel();
    this.seats = planeRequest.getSeats();
    this.notes = planeRequest.getNotes();
    return this;
  }

}
```

The interesting point is the `@Document` annotation. It enables us to configure the name of the MongoDB collection for our domain. The `@Builder` annotation creates an implementation of the Builder pattern using the annotated method. The `Project Lombok` library provides this feature (`https://projectlombok.org`). Also, the project has some exciting features, such as `@Data`, which creates `getters/setters`, `equals`, and `hashCode` implementation automatically for the annotated class.

As we can see, there are some domain models in this class. These models do not need explanation here, and the full source code can be found in the GitHub project at `https://github.com/PacktPublishing/Spring-5.0-By-Example/tree/master/Chapter08/airline-planes`.

The reactive repository

Our `Plane` class needs a repository to persist the data to a database. We will use a reactive repository for MongoDB provided by the Spring Reactive MongoDB implementation. We will use the `ReactiveCrudRepository` as it makes our repositories reactive. Our repository should be like this:

```
package springfive.airline.airlineplanes.repository;

import
org.springframework.data.repository.reactive.ReactiveCrudRepository;
import springfive.airline.airlineplanes.domain.Plane;

public interface PlaneRepository extends
ReactiveCrudRepository<Plane,String>{
}
```

The implementation is the same as it was in the previous Spring Data versions, except for the new reactive interface. Now, we can create our service layer in the next section.

Creating the Plane service

Our `PlaneService` will be responsible for creating a kind of glue between the `PlaneRepository` and `PlaneResource`; the latter one we will create in the next section. The implementation should be like this:

```
package springfive.airline.airlineplanes.service;
```

```
import lombok.NonNull;
import org.springframework.stereotype.Service;
import reactor.core.publisher.Flux;
import reactor.core.publisher.Mono;
import springfive.airline.airlineplanes.domain.Plane;
import springfive.airline.airlineplanes.repository.PlaneRepository;
import springfive.airline.airlineplanes.resource.data.PlaneRequest;

@Service
public class PlaneService {

  private final PlaneRepository planeRepository;

  public PlaneService(PlaneRepository planeRepository) {
    this.planeRepository = planeRepository;
  }

  public Flux<Plane> planes(){
    return this.planeRepository.findAll();
  }

  public Mono<Plane> plane(@NonNull String id){
    return this.planeRepository.findById(id);
  }

  public Mono<Void> deletePlane(@NonNull Plane plane){
    return this.planeRepository.delete(plane);
  }

  public Mono<Plane> create(@NonNull PlaneRequest planeRequest){
    final Plane plane = Plane.builder().owner(planeRequest.getOwner())
.planeModel(planeRequest.getModel()).seats(planeRequest.getSeats())
       .notes(planeRequest.getNotes()).build();
    return this.planeRepository.save(plane);
  }

  public Mono<Plane> update(@NonNull String id,@NonNull PlaneRequest
planeRequest){
    return this.planeRepository.findById(id)
       .flatMap(plane ->
Mono.just(plane.fromPlaneRequest(planeRequest)))
       .flatMap(this.planeRepository::save);
  }

}
```

There is nothing special in this class, and the `PlaneService` will invoke the `PlaneRepository` to persist the `Plane` in a database. As we can see, we have used lambdas extensively. Java 8 is a requirement to run Spring Boot 2 applications.

Take a look at how the Builder pattern enables us to write clean code. It is much easier to read this code; we did it using the `chaining` method provided by Lombok.

The REST layer

We will use Spring WebFlux to expose our REST endpoints, and then we need to return `Mono` or `Flux` in our methods. The REST implementation should be like this:

```
package springfive.airline.airlineplanes.resource;

import java.net.URI;
import javax.validation.Valid;
import org.springframework.http.HttpStatus;
import org.springframework.http.ResponseEntity;
import org.springframework.web.bind.annotation.DeleteMapping;
import org.springframework.web.bind.annotation.GetMapping;
import org.springframework.web.bind.annotation.PathVariable;
import org.springframework.web.bind.annotation.PostMapping;
import org.springframework.web.bind.annotation.PutMapping;
import org.springframework.web.bind.annotation.RequestBody;
import org.springframework.web.bind.annotation.RequestMapping;
import org.springframework.web.bind.annotation.RestController;
import org.springframework.web.util.UriComponentsBuilder;
import reactor.core.publisher.Flux;
import reactor.core.publisher.Mono;
import springfive.airline.airlineplanes.domain.Plane;
import springfive.airline.airlineplanes.resource.data.PlaneRequest;
import springfive.airline.airlineplanes.service.PlaneService;

@RestController
@RequestMapping("/planes")
public class PlaneResource {

  private final PlaneService planeService;

  public PlaneResource(PlaneService planeService) {
    this.planeService = planeService;
  }

  @GetMapping
  public Flux<Plane> planes() {
```

```
        return this.planeService.planes();
    }

    @GetMapping("/{id}")
    public Mono<ResponseEntity<Plane>> plane(@PathVariable("id") String
id) {
        return this.planeService.plane(id).map(ResponseEntity::ok)
            .defaultIfEmpty(ResponseEntity.notFound().build());
    }

    @PostMapping
    public Mono<ResponseEntity<Void>> newPlane(
        @Valid @RequestBody PlaneRequest planeRequest,
UriComponentsBuilder uriBuilder) {
        return this.planeService.create(planeRequest).map(data -> {
            URI location = uriBuilder.path("/planes/{id}")
                .buildAndExpand(data.getId())
                .toUri();
            return ResponseEntity.created(location).build();
        });
    }

    @DeleteMapping("/{id}")
    public Mono<ResponseEntity<Object>> deletePlane(@PathVariable("id")
String id) {
        return this.planeService.plane(id).flatMap(data ->
this.planeService.deletePlane(data)
            .then(Mono.just(ResponseEntity.noContent().build())))
            .defaultIfEmpty(new ResponseEntity<>(HttpStatus.NOT_FOUND));
    }

    @PutMapping("/{id}")
    public Mono<ResponseEntity<Object>> updatePlane(@PathVariable("id")
String id,@Valid @RequestBody PlaneRequest planeRequest) {
        return this.planeService.update(id,planeRequest)
            .then(Mono.just(ResponseEntity.ok().build()));
    }

}
```

Take a look at the `plane` method. When `planeService.plane(id)` returns the empty Mono, the REST endpoint will return `notFound` like this implementation: `ResponseEntity.notFound().build()`. It makes the code extremely easy to understand.

On the `newPlane` method, we will return the `location` HTTP header with the new entity ID recently created.

Running the plane microservice

Before we run the plane microservice, we will create the `plane` microservice's `main` class. It will be responsible for starting the application. To do that, we need to include a couple of Spring Annotations. The class implementation can be like this:

```
package springfive.airline.airlineplanes;

import org.springframework.boot.SpringApplication;
import org.springframework.boot.autoconfigure.SpringBootApplication;
import org.springframework.cloud.netflix.eureka.EnableEurekaClient;
import org.springframework.cloud.netflix.zuul.EnableZuulProxy;

@EnableZuulProxy
@EnableEurekaClient
@SpringBootApplication
public class AirlinePlanesApplication {

 public static void main(String[] args) {
  SpringApplication.run(AirlinePlanesApplication.class, args);
 }

}
```

The Spring Annotations will be connected with the Zuul proxy. Also, we need to connect the application with the Eureka server and configure the application automatically. These behaviors can be done using `@EnableZuulProxy`, `@EnableEurekaClient`, and `@SpringBootApplication`.

Now, we will create a `bootstrap.yaml` file to instruct the Spring Framework to search the configuration file on the Config Server, created in the previous chapter. The file should be like this:

```
spring:
  application:
    name: planes
  cloud:
    config:
      uri: http://localhost:5000
      label: master
```

We have configured the Config Server address; it was a piece of cake.

Now, we need to add the `application.yaml` file on the GitHub repository, because the Config Server will try to find the file in the repository.

The file can be found on GitHub at `https://github.com/PacktPublishing/Spring-5.0-By-Example/blob/master/config-files/flights.yaml`.

We can run the application on the IDE or via the command line; it is up to you. Check that the Config Server, Eureka, MongoDB, and RabbitMQ are up and running before trying to run it.

> We can use the Docker compose file located on GitHub (`https://github.com/PacktPublishing/Spring-5.0-By-Example/blob/master/Chapter07/docker/docker-compose-infra-full.yaml`). It contains RabbitMQ, Config Server, Eureka, MongoDB, MySQL, Redis, and Zipkin containers ready to use. If you are using it, run it using the following command: `docker-compose -f docker-compose-infra-full.yaml up -d`.

Let's check the output. We can check it in different ways: on a console, and on the Eureka server. Let's do it.

Check the console. Let's try to find a line about `DiscoveryClient`. The `planes` microservice is trying to connect to the Eureka server:

There is some important information on the log files here. The first line indicates which application is trying to register with the Eureka server. The next four lines are about Sleuth. The Sleuth framework is registering the RabbitMQ queues and channels.

We need to find the following line:

```
Started AirlinePlanesApplication in 17.153 seconds (JVM running for
18.25)
```

Also, we can check the Eureka server, and we can see the **PLANES** application there, like this:

Instances currently registered with Eureka			
Application	AMIs	Availability Zones	Status
PLANES	n/a (1)	(1)	UP (1) - 192.168.100.101:planes:50001

Awesome, our plane microservice is operational.

> **TIP**
> We can try our microservices using Postman. This application enables us to call our APIs using the intuitive IDE to interact with our microservice. The application permits us to group some HTTP calls into collections. The planes collection can be found on GitHub at `https://github.com/PacktPublishing/Spring-5.0-By-Example/blob/master/postman/planes.postman_collection`.

We have finished our first microservices. In the next section, we will create our `flights` microservice, which will consume the plane's data.

Flights microservice

Our plane's microservices are up and running. It will be important for now because the flight's microservice needs to get the plane's data to create the flight's entities.

We will introduce the Netflix Ribbon, which will act as a client load balancer for our applications, and we will consume the service discovery to look up the service's address from the service registry.

Cloning the Flight microservice project

We did this task many times in the previous chapter. We can download the project source code on GitHub at `https://github.com/PacktPublishing/Spring-5.0-By-Example/tree/master/Chapter08/airline-flights`. In the next section, we will dive deep into Ribbon and how it can help us on distributed systems.

Netflix Ribbon

The Ribbon is an open source project created and maintained by the Netflix company. The project is licensed under Apache 2.0 and can be used for commercial purposes.

The Ribbon provides a client-side software load balancing algorithm for the **IPC** (**Inter-Process Communication**). The project supports most popular protocols, such as TCP, UDP, and HTTP in an asynchronous manner.

There are more interesting features, such as service discovery integration, which enables integration in dynamic and elastic environments such as the cloud. For this purpose, we will look at our Eureka server. Both projects are maintained by the Netflix team. It fits well for our use case.

Another interesting feature is fault tolerance. The Ribbon client can find the live servers on the configured list and send the request. Also, the down servers will not receive any request.

The following diagram explains how the Ribbon works:

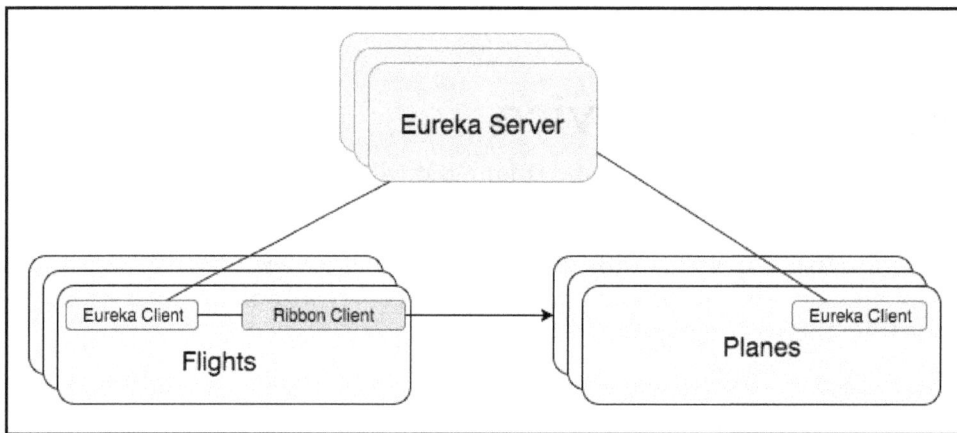

As we can see, the **Ribbon Client** can communicate with Eureka and then redirect the request for the desired microservice. In our case, the `flights` microservice will use the Ribbon client and get the service registry from Eureka and redirect the call to a live `planes` microservice instance. It sounds like an amazing solution.

Understanding the discovery client

Now, we will learn about service discovery and how it works in complex and dynamic environments. The basic idea of service discovery is to maintain the services repository and provide service addresses for the callers.

It requires some complex tasks to achieve this goal. There are two main behaviors to understand:

- The first one is the register. As we know, the service discovery needs to store the services information, such as the address and name, and then during the service bootstrap, it needs to send the information to the service registry.
- In the the second operation, the service discovery clients need to query the service registry, asking for the desired service name, for instance. Then the service registry will send the service information to the client.

Now we understand the basics, as illustrated in the following diagram:

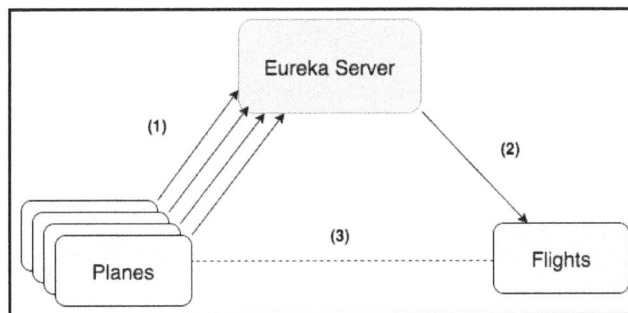

As you can see in the preceding diagram:

1. The first part is the service registration.
2. At the second stage, the service client will get the service address from the Eureka server.
3. Then the client can call based on the service information.

Let's do it in the code.

Service discovery and load balancing in practice

Now we will write some code to interact with our service discovery and load balance infrastructure. Now we know how it works, it will help us to understand the source code.

We will create a `DiscoveryService` class which will discover the addresses from a requested service name. The class code should be like this:

```
package springfive.airline.airlineflights.service;

import org.springframework.cloud.client.discovery.DiscoveryClient;
import
org.springframework.cloud.client.loadbalancer.LoadBalancerClient;
import org.springframework.stereotype.Service;
import reactor.core.publisher.Flux;
import reactor.core.publisher.Mono;

@Service
public class DiscoveryService {

  private final LoadBalancerClient lbClient;

  private final DiscoveryClient dClient;

  public DiscoveryService(LoadBalancerClient lbClient, DiscoveryClient
dClient) {
    this.lbClient = lbClient;
    this.dClient = dClient;
  }

  public Flux<String> serviceAddressFor(String service) {
    return Flux.defer(() ->
Flux.just(this.dClient.getInstances(service)).flatMap(srv ->
      Mono.just(this.lbClient.choose(service))
    ).flatMap(serviceInstance ->
      Mono.just(serviceInstance.getUri().toString())
    ));
  }

}
```

As we can see, we inject two objects: the `LoadBalanceClient`, which acts as a client load balancer, that is, Netflix Ribbon; and the `DiscoveryClient`, which will find the instance from a requested service.

We use the lambda `Flux.defer()` to organize the flow, and then we will look up the service instances from Eureka server. We use `this.dClient.getInstances(service)` for that. It will return a list of service names after we look up the service URI from the load balancing. This will be done using `this.lbClient.choose(service)`. Then we will return the `Flux` of service instances addresses.

It is time to see how the client code can use the `DiscoveryService` object. The client code can be like this:

```
public Mono<Plane> plane(String id) {
  return
discoveryService.serviceAddressFor(this.planesService).next().flatMap(
      address -> this.webClient.mutate().baseUrl(address + "/" +
this.planesServiceApiPath + "/" + id).build().get().exchange()
      .flatMap(clientResponse ->
clientResponse.bodyToMono(Plane.class)));
}
```

This code can be found in the `PlaneService` class on the project. Remember the `serviceAddressFor()` method returns a `Flux` of service addresses. We will get the first one, using the `next()` method. Then we are able to transform the service address to a valid address to reach the plane microservice.

Now, we will test the service connections. We need to do the following tasks:

1. Run the Config Server, Eureka, the `planes` microservice, and the `flights` microservice
2. Create a `plane` entity on the `planes` microservice
3. Create a `flight` entity on the `flights` microservice

Check whether all services listed previously are up and running. Then we will create a `plane` entity using the following JSON:

```
{
  "owner" : "Spring Framework Company",
  "model" : {
    "factory" : "Pivotal",
    "model" : "5.0",
    "name" : "Spring 5.0",
    "reference_name" : "S5.0"
  },
  "seats" : [
    {
      "identity" : "1A",
      "row" : "1",
      "right_side" : { "seat_identity" : "2A"},
      "category" : {
        "id" : "A",
        "name": "First Class"
      }
    },
    {
```

```
            "identity" : "2A",
            "row" : "1",
            "left_side" : { "seat_identity" : "1A"},
            "category" : {
              "id" : "A",
              "name": "First Class"
            }
          },
          {
            "identity" : "3A",
            "row" : "1",
            "left_side" :{ "seat_identity" : "2A"},
            "category" : {
              "id" : "A",
              "name": "First Class"
            }
          }
        ],
      "notes": "The best company airplane"
    }
```

We need to call the `planes` microservice in `http://localhost:50001/planes` using the HTTP `POST` method. We can find the request to create planes in the `Planes Collection` on Postman. When we have called the create plane API, we will get a new plane ID. It can be found in the HTTP response headers, as shown in the following image, on Postman:

> Postman is a tool that helps developers to test APIs. Postman provides a friendly **GUI (Graphic User Interface)** to make requests. Also, the tool supports environments and it can be helpful to test different environments, such as development, test, and production.

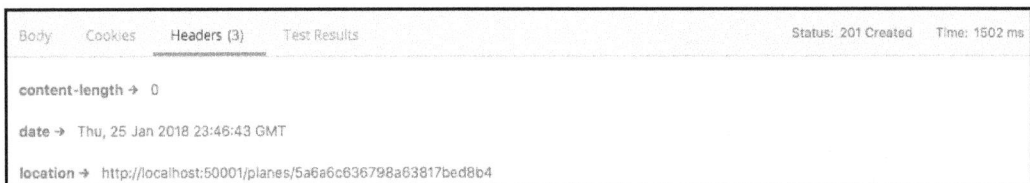

Body Cookies Headers (3) Test Results	Status: 201 Created Time: 1502 ms
content-length → 0	
date → Thu, 25 Jan 2018 23:46:43 GMT	
location → http://localhost:50001/planes/5a6a6c636798a63817bed8b4	

Take a look at the `location` HTTP response header. The HTTP status code is important as well. We will use the plane ID `5a6a6c636798a63817bed8b4`, created just now, to create a new flight.

> **TIP**
> We can find the list of HTTP status code at *W3 Org* (`https://www.w3.org/Protocols/rfc2616/rfc2616-sec10.html`). Keep this in mind, as it is very important to follow the correct status code. It is considered a best practice when we are creating REST APIs.

The Flight Collection can be found on GitHub at `https://github.com/PacktPublishing/Spring-5.0-By-Example/blob/master/postman/flights.postman_collection`. There is a **Create Flight** request we want to execute, but before that, we need to change our plane ID created previously. Take a look at the following screenshot:

```
▸ Create Flight

   POST ∨        http://localhost:50005/flights

   Authorization    Headers (1)    Body ●    Pre-request Script    Tests

   ⊚ form-data   ⊚ x-www-form-urlencoded   ⦿ raw   ⊚ binary   JSON (application/json) ∨

   1 ▾ {
   2 ▾     "from":{
   3            "name":"Viracopos International Airport",
   4            "code":"VCP",
   5            "city":"Campinas",
   6            "country":"Brazil"
   7        },
   8 ▾     "to":{
   9            "name":"Gov. André Franco Montoro International Airport (Cumbica)",
   10           "code":"GRU",
   11           "city":"Sao Paulo",
   12           "country":"Brazil"
   13       },
   14       "departure_at":"2018-08-08 08:00",
   15       "arrive_at":"2018-08-08 09:00",
   16       "plane_id":"5a6a6c636798a63817bed8b4",
   17 ▾     "prices" :[
```

The plane ID has changed to that of our plane previously created. Now we can execute the request. The `flights` microservices has the same behavior as a `planes` microservice. It will return the location response with the new flight ID. In my case, the new ID generated is like the following image:

Now, we can find the flight by ID. The request can be found at Flight Collection; the name is Flight by Id. We can execute this request, and the result should be like this:

```
{
    "id": "5a6a6f1e6798a6383a89fb09",
    "from": {
        "name": "Viracopos International Airport",
        "code": "VCP",
        "city": "Campinas",
        "country": "Brazil"
    },
    "to": {
        "name": "Gov. André Franco Montoro International Airport (Cumbica)",
        "code": "GRU",
        "city": "Sao Paulo",
        "country": "Brazil"
    },
    "departureAt": "2018-08-08T08:00:00",
    "arriveAt": "2018-08-08T09:00:00",
    "plane": {
        "id": "5a6a6c636798a63817bed8b4",
        "model": {
            "factory": "Pivotal",
            "model": "5.0",
            "name": "Spring 5.0"
        }
    },
```

Take a look at the `plane` JSON node. We don't have any data about a plane in the `flight` microservice. This information came in from the `planes` microservice. We have used service discovery and client load balancing. Well done!

Let's take a look at the debug provided by the IDE. We want to see the plane service address:

On the **Variables** panel, we can see the **address** variable. The value came in from service discovery and client load balancing. It is the **Service IP** or **Domain Name**. Now we are able to call the requested service transforming the URL.

Awesome, our infrastructure works very well, now we are able to find services using the infrastructure, but there is something important to pay attention to. We will discover it in the next section.

When the services fail, hello Hystrix

Sometimes the infrastructure can fail, especially the network. It can cause some problems in microservices architecture because in general there are many connections between services. It means at runtime that the microservices depend on other microservices. Normally these connections are done using the REST APIs through the HTTP protocol.

It can cause a behavior called **cascade failure**; that is, when one part of the microservices system fails, it can trigger the other microservices failure, because of the dependencies. Let's illustrate this:

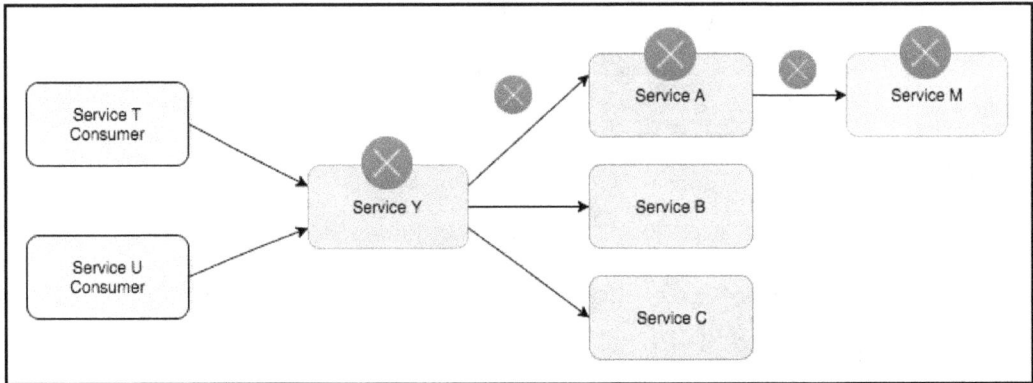

If **Service Y** fails, **Service A** and **Service M** potentially can fail as well.

We have a pattern to help us when this happens: the Circuit Breaker.

Hystrix in a nutshell

`Hystrix` is a library that helps developers to manage interactions between services. The project is open source, maintained by the community, and is under the Netflix GitHub.

The Circuit Breaker pattern is a pattern that helps to control the system integrations. The idea is quite simple: we will wrap the remote call in a function or object, and we will monitor these calls to keep track of the failures. If the calls reach the limit, the circuit will open. The behavior is like that of an electrical circuit breaker, and the idea is the same—protect something to avoid breaking the electrical system:

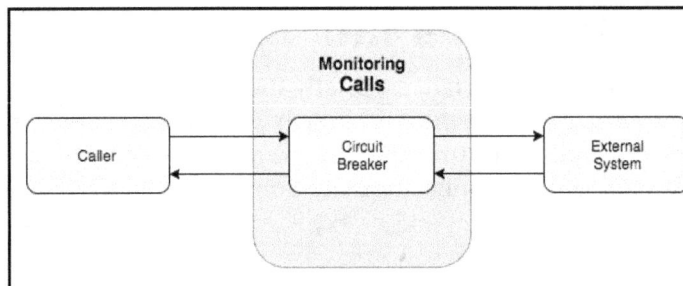

`Hystrix` implements the Circuit Breaker pattern and has some interesting behaviors, such as fallback options. `Hystrix` provides resilience for our applications. We are able to provide a fallback, stop cascading failures, and give the operational control.

The library provides high-level configurations and it can be configured through an annotation if we are using `Spring Cloud Hystrix`.

> The Circuit Breaker pattern was described by Martin Fowler. You can find more information about it on Martin Fowler's Page at https://martinfowler.com/bliki/CircuitBreaker.html

Spring Cloud Hystrix

As we expected, Spring Boot integrates with `Netflix Hystrix`. The integration can be done using a couple of annotations and by configuring the annotations with Hystrix properties. We will protect the `planes` microservice interactions we are coding in the `flight` service. We now have a method that tries to get the plane's data.

Let's take a look at that method:

```
@HystrixCommand(commandKey = "plane-by-id",groupKey = "airline-
flights",fallbackMethod = "fallback",commandProperties = {
@HystrixProperty(name="circuitBreaker.requestVolumeThreshold",value="1
0"),
        @HystrixProperty(name =
"circuitBreaker.errorThresholdPercentage", value = "10"),
@HystrixProperty(name="circuitBreaker.sleepWindowInMilliseconds",value
="10000"),
        @HystrixProperty(name =
"execution.isolation.thread.timeoutInMilliseconds", value = "800"),
        @HystrixProperty(name =
"metrics.rollingStats.timeInMilliseconds", value = "10000")
   })
public Mono<Plane> plane(String id) {
  return
discoveryService.serviceAddressFor(this.planesService).next().flatMap(
        address -> this.webClient.mutate().baseUrl(address + "/" +
this.planesServiceApiPath + "/" + id).build().get().exchange()
        .flatMap(clientResponse ->
clientResponse.bodyToMono(Plane.class)));
  }
```

There are some configurations for this command. The first configuration is `commandKey`. The basic idea here is to create a name for the command. It will be useful for panel control. The second one, `groupKey`, is the command used to group the commands. It also helps in grouping commands data together on dashboards. There is the concept of a rolling window. The idea is to group the request in a gap of time; it is used to enable metrics and statistics.

`circuitBreaker.requestVolumeThreshold` configures the number of requests in a rolling window that will trip at the circuit. For example, if we have a rolling window configured to be open for 10 seconds, if we have nine requests in a gap of 10 seconds, the circuit will not open because we have configured it to 10 in our command. Another configuration is `circuitBreaker.sleepWindowInMilliseconds`, where the basic idea is to give an amount of time, after tripping the circuit, to reject requests before trying again to allow attempts.

The last one is `execution.isolation.thread.timeoutInMilliseconds`. This property configures the timeout for the command. It means that if the time configured is reached, the circuit breaker system will perform a fallback logic and mark the command as a timeout.

> The `Hystrix` library is highly customizable, and there are a lot of properties to use. The full documentation can be found at `https://github.com/Netflix/Hystrix/wiki/configuration`. We can use these properties for different use cases.

Spring Boot Admin

The Spring Boot Admin project is a tool that helps developers in production environments. The tool shows Spring Boot application metrics in an organized dashboard, and it makes it extremely easy to see application metrics and much more information.

The tool uses the data from the Spring Boot Actuator as an information source. The project is open source and has a lot of contributors and is an active project in the community as well.

Running Spring Boot Admin

It is a piece of cake to set up the application. We will need a new Spring Boot application, and to connect this new application with our service discovery implementation. Let's do it right now.

We can find the code on GitHub at `https://github.com/PacktPublishing/Spring-5.0-By-Example/tree/master/Chapter08/admin`. If you want to create a new application, go ahead; the process is similar to what we did in the previous chapters.

The project is a Spring Boot regular application, with two new dependencies:

```
<dependency>
  <groupId>de.codecentric</groupId>
  <artifactId>spring-boot-admin-server</artifactId>
  <version>1.5.6</version>v
</dependency>

<dependency>
  <groupId>de.codecentric</groupId>
  <artifactId>spring-boot-admin-server-ui</artifactId>
  <version>1.5.6</version>
</dependency>
```

These dependencies are about `admin-server` and `admin-server-ui`. The project does not support Spring Boot 2 yet, but this is not a problem as we do not need reactive stuff for this; it is a monitoring tool.

We have configured our mandatory dependencies. We will need a service discovery because we have one in our infrastructure. We need it to provide the service discovery feature, and minimize the configurations for our Spring Boot Admin application. Let's add the Eureka client dependency:

```
<dependency>
  <groupId>org.springframework.cloud</groupId>
  <artifactId>spring-cloud-starter-netflix-eureka-client</artifactId>
</dependency>
```

Awesome, our dependencies are configured properly. Then we can create our main class. The main class should be like this:

```
package springfive.airline.admin;

import de.codecentric.boot.admin.config.EnableAdminServer;
import org.springframework.boot.SpringApplication;
import org.springframework.boot.autoconfigure.SpringBootApplication;
```

```
import org.springframework.cloud.netflix.eureka.EnableEurekaClient;

@EnableAdminServer
@EnableEurekaClient
@SpringBootApplication
public class AdminApplication {

   public static void main(String[] args) {
     SpringApplication.run(AdminApplication.class, args);
   }

}
```

The main difference here is that `@EnableAdminServer` will configure the Spring Boot Admin application and set up the server for us. As we expected, we will use the Config Server application to store our `application.yaml`. In order to achieve this, we need to create our `bootstrap.yaml`, which should be like this:

```
spring:
  application:
    name: admin
  cloud:
    config:
      uri: http://localhost:5000
      label: master
```

No difference at all, `bootstrap.yaml` is configured to look up the configuration file from the Config Server.

Time to create our `application.yaml` file, to which we need to add some configuration to set the new health check URL, since the actuator on Spring Boot 2 was moved, prefixed by *actuator*. Our new health check URL should be `/actuator/health`.

Our configuration file should be like this:

```
server:
  port: 50015

eureka:
  client:
    serviceUrl:
      defaultZone: http://localhost:8761/eureka/
spring:
  boot:
    admin:
      discovery:
```

```
converter:
    health-endpoint-path: /actuator/health
```

We have configured the Eureka server address and set the health check URL.

Now we can run our main class called `AdminApplication`. We can use the Java command line or IDE; there is no difference at all.

Run it!

We should see the following line at the log file:

Awesome, our application is ready to use. Now we can go to the main page. Go to `http://localhost:50015/#/` (main page), then we can see the following page:

Look how it is easier to see any outage or strange behaviors in our microservices. Remember the key point in microservices architecture is monitoring. It is really necessary in order to have a good environment.

Spring Cloud Zuul

The Spring Cloud Gateway is the natural choice when we adopt the microservices architecture, but nowadays the Spring Cloud Gateway does not have support enabled for service discovery features, such as the Eureka server. It means we will have to configure it route by route. This does not sound good.

We have the Zuul proxy as a gateway for our microservices environment, but keep in mind the Spring Cloud Gateway is the best choice when the project has support for service discovery.

Let's create the Zuul proxy project.

Understanding the EDGE service project

The EDGE service is a service that provides dynamic routing, monitoring, resiliency, and security. The basic idea here is to create a reverse proxy for our microservices.

This service will act as a proxy for our microservices and will be exposed as a central access point. The Spring Cloud Zuul integrates with the Eureka server. It will increase our resiliency because we will use the service discovery feature provided by the Eureka server.

The following image demonstrates how we will use the **Edge Service** in our architecture:

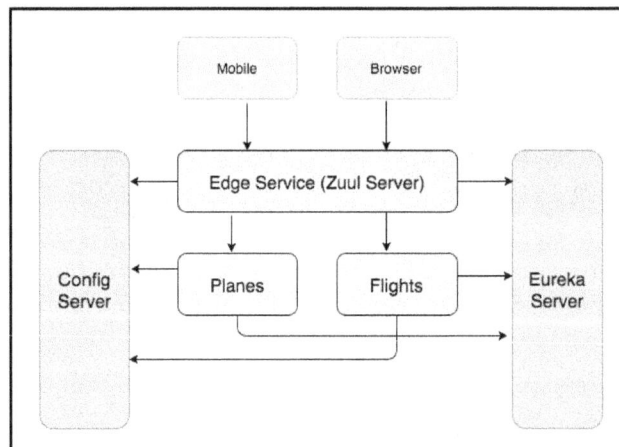

As we can see, the **Zuul Server** will connect to the service discovery server, to get the list of available services. After that the Zuul service will redirect to the requested service.

Look at the diagram. There is no interaction with the clients, that is, **Mobile** and **Browser**, and our microservices.

Spring Cloud Zuul also supports interesting features, such as:

- **pre**: This can be used to set some data in RequestContext; it is executed before the request is routed
- **route**: This handles the request routing
- **post**: This filters which one acts after the request is routed
- **error**: When some errors happen, we can use the error feature to handle the request

We will not use these features, but keep in mind that they can be very useful. Remember, our Zuul server is our gateway to the internet.

Creating the EDGE server

We will use the Zuul server to act as an API gateway for our applications. Now it's time to create our project. As there is no relevant difference involved in creating this project, we will take a look at specific Zuul parts.

The dependency required is:

```
<dependency>
  <groupId>org.springframework.cloud</groupId>
  <artifactId>spring-cloud-starter-netflix-zuul</artifactId>
</dependency>
```

It will configure for us the Zuul server dependencies.

Now we can add the project's main class. The class should be like this:

```
package springfive.airline.edge;

import org.springframework.boot.SpringApplication;
import org.springframework.boot.autoconfigure.SpringBootApplication;
import org.springframework.cloud.netflix.eureka.EnableEurekaClient;
import org.springframework.cloud.netflix.zuul.EnableZuulProxy;
import org.springframework.stereotype.Controller;
```

```
@Controller
@EnableZuulProxy
@EnableEurekaClient
@SpringBootApplication
public class EdgeServerApplication {

  public static void main(String[] args) {
    SpringApplication.run(EdgeServerApplication.class, args);
  }

}
```

The new thing here is `@EnableZuulProxy`. It will set up a Zuul server endpoint and configure reverse proxy filters. Then we will be able to forward a request to microservices applications. Zuul integrates with the Eureka server, so we do not need to configure it manually. The auto-configuration will find the services at the time of the discovery client implementation.

We can run the application via the command line or IDE, it is up to you.

Then we can see the routes configured. Go to `http://localhost:8888/routes` and we will able to see the routes:

```
← → C  ⓘ localhost:8888/routes

{
    "/api/v1/planes/**": "planes",
    "/api/v1/flights/**": "flights",
    "/api/v1/fares/**": "fares",
    "/api/v1/passengers/**": "passengers",
    "/api/v1/payments/**": "payments",
    "/api/v1/auth/**": "auth",
    "/planes/**": "planes"
}
```

We have some routes configured. We did this using the `application.yaml` file. The file should be like this:

```
zuul:
  routes:
    planes:
      path: /api/v1/planes/**
      serviceId: planes
    flights:
      path: /api/v1/flights/**
```

```
      serviceId: flights
    fares:
      path: /api/v1/fares/**
      serviceId: fares
    passengers:
      path: /api/v1/passengers/**
      serviceId: passengers
```

Let's understand this configuration. We have created a node called `planes`. This node configures a `path` (that is the URI) and configures the service name, by `serviceId`, registered in the Eureka server.

Let's do a simple test. We will:

- Configure the new URL path for the planes service
- Test the request using the Zuul server

Open the `PlaneResource` class located in the `planes` microservice project.

The `RequestMapping` is configured like this:

```
@RequestMapping("/planes")
```

Change it to something like this:

```
@RequestMapping("/")
```

Remember we can use the Zuul server as a router, so we do not need this information anymore. With the URI path on the source code, we are able to use the configuration file.

Run the `planes` microservice again. The following services need to be running:

- Config Server
- Eureka server
- Planes microservice
- API Edge

Then we can call the `planes` microservices using the Zuul proxy. Let's do it using cURL:

```
curl http://localhost:8888/api/v1/planes
```

Let's understand this a little bit. The port `8888` points to the **Zuul Server**, and we have configured it in `application.yaml`. When the path is `/api/v1/planes/**`, the **Zuul Server** will redirect to the `planes` microservices. The basic flow is:

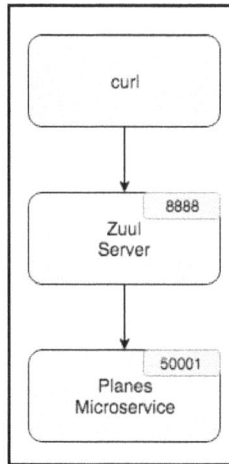

The request is coming to the **Zuul Server**, and then the **Zuul Server** will redirect it to the requested microservice. The result should be like this; in my case, I have some planes in the database:

[{"id":"5a633a556798a675a9a671a5","owner":"Spring Framework Company","model":{"factory":"Pivotal","model":"5.0","name":"Spring 5.0","reference_name":"55.0"},"seats":[{"identity":"1A","row":1,"category":{"id":"A","name":"F irst Class"},"right_side":{"seat_identity":"2A"},{"identity":"2A","row":1,"category":{"id":"A","name":"First Class"},"left_side":{"seat_identity":"1A"}},{"identity":"3A","row":1,"category":{"id":"A","name":"First Class"} ,"left_side":{"seat_identity":"2A"}}],"notes":"The best company airplane"},{"id":"5a6a6c636798a63817bed8b4","owner":"Spring Framework Company","model":{"factory":"Pivotal","model":"5.0","name":"Spring 5.0","reference_name ":"55.0"},"seats":[{"identity":"1A","row":1,"category":{"id":"A","name":"First Class"},"right_side":{"seat_identity":"2A"}},{"identity":"2A","row":1,"category":{"id":"A","name":"First ClassMacBook-Pro-de-Claudio:Library c

Awesome, our API Gateway is fully operational. We will use it for all services in the same port, and only the URI will be changed to point to the desired `serviceId`.

> We can configure the port like in other Spring Boot applications. We chose the `8888` port in this case.

Summary

In this chapter, we have learned about some important microservice patterns and how they can help us to deliver a fault-tolerant, resilient, and error-prone application.

We have practiced how to use the service discovery feature provided by the Spring Framework and how it works at the application runtime, and we made some debug tasks to help us to understand how it works under the hood.

The Hystrix project, hosted by Netflix, can increase our application's resilience and fault tolerance. When working with remote calls, in this section, we made some Hystrix commands and understood how Hystrix is a useful implementation of the Circuit Breaker pattern.

At the end of the chapter, we are able to understand the microservices drawbacks and how to solve the common problems in a distributed environment.

Now we know how to solve the common problems of microservices architectural style using the Spring Framework.

In the next chapter, we will finish our *Airline Ticket System*, using the configured tools to monitoring the microservices' health and look at how it helps developers during the operation time when the microservices are running in the production stage.

See you there.

Putting It All Together

9

There are some challenges to face when we adopt the microservices architectural style. The first one handles operational complexity; services such as service discovery and load balancer help us to tackle these points. We solved these challenges in the previous chapters and got to know some important tools while doing so.

There are some other important key points to handle in microservices adoption. The effective way to monitor what happens in our microservices environments is to monitor how many times microservices consume other microservices resources, such as HTTP APIs, and how many times they fail. If we have near real-time statistics, it can save the developer days of troubleshooting and error investigations.

In this chapter, we will create some services which help us monitor the Hystrix commands and aggregate the command's statistics in a distributed environment.

Security is an important characteristic in microservices architecture, especially because of the distributed characteristic adopted by the microservices architecture. There are a lot of microservices in our architecture; we cannot share state between services, so the stateless security fits well for our environment.

The OAuth 2.0 protocol specification has this important characteristic: the stateless implementation. Spring Cloud Security provides support for OAuth 2.0.

Finally, we will Dockerize our microservices to use the images in Docker compose files.

In this chapter, we will learn about:

- Implementing the Turbine server to aggregate Hystrix streams
- Configuring the Hystrix Dashboard to use Turbine and input data

- Creating a mail service that will integrate an email API
- Understanding Spring Cloud Security
- Dockerizing our microservices

The airline Bookings microservice

The airline `Bookings` microservice is a standard Spring Boot Application. There are some interactions with other services, such as the `flights` microservice.

These interactions were created using Hystrix to bring some desired behaviors, such as fault-tolerance and resilience, to the airline `Bookings` microservice.

There are some business rules on this service, they are is not important to the learning context now, so we will skip the project creation and execution sections.

> The full source code can be found at GitHub (`https://github.com/`
> `PacktPublishing/Spring-5.0-By-Example/tree/master/`
> `Chapter09/airline-booking`); let's check it out and take a look at
> some code.

The airline Payments microservice

The Airline `Payments` is a microservice that gives payments confirmation for our Airline Ticket System. For learning purposes, we will jump this project because there are some business rules, nothing important in the Spring Framework context.

We can find the full source code on GitHub (`https://github.com/PacktPublishing/`
`Spring-5.0-By-Example/tree/master/Chapter09/airline-payments`).

Learning about the Turbine server

There are some integrations in our microservices group; the `Bookings` microservice calls the `Fares` microservice and the `Passengers` microservice, these integrations are done using Hystrix to make it more resilient and fault tolerant.

However, in the microservices world, there are several instances of service. This will require us to aggregate the Hystrix command metrics by instance. Managing the instances panel by panel is not a good idea. The Turbine server helps developers in this context.

By default, Turbine pulls metrics from servers run by Hystrix, but it is not recommended for cloud environments because it can consume high values of network bandwidth and it will increase the traffic costs. We will use Spring Cloud Stream RabbitMQ to push metrics to Turbine via the **Advanced Message Queuing Protocol** (**AMQP**). Due to this, we will need to configure the RabbitMQ connections and put two more dependencies in our microservices, the dependencies are:

```xml
<dependency>
  <groupId>org.springframework.cloud</groupId>
  <artifactId>spring-cloud-netflix-hystrix-stream</artifactId>
</dependency>

<dependency>
  <groupId>org.springframework.cloud</groupId>
  <artifactId>spring-cloud-starter-stream-rabbit</artifactId>
</dependency>
```

These dependencies will enable the metrics to be sent to the Turbine server via the AMQP protocol.

The Turbine stream, by default, uses the port `8989`. We will configure it to run at `8010`, and we can use the `turbine.stream.port` property in the `application.yaml` to customize it.

The Turbine stream will be a Hystrix Dashboard data input to show the commands metrics.

> The full source code can be found on GitHub (`https://github.com/PacktPublishing/Spring-5.0-By-Example/tree/master/Chapter09/turbine`).

There are many configurations to customize the Turbine server. They make the server extremely adaptable for different use cases.

We can find the Turbine documentation in the *Spring Cloud Turbine* section (`https://cloud.spring.io/spring-cloud-netflix/ single/spring-cloud-netflix.html#_turbine`). There is a great deal of information, especially if you need to customize some configurations.

Creating the Turbine server microservice

Let's create our Turbine server. We will create a standard Spring Boot Application with a couple of annotations to enable Turbine stream and discovery client, as well.

The main class should be:

```
package springfive.airline.turbine;

import org.springframework.boot.SpringApplication;
import
org.springframework.boot.autoconfigure.SpringBootApplication;
import
org.springframework.cloud.netflix.eureka.EnableEurekaClient;
import
org.springframework.cloud.netflix.turbine.stream.EnableTurbineStre
am;

@EnableEurekaClient
@EnableTurbineStream
@SpringBootApplication
public class AirlineTurbineApplication {

  public static void main(String[] args) {
     SpringApplication.run(AirlineTurbineApplication.class, args);
  }

}
```

As we can see, `@EnableTurbineStream` will enable us to push Hystrix commands metrics via the RabbitMQ message broker, which is enough for us.

The Turbine server `application.yaml` file can be found on GitHub (`https:// github.com/PacktPublishing/Spring-5.0-By-Example/blob/master/config-files/ turbine.yaml`). There are a couple of configurations, such as discovery client and Turbine server configuration.

We can run the application, via the command line or IDE. Run it!

Make some calls to the `flights` microservice. The Create Flight API will call the `planes` microservice, which uses the Hystrix command, and will trigger some Hystrix command calls.

> **TIP**
>
> We can use the Postman Collection located at GitHub (`https://github.com/PacktPublishing/Spring-5.0-By-Example/blob/master/postman/flights.postman_collection`). This collection has a Create Flight request, which will call the `planes` microservices to get plane details. It is enough to collect metrics.

Now, we can test whether our Turbine server is running correctly. Go to the Turbine stream endpoint and then the JSON data with metrics should be displayed like this:

There are some Hystrix commands information, but as we can see, this information needs to be organized to make it useful for us. Turbine uses the **Server-Sent Events** (**SSE**) technology, which was introduced in `Chapter 6`, *Playing with Server-Sent Events*.

In the next section, we will introduce the Hystrix Dashboard. It will help us to organize and make this information useful for us.

Let's jump to the next section.

Hystrix Dashboard

The Hystrix Dashboard will help us to organize the Turbine stream information. As we saw in the previous section, the Turbine server sends information via SSE. It is done using JSON objects.

The Hystrix stream provides a dashboard for us. Let's create our Hystrix Dashboard microservice. The application is a standard Spring Boot Application annotated with `@EnableHystrixDashboard`. Let's add the dependency to enable it:

```
<dependency>
    <groupId>org.springframework.cloud</groupId>
    <artifactId>spring-cloud-starter-netflix-hystrix-
dashboard</artifactId>
</dependency>
```

Good, now we can create the main class for our application. The main class should look like this:

```
package springfive.airline.hystrix.ui;

import org.springframework.boot.SpringApplication;
import
org.springframework.boot.autoconfigure.SpringBootApplication;
import
org.springframework.cloud.netflix.eureka.EnableEurekaClient;
import
org.springframework.cloud.netflix.hystrix.dashboard.EnableHystrixD
ashboard;

@EnableEurekaClient
@SpringBootApplication
@EnableHystrixDashboard
public class HystrixApplication {

    public static void main(String[] args) {
        SpringApplication.run(HystrixApplication.class, args);
    }

}
```

The full source code can be found at GitHub: `https://github.com/ PacktPublishing/Spring-5.0-By-Example/tree/master/ Chapter09/hystrix-ui`.

As we can see, this is a pretty standard Spring Boot Application annotated with @EnableHystrixDashboard. It will provide the Hystrix Dashboard for us.

Now, we can run the application via IDE or the Java command line. Run it!

> The Hystrix Dashboard can be accessed using the following URL :
> http://localhost:50010/hystrix.

Then, go to the **Hystrix Dashboard** main page. The following page should be displayed:

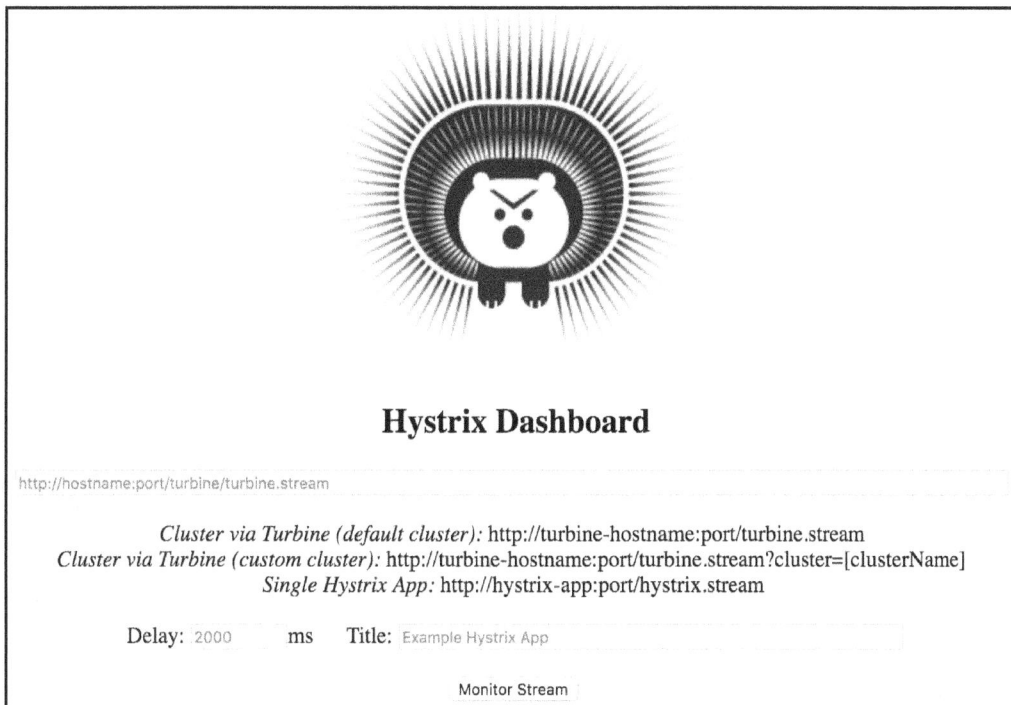

Hystrix Dashboard

http://hostname:port/turbine/turbine.stream

Cluster via Turbine (default cluster): http://turbine-hostname:port/turbine.stream
Cluster via Turbine (custom cluster): http://turbine-hostname:port/turbine.stream?cluster=[clusterName]
Single Hystrix App: http://hystrix-app:port/hystrix.stream

Delay: 2000   ms   Title: Example Hystrix App

Monitor Stream

Awesome – our **Hystrix Dashboard** is up and running. On this page, we can point to `hystrix.stream` or `turbine.stream` to consume and show the commands' metrics.

Keep this application running, we will use it later in this chapter.

Awesome job, guys, let's move to the next section.

Creating the Mail microservice

Now, we will create our `Mail` microservice. The name is self-explanatory, this component will be responsible for sending emails. We will not configure an **SMTP** (**Simple Mail Transfer Protocol**) server, we will use SendGrid.

SendGrid is an **SaaS** (**Software as a Service**) service for emails, we will use this service to send emails to our Airline Ticket System. There are some triggers to send email, for example, when the user creates a booking and when the payment is accepted.

Our `Mail` microservice will listen to a queue. Then the integration will be done using the message broker. We choose this strategy because we do not need the feature that enables us to answer synchronously. Another essential characteristic is the retry policy when the communication is broken. This behavior can be done easily using the message strategy.

We are using RabbitMQ as a message broker. For this project, we will use RabbitMQ Reactor, which is a reactive implementation of RabbitMQ Java client.

Creating the SendGrid account

Before we start to code, we need to create a SendGrid account. We will use the trial account which is enough for our tests. Go to the SendGrid portal (`https://sendgrid.com/`) and click on the **Try for Free** button.

Fill in the required information and click on the **Create Account** button.

In the main page, on the left side, click on **Settings**, then go to the **API Key** section, follow the image shown here:

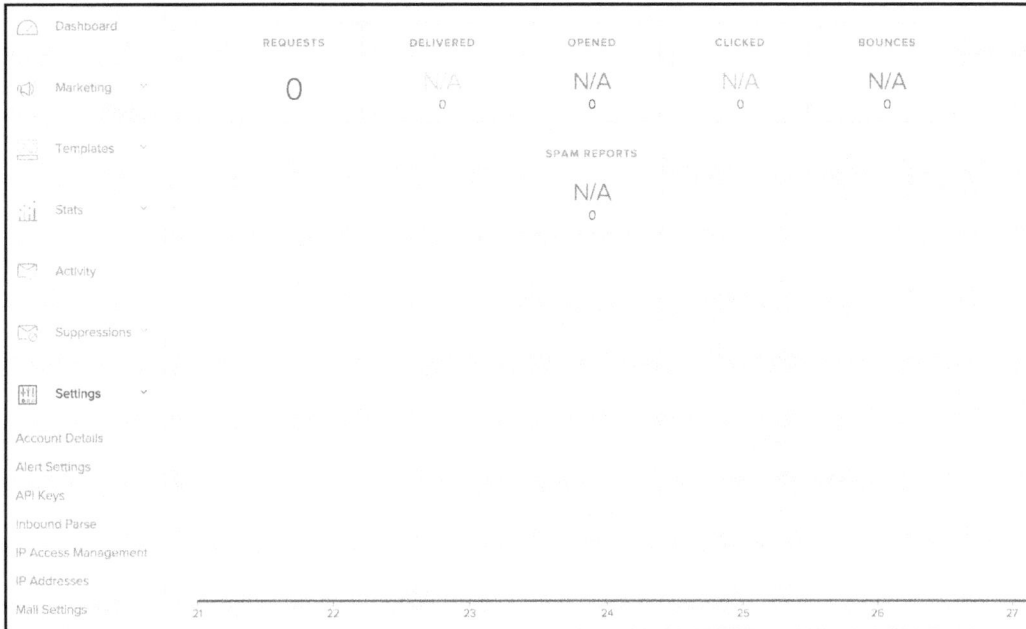

Then, we can click on the **Create API Key** button at the top-right corner. The page should look like this:

Fillin the **API Key** information and choose **Full Access**. After that the **API Key** will appear on your screen. Take a note of it in a safe place, as we will use it as an environment variable soon.

Goob job, our SendGrid account is ready to use, now we can code our `Mail` microservice.

Let's do it in the next section.

Creating the Mail microservice project

As we did in `Chapter 8`, *Circuit Breakers and Security,* we will take a look at essential project parts. We will be using Spring Initializr, as we have several times in the previous chapters.

> The full source code can be found at GitHub (`https://github.com/PacktPublishing/Spring-5.0-By-Example/tree/master/Chapter09/mail-service`).

Adding RabbitMQ dependencies

Let's add the RabbitMQ required dependencies. The following dependencies should be added:

```xml
<dependency>
    <groupId>io.projectreactor.rabbitmq</groupId>
    <artifactId>reactor-rabbitmq</artifactId>
    <version>1.0.0.M1</version>
</dependency>

<dependency>
    <groupId>org.springframework.boot</groupId>
    <artifactId>spring-boot-starter-amqp</artifactId>
</dependency>
```

The first one is about the reactive implementation for RabbitMQ and the second one is the starter AMQP, which will set up some configurations automatically.

Configuring some RabbitMQ stuff

We want to configure some RabbitMQ exchanges, queues, and bindings. It can be done using the RabbitMQ client library. We will configure our required infrastructure for the `Mail` microservice.

Our configuration class should look like this:

```java
package springfive.airline.mailservice.infra.rabbitmq;

// imports are omitted

@Configuration
public class RabbitMQConfiguration {
```

```
   private final String pass;

   private final String user;

   private final String host;

   private final Integer port;

   private final String mailQueue;

   public RabbitMQConfiguration(@Value("${spring.rabbitmq.password}")
String pass,
      @Value("${spring.rabbitmq.username}") String user,
      @Value("${spring.rabbitmq.host}") String host,
      @Value("${spring.rabbitmq.port}") Integer port,
      @Value("${mail.queue}") String mailQueue) {
    this.pass = pass;
    this.user = user;
    this.host = host;
    this.port = port;
    this.mailQueue = mailQueue;
   }

   @Bean("springConnectionFactory")
   public ConnectionFactory connectionFactory() {
     CachingConnectionFactory factory = new CachingConnectionFactory();
     factory.setUsername(this.user);
     factory.setPassword(this.pass);
     factory.setHost(this.host);
     factory.setPort(this.port);
     return factory;
   }

   @Bean
   public AmqpAdmin amqpAdmin(@Qualifier("springConnectionFactory")
ConnectionFactory connectionFactory) {
     return new RabbitAdmin(connectionFactory);
   }

   @Bean
   public TopicExchange emailExchange() {
     return new TopicExchange("email", true, false);
   }

   @Bean
   public Queue mailQueue() {
     return new Queue(this.mailQueue, true, false, false);
   }
```

```
    @Bean
    public Binding mailExchangeBinding(Queue mailQueue) {
        return
BindingBuilder.bind(mailQueue).to(emailExchange()).with("*");
    }

    @Bean
    public Receiver receiver() {
        val options = new ReceiverOptions();
        com.rabbitmq.client.ConnectionFactory connectionFactory = new
com.rabbitmq.client.ConnectionFactory();
        connectionFactory.setUsername(this.user);
        connectionFactory.setPassword(this.pass);
        connectionFactory.setPort(this.port);
        connectionFactory.setHost(this.host);
        options.connectionFactory(connectionFactory);
        return ReactorRabbitMq.createReceiver(options);
    }

}
```

There is interesting stuff here, but all of it is about infrastructure in RabbitMQ. It is important because when our application is in bootstrapping time, it means our application is preparing to run. This code will be executed and create the necessary queues, exchanges, and bindings. Some configurations are provided by the `application.yaml` file, look at the constructor.

Modeling a Mail message

Our `Mail` service is abstract and can be used for different purposes, so we will create a simple class to represent a mail message in our system. Our `Mail` class should look like this:

```
package springfive.airline.mailservice.domain;

import lombok.Data;

@Data
public class Mail {

    String from;

    String to;

    String subject;
```

```
String message;

}
```

Easy, this class represents an abstract message on our system.

The MailSender class

As we can expect, we will integrate with the SendGrid services through the REST APIs. In our case, we will use the reactive `WebClient` provided by Spring WebFlux.

Now, we will use the SendGrid API Key created in the previous section. Our `MailSender` class should look like this:

```
package springfive.airline.mailservice.domain.service;

import org.springframework.beans.factory.annotation.Value;
import org.springframework.http.HttpStatus;
import org.springframework.http.ReactiveHttpOutputMessage;
import org.springframework.stereotype.Service;
import org.springframework.web.reactive.function.BodyInserter;
import org.springframework.web.reactive.function.BodyInserters;
import org.springframework.web.reactive.function.client.WebClient;
import reactor.core.publisher.Flux;
import reactor.core.publisher.Mono;
import springfive.airline.mailservice.domain.Mail;
import
springfive.airline.mailservice.domain.service.data.SendgridMail;

@Service
public class MailSender {

  private final String apiKey;

  private final String url;

  private final WebClient webClient;

  public MailSender(@Value("${sendgrid.apikey}") String apiKey,
      @Value("${sendgrid.url}") String url,
      WebClient webClient) {
    this.apiKey = apiKey;
    this.webClient = webClient;
    this.url = url;
  }
```

```
    public Flux<Void> send(Mail mail){
        final BodyInserter<SendgridMail, ReactiveHttpOutputMessage> body =
BodyInserters
.fromObject(SendgridMail.builder().content(mail.getMessage()).from(mai
l.getFrom()).to(mail.getTo()).subject(mail.getSubject()).build());
        return this.webClient.mutate().baseUrl(this.url).build().post()
            .uri("/v3/mail/send")
            .body(body)
            .header("Authorization","Bearer " + this.apiKey)
            .header("Content-Type","application/json")
            .retrieve()
            .onStatus(HttpStatus::is4xxClientError, clientResponse ->
                Mono.error(new RuntimeException("Error on send email"))
            ).bodyToFlux(Void.class);
    }

}
```

We received the configurations in the constructor, that is, the `sendgrid.apikey` and `sendgrid.url`. They will be configured soon. In the `send()` method, there are some interesting constructions. Look at `BodyInserters.fromObject()`: it allows us to send a JSON object in the HTTP body. In our case, we will create a `SendGrid` mail object.

In the `onStatus()` function, we can pass a predicate to handle the HTTP errors family. In our case, we are interested in the 4xx error family.

This class will process sending the mail messages, but it is necessary to listen to the RabbbitMQ queue, which we will do in the next section.

Creating the RabbitMQ queue listener

Let's create our `MailQueueConsumer` class, which will listen to the RabbitMQ queue. The class should look like this:

```
package springfive.airline.mailservice.domain.service;

import com.fasterxml.jackson.databind.ObjectMapper;
import java.io.IOException;
import javax.annotation.PostConstruct;
import lombok.extern.slf4j.Slf4j;
import lombok.val;
import org.springframework.beans.factory.annotation.Value;
import org.springframework.stereotype.Service;
import reactor.rabbitmq.Receiver;
```

```
import springfive.airline.mailservice.domain.Mail;

@Service
@Slf4j
public class MailQueueConsumer {

  private final MailSender mailSender;

  private final String mailQueue;

  private final Receiver receiver;

  private final ObjectMapper mapper;

  public MailQueueConsumer(MailSender mailSender,
@Value("${mail.queue}") String mailQueue,
      Receiver receiver, ObjectMapper mapper) {
    this.mailSender = mailSender;
    this.mailQueue = mailQueue;
    this.receiver = receiver;
    this.mapper = mapper;
  }

  @PostConstruct
  public void startConsume() {
    this.receiver.consumeAutoAck(this.mailQueue).subscribe(message ->
{
      try {
        val mail = this.mapper.readValue(new
String(message.getBody()), Mail.class);
        this.mailSender.send(mail).subscribe(data ->{
          log.info("Mail sent successfully");
        });
      } catch (IOException e) {
        throw new RuntimeException("error on deserialize object");
      }
    });
  }

}
```

The method annotated with @PostConstruct will be invoked after
MailQueueConsumer is ready, which will mean that the injections are processed.
Then Receiver will start to process the messages.

Running the Mail microservice

Now, we will run our `Mail` microservice. Find the `MailServiceApplication` class, the main class of our project. The main class should look like this:

```
package springfive.airline.mailservice;

import org.springframework.boot.SpringApplication;
import org.springframework.boot.autoconfigure.SpringBootApplication;
import org.springframework.cloud.netflix.eureka.EnableEurekaClient;
import org.springframework.cloud.netflix.hystrix.EnableHystrix;
import org.springframework.cloud.netflix.zuul.EnableZuulProxy;

@EnableHystrix
@EnableZuulProxy
@EnableEurekaClient
@SpringBootApplication
public class MailServiceApplication {

  public static void main(String[] args) {
    SpringApplication.run(MailServiceApplication.class, args);
  }

}
```

It is a standard Spring Boot Application.

We can run the application in IDE or via the Java command line.

Run it!

> We need to pass `${SENDGRID_APIKEY}` and `${SENDGRID_URL}` as environment variables. If you are running the application with the Java command line, the `-D` option allows us to pass environment variables. If you are using the IDE, you can configure in the **Run/Debug Configurations**.

Creating the Authentication microservice

We want to secure our microservices. Security is essential for microservices applications, especially because of the distributed characteristics.

On the microservices architectural style, usually, there is a service that will act as an authentication service. It means this service will authenticate the requests in our microservices group.

Spring Cloud Security provides a declarative model to help developers enable security on applications. There is support for commons patterns such as OAuth 2.0. Also, Spring Boot Security enables **Single Sign-On (SSO)**.

Spring Boot Security also supports relay SSO tokens integrating with Zuul proxy. It means the tokens will be passed to downstream microservices.

For our architecture, we will use the OAuth 2.0 and JWT patterns, both integrate with Zuul proxy.

Before we do so, let's understand the main entities in OAuth 2.0 flow:

- **Protected resource**: This service will apply security rules; the microservices applications, in our case
- **OAuth authorization server**: The authentication server is a service between the application, which can be a frontend or a mobile, and a service that applications want to call
- **Application**: The application that will call the service, the client.
- **Resource Owner**: The user or machine that will authorize the client application to access their account

Let's draw the basic OAuth flow:

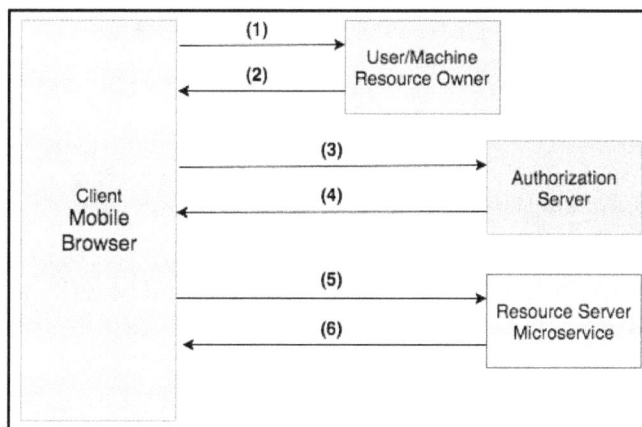

We can observe the following in this diagram:

1. The **Client** requests the authorization
2. The **Resource Owner** sends the authorization grant
3. The application client requests the access token from the **Authorization Server**
4. If the authorization grant is valid, the **Authorization Server** will provide the access token
5. The application calls the protected resource and sends the access token
6. If the **Resource Server** recognizes the token, the resource will serve for the application

These are the basics of the OAuth 2.0 authorization flow. We will implement this flow using Spring Cloud Security. Let's do it.

Creating the Auth microservice

As we have been doing in this chapter, we will take a look at the important parts. Let's start with our dependencies. We need to put in the following dependencies:

```
<dependency>
<groupId>org.springframework.cloud</groupId>
<artifactId>spring-cloud-starter-oauth2</artifactId>
</dependency>

<dependency>
  <groupId>org.springframework.security</groupId>
  <artifactId>spring-security-core</artifactId>
</dependency>

<dependency>
  <groupId>org.springframework.security</groupId>
  <artifactId>spring-security-config</artifactId>
</dependency>
```

These dependencies will enable us to use the Spring Cloud Security features. Let's start to code our Authentication microservice.

Configuring the security

Let's start coding our `Auth` microservice. We will start with the authorization and authentication, as we want to protect all resources in our microservices, then we will configure `WebSecurityConfigureAdapter`. The class should look like this:

```
package springfive.airline.authservice.infra.security;

import org.springframework.beans.factory.annotation.Autowired;
import org.springframework.context.annotation.Configuration;
import
org.springframework.security.config.annotation.authentication.builders
.AuthenticationManagerBuilder;
import
org.springframework.security.config.annotation.method.configuration.En
ableGlobalMethodSecurity;
import
org.springframework.security.config.annotation.web.builders.HttpSecuri
ty;
import
org.springframework.security.config.annotation.web.configuration.Enabl
eWebSecurity;
import
org.springframework.security.config.annotation.web.configuration.WebSe
curityConfigurerAdapter;
import org.springframework.security.crypto.password.PasswordEncoder;
import
springfive.airline.authservice.service.CredentialsDetailsService;

@Configuration
@EnableWebSecurity
@EnableGlobalMethodSecurity(prePostEnabled = true)
public class SecurityConfig extends WebSecurityConfigurerAdapter {

  private final PasswordEncoder passwordEncoder;

  private final CredentialsDetailsService credentialUserDetails;

  public SecurityConfig(PasswordEncoder passwordEncoder,
      CredentialsDetailsService credentialUserDetails) {
    this.passwordEncoder = passwordEncoder;
    this.credentialUserDetails = credentialUserDetails;
  }

  @Override
  @Autowired
  protected void configure(AuthenticationManagerBuilder auth) throws
```

```
Exception {
auth.userDetailsService(this.credentialUserDetails).passwordEncoder(th
is.passwordEncoder);
  }

  @Override
  protected void configure(HttpSecurity http) throws Exception {
    http.csrf().disable()
        .authorizeRequests()
        .antMatchers("/login", "/**/register/**").permitAll()
        .anyRequest().authenticated()
        .and()
        .formLogin().permitAll();
  }


}
```

There is a lot of stuff here. Let's start with the @EnableWebSecurity, this annotation enables Spring Security integrations with Spring MVC. @EnableGlobalMethodSecurity provides AOP interceptors to enable methods security using the annotations. We can use this feature by annotating the methods on a controller, for instance. The basic idea is to wrap the methods call in AOP interceptors and apply security on the methods.

WebSecurityConfigurerAdapter enables us to configure the secure endpoints and some stuff about how to authenticate users, which can be done using the configure(AuthenticationManagerBuilder auth) method. We have configured our CredentialsDetailsService and our PasswordEncoder to avoid plane password between application layers. In this case, CredentialsDetailsService is the source of our user's data.

In our method, configure(HttpSecurity http), we have configured some HTTP security rules. As we can see, all users can access /login and /**/register/**. It's about *Sign In* and *Sign Up* features. All other requests need to be authenticated by the Authorization server.

The CredentialsDetailsService should look like this:

```
package springfive.airline.authservice.service;

import
org.springframework.security.core.userdetails.UserDetailsService;
import
org.springframework.security.core.userdetails.UsernameNotFoundExceptio
n;
```

```
import org.springframework.stereotype.Component;
import springfive.airline.authservice.domain.Credential;
import springfive.airline.authservice.domain.data.CredentialData;
import springfive.airline.authservice.repository.CredentialRepository;

@Component
public class CredentialsDetailsService implements UserDetailsService {

  private final CredentialRepository credentialRepository;

  public CredentialsDetailsService(CredentialRepository
credentialRepository) {
    this.credentialRepository = credentialRepository;
  }

  @Override
  public CredentialData loadUserByUsername(String email) throws
UsernameNotFoundException {
    final Credential credential =
this.credentialRepository.findByEmail(email);
    return
CredentialData.builder().email(credential.getEmail()).password(credent
ial.getPassword()).scopes(credential.getScopes()).build();
  }

}
```

There is nothing special here. We need to override the
`loadUserByUsername(String email)` method to provide the user data to Spring
Security.

Let's configure our token signer and our token store. We will provide these beans
using the `@Configuration` class, as we did in the previous chapters:

```
package springfive.airline.authservice.infra.oauth;

import org.springframework.beans.factory.annotation.Value;
import org.springframework.context.annotation.Bean;
import org.springframework.context.annotation.Configuration;
import
org.springframework.security.crypto.bcrypt.BCryptPasswordEncoder;
import org.springframework.security.crypto.password.PasswordEncoder;
import
org.springframework.security.oauth2.provider.token.store.JwtAccessToke
nConverter;
import
org.springframework.security.oauth2.provider.token.store.JwtTokenStore
;
```

```
@Configuration
public class OAuthTokenProducer {

    @Value("${config.oauth2.privateKey}")
    private String privateKey;

    @Value("${config.oauth2.publicKey}")
    private String publicKey;

    @Bean
    public JwtTokenStore tokenStore(JwtAccessTokenConverter
tokenEnhancer) {
        return new JwtTokenStore(tokenEnhancer);
    }

    @Bean
    public PasswordEncoder passwordEncoder() {
        return new BCryptPasswordEncoder();
    }

    @Bean
    public JwtAccessTokenConverter tokenEnhancer() {
        JwtAccessTokenConverter converter = new
JwtAccessTokenConverter();
        converter.setSigningKey(privateKey);
        converter.setVerifierKey(publicKey);
        return converter;
    }

}
```

We have configured our private and public keys in the application.yaml file. Optionally, we can read the jks files from the classpath as well. Then, we provided our token signer or token enhancer using the JwtAccessTokenConverter class, where we have used the private and public key.

In our token store, Spring Security Framework will use this object to read data from tokens, then set up the JwtAccessTokenConverter on the JwtTokenStore instance.

Finally, we have provided the password encoder class using the BCryptPasswordEncoder class.

Our last class is the Authorization server configuration. The configuration can be done using the following class:

Look at the `OAuth2AuthServer` class located on GitHub (`https://github.com/ PacktPublishing/Spring-5.0-By-Example/blob/master/Chapter09/auth-service/ src/main/java/springfive/airline/authservice/infra/oauth/OAuth2AuthServer. java`).

We have used `@EnableAuthorizationServer` to configure the Authorization server mechanism in our `Auth` microservice. This class works together with `AuthorizationServerConfigurerAdapter` to provide some customizations.

On `configure(AuthorizationServerSecurityConfigurer oauthServer)`, we have configured the security for token endpoints.

At `configure(AuthorizationServerEndpointsConfigurer endpoints)`, we have configured the endpoints of the token service such as, `/oauth/token` and `/oauth/authorize`.

Finally, on `configure(ClientDetailsServiceConfigurer clients)`, we have configured the client's ID and secrets. We used in-memory data, but we can use JDBC implementations as well.

The `Auth` microservice main class should be:

```
package springfive.airline.authservice;

import org.springframework.boot.SpringApplication;
import org.springframework.boot.autoconfigure.SpringBootApplication;
import org.springframework.cloud.netflix.eureka.EnableEurekaClient;
import org.springframework.cloud.netflix.zuul.EnableZuulProxy;

@EnableZuulProxy
@EnableEurekaClient
@SpringBootApplication
public class AuthServiceApplication {

  public static void main(String[] args) {
    SpringApplication.run(AuthServiceApplication.class, args);
  }

}
```

Here, we have created a standard Spring Boot Application with service discovery and Zuul proxy enabled.

Testing the Auth microservice

As we can see, the `Auth` microservice is ready for testing. Our microservice is listening to port `7777`, which we configured using the `application.yaml` file on GitHub.

Client credentials flow

Let's start with the client credentials flow.

Our application needs to be up on port `7777`, then we can use the following command line to get the token:

```
curl -s
442cf4015509eda9c03e5ca3aceef752:4f7ec648a48b9d3fa239b497f7b6b4d801969
7bd@localhost:7777/oauth/token   -d grant_type=client_credentials   -d
scope=trust | jq .
```

As we can see, this *client ID* and *client secret* are from the `planes` microservice. We did this configuration at the `OAuth2AuthServer` class. Let's remember the exact point:

```
....
@Override
public void configure(ClientDetailsServiceConfigurer clients)throws
Exception {
  clients
      .inMemory()
      .withClient("ecommerce") // ecommerce microservice
      .secret("9ecc8459ea5f39f9da55cb4d71a70b5d1e0f0b80")
      .authorizedGrantTypes("authorization_code", "refresh_token",
"implicit",
          "client_credentials")
      .authorities("maintainer", "owner", "user")
      .scopes("read", "write")
      .accessTokenValiditySeconds(THREE_HOURS)
      .and()
      .withClient("442cf4015509eda9c03e5ca3aceef752") // planes
microservice
      .secret("4f7ec648a48b9d3fa239b497f7b6b4d8019697bd")
      .authorizedGrantTypes("authorization_code", "refresh_token",
"implicit",
          "client_credentials")
      .authorities("operator")
      .scopes("trust")
```

```
        .accessTokenValiditySeconds(ONE_DAY)
....
```

After you call the preceding command, the result should be:

```
{
  "access_token": "eyJhbGciOiJSUzI1NiIsInR5cCI6IkpXVCJ9.eyJzY29wZSIGWyJ0cnVzdCJdLCJleHAiOjE1MTczNTk4MjIsImF1dGhvcml0aWVzIjpbIm9wZXJhdGlvbl0sImp0aSI6IjM0N2YwYTg5LTgyODMtNDc3ZC05YmYyLT
ZhMTNiYThnYWQ2YyIsImNsaWVudF9pZCI6IjQ0MmNmNDAxNTUwOWVkYTljJMUNLNWNhM2FjZWVnNzUyIn0.UsMLHlEIS3Urx_IMoif7foLqUK5Xl4htzAusdii9D2GsVnxUn2lYlfnwT7341QG50rHQeSGGZA8cQSN0yITYvoY5ytBqSifiOdHJ
OglwiN8OQf_I_eSbtp5tqqy7T_tP-SkoyGATnkUqAz13n1TmqN1Je-Mb3Iy8-PlATsn9x5E",
  "token_type": "bearer",
  "expires_in": 86399,
  "scope": "trust",
  "jti": "347f0a89-8283-477d-9bf2-6a13ba8aad6c"
}
```

As we can see, the token was obtained with success. Well done, our client credentials flow was configured successfully. Let's move to the implicit flow, which will be covered in the next section.

Implicit grant flow

In this section, we will take a look at how to authenticate in our `Auth` microservice using the implicit flow.

Before we test our flow, let's create a user to enable authentication in the `Auth` microservice. The following command will create a user in the `Auth` service:

```
curl -H "Content-Type: application/json" -X POST -d '{"name":"John
Doe","email":"john@doe.com", "password" : "john"}'
http://localhost:7777/register
```

As we can see, the email is `john@doe.com` and the password is `john`.

We will use the browser to do this task. Let's go to the following URL:

```
http://localhost:7777/oauth/authorize?client_id=ecommerce&response
_type=token&scope=write&state=8777&redirect_uri=https://httpbin.or
g/anything
```

Let's understand the parameters:

The first part is the service address. To use the implicit grant flow, we need the path `/oauth/authorize`. Also we will use `ecommerce` as a client ID because we have configured it previously. `response_type=token` informs the implicit flow, `scope` is the scope as what we want in our case is write, `state` is a random variable, and `redirect_uri` is the URI to go after the `oauth` login process.

Put the URL in a web browser, and the following page should be displayed:

After typing the **User** and **Password**, the following page will be displayed to authorize our protected resources:

Click on the **Authorize** button. Then we will see the token in the browser URL like this:

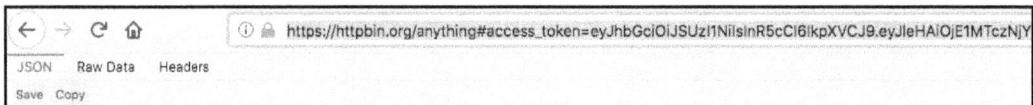

The full token can be viewed if we copy the browser URL.

Awesome job, guys, our `Auth` microservice is fully operational.

In the next sections, we will configure the `Auth` microservice to protect Zuul proxy downstream microservices, such as the `planes` microservices. Let's jump to the next section.

Protecting the microservices with OAuth 2.0

Now we will configure OAuth 2.0 to protect our microservices; in our case, our microservices are the resource servers. Let's start with the `planes` microservices. We will add the new dependency and configure the private and public keys. Also, we will configure our `JwtTokenStore`.

Let's do it.

Adding the security dependency

To add the newly required dependency, we will change the `pom.xml` of the `planes` microservice. We will add the following dependency:

```
<dependency>
  <groupId>org.springframework.cloud</groupId>
  <artifactId>spring-cloud-starter-oauth2</artifactId>
</dependency>
```

A piece of cake – our required dependency is configured properly.

In the next section, we will configure the `application.yaml` file.

Configuring the application.yaml file

To configure our private and public keys, we will use the `application.yaml` file. We did this configuration in the `Auth` microservice. The configuration is pretty easy. We need to add the following snippet:

```
config:
  oauth2:
    privateKey: |
      -----BEGIN RSA PRIVATE KEY-----
      MIICXQIBAAKBgQDNQZKqTlO/+2b4ZdhqGJzGBDltb5PZmBz1ALN2YLvt341pH6i5
      mO1V9cX5Ty1LM70fKfnIoYUP4KCE33dPnC7LkUwE/myh1zM6m8cbL5cYFPyP099t
      hbVxzJkjHWqywvQih/qOOjliomKbM9pxG8Z1dB26hL9dSAZuA8xExjlPmQIDAQAB
      AoGAImnYGU3ApPOVtBf/TOqLfne+2SZX96eVU06myDY3zA4rO3DfbR7CzCLE6qPn
      yDAIiW0UQBsOoBDdWOnOqz5YaePZu/yrLyj6KM6Q2e9ywRDtDh3ywrSfGpjdSvvo
      aeL1WesBWsgWv1vFKKvES7ILFLUxKwyCRC2Lgh7aI9GGZfECQQD84m98Yrehhin3
      fZuRaBNIu348Ci7ZFZmrvyxAIxrV4jBjpACW0RM2BvF5oYM2gOJqIfBOVjmPwUro
      bYEFcHRvAkEAz8jsfmxsZVwh3Y/Y47BzhKIC5FLaads541jNjVWfrPirljyCy1n4
      sg3WQH2IEyap3WTP84+csCtsfNfyK7fQdwJBAJNRyobY74cupJYkW5OK4OkXKQQL
      Hp2iosJV/Y5jpQeC3JO/gARcSmfIBbbI66q9zKjtmpPYUXI4tc3PtUEY8QsCQQCc
      xySyC0sKe6bNzyC+Q8AVvkxiTKWiI5idEr8duhJd589H72Zc2wkMB+a2CEGo+Y5H
```

```
        jy5cvuph/pG/7Qw7sljnAkAy/feClt1mUEiAcWrHRwcQ71AoA0+21yC9VkqPNrn3
        w7OEg8gBqPjRlXBNb00QieNeGGSkXOoU6gFschR22Dzy
        -----END RSA PRIVATE KEY-----
    publicKey: |
        -----BEGIN PUBLIC KEY-----
        MIGfMA0GCSqGSIb3DQEBAQUAA4GNADCBiQKBgQDNQZKqTlO/+2b4ZdhqGJzGBDlt
        b5PZmBz1ALN2YLvt341pH6i5mO1V9cX5Ty1LM70fKfnIoYUP4KCE33dPnC7LkUwE
        /myh1zM6m8cbL5cYFPyP099thbVxzJkjHWqywvQih/qOOjliomKbM9pxG8Z1dB26
        hL9dSAZuA8xExjlPmQIDAQAB
        -----END PUBLIC KEY-----
```

Moreover, the user info URI will be done using the following configuration in YAML:

```
oauth2:
  resource:
    userInfoUri: http://localhost:7777/credential
```

Awesome – our application is fully configured. Now, we will do the last part: configuring to get the information token.

Let's do that.

Creating the JwtTokenStore Bean

We will create the `JwtTokenStore`, which will be used to get token information. The class should look like this:

```
package springfive.airline.airlineplanes.infra.oauth;

import org.springframework.beans.factory.annotation.Value;
import org.springframework.context.annotation.Bean;
import org.springframework.context.annotation.Configuration;
import
org.springframework.security.oauth2.provider.token.store.JwtAccessToke
nConverter;
import
org.springframework.security.oauth2.provider.token.store.JwtTokenStore
;

@Configuration
public class OAuthTokenConfiguration {

  @Value("${config.oauth2.privateKey}")
  private String privateKey;

  @Value("${config.oauth2.publicKey}")
  private String publicKey;
```

```
@Bean
public JwtTokenStore tokenStore() throws Exception {
  JwtAccessTokenConverter enhancer = new JwtAccessTokenConverter();
  enhancer.setSigningKey(privateKey);
  enhancer.setVerifierKey(publicKey);
  enhancer.afterPropertiesSet();
  return new JwtTokenStore(enhancer);
}

}
```

Awesome – our token signer is configured.

Finally, we will add the following annotation to the main class, which should look like this:

```
package springfive.airline.airlineplanes;

import org.springframework.boot.SpringApplication;
import org.springframework.boot.autoconfigure.SpringBootApplication;
import org.springframework.cloud.netflix.eureka.EnableEurekaClient;
import org.springframework.cloud.netflix.zuul.EnableZuulProxy;
import
org.springframework.security.oauth2.config.annotation.web.configuratio
n.EnableResourceServer;

@EnableZuulProxy
@EnableEurekaClient
@EnableResourceServer
@SpringBootApplication
public class AirlinePlanesApplication {

  public static void main(String[] args) {
    SpringApplication.run(AirlinePlanesApplication.class, args);
  }

}
```

It will protect our application, and it will require the access token to access the application endpoints.

Remember, we need to do the same task for all microservices that we want to protect.

Monitoring the microservices

In the microservice architectural style, monitoring is a crucial part. There are a lot of benefits when we adopt this architecture, such as time to market, source maintenance, and an increase of business performance. This is because we can divide the business goals for different teams, and each team will be responsible for some microservices. Another important characteristic is optimization of computational resources, such as cloud computing costs.

As we know, there is no such thing as a free lunch, and this style brings some drawbacks, such as operational complexity. There are a lot of *small services* to monitor. There are potentially hundreds of different service instances.

We have implemented some of these services in our infrastructure but until now, we did not have the data to analyze our system health. In this section, we will explore our configured services.

Let's analyze right now!

Collecting metrics with Zipkin

We have configured our Zipkin server in the previous chapter. Now we will use this server to analyze our microservices data. Let's do it.

Make some calls to create a flight. The Create Flight API will call the **Auth Service** and the **Flight Service**. Look at the following diagram:

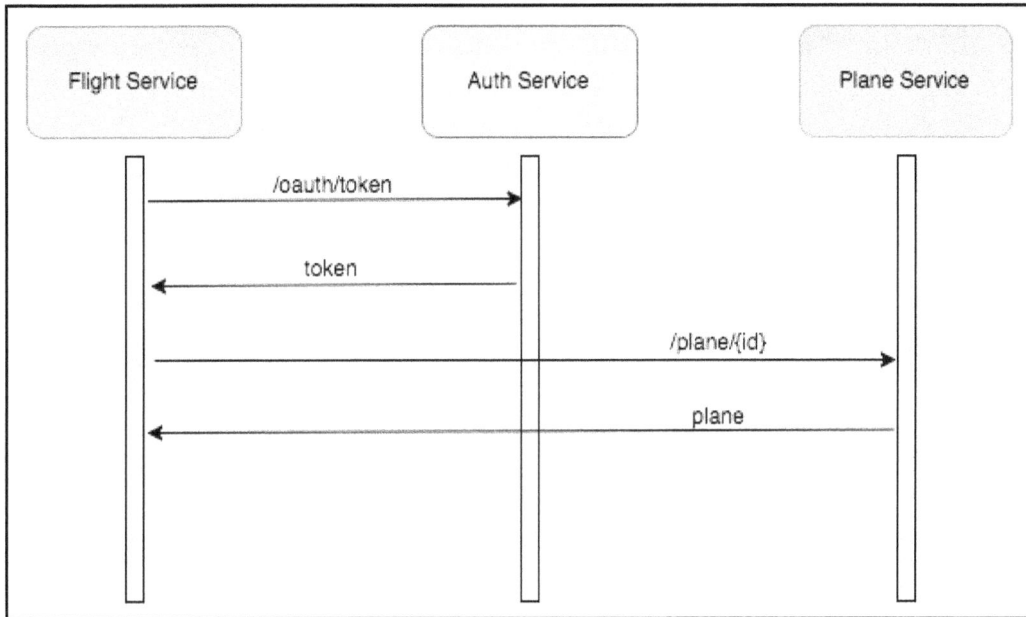

We will take a look at the `flights` microservice and the `planes` microservice communications. Let's analyze it:

Go to the Zipkin main page, `http://localhost:9999/`, select **flights**, and then click on **Find a trace**. The page should look like this:

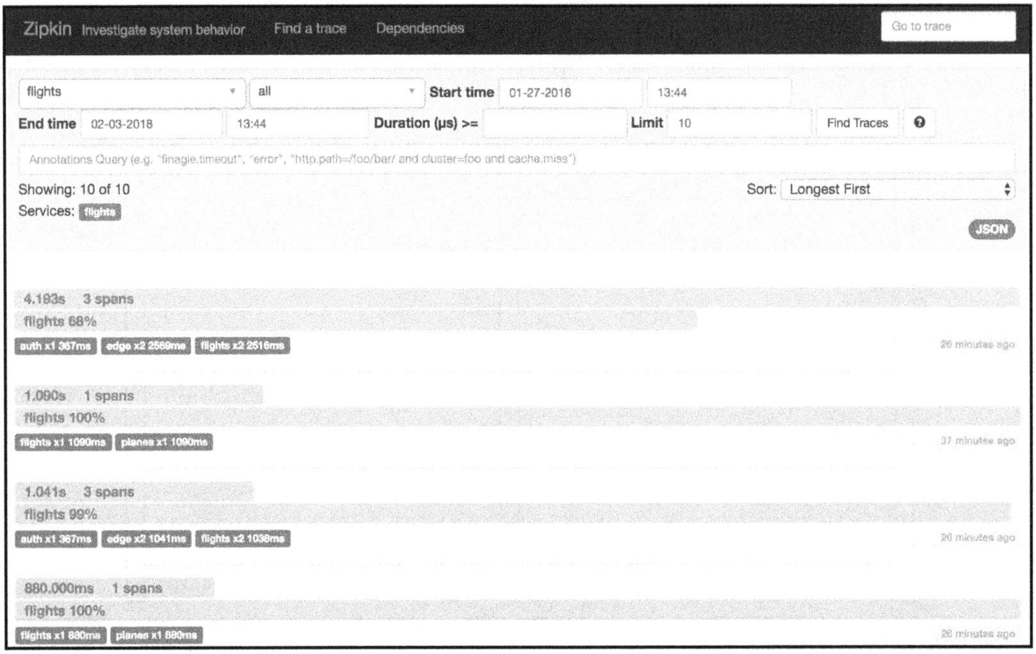

As we can see, there is some data on our Zipkin server. Click on **Span**, which has the `flights` and `planes` tags, then we will take a look at this specific trace, and we will be redirected to another page with specific span data, like this:

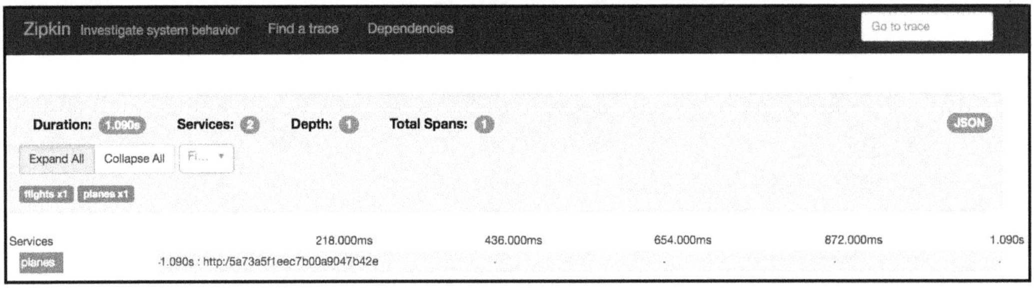

On this page, we can see important information, such as the total request time. Then click on the **planes** row, where we will be able to see detailed information, as in the following image:

```
planes.http:/5a73a5f1eec7b00a9047b42e: 1.090s
AKA: flights,planes
```

Date Time	Relative Time	Annotation	Address
2/3/2018, 1:08:28 PM		Client Send	192.168.100.100:50005 (flights)
2/3/2018, 1:08:28 PM	36.000ms	Server Receive	192.168.100.100:50001 (planes)
2/3/2018, 1:08:28 PM	93.000ms	Server Send	192.168.100.100:50001 (planes)
2/3/2018, 1:08:29 PM	1.090s	Client Receive	192.168.100.100:50005 (flights)

Key	Value
http.host	192.168.100.100
http.method	GET
http.path	/5a73a5f1eec7b00a9047b42e
http.url	http://192.168.100.100:50001/5a73a5f1eec7b00a9047b42e
mvc.controller.class	PlaneResource
mvc.controller.method	plane
spring.instance_id	192.168.100.100:flights:50005
spring.instance_id	192.168.100.100:planes:50001

More Info

Look at the request information. There are some interesting things, such as `mvc.controller.class` and `mvc.controller.method`. These help developers to troubleshoot errors. Also in the first panel, we have the times of the service's interactions. It is very helpful to find microservices network latencies; for example, it makes environment management easier because we have visual tools to understand data better.

Also, the Zipkin server provides others interesting features to find microservices statistics, such as finding requests that have delayed for more than a specific time. It is very helpful for the operations guys.

We can find more information about Spring Cloud Sleuth on the documentation page (`http://cloud.spring.io/spring-cloud-static/spring-cloud-sleuth/2.0.0.M5/single/spring-cloud-sleuth.html`) or in the GitHub (`https://github.com/spring-cloud/spring-cloud-sleuth`) project page.

Collection commands statistics with Hystrix

Now, we want to monitor our Hystrix commands. There are several commands in our microservices and probably the most used will be the OAuth token requester, because we always need to have a token to call any microservice in our system. Our Turbine server and Hystrix UI were configured at the beginning of this chapter and we will use these services right now.

Remember, we are using `spring-cloud-netflix-hystrix-stream` as an implementation to send Hystrix data to the Turbine server, as it performs better than HTTP and also brings some asynchronous characteristics.

Asynchronous calls can make the microservice more resilient. In this case, we will not use HTTP calls (synchronous calls) to register Hystrix Commands statistics. We will use the RabbitMQ queue to register it. In this case, we will put the message in the queue. Also, asynchronous calls make our application more optimized to use computational resources.

Run the Turbine server application and Hystrix UI application. Turbine will aggregate the metrics from the servers. Optionally, you can run several instances of the same service, such as `flights`. Turbine will aggregate the statistics properly.

Let's call the Create Flights API; we can use the Postman to do that.

Then we can see the real-time commands statistics. Before that, we will configure `turbine.stream` in our Hystrix Dashboard.

Go to the Hystrix Dashboard page: `http://localhost:50010/hystrix/`. The
following page will be displayed:

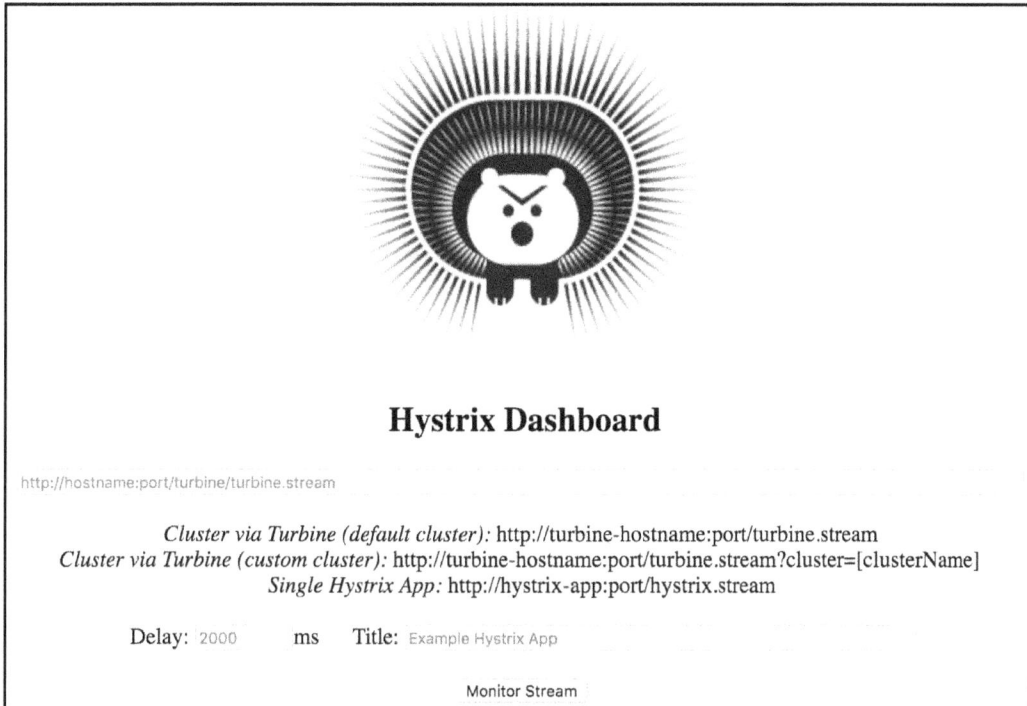

Hystrix Dashboard

http://hostname:port/turbine/turbine.stream

Cluster via Turbine (default cluster): http://turbine-hostname:port/turbine.stream
Cluster via Turbine (custom cluster): http://turbine-hostname:port/turbine.stream?cluster=[clusterName]
Single Hystrix App: http://hystrix-app:port/hystrix.stream

Delay: 2000   ms   Title: Example Hystrix App

Monitor Stream

Then we have some work to do. Let's configure our Turbine server stream. Our
Turbine stream is running at `http://localhost:8010/turbine.stream`. Put this
information below the **Hystrix Dashboard** information, and then we can click on the
Monitor Stream button.

We will redirect to the Hystrix Commands Dashboard; we called the Create Flights API a few times ago. The commands metrics will be displayed, like the following image:

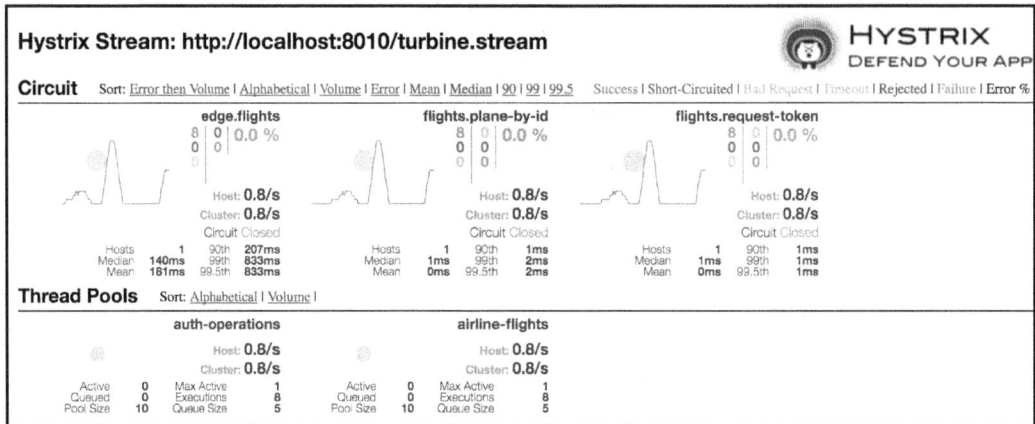

As we can see, we called the Create Flights API eight times. This API uses some commands, such as `flights.plane-by-id`, it calls the planes microservice, and the `flights.request-token` calls the `Auth` service.

Look how easy it is to monitor the commands. Operation guys like the Zipkin server can use this page.

Awesome job, guys, our services integrations are adequately monitored, which makes our microservices adoption more comfortable because we have useful applications to monitor our services instances.

Dockerizing the microservices

In the previous chapters, we have used the Fabric8 Maven Docker plugin to enable us to create Docker images, using the Maven goals.

Now, we need to configure our microservices to use this plugin to easily create images for us. It can be helpful to integrate with some Continuous Integration and Delivery tools, such as Jenkins, because we can call the `docker: build` goal easily.

Each project has the custom configurations, such as port and image name. We can find the configuration at the GitHub repository. Remember, the configuration is done using the `pom.xml`.

The following list has the GitHub repository addresses for all projects; the `pom.xml` has the Maven Docker plugin configuration:

- **Flights**: `https://github.com/PacktPublishing/Spring-5.0-By-Example/blob/master/Chapter09/airline-flights/pom.xml`
- **Planes**: `https://github.com/PacktPublishing/Spring-5.0-By-Example/blob/master/Chapter09/airline-planes/pom.xml`
- **Fares**: `https://github.com/PacktPublishing/Spring-5.0-By-Example/blob/master/Chapter09/airline-fare/pom.xml`
- **Bookings**: `https://github.com/PacktPublishing/Spring-5.0-By-Example/blob/master/Chapter09/airline-booking/pom.xml`
- **Admin**: `https://github.com/PacktPublishing/Spring-5.0-By-Example/blob/master/Chapter09/admin/pom.xml`
- **EDGE**: `https://github.com/PacktPublishing/Spring-5.0-By-Example/blob/master/Chapter09/api-edge/pom.xml`
- **Passengers**: `https://github.com/PacktPublishing/Spring-5.0-By-Example/blob/master/Chapter09/airline-passengers/pom.xml`
- **Auth**: `https://github.com/PacktPublishing/Spring-5.0-By-Example/blob/master/Chapter09/auth-service/pom.xml`
- **Mail**: `https://github.com/PacktPublishing/Spring-5.0-By-Example/blob/master/Chapter09/mail-service/pom.xml`
- **Turbine**: `https://github.com/PacktPublishing/Spring-5.0-By-Example/blob/master/Chapter09/turbine/pom.xml`
- **Zipkin**: `https://github.com/PacktPublishing/Spring-5.0-By-Example/blob/master/Chapter09/zipkin-server/pom.xml`
- **Payments**: `https://github.com/PacktPublishing/Spring-5.0-By-Example/blob/master/Chapter09/airline-payments/pom.xml`
- **Hystrix-dashboard**: `https://github.com/PacktPublishing/Spring-5.0-By-Example/blob/master/Chapter09/hystrix-ui/pom.xml`
- **Discovery**: `https://github.com/PacktPublishing/Spring-5.0-By-Example/blob/master/Chapter09/eureka/pom.xml`
- **Config Server**: `https://github.com/PacktPublishing/Spring-5.0-By-Example/blob/master/Chapter09/config-server/pom.xml`

Running the system

Now we can run our Docker containers using our images, which were created in the previous section.

We will split the services into two Docker compose files. The first one is about infrastructure services. The second one is about our microservices.

The stacks must be run on the same Docker network, because the service should be connected by the container hostname.

The Docker compose file for infrastructure can be found at GitHub: `https://github.com/PacktPublishing/Spring-5.0-By-Example/blob/master/stacks/docker-compose-infra.yaml`.

The Docker compose file for microservices can be found at GitHub: `https://github.com/PacktPublishing/Spring-5.0-By-Example/blob/master/stacks/docker-compose-micro.yaml`.

Now, we can run these files using the `docker-compose` commands. Type the following commands:

```
docker-compose -f docker-compose-infra.yaml up -d
docker-compose -f docker-compose-micro.yaml up -d
```

Then the full application will be up and running.

Well done, guys.

Summary

In this chapter, we have learned some important points on microservices architecture.

We were introduced to some important tools for monitoring the microservices environment. We have learned how the Turbine server can help us to monitor our Hystrix commands in distributed environments.

We were also introduced to the Hystrix Dashboard feature, which helps the developers and operations guys provide a rich dashboard with the commands statistics in near real time.

We learned how Spring Cloud Security enables security features for our microservices, and we implemented the OAuth 2 server, using JWT to enable resilience for our security layer.

Learning Spring Boot 2.0

*Simplify the development of lightning fast applications
based on microservices and reactive programming*

10
Quick Start with Java

Working with Spring Boot is like pair-programming with the Spring developers.

– Josh Long @starbuxman

Perhaps you've heard about Spring Boot? It's cultivated the most popular explosion in software development in years. Clocking millions of downloads *per month*, the community has exploded since its debut in 2013.

I hope you're ready for some fun, because we are going to take things to the next level as we use Spring Boot to build a social media platform. We'll explore its many valuable features, all the way from the tools designed to speed up development efforts to production-ready support as well as cloud-native features.

Despite some rapid fire demos you might have caught on YouTube, Spring Boot isn't just for quick demos. Built atop the de facto standard toolkit for Java, the Spring Framework, Spring Boot will help us build this social media platform with lightning speed and stability.

Also, this book will explore a new paradigm introduced in Spring Framework 5, **reactive programming**. In this day and age, as we build bigger systems, iterate faster, and host fleets of distributed microservices, it has become critical that we switch from a classic blocking programming style. As Josh Long would point out, this is nothing new. The network stacks of today's OSs are inherently asynchronous, but the JVM is *not*. Only in recent years have people realized the need to chop up tasks in a asynchronous, non-blocking fashion. However, the programming paradigm to handle potentially unlimited streams of data coming at fluctuating times requires a new programming model, which we will explore carefully alongside the power of Spring Boot itself.

In this chapter, we'll get a quick kick off with Spring Boot using the Java programming language. Maybe that makes you chuckle? People have been dissing Java for years as being slow, bulky, and not a good language for agile shops. In this chapter, we'll see how that is *not* the case.

In this chapter, we will cover the following topics:

- Creating a bare project using the Spring Initializr found at `http://start.spring.io`
- Exploring Spring Boot's management of third-party libraries
- Seeing how to run our app straight inside our **Integrated Development Environment (IDE)** with no standalone containers
- Using Spring Boot's property support to make external adjustments
- Packaging our app into a self-contained, runnable JAR file
- Deploying our app into the cloud
- Adding out-of-the-box production-grade support tools

> At any time, if you're interested in a more visual medium, feel free to check out my *Learning Spring Boot [Video]* at `https://www.packtpub.com/application-development/learning-spring-boot-video`.

Getting started

What is step one when we get underway with a project? We visit Stack Overflow and look for an example project to help us build our project!

Seriously, the amount of time spent adapting another project's build file, picking dependencies, and filling in other details adds up to a lot of wasted time.

No more.

At the **Spring Initializr** (`https://start.spring.io`), we can enter minimal details about our app, pick our favorite build system and the version of Spring Boot we wish to use, and then choose our dependencies off a menu. Click the **Generate Project** button, and we have a free-standing, ready-to-run application.

In this chapter, we'll take a quick test drive, and build a small web app. We can start by picking **Gradle** from the drop-down menu. Then select **2.0.0.M5** as the version of Spring Boot we wish to use.

Next, we need to pick our application's coordinates, as follows:

- Group - `com.greglturnquist.learningspringboot`
- Artifact - `learning-spring-boot`

Now comes the fun part. We pick the ingredients for our application, like picking off a delicious menu. If we start typing, say, `Web`, into the **Dependencies** box, we'll see several options appear. To see all the available options, click on the **Switch to the full version** link toward the bottom.

> There are lots of overrides, such as switching from JAR to WAR, or using an older version of Java. You can also pick Kotlin or Groovy as the primary language for your application. For starters, in this day and age, there is no reason to use anything older than Java 8. JAR files are the way to go. WAR files are only needed when applying Spring Boot to an old container.

To build our social media platform, we need these few ingredients:

- Reactive Web (embedded Netty + Spring WebFlux)
- Reactive MongoDB (Spring Data MongoDB)
- Thymeleaf template engine
- Lombok (to simplify writing POJOs)

The following screenshot shows us picking these options:

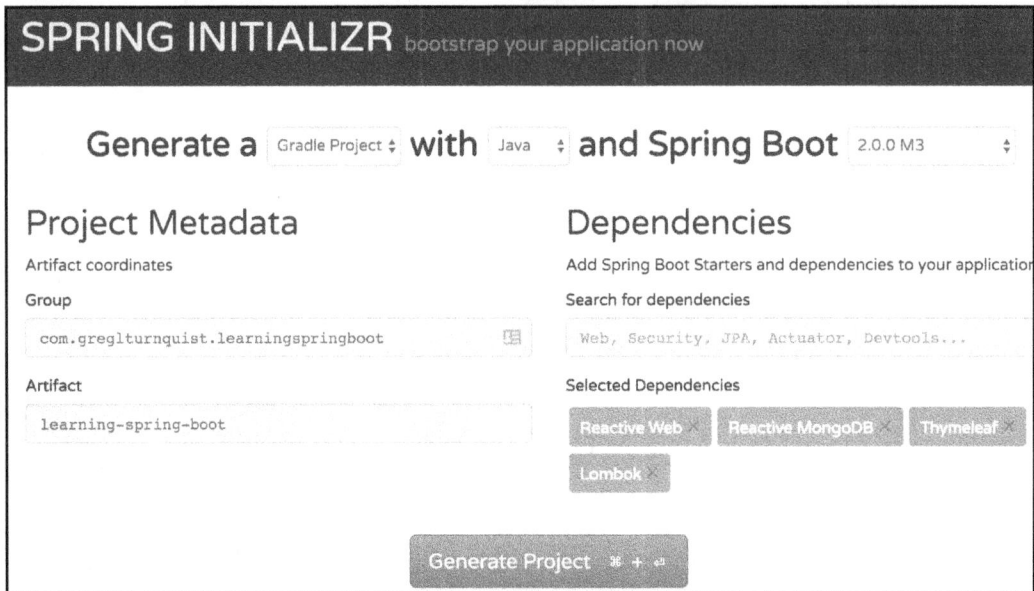

With these items selected, click on **Generate Project**.

> There are *lots* of other tools that leverage this site. For example, IntelliJ IDEA lets you create a new project inside the IDE, giving you the same options shown here. It invokes the website's REST API, and imports your new project. You can also interact with the site via curl or any other REST-based tool.

Now, let's unpack that ZIP file, and see what we've got. You will find the following:

- A `build.gradle` build file
- A Gradle wrapper, so there's no need to install Gradle
- A `LearningSpringBootApplication.java` application class
- An `application.properties` file
- A `LearningSpringBootApplicationTests.java` test class

We built an empty Spring Boot project. Now what? Before we sink our teeth into writing code, let's take a peek at the build file. It's quite terse, but carries some key bits.

Let's take a look, starting from the top:

```
buildscript {
  ext {
    springBootVersion = '2.0.0.M5'
  }
  repositories {
    mavenCentral()
    maven { url "https://repo.spring.io/snapshot" }
    maven { url "https://repo.spring.io/milestone" }
  }
  dependencies {
    classpath(
        "org.springframework.boot:spring-boot-gradle-
        plugin:${springBootVersion}")
  }
}
```

This preceding build file contains the basis for our project:

- `springBootVersion` shows us we are using Spring Boot **2.0.0.M5**
- The Maven repositories it will pull from are listed next (Maven central plus Spring's snapshot and milestone repositories)
- Finally, we see the `spring-boot-gradle-plugin`, a critical tool for any Spring Boot project

The first piece, the version of Spring Boot, is important. That's because Spring Boot comes with a curated list of 140 third-party library versions, extending well beyond the Spring portfolio and into some of the most commonly used libraries in the Java ecosystem. By simply changing the version of Spring Boot, we can upgrade all these libraries to newer versions known to work together. (See `https://github.com/ spring-projects/spring-boot/blob/master/spring-boot-project/spring-boot- dependencies/pom.xml` for a complete list.)

> There is an extra project, the Spring IO Platform (`http://platform.spring.io/platform/`), which includes an additional 134 curated versions, bringing the total to 274.

The repositories aren't as critical, but it's important to add milestones and snapshots if fetching a library that hasn't been released to Maven central, or is hosted on some vendor's local repository. Thankfully, Spring Initializr does this for us based on the version of Spring Boot selected on the site.

Finally, we have `spring-boot-gradle-plugin` (and there is a corresponding `spring-boot-maven-plugin` for Maven users). This plugin is responsible for linking Spring Boot's curated list of versions with the libraries we select in the build file. That way, we don't have to specify the version number.

Additionally, this plugin hooks into the build phase and bundles our application into a runnable über JAR, also known as a shaded or fat JAR.

> **TIP**
>
> Java doesn't provide a standardized way of loading nested JAR files into the classpath. Spring Boot provides the means to bundle up third-party JARs inside an enclosing JAR file, and properly load them at runtime. Read more at `http://docs.spring.io/spring-boot/docs/2.0.0.M5/reference/h tmlsingle/#executable-jar`.

With an über JAR in hand, we only need put it on a thumb drive. We can carry it to another machine, to a hundred virtual machines in the cloud, our data center, or anywhere else. It runs anywhere we can find a JVM.

Peeking a little further down in `build.gradle`, we can see the plugins that are enabled by default:

```
apply plugin: 'java'
apply plugin: 'eclipse'
apply plugin: 'org.springframework.boot'
apply plugin: 'io.spring.dependency-management'
```

- The `java` plugin indicates the various tasks expected for a Java project
- The `eclipse` plugin helps generate project metadata for Eclipse users
- The `org.springframework.boot` plugin is where the actual `spring-boot-gradle-plugin` is activated
- The `io.spring.dependency-management` plugin supports Maven **Bill of Materials** (**BOM**) manifests, allowing usage of libraries that manage the sets of library versions in our Gradle build. (Because Maven supports this natively, there is no Maven equivalent plugin.)

> **i**
>
> An up-to-date copy of IntelliJ IDEA can read a plain old Gradle-build file just fine without extra plugins.

This brings us to the final ingredient used to build our application--**Dependencies**.

Spring Boot starters

No application is complete without specifying dependencies. A valuable feature of Spring Boot is its virtual packages. These are published packages that don't contain any code, but simply list other dependencies instead.

The following code shows all the dependencies we selected on the Spring Initializr site:

```
dependencies {
    compile('org.springframework.boot:spring-boot-starter-data-
      mongodb-reactive')
    compile('org.springframework.boot:spring-boot-starter-
thymeleaf')
    compile('org.springframework.boot:spring-boot-starter-webflux')

    compile('org.projectlombok:lombok')
    compile('de.flapdoodle.embed:de.flapdoodle.embed.mongo')
    testCompile('org.springframework.boot:spring-boot-starter-test')
}
```

You might have noticed that most of these packages are Spring Boot starters:

- `spring-boot-starter-data-mongodb-reactive` pulls in Spring Data MongoDB with the reactive bits enabled
- `spring-boot-starter-thymeleaf` pulls in the Thymeleaf template engine
- `spring-boot-starter-webflux` pulls in Spring WebFlux, Jackson JSON support, and embedded Netty

These starter packages allow us to quickly grab the bits we need to get up and running. Spring Boot starters have become so popular that many other third-party library developers are crafting their own.

In addition to starters, we have the following three extra libraries:

- Project Lombok (`https://projectlombok.org`) makes it dead simple to define POJOs without getting bogged down in getters, setters, and other details.
- Flapdoodle is an embedded MongoDB database that allows us to write tests, tinker with a solution, and get things moving before getting involved with an external database.

At the time of writing, Flapdoodle isn't listed on the website. We must add it manually, as shown previously.

- `spring-boot-starter-test` pulls in Spring Boot Test, JSONPath, JUnit, AssertJ, Mockito, Hamcrest, JSONassert, and Spring Test, all within test scope.

The value of this last starter, `spring-boot-starter-test`, cannot be overstated. With a single line, the most powerful test utilities are at our fingertips, allowing us to write unit tests, slice tests, and full-blown our-app-inside-embedded-Netty tests. It's why this starter is included in all projects without checking a box on the Spring Initializr site.

Now, to get things off the ground, we need to shift focus to the tiny bit of code written for us by the Spring Initializr.

Running a Spring Boot application

The fabulous `https://start.spring.io` website created a tiny class, `LearningSpringBootApplication`, as shown here:

```
package com.greglturnquist.learningspringboot;

import org.springframework.boot.SpringApplication;
import
 org.springframework.boot.autoconfigure.SpringBootApplication;

@SpringBootApplication
public class LearningSpringBootApplication {

  public static void main(String[] args) {
    SpringApplication.run(
      LearningSpringBootApplication.class, args);
  }
}
```

This preceding tiny class is actually a fully operational web application!

- The @SpringBootApplication annotation tells Spring Boot, when launched, to scan recursively for Spring components inside this package and register them. It also tells Spring Boot to enable **autoconfiguration**, a process where beans are automatically created based on classpath settings, property settings, and other factors. We'll see more of this throughout the book. Finally, it indicates that this class itself can be a source for Spring bean definitions.
- It holds public static void main(), a simple method to run the application. There is no need to drop this code into an application server or servlet container. We can just run it straight up, inside our IDE. The amount of time saved by this feature, over the long haul, adds up fast.
- SpringApplication.run() points Spring Boot at the leap-off point--in this case, this very class. But it's possible to run other classes.

This little class is runnable. Right now! In fact, let's give it a shot:

```
  .   ____          _            __ _ _
 /\\ / ___'_ __ _ _(_)_ __  __ _ \ \ \ \
( ( )\___ | '_ | '_| | '_ \/ _` | \ \ \ \
 \\/  ___)| |_)| | | | | || (_| |  ) ) ) )
  '  |____| .__|_| |_|_| |_\__, | / / / /
 =========|_|==============|___/=/_/_/_/
 :: Spring Boot ::   (v2.0.0.M5)
2017-08-02 15:34:22.374: Starting LearningSpringBootApplication
 on ret...
2017-08-02 15:34:22.377: Running with Spring Boot
 v2.0.0.BUILD-SNAPSHO...
2017-08-02 15:34:22.378: No active profile set, falling back
 to defaul...
2017-08-02 15:34:22.433: Refreshing
 org.springframework.boot.web.react...
2017-08-02 15:34:23.717: HV000184: ParameterMessageInterpolator
 has be...
2017-08-02 15:34:23.815: HV000184: ParameterMessageInterpolator
 has be...
2017-08-02 15:34:23.953: Cannot find template location:
 classpath:/tem...
2017-08-02 15:34:24.094: Mapped URL path [/webjars/**] onto
 handler of...
2017-08-02 15:34:24.094: Mapped URL path [/**] onto handler of
 type [c...
2017-08-02 15:34:24.125: Looking for @ControllerAdvice:
 org.springfram...
```

```
2017-08-02 15:34:24.501: note: noprealloc may hurt performance
in many...
2017-08-02 15:34:24.858: 2017-08-02T15:34:24.858-0500 I
NETWORK  [init...
2017-08-02 15:34:24.858: start
de.flapdoodle.embed.mongo.config.Mongod...
2017-08-02 15:34:24.908: Cluster created with settings
{hosts=[localho...
2017-08-02 15:34:24.908: Adding discovered server
localhost:65485 to c...
2017-08-02 15:34:25.007: 2017-08-02T15:34:25.006-0500 I
NETWORK  [init...
2017-08-02 15:34:25.038: Opened connection
[connectionId{localValue:1,...
2017-08-02 15:34:25.040: Monitor thread successfully
connected to serv...
2017-08-02 15:34:25.041: Discovered cluster type of STANDALONE
2017-08-02 15:34:25.145: Cluster created with settings
{hosts=[localho...
2017-08-02 15:34:25.145: Adding discovered server
localhost:65485 to c...
2017-08-02 15:34:25.153: Opened connection
[connectionId{localValue:2,...
2017-08-02 15:34:25.153: Monitor thread successfully connected
to serv...
2017-08-02 15:34:25.153: Discovered cluster type of STANDALONE
2017-08-02 15:34:25.486: Registering beans for JMX exposure
on startup
2017-08-02 15:34:25.556: Started HttpServer on
/0:0:0:0:0:0:0:0:8080
2017-08-02 15:34:25.558: Netty started on port(s): 8080
2017-08-02 15:34:25.607: Started in 3.617 seconds (JVM
running for 4.0...
```

Scrolling through the preceding output, we can see these several things:

- The banner at the top gives us a read-out of the version of Spring Boot. (By the way, you can create your own ASCII art banner by creating either `banner.txt` or `banner.png` and putting it in the `src/main/resources/` folder.)
- Embedded Netty is initialized on port `8080`, indicating that it's ready for web requests.
- It's slightly cut off, but there are signs that Flapdoodle, our embedded MongoDB data store, has come up.
- And the wonderful **Started LearningSpringBootApplication in 3.617 seconds** message can be seen too.

Spring Boot uses embedded Netty, so there's no need to install a container on our target machine. Non-web apps don't even require that. The JAR itself is the new container that allows us to stop thinking in terms of old-fashioned servlet containers. Instead, we think in terms of apps. All these factors add up to maximum flexibility in application deployment.

How does Spring Boot use embedded Netty among other things? As mentioned earlier, it has autoconfiguration, which means that it defines Spring beans based on different conditions. When Spring Boot sees Netty on the classpath, it creates an embedded Netty instance along with several beans to support it.

When it spots Spring WebFlux on the classpath, it creates view resolution engines, handler mappers, and a whole host of other beans needed to help us write a web application. This lets us focus writing routes, not doddling around configuring infrastructure.

With Flapdoodle on the classpath as well as the Reactive MongoDB drivers, it spins up an in-memory, embedded MongoDB data store and connects to it with its state-of-the-art drivers.

Spring Data MongoDB will cause Spring Boot to craft a `MongoOperations` bean along with everything else needed to start speaking Mongo Query Language and make it available if we ask for it, letting us focus on defining repositories.

At this stage, we have a running web application, albeit an empty one. There are no custom routes, and no means to handle data. But we can add some real fast.

Let's start by drafting a simple REST controller as follows:

```
package com.greglturnquist.learningspringboot;

import org.springframework.web.bind.annotation.GetMapping;
import org.springframework.web.bind.annotation.RequestParam;
import org.springframework.web.bind.annotation.RestController;

@RestController
public class HomeController {

  @GetMapping
  public String greeting(@RequestParam(required = false,
  defaultValue = "") String name) {
    return name.equals("") ? "Hey!" : "Hey, " + name + "!";
  }

}
```

Let's examine this tiny REST controller in detail:

- The `@RestController` annotation indicates that we don't want to render views, but write the results straight into the response body instead.
- `@GetMapping` is Spring's shorthand annotation for `@RequestMapping(method = RequestMethod.GET)`. In this case, it defaults the route to `/`.

- Our `greeting()` method has one argument--`@RequestParam(required=false, defaultValue="")` `String name`. It indicates that this value can be requested via an HTTP query (`?name=Greg`)--the query isn't required, and in case it's missing, it will supply an empty string.
- Finally, we return one of two messages depending on whether or not the `name` is an empty string, using Java's ternary operator.

If we relaunch `LearningSpringBootApplication` in our IDE, we'll see this new entry in the console:

```
2017-08-02 15:40:00.741: Mapped "{[],methods=[GET]}" onto
public java....
```

We can then ping our new route in the browser at `http://localhost:8080` and `http://localhost:8080?name=Greg`. Try it out!

(By the way, it sure would be handy if the system could detect this change and relaunch automatically, right? Check out `Chapter 14`, *Developer Tools for Spring Boot Apps* to find out how.)

That's nice, but since we picked Spring Data MongoDB, how hard would it be to load some sample data and retrieve it from another route? (Spoiler alert--Not hard at all.)

We can start out by defining a simple `Chapter` entity to capture book details, as follows:

```
package com.greglturnquist.learningspringboot;

import lombok.Data;

import org.springframework.data.annotation.Id;
import org.springframework.data.mongodb.core.mapping.Document;

@Data
@Document
```

```
public class Chapter {

  @Id
  private String id;
  private String name;

  public Chapter(String name) {
    this.name = name;
  }

}
```

This preceding little POJO lets us look at the details about the chapter of a book as follows:

- The @Data annotation from Lombok generates getters, setters, a toString() method, an equals() method, a hashCode() method, and a constructor for all required (that is, final) fields
- The @Document annotation flags this class as suitable for storing in a MongoDB data store
- The id field is marked with Spring Data's @Id annotation, indicating this is the primary key of our Mongo document
- Spring Data MongoDB will, by default, create a collection named chapters with two fields, id and name
- Our field of interest is name, so let's create a constructor call to help insert some test data

To interact with this entity and its corresponding collection in MongoDB, we could dig in and start using the autoconfigured MongoOperations supplied by Spring Boot. But why do that when we can declare a repository-based solution?

To do this, we'll create an interface defining the operations we need. Check out this simple interface:

```
package com.greglturnquist.learningspringboot;

import org.springframework.data.repository
  .reactive.ReactiveCrudRepository;

public interface ChapterRepository
  extends ReactiveCrudRepository<Chapter, String> {

}
```

This last declarative interface creates a Spring Data repository as follows:

- `ReactiveCrudRepository` extends `Repository`, a Spring Data Commons marker interface that signals Spring Data to create a concrete implementation based on the reactive paradigm while also capturing domain information. It also comes with some predefined CRUD operations (`save`, `delete`, `deleteById`, `deleteAll`, `findById`, `findAll`, and more).
- It specifies the entity type (`Chapter`) and the type of the primary key (`String`).
- We could also add custom finders, but we'll save that for *Chapter 3, Reactive Data Access with Spring Boot.*

Spring Data MongoDB will automatically wire up a concrete implementation of this interface.

Spring Data doesn't engage in code generation. Code generation has a sordid history of being out of date at some of the worst times. Instead, Spring Data uses proxies and other mechanisms to support these operations. Never forget--the code you don't write has no bugs.

With `Chapter` and `ChapterRepository` defined, we can now preload the database, as shown in the following code:

```
package com.greglturnquist.learningspringboot;

import reactor.core.publisher.Flux;

import org.springframework.boot.CommandLineRunner;
import org.springframework.context.annotation.Bean;
import org.springframework.context.annotation.Configuration;

@Configuration
public class LoadDatabase {

  @Bean
  CommandLineRunner init(ChapterRepository repository) {
    return args -> {
      Flux.just(
        new Chapter("Quick Start with Java"),
        new Chapter("Reactive Web with Spring Boot"),
        new Chapter("...and more!"))
        .flatMap(repository::save)
        .subscribe(System.out::println);
    };
```

```
        }

    }
```

This preceding class will be automatically scanned by Spring Boot and run in the following way:

- @Configuration marks this class as a source of beans.
- @Bean indicates that the return value of init() is a Spring Bean--in this case, a CommandLineRunner (utility class from Spring Boot).
- Spring Boot runs all CommandLineRunner beans after the entire application is up and running. This bean definition requests a copy of ChapterRepository.

- Using Java 8's ability to coerce the args → {} lambda function into CommandLineRunner, we are able to gather a set of Chapter data, save all of them and then print them out, preloading our data.

> We aren't going to delve into the intricacies of Flux, flatMap, and subscribe yet. We'll save that for Chapter 11, *Reactive Web with Spring Boot* and Chapter 12, *Reactive Data Access with Spring Boot*.

With all this in place, the only thing left is to write a REST controller to serve up the data!

```
package com.greglturnquist.learningspringboot;

import reactor.core.publisher.Flux;

import org.springframework.web.bind.annotation.GetMapping;
import org.springframework.web.bind.annotation.RestController;

@RestController
public class ChapterController {

  private final ChapterRepository repository;

  public ChapterController(ChapterRepository repository) {
    this.repository = repository;
  }

  @GetMapping("/chapters")
  public Flux<Chapter> listing() {
```

```
        return repository.findAll();
    }
}
```

This preceding controller is able to serve up our data as follows:

- `@RestController` indicates that this is another REST controller.
- Constructor injection is used to automatically load it with a copy of `ChapterRepository`. With Spring, if there is only one constructor call, there is no need to include an `@Autowired` annotation.
- `@GetMapping` tells Spring that this is the place to route `/chapters` calls. In this case, it returns the results of the `findAll()` call found in `ReactiveCrudRepository`. Again, if you're curious what `Flux<Chapter>` is, we'll tackle that at the top of the next chapter. For now, think of it being like a `Stream<Chapter>`.

If we relaunch our application and visit `http://localhost:8080/chapters`, we can see our preloaded data served up as a nicely formatted JSON document, as seen in this screenshot:

```
[
  - {
        id: 1,
        name: "Quick start with Java"
    },
  - {
        id: 2,
        name: "Reactive Web with Spring Boot"
    },
  - {
        id: 3,
        name: "...and more!"
    }
]
```

This may not be very elaborate, but this small collection of classes has helped us quickly define a slice of functionality. And, if you'll notice, we spent zero effort configuring JSON converters, route handlers, embedded settings, or any other infrastructure.

Spring Boot is designed to let us focus on functional needs, not low-level plumbing.

Delving into Spring Boot's property support

We just got things off the ground with an operational application, but that isn't the only killer feature of Spring Boot.

Spring Boot comes with a fistful of prebuilt properties. In fact, just about every autoconfigured component has some property setting (`http://docs.spring.io/spring-boot/docs/2.0.0.M5/reference/htmlsingle/#common-application-properties`) allowing you to override just the parts you like.

Many of these autoconfigured beans will back off if Boot spots us creating our own. For example, when Spring Boot spots reactive MongoDB drivers on the classpath, it automatically creates a reactive `MongoClient`. However, if we define our own `MongoClient` bean, then Spring Boot will back off and accept ours.

This can lead to other components switching off. But sometimes, we don't need to swap out an entire bean. Instead, we may wish to merely tweak a single property of one of these autoconfigured beans.

Let's try to make some adjustments to `src/main/resources/application.properties` as follows:

```
# Override the port Tomcat listens on
server.port=9000

# Customize log levels
logging.level.com.greglturnquist=DEBUG
```

This preceding changes will cause Spring Boot to launch Netty on port `9000`, as shown here:

```
2017-08-02 15:40:02.489: Netty started on port(s): 9000
```

It will also bump up the log level for package `com.greglturnquist` to `DEBUG`.

> Many modern IDEs include **code completion** to find various properties.

While it's handy to externalize configuration settings into property files, it wouldn't be a big advantage if they were only embeddable inside our app's JAR file.

That's why, Spring Boot comes with property override support. The following list shows all the locations from which we can override properties, the first being the highest priority:

- The `@TestPropertySource` annotation on test classes
- Command-line arguments
- The properties found inside `SPRING_APPLICATION_JSON` (inline JSON embedded in an `env` variable or system property)
- The `ServletConfig` init parameters
- The `ServletContext` init parameters
- The JNDI attributes from `java:comp/env`
- The Java System properties (`System.getProperties()`)
- The OS environment variables
- A `RandomValuePropertySource` that only has properties in `random.*`
- Profile-specific properties outside the packaged JAR file (`application-{profile}.properties` and YAML variants)
- Profile-specific properties inside the packaged JAR file (`application-{profile}.properties` and YAML variants)
- Application properties outside the package JAR file (`application.properties` and YAML variants)
- Application properties inside the packaged JAR file (`application.properties` and YAML variants)
- The `@PropertySource` annotation on any `@Configuration` classes
- Default properties (specified using `SpringApplication.setDefaultProperties`)

For an example of the same overrides in YAML format as our `application.properties` file, we could put the following in `application.yml` in `src/main/resources`:

```
server:
  port: 9000
logging:
  level:
    com:
      greglturnquist: DEBUG
```

This would do the exact same thing that we already saw with `application.properties`. The only difference is the formatting.

What are the benefits of YAML over properties? If we need to override lots of settings, it avoids duplication of various keys.

Spring properties can also reference other properties, as shown in this fragment:

```
app.name=MyApp
app.description=${app.name} is a Spring Boot application
```

In this preceding example, the second property, `app.description`, references the first property, `app.name`.

This isn't the end of options with property overrides. It's just the beginning. Throughout this book, we'll expand on the options provided by Spring Boot's property support.

For now, let's focus on getting our app to production!

Bundling up the application as a runnable JAR file

We've hacked out a suitable application. Now it's time to take it to production. As Spring Developer Advocate Josh Long likes to say, production is the happiest place on earth.

The good ol' `spring-boot-gradle-plugin` has built-in hooks to handle that for us. By invoking Gradle's `build` task, it will insert itself into the build process, and create a JAR file.

```
$ ./gradlew clean build
:clean
:compileJava
:processResources
:classes
:findMainClass
:jar
:bootRepackage
:assemble
:compileTestJava
```

```
:processTestResources UP-TO-DATE
:testClasses
:test
... test output ...
:check
:build
BUILD SUCCESSFUL
Total time: 10.946 secs
```

If we peek at the output, we'll find the original JAR file (non-FAT) along with the rebundled one containing our application code as well as the third-party dependencies, as shown here:

```
$ ls build/libs
learning-spring-boot-0.0.1-SNAPSHOT.jar
learning-spring-boot-0.0.1-SNAPSHOT.jar.original
```

> If you wish to check out the newly minted JAR's contents, type `jar tvf build/libs/learning-spring-boot-0.0.1-SNAPSHOT.jar`. We won't show it here because of space constraints.

The über JAR is nicely loaded up with our custom code, all of our third-party dependencies, and a little Spring Boot code to allow us to run it. Why not try that out right here?

Let's type the following command:

```
$ java -jar build/libs/learning-spring-boot-0.0.1-SNAPSHOT.jar
```

We can expect the same output as before, which is as seen in this image:

```
  .   ___          _            __ _ _
 /\ / ___'_ __ _ _(_)_ __  __ _ \ \ \ \
( ( )___ | '_ | '_| | '_ / _` |  \ \ \ \
 \/  ___)| |_)| | | | | || (_| |  ) ) ) )
  '  |____| .__|_| |_|_| |_\__, | / / / /
 =========|_|==============|___/=/_/_/_/
 :: Spring Boot ::   (v2.0.0.M5)
2017-09-19 20:41:20.036: Starting LearningSpringBootApplication
 on ret...
 ...
 ... the rest has been cut for space ...
```

By invoking the JAR using Java's `-jar` option, we can launch the application with nothing more than the JVM on our machine.

With our JAR file in hand, we can take our application anywhere. If we need to override any settings, we can do it without cracking it open and making alterations.

Suppose we alter our command slightly, like this:

```
$ SERVER_PORT=8000 java
  -jar build/libs/learning-spring-boot-0.0.1-SNAPSHOT.jar
```

We can now expect the results to be a little different, as seen in this image:

```
  .   ____          _            __ _ _
 /\\ / ___'_ __ _ _(_)_ __  __ _ \ \ \ \
( ( )\___ | '_ | '_| | '_ \/ _` | \ \ \ \
 \\/  ___)| |_)| | | | | || (_| |  ) ) ) )
  '  |____| .__|_| |_|_| |_\__, | / / / /
 =========|_|==============|___/=/_/_/_/
 :: Spring Boot ::    (v2.0.0.M5)
 . . .
 2017-08-03 15:40:02.489: Netty started on port(s): 8000
 . . .
```

From the command line, we override `server.port` using an alternative notation (`SERVER_PORT`) and run it on port `8000`.

This lends us the ability to deploy it into the cloud.

Deploying to Cloud Foundry

Cloud-native applications are becoming the norm, as companies accelerate their rate of releasing to production (`https://pivotal.io/cloud-native`).

> *Cloud Native describes the patterns of high performing organizations delivering software faster, consistently and reliably at scale. Continuous delivery, DevOps, and microservices label the why, how and what of the cloud natives. In the the most advanced expression of these concepts they are intertwined to the point of being inseparable. Leveraging automation to improve human performance in a high trust culture, moving faster and safer with confidence and operational excellence.*

Many cloud platforms thrive under releasing self-contained applications. The open source Cloud Foundry platform, with its support for many technologies and runnable JAR files, is one of the most popular ones.

To get started, we need either a copy of Cloud Foundry installed in our data center, or an account at **Pivotal Web Services** (**PWS**), a Cloud Foundry hosting provider (`https://run.pivotal.io/`). Assuming we have a PWS account (pronounced *p-dubs*), let's install the tools and deploy our app.

On macOS X, we can type this:

```
$ brew tap cloudfoundry/tap
$ brew install cf-cli
=> Installing cf-cli from cloudfoundry/tap
==> Downloading
    https://cli.run.pivotal.io/stable?release=macosx64-bin...
==> Downloading from
    https://s3-us-west-1.amazonaws.com/cf-cli-release...
    #################################################
    ####################...
==> Caveats
    Bash completion has been installed to:
    /usr/local/etc/bash_completion.d
==> Summary
    /usr/local/Cellar/cf-cli/6.32.0: 6 files, 16.7MB,
    built in 10 seco...
```

For Linux, we can fetch a tarball like this:

```
$ wget -O cf-linux.tgz "https://cli.run.pivotal.io/stable?
  release=linux64-binary&source=github"
$ tar xvfz cf-linux.tgz
$ chmod 755 ./cf
```

This preceding code will download and enable a Linux-based `cf` tool.

> Before using the `cf` tool, you must register for an account at PWS.

For more installation details, visit
`https://docs.run.pivotal.io/cf-cli/install-go-cli.html`.

Using the `cf` tool, let's deploy our application. To kick things off, we need to log into PWS, as follows:

```
$ cf login
API endpoint: https://api.run.pivotal.io
Email> gturnquist@pivotal.io
Password>
```

```
Authenticating...
OK
Select an org (or press enter to skip):
... your organizations will be listed here ...
Org> 2
Targeted org FrameworksAndRuntimes
Select a space (or press enter to skip):
... your spaces will be listed here ...
Space> 1
Targeted space development
API endpoint:    https://api.run.pivotal.io (API version: 2.62.0)
User:            gturnquist@pivotal.io
Org:             FrameworksAndRuntimes
Space:           development
```

We are logged in and targeting a logical space inside an organization.

> Your Org and Space will certainly be different.

Time to deploy! We can do so with the cf push command. At a minimum, we specify the name of our application and the artifact with the -p option (and use a different name than learning-spring-boot, since it's been taken by this book!):

```
$ cf push learning-spring-boot -p build/libs/learning-spring-boot-
  0.0.1-SNAPSHOT.jar
Creating app learning-spring-boot in org FrameworksAndRuntimes
/ space development as gturnquist@pivotal.io...
OK
Creating route learning-spring-boot.cfapps.io...
OK
Binding learning-spring-boot.cfapps.io to learning-spring-boot...
OK
Uploading learning-spring-boot...
...
...
Staging complete
Uploading droplet, build artifacts cache...
Uploading build artifacts cache...
Uploading droplet...
Uploaded build artifacts cache (108B)
Uploaded droplet (76.7M)
Uploading complete
Destroying container
Successfully destroyed container
```

```
0 of 1 instances running, 1 starting
0 of 1 instances running, 1 starting
0 of 1 instances running, 1 starting
1 of 1 instances running
App started
OK
...
...
requested state: started
instances: 1/1
usage: 1G x 1 instances
urls: learning-spring-boot.cfapps.io
last uploaded: Tue Sep 20 02:01:13 UTC 2017
stack: cflinuxfs2
buildpack: java-buildpack=v3.9-offline-
https://github.com/cloudfoundry/java-buildpack.git#b050954 java-main
open-jdk-like-jre=1.8.0_101 open-jdk-like-memory-
calculator=2.0.2_RELEASE spring-auto-reconfiguration=1.10.0_RELEASE
     state     since                    cpu      memory         disk
#0  running  2017-09-19 09:01:59 PM    243.7%   503.5M of 1G    158.1M
of 1G

    details
```

We have pushed our JAR file to PWS, let the Java buildpack (automatically selected) register it with a URL, and start it up. Now, we can visit its registered URL at `http://learning-spring-boot.cfapps.io`:

```
$ curl http://learning-spring-boot.cfapps.io?name=Greg
  Hey, Greg!
```

We've taken our application to production.

The next step is to handle what are sometimes referred to as *Day 2 situations*. This is where we must now monitor and maintain our application, and Spring Boot is ready to provide us just what we need.

Adding production-ready support

We've created a Spring web app with minimal code and released it to production. This is the perfect time to introduce production-grade support features.

There are some questions that often arise in production, and these are as follows:

- What do we do when the system administrator wants to configure his or her monitoring software to ping our app to see if it's up?
- What happens when our manager wants to know the metrics of people hitting our app?
- What are we going to do when the ops center supervisor calls us at 2:00 a.m. and we have to figure out what went wrong?

The last feature we are going to introduce in this chapter is Spring Boot's **Actuator** module. This module provides some super slick Ops-oriented features that are incredibly valuable in a production environment.

We start by adding this dependency to our `build.gradle` as follows:

```
compile('org.springframework.boot:spring-boot-starter-actuator')
```

When you run this version of our app, the same business functionality is available that we saw earlier, but there are additional HTTP endpoints; these are listed in the following table:

Actuator Endpoint	Description
`/application/autoconfig`	This reports what Spring Boot did and didn't autoconfigure, and why
`/appplication/beans`	This reports all the beans configured in the application context (including ours as well as the ones autoconfigured by Boot)
`/application/configprops`	This exposes all configuration properties
`/application/dump`	This creates thread dump report
`/application/env`	This reports on the current system environment
`/application/health`	This is a simple endpoint to check the life of the app
`/application/info`	This serves up custom content from the app
`/application/metrics`	This shows counters and gauges on web usage
`/application/mappings`	This gives us details about all Spring WebFlux routes
`/application/trace`	This shows the details about past requests

Endpoints, by default, are disabled. We have to *opt in*. This is accomplished by setting `endpoints.{endpoint}.enabled=true` inside `src/main/resources/application.properties`, like this:

```
endpoints.health.enabled=true
```

This line added to `application.properties` mentions the endpoint, health, and enables it. If we restart the application, we can ping for its health, as shown in the next section.

Pinging our app for general health

Each of these endpoints can be visited using our browser or using other tools like `curl`:

```
$ curl localhost:9000/application/health
{
  "status": "UP",
  "details": {
    "mongo": {
      "status": "UP",
      "details": {
        "version": "3.2.2"
      }
    },
    "diskSpace": {
      "status": "UP",
      "details": {
        "total": 498937626624,
        "free": 66036432896,
        "threshold": 10485760
      }
    }
  }
}
```

This preceding health status gives us the following:

- An overall UP status
- The status of MongoDB
- The status of the diskspace

When other components are added, they may, optionally, add their own health checks.

This immediately solves our first need listed previously. We can inform the system administrator that he or she can write a management script to interrogate our app's health.

Be warned that each of these endpoints serve up a compact JSON document. Generally speaking, command-line `curl` probably isn't the best option. While it's convenient on *nix and Mac systems, the content is dense and hard to read. It's more practical to have the following:

- a JSON plugin installed in our browser (such as JSON Viewer at `https://github.com/tulios/json-viewer`)
- a script that uses a JSON parsing library if we're writing a management script (such as Groovy's JsonSlurper at `http://docs.groovy-lang.org/latest/html/gapi/groovy/json/JsonSlurper.html` or JsonPath at `https://code.google.com/p/json-path`)

Metrics

To really get operational, we need metrics. Most production systems have metrics in one form or another. Thankfully, we don't have to start from scratch. There is a metric endpoint in Spring Boot Actuator. If we add this following setting to `application.properties`:

```
endpoints.metrics.enabled=true
```

With this property setting, if we restart the application, we can get a quick read out on thing.

Assuming we have JSON Viewer installed, it's easy to surf to `http://localhost:9000/application/metrics` and get a listing on all sorts of metrics. We even have counters for every good/bad web hit, broken down on a per-page basis, as shown here:

```
{
    "names": [
        "jvm.buffer.memory.used",
        "jvm.memory.used",
        "jvm.buffer.count",
        "logback.events",
        "process.uptime",
```

```
            "jvm.memory.committed",
            "jvm.buffer.total.capacity",
            "jvm.memory.max",
            "process.starttime",
            "http.server.requests"
        ]
    }
```

We can visit any one of these metrics by appending it's name to the metrics URL. For example, to view the `http.server.requests`, visit `http://localhost:9000/application/metrics/http.server.requests`:

```
    {
      "name": "http.server.requests",
      "measurements": [
        {
          "statistic": "TotalTime",
          "value": 3.53531643E8
        },
        {
          "statistic": "Count",
          "value": 57.0
        }
      ],
      "availableTags": [
        {
          "tag": "exception",
          "values": [
            "none",
            "none",
            "none",
            "none"
          ]
        },
        {
          "tag": "method",
          "values": [
            "GET",
            "GET",
            "GET",
            "GET"
          ]
        },
        {
          "tag": "uri",
          "values": [
            "/application/metrics/{requiredMetricName}",
            "/application/metrics/{requiredMetricName}",
```

```
        "/application/metrics",
        "/favicon.ico"
      ]
    },
    {
      "tag": "status",
      "values": [
        "200",
        "404",
        "200",
        "200"
      ]
    }
  ]
}
```

This provides a basic framework of metrics to satisfy our manager's needs. It's important to understand that metrics gathered by Spring Boot Actuator aren't persistent across application restarts. To gather long-term data, we have to write them elsewhere (`http://docs.spring.io/spring-boot/docs/2.0.0.M5/reference/htmlsingle/#production-ready-metrics`).

> If you have used Spring Boot 1.x, then this may look very different. That's because a newer, more sophisticated version of metrics has arrived--**Micrometer**. It's currently in development, and may change quite a bit, so stay tuned at `http://micrometer.io/`, and be sure to follow `@micrometerio` on Twitter, as the ability to craft highly detailed and advanced metrics comes to Spring Boot.

Summary

In this chapter, we rapidly crafted a Spring Web application using the Spring stack on top of Netty with little configuration from our end. We plugged in Spring Boot's Actuator module, configuring it with metrics, health, and management features so that we can monitor it in production by merely adding two lines of extra code.

In the next chapter, we'll get underway building our social media platform using these scalable APIs built on top of Reactive Streams.

Reactive Web with Spring Boot

11

The more and more I use #SpringBoot the more I like it.

– Derek Stainer @dstainer

In the previous chapter, we saw how quickly an application can be created with just a few lines of code. In this chapter, we are going to embark upon a journey. We will build a social media application where users can upload pictures and write comments.

In this chapter, we will build the web layer for our social media application doing the following:

- Creating a reactive web application with Spring Initializr
- Learning the tenets of reactive programming
- Introducing Reactor types
- Switching from Apache Tomcat to Embedded Netty
- Comparing reactive **Spring WebFlux** against classic Spring MVC
- Showing some Mono/Flux-based endpoints
- Creating a reactive ImageService
- Creating a reactive file controller
- Showing how to interact with a Thymeleaf template
- Illustrating how going from async to sync can be easy, but the opposite is not

Creating a reactive web application with Spring Initializr

In the last chapter, we took a quick tour through the Spring Initializr site at `http://start.spring.io`. Let's go back there and pick some basic ingredients to start building our social media site by picking the options needed as shown in the following screenshot:

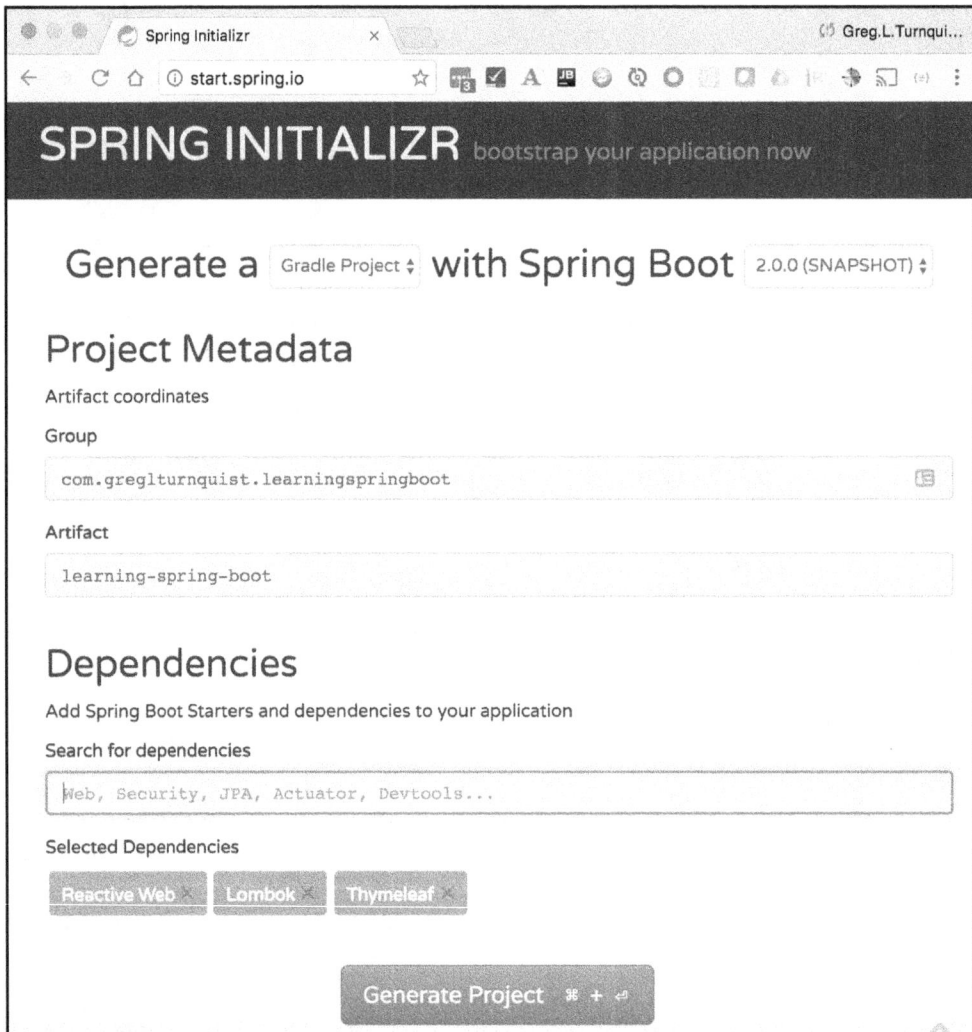

As shown in the preceding screenshot, we've picked the following options:

- **Build system**: Gradle
- **Spring Boot Version**: 2.0
- **Group**: com.greglturnquist.learningspringboot
- **Artifact**: learning-spring-boot

For dependencies, we are going to use these:

- **Reactive Web**: This pulls in Reactive Spring, something we'll explore here and through the rest of this book
- **Lombok**: This is a tiny library that keeps Java interesting by handling getters, setters, toString, equals, hashCode, and more
- **Thymeleaf**: This is not Boot's only supported template library, but a powerful one that includes reactive support as well as strict HTML compliance.

From here, we merely need to click on the **Generate Project** button and a zipped up project will be downloaded. Import it into our IDE, and we're ready to get rolling.

(We will add more dependencies to our project in later chapters.)

We won't list the entire Gradle build file generated by the site, but the dependencies are listed as follows:

```
dependencies {
    compile('org.springframework.boot:spring-boot-starter-webflux')
    compile("org.springframework.boot:spring-boot-starter-
thymeleaf")
    compile('org.synchronoss.cloud:nio-multipart-parser:1.1.0')
    compile('org.projectlombok:lombok')
    testCompile('org.springframework.boot:spring-boot-starter-test')
}
```

The following dependencies are included in the build file:

- spring-boot-starter-webflux: This is the foundation for a Reactive Spring web applications
- spring-boot-starter-thymeleaf: This brings in Thymeleaf's template engine
- nio-multipart-parser: This is a third-party library from Synchronoss, which supports reactive multipart file uploads

- `lombok`: This is a convenient library to create mutable and immutable value objects among other things
- `spring-boot-starter-test`: This is a collection of test libraries including JUnit, Spring Boot Test, Mockito, AssertJ, JSONassert, and Hamcrest

What version of Spring Boot are we using? That can be spotted toward the top of `build.gradle` inside the `buildscript` fragment, as seen here:

```
ext {
    springBootVersion = '2.0.0.M5'
}
```

The version is specified at the top to feed both `spring-boot-gradle-plugin` as well as in the dependencies.

The Gradle build additionally uses the Spring team's Dependency Management Gradle plugin (available here: `https://github.com/spring-gradle-plugins/dependency-management-plugin`), which includes several Maven-like dependency management features. It includes the ability to consume any Maven **Bills of Materials** (**BOMs**) while also handling direct and transitive dependencies.

With our build file in place, we can now dive into *reactive programming*.

Learning the tenets of reactive programming

To launch things, we are going to take advantage of one of Spring Boot's hottest new features--Spring Framework 5's reactive support. The entire Spring portfolio is embracing the paradigm of reactive applications, and we'll focus on what this means and how we can cash in without breaking the bank.

Before we can do that, the question arises--what *is* a reactive application?

In simplest terms, reactive applications engage in the concept of non-blocking, asynchronous operations. Asynchronous means that the answer comes later, whether by polling or by an event pushed backed to us. Non-blocking means not waiting for a response, implying we may have to poll for the results. Either way, while the result is being formed, we don't hold up the thread, allowing it to service other calls.

The side effect of these two characteristics is that applications are able to accomplish more with existing resources.

There are several flavors of reactive applications going back to the 1970s, but the current one gaining resonance is **Reactive Streams** due its introduction of **backpressure**.

Backpressure is another way of saying volume control. The consumer controls how much data is sent by using a pull-based mechanism instead of a traditional push-based solution. For example, imagine requesting a collection of images from the system. You could receive one or a hundred thousand. To prevent the risk of running out of memory in the latter case, people often code page-based solutions. This ripples across the code base, causing a change in the API. And it introduces another layer of handling.

To expand on this example, the following solution would depict that risky collection:

```
public interface MyRepository {
    List<Image> findAll();
}
```

This preceding repository could indeed return one `Image` or a hundred thousand. There's no way to tell. The most common solution, as mentioned, would be to switch to something like this instead:

```
public interface MyRepository {
    Page<Image> findAll(Pageable p);
}
```

The first solution is simple. We know how to iterate over it. The second solution is also iterable (Spring Data Commons's `Page` type implements Java's `Iterable` interface), but requires passing in a parameter to our API, specifying how big a page is and which page we want. While not hard, it introduces a fundamental change in our API.

Reactive Streams is much simpler--return a container that lets the client choose how many items to take. Whether there is one or thousands, the client can use the exact same mechanism and take however many it's ready for. To do this, we would use the following method signature:

```
public interface MyRepository {
    Flux<Image> findAll();
}
```

A `Flux`, which we'll explore in greater detail in the next section, is very similar to a Java 8 `Stream`. We can take as many as we want and it lazily waits until we subscribe to it to yield anything. There is no need to put together a `PageRequest`, making it seamless to chain together controllers, services, and even remote calls.

Introducing Reactor types

We've mentioned Reactive Streams with little detail. There is a spec for Reactive Streams (`http://www.reactive-streams.org/`), but it's important to understand that it is quite primitive. In fact, it's so primitive that it's not very effective for building applications. That may sound counterintuitive, but it wasn't written so much for end users as it was for framework developers. To build reactive applications, we'll use Project Reactor (`http://projectreactor.io/`), the core library that Spring Framework 5 uses for its reactive programming model.

To introduce Reactor's core types, we'll begin with the one we just saw in the previous section, `Flux`, and some code like this:

```
Flux.just("alpha", "bravo", "charlie");
```

This simple creation of a Reactor `Flux` can be detailed as follows:

- `Flux` is Reactor's base type, a container holding *0..N* items, none of which will be reached until the client calls the reactive stream's `subscribe()` method. In this case, the container holds a set of strings.
- `just()` is a static helper method to construct a fixed collection. Other static helpers are also available, like `fromArray()`, `fromIterable()`, and `fromStream()`. This makes it easy to bridge existing Java collections.

> There are additional methods to convert a `Flux` to a Java `Stream` and an `Iterable`. But since these types are generally blocking, it's best to avoid them if possible.

Exactly what does a `Flux` embody? How is it different from a Java `List` or `Stream`? A `Flux` keenly represents multiple values coming, in the future, asynchronously. When those values are coming is not specified nor can it be assumed they are all arriving on the same thread.

In the past, Java has made it possible to represent either a single value or a collection of values that are coming right now in synchronous, blocking APIs. We've also had single value types for asynchronous values (`Future` and `CompletableFuture`). But Java has yet to create a value type for multiple, asynchronous values. That is what Project Reactor and Reactive Streams is all about--processing multiple, asynchronous, non-blocking values in a cohesive fashion.

To consume a `Flux`, we have to either `subscribe` or let the framework do it for us. Here's an example of subscribing for the results:

```
Flux.just("alpha", "bravo", "charlie")
    .subscribe(System.out::println);
```

This last code creates a `Flux` with three items, subscribes for the results, and prints each value out to the screen as follows:

```
alpha
bravo
charlie
```

This may not appear impressive, especially when compared to the existing Java collection builders like `Arrays.asList("alpha", "bravo", "charlie")`. Looks the same, right?

A difference can be seen when we start leveraging Java 8 lambdas and function types. That's when we can chain together a series of function calls, all of which are delayed until that exact element is extracted. Look at the following fragment:

```
Flux.just(
    (Supplier<String>) () -> "alpha",
    (Supplier<String>) () -> "bravo",
    (Supplier<String>) () -> "charlie")
      .subscribe(supplier -> System.out.println(supplier.get()));
```

This `Flux` contains the equivalent in values of our earlier `Flux.just()` except that each one is wrapped inside a Java 8 `Supplier`. This means that, actually, **retrieving** each value is delayed until subscription and only when each individual value is fetched through Reactor's `onNext()` method. This is also known as **lazy**.

Sure this example is contrived, but we'll see more of this paradigm as we explore reactive programming throughout this book.

Another facet of Project Reactor is over 160 operations rooted in functional programming including some of the most well known ones such as `map`, `flatMap`, `filter`, and `then`.

To wrap up this section, let's pick an example a little more complex in nature. What if we took the sample data that we have been poking at and count up how many of each letter we have. Check it out:

```
Flux.just("alpha", "bravo", "charlie")
  .map(String::toUpperCase)
  .flatMap(s -> Flux.fromArray(s.split("")))
  .groupBy(String::toString)
  .sort((o1, o2) -> o1.key().compareTo(o2.key()))
  .flatMap(group -> Mono.just(group.key()).and(group.count()))
  .map(keyAndCount ->
    keyAndCount.getT1() + " => " + keyAndCount.getT2())
    .subscribe(System.out::println);
```

We can take apart this preceding flow as follows:

- This **flow** starts with the same values as shown earlier in this chapter, `alpha`, `bravo`, and `charlie` bundled into a Reactor `Flux`.
- Each entry is converted to uppercase using `String::toUpperCase` ensuring we'll count lowers and uppers together.
- The entries are then flatMapped into individual letters. To visualize flatMapping, look at this example--`["alpha", "bravo"]` is mapped by `s.split("")` into a collection of collections, `[["a", "l", "p", "h", "a"], ["b", "r", "a", "v", "o"]]`, and then flattened into a single collection, `["a", "l", "p", "h", "a", "b", "r", "a", "v", "o"]`.
- Then we group by the string value, which will combine all the `"a"` entries into one subgroup, and so on and so forth.
- Next, we sort by the key value, because the group type doesn't implement `Comparable`.

The underlying type of `groupBy()` is a `GroupedFlux`, a `Flux` with a key value that doesn't implement `Comparable`.

- We flatMap the group's key and count value into a pair of `Mono` objects. (More on `Mono` further in this chapter.)
- We unpack the tuple, and convert it into a string showing key and count.
- We subscribe to the entire flow, printing out the results.

The output can be seen as follows:

```
A => 4
B => 1
C => 1
E => 1
H => 2
I => 1
L => 2
O => 1
P => 1
R => 2
V => 1
```

> **TIP**
> Now that's a lot to take in all at once. Reactor flows, much like Java 8 streams, can pack a lot of functionality. But that is their key benefit. By spending little time on language ceremony, we, instead, focus on strong functional definitions. If needed, it can be handy to read each step in that flow again, using the bullet points to help decode it.

After chatting about `Flux` and all of its operations, something else has leaked into our code--Mono. What is that? It's a Reactor container for *0..1* items, a subset of `Flux`. It implements the same Reactive Streams interface, `Publisher`, which means that we only get its results when we invoke `subscribe()`. It has a few API differences from `Flux` like `flatMap()` versus `flatMapMany()`, but apart from that, it is not hard to grok.

It turns out, a lot of use cases involve handling single values, making it worthwhile capturing this type. In the flow we just walked through, it turns out that the `count()` of a group is stored in a `Mono<Long>`, indicating that we can't know the value until the subscribe is applied at the end. So we have to bundle it up along with the key and map over it to effectively unpack it.

Given that we just walked through a chain of Reactor operations, it's handy to review some of the most commonly used ones. Look at this quick guide:

Operation	Description
`map()`	Converts one `Flux` into another `Flux` of identical size using a function applied to each element
`flatMap()`	Converts one `Flux` into another `Flux` of a different size by first mapping, and then removing any nesting
`filter()`	Converts one `Flux` into a smaller `Flux` with elements removed based on a filtering function
`groupBy()`	Converts the `Flux` into a bundled set of subgroups based on the grouping function
`sort()`	Converts one `Flux` into a sorted `Flux` based on the sorting function

Several of these operations listed in the previous table also exist for `Mono`. There are others, but these are the big ones.

What's the big picture in all this? Essentially, every step of this flow *could* be an asynchronous, non-blocking, remote call to another service. With Reactor, we don't have to worry about thread management unless we really want to get into it. It's handled for us. And soon, we'll start doing just that.

There's a myth that is possibly as old as Java itself: **To make things run faster, we must use threads**. And the corollary would be: **The more threads, the faster**. But this is not born out of empirical research. In fact, using threads can lead to concurrent faults and using too many threads can introduce context switching overhead. JavaScript developers, in an environment where there is but one thread, have developed many reactive solutions that are very efficient at handling things. That is because using queues and event loops combined with asynchronous, non-blocking APIs that don't hold up the thread, actually results in accomplishing a lot with few resources.

If this introductory taste of Project Reactor, `Flux`, and `Mono` is still confusing, please read the following blog articles for more detailed information on reactive programming:

- http://bit.ly/reactive-part-1
- http://bit.ly/reactive-part-2
- http://bit.ly/reactive-part-3
- http://bit.ly/reactive-types

Switching from Embedded Netty to Apache Tomcat

By default, Spring Boot is geared up to use embedded Netty (http://netty.io). Why? Because it's one of the most popular solutions for reactive applications. And when it comes to reactive applications, it's critical that the entire stack be reactive.

However, it's possible to switch to another embedded container. We can experiment with using Apache Tomcat and its asynchronous Servlet 3.1 API. All we have to do is to make some tweaks to the dependency settings in `build.gradle`, as follows:

```
compile('org.springframework.boot:spring-boot-starter-webflux') {
    exclude group: 'org.springframework.boot',
    module: 'spring-boot-starter-reactor-netty'
}
compile('org.springframework.boot:spring-boot-starter-tomcat')
```

What's happening in the preceding code? This can be explained as follows:

- `spring-boot-starter-webflux` excludes `spring-boot-starter-reactor-netty`, taking it off the classpath
- `spring-boot-starter-tomcat` is added to the classpath
- Spring Boot's `TomcatAutoConfiguration` kicks in, and configures the container to work using `TomcatReactiveWebServerFactory`

It's important to point out that there are these other containers available:

- Jetty
- Undertow

For the rest of this title, we'll stick with Spring Boot's default, Netty.

> It's interesting to refer to these as containers given that they are *contained* inside our application. It used to be standard practice to install Apache Tomcat (or whatever container we picked) and install the application into it. But Spring Boot has made embedded containers a core feature, inverting this concept of apps inside containers and putting the container inside the app instead. For an entertaining presentation on how this change has swept the Java community, check out Eberhard Wolff's Java Application Servers Are Dead (`http://www.slideshare.net/ewolff/java-application-servers-are-dead`) presentation.

Comparing reactive Spring WebFlux against classic Spring MVC

Ever heard of Spring MVC? It's one of the most popular web frameworks used by the Java community. Since Spring Framework 3, it has utilized an annotation-driven programming style, sometimes known as `@MVC`.

But we aren't going to use that in this book. Instead, we are going to use something new, Spring WebFlux. WebFlux is an alternative module in the Spring Framework focused on reactive handling of web requests. A huge benefit is that it uses the same annotations as `@MVC`, along with many of the same paradigms while also supporting Reactor types (`Mono` and `Flux`) on the inputs and outputs. This is NOT available in Spring MVC. The big thing to understand is that it's just a module name--`spring-webflux` versus `spring-webmvc`.

Why is Spring doing this?

Spring MVC is built on top of Java EE's Servlet spec. This specification is inherently blocking and synchronous. Asynchronous support has been added in later versions, but servlets can still hold up threads in the pool while waiting for responses, defying our need for non-blocking. To build a reactive stack, things need to be reactive from top to bottom, and this requires new contracts and expectations.

Certain things, like HTTP status codes, a `ResponseBody`, and the `@GetMapping`/`@PostMapping`/`@DeleteMapping`/`@PutMapping` annotations are used by both modules. But other things under the hood must be rewritten from scratch. The important point is that this doesn't impact the end developer.

By switching to Reactive Spring, we can immediately start coding with `Flux` and `Mono`, and don't have to stop and learn a totally new web stack. Instead, we can use the popular annotation-based programming model while we invest our effort in learning how to make things reactive. It's also important to know that Spring MVC isn't going away or slated for end of life. Both Spring WebFlux *and* Spring MVC will stay as actively supported options inside the Spring portfolio.

Showing some Mono/Flux-based endpoints

Let's start with a simple HTTP `GET`. Similar to Spring MVC endpoints, Spring WebFlux supports Flux operations as shown here:

```
@GetMapping(API_BASE_PATH + "/images")
Flux<Image> images() {
  return Flux.just(
    new Image("1", "learning-spring-boot-cover.jpg"),
    new Image("2", "learning-spring-boot-2nd-edition-cover.jpg"),
    new Image("3", "bazinga.png")
  );
}
```

This preceding controller can be described as follows:

- Using the same `Flux.just()` helper, we return a rather contrived list
- The Spring controller returns a `Flux<Image>` Reactor type, leaving Spring in charge of properly subscribing to this flow when the time is right

Before we can move forward, we need to define this `Image` data type like this:

```
@Data
@NoArgsConstructor
public class Image {

  private String id;
  private String name;

  public Image(String id, String name) {
    this.id = id;
    this.name = name;
  }
}
```

The preceding POJO class can be described as follows:

- `@Data` is a Lombok annotation that generates getters, `toString`, `hashCode`, `equals` as well as setters for all non-final fields
- `@NoArgsConstructor` is a Lombok annotation to generate a no-argument constructor
- It has `id` and `name` fields for storing data
- We have crafted a custom constructor to load up fields of data

With this simple data type, we can now focus on reactively interacting with them.

Nothing is simple without creating new data. To do that, we can write an HTTP POST operation as follows:

```
@PostMapping(API_BASE_PATH + "/images")
Mono<Void> create(@RequestBody Flux<Image> images) {
  return images
    .map(image -> {
      log.info("We will save " + image +
        " to a Reactive database soon!");
      return image;
    })
    .then();
}
```

The last code can be described as follows:

- @PostMapping indicates this method will respond to HTTP POST calls. The route is listed in the annotation.
- @RequestBody instructs Spring to fetch data from the HTTP request body.
- The container for our incoming data is another Flux of Image objects.
- To consume the data, we map over it. In this case, we simply log it and pass the original Image onto the next step of our flow.
- To wrap this logging operation with a promise, we invoke Flux.then(), which gives us Mono<Void>. Spring WebFlux will make good on this promise, subscribing to the results when the client makes a request.

If we run this code and submit some JSON, we can check out the results.

First, let's use HTTPie (https://httpie.org):

```
http --json -v POST localhost:8080/api/images id=10 name=foo
```

The verbose results are easy to read and are as follows:

```
POST /api/images HTTP/1.1
Accept: application/json, */*
Accept-Encoding: gzip, deflate
Connection: keep-alive
Content-Length: 27
Content-Type: application/json
Host: localhost:8080
User-Agent: HTTPie/0.9.8
{
    "id": "10",
    "name": "foo"
}
HTTP/1.1 200
Content-Length: 0
Date: Sat, 28 Jan 2017 20:14:35 GMT
```

In this case, HTTPie nicely sent a single item and our Spring WebFlux controller parsed it perfectly, like this:

```
... c.g.learningspringboot.ApiController ... We will save
    Image(id=10, name=foo) to a Reactive database soon!
```

Single entry Flux has been nicely handled.

If we want to send a JSON array, we can either embed the JSON array in a file or just send it directly with `curl`, as follows:

```
curl -v -H 'Content-Type:application/json' -X POST -d '[{"id":10,
"name": "foo"}, {"id":11, "name":"bar"}]' localhost:8080/api/images
```

Ta-dah!

```
c.g.learningspringboot.ApiController ... We will save Image(id=10,
name=foo) to a Reactive database soon!
c.g.learningspringboot.ApiController ... We will save Image(id=11,
name=bar) to a Reactive database soon!
```

> **TIP**
> Whether we send a single JSON item or an array of JSON items,
> Spring WebFlux maps both onto Reactor's `Flux` with no issue. In
> classic Spring MVC, we'd have to choose either `Image` or
> `List<Image>` and encode things properly or write two handlers.

Want to dial up the log levels? With Spring Boot, adjusting logging levels is a snap. Rename the `application.properties` file supplied by `start.spring.io` as `application.yml`, and edit it to look like this:

```
logging:
  level:
    io:
      netty: DEBUG
    reactor: DEBUG
```

The preceding code will punch up Netty and Project Reactor to spit out DEBUG level messages.

If we fetch the list of images again (`http localhost:8080/api/images`), we can see stuff like this in the server logs:

```
    2017-01-28 15:46:23.470 DEBUG 28432 --- [ctor-http-nio-4]
r.i.n.http.server.HttpServerOperations   : New http connection,
requesting read
    2017-01-28 15:46:23.471 DEBUG 28432 --- [ctor-http-nio-4]
r.ipc.netty.http.server.HttpServer       : [id: 0x9ddcd1ba,
L:/0:0:0:0:0:0:0:1:8080 - R:/0:0:0:0:0:0:0:1:65529] RECEIVED: 145B
         +-------------------------------------------------+
         | 0  1  2  3  4  5  6  7  8  9  a  b  c  d  e  f |
  +--------+-------------------------------------------------+------
----------+
  |00000000| 47 45 54 20 2f 61 70 69 2f 69 6d 61 67 65 73 20 |GET
/api/images |
  |00000010| 48 54 54 50 2f 31 2e 31 0d 0a 48 6f 73 74 3a 20
```

```
|HTTP/1.1..Host: |
    |00000020| 6c 6f 63 61 6c 68 6f 73 74 3a 38 30 38 30 0d 0a
|localhost:8080..|
    |00000030| 55 73 65 72 2d 41 67 65 6e 74 3a 20 48 54 54 50 |User-
Agent: HTTP|
    |00000040| 69 65 2f 30 2e 39 2e 38 0d 0a 41 63 63 65 70 74
|ie/0.9.8..Accept|
    |00000050| 2d 45 6e 63 6f 64 69 6e 67 3a 20 67 7a 69 70 2c |-
Encoding: gzip,|
    |00000060| 20 64 65 66 6c 61 74 65 0d 0a 41 63 63 65 70 74 |
deflate..Accept|
    |00000070| 3a 20 2a 2f 2a 0d 0a 43 6f 6e 6e 65 63 74 69 6f |:
*/*..Connectio|
    |00000080| 6e 3a 20 6b 65 65 70 2d 61 6c 69 76 65 0d 0a 0d |n:
keep-alive...|
    |00000090| 0a                                              |.
|
    +--------+-------------------------------------------------+------
----------+
    2017-01-28 15:46:23.471 DEBUG 28432 --- [ctor-http-nio-4]
r.ipc.netty.channel.ChannelOperations   : [HttpServer] handler is
being applied:
org.springframework.http.server.reactive.ReactorHttpHandlerAdapter@3a9
50f21
```

This shows the incoming web request to GET /api/images, headers and all. The output can also be read, but given the volume of data from Netty, its verbose output is not shown. Nevertheless, these log levels provide a handy means to debug traffic on the wire.

> *DON'T DO THIS if the request or the results are HUGE! I once switched this on when I was uploading a 300 MB JAR file. The logging broke the application.*

Creating a reactive ImageService

The first rule of thumb when building web apps is to keep Spring controllers as light as possible. We can think of them as converters between HTTP traffic and our system.

To do that, we need to create a separate `ImageService`, as shown here, and let it do all the work:

```
@Service
public class ImageService {

  private static String UPLOAD_ROOT = "upload-dir";

  private final ResourceLoader resourceLoader;

  public ImageService(ResourceLoader resourceLoader) {
    this.resourceLoader = resourceLoader;
  }
  ...
}
```

This last Spring service can be described as follows:

- `@Service`: This indicates this is a Spring bean used as a service. Spring Boot will automatically scan this class and create an instance.
- `UPLOAD_ROOT`: This is the base folder where images will be stored.
- `ResourceLoader`: This is a Spring utility class used to manage files. It is created automatically by Spring Boot and injected to our service via **constructor injection**. This ensures our service starts off with a consistent state.

Now we can start creating various utility methods needed to service our application.

Let's kick things off by loading up some mock image files loaded with test data. To do that, we can add the following method to the bottom of our newly minted `ImageService` class:

```
/**
 * Pre-load some test images
 *
 * @return Spring Boot {@link CommandLineRunner} automatically
 *         run after app context is loaded.
 */
@Bean
CommandLineRunner setUp() throws IOException {
  return (args) -> {
    FileSystemUtils.deleteRecursively(new File(UPLOAD_ROOT));

    Files.createDirectory(Paths.get(UPLOAD_ROOT));

    FileCopyUtils.copy("Test file",
```

```
        new FileWriter(UPLOAD_ROOT +
          "/learning-spring-boot-cover.jpg"));

      FileCopyUtils.copy("Test file2",
        new FileWriter(UPLOAD_ROOT +
          "/learning-spring-boot-2nd-edition-cover.jpg"));

      FileCopyUtils.copy("Test file3",
        new FileWriter(UPLOAD_ROOT + "/bazinga.png"));
    };
  }
```

The preceding little nugget of initializing code is described as follows:

- `@Bean` indicates that this method will return back an object to be registered as a Spring bean at the time that `ImageService` is created.
- The bean returned is a `CommandLineRunner`. Spring Boot runs ALL `CommandLineRunners` after the application context is fully realized (but not in any particular order).
- This method uses a Java 8 lambda, which gets automatically converted into a `CommandLineRunner` via Java 8 **SAM (Single Abstract Method)** rules.
- The method deletes the `UPLOAD_ROOT` directory, creates a new one, then creates three new files with a little bit of text.

With test data in place, we can start interacting with it by fetching all the existing files in `UPLOAD_ROOT` *reactively* by adding the following method to our `ImageService`:

```
public Flux<Image> findAllImages() {
  try {
    return Flux.fromIterable(
      Files.newDirectoryStream(Paths.get(UPLOAD_ROOT)))
        .map(path ->
         new Image(path.hashCode(),
                   path.getFileName().toString()));
  } catch (IOException e) {
    return Flux.empty();
  }
}
```

Let's explore the preceding code:

- This method returns `Flux<Image>`, a container of images that only gets created when the consumer subscribes.

- The Java NIO APIs are used to create a `Path` from `UPLOAD_ROOT`, which is used to open a lazy `DirectoryStream` courtesy of `Files.newDirectoryStream()`. `DirectoryStream` is a lazy iterable, which means that nothing is fetched until `next()` is called, making it a perfect fit for our Reactor `Flux`.
- `Flux.fromIterable` is used to wrap this lazy iterable, allowing us to only pull each item as demanded by a reactive streams client.
- The `Flux` maps over the paths, converting each one to an `Image`.
- In the event of an exception, an empty `Flux` is returned.

It's important to repeat that the stream of directory paths is lazy as well as the `Flux` itself. This means that nothing happens until the client subscribes, that is, starts pulling for images. At that point, the flow we just wrote will *react*, and start performing our data transformation. And it will only process each entry as each entry is pulled.

The next piece we need in our `ImageService` is the ability to fetch a single image so it can be displayed, and we can use this to do so:

```
public Mono<Resource> findOneImage(String filename) {
  return Mono.fromSupplier(() ->
    resourceLoader.getResource(
      "file:" + UPLOAD_ROOT + "/" + filename));
}
```

This last code can easily be described as follows:

- Since this method only handles one image, it returns a `Mono<Resource>`. Remember, `Mono` is a container of one. `Resource` is Spring's abstract type for files.
- `resourceLoader.getResource()` fetches the file based on `filename` and `UPLOAD_ROOT`.
- To delay fetching the file until the client subscribes, we wrap it with `Mono.fromSupplier()`, and put `getResource()` inside a lambda.

Until now, we've seen `Mono.just()` used to illustrate Reactor's way of initializing single items. However, if we wrote `Mono.just(resourceLoader.getResource(...))`, the resource fetching would happen immediately when the method is called. By putting it inside a Java 8 `Supplier`, that won't happen until the lambda is invoked. And because it's wrapped by a `Mono`, invocation won't happen until the client subscribes.

There is another `Mono` operation that is very similar to `fromSupplier()`--`defer()`. The difference is that `Mono.defer()` is invoked individually by every downstream subscriber. It's best used not for fetching resources like our situation but for something like polling status instead.

Having written code to fetch all images and a single image, it's time we introduce the ability to create new ones. The following code shows a reactive way to handle this:

```
public Mono<Void> createImage(Flux<FilePart> files) {
  return files.flatMap(file -> file.transferTo(
    Paths.get(UPLOAD_ROOT, file.filename()).toFile())).then();
}
```

The last code can be described as follows:

- This method returns a `Mono<Void>` indicating that it has no resulting value, but we still need a handle in order to subscribe for this operation to take place
- The incoming `Flux` of `FilePart` objects are flatMapped over, so we can process each one
- Each file is tested to ensure it's not empty
- At the heart of our chunk of code, Spring Framework 5's `FilePart` transfers the content into a new file stored in `UPLOAD_ROOT`
- `then()` lets us wait for the entire `Flux` to finish, yielding a `Mono<Void>`

Our last image-based operation to add to `ImageService` is to implement the means to delete images, as shown here:

```
public Mono<Void> deleteImage(String filename) {
  return Mono.fromRunnable(() -> {
    try {
      Files.deleteIfExists(Paths.get(UPLOAD_ROOT, filename));
    } catch (IOException e) {
      throw new RuntimeException(e);
    }
  });
}
```

The preceding code can be described as follows:

- Because this method doesn't care about return values, its return type is `Mono<Void>`.

- To hold off until subscribe, we need to wrap our code with `Mono.fromRunnable()`, and use a lambda expression to coerce a `Runnable`. This lets us put our code off to the side until we're ready to run it.
- Inside all of that, we can use Java NIO's handy `Files.deleteIfExists()`.

> If wrapping every return type in either a `Flux` or a `Mono` is starting to bend your brain, you are not alone. This style of programming may take a little getting used to but it's not that big of a leap. Once you get comfortable with it, I guarantee you'll spot blocking code all over the place. Then you can set out to make it reactive without descending into **callback hell**.

Creating a reactive file controller

With our reactive image service in place, we can start to work on the reactive file controller.

For starters, let's create a `HomeController` as shown here:

```
@Controller
public class HomeController {

  private static final String BASE_PATH = "/images";
  private static final String FILENAME = "{filename:.+}";

  private final ImageService imageService;

  public HomeController(ImageService imageService) {
    this.imageService = imageService;
  }
```

The preceding code can be described as follows:

- `@Controller`: This indicates that it is a web controller, and will be registered by Spring Boot to handle web requests.
- `BASE_PATH`: This is a static string used to define the base of many routes.

- `FILENAME`: This is a pattern for filenames where the "`.`" is included. Otherwise, Spring WebFlux will use the suffix as part of content negotiation (for example, `.json` would try to fetch a JSON response, while `.xml` would try to fetch an XML response).
- `ImageService`: This is injected via constructor injection so that we can tap our reactive image handling code we just wrote.

With this in place, we can code the handler for displaying a single image on the web page like this:

```
@GetMapping(value = BASE_PATH + "/" + FILENAME + "/raw",
 produces = MediaType.IMAGE_JPEG_VALUE)
@ResponseBody
public Mono<ResponseEntity<?>> oneRawImage(
  @PathVariable String filename) {
    return imageService.findOneImage(filename)
     .map(resource -> {
       try {
         return ResponseEntity.ok()
          .contentLength(resource.contentLength())
          .body(new InputStreamResource(
            resource.getInputStream()));
       } catch (IOException e) {
         return ResponseEntity.badRequest()
          .body("Couldn't find " + filename +
           " => " + e.getMessage());
       }
    });
  }
```

The last code can be explained as follows:

- `@GetMapping` defines a route mapping for `GET BASE_PATH + "/" + FILENAME + "/raw"`. It also sets the `Content-Type` header to properly render it as an image.
- `@ResponseBody` indicates that this method's response will be written directly into the HTTP response body.
- `@PathVariable` flags that the input `filename` will be extracted from the route's `{filename}` attribute.
- `Mono<ResponseEntity<?>>` shows that we are returning a single response, reactively. `ResponseEntity<?>` describes a generic HTTP response.
- The code taps our image service's `findOneImage()` using `filename`.

> It's possible to have incoming arguments wrapped in Reactor types such as `Mono<String>`. Since this argument comes from the route and not the request body, there is nothing gained in this situation.

- Since `findOneImage` returns a `Mono<Resource>`, we map over it, transforming this Spring `Resource` into a `ResponseEntity` including a `Content-Length` response header as well as the data embedded in the body.
- In the event of an exception, it will return an *HTTP Bad Response*.

This one controller handler method demonstrates many features provided by Reactive Spring. We see route handling, delegating to a separate service, converting the response into a suitable format for clients, and error handling.

This code also shows it being done reactively. Generating the *HTTP OK / HTTP BAD REQUEST* response doesn't happen until `map()` is executed. This is chained to the image service fetching the file from disk. And none of that happens until the client subscribes. In this case, subscribing is handled by the framework when a request comes in.

> *I thought you said to keep controllers light!* That is true. Maybe this looks not so light? To take the `ResponseEntity` wrapping and move it into the `ImageService` would be wrong, because that service doesn't know anything about the web layer. This controller's focus is to make the data presentable to web clients, which is exactly what we've coded.

The next controller method we can add to `HomeController` is the handler for uploading new files, as shown here:

```
@PostMapping(value = BASE_PATH)
public Mono<String> createFile(@RequestPart(name = "file")
 Flux<FilePart> files) {
    return imageService.createImage(files)
    .then(Mono.just("redirect:/"));
}
```

The preceding method is described as follows:

- A collection of incoming `FilePart` objects is represented as a `Flux`
- The flux of files is handed directly to the image service to be processed
- `.then()` indicates that once the method is complete, it will then return a `redirect:/` directive (wrapped in a `Mono`), issuing an HTML redirect to `/`

It's important to remember that we aren't issuing `.then()` against the flux of files. Instead, the image service hands us back a `Mono<Void>` that signals when it has completed processing all the files. It is that `Mono` which we are chaining an additional call to return back the redirect.

The next thing we need to add to our `HomeController` is the ability to handle requests for deleting images. This is done as follows:

```
@DeleteMapping(BASE_PATH + "/" + FILENAME)
public Mono<String> deleteFile(@PathVariable String filename) {
    return imageService.deleteImage(filename)
      .then(Mono.just("redirect:/"));
}
```

The previous code can be described like this:

- Using Spring's `@DeleteMapping` annotation, this method is ready for HTTP `DELETE` operations
- It's keyed to the same `BASE_PATH + "/" + FILENAME` pattern
- It taps the image service's `deleteImage()` method
- It uses `then()` to wait until the delete is done before returning back a mono-wrapped `redirect:/` directive

The last bit to add to our `HomeController` is the call to serve up a list of images in a template. For that, we need this general `GET` handler for the root:

```
@GetMapping("/")
public Mono<String> index(Model model) {
  model.addAttribute("images", imageService.findAllImages());
  return Mono.just("index");
}
```

The preceding handler can be described as follows:

- `@GetMapping` is used to explicitly map the `"/"` route.
- It accepts a `Model` object, giving us a place to load data *reactively*.
- `addAttribute()` lets us assign the image service's `findAllImages()` `Flux` to the template model's `images` attribute.
- The method returns `"index"` wrapped in a `Mono`, ensuring the whole thing is chained together, top to bottom, to kick off when Spring WebFlux subscribes to render the template.

It's important to understand that we don't assign a list of images to the template model's `images` attribute. We assign a lazy `Flux` of images, which means that the model won't be populated with real data until Reactive Spring subscribes for the data. Only then will the code actually start fetching image data.

> Perhaps, at this stage, you're wondering amidst all the lambdas, Fluxes, Monos, and subscriptions, exactly what is happening from a threading perspective. Project Reactor is **concurrency agnostic**. It doesn't enforce a certain concurrency model, but leaves you in command instead. Reactor has several schedulers that support a multitude of options. This includes running in the current thread, running in a single worker thread, running on a per-call dedicated thread, an elastic pool of threads, a fixed pool of worker threads tuned for parallel work, and a time-aware scheduler capable of scheduling tasks in the future. Additionally, Reactor allows creating a scheduler out of any `ExecutorService`. We aren't going to delve into that in this work, but it's definitely something to investigate when you build a real application and want to govern how things scale.

Why use reactive programming?

At this stage, you've gotten a good taste of how to whip up a file-handling controller, and hitch it to a service that reads and writes files to disk. But the question that often arises is *why do I need to do this reactively?*

With imperative programming, the process of taking inputs, building intermediate collections and other steps often leaves us with lots of intermediate states--some of it potentially blocking in bad places.

Using the functional style as we've explored so far moves away from the risk of inefficiently building up this state, and switches to building a stream of data instead. And Reactor's operations let us have one stream feed another in lots of different ways. We can merge streams, filter streams, and transform streams.

When we engage in reactive programming, the level of abstraction moves up a level. We find ourselves focusing on creating tiny functions to perform various operations, and chaining them together. We think more along integration of the items in our streams rather than the lower-level implementation details.

By building up these flows of chained operations, tying inputs to outputs, Reactor is able to do the heavy lifting of invoking code when needed, and requesting/releasing resources as effectively as possible.

Additionally, by having an inherently asynchronous, non-blocking nature, our framework of choice (Reactor) is able to manage talking to the scheduler for us. We can focus on *what* happens during the flow while the framework handles *when* it happens.

For yet another metaphor to describe reactive operations chained together, imagine a train with lots of cars. Each car is a different operation to be applied to our data, and we can easily see the order in which things must happen. We can carefully lay out each car with its defined purpose, but nothing moves until the locomotive moves. And then, the whole chain of cars moves as expected. Adding/removing/inserting cars is the nature of building a reactive data flow.

To summarize, reactive programming helps us in the following:

- Avoid inefficient, intermediate state
- Focus on building streams of data
- Gives us ability to merge, filter, and transform streams of data
- Focus on *what* happens at each step while Reactor decides *when*

Interacting with a Thymeleaf template

Having put Thymeleaf on the classpath, an entire reactive view resolver has already been configured for us. The last step in putting together the web layer for our social media platform is to create the Thymeleaf template itself. We can do that by putting the following content into `index.html` underneath
`/src/main/resources/templates`:

```
<!DOCTYPE html>
<html xmlns:th="http://www.thymeleaf.org">
<head>
  <meta charset="UTF-8" />
  <title>Learning Spring Boot: Spring-a-Gram</title>
  <link rel="stylesheet" href="/main.css" />
</head>
<body>

<h1>Learning Spring Boot - 2nd Edition</h1>

<div>
  <table>
    <thead>
    <tr>
        <th>Id</th><th>Name</th><th>Image</th><th></th>
    </tr>
    </thead>
    <tbody>
    <tr th:each="image : ${images}">
        <td th:text="${image.id}" />
        <td th:text="${image.name}" />
        <td>
            <a th:href="@{'/images/' + ${image.name} + '/raw'}">
                <img th:src="@{'/images/'+${image.name}+'/raw'}"
                    class="thumbnail" />
            </a>
        </td>
        <td>
            <form th:method="delete"
                    th:action="@{'/images/' + ${image.name}}">
                <input type="submit" value="Delete" />
            </form>
        </td>
    </tr>
    </tbody>
  </table>

  <form method="post" enctype="multipart/form-data"
```

```
                                    action="/images">
    <p><input type="file" name="file" /></p>
    <p><input type="submit" value="Upload" /></p>
  </form>
</div>

</body>
</html>
```

Key parts of the preceding template are described here:

- All of the Thymeleaf directives are tagged with a `th` prefix, making the entire template HTML compliant
- `<tr th:each="image : ${images}" />` is Thymeleaf's `for-each` directive, where we read `images` from the template model and iterate over it, forming one table row element per image
- `<a th:href="@{'/images/' + ${image.name} + '/raw'}">` shows how to create a link by splicing together strings with the `image.name` attribute
- The whole thing builds a table with a row for each image, showing ID, name, image, and a delete button
- At the bottom is a single upload form for creating new images

A critical thing to remember is that the name of the template must be `index.html`, matching our controller's return of `Mono.just("index")` combined with the default configuration settings of Spring Boot for Thymeleaf.

> Spring Boot autoconfigures view resolvers based on the templating solution we pick. Spring Boot supports many including Thymeleaf, Mustache, Groovy Templates, and even Apache FreeMarker. By default, they all come with a conventional location to put templates, in this case, `src/main/resources/templates/<template name>.html`.

Since we want a bare amount of CSS, we can drop the following into `src/main/resources/static/main.css`:

```
table {
  border-collapse: collapse;
}

td, th {
  border: 1px solid #999;
  padding: 0.5rem;
```

```
      text-align: left;
}

.thumbnail {
  max-width: 75px;
  max-height: 75px;
}
```

Let's tear the preceding small bit of CSS apart:

- The borders of the table are collapsed
- A little spacing is defined for the table entries
- A special class is created to render images with a small thumbnail size

Of course, this is primitive CSS, but our focus is to learn about Spring Boot not CSS3. The important thing to observe here is that Spring Boot will automatically serve up all content underneath `src/main/resources/static` as web resources. We can put CSS, JavaScript, favicons, and images for our site. Anything that needs to be statically served can be put here, and will be available from the root of the web application's context path.

Throughout this book, we'll add to this web page, enhancing the user experience. But for now, we should have enough to get off the ground.

The only thing remaining is to code a `public static void main()`; however, we don't have to! The Spring Initializr site has already created one for us, which is as follows:

```
@SpringBootApplication
public class LearningSpringBootApplication {

  public static void main(String[] args) {
    SpringApplication.run(
      LearningSpringBootApplication.class, args);
  }

  @Bean
  HiddenHttpMethodFilter hiddenHttpMethodFilter() {
    return new HiddenHttpMethodFilter();
  }

}
```

This last code is almost identical to the application class we created in Chapter 10, *Quick Start with Java*. But there is one difference--we must add a HiddenHttpMethodFilter Spring bean to make the HTTP DELETE methods work properly.

> DELETE is not a valid action for an HTML5 FORM, so Thymeleaf creates a hidden input field containing our desired verb while the enclosing form uses an HTML5 POST. This gets transformed by Spring during the web call, resulting in the @DeleteMapping method being properly invoked with no effort on our end.

Illustrating how going from async to sync can be easy, but the opposite is not

Invariably, the question comes along--*Do I need a synchronous or asynchronous API?*

It's important to understand that reactive programming is not very effective unless the *entire* stack is reactive. Otherwise, we're simply blocking at some point, which causes the backpressure to not achieve much. That's a long-winded way of saying there is little value in making the web layer reactive if the underlying services are not.

However, it is *very* likely that we may produce a chunk of code that must be tapped by a non-reactive layer, hence, we have to wrap our asynchronous, non-blocking code with the means to block.

Let's explore async-to-sync by creating a BlockingImageService. This service will, basically, leverage the already written ImageService, but *not* include any of Reactor's Flux or Mono types in its method signatures.

We can start with a class definition as follows:

```
public class BlockingImageService {

  private final ImageService imageService;

  public BlockingImageService(ImageService imageService) {
    this.imageService = imageService;
  }
```

This preceding class definition can be described as follows:

- The class has no annotation, hence, it won't be automatically scanned and activated by Spring Boot. However, it can appear in a configuration class somewhere via a @Bean-annotated method.
- It will contain a constructor injected ImageService.

With this in place, we can look at wrapping the findAllImages() method with blocking semantics, like this:

```
public List<Image> findAllImages() {
  return imageService.findAllImages()
    .collectList()
    .block(Duration.ofSeconds(10));
}
```

Let's dig into the details of the last code:

- ImageService.findAllImages() has no arguments, and returns a Flux<Image>. The simplest mechanism is collectList(), which transforms it into a Mono<List<Image>>. This means that instead of signaling the arrival of each image, there is one single (Mono) for a list of ALL images.
- To ask for the result, we use block(). Reactor's block() can either wait forever for the next signal, or we can supply it with a timeout limit. In this case, we have selected ten seconds as the longest that we'll wait.

Reactor's block() API is what we do when we want to transform a Mono<T> into just T. It's a simple one-to-one concept. Inside the method, it invokes the reactive streams' subscribe() API, meaning it will cause any chain of operations to take effect.

Flux has no block() because it represents multiple values. Flux *does* come with blockFirst() and blockLast() if we wanted the first or the last item. But to get the whole collection entails a bigger semantic scope. Hence, the need to collectList() into a Mono followed by blocking for it.

It's usually a good idea to set a timeout limit for *any* async call to
avoid deadlock situations or waiting for a response that may never
come.

Fetching a single image is a bit simpler and can be done using the following code:

```
public Resource findOneImage(String filename) {
    return imageService.findOneImage(filename)
      .block(Duration.ofSeconds(30));
}
```

`ImageService.findOneImage()` has one argument, the filename, but it isn't
wrapped with any Reactor types. The return type is `Mono<Resource>`, so a simple
`block()` is all we need to transform it into a `Resource`. In this case, we've picked
thirty seconds as the maximum time to wait for an answer.

When it comes to uploading new images, that is a little more complicated.

```
public void createImage(List<FilePart> files) {
    imageService.createImage(Flux.fromIterable(files))
      .block(Duration.ofMinutes(1));
}
```

The last code can be described as follows:

- The image service's input is `Flux<FilePart>` and the return type is
  `Mono<Void>`. This makes things doubly interesting, having to massage
  both the input *and* the output.
- The preceding code assumes we are uploading multiple files. To transform
  it into a `Flux`, we use `Flux.fromIterable(files)`. If the input had been
  a single `FilePart`, we could have used `Flux.just(file)`.
- The return type is `void`, meaning we don't have to return anything. Simply
  invoking image service's `create()` method may seem hunky dory. But
  remember--*nothing* happens with Reactor types until we subscribe, so it's
  critical that we invoke `block()` even if we aren't going to return it.

We'll leave it as an exercise for the reader to implement a blocking version of
`deleteImage()`.

Summary

We're off to a good start by building the web layer of our social media platform. We used the Spring Initializr to create a bare bones Reactive Spring application with Gradle support. Then we explored the basics of reactive programming by creating a reactive image handling service and wrapping it with a reactive web layer. And we drafted a Thymeleaf template to show thumbnails, allow deleting of images and uploading of new images.

In the next chapter, we will see how to build a data layer and make it reactive as well.

12
Reactive Data Access with Spring Boot

Very impressed with @springboot so far, 10 mins to get a REST service up and running, now to add MongoDB. No black magic under the covers!

– Graham Rivers-Brown @grahamrb

In the previous chapter, we started putting together the frontend bits of our social media platform using Spring WebFlux. The missing critical ingredient was a data store. Few applications exist that don't touch a database. In fact, data storage is arguably one of the most critical components we encounter with app development. In this chapter, we'll learn how to persist information in a reactive data store (MongoDB), and learn how to interact with it.

In this chapter, we will be doing the following:

- Getting underway with a reactive data store
- Wiring up Spring Data repositories with Spring Boot
- Creating a reactive repository
- Pulling data through a Mono/Flux and chain of operations
- Creating custom finders
- Querying by example
- Querying with MongoOperations
- Logging reactive operations

Getting underway with a reactive data store

Since this book is aimed at the cutting edge of Spring Boot 2.0 and its Reactive Streams support, we have to pick something a little more up to date than JPA. The JPA spec doesn't cover reactive programming. Hence, its APIs are not reactive. However, MongoDB has reactive drivers, and will be perfect.

To get going, we need to install the latest version of MongoDB 3.4 (for reactive support).

If you're using macOS X, installing MongoDB is as simple as this:

```
$ brew install mongodb
==> Installing mongodb
==> Downloading https://homebrew.bintray.com/bottles/mongodb-
3.4.6.el_capitan.bottle.tar.gz
######################################################## 100.0%
==> Pouring mongodb-3.4.6.el_capitan.bottle.tar.gz
==> Summary
/usr/local/Cellar/mongodb/3.4.6: 18 files, 267.5MB
```

With MongoDB installed, we can launch it as a service, like this:

```
$ brew services start mongodb
==> Successfully started `mongodb` (label: homebrew.mxcl.mongodb)
```

> For other operating systems, check out the download links at
> `https://www.mongodb.com/download-center`. For more details
> about installing MongoDB, visit
> `https://docs.mongodb.com/manual/installation/`.

Assuming that we have MongoDB installed and running, we can now delve into writing a little code.

To write any MongoDB code, we need to add Spring Data MongoDB to our classpath. We can do so by updating our build file with the following:

```
compile('org.springframework.boot:spring-boot-starter-
    data-mongodb-reactive')
```

The preceding, new compile-time dependency pulls in the following:

- Spring Data MongoDB
- MongoDB's core components + Reactive Stream drivers

It's important to point out that both `spring-boot-starter-webflux` *and* `spring-boot-starter-data-mongodb-reactive` transitively bring in Project Reactor. Spring Boot's `dependency-management` plugin is responsible for ensuring they both pull in the same version.

With all these things on the classpath, Spring Boot will get busy configuring things for us. But first, what *is* the problem we are trying to solve?

Solving a problem

In this day and age, why are we still writing queries like this:

```
SELECT *
FROM PERSON
WHERE FIRST_NAME = %1
```

That type of query must be thirty years old! The ANSI spec for SQL was released in 1986, and its effects can be seen in countless languages.

So, is it any better to write something more like this:

```
SELECT e
FROM Employee e
WHERE e.firstName = :name
```

The last bit of code is **JPA (Java Persistence API)**, based upon the open source Hibernate project (which has become JPA's reference implementation). Is this Java's improvement over writing pure SQL?

Maybe this fragment below is an enhancement?

```
create
  .select()
  .from(EMPLOYEE)
  .where(EMPLOYEE.FIRST_NAME.equal(name))
  .fetch()
```

That last code snippet is **jOOQ**, and can help with code completion, but it seems that we are, basically, doing the same thing we've been doing for decades.

Especially, considering that we could do the same thing by merely creating this:

```
interface EmployeeRepository
 extends ReactiveCrudRepository<Employee, Long> {

   Flux<Employee> findByFirstName(Mono<String> name);
}
```

This preceding declarative interface does the exact same thing, but without writing a single query in any language.

By extending Spring Data's `ReactiveCrudRepository`, we are granted an out-of-the-box set of CRUD operations (`save`, `findById`, `findAll`, `delete`, `deleteById`, `count`, `exists`, and more). We also have the ability to add custom finders purely by method signature (`findByFirstName` in this example).

When Spring Data sees an interface extending its `Repository` marker interface (which `ReactiveCrudRepository` does), it creates a concrete implementation. It scans every method, and parses their method signatures. Seeing `findBy`, it knows to look at the rest of the method name, and start extracting property names based on the domain type (`Employee`). Because it can see that `Employee` has `firstName`, it has enough information to fashion a query. This also tips it off about expected criteria in the arguments (`name`). Finally, Spring Data looks at the return type to decide what result set to assemble--in this case, a Reactor `Flux` that we started to explore in the previous chapter. The entire query (*not* the query *results*), once assembled, is cached, so, there is no overhead in using the query multiple times.

In a nutshell, by following a very simple convention, there is no need to handwrite a query at all. And while this book is focused on MongoDB and its corresponding Mongo Query Language, this concept applies to SQL, JPA, Cassandra Query Language, or any other supported data store.

> Spring Data does not engage in **code generation** of any code. Code generation has had a flaky history. Instead, it uses various tactics to pick a base class that handles the minimum set of operations while wrapping it with a proxy that implements the declared interface, bringing onboard the dynamic query handler.

This mechanism of managing data is revolutionary, making Spring Data one of the most popular Spring portfolio projects, second only to the Spring Framework itself and Spring Security (and of course Spring Boot).

Wait a second, didn't we just mention using MongoDB earlier?

Yup. That's why Spring Data's query-neutral approach is even better. Changing data stores doesn't require throwing away absolutely everything and starting over. The interface declared previously extends Spring Data Commons, not Spring Data MongoDB. The only data store details are in the domain object itself.

Instead of `Employee` being some JPA-based entity definition, we can work on a MongoDB document-based one instead, like this:

```
@Data
@Document(collection="employees")
public class Employee {
  @Id String id;
  String firstName;
  String lastName;
}
```

This preceding MongoDB POJO can be described as follows:

- The `@Data` Lombok annotation takes care of getters, setters, `toString`, `equals`, and `hashCode` functions.
- `@Document` is an optional annotation that lets us spell out the MongoDB collection that this domain object will be stored under (`"employees"`).
- `@Id` is a Spring Data Commons annotation that flags which field is the key. (NOTE: When using Spring Data JPA, the required annotation is `javax.persistence.Id`, whereas, all other Spring-Data-supported stores utilize `org.springframework.data.annotation.Id`).

> What is Spring Data Commons? It's the parent project for all Spring Data implementations. It defines several concepts implemented by every solution. For example, the concept of parsing finder signatures to put together a query request is defined here. But the bits where this is transformed into a native query is supplied by the data store solution itself. Spring Data Commons also provides various interfaces, allowing us to reduce coupling in our code to the data store, such as `ReactiveCrudRepository`, and others that we'll soon see.

Nothing else is needed to start writing `Employee` objects into the `employees` collection of our MongoDB database.

Wiring up Spring Data repositories with Spring Boot

Normally, wiring up a repository requires not only defining a domain object and a repository, but also activating Spring Data. Each data store comes with an annotation to activate it for repository support. In our case, that would be `@EnableReactiveMongoRepositories`, since we are using MongoDB's reactive drivers.

However, with Spring Boot, we don't have to lift a finger!

Why?

Because the following code, lifted from Spring Boot itself, shows how MongoDB reactive repository support is enabled:

```
@Configuration
@ConditionalOnClass({ MongoClient.class,
 ReactiveMongoRepository.class })
@ConditionalOnMissingBean({
    ReactiveMongoRepositoryFactoryBean.class,
     ReactiveMongoRepositoryConfigurationExtension.class })
@ConditionalOnProperty(prefix = "spring.data.mongodb.reactive-
    repositories", name = "enabled",
    havingValue = "true", matchIfMissing = true)
@Import(MongoReactiveRepositoriesAutoConfigureRegistrar.class)
@AutoConfigureAfter(MongoReactiveDataAutoConfiguration.class)
public class MongoReactiveRepositoriesAutoConfiguration {

}
```

The preceding autoconfiguration policy can be described as follows:

- `@Configuration`: This indicates that this class is a source of bean definitions.
- `@ConditionalOnClass`: This lists ALL the classes that must be on the classpath for this to kick in--in this case, MongoDB's reactive `MongoClient` (Reactive Streams version) and `ReactiveMongoRepository`, which means that it only applies if Reactive MongoDB and Spring Data MongoDB 2.0 are on the classpath.
- `@ConditionalOnMissingBean`: This indicates that it only applies if there isn't already a `ReactiveMongoRepositoryFactoryBean` and a `ReactiveMongoRepositoryConfigurationExtension` bean.

- `@ConditionalOnProperty`: This means that it requires that the `spring.data.mongodb.reactive-repositories` property must be set to `true` for this to apply (which is the default setting if no such property is provided).
- `@Import`: This delegates all bean creation for reactive repositories to `MongoReactiveRepositoriesAutoConfigureRegistrar`.
- `@AutoConfigureAfter`: This ensures that this autoconfiguration policy is only applied after `MongoReactiveDataAutoConfiguration` has been applied. That way, we can count on certain infrastructure being configured.

When we added `spring-boot-starter-data-mongodb-reactive` to the classpath, this policy kicked in, and created critical beans for interacting reactively with a MongoDB database.

It's left as an exercise for the reader to pull up `MongoReactiveRepositoriesAutoConfigureRegistrar`, and see how it works. What's important to note is that nestled at the bottom of that class is the following:

```
@EnableReactiveMongoRepositories
private static class EnableReactiveMongoRepositoriesConfiguration
{
}
```

This aforementioned little class means that we don't have to enable reactive MongoDB repositories. Spring Boot will do it for us automatically when Reactive MongoDB and Spring Data MongoDB 2.0+ are on the classpath.

Creating a reactive repository

So far, we have been dabbling with Spring Data using our sample domain of employees. We need to shift our focus back to the social media platform that we started building in the previous chapter.

Before we can work on a reactive repository, we need to revisit the `Image` domain object we defined in the last chapter. Let's adjust it so that it works nicely with MongoDB:

```
@Data
@Document
public class Image {
```

```
    @Id final private String id;
    final private String name;
}
```

This preceding definition is almost identical to what we saw in the previous chapter, with the following differences:

- We use `@Document` to identify this is a MongoDB domain object, but we accept Spring Data MongoDB's decision about what to name the collection (it's the short name of the class, lowercase, that is, `image`)
- `@Data` creates a constructor for all final fields by default, hence, we've marked both `id` and `name` as `final`
- We have also marked both fields `private` for proper encapsulation

With that in place, we are ready to declare our social media platform's reactive repository as follows:

```
public interface ImageRepository
  extends ReactiveCrudRepository<Image, String> {

  Mono<Image> findByName(String name);
}
```

This code for the reactive repository can be described as follows:

- Our interface extends `ReactiveCrudRepository`, which, as stated before, comes with a prepackaged set of reactive operations including `save`, `findById`, `exists`, `findAll`, `count`, `delete`, and `deleteAll`, all supporting Reactor types
- It includes a custom **finder** named `findByName` that matches on `Image.name` based on parsing the name of the method (not the input argument)

Each of the operations inherited from `ReactiveCrudRepository` accepts direct arguments or a Reactor-friendly variant. This means, we can invoke either `save(Image)` or `saveAll(Publisher<Image>)`. Since `Mono` and `Flux` both implement `Publisher`, `saveAll()` can be used to store either.

`ReactiveCrudRepository` has ALL of its methods returning either a `Mono` or a `Flux` based on the situation. Some, like `delete`, simply return `Mono<Void>`, meaning, there is no data to return, but we need the operation's handle in order to issue the Reactive Streams' `subscribe` call. `findById` returns a `Mono<Image>`, because there can be only one. And `findAll` returns a `Flux<Image>`.

Before we can get our feet wet in using this reactive repository, we need to preload our MongoDB data store. For such operations, it's recommended to actually use the *blocking* API. That's because when launching an application, there is a certain risk of a thread lock issue when both the web container as well as our hand-written loader are starting up. Since Spring Boot also creates a `MongoOperations` object, we can simply grab hold of that, as follows:

```
@Component
public class InitDatabase {
  @Bean
  CommandLineRunner init(MongoOperations operations) {
    return args -> {
      operations.dropCollection(Image.class);

      operations.insert(new Image("1",
        "learning-spring-boot-cover.jpg"));
      operations.insert(new Image("2",
        "learning-spring-boot-2nd-edition-cover.jpg"));
      operations.insert(new Image("3",
        "bazinga.png"));

      operations.findAll(Image.class).forEach(image -> {
        System.out.println(image.toString());
      });
    };
  }
}
```

The preceding code is detailed as follows:

- `@Component` ensures that this class will be picked up automatically by Spring Boot, and scanned for bean definitions.
- `@Bean` marks the `init` method as a bean definition requiring a `MongoOperations`. In turn, it returns a Spring Boot `CommandLineRunner`, of which all are run after the application context is fully formed (though in no particular order).

- When invoked, the command-line runner will use `MongoOperations`, and request that all entries be deleted (`dropCollection`). Then it will insert three new `Image` records. Finally, it will fetch with (`findAll`) and iterate over them, printing each out.

With sample data loaded, let's hook things into our reactive `ImageService` in the next section.

Pulling data through a Mono/Flux and chain of operations

We have wired up a repository to interface with MongoDB through Spring Data. Now we can start hooking it into our `ImageService`.

The first thing we need to do is inject our repository into the service, like this:

```
@Service
public class ImageService {
  ...
  private final ResourceLoader resourceLoader;

  private final ImageRepository imageRepository;

  public ImageService(ResourceLoader resourceLoader,
    ImageRepository imageRepository) {
      this.resourceLoader = resourceLoader;
      this.imageRepository = imageRepository;
  }
  ...
}
```

In the previous chapter, we loaded Spring's `ResourceLoader`. In this chapter, we are adding `ImageRepository` to our constructor.

Previously, we looked up the names of the existing uploaded files, and constructed a `Flux` of `Image` objects. That required coming up with a contrived `id` value.

Now that we have a real data store, we can simply fetch them all, and return them to the client, like this:

```
public Flux<Image> findAllImages() {
  return imageRepository.findAll();
}
```

In this last bit of code, we leverage `imageRepository` to do all the work with its `findAll()` method. Remember--`findAll` was defined inside `ReactiveCrudRepository`. We didn't have to write it ourselves. And since it already gives us a `Flux<Image>`, there is no need to do anything else.

It's good to remember that the `Flux` of images being returned is *lazy*. That means that only the number of images requested by the client is pulled from the database into memory and through the rest of the system at any given time. In essence, the client can ask for one or as many as possible, and the database, thanks to reactive drivers, will comply.

Let's move on to something a little more complex--storing a `Flux` of images as follows:

```
public Mono<Void> createImage(Flux<FilePart> files) {
  return files
    .flatMap(file -> {
      Mono<Image> saveDatabaseImage = imageRepository.save(
        new Image(
          UUID.randomUUID().toString(),
          file.filename())));

      Mono<Void> copyFile = Mono.just(
        Paths.get(UPLOAD_ROOT, file.filename())
          .toFile())
          .log("createImage-picktarget")
          .map(destFile -> {
            try {
              destFile.createNewFile();
              return destFile;
            } catch (IOException e) {
                throw new RuntimeException(e);
            }
          })
          .log("createImage-newfile")
          .flatMap(file::transferTo)
          .log("createImage-copy");

      return Mono.when(saveDatabaseImage, copyFile);
    })
    .then();
}
```

The preceding code can be described as follows:

- With a `Flux` of multipart files, `flatMap` each one into two independent actions: saving the image and copying the file to the server.
- Using `imageRepository`, put together a `Mono` that stores the image in MongoDB, using `UUID` to create a unique key and the filename.
- Using `FilePart`, WebFlux's reactive multipart API, build another `Mono` that copies the file to the server.
- To ensure both of these operations are completed, join them together using `Mono.when()`. This means that each file won't be completed until the record is written to MongoDB *and* the file is copied to the server.
- The entire flow is terminated with `then()` so we can signal when all the files have been processed.

> Ever worked with promises? They are quite popular in the JavaScript world. Project Reactor's `Mono.when()` is akin to the A+ Promise spec's `promise.all()` API, that waits until all sub-promises are completed before moving forward. Project Reactor can be thought of as promises on steroids with many more operations available. In this case, by stringing several operations together using `then()`, you can avoid *callback hell* while ensuring the flow of how things unfold.

On a fundamental level, we need **creating an image** to involve two things--copying the file's contents to the server, and writing a record of it in MongoDB. That is on par with what we've declared in the code by using `Mono.when()` to combine two separate actions.

`imageRepository.save()` is already a reactive operation, so we can capture it straight up as a `Mono`. Because `MultipartFile` is, inherently, tied to the blocking servlet paradigm, WebFlux has a new interface, `FilePart`, meant to handle file uploads reactively. Its `transferTo()` API returns a `Mono<Void>` letting us signal when to carry out the transfer.

Is this a transaction? Certainly not an **ACID**-style one (**Atomic, Consistent, Isolated, Durable**) traditionally found with relational data stores. Those types of transactions have a long history of not scaling well. When more clients try to alter the same rows of data, traditional transactions block with increasing frequency. And blocking in, and of itself, is not congruent with reactive programming.

However, semantically, perhaps we are engaged in a transaction. After all, we are saying that both of these actions must *complete* from a Reactive Streams perspective before the given `FilePart` is considered to be processed in the middle of the `Flux`. Given the long history of assumptions made regarding **transactions**, it might be best to leave that term behind, and refer to this as a **reactive promise**.

> While it's possible to inline both the `saveDatabaseImage` operation and the `copyFile` operation inside the `Mono.when()`, they were pulled out as separate variables for readability. The more flows you write, the more you may be tempted to streamline things in a single, chained statement. If you're feeling lucky, go for it!

When it comes to order of processing, which goes first? Saving the document in MongoDB, or storing the file on the server? It's actually not specified in the API. All that is declared is that both of these operations must be completed to move on, and Reactor guarantees that if any asynchronous threading is being used, the framework will handle any and all coordination.

This is why `Mono.when()` is the perfect construct when two or more tasks need to be completed, and **the order doesn't matter**. The first time the code is run, perhaps, MongoDB is able to store the record first. It's quite possible that the next time this code is exercised, MongoDB may be slightly delayed due to external factors such as responding to another operation, hence allowing the file to be copied first. And the time after that, other factors may cause the order to swap. But the key point of this construct is to ensure that we use resources with maximum efficiency while still having a consistent result--both are completed before moving on.

> Notice how we used `flatMap` to turn each file into a promise to both copy the file and save a MongoDB record? `flatMap` is kind of like `map` and `then`, but on steroids. `map` has a signature of map(T → V) : V, while `flatMap` has flatMap(T → Publisher<V>) : V, meaning, it can unwrap the `Mono` and produce the contained value. If you're writing a reactive flow that isn't clicking, check if one of your `map` or `then` calls needs to be replaced with a `flatMap`.

If we wanted a certain order to happen, the best construct would be `Mono.then()`. We can chain multiple `then` calls together, ensuring that a certain uniform state is achieved at each step before moving forward.

Let's wrap up this section by making adjustments to `deleteImage` as follows:

```
public Mono<Void> deleteImage(String filename) {
  Mono<Void> deleteDatabaseImage = imageRepository
    .findByName(filename)
    .flatMap(imageRepository::delete);

  Mono<Void> deleteFile = Mono.fromRunnable(() -> {
    try {
      Files.deleteIfExists(
        Paths.get(UPLOAD_ROOT, filename));
    } catch (IOException e) {
        throw new RuntimeException(e);
    }
  });

  return Mono.when(deleteDatabaseImage, deleteFile)
    .then();
}
```

The previous code can be explained as follows:

- First we create a `Mono` to delete the MongoDB image record. It uses `imageRepository` to first `findByName`, and then it uses a Java 8 method handle to invoke `imageRepository.delete`.
- Next, we create a `Mono` using `Mono.fromRunnable` to delete the file using `Files.deleteIfExists`. This delays deletion until `Mono` is invoked.
- To have both of these operations completed together, we join them with `Mono.when()`.
- Since we're not interested in the results, we append a `then()`, which will be completed when the combined `Mono` is done.

We repeat the same coding pattern as `createImage()` where we collect operations into multiple `Mono` definitions, and wrap them with a `Mono.when()`. This is the promise pattern, and when coding reactively, we'll use it often.

Traditionally, `Runnable` objects are started in some multithreaded fashion, and are meant to run in the background. In this situation, Reactor is in full control of how it gets started through the use of its scheduler. Reactor is also able to ensure that the reactive streams **complete** signal is issued when the `Runnable` object is done with its work.

At the end of the day, that is the whole point of these various operations from Project Reactor. We declare the desired state, and offload all the work scheduling and thread management to the framework. We use a toolkit that is designed from the ground up to support asynchronous, non-blocking operations for maximum resource usage. This gives us a consistent, cohesive way to define expected results while getting maximum efficiency.

Creating custom finders

With Spring Data repositories, we are able to create queries to suit any situation. Earlier in this chapter, we saw `findByName`, which merely queries based on the domain object's `name` attribute.

The following table shows a more comprehensive collection of finders we can write with Spring Data MongoDB. To illustrate the breadth of these keywords, it presumes a domain model bigger than the `Image` class we defined earlier:

Finder Method	Description
`findByLastName(...)`	Query based on `lastName`
`findByFirstNameAndLastName(...)`	Query based on `firstName` and `lastName`
`findByFirstNameAndManagerLastName(...)`	Query based on `firstName` and by a related manager's `lastName`
`findTop10ByFirstName(...)` or `findFirst10ByFirstName(...)`	Query based on `firstName`, but only return the first ten entries
`findByFirstNameIgnoreCase(...)`	Query by `firstName`, but ignore the case of the text
`findByFirstNameAndLastNameAllIgnoreCase(...)`	Query by `firstName` and `lastName`, but ignore the case of the text in ALL fields

`findByFirstNameOrderByLastNameAsc(...)`	Query by `firstName`, but order the results based on `lastName` in ascending order (or use `Desc` for descending order)
`findByBirthdateAfter(Date date)`	Query based on `birthdate` being after the `date`
`findByAgeGreaterThan(int age)`	Query based on `age` attribute being greater than `age` parameter.
`findByAgeGreaterThanEqual(int age)`	Query based on `age` attribute being greater than or equal to `age` parameter.
`findByBirthdateBefore(Date date)`	Query based on `birthdate` being before the `date`
`findByAgeLessThan(int age)`	Query based on `age` attribute being less than `age` parameter.
`findByAgeLessThanEqual(int age)`	Query based on `age` attribute being less than or equal to `age` parameter.
`findByAgeBetween(int from, int to)`	Query based on `age` being between `from` and `to`
`findByAgeIn(Collection ages)`	Query based on `age` being found in the supplied collection
`findByAgeNotIn(Collection ages)`	Query based on `age` NOT being found in the supplied collection
`findByFirstNameNotNull()` or `findByFirstNameIsNotNull()`	Query based on `firstName` not being null

`findByFirstNameNull()` or `findByFirstNameIsNull()`	Query based on `firstName` being null
`findByFirstNameLike(String f)` or `findByFirstNameStartingWith(String f)` or `findByFirstNameEndingWith(String f)`	Query based on input being a regular expression
`findByFirstNameNotLike(String f)` or `findByFirstNameIsNotLike(String f)`	Query based on input being a regex, with a MongoDB `$not` applied
`findByFirstnameContaining(String f)`	For a string input, query just like `Like`; for a collection, query testing membership in the collection
`findByFirstnameNotContaining(String f)`	For a string input, query like like `NotLike`; for a collection, query testing lack of membership in the collection
`findByFirstnameRegex(String pattern)`	Query using `pattern` as a regular expression
`findByLocationNear(Point p)`	Query by geospatial relation using MongoDB's `$near`
`findByLocationNear(Point p, Distance max)`	Query by geospatial relation using MongoDB's `$near` and `$maxDistance`
`findByLocationNear(Point p, Distance min, Distance max)`	Query by geospatial relation using MongoDB's `$near`, `$minDistance`, and `$maxDistance`

`findByLocationWithin(Circle c)`	Query by geospatial relation using MongoDB's `$geoWithin`, `$circle`, and distance
`findByLocationWithin(Box b)`	Query by geospatial relation using MongoDB's `$geoWithin`, `$box`, and square coordinates
`findByActiveIsTrue()`	Query by `active` being true
`findByActiveIsFalse()`	Query by `active` being false
`findByLocationExists(boolean e)`	Query by `location` having the same Boolean value as the input

All of these aforementioned keywords can also be used to construct `deleteBy` methods.

> Many of these operators also work with other supported data stores including JPA, Apache Cassandra, Apache Geode, and GemFire to name a few. However, be sure to check the specific reference guide.

While the previous table shows all the keywords supported for MongoDB repository queries, the following list shows the various supported return types:

- `Image` (or Java primitive types)
- `Iterable<Image>`
- `Iterator<Image>`
- `Collection<Image>`
- `List<Image>`
- `Optional<Image>` (Java 8 or Guava)
- `Option<Image>` (Scala or Vavr)
- `Stream<Image>`
- `Future<Image>`

- `CompletableFuture<Image>`
- `ListenableFuture<Image>`
- `@Async Future<Image>`
- `@Async CompletableFuture<Image>`
- `@Async ListenableFuture<Image>`
- `Slice<Image>`
- `Page<Image>`
- `GeoResult<Image>`
- `GeoResults<Image>`
- `GeoPage<Image>`
- `Mono<Image>`
- `Flux<Image>`

> **TIP**
> Spring Data blocking APIs support `void` return types as well. In Reactor-based programming, the equivalent is `Mono<Void>`, because the caller needs the ability to invoke `subscribe()`.

In a nutshell, just about every container type is covered by Spring Data, which means that we can pick the right solution to suit our needs. Since this book's focus is reactive programming, we'll stick with `Mono` and `Flux`, considering they encapsulate asynchronous + non-blocking + lazy, without impacting the client, and regardless of quantity.

Querying by example

So far, we've built up several reactive queries using property navigation. And we've updated `ImageService` to reactively transform our queried results into operations needed to support our social media platform.

But something that may not be apparent in the design of our data API is the fact that our method signatures are tied to the properties directly. This means that if a domain field changes, we would have to update the queries, or they will break.

There are other issues we might run into, such as offering the ability to put a filter on our web page, and letting the user fetch a subset of images based on their needs.

What if we had a system that listed information about employees. If we imagined writing a finder that lets a user enter `firstName`, `lastName`, and age range, it would probably look like this:

```
interface PersonRepository
  extends ReactiveCrudRepository<Person, Long> {

    List<Person> findByFirstNameAndLastNameAndAgeBetween(
      String firstName, String lastName, int from, int to);
}
```

Yikes! That's ugly. (Even worse, imagine making all the strings case insensitive!)

All of these things lead us toward an alternative Spring Data solution--**Query by Example**.

Query by Example, simply stated, has us assemble a domain object with the criteria provided, and submit them to a query. Let's look at an example. Assume we were storing `Employee` records like this:

```
@Data
@Document
public class Employee {

  @Id private String id;
  private String firstName;
  private String lastName;
  private String role;
}
```

This preceding example is a very simple domain object, and can be explained as follows:

- Lombok's `@Data` annotation provides getters, setters, `equals`, `hashCode`, and `toString` methods
- Spring Data MongoDB's `@Document` annotation indicates this POJO is a target for storage in MongoDB
- Spring Data Commons' `@Id` annotation indicates that the `id` field is the identifier
- The rest of the fields are simple strings

Next, we need to define a repository as we did earlier, but we must also mix in another interface that gives us a standard complement of Query by Example operations. We can do that with the following definition:

```
public interface EmployeeRepository extends
  ReactiveCrudRepository<Employee, String>,
  ReactiveQueryByExampleExecutor<Employee> {

}
```

This last repository definition can be explained as follows:

- It's an interface declaration, meaning, we don't write any implementation code
- `ReactiveCrudRepository` provides the standard CRUD operations with reactive options (`Mono` and `Flux` return types, and more)
- `ReactiveQueryByExampleExecutor` is a **mix-in** interface that introduces the **Query by Example** operations which we'll poke at shortly

Once again, with just a domain object and a Spring Data repository defined, we have all the tools to go forth and query MongoDB!

First things first, we should again use blocking `MongoOperations` to preload some data like this:

```
mongoOperations.dropCollection(Employee.class);

Employee e1 = new Employee();
e1.setId(UUID.randomUUID().toString());
e1.setFirstName("Bilbo");
e1.setLastName("Baggins");
e1.setRole("burglar");

mongoOperations.insert(e1);

Employee e2 = new Employee();
e2.setId(UUID.randomUUID().toString());
e2.setFirstName("Frodo");
e2.setLastName("Baggins");
e2.setRole("ring bearer");

mongoOperations.insert(e2);
```

The preceding setup can be described as follows:

- Start by using `dropCollection` to clean things out
- Next, create a new `Employee`, and insert it into MongoDB
- Create a second `Employee` and insert it as well

> Only use `MongoOperations` to preload test data. Do NOT use it for production code, or your efforts at building reactive apps will be for nothing.

With our data preloaded, let's take a closer look at that `ReactiveQueryByExampleExecutor` interface used to define our repository (provided by Spring Data Commons). Digging in, we can find a couple of key query signatures like this:

```
<S extends T> Mono<S> findOne(Example<S> example);
<S extends T> Flux<S> findAll(Example<S> example);
```

Neither of these aforementioned methods have any properties whatsoever in their names compared to finders like `findByLastName`. The big difference is the usage of `Example` as an argument. `Example` is a container provided by Spring Data Commons to define the parameters of a query.

What does such an `Example` object look like? Let's construct one right now!

```
Employee e = new Employee();
e.setFirstName("Bilbo");
Example<Employee> example = Example.of(e);
```

This construction of an `Example` is described as follows:

- We create an `Employee` probe named e
- We set the probe's `firstName` to `Bilbo`
- Then we leverage the `Example.of` static helper to turn the probe into an `Example`

> In this example, the probe is hard coded, but in production, the value would be pulled from the request whether it was part of a REST route, the body of a web request, or somewhere else.

Before we actually use the `Example` to conduct a query, it pays to understand *what* an `Example` object is. Simply put, an `Example` consists of a probe and a matcher. The probe is the POJO object containing all the values we wish to use as criteria. The matcher is an `ExampleMatcher` that governs how the probe is used. We'll see different types of matching in the following various usages.

Proceeding with our `Example` in hand, we can now solicit a response from the repository as follows:

```
Mono<Employee> singleEmployee = repository.findOne(example);
```

We no longer have to put `firstName` in the query's method signature. Instead, it has become a parameter fed to the query through the `Example` input.

Examples, by default, only query against non-null fields. That's a fancy way of saying that only the fields populated in the probe are considered. Also, the values supplied must match the stored records exactly. This is the default matcher used in the `Example` objects.

Since an exact match isn't always what's needed, let's see how we can adjust things, and come up with a different match criteria, as shown in this code:

```
Employee e = new Employee();
e.setLastName("baggins"); // Lowercase lastName

ExampleMatcher matcher = ExampleMatcher.matching()
  .withIgnoreCase()
  .withMatcher("lastName", startsWith())
  .withIncludeNullValues();

Example<Employee> example = Example.of(e, matcher);
```

This preceding example can be described as follows:

- We create another `Employee` probe
- We deliberately set the `lastName` value as lowercase
- Then we create a custom `ExampleMatcher` using `matching()`
- `withIgnoreCase` says to ignore the case of the values being checked
- `withMatcher` lets us indicate that a given document's `lastName` starts *with* the probe's value

- `withIncludeNullValues` will also match any entries that have nulled-out values
- Finally, we create an `Example` using our probe, but with this custom matcher

With this highly customized example, we can query for ALL employees matching these criteria:

```
Flux<Employee> multipleEmployees = repository.findAll(example);
```

This last code simply uses the `findAll` query, that returns a `Flux` using the same example criteria.

> Remember how we briefly mentioned that Query by Example can lend itself to a form on a web page where various fields are filled out? Based on the fields, the user can decide what to fetch. Notice how we used `withIgnoreCase`? By default, that flag flips to `true`, but it's possible to feed it a Boolean. It means we can put a checkbox on the web page allowing the user to decide whether or not to ignore case in their search.

Simple or complex, Query by Example provides flexible options to query for results. And using Reactor types, we can get just about anything we need with the two queries provided: `findOne` or `findAll`.

Querying with MongoOperations

So far, we have delved into the repository solution using both query by property and Query by Example. There is another angle we can use, `MongoTemplate`.

`MongoTemplate` mimics the Spring Framework's `JdbcTemplate`, the first data access mechanism implemented by Spring. `JdbcTemplate` allows us to focus on writing queries while delegating connection management and error handling to the framework.

`MongoTemplate` brings the same power to bear on crafting MongoDB operations. It's very powerful, but there is a critical tradeoff. All code written using `MongoTemplate` is MongoDB-specific. Porting solutions to another data store is very difficult. Hence, it's not recommended as the first solution, but as a tool to keep in our back pocket for critical operations that require highly tuned MongoDB statements.

To perform reactive `MongoTemplate` operations, there is a corresponding `ReactiveMongoTemplate` that supports Reactor types. The recommended way to interact with `ReactiveMongoTemplate` is through its interface, `ReactiveMongoOperations`.

> The tool that actually conducts MongoDB repository operations under the hood is, in fact, a `MongoTemplate` (or a `ReactiveMongoTemplate` depending on the nature of the repository).

Additionally, Spring Boot will automatically scan the classpath, and if it spots Spring Data MongoDB 2.0 on the classpath along with MongoDB itself, it will create a `ReactiveMongoTemplate`. We can simply request a copy autowired into our class, whether by constructor injection or field injection, as follows:

```
@Autowired
ReactiveMongoOperations operations;
```

`@Autowired` in the last code snippet indicates this field will be injected when the class is loaded, and we'll get a copy of the bean that implements `ReactiveMongoOperations`.

> For test cases, field injection is fine. But for actual running components, the Spring team recommends constructor injection, as will be shown throughout this book. For more details about the benefits of constructor injection, read Spring Data lead Oliver Gierke's blog post at
> `http://olivergierke.de/2013/11/why-field-injection-is-evil/`.

Using `ReactiveMongoOperations` along with `Query byExample`, we can see the previous query rewritten as follows:

```
Employee e = new Employee();
e.setFirstName("Bilbo");
Example<Employee> example = Example.of(e);

Mono<Employee> singleEmployee = operations.findOne(
   new Query(byExample(example)), Employee.class);
```

We can tear apart this latest wrinkle in MongoDB querying as follows:

- The declaration of the probe and its example is the same as shown earlier
- To create a query for one entry, we use `findOne` from `ReactiveMongoOperations`
- For the first parameter, we create a new `Query`, and use the `byExample` static helper to feed it the example
- For the second parameter, we tell it to return an `Employee`

Because this is `ReactiveMongoOperations`, the value is returned wrapped inside a `Mono`.

A similar tune-up can be made to fetch multiple entries with custom criteria, as follows:

```
Employee e = new Employee();
e.setLastName("baggins"); // Lowercase lastName

ExampleMatcher matcher = ExampleMatcher.matching()
  .withIgnoreCase()
  .withMatcher("lastName", startsWith())
  .withIncludeNullValues();

Example<Employee> example = Example.of(e, matcher);

Flux<Employee> multipleEmployees = operations.find(
    new Query(byExample(example)), Employee.class);
```

Now let's check out the details of this preceding query:

- The example is the same as the previous `findAll` query
- This time we use `find`, which accepts the same parameters as `findOne`, but returns a `Flux`

`ReactiveMongoOperations` and its `Query` input opens up a world of powerful operations, like this:

```
reactiveMongoOperations
  .findOne(
    query(
      where("firstName").is("Frodo")), Employee.class)
```

Beyond that, there is support for updating documents, finding-then-updating, and upserting, all supporting the rich, native MongoDB operators through a fluent API.

Delving into more MongoDB operations is beyond the scope of this book, but it's within your grasp should the need arise.

Logging reactive operations

So far, we have crafted a domain object for MongoDB, defined a reactive repository, and updated our `ImageService` to use it. If we fire things up, though, how can we see what's happening? Apart from viewing the web page, what can we expect to see in the console logs?

So far, this appears to be the most we get:

```
org.mongodb.driver.cluster       : Cluster created with settings {hosts=[localhost:27017], mode=SINGLE, requiredCluste
org.mongodb.driver.connection    : Opened connection [connectionId{localValue:1, serverValue:202}] to localhost:27017
org.mongodb.driver.cluster       : Monitor thread successfully connected to server with description ServerDescription{
org.mongodb.driver.cluster       : Cluster created with settings {hosts=[localhost:27017], mode=SINGLE, requiredCluste
org.mongodb.driver.connection    : Opened connection [connectionId{localValue:2, serverValue:203}] to localhost:27017
org.mongodb.driver.cluster       : Monitor thread successfully connected to server with description ServerDescription{
o.s.j.e.a.AnnotationMBeanExporter : Registering beans for JMX exposure on startup
r.ipc.netty.tcp.BlockingNettyContext : Started HttpServer on /0:0:0:0:0:0:0:0:8080
o.s.b.web.embedded.netty.NettyWebServer : Netty started on port(s): 8080
org.mongodb.driver.connection    : Opened connection [connectionId{localValue:3, serverValue:204}] to localhost:27017
```

We see some log messages about connecting to an instance of MongoDB, but that's it! Not much there to debug things, ehh? Never fear, Spring Boot to the rescue.

Spring Boot comes with extensive logging support. Off the cuff, we can create a `logback.xml` file, and add it to our configuration in `src/main/resources`. Spring Boot will read it, and override its default logging policy. That's nice if we want to totally overhaul the log settings.

But often times, we just want to adjust some logging levels for specific packages. Spring Boot grants us a more fine-grained way to alter *what* gets logged.

Simply add this to `src/main/resources/application.properties`:

```
logging.level.com.greglturnquist=DEBUG
logging.level.org.springframework.data=TRACE
logging.level.reactor.core=TRACE
logging.level.reactor.util=TRACE
```

These adjustments can be described as follows:

- `logging.level` tells Spring Boot to adjust log levels with the name of the package tacked on followed by a level
- The application code, `com.greglturnquist`, is set to `DEBUG`
- Spring Data, `org.springframework.data`, is set to `TRACE`
- Project Reactor, `reactor.core` and `reactor.util`, are set to `TRACE`

With these adjustments, if we launch our application, this is part of the output we get:

```
org.mongodb.driver.cluster          : Cluster created with settings {hosts=[localhost:27017], mode=SINGLE, requiredClust
org.mongodb.driver.connection       : Opened connection [connectionId{localValue:1, serverValue:205}] to localhost:27017
org.mongodb.driver.cluster          : Monitor thread successfully connected to server with description ServerDescription
org.mongodb.driver.cluster          : Cluster created with settings {hosts=[localhost:27017], mode=SINGLE, requiredClust
org.mongodb.driver.connection       : Opened connection [connectionId{localValue:2, serverValue:206}] to localhost:27017
org.mongodb.driver.cluster          : Monitor thread successfully connected to server with description ServerDescription
.m.c.i.MongoPersistentEntityIndexCreator : Analyzing class class com.greglturnquist.learningspringboot.Image for index inform
.m.c.i.MongoPersistentEntityIndexCreator : Analyzing class class com.greglturnquist.learningspringboot.Image for index inform
o.s.j.e.a.AnnotationMBeanExporter    : Registering beans for JMX exposure on startup
r.ipc.netty.tcp.BlockingNettyContext : Started HttpServer on /0:0:0:0:0:0:0:0:8080
o.s.b.web.embedded.netty.NettyWebServer : Netty started on port(s): 8080
org.mongodb.driver.connection       : Opened connection [connectionId{localValue:3, serverValue:207}] to localhost:27017
o.s.data.mongodb.core.MongoTemplate  : Dropped collection [image]
o.s.data.mongodb.core.MongoTemplate  : Inserting Document containing fields: [_id, name, _class] in collection: image
o.s.data.mongodb.core.MongoTemplate  : Inserting Document containing fields: [_id, name, _class] in collection: image
o.s.data.mongodb.core.MongoTemplate  : Inserting Document containing fields: [_id, name, _class] in collection: image
```

This preceding output shows some MongoDB activity including cluster configuration, connections, and domain analysis. Toward the end, the effects of `InitDatabase` preloading our data can be seen to some degree, and can be explained as follows:

- `Dropped collection [image]`: This indicates all the entries being deleted by our `dropCollection`
- `Inserting Document containing fields...`: This indicates entries being saved using our `insert`

This is definitely an improvement, but something that's missing is the role that Reactor plays in handling all of this. While we've dialed up the log levels for Reactor, nothing has been output.

If we look at `ImageService`, the question arises, where *can* we add more logging? In traditional imperative programming, we would, typically, write `log.debug("blah blah")` at several spots along the way. But in this reactive flow, there are no "stops" to put them.

Project Reactor comes with a declarative log statement we can add along the way. Here is how we can decorate `findAllImages`:

```
public Flux<Image> findAllImages() {
    return imageRepository.findAll()
      .log("findAll");
}
```

This preceding service operation has but one reactive step, so we can only slip in a single `log` statement. `ImageService.findOneImage` has the same story, so no need to show that.

However, `createImage` has several steps, which are seen in this code:

```
public Mono<Void> createImage(Flux<FilePart> files) {
    return files
      .log("createImage-files")
      .flatMap(file -> {
        Mono<Image> saveDatabaseImage = imageRepository.save(
          new Image(
            UUID.randomUUID().toString(),
            file.filename())))
          .log("createImage-save");

        Mono<Void> copyFile = Mono.just(
          Paths.get(UPLOAD_ROOT, file.filename())
          .toFile())
          .log("createImage-picktarget")
          .map(destFile -> {
            try {
              destFile.createNewFile();
              return destFile;
            } catch (IOException e) {
                throw new RuntimeException(e);
            }
          })
          .log("createImage-newfile")
          .flatMap(file::transferTo)
          .log("createImage-copy");

        return Mono.when(saveDatabaseImage, copyFile)
          .log("createImage-when");
      })
      .log("createImage-flatMap")
      .then()
      .log("createImage-done");
}
```

This last code is identical to what we had before except that each Reactor operation is tagged with a `log` statement. And each one has a unique tag appended, so, we can tell *exactly* what is happening and where.

If we exercise this code from a unit test that uploads two mock multipart files (a test we'll look closer at in the next chapter, `Chapter 13`, *Testing with Spring Boot*), we can spot each tag in the console output as follows:

```
createImage-files              : | onSubscribe([Synchronous Fuseable] FluxArray.ArraySubscription)
createImage-flatMap            : onSubscribe(FluxFlatMap.FlatMapMain)
createImage-done               : onSubscribe(MonoIgnoreElements.IgnoreElementsSubscriber)
createImage-done               : request(unbounded)
createImage-flatMap            : request(unbounded)
createImage-files              : | request(256)
createImage-files              : | onNext(Mock for FilePart, hashCode: 154449199)
createImage-when               : onSubscribe([Fuseable] MonoWhen.WhenCoordinator)
createImage-when               : request(32)
o.s.d.m.core.ReactiveMongoTemplate : Saving Document containing fields: [_id, name, _class]
createImage-save               : onSubscribe(FluxOnErrorResume.ResumeSubscriber)
createImage-save               : request(unbounded)
createImage-copy               : | onSubscribe([Fuseable] MonoFlatMap.FlatMapMain)
createImage-copy               : | request(unbounded)
createImage-picktarget         : | onSubscribe([Synchronous Fuseable] Operators.ScalarSubscription)
createImage-newfile            : | onSubscribe([Fuseable] FluxMapFuseable.MapFuseableSubscriber)
createImage-newfile            : | request(unbounded)
createImage-picktarget         : | request(unbounded)
createImage-picktarget         : | onNext(upload-dir/alpha.jpg)
createImage-newfile            : | onNext(upload-dir/alpha.jpg)
createImage-copy               : | onComplete()
createImage-picktarget         : | onComplete()
createImage-newfile            : | onComplete()
createImage-files              : | onNext(Mock for FilePart, hashCode: 430329518)
createImage-when               : onSubscribe([Fuseable] MonoWhen.WhenCoordinator)
createImage-when               : request(32)
o.s.d.m.core.ReactiveMongoTemplate : Saving Document containing fields: [_id, name, _class]
createImage-save               : onSubscribe(FluxOnErrorResume.ResumeSubscriber)
createImage-save               : request(unbounded)
createImage-copy               : | onSubscribe([Fuseable] MonoFlatMap.FlatMapMain)
createImage-copy               : | request(unbounded)
createImage-picktarget         : | onSubscribe([Synchronous Fuseable] Operators.ScalarSubscription)
createImage-newfile            : | onSubscribe([Fuseable] FluxMapFuseable.MapFuseableSubscriber)
createImage-newfile            : | request(unbounded)
createImage-picktarget         : | request(unbounded)
createImage-picktarget         : | onNext(upload-dir/bravo.jpg)
org.mongodb.driver.connection  : Opened connection [connectionId{localValue:4, serverValue:220}] to lo
createImage-newfile            : | onNext(upload-dir/bravo.jpg)
createImage-copy               : | onComplete()
createImage-picktarget         : | onComplete()
createImage-newfile            : | onComplete()
createImage-files              : | onComplete()
org.mongodb.driver.connection  : Opened connection [connectionId{localValue:5, serverValue:221}] to lo
createImage-save               : onNext(Image{id=85c62c00-c315-4a6b-914b-059e1020ee6b, name=bravo.jpg})
createImage-save               : onNext(Image{id=7f4fb639-8b0d-4791-b88a-366b2cce0b55, name=alpha.jpg})
createImage-when               : onComplete()
createImage-when               : onComplete()
createImage-save               : onComplete()
createImage-flatMap            : onComplete()
createImage-done               : onComplete()
```

This preceding output shows each of the steps, and how they play together in the reactive streams' dance of subscribe, request, next, and complete. Most notably, the outer operations (`files`, `flatMap`, and `done`) are shown at the top when subscriptions are made. Each file causes a filter operation to occur followed by a save and a copy. And at the bottom, the same outer operations (again `files`, `flatMap`, and `done`) issue a reactive streams **complete**.

To mark up `deleteImage` with logs, let's make these changes:

```
public Mono<Void> deleteImage(String filename) {
  Mono<Void> deleteDatabaseImage = imageRepository
    .findByName(filename)
    .log("deleteImage-find")
    .flatMap(imageRepository::delete)
    .log("deleteImage-record");

  Mono<Object> deleteFile = Mono.fromRunnable(() -> {
    try {
      Files.deleteIfExists(
        Paths.get(UPLOAD_ROOT, filename));
    } catch (IOException e) {
      throw new RuntimeException(e);
    }
  })
  .log("deleteImage-file");

  return Mono.when(deleteDatabaseImage, deleteFile)
    .log("deleteImage-when")
    .then()
    .log("deleteImage-done");
}
```

This is the same `deleteImage` code we wrote earlier, only, we've sprinkled in log statements everywhere to indicate exactly what is happening.

With everything set up, we should be able to test things out. For starters, we can launch the code by either running the `LearningSpringBootApplication` class's `public static void main()` method, or we can run it from the command line using Gradle like this:

```
$ ./gradlew clean bootRun
```

If we launch the application and navigate to `http://localhost:8080`, we can see our preloaded images, as seen in this screenshot:

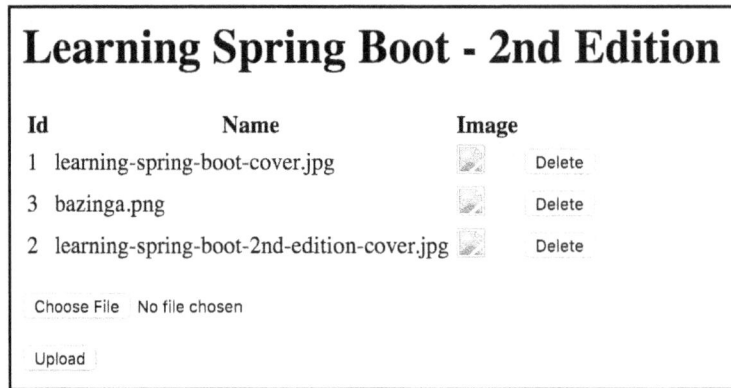

Learning Spring Boot - 2nd Edition

Id	Name	Image	
1	learning-spring-boot-cover.jpg		Delete
3	bazinga.png		Delete
2	learning-spring-boot-2nd-edition-cover.jpg		Delete

Choose File No file chosen

Upload

We can click on a single image, and see some comparable log messages like this:

```
findOneImage :  | onSubscribe([Fuseable] Operators.MonoSubscriber)
findOneImage :  | request(unbounded)
findOneImage :  | onNext(URL [file:upload-dir/learning-spring-boot-
    cover.jpg])
findOneImage :  | onComplete()
```

This very simple flow illustrates the Reactive Streams pattern. We subscribe for an image. A request is sent--in this case, unbounded (even though we know in advance there is only one result). `onNext` is the answer, and it's a file-based URL (a Spring `Resource`) being returned. Then the `complete` is issued.

> This logging is confined to `ImageService`, which means we don't see it transformed into an HTTP response. If you wish to explore this further, feel free to add extra `log` statements to `HomeController.oneRawImage`.

If we click on the **Delete** button, it deletes the image and refreshes the page, as follows:

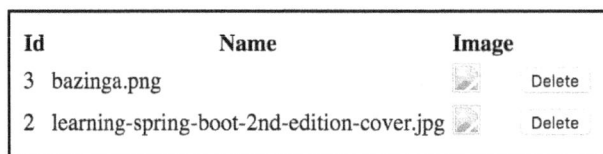

Id	Name	Image	
3	bazinga.png		Delete
2	learning-spring-boot-2nd-edition-cover.jpg		Delete

After completing the deletion, if we look at the console logs and focus on what happened, we will see something like this:

```
o.s.d.m.r.query.MongoQueryCreator        : Created query Query: { "name" : "learning-spring-boot-cover.jpg"}, Fields:
o.s.d.m.core.ReactiveMongoTemplate       : findOne using query: { "name" : "learning-spring-boot-cover.jpg"} fields:
deleteImage-when                         : onSubscribe([Fuseable] MonoWhen.WhenCoordinator)
deleteImage-done                         : onSubscribe(MonoIgnoreElements.IgnoreElementsSubscriber)
deleteImage-done                         : request(unbounded)
deleteImage-when                         : request(unbounded)
deleteImage-record                       :  | onSubscribe([Fuseable] MonoFlatMap.FlatMapMain)
deleteImage-record                       :  | request(unbounded)
o.s.d.m.core.ReactiveMongoTemplate       : findOne using query: { "name" : "learning-spring-boot-cover.jpg"} fields:
deleteImage-find                         : onSubscribe(FluxOnErrorResume.ResumeSubscriber)
deleteImage-find                         : request(unbounded)
deleteImage-file                         : onSubscribe([Fuseable] Operators.EmptySubscription)
deleteImage-file                         : request(unbounded)
deleteImage-file                         : onComplete()
deleteImage-find                         : onNext(Image(id=1, name=learning-spring-boot-cover.jpg))
o.s.d.m.core.ReactiveMongoTemplate       : Remove using query: { "_id" : "1"} in collection: image.
deleteImage-find                         : onComplete()
deleteImage-record                       :  | onComplete()
deleteImage-when                         : onComplete()
deleteImage-done                         : onComplete()
```

At the very top, we can see a MongoDB query issued to find the desired image with the `findOne using query` output. A `Mono.when` is set up, and then, a `Remove using query` is issued to delete the record. The actual deletion of the file is logged with little details except the complete signal. The whole thing is wrapped up when we see `deleteImage-done` issue a complete.

> We haven't begun to mark up the `HomeController` with log messages, but we don't need to at this stage. If you wish to explore that area, feel free to do so. Using these log statements, you can get a real feel for how Reactor arranges tasks, and even spot cases where the order of operations fluctuates at different times. The key thing is we have a real tool for debugging reactive flows.

With this, we have successfully coded a reactive `ImageService` that both copies files to the server and writes records in MongoDB; and we did it letting Spring Boot autoconfigure all the beans needed to make Spring Data MongoDB work seamlessly with Spring WebFlux and MongoDB.

Summary

In this chapter, we wrote several data access operations using a repository-based solution. We explored alternative querying options. Then we showed how to wire that into our controller, and store live data. We wrapped things up by exploring logging options in a functional, reactive nature.

In the next chapter, we will discover all the various ways Spring Boot makes testing super easy, combined with the utilities provided by Project Reactor to test async, non-blocking flows.

13
Testing with Spring Boot

Most innovative contribution to the java ecosystem: spring Boot #jaxlondon

– @JAXenter

If we go back more than 10 years, we would find testing a process mostly conducted by legions of test engineers. But with the rise of JUnit, the adoption of **continuous integration** (**CI**) servers, a plethora of test assertion libraries, and integrated test coverage services, we can see widespread adoption of automated testing.

In this chapter, we will see how critical Spring Boot views automated testing by providing multiple levels of support. We shall do the following:

- Write some basic unit tests
- Introduce **slice** testing
- Embark upon WebFlux testing
- Leverage complete embedded container testing
- Draft some autoconfiguration tests

Test dependencies

So far, we have used the Spring Initializr (`http://start.spring.io`) to create our social media platform. We picked several dependencies and added others along the way. But we haven't investigated test libraries.

It turns out, Spring Boot takes testing so seriously that it's not an option on the website. All projects created automatically have this test-scoped dependency:

```
testCompile('org.springframework.boot:spring-boot-starter-test')
```

So what's included with that single line?

- **JUnit**: De-facto standard for testing Java apps
- **JSON Path**: XPath for JSON
- **AssertJ**: Fluent assertion library
- **Mockito**: Java mocking library
- **Hamcrest**: Library of matcher objects
- **JSONassert**: Assertion library for JSON
- **Spring Test** and **Spring Boot Test**: Test libraries provided by the Spring Framework and Spring Boot

In addition to these various testing libraries being automatically supplied, many optional dependencies are also included. This means that they can be added to our project's list of dependencies without specifying the version. The optional dependencies are listed as follows:

- **HTMLUnit**: Testing toolkit for HTML outputs
- **Selenium**: Browser automation for UI testing
- **Flapdoodle**: Embedded MongoDB database for testing
- **H2**: Embedded SQL database for testing
- **Spring REST Docs**: Generates REST documentation using automated tests

> Before we dig any deeper, it's important to understand that entire books have been written about testing applications. We'll attempt to get a good cross-section of testing and look at how Spring Boot makes certain types of tests even easier, but don't consider this chapter to be the end-all of what's possible.

Unit testing

The smallest scoped tests we can write are referred to as unit tests. In fact, people have been writing tiny tests for years. A common paradigm is to try and test just one class in a given unit test.

To get going, let's test the smallest unit of code we have: our Lombok-enabled `Image` domain object.

As a reminder, here is what that code looks like:

```
@Data
@Document
public class Image {
    @Id final private String id;
    final private String name;
}
```

This tiny little POJO is flagged with Spring Data MongoDB annotations as well as Lombok's `@Data` annotation providing getters and setters.

A unit test shouldn't be too hard. We can start by creating `ImageTests.java` in `/src/test/java`, and in the same package as the original class (`com.greglturnquist.learningspringboot`), as follows:

```
public class ImageTests {
  @Test
  public void imagesManagedByLombokShouldWork() {
    Image image = new Image("id", "file-name.jpg");
    assertThat(image.getId()).isEqualTo("id");
    assertThat(image.getName()).isEqualTo("file-name.jpg");
  }
}
```

This preceding unit test can easily be explained, as follows:

- `@Test` indicates that `imagesManagedByLombokShouldWork` is a JUnit test case, ensuring it is automatically picked up and run either from our IDE when we choose or from Gradle when we build the system
- The test creates a new `Image` object
- Then it uses AssertJ's `assertThat()` method to prove the values are as expected

Let's run it!

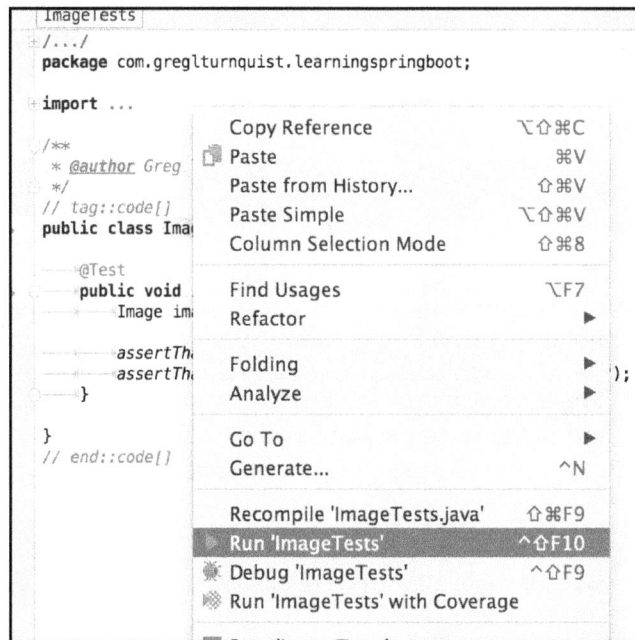

As shown in the preceding screenshot, we merely right-click on the class
`ImageTests`, select **Run 'ImageTests'**, and watch for the output (shown next):

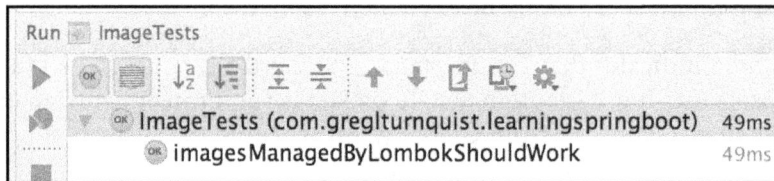

Hooray! There is always a little happiness when our automated tests go green.

> I know that in print, the color green turns to grey. But we can also
> see the **OK** text in the bubble next to the test case, indicating that it
> passed.

So far, so good. With our first test written, we have gotten off the ground with a test-based approach to things. But testing can get more complicated, quickly.

Slice-based testing

Across the industry, many express an interest in testing. Yet, when push comes to shove and we run into tricky situations, it's quite easy to throw up our hands and shout, *This is too hard!*

Spring Boot aims to help!

JUnit, all by itself, gives us the power to declare tests and assert pass/fail scenarios. But in reality, not everything works straight out of the box. For example, parts of our code will easily come to rely upon Boot autoconfiguring various beans as well as having that powerful property support.

A keen example is the need to do some MongoDB operations. It would be quite handy if we could ask Spring Boot to autoconfigure just enough beans to support MongoDB for our tests but nothing else.

Well, today's our lucky day.

Spring Boot 1.5 introduced slice testing. This is where a subset of Spring Boot's autoconfiguration power can be switched on, while also having full access to its property support. The following list of test annotations each enable a different slice of code:

- @DataMongoTest
- @DataJpaTest
- @JdbcTest
- @JsonTest
- @RestClientTest
- @WebFluxTest
- @WebMvcTest

Each of these annotations enables a different slice of beans to be configured. For example, `@DataJpaTest` will:

- Enable transactions by applying Spring's `@Transactional` annotation to the test class
- Enable caching on the test class, defaulting to a `NoOp` cache instance
- Autoconfigure an embedded test database in place of a real one
- Create a `TestEntityManager` bean and add it to the application context
- Disable the general Spring Boot autoconfiguration, confining things to the autoconfiguration policies found in `spring-boot-test-autoconfigure`

> All of these annotations require additionally annotating our test class with `@RunWith(SpringRunner.class)`.

An important point to understand is that tests work best when confined to a relatively narrow scope. Hence, using more than one of these `@...Test` annotations is not recommended. Instead, break things up into multiple test classes.

Testing with embedded MongoDB

The first annotation listed above for slice testing is `@DataMongoTest`. In this section, we want to write some test methods that involve our MongoDB-specific code.

When it comes to testing MongoDB code, we have the following two options provided by Spring Boot:

- Testing against an embedded MongoDB instance
- Testing against a live MongoDB instance

Spring Boot, by default, will check if Flapdoodle, the embedded MongoDB database, is on the classpath. If so, it will attempt to run the test using it. If Flapdoodle is NOT on our classpath, it will attempt to connect to a real MongoDB instance.

So let's get started by adding `flapdoodle` to our project's list of dependencies as follows:

```
testCompile("de.flapdoodle.embed:de.flapdoodle.embed.mongo")
```

Since we are going to test our Reactor-based APIs, we also want to leverage Reactor Test, a library of utilities provided by Project Reactor. Let's add the following test dependency:

```
testCompile("io.projectreactor:reactor-test")
```

With this last dependency added to our project, we can now start writing `EmbeddedImageRepositoryTests.java` inside `src/test/java`, in the `com.greglturnquist.learningspringboot` package, like this:

```
@RunWith(SpringRunner.class)
@DataMongoTest
public class EmbeddedImageRepositoryTests {

    @Autowired
    ImageRepository repository;

    @Autowired
    MongoOperations operations;
```

The preceding code for the first part of this test class can be described as follows:

- `@RunWith(SpringRunner.java)` is needed to ensure that Spring Boot test annotations run properly within JUnit
- `@DataMongoTest` will disable the general Spring Boot autoconfiguration, and instead, use Spring Boot's test-based autoconfigurations to create a `MongoTemplate`, a MongoDB connection, MongoDB property settings, a `ReactiveMongoTemplate` and an embedded MongoDB instance; it will also enable the MongoDB repositories
- With the Spring Data MongoDB repositories enabled, Spring Boot will automatically instantiate an `ImageRepository`, and inject it into our autowired `repository` field

> **TIP**
>
> In general, it's recommended to use constructor injection for production code. But for test code where constructors are limited due to JUnit, autowiring as we've just done is fine.

With access to a clean MongoDB instance (embedded), we can now perform a little setup work as follows:

```
/**
 * To avoid {@code block()} calls, use blocking
 * {@link MongoOperations} during setup.
```

```
*/
@Before
public void setUp() {
  operations.dropCollection(Image.class);
  operations.insert(new Image("1",
    "learning-spring-boot-cover.jpg"));
  operations.insert(new Image("2",
    "learning-spring-boot-2nd-edition-cover.jpg"));
  operations.insert(new Image("3",
    "bazinga.png"));
  operations.findAll(Image.class).forEach(image -> {
    System.out.println(image.toString());
  });
}
```

This preceding setup method can be described as follows:

- The `@Before` flags this method to be run before every single `@Test` method in this class
- The `operations` is used to `dropCollection` and then insert three new entries in the database, turn around and fetch them all, and print them to the console

With things preloaded properly, we can start writing our first test case, as shown next:

```
@Test
public void findAllShouldWork() {
  Flux<Image> images = repository.findAll();
  StepVerifier.create(images)
    .recordWith(ArrayList::new)
    .expectNextCount(3)
    .consumeRecordedWith(results -> {
      assertThat(results).hasSize(3);
      assertThat(results)
      .extracting(Image::getName)
      .contains(
        "learning-spring-boot-cover.jpg",
        "learning-spring-boot-2nd-edition-cover.jpg",
        "bazinga.png");
    })
    .expectComplete()
    .verify();
}
```

This preceding test case can be described as follows:

- `@Test` indicates this is a test method and the method name describes our overall goal.
- We use Reactor Test's `StepVerifier` to subscribe to the `Flux` from the repository and then assert against it.
- Because we want to assert against the whole collection, we need to pipe it through Reactor Test's `recordWith` method, which fetches the entire `Flux` and converts it into an `ArrayList` via a method handle.
- We verify that there were indeed three entries.
- We write a lambda to peek inside the recorded `ArrayList`. In it, we can use AssertJ to verify the size of `ArrayList` as well as extract each image's name with `Image::getName` and verify them.
- Finally, we can verify that `Flux` emitted a **Reactive Streams** complete signal, meaning that it finished correctly.

`StepVerifier` speaks Reactive Streams and will execute all the various signals to talk to the enclosed `Publisher`. In this case, we interrogated a `Flux` but this can also be used on a `Mono`.

To wrap things up, we are going to test our custom finder, `findByName`, as shown here:

```
@Test
public void findByNameShouldWork() {
  Mono<Image> image = repository.findByName("bazinga.png");
  StepVerifier.create(image)
    .expectNextMatches(results -> {
      assertThat(results.getName()).isEqualTo("bazinga.png");
      assertThat(results.getId()).isEqualTo("3");
      return true;
    });
}
```

This last test case can be described as follows:

- `repository.findByName()` is used to fetch one record
- We again use `StepVerifier` to create a subscriber for our `Mono` and then expect the next signal to come through, indicating that it was fetched
- Inside the lambda, we perform a couple of AssertJ assertions to verify the state of this `Image`

Due to the functional nature of `StepVerifier`, we need to return a Boolean representing pass/fail.

By the way, exactly how many CRUD methods do we need to test? We covered `findAll` and `findByName`. In principle, we could sidestep `findAll` since that can be considered a part of Spring Data MongoDB. But it makes a good example in this book for testing a Reactor `Flux` result.

In general, we shouldn't bite off testing framework code. But verifying our custom finder makes perfect sense. And there's always room for end-to-end testing, which we'll explore further in this chapter.

Testing with a real MongoDB database

Testing against an embedded MongoDB instance is quite handy. But there are times when we need to work with a real instance, and for multiple reasons: security settings, a batch of live data, a customized configuration. Whatever the reason, there is no need for that to derail our testing efforts.

We can write another test class, `LiveImageRepositoryTests`, and make it look like this:

```
@RunWith(SpringRunner.class)
@DataMongoTest(excludeAutoConfiguration =
  EmbeddedMongoAutoConfiguration.class)
  public class LiveImageRepositoryTests {
    @Autowired
    ImageRepository repository;
    @Autowired
    MongoOperations operations;
```

The details for this preceding live test are as follows:

- `@RunWith(SpringRunner.class)` is our familiar annotation to integrate Spring with JUnit.
- `@DataMongoTest` (and the other `@...Test` annotations) lets us exclude explicit autoconfiguration classes. To switch off Flapdoodle, all we need to do is exclude `EmbeddedMongoAutoConfiguration`

The rest of the code in this class is the same as `EmbeddedImageRepositoryTests`, so there's no need to show it here. (In fact, it would be quite nice if the exact same tests ran on both embedded as well as a live MongoDB instance.)

Let's run our latest batch of both embedded and live MongoDB tests:

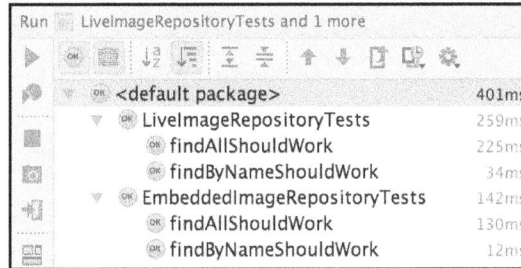

All green (along with the **OK** icon)!

> Keeping identical test code in two different classes violates the **DRY** (**Don't Repeat Yourself**) principle. If we altered one test class, we should presumably alter the matching test case in the other class. But a new teammate may not be aware of this. It's left as an exercise for the reader to extract an abstract set of test methods to be used by both `LiveImageRepositoryTests` and `EmbeddedImageRepositoryTests`.

Testing WebFlux controllers

So far, we've looked at unit testing as well as slice testing for MongoDB. These are good for covering services and backend logic. The last part we need to ensure is whether the web controllers are working properly.

Spring Boot comes with automated support to help us pick the exact type of test that we want to run. Let's start with an example:

```
@RunWith(SpringRunner.class)
@WebFluxTest(controllers = HomeController.class)
@Import({ThymeleafAutoConfiguration.class})
public class HomeControllerTests {
  @Autowired
  WebTestClient webClient;
  @MockBean
  ImageService imageService;
```

```
        . . .
    }
```

This preceding beginning of a controller test case can be described as follows:

- `@RunWith(SpringRunner.class)` ensures all of our Spring Framework and Spring Boot test annotations integrate properly with JUnit.
- `@WebFluxTest(controllers = HomeController.class)` is another slice of testing which focuses on Spring WebFlux. The default configuration enables all `@Controller` beans and `@RestController` beans as well as a mock web environment, but with the rest of the autoconfiguration disabled. However, by using the `controllers` argument, we have confined this test case to ONLY enable `HomeController`.
- `@Import(...)` specifies what additional bits we want configured outside of any Spring WebFlux controllers. In this case, the Thymeleaf autoconfiguration is needed.
- A `WebTestClient` bean is autowired into our test case, giving us the means to make mock web calls.
- `@MockBean` signals that the `ImageService` collaborator bean needed by our `HomeController` will be replaced by a mock, which we'll configure shortly.

> Even though `@WebFluxTest` is another slice similar to `@DataMongoTest`, we broke it out of the previous section, Slice Testing, because WebFlux testing comes with an extensive range of configuration options, which we will explore later in more detail.

Let's look at a test case where we get the base URL `/`:

```
@Test
public void baseRouteShouldListAllImages() {
  // given
  Image alphaImage = new Image("1", "alpha.png");
  Image bravoImage = new Image("2", "bravo.png");
  given(imageService.findAllImages())
    .willReturn(Flux.just(alphaImage, bravoImage));

  // when
  EntityExchangeResult<String> result = webClient
    .get().uri("/")
    .exchange()
    .expectStatus().isOk()
    .expectBody(String.class).returnResult();
```

```
// then
verify(imageService).findAllImages();
verifyNoMoreInteractions(imageService);
assertThat(result.getResponseBody())
  .contains(
    "<title>Learning Spring Boot: Spring-a-Gram</title>")
  .contains("<a href=\"/images/alpha.png/raw\">")
  .contains("<a href=\"/images/bravo.png/raw\">");
}
```

We can cover the details of this last test case as follows:

- `@Test` marks this method as a JUnit test case.
- The method name, `baseRouteShouldListAllImages`, gives us a quick summary of what this method should verify.
- The first three lines mock up the `ImageService` bean to return a `Flux` of two images when `findAllImages` gets called.
- `webClient` is then used to perform a `GET /` using its fluent API.
- We verify the HTTP status to be a 200 OK, and extract the body of the result into a string.
- We use Mockito's `verify` to prove that our `ImageService` bean's `findAllImages` was indeed called.
- We use Mockito's `verifyNoMoreInteractions` to prove that no other calls are made to our mock `ImageService`.
- Finally, we use AssertJ to inspect some key parts of the HTML page that was rendered.

This test method gives us a pretty good shake out of `GET /`. We are able to verify that the web page was rendered with the right content. We can also verify that our `ImageService` bean was called as expected. And both were done without involving a real MongoDB engine and without a fully running web container.

Spring's WebFlux machinery is verified since it still includes the bits that take an incoming request for / and routes it to `HomeController.index()`, yielding a Thymeleaf-generated HTML page. This way, we know our controller has been wired properly. And oftentimes, this is enough to prove the web call works.

A key scenario to explore is actually fetching a file, mockingly. It's what our app does when requesting a single image. Check out the following test case:

```
@Test
public void fetchingImageShouldWork() {
  given(imageService.findOneImage(any()))
```

```
      .willReturn(Mono.just(
        new ByteArrayResource("data".getBytes())));

    webClient
      .get().uri("/images/alpha.png/raw")
      .exchange()
      .expectStatus().isOk()
      .expectBody(String.class).isEqualTo("data");
    verify(imageService).findOneImage("alpha.png");
    verifyNoMoreInteractions(imageService);
  }
```

This preceding test case can be described as follows:

- @Test flags this method as a JUnit test case.
- The method name, fetchingImageShouldWork, hints that this tests successful file fetching.
- The ImageService.findOneImage method returns a Mono<Resource>, so we need to assemble a mock resource. That can be achieved using Spring's ByteArrayResource, which takes a byte[]. Since all Java strings can be turned into byte arrays, it's a piece of cake to plug it in.
- webClient calls GET /images/alpha.png/raw.
- After the exchange() method, we verify the HTTP status is OK.
- We can even check the data content in the body of the HTTP response given that the bytes can be curried back into a Java string.
- Lastly, we use Mockito's verify to make sure our mock was called once and in no other way.

Since we're coding against a very simple interface, Resource, we don't have to go through any complicated ceremony of staging a fake test file and having it served up. While that's possible, Mockito makes it easy to stand up stubs and mocks. Additionally, Spring's assortment of Resource implementations lets us pick the right one. This reinforces the benefit of coding services against interfaces and not implementations when possible.

The other side of the coin when testing file retrieval is to verify that we properly handle file errors. What if we attempted to fetch an image but for some reason the file on the server was corrupted? Check it out in the following test code:

```
@Test
public void fetchingNullImageShouldFail() throws IOException {
  Resource resource = mock(Resource.class);
  given(resource.getInputStream())
```

```
    .willThrow(new IOException("Bad file"));
  given(imageService.findOneImage(any()))
    .willReturn(Mono.just(resource));

  webClient
    .get().uri("/images/alpha.png/raw")
    .exchange()
    .expectStatus().isBadRequest()
    .expectBody(String.class)
    .isEqualTo("Couldn't find alpha.png => Bad file");

  verify(imageService).findOneImage("alpha.png");
  verifyNoMoreInteractions(imageService);
}
```

This preceding test of a failure can be described as follows:

- @Test flags this method as a JUnit test case.
- The method name, fetchingNullImageShouldFail, hints that this test is aimed at a failure scenario.
- We need to mock out the file on the server, which is represented as a Spring Resource. That way, we can force it to throw an IOException when getInputStream is invoked.
- That mock is returned when ImageService.findOneImage is called. Notice how we use Mockito's any() to simplify inputs?
- webClient is again used to make the call.
- After the exchange() method is made, we verify that the HTTP status is a 400 Bad Request.
- We also check the response body and ensure it matches the expected body from our controller's exception handler.
- Finally, we use Mockito to verify that our mock ImageService.findOneImage() was called once (and only once!) and that no other calls were made to this mock bean.

This test case shows a critical skill we all need to polish: verifying that the path of failure is handled properly. When a manager asks *what if the file isn't there?*, we can show them a test case indicating that we have covered it. Say we write a try...catch clause in the our code, like this one in HomeController.oneRawImage():

```
    return imageService.findOneImage(filename)
  .map(resource -> {
    try {
```

```
        return ResponseEntity.ok()
        .contentLength(resource.contentLength())
        .body(new InputStreamResource(
          resource.getInputStream()));
      } catch (IOException e) {
      return ResponseEntity.badRequest()
      .body("Couldn't find " + filename +
        " => " + e.getMessage());
      }
    });
```

We should immediately start thinking of two test cases: one test case for the try part when we can find the file and return an OK, and another test case for the catch part when IOException gets thrown and we return a Bad Request.

While it's not hard to think up all the successful scenarios, capturing the failure scenarios and testing them is important. And Mockito makes it quite easy to mock failing behavior. In fact, it's a common pattern to have one mock return another, as we did in this test case.

Mockito makes it easy to mock things left and right. Just keep sight of what you're really trying to test. One can get so caught up in mocking so that all that gets tested are the mocks. We must be sure to verify the actual behavior of the code, or the test will be meaningless.

Another webish behavior that happens all the time is processing a call and then redirecting the client to another web location. This is exactly the behavior when we issue an HTTP DELETE to our site. The URL is expected to carry the resource that must be deleted. Once completed, we need to instruct the browser to go back to the home page.

Check out the following test case:

```
@Test
public void deleteImageShouldWork() {
  Image alphaImage = new Image("1", "alpha.png");
  given(imageService.deleteImage(any())).willReturn(Mono.empty());

  webClient
    .delete().uri("/images/alpha.png")
    .exchange()
    .expectStatus().isSeeOther()
    .expectHeader().valueEquals(HttpHeaders.LOCATION, "/");

  verify(imageService).deleteImage("alpha.png");
```

```
        verifyNoMoreInteractions(imageService);
    }
```

We can describe this preceding redirecting web call as follows:

- The `@Test` flags this method as a JUnit test case.
- We prep our `ImageService` mock bean to handle a `deleteImage` by returning `Mono.empty()`. This is the way to construct a `Mono<Void>` object, which represents the promise that our service hands us when deletion of the file and its corresponding MongoDB record are both completed.
- `webClient` performs a `DELETE /images/alpha.png`.
- After the `exchange()` is complete, we verify the HTTP status is `303 See Other`, the outcome of a Spring WebFlux `redirect:/` directive.
- As part of the HTTP redirect, there should also be a `Location` header containing the new URL, `/`.
- Finally, we confirm that our `ImageService` mock bean's `deleteImage` method was called and nothing else.

This proves that we have properly invoked our service and then followed it up with a redirect back to the home page. It's actually possible to grab that Location header and issue another `webClient` call, but there is no point in this test case. We have already verified that behavior.

However, imagine that the redirect included some contextual thing like `redirect:/?msg=Deleted` showing a desire to bounce back to the home page but with extra data to be shown. That would be a great time to issue a second call and prove that this special message was rendered properly.

Now we can run the entire test case and see green bubbles all the way down:

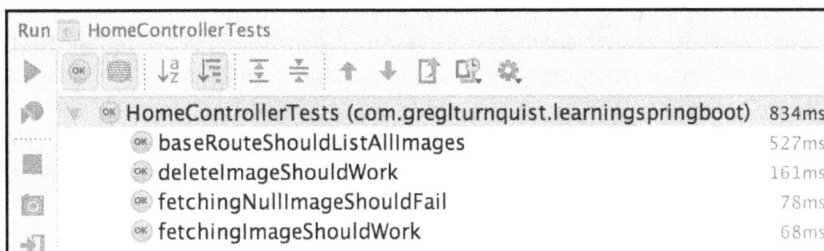

Run	HomeControllerTests	
▶ ⊙ ■ ↓ᵃ⁻ᶻ ⌱ᵃ⁻ᶻ ⌧ ⌹ ↑ ↓ ⌸ ⌺ ⚙		
▸	HomeControllerTests (com.greglturnquist.learningspringboot)	834ms
	baseRouteShouldListAllImages	527ms
	deleteImageShouldWork	161ms
	fetchingNullImageShouldFail	78ms
	fetchingImageShouldWork	68ms

We have used Mockito quite a bit but we aren't going to delve into all its features. For that, I recommend reading *Mockito Cookbook* written by Spring teammate Marcin Grzejszczak (@MGrzejszczak).

Fully embedded Spring Boot app tests

We did some nice testing of the web controller and verified that it behaves properly. But that was just another slice. At some point, it's good to test the whole thing, end-to-end. And with today's modern suite of test tools, it's totally doable.

Spring Boot doesn't always support every tool. For example, Selenium WebDriver, a popular browser automation toolkit, is not yet supported outside of servlets.

No problem! What we really need is for Spring Boot to launch our application, preferably on an unoccupied port, and get out of the way while we do some testing. So let's do just that.

We can start by crafting a new test case like this:

```
@RunWith(SpringRunner.class)
@SpringBootTest(
   webEnvironment = SpringBootTest.WebEnvironment.RANDOM_PORT)
   public class EndToEndTests {
```

This preceding test class can be described as follows:

- `@RunWith(SpringRunner.class)` ensures the Spring Boot annotations integrate with JUnit.
- `@SpringBootTest` is the test annotation where we can activate all of Spring Boot in a controlled fashion. With `webEnvironment` switched from the default setting of a mocked web environment to `SpringBootTest.WebEnvironment.RANDOM_PORT`, a real embedded version of the app will launch on a random available port.

This configuration will spin up a copy of our application on an open port, with a full-blown autoconfiguration, and all of our `CommandLineRunners` will run. That means our `InitDatabase` class that pre-loads MongoDB will kick in.

By the way, Flapdoodle will also run an embedded MongoDB instance because we are in the test scope.

First of all, we need a handful of test objects declared as fields of our test class. These are obtained as follows:

```
static ChromeDriverService service;
static ChromeDriver driver;
@LocalServerPort
int port;
```

These attributes of `EndToEndTests` can be described as follows:

- `ChromeDriverService`: This gives us a handle on the bridge between Selenium and the Chrome handling library
- `ChromeDriver`: This is an implementation of the `WebDriver` interface, giving us all the operations to drive a test browser
- `@LocalServerPort`: This is a Spring Boot annotation that instructs Boot to autowire the port number of the web container into `port`

To use `ChromeDriver`, not only do we need the browser Chrome downloaded and installed in its default location, we also need a separate executable: `chromedriver`. Assuming you have visited `https://sites.google.com/a/chromium.org/chromedriver/downloads`, downloaded the bundle (macOS in my case), unzipped it, and put the executable in a folder named `ext`, you can proceed.

With `chromedriver` installed in `ext`, we can configure it to start and stop as follows:

```
@BeforeClass
public static void setUp() throws IOException {
  System.setProperty("webdriver.chrome.driver",
    "ext/chromedriver");
  service = createDefaultService();
  driver = new ChromeDriver(service);
  Path testResults = Paths.get("build", "test-results");
  if (!Files.exists(testResults)) {
    Files.createDirectory(testResults);
  }
}

@AfterClass
public static void tearDown() {
```

```
      service.stop();
    }
```

This setup/teardown behavior can be described as follows:

- `@BeforeClass` directs JUnit to run this method before any test method inside this class runs and to only run this method once
- Inside the `setUp` method, it sets the `webdriver.chrome.driver` property to the relative path of `chromedriver`
- Next, it creates a default service
- Then it creates a new `ChromeDriver` to be used by all the test methods
- Finally, it creates a test directory to capture screenshots (as we'll soon see)
- `@AfterClass` directs JUnit to run the `tearDown` method after ALL tests have run in this class
- It commands `ChromeDriverService` to shut down. Otherwise, the server process will stay up and running

Is this starting to sound a bit convoluted? We'll explore options to simplify this later on in this chapter.

For now, let's focus on writing this test case:

```
@Test
public void homePageShouldWork() throws IOException {
  driver.get("http://localhost:" + port);

  takeScreenshot("homePageShouldWork-1");

  assertThat(driver.getTitle())
    .isEqualTo("Learning Spring Boot: Spring-a-Gram");

  String pageContent = driver.getPageSource();

  assertThat(pageContent)
    .contains("<a href="/images/bazinga.png/raw">");
  WebElement element = driver.findElement(
      By.cssSelector("a[href*="bazinga.png"]"));
  Actions actions = new Actions(driver);
  actions.moveToElement(element).click().perform();

  takeScreenshot("homePageShouldWork-2");
  driver.navigate().back();
}
```

This preceding test case can be detailed as follows:

- `@Test` indicates this is a JUnit test case
- `driver` navigates to the home page using the injected `port`
- It takes a screenshot so we can inspect things after the fact
- We verify the title of the page is as expected
- Next, we grab the entire page's HTML content and verify one of the links
- Then we hunt down that link using a W3C CSS selector (there are other options as well), move to it, and click on it
- We grab another snapshot and then click on the back button

This is a pretty basic test. It doesn't do a lot apart from verifying the home page and checking out one link. However, it demonstrates that we can automatically test the entire system. Remember, we have the whole system up, including a live MongoDB database (if you count an embedded one as being real). This verifies not only our own code, but our assumptions regarding what gets autoconfigured, autowired, and initialized.

As a culmination of testing nirvana, we can even grab screen snapshots to prove we were here. Or at least that our test case was here. That code is shown here:

```
private void takeScreenshot(String name) throws IOException {
  FileCopyUtils.copy(
    driver.getScreenshotAs(OutputType.FILE),
    new File("build/test-results/TEST-" + name + ".png"));
}
```

Snapping a screenshot can be explained as follows:

- `driver.getScreenshotAs(OutputType.FILE)` taps the `TakesScreenshot` subinterface to grab a snapshot of the screen and put it into a `temp` file
- Spring's `FileCopyUtils` utility method is used to copy that `temp` file into the project's `build/test-results` folder using the input argument to give it a custom name

Taking screenshots is a key reason to use either `ChromeDriver`, `FirefoxDriver`, or `SafariDriver`. All of these real-world browser integrations support this feature. And thanks to that, we have the following snapshot results:

That first shot shows the whole web page. The following screenshot shows a single image after being clicked:

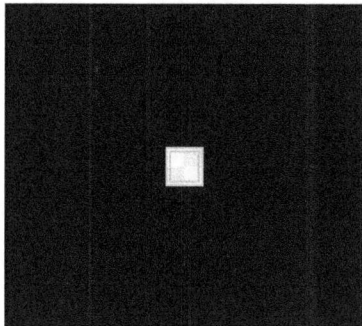

The screenshot of this image may look a little awkward, but remember; these images aren't real JPGs. Instead, they are strings stuffed into the filesystem.

If we run our entire suite of test cases, we can see the whole thing takes just shy of 2.5 seconds:

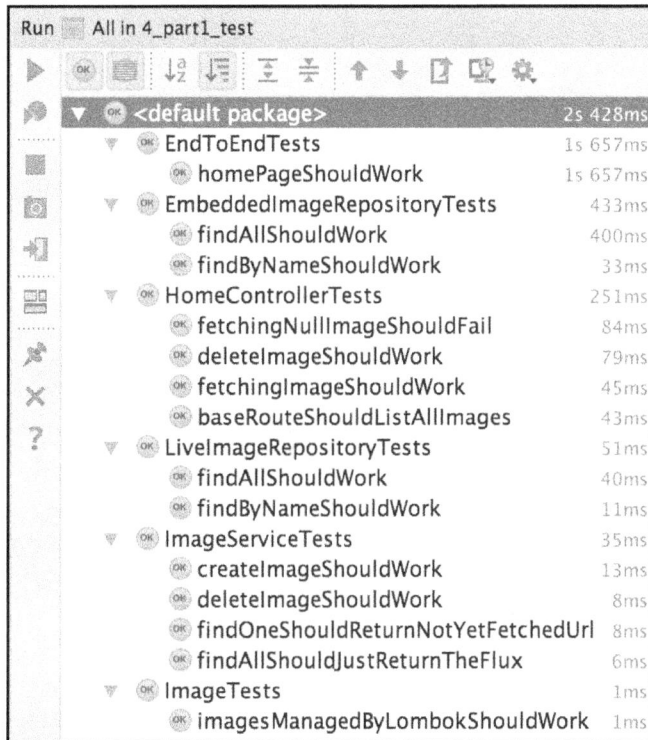

Impressive, huh?

How good a test suite is that? Using the IDE, we can run the same test suite but with coverage analysis turned on:

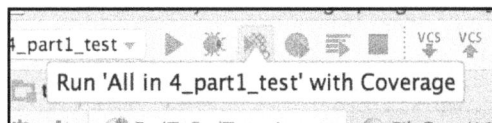

After running the same test suite but with the IDE's coverage tools enabled, we can get a read out in the source code listing, as seen in this screenshot:

```
▼ ☐ src
    ▼ ☐ main
        ▼ ☐ java 85% classes, 88% lines covered
            ▼ ☐ com.greglturnquist.learningspringboot 85% classes, 88% lines covered
                © ☐ ApiController 25% methods, 25% lines covered
                © ☐ HomeController 83% methods, 90% lines covered
                © ☐ Image 100% methods, 100% lines covered
                ① ☐ ImageRepository
                © ☐ ImageService 100% methods, 92% lines covered
                © ☐ InitDatabase 100% methods, 100% lines covered
                © ☐ LearningSpringBootApplication 0% methods, 33% lines covered
                © ☐ ReactiveThymeleafConfig 100% methods, 100% lines covered
```

That's quite handy. We can even drill into each class and see what's missing. As deft as this is, we aren't going to delve any more into test coverage. That's something best left to a more test-oriented book.

> **TIP**
>
> Don't let test coverage consume you. As mentioned in my other book, *Python Testing Cookbook,* in *Chapter 9* under the *Coverage isn't everything* section, the test coverage should be used to identify new, reasonable scenarios that should be checked out, not gaming the system to squeeze out another percentage point or two. And coverage reports should never be used to compare one system or test regimen against another, let alone be used as a gate for release. We should all seek to increase test coverage over time as the means to increase confidence and reduce risk, not as a gate to make releases.

We just mentioned all the ceremony invested into getting Chrome to operate. Why did we do that? Because the one `WebDriver` implementation that requires no such effort to bring online *doesn't support taking screenshots*. There is also no way of knowing if the person checking out your code has the same browser installed.

If we coded everything around Chrome because we don't like Firefox but another teammate doesn't have Chrome, we've got a problem.

On one hand, if screenshots aren't important, then `HtmlUnitDriver` is the way to go. It comes out of the box, works as good as any other `WebDriver`, and doesn't require any third-party executables or drivers. But that is the penalty of going by the least common denominator.

Wouldn't it be preferable to have *whatever* WebDriver we can get based on whatever we have installed on our system and automatically load that into our test case? After all, Spring Boot is about reducing Java complexity when building apps.

If you sense a slow walk toward a Spring Boot-oriented solution to this craziness, you're right. In the next section, we'll explore how to autoconfigure a WebDriver based on what's available and then we'll unit test that autoconfiguration policy.

Testing your custom Spring Boot autoconfiguration

If picking between several WebDriver implementations sounds hokey and unnecessarily complicated, then let's do what Spring Boot does best: autoconfigure it!

Okay, if we're going to autoconfigure something, we sure as heck want to *test* what we're doing. That way, we can make sure it performs as expected. To do so requires a little bit of test setup. Check it out:

```
public class WebDriverAutoConfigurationTests {
  private AnnotationConfigApplicationContext context;
  @After
  public void close() {
    if (this.context != null) {
      this.context.close();
    }
  }

  private void load(Class<?>[] configs, String... environment) {
    AnnotationConfigApplicationContext applicationContext =
      new AnnotationConfigApplicationContext();
    applicationContext
      .register(WebDriverAutoConfiguration.class);
    if (configs.length > 0) {
      applicationContext.register(configs);
    }
    EnvironmentTestUtils
      .addEnvironment(applicationContext, environment);
    applicationContext.refresh();
    this.context = applicationContext;
  }

  ...more coming later...
}
```

This preceding test case is set up as follows:

- It starts off very different from what we've seen up until now. Instead of using various Spring Boot test annotations, this one starts with nothing. That way, we can add only the bits of Boot that we want in a very fine-grained fashion.
- We'll use Spring's `AnnotationConfigApplicationContext` as the DI container of choice to programmatically register beans.
- The `@After` annotation flags the `close()` method to run after every test case and close the application context, ensuring the next test case has a clean start.
- `load()` will be invoked by each test method as part of its setup, accepting a list of Spring configuration classes as well as optional property settings, as it creates a new application context.
- `load()` then registers a `WebDriverAutoConfiguration` class (which we haven't written yet).
- After that, it registers any additional test configuration classes we wish.
- It then uses Spring Boot's `EnvironmentTestUtils` to add any configuration property settings we need to the application context. This is a convenient way to programmatically set properties without mucking around with files or system settings.
- It then uses the application context's `refresh()` function to create all the beans.
- Lastly, it assigns the application context to the test class's `context` field.

In this bit of code, we programmatically build up a Spring application context from scratch. In this test class, we register our brand new `WebDriverAutoConfiguration` class to be at the heart of all of our tests. Then we are free to run all kinds of test cases, ensuring it acts properly. We can even register different configuration classes to override any of the autoconfiguration beans.

Now let's noodle out our first test case. What's a good place to start? What if we were to disable all the browser-based `WebDriver` instances (like Firefox and Chrome), and instead, expect the thing to fall back to the universal `HtmlUnitDriver`? Let's try it:

```
@Test
public void fallbackToNonGuiModeWhenAllBrowsersDisabled() {
  load(new Class[]{},
    "com.greglturnquist.webdriver.firefox.enabled:false",
    "com.greglturnquist.webdriver.safari.enabled:false",
    "com.greglturnquist.webdriver.chrome.enabled:false");
```

```
WebDriver driver = context.getBean(WebDriver.class);
assertThat(ClassUtils.isAssignable(TakesScreenshot.class,
  driver.getClass())).isFalse();
assertThat(ClassUtils.isAssignable(HtmlUnitDriver.class,
  driver.getClass())).isTrue();
}
```

This test case can be explained as follows:

- `@Test` **marks** `fallbackToNonGuiModeWhenAllBrowsersDisabled` as a JUnit test method.
- To start things, it uses the `load()` method. Since we don't have any custom overrides, we supply it with an empty array of configuration classes. We also include a slew of properties, the first one being `com.greglturnquist.webdriver.firefox.enabled:false`. From a design perspective, it's nice to optionally exclude certain types, so having a well-qualified property (using a domain we own) and setting them all to false sounds like a good start.
- Now we can ask the application context to give us a `WebDriver` bean.
- If it bypassed all those browser-specific ones and landed on `HtmlUnitDriver`, then it shouldn't support the `TakesScreenshot` interface. We can verify that with the AssertJ `assertThat()` check, using Spring's `ClassUtils.isAssignable` check.
- To make it crystal clear that we're getting an `HtmlUnitDriver`, we can also write another check verifying that.

Since we aren't actually testing the guts of Selenium WebDriver, there is no need to examine the object anymore. We have what we want, an autoconfigured `WebDriver` that should operate well.

Having captured our first expected set of conditions, it's time to roll up our sleeves and get to work. We'll start by creating `WebDriverAutoConfiguration.java` as follows:

```
@Configuration
@ConditionalOnClass(WebDriver.class)
@EnableConfigurationProperties(
  WebDriverConfigurationProperties.class)
@Import({ChromeDriverFactory.class,
  FirefoxDriverFactory.class, SafariDriverFactory.class})
public class WebDriverAutoConfiguration {
    ...
}
```

This preceding Spring Boot autoconfiguration class can be described as follows:

- `@Configuration`: This indicates that this class is a source of beans' definitions. After all, that's what autoconfiguration classes do--create beans.
- `@ConditionalOnClass(WebDriver.class)`: This indicates that this configuration class will only be evaluated by Spring Boot if it detects `WebDriver` on the classpath, a telltale sign of Selenium WebDriver being part of the project.
- `@EnableConfigurationProperties(WebDriverConfigurationPrope rties.class)`: This activates a set of properties to support what we put into our test case. We'll soon see how to easily define a set of properties that get the rich support Spring Boot provides of overriding through multiple means.
- `@Import(...)`: This is used to pull in extra bean definition classes.

This class is now geared up for us to actually define some beans pursuant to creating a `WebDriver` instance. To get an instance, we can imagine going down a list and trying one such as Firefox. If it fails, move on to the next. If they all fail, resort to using `HtmlUnitDriver`.

The following class shows this perfectly:

```
@Primary
@Bean(destroyMethod = "quit")
@ConditionalOnMissingBean(WebDriver.class)
public WebDriver webDriver(
  FirefoxDriverFactory firefoxDriverFactory,
  SafariDriverFactory safariDriverFactory,
  ChromeDriverFactory chromeDriverFactory) {
    WebDriver driver = firefoxDriverFactory.getObject();

    if (driver == null) {
      driver = safariDriverFactory.getObject();
    }

    if (driver == null) {
      driver = chromeDriverFactory.getObject();
    }

    if (driver == null) {
      driver = new HtmlUnitDriver();
    }

    return driver;
}
```

This `WebDriver` creating code can be described as follows:

- `@Primary`: This indicates that this method should be given priority when someone is trying to autowire a `WebDriver` bean over any other method (as we'll soon see).
- `@Bean(destroyMethod = "quit")`: This flags the method as a Spring bean definition, but with the extra feature of invoking `WebDriver.quit()` when the application context shuts down.
- `@ConditionalOnMissingBean(WebDriver.class)`: This is a classic Spring Boot technique. It says to skip this method if there is already a defined `WebDriver` bean. HINT: There should be a test case to verify that Boot backs off properly!
- `webDriver()`: This expects three input arguments to be supplied by the application context--a `FirefoxDriver` factory, a `SafariDriver` factory, and a `ChromeDriver` factory. What is this for? It allows us to swap out `FirefoxDriver` with a mock for various test purposes. Since this doesn't affect the end user, this form of indirection is suitable.
- The code starts by invoking `firefoxDriver` using the `FirefoxDriver` factory. If null, it will try the next one. It will continue doing so until it reaches the bottom, with `HtmlUnitDriver` as the last choice. If it got a hit, these `if` clauses will be skipped and the `WebDriver` instance returned.

This laundry list of browsers to try out makes it easy to add new ones down the road should we wish to do so. But before we investigate, say `firefoxDriver()`, let's first look at `FirefoxDriverFactory`, the input parameter to that method:

```
class FirefoxDriverFactory implements ObjectFactory<FirefoxDriver>
{
    private WebDriverConfigurationProperties properties;

    FirefoxDriverFactory(WebDriverConfigurationProperties
properties)
    {
      this.properties = properties;
    }

    @Override
    public FirefoxDriver getObject() throws BeansException {
      if (properties.getFirefox().isEnabled()) {
        try {
          return new FirefoxDriver();
        } catch (WebDriverException e) {
          e.printStackTrace();
```

```
            // swallow the exception
        }
      }
      return null;
    }
}
```

This preceding driver factory can be described as follows:

- This class implements Spring's `ObjectFactory` for the type of `FirefoxDriver`. It provides the means to create the named type.
- With constructor injection, we load a copy of `WebDriverConfigurationProperties`.
- It implements the single method, `getObject()`, yielding a new `FirefoxDriver`.
- If the `firefox` property is enabled, it attempts to create a `FirefoxDriver`. If not, it skips the whole thing and returns null.

This factory uses the *old trick of try to create the object* to see if it exists. If successful, it returns it. If not, it swallows the exception and returns a null. This same tactic is used to implement a `SafariDriver` bean and a `ChromeDriver` bean. Since the code is almost identical, it's not shown here.

Why do we need this factory again? Because later in this chapter when we wish to prove it will create such an item, we don't want the test case to require installing Firefox to work properly. Thus, we'll supply a mocked solution. Since this doesn't impact the end user receiving the autoconfigured `WebDriver`, it's perfectly fine to use such machinery.

Notice how we used `properties.getFirefox().isEnabled()` to decide whether or not we would try? That was provided by our `com.greglturnquist.webdriver.firefox.enabled` property setting. To create a set of properties that Spring Boot will let consumers override as needed, we need to create a `WebDriverConfigurationProperties` class like this:

```
@Data
@ConfigurationProperties("com.greglturnquist.webdriver")
public class WebDriverConfigurationProperties {

  private Firefox firefox = new Firefox();
  private Safari safari = new Safari();
  private Chrome chrome = new Chrome();

  @Data
```

```
static class Firefox {
  private boolean enabled = true;
}

@Data
static class Safari {
  private boolean enabled = true;
}

@Data
static class Chrome {
  private boolean enabled = true;
}
}
```

This last property-based class can be described as follows:

- `@Data` is the Lombok annotation that saves us from creating getters and setters.
- `@ConfigurationProperties("com.greglturnquist.webdriver")` marks this class as a source for property values with `com.greglturnquist.webdriver` as the prefix.
- Every field (`firefox`, `safari`, and `chrome`) is turned into a separately named property.
- Because we want to nest subproperties, we have `Firefox`, `Safari`, and `Chrome`, each with an `enabled` Boolean property defaulted to `True`.
- Each of these subproperty classes again uses Lombok's `@Data` annotation to simplify their definition.

> It's important to point out that the name of the property class, `WebDriverConfigurationProperties`, and the names of the subclasses such as `Firefox` are not important. The prefix is set by `@ConfigurationProperties`, and the individual properties use the field's name to define themselves.

With this class, it's easy to inject this strongly typed POJO into any Spring-managed bean and access the settings.

At this stage, our first test case, `fallbackToNonGuiModeWhenAllBrowsersDisabled`, should be operational. We can test it out.

Assuming we verified it, we can now code another test, verifying that
`FirefoxDriver` is created under the right circumstances. Let's start by defining our
test case. We can start by deliberately disabling the other choices:

```
@Test
public void testWithMockedFirefox() {
  load(new Class[]{MockFirefoxConfiguration.class},
    "com.greglturnquist.webdriver.safari.enabled:false",
    "com.greglturnquist.webdriver.chrome.enabled:false");
  WebDriver driver = context.getBean(WebDriver.class);
  assertThat(ClassUtils.isAssignable(TakesScreenshot.class,
    driver.getClass())).isTrue();
  assertThat(ClassUtils.isAssignable(FirefoxDriver.class,
    driver.getClass())).isTrue();
}
```

This preceding test case is easily described as follows:

- `@Test` marks `testWithMockedFirefox` as a JUnit test method
- `load` is used to add `MockFirefoxConfiguration`, a configuration class
  we'll soon write to help us mock out the creation of a real `FirefoxDriver`
- We also disable Chrome and Safari using the property settings
- Fetching a `WebDriver` from the application context, we verify that it
  implements the `TakesScreenshot` interface and is actually a
  `FirefoxDriver` class

As one can imagine, this is tricky. We can't assume the developer has the Firefox
browser installed. Hence, we can never create a real `FirefoxDriver`. To make this
possible, we need to introduce a little indirection. When Spring encounters multiple
bean definition methods, the last one wins. So, by adding another config class,
`MockFirefoxConfiguration`, we can sneak in and change how our default factory
works.

The following class shows how to do this:

```
@Configuration
protected static class MockFirefoxConfiguration {
  @Bean
  FirefoxDriverFactory firefoxDriverFactory() {
    FirefoxDriverFactory factory =
        mock(FirefoxDriverFactory.class);
    given(factory.getObject())
        .willReturn(mock(FirefoxDriver.class));
```

```
        return factory;
    }
}
```

The previous class can be described as follows:

- @Configuration marks this class as a source of bean definitions.
- @Bean shows that we are creating a FirefoxDriverFactory bean, the same type pulled into the top of our WebDriverAutoConfiguration class via the @Import annotation. This means that this bean definition will overrule the one we saw earlier.
- We use Mockito to create a mock FirefoxDriverFactory.
- We instruct this mock factory to create a mock FirefoxDriver when it's factory method is invoked.
- We return the factory, so it can be used to run the actual test case.

With this code, we are able to verify things work pretty well. There is a slight bit of hand waving. The alternative would be to figure out the means to *ensure* every browser was installed. Including the executables in our test code for every platform and running them all, may yield a little more confidence. But at what price? It could possibly violate the browser's license. Ensuring that every platform is covered, just for a test case, is a bit extreme. So, all in all, this test case hedges such a risk adequately by avoiding all that extra ceremony.

It's left as an exercise for the reader to explore creating Safari and Chrome factories along with their corresponding test cases.

If we run all the test cases in WebDriverAutoConfigurationTests, what can we hope to find?

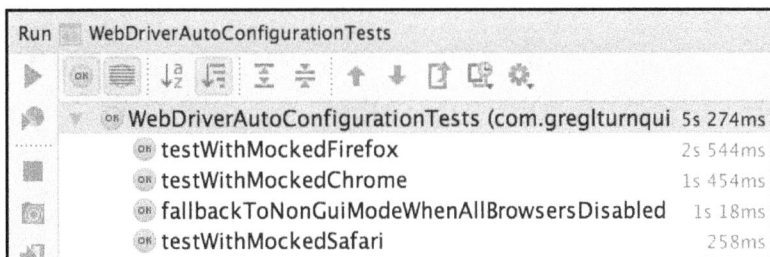

Using Spring Boot and Spring Framework test modules along with JUnit and Flapdoodle, we have managed to craft an autoconfiguration policy for Selenium WebDriver with a complete suite of test methods. This makes it possible for us to release our own third-party autoconfiguration module that autoconfigures Selenium WebDriver.

So what have we covered? Unit tests, MongoDB-oriented slice tests, WebFlux-oriented slice tests, full container end-to-end tests, and even autoconfiguration tests.

This is a nice collection of tests that should deliver confidence to any team. And Spring Boot made it quite easy to execute.

Summary

In this chapter, we crafted unit tests using JUnit and AssertJ. Then we performed slice-based tests against MongoDB using Spring Boot's `@DataMongoTest` annotation, with and without embedded MongoDB. We tested WebFlux controllers, ensuring they operated correctly. We also wrote end-to-end tests with Spring Boot spinning up an entire embedded web container so that Selenium WebDriver could drive it from the browser. Finally, we put together an autoconfiguration policy for Selenium WebDriver using test-first practices to verify that it worked.

In the next chapter, we will explore the developer tools provided by Spring Boot to ease the tasks we all must deal with.

14
Developer Tools for Spring Boot Apps

I owe @springboot a lot. #productivity #engineering #sota #minimalist #microservices #performance #quality #bestpractises

– Amir Sedighi @amirsedighi

In the previous chapter, you learned how to use Spring Boot's various testing features. We saw how to craft simple unit tests, slice tests, mock WebFlux tests, and even fully spun-up embedded Netty integration tests.

When we get into the swing of things, anything that can bend the curve of time spent building an app is appreciated. We will explore the various tools Spring Boot brings to the table to help us hack away at our applications.

In this chapter, we will do the following:

- Using Spring Boot's DevTools for hot code reloading and decaching
- Glean what Spring Boot did with its autoconfiguration report
- Make local changes and see them on the target system
- Write a custom health check
- Add build data to the `/application/info` endpoint
- Create custom metrics

Using Spring Boot's DevTools for hot code reloading

Developers are *always* looking for ways to speed things up. Long ago, one of the biggest speedups was incremental compilers and having them run every time we saved a file. Now that it's permeated modern tools, no one thinks twice about such a feature.

Something critically needed when it comes to building Spring Boot apps is the ability to detect a change in our code and relaunch the embedded container.

Thankfully, we just need one addition to our code we built in the previous chapter:

```
compile("org.springframework.boot:spring-boot-devtools")
```

> If you happen to be using Maven, you would want to include the `optional` flag.

So, this tiny module performs the following activities:

- Disables cache settings for autoconfigured components
- When it detects a change in code, it restarts the application, holding onto third-party classes and simply throwing away and reloading custom classes
- Activates an embedded **LiveReload** (http://livereload.com/) server that can trigger the browser to refresh the page automatically

For a listing of all the disabled components, look at the following code snippet:

```
properties.put("spring.thymeleaf.cache", "false");
properties.put("spring.freemarker.cache", "false");
properties.put("spring.groovy.template.cache", "false");
properties.put("spring.mustache.cache", "false");
properties.put("server.session.persistent", "true");
properties.put("spring.h2.console.enabled", "true");
properties.put("spring.resources.cache-period", "0");
properties.put("spring.resources.chain.cache", "false");
```

```
properties.put("spring.template.provider.cache", "false");
properties.put("spring.mvc.log-resolved-exception", "true");
properties.put("server.servlet.jsp.init-parameters.development",
 "true");
properties.put("spring.reactor.stacktrace-mode.enabled", "true");
```

> **TIP**
>
> Many IDEs also come with additional reloading support when apps are run in the debug mode, a highly recommended option to use in conjunction with Spring Boot DevTools.

What is the net benefit, you ask?

When we make a change to our code and either issue a **Save** or a **Make Project**, DevTools will throw away the class loader holding our custom code and launch a new application context. This makes for a relatively speedy restart.

> **TIP**
>
> Save or Make Project? Spring Boot DevTools listens for file updates. For certain IDEs, such as Eclipse, ⌘-S is used to perform a **Save** operation. IntelliJ IDEA autosaves, so an alternative signal is Make Project, ⌘-F9, which refreshes the environment.

With the LiveReload server running and a LiveReload plugin (http://livereload.com/extensions/) installed in our browser, we can enable LiveReloading upon visiting the site. Anytime we update the code, the plugin will essentially click the browser's refresh button for us.

> **Restarting** versus **reloading**: DevTools provides the ability to restart the application quickly, but it is limited in various ways. For example, updating the classpath by adding new dependencies is not picked up. Adding new classes isn't supported. For more sophisticated tools that handle these complex use cases, you may wish to investigate something such as Spring Loaded (https://github.com/spring-projects/spring-loaded) or JRebel (http://zeroturnaround.com/software/jrebel/).

With all these caches cleared out, we can see changes propagate much faster. Let's test it out by launching `LearningSpringBootApplication` in the debug mode. If we visit the site, things look as expected:

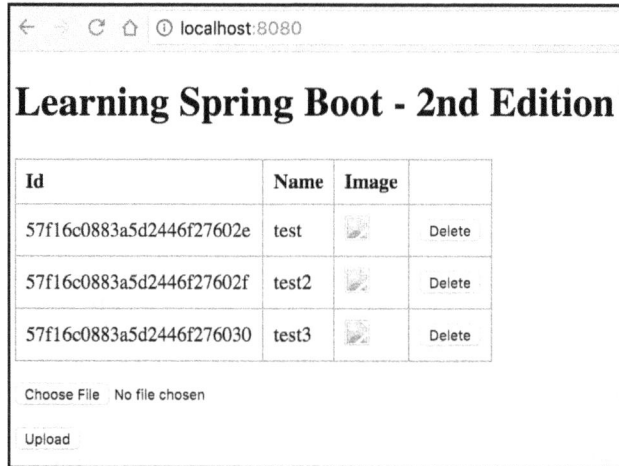

The site starts off with our pre-loaded test data. To have the browser listen for updates, we need to click the LiveReload icon:

At first, the dot in the center is hollow. When enabled, the dot turns solid, as shown in the preceding screenshot.

Let's make some edits to our template:

```
<body>

    <h1>Learning Spring Boot - 2nd Edition</h1>
    <h3>Using the LiveReload plugin in your browser will speed up efforts.</h3>
```

With this extra sub-header, we just need to hit Save or Make Project in our IDE. Switching to the browser will show the results instantly:

> ## Learning Spring Boot - 2nd Edition
>
> **Using the LiveReload plugin in your browser will speed up efforts.**

Let's make some tweaks to `HomeController` as shown here:

```
@GetMapping("/")
public Mono<String> index(Model model) {
  model.addAttribute("images",
    imageService.findAllImages());
  model.addAttribute("extra",
    "DevTools can also detect code changes too");
  return Mono.just("index");
}
```

This is the same as the previous chapter, except that we have added a new attribute, `extra`, to the model. We can display it with an adjustment to our template:

```
<h4 th:text="${extra}"></h4>
```

This displays the new `extra` model attribute as an H4 header, all without clicking a thing in our browser:

> ## Learning Spring Boot - 2nd Edition
>
> **Using the LiveReload plugin in your browser will speed up efforts.**
>
> **DevTools can also detect code changes too**

There is one key side effect when using Spring Boot DevTools for restarts-- any in-memory data or state will be lost.

That can be good or bad. It certainly encourages you to create a pre-loader, perhaps with a `@Profile("dev")` annotation such that it only runs when `spring.profiles.active=dev` is switched on.

This can become an issue if our use case takes a lot of steps to set up, and restarting the app makes us repeat these steps again and again. This is amplified by in-memory database solutions such as H2. In our situation, the start-up code that cleans out the uploaded files will cause a similar refresh of data.

Another reason to consider NOT switching on LiveReload in the browser (yet let the app restart) is if we are working on a JavaScript-heavy frontend and don't want every change to force a reload. For example, we might have a page with a lot of fields filled out. A triggered restart may clean out our form and force us to re-enter the data.

Nevertheless, this is a good problem to have. Having the option to refresh the browser and stay in sync with code changes is a powerful tool.

Using Spring Boot's autoconfiguration report

As we've seen in this book so far, Spring Boot autoconfigures beans to help us avoid configuring infrastructure and instead focus on coding business requirements. However, sometimes, we may want to know *what* Spring Boot did (or didn't) do for us.

That's why it has an **autoconfiguration report**. Essentially, every time a bean is selected based on some conditional check, Spring Boot logs the decision (yea or nay) and offers it to us in many different ways.

The simplest approach is to add --debug to the run configuration. In the following screenshot, we can see how to set it in IntelliJ:

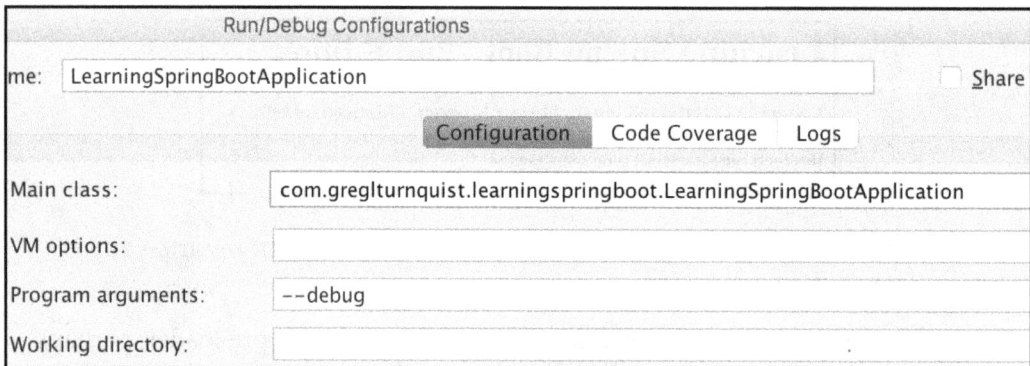

Run/Debug Configurations			
me: LearningSpringBootApplication			□ Share
	Configuration	Code Coverage	Logs
Main class:	com.greglturnquist.learningspringboot.LearningSpringBootApplication		
VM options:			
Program arguments:	--debug		
Working directory:			

If we launch our app with --debug as a program argument, an autoconfiguration report is printed out to the console:

```
2016-09-30 14:57:52.106 DEBUG 50763 --- [  restartedMain] o.s.b.a.e.jmx.Endpo
2016-09-30 14:57:52.128 DEBUG 50763 --- [  restartedMain] utoConfigurationRep


===========================
AUTO-CONFIGURATION REPORT
===========================


Positive matches:
-----------------

    AuditAutoConfiguration#auditListener matched
      - @ConditionalOnMissingBean (types: org.springframework.boot.actuate.au

    AuditAutoConfiguration.AuditEventRepositoryConfiguration matched
      - @ConditionalOnMissingBean (types: org.springframework.boot.actuate.au
```

That's nice, and during certain failure scenarios, the report will print out automatically to help with postmortem analysis. However, scraping the console for a report isn't very effective.

If we use **Spring Boot Actuator**, we can consume this report in a nicer JSON structure. If you'll recall, we included **Actuator** in our list of dependencies back in Chapter 10, *Quick Start with Java*:

```
compile('org.springframework.boot:spring-boot-starter-actuator')
```

> If you're building a new application and *didn't* pick it on
> http://start.spring.io, this dependency is quite valuable.

In addition to adding Spring Boot's Actuator module, we have to *opt in* or rather enable its features. In Spring Boot 2.0, Actuator supports many technologies including Spring MVC, Spring WebFlux, and JMX. We have to signal what platforms we wish to enable instead of expecting Spring Boot to guess. To do so, we need to add the following line of code to our application.properties file:

endpoints.default.web.enabled=true

This will make Actuator's endpoints active from an HTTP perspective; (to enable Actuator for JMX, we would want to set endpoints.default.jmx.enabled to true).

When we launch our application, several Spring WebFlux endpoints are added, providing additional information. To get a quick glance at all the available endpoints, we can visit `http://localhost:8080/application`, as shown in the following screenshot:

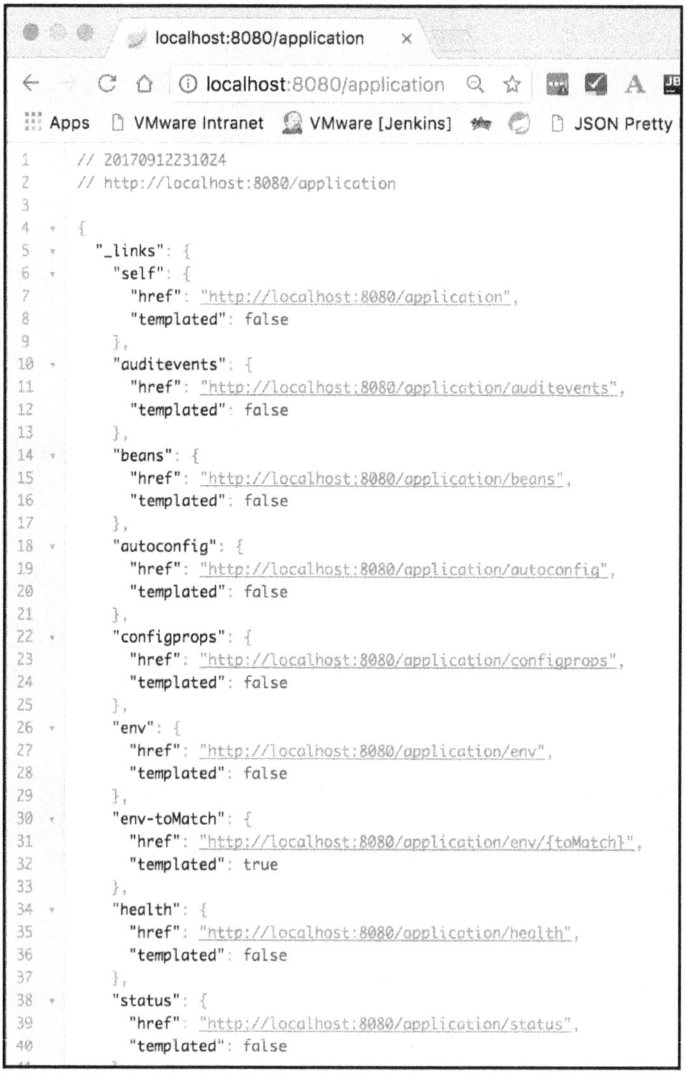

This screenshot doesn't capture them all, but there is a long list of endpoints serving up detailed information about our application. (By the way, earlier in the book, we enabled just one actuator endpoint, `/application/health`. This flag lets us switch on all the default endpoints.)

From there, we can easily find the autoconfiguration report at `http://localhost:8080/application/autoconfig`, click on it, and thanks to JSON Viewer (`https://github.com/tulios/json-viewer`), see this nicely formatted report:

Okay, so we've seen a couple ways to generate this report. But what does it *say*?

If we zoom into one fragment, we can figure something out:

```
"ReactiveWebServerConfiguration.ReactorNettyAutoConfiguration": [
  {
    "condition": "OnClassCondition",
    "message": "@ConditionalOnClass found required class
    'reactor.ipc.netty.http.server.HttpServer';
    @ConditionalOnMissingClass did not find unwanted class"
  },
  {
    "condition": "OnBeanCondition",
    "message": "@ConditionalOnMissingBean (types:
      org.springframework.boot.web.reactive
```

```
        .server.ReactiveWebServerFactory; SearchStrategy: all) did
        not find any beans"
}
]
```

This fragment of JSON in the autoconfiguration report can be described as follows:

- `ReactiveWebServerConfiguration.ReactorNettyAutoConfigurati on` is a Spring Boot autoconfiguration policy that was evaluated, specifically on the subject of Netty.
- `@ConditionalOnClass` matched on spotting Reactor's `HttpServer` class, glue code used by Reactor to embed the Netty container. This shows that Netty was on the classpath.
- `@ConditionalOnMissingBean` is the second condition, and was negative, indicating there is no overriding, user-defined `ReactiveWebServerFactory` defined. Therefore, Spring Boot is activating its default policy for Reactor Netty.

To divine exactly what this autoconfiguration policy was, we can open the code and inspect it ourselves. Using our IDE, we merely need to look for the parent class, `ReactiveWebServerConfiguration`:

```
abstract class ReactiveWebServerConfiguration {

  @ConditionalOnMissingBean(ReactiveWebServerFactory.class)
  @ConditionalOnClass({ HttpServer.class })
  static class ReactorNettyAutoConfiguration {

    @Bean
    public NettyReactiveWebServerFactory
     NettyReactiveWebServerFactory() {
        return new NettyReactiveWebServerFactory();
    }

  }
  ...
}
```

This fragment from Spring Boot's Reactive web server configuration code can be explained as follows:

- `ReactiveWebServerConfiguration` is an abstract class that is merely used as a container for other policies

- `@ConditionalOnMissingBean(ReactiveWebServerFactory.class)` tells Spring Boot to back off and not use this if the user has declared such a bean elsewhere
- `@ConditionalOnClass({HttpServer.class})` tells Spring Boot to only consider this if Reactor Netty is on the classpath
- `static class ReactorNettyAutoConfiguration` names this rule used to autoconfigure Reactor Netty
- `@Bean` flags the code as a Spring bean
- `return new NettyReactiveWebServerFactory()` actually creates the Spring bean for Reactor Netty

All this comes together to allow Reactor Netty to be configured automatically when put on the classpath. And we spotted it in the autoconfiguration report.

> There are other bean definitions in `ReactiveWebServerConfiguration`, including support for Jetty, Apache Tomcat, and Undertow, but aren't shown due to space constraints.

What is this good for?

If we are attempting to use some feature of Spring Boot and it's not going as desired, one thing to debug is whether or not the expected beans are being created. Another usage is if we are working on our own autoconfiguration module for a given project and need to see if the right beans are being created.

You see, the autoconfiguration report isn't confined to what is released by the Spring team. It looks at *everything*.

Speaking of making a change, notice how we have Netty running under the hood. We can tell both from the console output as well as the autoconfiguration report we just looked at.

What if we wanted to change containers? It's quite easy with Spring Boot. We simply have to tweak the build file.

By default, Spring Boot uses Netty for Reactive apps, but it's not hard to switch:

```
compile('org.springframework.boot:spring-boot-starter-webflux') {
  exclude module: 'spring-boot-starter-reactor-netty'
}
compile('org.springframework.boot:spring-boot-starter-undertow')
```

The changes to `build.gradle` are as follows:

- Excludes `spring-boot-starter-reactor-netty` from the reactive web dependency
- Introduces `spring-boot-starter-undertow` as an alternative container

If we relaunch our application and look at the autoconfiguration report again and look for the `ReactorNettyAutoConfiguration` entry, we will find this:

```
"ReactiveWebServerConfiguration.ReactorNettyAutoConfiguration": {
  "notMatched": [
    {
      "condition": "OnClassCondition",
      "message": "@ConditionalOnClass did not find required class
      'reactor.ipc.netty.http.server.HttpServer'"
    }
  ],
  "matched": [

  ]
}
```

The new fragment of JSON from the autoconfiguration report shows that the same policy we just looked at has now switched to `notMatched`. In the details, it failed because `@ConditionalOnClass` didn't spot `HttpServer` on the classpath.

In light of switching from Reactor Netty to Undertow, searching for `Undertow` in the autoconfiguration report will lead us to this:

```
"ReactiveWebServerConfiguration.UndertowAutoConfiguration": [
  {
    "condition": "OnClassCondition",
    "message": "@ConditionalOnClass found required class
    'io.undertow.Undertow'; @ConditionalOnMissingClass did not
     find unwanted class"
  },
  {
    "condition": "OnBeanCondition",
    "message": "@ConditionalOnMissingBean (types:
    org.springframework.boot.web.reactive.server
    .ReactiveWebServerFactory; SearchStrategy: all) did not
     find any beans"
  }
]
```

This fragment of JSON reveals that `UndertowAutoConfiguration` is now in effect as follows:

- `@ConditionalOnClass` has found `Undertow` on the classpath
- `@ConditionalOnMissingBean` has not found a user-defined `ReactiveWebServerFactory` bean; hence, Spring Boot did not back off with its autoconfiguration of Undertow.

On further digging into `UndertowReactiveWebServerFactory`, we will find all the details needed to run Undertow for a Reactor-based application.

Making local changes and seeing them on the target system

So far, we've seen how to speed up developer time by using automatic restarts, and we have gathered information on what Spring Boot is up to, courtesy of its autoconfiguration report.

The next step for developers is often using the debugger of their IDE. We won't go into profuse detail about that because it's highly specific to which IDE you use. However, something of extended value offered by Spring Boot is the opportunity to remotely connect to an application and make changes.

Imagine we have built up our application and pushed it to the cloud. We test a key feature in this environment because it's the only way to tie it to a particular resource or in a certain configuration. Well, the process for making changes is much more expensive. We would have to bundle things up, redeploy, restart, and re-navigate. All for a few lines of code!

Spring Boot's DevTools provide the means to connect our IDE to our remotely running application and push code changes over the wire, allowing us to automatically make mods and test them immediately.

To get geared up, we must execute the following steps:

1. Add `spring.devtools.remote.secret=learning-spring-boot` to `application.properties`.
2. Build the application using `./gradlew build`.

3. Push the application to the cloud (Pivotal Web Services in this case with `cf push learning-spring-boot -p build/libs/learning-spring-boot-0.0.1-SNAPSHOT.jar`).

4. Instead of running the app locally in our IDE, run Spring Boot's `RemoteSpringApplication` class instead.

5. Add `https://learning-spring-boot.cfapps.io` (or whatever the app's remote URL is) as a program argument.

5. Launch the `RemoteSpringApplication` configured runner.

The following screenshot shows how to configure it in IntelliJ IDEA:

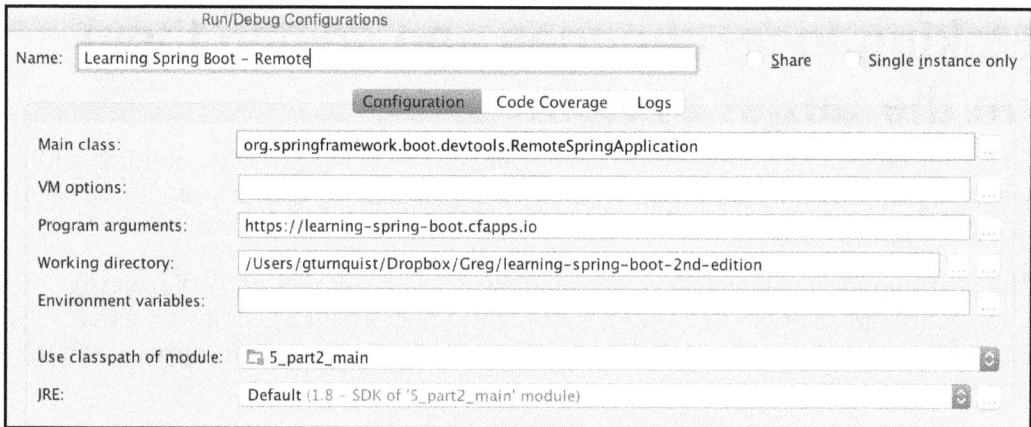

After it launches, the console in our IDE shows a remote banner:

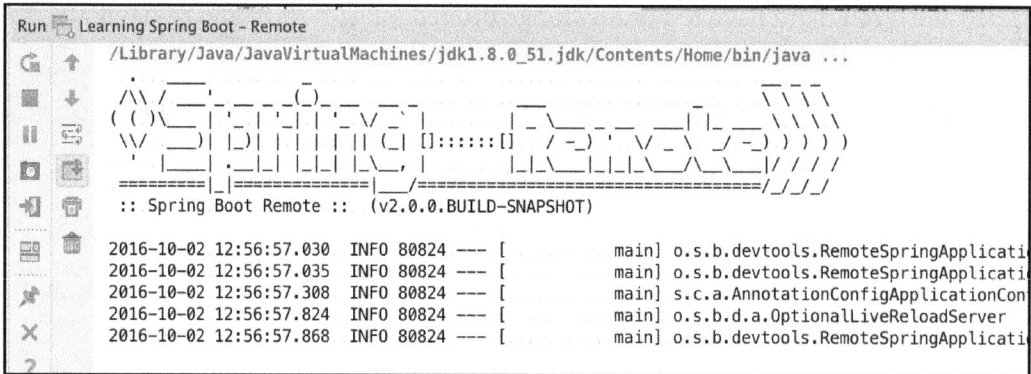

Now, we are free to make changes in our IDE, Save/Make Project, and watch them propagate to our cloud-based app running at `https://learning-spring-boot.cfapps.io`.

First of all, let's tweak our template at `src/main/resources/templates/index.html`. We can add a sub-header below the main header similar to what we did earlier in this chapter:

```
<h1>Learning Spring Boot - 2nd Edition</h1>

<h2>It's really handy to make local edits and watch them go out
  to the cloud automatically</h2>

<h4 th:text="${extra}"></h4>
```

Hitting Save or Make Project, the code change will be uploaded to the cloud and trigger a restart (this is a great opportunity to use the LiveReload server and automatically refresh the page):

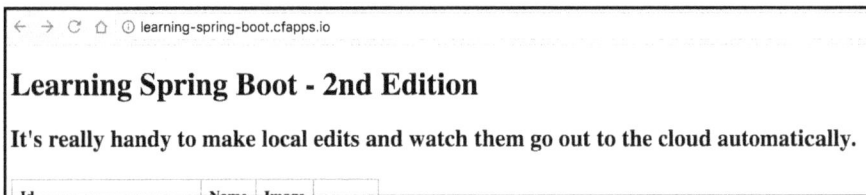

With this flow, we can make all sorts of changes. When ready, we can commit them locally, build a newer JAR file, push to the cloud, and continue forward.

> It's *always* recommended to use `https://` when connecting to a remote application. It prevents other users from snooping the network for secrets.

> Enabling Spring Boot DevTools on a remote application is a risk. The only thing protecting the application from code updates is the simple secret the two share. You should never enable this on a production deployment.

Writing a custom health check

Another critical feature needed when we take our application to production is monitoring it. In the olden days, people would set up a CRON job to ping a server and see if it was up. More intricate systems would track disk usage, memory usage, and ideally page someone when the database was at 95%, so it could be saved before falling over.

Spring Boot provides a new era in health check monitoring. To kick things off, launch the application and visit `/application/health`:

```
{
    status: "UP",
    diskSpace: {
        status: "UP",
        total: 498937626624,
        free: 96519303168,
        threshold: 10485760
    },
    mongo: {
        status: "UP",
        version: "3.4.6"
    }
}
```

Out of the box, this provides us with an endpoint we can ping and additionally, gives us some information regarding disk space. It also includes an automatically included MongoDB health check.

But what if we needed to write our own health check? Perhaps, there is a system we are dependent upon. Knowing if this upstream service is unavailable could prove valuable.

To write our own health check, we merely need to write a Spring component that implements Spring Boot's `HealthIndicator` interface:

```
@Component
public class LearningSpringBootHealthIndicator
  implements HealthIndicator {

    @Override
    public Health health() {
      try {
        URL url =
          new URL("http://greglturnquist.com/books/learning-spring-
            boot");
```

```
        HttpURLConnection conn =
          (HttpURLConnection) url.openConnection();
        int statusCode = conn.getResponseCode();
        if (statusCode >= 200 && statusCode < 300) {
          return Health.up().build();
        } else {
            return Health.down()
              .withDetail("HTTP Status Code", statusCode)
              .build();
        }
      } catch (IOException e) {
        return Health.down(e).build();
      }
    }
  }
}
```

Let's dissect this custom health indicator:

- `@Component` marks this class so that Spring Boot picks it up and registers it automatically.
- By implementing the `HealthIndicator` interface, Spring Boot will include it along with the pre-built health checks when we hit `/application/health`.
- The name `LearningSpringBootHealthIndicator` is used to create the indicator. `HealthIndicator` will be trimmed off, and the remaining text will be formatted with lazy camel style.
- There is but one method in this interface (meaning you *could* implement it using a Java 8 lambda), `health()`. It uses some plain old Java APIs to open a connection to a remote URL and fetch a status code. If the status code is good, it will build a `Health` status code of `UP`. Otherwise, it will build a `Health` status code of `DOWN` while also giving us the failed HTTP status code.
- Finally, if any other exceptions occur, we will also get a `Health` status code of `DOWN` but with the information from the exception instead of a commonly coded error path.

Let's relaunch the application and see what our `/application/health` endpoint reports:

```
{
  "status": "UP",
  "details": {
    "mongo": {
      "status": "UP",
```

```
        "details": {
          "version": "3.4.6"
        }
      },
      "diskSpace": {
        "status": "UP",
        "details": {
          "total": 498937626624,
          "free": 43632435200,
          "threshold": 10485760
        }
      },
      "learningSpringBoot": {
        "status": "UP"
      }
    }
  }
}
```

We can see our new health indicator, `learningSpringBoot`, listed with its status of
UP.

To simulate a failure, let's alter the URL by switching the domain in the code to
`greglturnquist.io` and see what happens:

```
URL url = new URL("http://greglturnquist.io/books/learning-spring-
boot");
```

When we restart and ping `/application/health`, this is the outcome:

```
{
  "status": "DOWN",
  "details": {
    "mongo": {
      "status": "UP",
      "details": {
        "version": "3.4.6"
      }
    },
    "diskSpace": {
      "status": "UP",
      "details": {
        "total": 498937626624,
        "free": 43629961216,
        "threshold": 10485760
      }
    },
    "learningSpringBoot": {
      "status": "DOWN",
```

```
        "details": {
            "error": "java.net.UnknownHostException:
greglturnquist.io"
            }
        }
    }
}
```

A few things have happened:

- Our `learningSpringBoot` indicator now reports `DOWN`. It's not due to some HTTP status code, but instead `ConnectionException` caused by not being able to form a connection.
- While `diskSpace` and `mongo` are `UP`, the `DOWN` status of this indicator percolates to the top-level status, switching it to `DOWN`.

If we change the URL to simply `http://greglturnquist.com/foo` and restart, we can see a different status:

In this situation, we still have a DOWN status, but the HTTP status code 404 is reported. Both of these indicators can be quite informative for the DevOps team watching our application.

Adding build data to /application/info

One of the biggest issues in getting to the heart of problems is knowing what version is running! Have you ever gotten a 3:00 a.m. call from a customer reporting that the system is broken? In a half-awake state, it's easy to start trying to solve the problem only to discover two hours later, the customer is running an older version and that their issue was patched last week.

The solution is embedding precise versions in every release so that the customer can relay this over the phone. Then, we can quickly figure out if this issue is new, fixed, or a regression. Interested?

Just add this to the `build.gradle` file, right below the `buildscripts` section:

```
id "com.gorylenko.gradle-git-properties" version "1.4.17"
```

This will add a new task, `generateGitProperties`, to our system. Anytime we engage Gradle to build the app, whether it's to package up a runnable JAR or simply to bootRun it, a new `build/resources/main/git.properties` file will be generated and served up via Spring Boot Actuator's `/application/info` endpoint:

```
{
    git: {
        commit: {
            time: 1474434957000,
            id: "3ac9c1c"
        },
        branch: "master"
    }
}
```

This report gives us the timestamp, git commit hash, and branch. That tiny nugget of knowledge has the potential to save us *hours* of effort over the long haul.

Using Maven? There is a similar plugin:

```
<build>
    <plugins>
        <plugin>
            <groupId>pl.project13.maven</groupId>
```

```
        <artifactId>git-commit-id-plugin</artifactId>
      </plugin>
    </plugins>
  </build>
```

It works the same.

One extra tidbit--Spring Boot has two different modes of git information. The format shown is the **SIMPLE** mode. To get more details, add this to `application.properties`:

```
management.info.git.mode=full
```

This will produce a much more detailed report:

```
{
    git: {
        commit: {
            message: {
                full: "Move images back to 1/image",
                short: "Move images back to 1/image"
            },
            time: 1474434957000,
            id: "3ac9c1c7875d7378d6fbd607d0af5ef206e21ede",
            id.abbrev: "3ac9c1c",
            user: {
                email: "gturnquist@pivotal.io",
                name: "Greg Turnquist"
            }
        },
        branch: "master"
    }
}
```

It's up to each team to decide which version is the most useful and which version doesn't leak out unnecessary details.

Additionally, we can grab more details about the build by adding this to our `build.gradle` file:

```
springBoot {
  buildInfo()
}
```

This little addition, when we run Gradle's `build` task, will add a `build-info.properties` file to our JAR file, showing content like this:

```
#Properties
#Tue Sep 12 23:53:05 CDT 2017
build.time=2017-09-12T23:53:05-0500
build.artifact=5/part2
build.group=learning-spring-boot
build.name=5/part2
build.version=unspecified
```

Both of these reports (a simple git report + build info details) would give us this nice bit of information useful to start debugging an issue by visiting `localhost:8080/application/info`.

Creating custom metrics

Every program manager loves metrics. In fact, a popular company (Netflix) is so well known in this arena that people describe it as a metrics-gathering company that happens to stream video.

When it comes to Spring Boot, metrics are a prime piece of **Spring Boot Actuator** functionality. If we visit `/application/metrics`, we can see a list of metrics:

```
{
  "names": [
    "jvm.buffer.memory.used",
    "jvm.memory.used",
    "jvm.buffer.count",
    "logback.events",
    "process.uptime",
    "jvm.memory.committed",
    "http.server.requests",
    "jvm.buffer.total.capacity",
    "jvm.memory.max",
    "process.starttime"
  ]
}
```

This lists all sorts of stuff--memory, garbage collection, heap versus nonheap, threads, and more. That's nice, but what's usually needed is the ability to create our own metrics.

Spring Boot provides an interface to register our own metrics and have them appear on the same page. Supplied immediately is the ability to grab a `MeterRegistry`.

To make use of this three meter registry, we need to inject it into `ImageService` we built in `Chapter 12`, *Reactive Data Access with Spring Boot*:

```
@Service
public class ImageService {

    ...

    private final MeterRegistry meterRegistry;

    public ImageService(ResourceLoader resourceLoader,
        ImageRepository imageRepository,
        MeterRegistry meterRegistry) {

        this.resourceLoader = resourceLoader;
        this.imageRepository = imageRepository;
        this.meterRegistry = meterRegistry;
    }
    ...
```

This code shows the following:

- Three metric services, `CounterService`, `GaugeService`, and `InMemoryMetricRepository` declared as final attributes
- These three fields are populated by **constructor injection**, ensuring they are supplied when the service is created

With that in place, further down inside `createImage`, we can define custom metrics:

```
public Mono<Void> createImage(Flux<FilePart> files) {
  return files
    .log("createImage-files")
    .flatMap(file -> {
      Mono<Image> saveDatabaseImage = imageRepository.save(
        new Image(
          UUID.randomUUID().toString(),
          file.filename()))
          .log("createImage-save");
```

```
Mono<Void> copyFile = Mono.just(Paths.get(UPLOAD_ROOT,
file.filename()).toFile())
.log("createImage-picktarget")
.map(destFile -> {
  try {
    destFile.createNewFile();
    return destFile;
  } catch (IOException e) {
      throw new RuntimeException(e);
  }
})
.log("createImage-newfile")
.flatMap(file::transferTo)
.log("createImage-copy");

Mono<Void> countFile = Mono.fromRunnable(() -> {
  meterRegistry
    .summary("files.uploaded.bytes")
    .record(Paths.get(UPLOAD_ROOT,
    file.filename()).toFile().length())
});

return Mono.when(saveDatabaseImage, copyFile, countFile)
  .log("createImage-when");
})
.log("createImage-flatMap")
.then()
.log("createImage-done");
}
```

The first part of the code where a new image is created is the same, but following that
is `meterRegistry.summary("files.uploaded.bytes").record(... )`, which
creates a new **distribution summary** named `files.uploaded.bytes`. A distribution
summary includes both a name, optional tags, and a value. What is registered is both
a value and an occurrence. Each time a meter is added, it counts it, and the running
total is tabulated.

With these adjustments, we can refresh the application, wait for it to reload, and then upload a few images, as shown here:

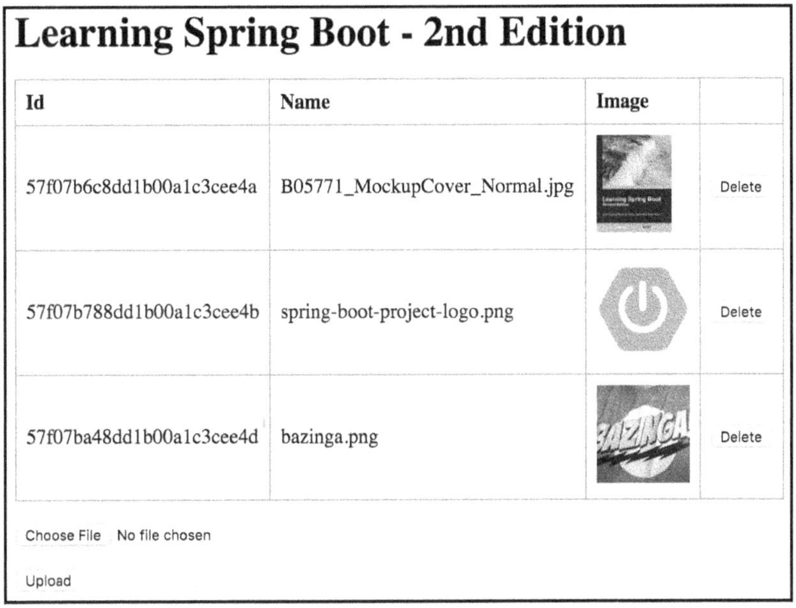

After uploading these images, if we revisit `/application/metrics`, we can see our new metric at the bottom of the list:

```
{
  "names": [
    "jvm.buffer.memory.used",
    "jvm.memory.used",
    "jvm.buffer.count",
    "logback.events",
    "process.uptime",
    "jvm.memory.committed",
    "http.server.requests",
    "jvm.buffer.total.capacity",
    "jvm.memory.max",
    "process.starttime",
    "files.uploaded.bytes"
  ]
}
```

If we navigate to
`http://localhost:8080/application/metrics/files.uploaded.bytes`, we
can view it:

```
{
  "name": "files.uploaded.bytes",
  "measurements": [
    {
      "statistic": "Count",
      "value": 3.0
    },
    {
      "statistic": "Total",
      "value": 208020.0
    }
  ],
  "availableTags": [

  ]
}
```

This JSON shows that **three** measurements have been registered with
`files.uploaded.bytes`, totaling `208020` bytes. What's not immediately shown is
also the time when these metrics were posted. It's possible to calculate upload trends
using the new Micrometer module (`http://micrometer.io`).

Micrometer is a new project at Pivotal. It's a facade for metrics
gathering. Think SLF4J, but for metrics instead. It is designed to
integrate with lots of metric-gathering systems, including Atlas,
Prometheus, Datadog, Influx, Graphite, and more. In this case, it's
using a memory-based solution. Since it's currently under
development and could warrant its *own* book, we will not delve too
deep.

This is but a sampling of the possible metrics that can be defined. Feel free to dig in
and experiment with the data.

Working with additional Actuator endpoints

Spring Boot Actuator provides *lots* of extra data. The following table is a quick summary:

Actuator Endpoint	Description
auditevents	Exposes audit events for the current application
autoconfig	Reports what Spring Boot did and didn't autoconfigure and why
beans	Reports all the beans configured in the application context (including ours as well as the ones autoconfigured by Boot)
configprops	Exposes all configuration properties
env	Reports on the current system environment
health	A simple endpoint to check the life of the app
heapdump	Returns a GZip-compressed **hprof** heap dump file (hprof is a tool by every JDK)
info	Serves up custom content from the app
logfile	Returns the contents of the logfile (assuming `logging.file` or `logging.path` has been set)
loggers	Lists all configured loggers and their levels. Also supports updating log levels through `POST` operations.
metrics	Shows counters and gauges on web usage
mappings	Gives us details about all Spring WebFlux routes
status	threaddump
Creates thread dump report	trace

Every one of these is prefixed (by default) with `/application/`. For example, `health` is found at `/application/health`. To override this prefix, just add `management.context-path` to `application.properties` and swap out your preferred prefix (such as `/manager`). Also, `management.context-path` is relative to `server.context-path`.

It's possible to adjust the port that Actuator endpoints are served on. Setting the `management.port` property to `8081` will change the port for all these endpoints to `8081`. We can even adjust the network address used by setting `management.address=127.0.0.1`. This setting would make these information-rich endpoints only visible to the local box and curtail visibility to outside connections.

Summary

In this chapter, we hooked up Spring Boot's DevTools module. This made it possible to use an embedded LiveReload server as well as decache the templates. We used Spring Boot's autoconfiguration report to glean information about the embedded container. Then, we swapped out Netty with Undertow and verified it through the same report. We dabbled with writing a custom health check and a custom metric. Then, we buttoned things up by embedding our build information into the application to spot the version in operations should we get a late night phone call from our Ops center.

In the next chapter, we'll learn how to communicate between processes using fault-tolerant **Advanced Message Queuing Protocol (AMQP)** messaging.

15
AMQP Messaging with Spring Boot

I should add that we are @springboot / @SpringCloudOSS from top to bottom.

– DaShaun Carter @dashaun

In the previous chapter, we added some tools to our social media application to speed up developer time as well as to provide basic operational support features.

But nothing stands still. In various social media platforms, there is some form of messaging between the users. Why not create one for ours?

In this chapter, we will learn the following topics:

- Getting started with RabbitMQ, an AMQP broker
- Creating a message-based module for our social media app
- Adding customized metrics to track message flow
- Creating dynamically routed messages
- Taking a peek at Spring Cloud Stream and its RabbitMQ bindings

Getting started with RabbitMQ

RabbitMQ is an open source AMQP broker. **Advanced Message Queuing Protocol (AMQP)** is an open protocol that includes the format of messages sent over the wire. This has risen in popularity compared to other messaging solutions like JMS. Why?

JMS is an API, whereas AMQP is a protocol. JMS defines how to talk to the broker but not the format of its messages. And it's confined to Java apps. AMQP doesn't speak about how to talk to a broker but about how messages are put on the wire and how they are pulled down.

To illustrate this point, imagine two different applications. If they were both Java, they could communicate via JMS. But if one of them were Ruby, JMS would be off the table.

To further demonstrate the differences between JMS and AMQP, a JMS-speaking broker can actually use AMQP under the hood to transport the messages.

> In fact, I have contributed to the RabbitMQ JMS Client developed by Pivotal Software found at
> `https://github.com/rabbitmq/rabbitmq-jms-client`.

For this chapter, we will explore using RabbitMQ in the spirit of maximum options.

Installing RabbitMQ broker

To do this, we need to install the RabbitMQ broker.

On a macOS, if we are using Homebrew (`http://brew.sh/`), it's as simple as this:

```
$ brew install rabbitmq
==> Installing dependencies for rabbitmq: openssl, libpng, libtiff,
    wx...
==> Pouring openssl-1.0.2j.el_capitan.bottle.tar.gz
    /usr/local/Cellar/openssl/1.0.2j: 1,695 files, 12M
==> Pouring libpng-1.6.25.el_capitan.bottle.tar.gz
    /usr/local/Cellar/libpng/1.6.25: 25 files, 1.2M
==> Pouring libtiff-4.0.6_2.el_capitan.bottle.tar.gz
    /usr/local/Cellar/libtiff/4.0.6_2: 261 files, 3.4M
==> Pouring wxmac-3.0.2_3.el_capitan.bottle.tar.gz
    /usr/local/Cellar/wxmac/3.0.2_3: 809 files, 23.6M
==> Pouring erlang-19.1.el_capitan.bottle.tar.gz
    /usr/local/Cellar/erlang/19.1: 7,297 files, 279.8M
==> Installing rabbitmq
    /usr/local/Cellar/rabbitmq/3.6.4: 187 files, 5.8M, built in 6
    seco...
```

On Debian Linux, you can use the following command:

```
$ sudo apt-get install rabbitmq-server
```

On any of the Red Hat Linux systems, the following command can be run:

```
$ yum install erlang
$ yum install rabbitmq-server-<version>.rpm
```

On various cloud solutions, including Cloud Foundry, RabbitMQ can be found as a service (including Pivotal's RabbitMQ for PCF at `https://network.pivotal.io/products/p-rabbitmq`), something we'll explore in `Chapter 19`, *Taking Your App to Production with Spring Boot*.

For more details on downloading and installing, visit `https://www.rabbitmq.com/download.html`.

Launching the RabbitMQ broker

With the RabbitMQ broker installed, we just need to launch it. There are these two approaches to doing that:

- Starting it in our current shell
- Having it start when the machine boots

To start in our current shell, we can execute the following command:

```
$ rabbitmq-server
RabbitMQ 3.6.4. Copyright (C) 2007-2016 Pivotal Software...
##  ##      Licensed under the MPL.  See http://www.rabbitmq.com/
##  ##
##########  Logs: /usr/local/var/log/rabbitmq/rabbit@localhost.log
######  ##        /usr/local/var/log/rabbitmq/rabbit@localhost-
sasl....
##########
Starting broker...
completed with 10 plugins.
```

On a macOS with Homebrew, use the following to launch as a daemon process and relaunch when we reboot:

```
$ brew services start rabbitmq
==> Tapping homebrew/services
Cloning into '/usr/local/Homebrew/Library/Taps/homebrew/homebrew-
services'...
remote: Counting objects: 10, done.
remote: Compressing objects: 100% (7/7), done.
remote: Total 10 (delta 0), reused 6 (delta 0), pack-reused 0
Unpacking objects: 100% (10/10), done.
```

```
Checking connectivity... done.
Tapped 0 formulae (36 files, 46K)
==> Successfully started `rabbitmq` (label: homebrew.mxcl.rabbitmq)
```

If you are using Homebrew, there is a feature to manage various *services*. Type `homebrew services` to see the commands available. For example, `brew services list` will list all services and their state:

```
$ brew services list
Name       Status  User        Plist
activemq   stopped
mongodb    started gturnquist
/Users/gturnquist/Library/LaunchAgents/hom...
mysql      stopped
neo4j      stopped
rabbitmq   started gturnquist
/Users/gturnquist/Library/LaunchAgents/hom...
redis      stopped
tor        stopped
```

Now we can see that RabbitMQ has joined MongoDB (which we installed in `Chapter 12`, *Reactive Data Access with Spring Boot*).

This, essentially, leverages macOS X's `launchctl` system with a Homebrew-supplied daemon control file.

For Windows, check out `https://www.rabbitmq.com/install-windows.html`. It has links to download the broker. Upon installation, it will configure it with various defaults and also start it up.

To control the broker, check out the `rabbitmqctl.bat` script found in the `sbin` folder (as administrator). Use the following commands:

- `rabbitmqctl start`
- `rabbitmqctl stop`
- `rabbitmqctl status`

> Want to poke around with the RabbitMQ broker in a more visual way? Run `rabbitmq-plugins enable rabbitmq_managment`, and visit `http://localhost:15672`. The default username/password for RabbitMQ is `guest`/`guest`. I suggest looking at *Exchanges* and *Queues* first.

With the RabbitMQ broker up and running, we can now shift focus to our application efforts.

Adding messaging as a new component to an existing application

What have we built so far for our social media platform? We have the ability to upload and delete pictures. However, a key piece of any social media platform is to allow users to interact with each other. This is commonly done by either commenting on the social media content or chatting directly with each other.

Let's start by adding the ability to comment on images. But before we get going, let's stop and discuss the architecture.

For years, people have used the layer approach to split up applications. Fundamentally, we don't want a big application with all the classes in one package because it's too hard to keep up with everything.

So far, we have everything located in `com.greglturnquist.learningspringboot`. Historically, the pattern has been to split things up in a domain layer, a services layer, and a controllers layer, as shown in the following screenshot:

```
📁 src
  ▼ 📁 main
    ▼ 📁 java
      ▼ 📁 com.greglturnquist.learningspringboot
          📁 controllers
          📁 domain
          📁 services
          🔧 MyCoolApplication
```

In this structure, we would put every service into the `services` subpackage and create further sub-subpackages if need be. We'd put all the domain objects in `domain` and all the controllers would go into `controllers`.

The idea was that controllers call services and services return domain objects. It prevented entanglements such as services invoking controllers, which made sense at the time.

But with the rise of microservices (something we'll dig into in Chapter 16, *Microservices with Spring Boot*), these layer-based approaches become an issue when the application gets really big. When refactoring is in order, services found in the same package that are functionally unrelated can get tricky due to needless coupling we may have created.

A more slim and trim approach is to break things up using vertical **slices** instead of horizontal **layers**:

```
▼ src
  ▼ main
    ▼ java
      ▼ com.greglturnquist.learningspringboot
          comments
          images
          MyCoolApplication
```

With the structure shown in the preceding screenshot, we have split things up into images and comments, a more function-based nature.

We would put everything related to handling images in the former and everything related to comments in the latter. If the need arises, either of these packages can be further split up into subpackages, as follows:

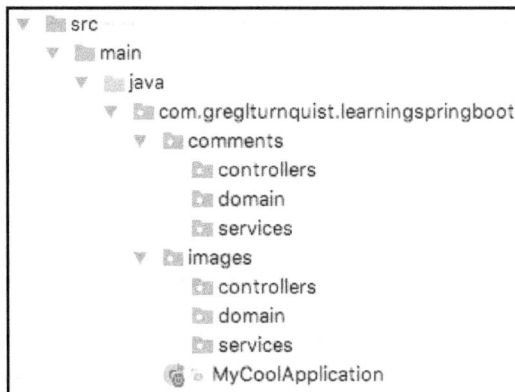

```
▼ src
  ▼ main
    ▼ java
      ▼ com.greglturnquist.learningspringboot
        ▼ comments
            controllers
            domain
            services
        ▼ images
            controllers
            domain
            services
            MyCoolApplication
```

Worried that this will cause an explosion of the domain/services/controllers trio all over our code? Don't panic! We only do this as needed, and given that each domain subpackage will be relatively small in scope as compared to the old layer approach, the functionality should be highly cohesive, that is, have much in common with each other.

Since we are about to create a separate piece of functionality (comments), it would make sense to go ahead and break up our application into images and comments. So let's do that!

First, let's create the images and comments subpackages. With that in place, the most obvious change is to move Image, ImageRepository, and ImageService into the image subpackage. Easy enough.

That leaves us with the following:

- LearningSpringBootApplication
- HomeController
- LearningSpringBootHealthIndicator

LearningSpringBootApplication embodies the entire app, so it should stay at the top level. This isn't just a semantic statement. That class contains our SpringBootApplication annotation, which enables the application's autoconfigured behaviors like component scanning. Component scanning should start at the top level and search all subpackages.

HomeController represents an interesting concept. Even though it calls into ImageService, since it serves the application's top-level view, let's leave it at the top level as well.

As for LearningSpringBootHealthIndicator, a similar case could be made to keep it at the root. Since we are shooting to keep things light at the top, why don't we create a separate module to encompass all Ops-based features that aren't specific to any one module, ops.

Given all these decisions, our new structure now looks like this:

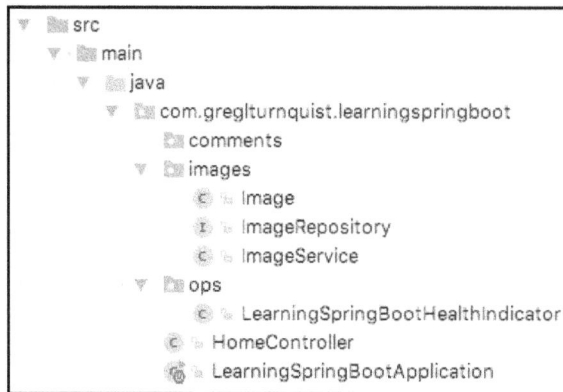

```
▼ 📁 src
  ▼ 📁 main
    ▼ 📁 java
      ▼ 📁 com.greglturnquist.learningspringboot
          📁 comments
        ▼ 📁 images
            © ⊾ Image
            I ⊾ ImageRepository
            © ⊾ ImageService
        ▼ 📁 ops
            © ⊾ LearningSpringBootHealthIndicator
          © ⊾ HomeController
          🎓 ⊾ LearningSpringBootApplication
```

> **TIP**
>
> Is spending this amount of time debating package structure worth it? In any agile environment, it's okay to try something if it doesn't cost two weeks of effort. Stopping to spend ten minutes thinking about a maintainable structure is an acceptable investment, especially if we're willing to change it later should the need arise.

Creating a message producer/message consumer

Having restructured our application to make room for comments, let's get to it!

First of all, we need to add a new dependency to our build file, which is done with the following code:

```
compile('org.springframework.boot:spring-boot-starter-amqp')
```

That will give us access to Spring AMQP, which includes RabbitMQ support.

Adding messaging technology to our application may make us clamor to, well, write some code that talks to RabbitMQ. But that isn't really a good flow. Instead, we should start from one of two perspectives--writing a unit test or writing some UI.

Either approach is aimed at figuring out the use case we are trying to solve. Before *solving* the problem at hand, we need to noodle out what our exact problem is. In this case, let's start from the UI perspective.

To do that, we can take advantage of **Spring Boot DevTools** from the last chapter and launch our application in the **Debug** mode with the LiveReload feature enabled. That way, as we make changes, we can see them right away:

```
o.s.b.d.a.OptionalLiveReloadServer        : LiveReload server is running on port 35729
o.s.j.e.a.AnnotationMBeanExporter         : Registering beans for JMX exposure on startup
o.s.j.e.a.AnnotationMBeanExporter         : Bean with name 'rabbitConnectionFactory' has been a
o.s.j.e.a.AnnotationMBeanExporter         : Located managed bean 'rabbitConnectionFactory': reg
o.s.c.support.DefaultLifecycleProcessor   : Starting beans in phase -2147482648
o.s.c.support.DefaultLifecycleProcessor   : Starting beans in phase 0
o.s.c.support.DefaultLifecycleProcessor   : Starting beans in phase 2147483647
o.s.a.r.c.CachingConnectionFactory        : Created new connection: rabbitConnectionFactory#168
o.s.amqp.rabbit.core.RabbitAdmin          : Auto-declaring a non-durable, auto-delete, or exclu
r.ipc.netty.tcp.BlockingNettyContext      : Started HttpServer on /0:0:0:0:0:0:0:0:8080
o.s.b.web.embedded.netty.NettyWebServer   : Netty started on port(s): 8080
org.mongodb.driver.connection             : Opened connection [connectionId{localValue:3, serve
boot-cover.jpg)
boot-2nd-edition-cover.jpg)

c.g.l.LearningSpringBootApplication       : Started LearningSpringBootApplication in 6.655 seco
```

With this preceding screenshot, we can see our application up and running with the LiveReload server enabled (and some sample data preloaded).

Displaying comments

Now we can make edits to our Thymeleaf template and create input fields for people to write comments:

```
<td>
    <ul>
        <li th:each="comment : ${image.comments}"
            th:text="${comment.comment}"></li>
    </ul>
</td>
<td>
    <form th:method="post" th:action="@{'/comments'}">
        <input name="comment" value="" type="text" />
        <input name="imageId" th:value="${image.id}"
         type="hidden" />
        <input type="submit" />
    </form>
</td>
```

The section of our preceding template where each row is rendered can be explained as follows:

- There is a new column containing an HTML unordered list to display each comment
- The unordered list consists of an HTML line item for each comment via Thymeleaf's `th:each` construct
- There is also a new column containing an HTML form to post a new comment
- The form contains an HTML text input for the comment itself
- The form also contains a hidden HTML element specifying the ID of the image that the comment will be associated with

To support this, we need to update `HomeController` as follows:

```
private final ImageService imageService;
private final CommentReaderRepository repository;

public HomeController(ImageService imageService,
  CommentReaderRepository repository) {
    this.imageService = imageService;
    this.repository = repository;
}
```

We have updated the class definition as follows:

- A new `repository` field is created for `CommentReaderRepository` (which we'll define further ahead in the chapter)
- This field is initialized by **constructor injection**

We need to look up the comments. To do that, we need a Spring Data repository that can read comments. And reading comments is ALL this repository needs to do at this stage of our social media app.

Let's take this new repository and use it inside the Spring WebFlux handler for GET /, like this:

```
@GetMapping("/")
public Mono<String> index(Model model) {
  model.addAttribute("images",
    imageService
    .findAllImages()
    .flatMap(image ->
      Mono.just(image)
```

```
      .zipWith(repository.findByImageId(
        image.getId()).collectList()))
    .map(imageAndComments -> new HashMap<String, Object>(){{
        put("id", imageAndComments.getT1().getId());
        put("name", imageAndComments.getT1().getName());
        put("comments",
          imageAndComments.getT2());
    }})
  );
  model.addAttribute("extra",
    "DevTools can also detect code changes too");
  return Mono.just("index");
}
```

This last code contains a slight adjustment to the model's `images` attribute:

- The code takes the `Flux` returned from our `ImageService.findAll()` method and flatMaps each entry from an Image into a call to find related comments.

- `repository.findByImageId(image.getId()).collectList()` actually fetches all `Comment` objects related to a given `Image`, but turns it into `Mono<List<Comment>>`. This waits for all of the entries to arrive and bundles them into a single object.

- The collection of comments and it's related image are bundled together via `Mono.zipWith(Mono)`, creating a tuple-2 or a pair. (This is the way to gather multiple bits of data and pass them on to the next step of any Reactor flow. Reactor has additional tuple types all the way up to `Tuple8`.)

- After flatMapping `Flux<Image>` into `Flux<Tuple2<Image, List<Comment>>>`, we then map each entry into a classic Java `Map` to service our Thymeleaf template.

- Reactor's `Tuple2` has a strongly typed `getT1()` and `getT2()`, with `T1` being the `Image` and `T2` being the list of comments, which is suitable for our needs since it's just a temporary construct used to assemble details for the web template.

- The image's `id` and `name` attributes are copied into the target map from `T1`.

- The `comments` attribute of our map is populated with the complete `List<Comment>` extracted from `T2`.

> **TIP**
> Since Thymeleaf templates operate on key-value semantics, there is no need to define a new domain object to capture this construct. A Java `Map` will work just fine.

As we continue working with Reactor types, these sorts of flows are, hopefully, becoming familiar. Having an IDE that offers code completion is a key asset when putting flows like this. And the more we work with these types of transformations the easier they become.

> If you'll notice, `ImageService` is fully reactive given that we use MongoDB's reactive drivers. The operation to retrieve comments is *also* reactive. Chaining reactive calls together, using Reactor's operators and hitching them to Thymeleaf's reactive solution, ensures that everything is being fetched as efficiently as possible and only when necessary. Writing reactive apps hinges on having a fully reactive stack.

To round out our feature of **reading comments**, we need to define `CommentReaderRepository` as follows:

```
public interface CommentReaderRepository
  extends Repository<Comment, String> {

  Flux<Comment> findByImageId(String imageId);
}
```

The preceding code can be described as follows:

- It's a declarative interface, similar to how we created `ImageRepository` earlier in this book.
- It extends Spring Data Commons' `Repository` interface, which contains no operations. We are left to define them all. This lets us create a read-only repository.
- It has a `findByImageId(String imageId)` method that returns a `Flux` of `Comment` objects.

This repository gives us a read-only readout on comments. This is handy because it lets us fetch comments and does not accidentally let people write through it. Instead, we intend to implement something different further in this chapter.

Our `CommentReaderRepository` needs one thing: a `Comment` domain object:

```
package com.greglturnquist.learningspringboot.images;

import lombok.Data;

import org.springframework.data.annotation.Id;
```

```
@Data
public class Comment {

  @Id private String id;
  private String imageId;
  private String comment;

}
```

This preceding domain object contains the following:

- The `@Data` annotation tells Lombok to generate getters, setters, `toString()`, `equals()`, and `hashCode()` methods
- The `id` field is marked with Spring Data Commons' `@Id` annotation so we know it's the key for mapping objects
- The `imageId` field is meant to hold an `Image.id` field, linking comments to images
- The `comment` field is the place to store an actual comment

> **TIP**
>
> For both `CommentReaderRepository` and `Comment`, the entire class is shown including the package. That's to show that it's located in the `images` subpackage we defined earlier in this chapter. This domain object provides the comment information **pertinent to images**. And this information is read-only, which means that this is not where updates regarding comments are made.

Producing comments

Having written the code to display comments, it's now time to craft the bits to create them.

We've already seen the changes to our template adding an HTML form to write a comment. Let's code the corresponding controller **in the comments subpackage**, as follows:

```
@Controller
public class CommentController {

  private final RabbitTemplate rabbitTemplate;

  public CommentController(RabbitTemplate rabbitTemplate) {
    this.rabbitTemplate = rabbitTemplate;
  }
```

```
@PostMapping("/comments")
public Mono<String> addComment(Mono<Comment> newComment) {
  return newComment.flatMap(comment ->
   Mono.fromRunnable(() -> rabbitTemplate
     .convertAndSend(
       "learning-spring-boot",
       "comments.new",
       comment)))
     .log("commentService-publish")
     .then(Mono.just("redirect:/"));
}


}
```

The code can be explained as follows:

- It's the first class we have put in the new `comments` subpackage.
- The `@Controller` annotation marks this as another Spring controller.
- It contains a `RabbitTemplate` initialized by constructor injection. This `RabbitTemplate` is created automatically by Spring Boot when it spots `spring-amqp` on the classpath.
- The `@PostMapping("/comments")` annotation registers this method to respond to the form submissions that we added earlier in the template with `th:action="@{'/comments'}"`.
- Spring will automatically convert the body of the POST into a `Comment` domain object. Additionally, since we are using WebFlux, deserializing the request body is wrapped in a `Mono`, hence that process will only occur once the framework subscribes to the flow.
- The incoming `Mono<Comment>` is unpacked using `flatMap` and then turned into a `rabbitTemplate.convertAndSend()` operation, which itself is wrapped in `Mono.fromRunnable`.
- The comment is published to RabbitMQ's `learning-spring-boot` exchange with a routing key of `comments.new`.
- We wait for this to complete with `then()`, and when done, return a Spring WebFlux **redirect** to send the webpage back to the home page.

Time out. That bullet point about the RabbitMQ exchange and routing key may have sounded a bit complex.

> The comment is published to RabbitMQ's `learning-spring-boot` exchange with a routing key of `comments.new`.

We need to take this apart to understand the basics of AMQP a little better.

AMQP fundamentals

If you've already used JMS, then you're aware that it has queues and topics. AMQP has queues as well but the semantics are different.

Each message sent by a JMS-based producer is consumed by just one of the clients of that queue. AMQP-based producers don't publish directly to queues but to **exchanges** instead. When queues are declared, they must be bound to an exchange. Multiple queues can be bound to the same exchange, emulating the concept of topics.

JMS has message selectors which allow consumers to be selective about the messages they receive from either queues or topics. AMQP has **routing keys** that behave differently based on the type of the exchange, as listed next.

A **direct exchange** routes messages based on a fixed routing key, often the name of the queue. For example, the last code that we just looked at mentioned `learning-spring-boot` as the name of exchange and `comments.new` as the routing key. Any consumer that binds their own queue to that exchange with a routing key of `comments.new` will receive a copy of each message posted earlier.

A **topic exchange** allows routing keys to have wildcards like `comments.*`. This situation best suits clients where the actual routing key isn't known until a user provides the criteria. For example, imagine a stock-trading application where the user must provide a list of ticker symbols he or she is interested in monitoring.

A **fanout exchange** blindly broadcasts every message to every queue that is bound to it, regardless of the routing key.

Regarding the semantics of AMQP, let's explore that further by looking at the
CommentService (also in comments subpackage) in chunks:

```
@Service
public class CommentService {

  private CommentWriterRepository repository;

  public CommentService(CommentWriterRepository repository) {
    this.repository = repository;
  }
  ... more to come below...
}
```

This preceding code can be described as follows:

- The @Service annotation marks it as a Spring service to be registered with
  the application context on startup
- CommentWriterRepository is a Spring Data repository used to write new
  comments and is initialized by the constructor injection

Which brings us to the meat of this service, which is as follows:

```
@RabbitListener(bindings = @QueueBinding(
  value = @Queue,
  exchange = @Exchange(value = "learning-spring-boot"),
  key = "comments.new"
))
public void save(Comment newComment) {
  repository
    .save(newComment)
    .log("commentService-save")
    .subscribe();
}
```

This last little function packs a punch, so let's take it apart:

- The @RabbitListener annotation is the easiest way to register methods to
  consume messages.
- The @QueueBinding annotation is the easiest way to declare the queue *and*
  the exchange it's bound to on-the-fly. In this case, it creates an anonymous
  queue for this method and binds to the learning-spring-boot
  exchange.

- The routing key for this method is `comments.new`, meaning any message posted to the `learning-spring-boot` exchange with that exact routing key will cause this method to be invoked.
- It's possible for the `@RabbitListener` methods to receive a Spring AMQP `Message`, a Spring Messaging `Message`, various message headers, as well as a plain old Java object (which is what we have here).
- The method itself invokes our `CommentWriterRepository` to actually save the comment in the data store.

To use RabbitMQ, we would normally need `@EnableRabbit`, but thanks to Spring Boot, it's automatically activated when `spring-boot-starter-amqp` is on the classpath. Once again, Boot knows what we want and just does it.

An important thing to understand is that `@RabbitListener` makes it possible to dynamically create all the exchanges and queues needed to operate. However, it only works if an instance of `AmqpAdmin` is in the application context. Without it, ALL exchanges and queues must be declared as separate Spring beans. But Spring Boot's RabbitMQ autoconfiguration policy provides one, so no sweat!

There is one slight issue with this method that will cause it to not operate--object serialization. If we had declared the method signature to provide us with a Spring AMQP `Message` object, we would pull down a byte array. However, out of the box, Spring AMQP has limited functionality in serializing custom domain objects. With no effort, it can handle simple strings and serializables.

But for custom domain objects, there is a more preferred solution--a Spring AMQP message converter, as shown next:

```
@Bean
Jackson2JsonMessageConverter jackson2JsonMessageConverter() {
    return new Jackson2JsonMessageConverter();
}
```

This preceding bean, listed right below the `save(Comment newComment)` method, can be described as follows:

- `@Bean` registers this as a bean definition.
- It creates `Jackson2JsonMessageConverter`, an implementation of Spring AMQP's `MessageConverter`, used to serialize and deserialize Spring AMQP `Message` objects. In this case, is uses Jackson to convert POJOs to/from JSON strings.

Spring Boot's RabbitMQ autoconfiguration policy will look for any implementation of Spring AMQP's `MessageConverter` instances and register them with both the `RabbitTemplate` we used earlier as well as the `SimpleMessageListenerContainer` that it creates when it spots `@RabbitListener` in our code.

To start our application with a clean slate, we have this code at the bottom of `CommentService`:

```
@Bean
CommandLineRunner setUp(MongoOperations operations) {
  return args -> {
    operations.dropCollection(Comment.class);
  };
}
```

The last code can be described as follows:

- The `@Bean` annotation will register this chunk of code automatically
- By implementing Spring Boot's `CommandLineRunner` interface, the Java 8 lambda expression will run itself when all beans have been created
- It receives a copy of `MongoOperations`, the blocking MongoDB object we can use to drop the entire collection based on `Comment`

> This code is handy for development, but should be either removed in production or wrapped in a `@Profile("dev")` annotation such that it ONLY runs when `spring.profiles.active=dev` is present.

To persist comments in our data store, we have the following Spring Data repository:

```
public interface CommentWriterRepository
  extends Repository<Comment, String> {

  Mono<Comment> save(Comment newComment);

  // Needed to support save()
  Mono<Comment> findById(String id);
}
```

This preceding repository isn't too difficult to dissect, and that can be done as follows:

- It's an interface, which means that we don't have to write any code. We just declare the semantics and Spring Data does the rest.
- By extending Spring Data Commons' `Repository` interface, it will be picked up as a repository. Being an empty interface, it comes with no predefined operations.
- It contains a `save()` operation to store a new comment (and return it after it gets saved). If the ID value is null, Spring Data MongoDB will automatically generate a unique string value for us.
- Spring Data requires a `findOne()` operation in order to perform saves because that's what it uses to fetch what we just saved in order to return it.
- All of these method signatures use Reactor `Mono` types.

This repository is focused on writing data into MongoDB and nothing more. Even though it has a `findOne()`, it's not built for reading data. That has been kept over in the `images` subpackage.

To finish things up in our `comments` subpackage, let's look at the core domain object:

```
package com.greglturnquist.learningspringboot.comments;

import lombok.Data;

import org.springframework.data.annotation.Id;
import org.springframework.data.mongodb.core.mapping.Document;

@Data
@Document
public class Comment {

  @Id private String id;
  private String imageId;
  private String comment;
}
```

This previous domain object contains the following:

- The `@Data` annotation tells Lombok to generate getters, setters, `toString()`, `equals()`, and `hashCode()` methods
- The `id` field is marked with Spring Data Common's `@Id` annotation so we know it's the key for mapping objects
- The `imageId` field is meant to hold an `Image.id` field linking comments to images
- The `comment` field is the place to store an actual comment

> Wait a second! Isn't this the *exact same code* found in `com.greglturnquist.learningspringboot.images.Comment`? It is right now. But it's important to recognize that different *slices* may need different attributes in the future. By keeping a slice-specific domain object, we can change one without the risk of changing the other. In fact, it's possible that we can (spoiler alert!), later in this book, move this entire comments system into a separate microservice. By keeping things in nicely divided slices, the risk of tight coupling can be reduced.

Another factor is that RabbitMQ is *not reactive*. Invoking `rabbitTemplate.convertAndSend()` is blocking. That may sound awkward given AMQP is a pub/sub technology. But the whole process of publishing the message to the RabbitMQ broker holds up our thread, and is, by definition, blocking.

So our code wraps that inside a Java `Runnable` and converts it into a `Mono` via Reactor's `Mono.fromRunnable`. That makes it possible to invoke this blocking task only when we're ready at the right time. It's important to know that a Mono-wrapped-Runnable doesn't act like a traditional Java `Runnable` and doesn't get launched in a separate thread. Instead, the `Runnable` interface provides a convenient wrapper where Reactor controls precisely when the `run()` method is invoked inside its scheduler.

If we refresh our code in the IDE and let it restart, we can now start creating comments. Check out the following screenshot:

Learning Spring Boot - 2nd Edition

1 of 1

20 item(s) per page

Id	Name	Image			
57f8641e83a5d272b18d4ce1	B05771_MockupCover_Normal.jpg		Delete	• I love the cover! • Can I order a copy yet?	Submit
57f8643b83a5d272b18d4ce3	bazinga.png		Delete		Submit
57f8645883a5d272b18d4ce5	spring-boot-project-logo.png		Delete		Spring Boot is awesome! Submit

Choose File No file chosen

Upload

The preceding screenshot shows a couple of comments added to the first image and a third being written. Cool, ehh?

But perhaps, you're wondering why we spent all that effort splitting up reading and writing comments? After all, Spring Data appears to make it easy enough to define a single repository that could handle both. That may even imply we didn't need RabbitMQ and could let `HomeController` and `CommentController` use the repository directly instead.

The reason to use messaging is to provide a reliable way to offload work to another system. A real system that grows to thousands, if not millions, of users will see a huge flow of traffic. Think about it. Are there any other social media platforms where people write comments constantly but only view a handful at a time?

This facet of our application is designed with scalability in mind. If we had one million users, they may be writing tens of millions of messages a day. Hitching our controller directly to MongoDB may cause it to keel over. But if we push all the writes to a separate service, we can tune suitably.

The number of reads is much smaller.

Adding customized metrics to track message flow

Having added the ability to comment on other people's posted images, it would be nice to start gathering metrics.

To do so, we can introduce metrics similar to those shown in Chapter 14, *Developer Tools for Spring Boot Apps*, as follows:

```
@Controller
public class CommentController {

    private final RabbitTemplate rabbitTemplate;

    private final MeterRegistry meterRegistry;

    public CommentController(RabbitTemplate rabbitTemplate,
      MeterRegistry meterRegistry) {
        this.rabbitTemplate = rabbitTemplate;
        this.meterRegistry = meterRegistry;
    }

    @PostMapping("/comments")
    public Mono<String> addComment(Mono<Comment> newComment) {
        return newComment.flatMap(comment ->
          Mono.fromRunnable(() ->
            rabbitTemplate
              .convertAndSend(
                "learning-spring-boot",
                "comments.new",
              comment))
              .then(Mono.just(comment)))
              .log("commentService-publish")
              .flatMap(comment -> {
                meterRegistry
                  .counter("comments.produced", "imageId",
comment.getImageId())
                    .increment();
                  return Mono.just("redirect:/");
              });
    }
}
```

This last code has these few changes compared to what we wrote earlier in this chapter:

- A `MeterRegistry` is injected through the constructor and captured as a field.
- It's used to increment a `comments.produced` metric with every comment.
- Each metric is also "tagged" with the related **imageId**.
- We have to tune the `Mono` wrapping our `rabbitTemplate.convertAndSend()`, and ensure that the **comment** is passed via `then()`. Then it must be unpacked via `flatMap` in the part of the flow that writes metrics.

> Should the code talking to the `meterRegistry` *also* be wrapped in `Mono.fromRunnable()`? Perhaps. The code blocks when writing, but in this incarnation, the metrics are stored in memory, so the cost is low. Nevertheless, the cost could rise, meaning it should be properly managed. If the service became external, the odds would increase quickly in favor of wrapping with a separate `Mono`.

In a similar vein, if we inject `MeterRegistry` into `CommentService`, we can then use it there as well:

```
@RabbitListener(bindings = @QueueBinding(
  value = @Queue,
  exchange = @Exchange(value = "learning-spring-boot"),
  key = "comments.new"
))
public void save(Comment newComment) {
  repository
    .save(newComment)
    .log("commentService-save")
    .subscribe(comment -> {
      meterRegistry
        .counter("comments.consumed", "imageId",
comment.getImageId())
          .increment();
    });
}
```

This lines up with what we added to `CommentController`. The preceding code can be explained as follows:

- Using the injected `MeterRegistry`, we increment a `comments.consumed` metric with every comment.
- It's also tagged with the comment's related **imageId**.
- The metrics are handled after the save is completed inside the `subscribe` method. This method grants us the ability to execute some code once the flow is complete.

> Spring AMQP doesn't yet support Reactive Streams. That is why `rabbitTemplate.convertAndSend()` must be wrapped in `Mono.fromRunnable`. Blocking calls such as this `subscribe()` method should be red flags, but in this situation, it's a necessary evil until Spring AMQP is able to add support. There is no other way to signal for this Reactor flow to execute without it.

The thought of relaunching our app and manually entering a slew of comments doesn't sound very exciting. So why not write a simulator to do it for us!

```
@Profile("simulator")
@Component
public class CommentSimulator {

  private final CommentController controller;
  private final ImageRepository repository;

  private final AtomicInteger counter;

  public CommentSimulator(CommentController controller,
            ImageRepository repository) {
    this.controller = controller;
    this.repository = repository;
    this.counter = new AtomicInteger(1);
  }

  @EventListener
  public void onApplicationReadyEvent(ApplicationReadyEvent event) {
    Flux
      .interval(Duration.ofMillis(1000))
      .flatMap(tick -> repository.findAll())
      .map(image -> {
        Comment comment = new Comment();
        comment.setImageId(image.getId());
        comment.setComment(
```

```
          "Comment #" + counter.getAndIncrement());
        return Mono.just(comment);
      })
      .flatMap(newComment ->
        Mono.defer(() ->
          controller.addComment(newComment)))
      .subscribe();
  }
}
```

Let's take this simulator apart:

- The @Profile annotation indicates that this only operates if
  spring.profiles.active=simulator is present when the app starts
- The @Component annotation will allow this class to get picked up by
  Spring Boot automatically and activated
- The class itself is located in the root package,
  com.greglturnquist.learningspring, given that it pulls bits from
  both subpackages
- The @EventListener annotation signals Spring to pipe application events
  issued to the app context. In this case, the method is interested in
  ApplicationReadyEvents, fired when the application is up and
  operational
- Flux.interval(Duration.ofMillis(1000)) causes a stream of lazy
  ticks to get fired every 1000 ms, lazily
- By flatMapping over this Flux, each tick is transformed into all images
  using the ImageRepository
- Each image is used to generate a new, related comment
- Using the injected CommentController, it simulates the newly minted
  comment being sent in from the web

If we reconfigure our runner with `spring.profiles.active=simulator`, we can see it run. IntelliJ IDEA provides the means to set Spring profiles easily:

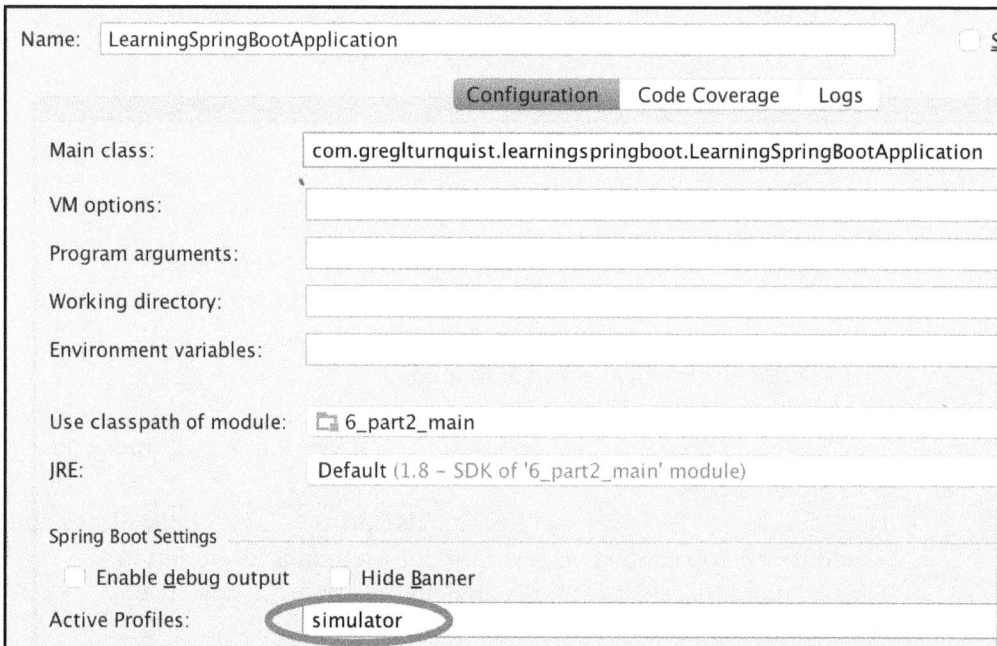

You can see the entry highlighted at the bottom of the previous screenshot.

If we kick things off after hearing our machine's fan move into high gear, we can check the metrics at
`http://localhost:8080/application/metrics/comments.consumed` and
`http://localhost:8080/application/metrics/comments.produced`, and
expect to see tallies.

In this last screenshot, we can clearly see `counter.comments.produced` and `counter.comments.consumed`, and they happen to be the same, which means that none were lost.

We can also see the unique image IDs with an equal number of messages spread between them (as expected with our simulator).

Peeking at Spring Cloud Stream (with RabbitMQ)

Linking lots of small services together via messaging is a very common pattern. It increases in popularity with the rise of microservices. Coding the same pattern over and over using `RabbitTemplate` or some other transport template (`KafkaTemplate` and others) is another level of complexity we shouldn't be saddled with.

Spring Cloud Stream (`http://cloud.spring.io/spring-cloud-stream/`) to the rescue!

Spring Cloud Stream takes the concept of **inputs**, **outputs**, and **transformers** from Spring Integration and makes it super easy to chain them together.

To alter our social media platform to do this, we can remove `spring-boot-starter-amqp` from our build file and add this instead:

```
compile(
  'org.springframework.cloud:spring-cloud-starter-stream-rabbit')
compile(
  'org.springframework.cloud:spring-cloud-stream-reactive')
```

This preceding dependency brings in the following:

- `spring-cloud-stream-binder-rabbit-core`
- `spring-cloud-stream-codec`
- `spring-cloud-stream`
- `spring-cloud-stream-reactive`
- `spring-boot-starter-amqp`
- `spring-integration-amqp`

Spring Cloud Stream has many starters. In essence, we must pick the underlying transport technology, but we don't have to interact with the transport technology directly.

Introduction to Spring Cloud

Spring Cloud? What is that?

Spring Cloud is an extension of Spring Boot provided through various libraries and aimed at addressing different cloud-native patterns. In this case, Spring Cloud Stream aims to simplify the chaining together of services via messaging.

To use any Spring Cloud library, we need to add the following chunk to the bottom of our `build.gradle` file:

```
dependencyManagement {
  imports {
    mavenBom "org.springframework.cloud:spring-cloud-
      dependencies:${springCloudVersion}"
  }
}
```

This preceding fragment of code is part of Spring's Dependency Management gradle plugin, pulling in Spring Cloud **BOM** (**Bill of Materials**). In this case, it has a variable, `springCloudVersion`, which we need to select.

Spring Cloud has release trains, which means that each library has a version but all the versions are coordinated. By picking one train, we get a fleet of tools to pick from (and we will throughout the rest of this book!).

The Spring Cloud release train tied to Spring Boot 2.0 is `Finchley`, so let's put that right next to our version of Boot at the top:

```
buildscript {
  ext {
    springBootVersion = '2.0.0.M5'
    springCloudVersion = 'Finchley.M3'
  }
  ...
}
```

If you're curious about the various release trains of Spring Cloud, check out its project page at `http://projects.spring.io/spring-cloud/`.

With Spring Cloud's BOM and Spring Cloud Stream added to our build, let's return to configuring messaging using Spring Cloud Stream's core interfaces, as follows:

```
@Controller
@EnableBinding(Source.class)
public class CommentController {

  private final CounterService counterService;
  private FluxSink<Message<Comment>> commentSink;
  private Flux<Message<Comment>> flux;

  public CommentController(CounterService counterService) {
    this.counterService = counterService;
    this.flux = Flux.<Message<Comment>>create(
      emitter -> this.commentSink = emitter,
      FluxSink.OverflowStrategy.IGNORE)
      .publish()
      .autoConnect();
  }

  @PostMapping("/comments")
  public Mono<String> addComment(Mono<Comment> newComment) {
    if (commentSink != null) {
      return newComment
       .map(comment -> commentSink.next(MessageBuilder
       .withPayload(comment)
       .build())))
       .then(Mono.just("redirect:/"));
    } else {
        return Mono.just("redirect:/");
    }
  }

  @StreamEmitter
  public void emit(@Output(Source.OUTPUT) FluxSender output) {
    output.send(this.flux);
  }

}
```

This last code is very similar to the `CommentController` that we created earlier in this chapter, but with the following differences:

- `@EnableBinding(Source.class)` flags this app as a **source** for new events. Spring Cloud Stream uses this annotation to signal the creation of **channels**, which, in RabbitMQ, translates to **exchanges** and **queues**.
- The constructor proceeds to set up a `FluxSink`, the mechanism to emit new messages into a downstream `Flux`. This sink is configured to ignore downstream backpressure events. It starts publishing right away, autoconnecting to its upstream source upon subscription.
- The objects being emitted are `Message<Comment>`, which is Spring's abstraction for a POJO wrapped as a transportable message. This includes the ability to add headers and other information.
- Inside `addComments`, if the sink has been established, it maps `newComment` into a `Message<Comment>` using Spring Messaging APIs. Finally, it transmits the message into the sink.
- When the message is successfully emitted to `Flux`, a redirect is issued.
- To transmit `Flux` of `Message<Comment>` objects, a separate method, `emit`, is wired up with an `@StreamEmitter` annotation. This method is fed a `FluxSender`, which provides us with a Reactor-friendly means to transmit messages into a channel. It lets us hook up the `Flux` tied to our `FluxSink`.
- The `@Output(Source.OUTPUT)` annotation marks up *which* channel it gets piped to (visiting `Source.OUTPUT` reveals the channel name as **output**).

That's a lot of stuff packed into this controller. To better understand it, there are some fundamental concepts to realize.

First of all, it's not common practice to create a `Flux` and then add to it. The paradigm is to wrap it around something else. To drive this point home, `Flux` itself is an abstract class. You can't instantiate it. Instead, you must use its various static helper methods to craft one. So, when we want to take a behavior that is tied to users clicking on a site and link it to a `Flux` that was created when the application started, we need something like `FluxSink` to bridge these two things together.

Spring Cloud Stream focuses on chaining together streams of messages with source/sink semantics. When it comes to Reactor, this means adapting a `Flux` of messages onto a channel, a concept curated for several years by Spring Integration. Given that the concrete nature of the channel is abstracted away, it doesn't matter what transport technology we use. Thanks to the power of Spring Boot, this is defined by dependencies on the classpath. Nevertheless, we'll continue using RabbitMQ because it's darn simple and powerful at the same time.

By the way, we'll see this concept of connecting a sink to `Flux` again when we visit `Chapter 17`, *WebSockets with Spring Boot*. It's a common Reactor pattern when connecting one-off objects to established flows.

To declare a Spring Cloud Stream consumer, we merely need to update our `CommentService` as follows:

```
@Service
@EnableBinding(CustomProcessor.class)
public class CommentService {
```

At the top of `CommentService`, we need to add `@EnableBinding(CustomProcessor.class)`. If this was the only Spring Cloud Stream component, we could have used `@EnableBinding(Processor.class)`, however, we can't share the same channel, output, with the `CommentController`. So we need to code a custom set of channels, `CustomProcessor` as shown below:

```
public interface CustomProcessor {

    String INPUT = "input";
    String OUTPUT = "emptyOutput";

    @Input(CustomProcessor.INPUT)
    SubscribableChannel input();

    @Output(CustomProcessor.OUTPUT)
    MessageChannel output();

}
```

This custom processor is quite similar to Spring Cloud Stream's `Processor`:

- It's a declarative interface.
- It has two channel names, `INPUT` and `OUTPUT`. The `INPUT` channel uses the same as `Processor`. To avoid colliding with the `OUTPUT` channel of `Source`, we create a different channel name, `emptyOutput`. (Why call it `emptyOutput`? We'll see in a moment!)
- The is a `SubscribableChannel` for inputs and a `MessageChannel` for outputs.

This flags our application as both a `Sink` as well as a `Source` for events. Remember how we had to `subscribe` earlier when consuming with `RabbitTemplate`?

Thankfully, Spring Cloud Stream is Reactor-friendly. When dealing with Reactive Streams, our code shouldn't be the termination point for processing. So, receiving an incoming `Flux` of `Comment` objects must result in an outgoing `Flux` that the framework can invoke as we'll soon see.

Further down in `CommentService`, we need to update our `save` method as follows:

```
@StreamListener
@Output(CustomProcessor.OUTPUT)
public Flux<Void> save(@Input(CustomProcessor.INPUT)
 Flux<Comment> newComments) {
    return repository
      .saveAll(newComments)
      .flatMap(comment -> {
        meterRegistry
          .counter("comments.consumed", "imageId",
comment.getImageId())
            .increment();
        return Mono.empty();
      });
 }
```

Let's tear apart this preceding updated version of `save`:

- The `@RabbitListener` annotation has been replaced with `@StreamListener`, indicating that it's transport-agnostic.
- The argument `newComments` is tied to the **input** channel via the `@Input()` annotation.
- Since we've marked it as `Flux`, we can immediately consume it with our MongoDB repository.

- Since we have to hand a stream back to the framework, we have marked up the whole method with `@Output`.
- From there, we can flatMap it to generate metrics and then transform it into a `Flux` of `Mono<Void>`s with `Mono.empty()`. This ensures that no more processing is done by the framework.

This method has the same concept as all Spring `@*Listener` annotations--invoke the method with optional domain objects. But this time, it receives them from whatever underlying technology we have configured Spring Cloud Stream to use. The benefit is that this is slim and easy to manage and our code is no longer bound to RabbitMQ directly.

That being said, we need to express to Spring Cloud Stream that our source and sink need to communicate through the same RabbitMQ exchange. To do so, we need to provide settings in `application.yml`:

```
spring:
  cloud:
    stream:
      bindings:
        input:
          destination: learning-spring-boot-comments
          group: learning-spring-boot
        output:
          destination: learning-spring-boot-comments
          group: learning-spring-boot
```

This last application configuration contains the following details:

- `spring.cloud.stream.bindings` is configured for both the `input` and the `output` channel's destination to be `learning-spring-boot`. When using RabbitMQ bindings, this is the name of the **exchange** and Spring Cloud Stream uses topic exchanges by default.
- We take advantage of Spring Cloud Streams' support for **consumer groups** by *also* setting the `group` property. This ensures that even if there are multiple stream listeners to a given channel, only one listener will consume any one message. This type of guarantee is required in cloud-native environments when we can expect to run multiple instances.

> As stated early in this book, you can use either `application.properties` or `application.yml`. If you find yourself configuring many settings with the same prefix, use YAML to make it easier to read and avoid repetition.

By the way, remember having to define a `Jackson2JsonMessageConverter` bean earlier in this chapter to handle serialization? No longer needed. Spring Cloud Stream uses Esoteric Software's Kryo library for serialization/deserialization (`https://github.com/EsotericSoftware/kryo`). That means, we can chuck that bean definition. Talk about thinning out the code!

If we run the simulator again (`spring.profiles.active=simulator`) and check `http://localhost:8080/application/metrics`, we can see our custom metrics tabulating everything.

With this, we have managed to change the **comments** solution and yet retain the same set of metrics.

However, by switching to Spring Cloud Stream, we have gathered a whole new fleet of metrics, as seen in this screenshot:

```
integration.channel.output.errorRate.mean: 0,
integration.channel.output.errorRate.max: 0,
integration.channel.output.errorRate.min: 0,
integration.channel.output.errorRate.stdev: 0,
integration.channel.output.errorRate.count: 0,
integration.channel.output.sendCount: 1080,
integration.channel.output.sendRate.mean: 33.2953175275134,
integration.channel.output.sendRate.max: 0.10356745398044587,
integration.channel.output.sendRate.min: 0.00007268595695495606,
integration.channel.output.sendRate.stdev: 127.44592804513556,
integration.channel.output.sendRate.count: 1080,
integration.channel.output.receiveCount: -1,
integration.channel.input.errorRate.mean: 0,
integration.channel.input.errorRate.max: 0,
integration.channel.input.errorRate.min: 0,
integration.channel.input.errorRate.stdev: 0,
integration.channel.input.errorRate.count: 0,
integration.channel.input.sendCount: 1080,
integration.channel.input.sendRate.mean: 30.60592083415993,
integration.channel.input.sendRate.max: 0.10221006900072098,
integration.channel.input.sendRate.min: 0.000672169029712677,
integration.channel.input.sendRate.stdev: 20.733646866079425,
integration.channel.input.sendRate.count: 1080,
integration.channel.input.receiveCount: -1,
```

This is a subset (too many to fill a book) covering the input and output channels.

Remember how we wrote a custom health check in the last chapter? It would be handy to have one for RabbitMQ and its bindings. Guess what? It's already done. Check it out:

```
{
    status: "UP",
  - learningSpringBoot: {
        status: "UP"
    },
  - diskSpace: {
        status: "UP",
        total: 498937626624,
        free: 89344151552,
        threshold: 10485760
    },
  - rabbit: {
        status: "UP",
        version: "3.6.4"
    },
  - mongo: {
        status: "UP",
        version: "3.2.6"
    },
  - binders: {
        status: "UP",
      - rabbit: {
            status: "UP",
          - binderHealthIndicator: {
                status: "UP",
                version: "3.6.4"
            }
        }
    }
}
```

In this last screenshot, we can see the following:

- The RabbitMQ broker is up and operational
- Our RabbitMQ binders are operational as well

With this in place, we have a nicely working **comment** system.

Logging with Spring Cloud Stream

To wrap things up, it would be nice to actually see how Spring Cloud Stream is handling things. To do so, we can dial up the log levels in `application.yml` like this:

```
logging:
  level:
    org:
      springframework:
        cloud: DEBUG
        integration: DEBUG
```

This last code dials up the log levels for both Spring Cloud Stream and its underlying technology, Spring Integration. It's left as an exercise for the reader to change `RabbitTemplate` log levels by setting `org.springframework.amqp=DEBUG` and see what happens.

With these levels dialed up, if we run our application, we can see a little of this:

```
o.s.a.r.c.CachingConnectionFactory        : Created new connection: rabbitConnectionFactory#1470a7b3:0/SimpleConnection@31792aa
o.s.integration.channel.DirectChannel     : Channel 'unknown.channel.name' has 1 subscriber(s).
o.s.c.s.binding.BindableProxyFactory      : Binding outputs for :interface org.springframework.cloud.stream.messaging.Processor
o.s.c.s.binding.BindableProxyFactory      : Binding :interface org.springframework.cloud.stream.messaging.Processor:output
o.s.integration.channel.DirectChannel     : Channel 'application.output' has 1 subscriber(s).
o.s.c.support.DefaultLifecycleProcessor   : Starting beans in phase 0
o.s.i.endpoint.EventDrivenConsumer        : Adding {logging-channel-adapter:_org.springframework.integration.errorLogger} as a
o.s.i.channel.PublishSubscribeChannel     : Channel 'application.errorChannel' has 1 subscriber(s).
o.s.i.endpoint.EventDrivenConsumer        : started _org.springframework.integration.errorLogger
o.s.c.support.DefaultLifecycleProcessor   : Starting beans in phase 2147482647
o.s.c.s.binding.BindableProxyFactory      : Binding inputs for :interface org.springframework.cloud.stream.messaging.Source
o.s.c.s.binding.BindableProxyFactory      : Binding inputs for :interface org.springframework.cloud.stream.messaging.Processor
o.s.c.s.binding.BindableProxyFactory      : Binding :interface org.springframework.cloud.stream.messaging.Processor:input
r.s.b.r.p.RabbitExchangeQueueProvisioner  : declaring queue for inbound: learning-spring-boot-comments.learning-spring-boot, bd
r.s.b.r.p.RabbitExchangeQueueProvisioner  : autoBindDLQ=false for: learning-spring-boot-comments.learning-spring-boot
o.s.i.a.i.AmqpInboundChannelAdapter       : started inbound.learning-spring-boot
o.s.i.endpoint.EventDrivenConsumer        : Adding {message-handler:inbound.learning-spring-boot-comments.learning-spring-boot}
o.s.i.endpoint.EventDrivenConsumer        : started inbound.learning-spring-boot-comments.learning-spring-boot
```

This previous screenshot shows a clear separation between Spring Cloud Stream involved in binding compared to Spring Integration dealing with channel settings as well as setting up AMQP exchanges and queues.

It's also nice to observe that the logging prefix `o.s.c.s` is short for `org.springframework.cloud.stream` or Spring Cloud Stream.

If we add a new comment on the web page, we can see the outcome, as seen here:

```
o.s.integration.channel.DirectChannel      : preSend on channel 'output', message: GenericMessage [payload=Comment(id=null, ima
tractMessageChannelBinder$SendingHandler    : org.springframework.cloud.stream.binder.AbstractMessageChannelBinder$SendingHandle
o.s.i.codec.kryo.CompositeKryoRegistrar     : registering [40, java.io.File] with serializer org.springframework.integration.cod
o.s.i.a.outbound.AmqpOutboundEndpoint       : org.springframework.integration.amqp.outbound.AmqpOutboundEndpoint@52038bac receiv
s.i.m.AbstractHeaderMapper$HeaderMatcher    : headerName=[contentType] WILL be mapped, matched pattern=*
o.s.i.a.outbound.AmqpOutboundEndpoint       : handler 'org.springframework.integration.amqp.outbound.AmqpOutboundEndpoint@52038b
o.s.integration.channel.DirectChannel       : postSend (sent=true) on channel 'output', message: GenericMessage [payload=Comment
s.i.m.AbstractHeaderMapper$HeaderMatcher    : headerName=[amqp_receivedDeliveryMode] WILL be mapped, matched pattern=*
s.i.m.AbstractHeaderMapper$HeaderMatcher    : headerName=[amqp_receivedRoutingKey] WILL be mapped, matched pattern=*
s.i.m.AbstractHeaderMapper$HeaderMatcher    : headerName=[amqp_receivedExchange] WILL be mapped, matched pattern=*
s.i.m.AbstractHeaderMapper$HeaderMatcher    : headerName=[amqp_deliveryTag] WILL be mapped, matched pattern=*
s.i.m.AbstractHeaderMapper$HeaderMatcher    : headerName=[amqp_correlationId] WILL be mapped, matched pattern=*
s.i.m.AbstractHeaderMapper$HeaderMatcher    : headerName=[amqp_redelivered] WILL be mapped, matched pattern=*
s.i.m.AbstractHeaderMapper$HeaderMatcher    : headerName=[contentType] WILL be mapped, matched pattern=*
s.i.m.AbstractHeaderMapper$HeaderMatcher    : headerName=[contentType] WILL be mapped, matched pattern=*
actMessageChannelBinder$ReceivingHandler    : org.springframework.cloud.stream.binder.AbstractMessageChannelBinder$ReceivingHand
findAll                                      : | onSubscribe([Fuseable] FluxOnAssembly.OnAssemblySubscriber)
findAll                                      : | request(256)
o.s.integration.channel.DirectChannel       : preSend on channel 'input', message: GenericMessage [payload=Comment(id=null, imag
findAll                                      : | onNext(Image(id=59894898c4d956e34025dacc, name=learning-spring-boot-cover.jpg))
findAll                                      : | request(1)
findAll                                      : | onNext(Image(id=59894898c4d956e34025dacd, name=learning-spring-boot-2nd-edition-
findAll                                      : | request(1)
findAll                                      : | onNext(Image(id=59894899c4d956e34025dace, name=bazinga.png))
findAll                                      : | onComplete()
o.s.integration.channel.DirectChannel       : postSend (sent=true) on channel 'input', message: GenericMessage [payload=Comment(
```

This screenshot nicely shows **Comment** being transmitted to the **output** channel and then received on the **input** channel later.

Also notice that the logging prefix `o.s.i` indicates Spring Integration, with `s.i.m` being Spring Integration's Message API.

Summary

In this chapter, we created a message-based solution for users to comment on images. We first used Spring AMQP and `RabbitTemplate` to dispatch writes to a separate *slice*. Then we replaced that with Spring Cloud Stream with RabbitMQ bindings. That let us solve the comments situation with messaging, but without our code being bound to a specific transport technology.

In the next chapter, we'll break up our quickly growing, monolithic application into smaller microservices and use Spring Cloud to simplify integration between these distributed components.

16
Microservices with Spring Boot

@SpringBoot and @SpringCloudOSS are making it way too easy to build advanced distributed systems. Shame on you! #ComplimentarySarcasm

– InSource Software @InSourceOmaha

In the previous chapter, we learned how to communicate between different systems using AMQP messaging with RabbitMQ as our broker.

In this day and age, teams around the world are discovering that constantly tacking on more and more functionality is no longer effective after a certain point. Domains become blurred, coupling between various systems makes things resistant to change, and different teams are forced to hold more and more meetings to avoid breaking various parts of the system, sometimes, for the tiniest of changes.

Emerging from all this malaise are **microservices**. The term microservice is meant to connote a piece of software that doesn't attempt to solve too many problems, but a targeted situation instead. Its scope is microscopic when compared with the existing behemoth monoliths that litter the horizon.

And that's where Spring Cloud steps in. By continuing the paradigm of autoconfiguration, Spring Cloud extends Spring Boot into the realm of cloud-native microservices, making the development of distributed microservices quite practical.

In this chapter, we will cover the following topics:

- A quick primer on microservices
- Dynamically registering and finding services with Eureka
- Introducing `@SpringCloudApplication`

- Calling one microservice from another with client-side load balancing
- Implementing microservice circuit breakers
- Monitoring circuits
- Offloading microservice settings to a configuration server

A quick primer on microservices

As we said, a microservice focuses on solving a problem and solving it right, much like the UNIX philosophy of *make each program do one thing well* [Doug McIlroy].

That said, too many people describe microservices as being less than a certain number of lines of code, or less than a certain number of megabytes in total size. Nothing could be further from the truth. In fact, microservices are more closely tied to **bounded contexts** as defined by Eric Evans in *Domain Driven Design*, a worthwhile read despite having been written in 2003.

In essence, a microservice should focus on solving a particular problem, and only use enough domain knowledge to tackle that specific problem. If other parts of the system wish to interact with the same domain, their own context might be different.

In case you missed it, we introduced Spring Cloud (`http://projects.spring.io/spring-cloud/`) in the previous chapter using Spring Cloud Stream. Spring Cloud is a collection of Spring projects that are aimed at solving cloud-native problems. These are problems observed time and again when systems grow in size and scope, and are often relegated to cloud platforms. Solving cloud-native problems with microservices has seen a high rate of success, hence making many of their tools a perfect fit for this chapter.

Suffice it to say, entire books have been written on the subject of microservices, so, to further explore this realm, feel free to look about. For the rest of this chapter, we'll see how Spring Boot and Spring Cloud make it super simple to engage in microservice development without paying a huge cost.

There are *hundreds* of books written on the subject of microservices. For more details, check out the free book, *Migrating to Cloud Native Application Architectures* by cloud native polymath Matt Stine (`http://mattstine.com`). It covers many concepts that underpin microservices.

Dynamically registering and finding services with Eureka

At a fundamental level, taking one big application (like we've built so far) and splitting it up into two or more microservices requires that the two systems communicate with each other. And to communicate, these systems need to find each other. This is known as **service discovery**.

The Netflix engineering team built a tool for this called **Eureka**, and open sourced it. Eureka provides the means for microservices to power up, advertise their existence, and shutdown as well. It supports multiple copies of the same service registering themselves, and allows multiple instances of Eureka to register with each other to develop a highly available service registry.

Standing up a Eureka Server is quite simple. We simply have to create a new application at `http://start.spring.io`:

Yes, that's correct. We create an entirely *separate* Spring Boot application using the Spring Initializr, apart from our functional application. And in the preceding screenshot, the arrows point out that we are calling it `learning-spring-boot-eureka-server` while also adding a single dependency, **Eureka Server**. This application will be dedicated to providing our microservices with a **service registry**.

If we peek at our Eureka Server's build file, we'll find a slim list of dependencies toward the bottom:

```
dependencies {
  compile('org.springframework.cloud:spring-cloud-starter-eureka-
    server')
}

dependencyManagement {
  imports {
    mavenBom "org.springframework.cloud:spring-cloud-
      dependencies:${springCloudVersion}"
  }
}
```

This short list has but one dependency--`spring-cloud-starter-eureka-server`. Following it is the same Spring Cloud **Bill of Materials** (**BOM**) used to provide the proper versions of the Spring Cloud components.

Toward the top of the build file, we can see the exact versions of both Spring Boot and Spring Cloud:

```
buildscript {
  ext {
    springBootVersion = '2.0.0.M5'
    springCloudVersion = 'Finchley.M3'
  }
  ...
}
```

> Spring Cloud's `Finchley` release train, also mentioned in the previous chapter, is the version compatible with Spring Boot 2.0.

With that in place, the only code we must write is shown here:

```
@SpringBootApplication
@EnableEurekaServer
public class LearningSpringBootEurekaServerApplication {
```

```
public static void main(String[] args) {
  SpringApplication.run(
    LearningSpringBootEurekaServerApplication.class);
  }
}
```

This preceding simple application can be described as follows:

- `@SpringBootApplication` marks this app as a Spring Boot application, which means that it will autoconfigure beans based on the classpath, and load properties as well.
- `@EnableEurekaServer` tells Spring Cloud Eureka that we want to run a Eureka Server. It proceeds to configure all the necessary beans to host a service registry.
- The code inside `public static void main` is the same as the previous chapters, simply loading the surrounding class.

Before we can launch our Eureka service registry, there are some key settings that must be plugged in. To do so, we need to create a `src/main/resources/application.yml` file as follows:

```
server:
  port: 8761

eureka:
  instance:
    hostname: localhost
  client:
    registerWithEureka: false
    fetchRegistry: false
    serviceUrl:
      defaultZone:
        http://${eureka.instance.hostname}:${server.port}/eureka/
```

The previous configuration file can be explained in detail as follows:

- `server.port` lets us run it on Eureka's standard port of `8761`.
- For a standalone Eureka Server, we have to configure it with a `eureka.instance.hostname` and a `eureka.client.serviceUrl.defaultZone` setting. This resolves to `http://localhost:8761/eureka`, the URI for this standalone version of Eureka. For a multi-node Eureka Server configuration, we would alter this configuration.

Eureka servers are also clients, which means that with multiple instances running, they will send heartbeats to each other, and also registry data. With a standalone instance, we would get bombarded with log messages about failing to reach peers unless we disable the Eureka server from being a client via `eureka.client.registerWithEureka=false` and `eureka.client.fetchRegistry=false` (as we just did).

To run things in a more resilient mode, we could run two instances, each with a different Spring profile (`peer1` and `peer2`) with the following configuration:

```
---
spring:
  profiles: peer1
eureka:
  instance:
    hostname: peer1
  client:
    serviceUrl:
      defaultZone: http://peer2/eureka/

---
spring:
  profiles: peer2
eureka:
  instance:
    hostname: peer2
  client:
    serviceUrl:
      defaultZone: http://peer1/eureka/
```

`spring.profiles`, in a YAML file with the triple-dash separators, lets us put multiple profiles in the same `application.yml` configuration file. To launch an application with a given profile, we merely need to run it with `spring.profiles.active=peer1` or `SPRING_PROFILES_ACTIVE=peer1`. As stated, this configuration file has two profiles, `peer1` and `peer2`.

Assuming we launched two separate copies of our Eureka Server, each on a different port running each profile, they would seek each other out, register as clients to each other, send heartbeats, and synchronize their registry data. It's left as an exercise for the reader to spin up a pair of Eureka Servers.

Going back to the original configuration file we wrote, we can now run `LearningSpringBootEurekaServerApplication`. With this service running in the background, we can now embark on converting our previous monolith into a set of microservices.

Introducing @SpringCloudApplication

If you haven't caught on by now, we plan to split up the system we've built so far so that one microservice focuses on images, and the other on comments. That way, in the future, we can scale each service with the appropriate number of instances based on traffic.

To make this break, let's basically grab all the code from the `comments` subpackage, and move it into an entirely different project. We'll call one project `images` and the other one `comments`.

Before we can copy all that code, we need a project for each. To do so, simply create two new folders, `learning-spring-boot-comments` and `learning-spring-boot-images`. We could go back to Spring Initializr to create them from scratch, but that's unnecessary. It's much easier to simply copy the existing build file of our monolith into both of our new microservices, and customize the name of the artifact. Since the `build.gradle` file is almost identical to the monolith, there's no need to inspect it here.

The new `comments` microservice file layout should look something like this:

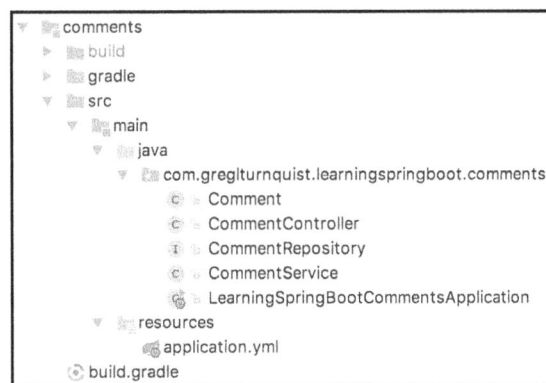

And the new `images` microservice file layout should appear something like this:

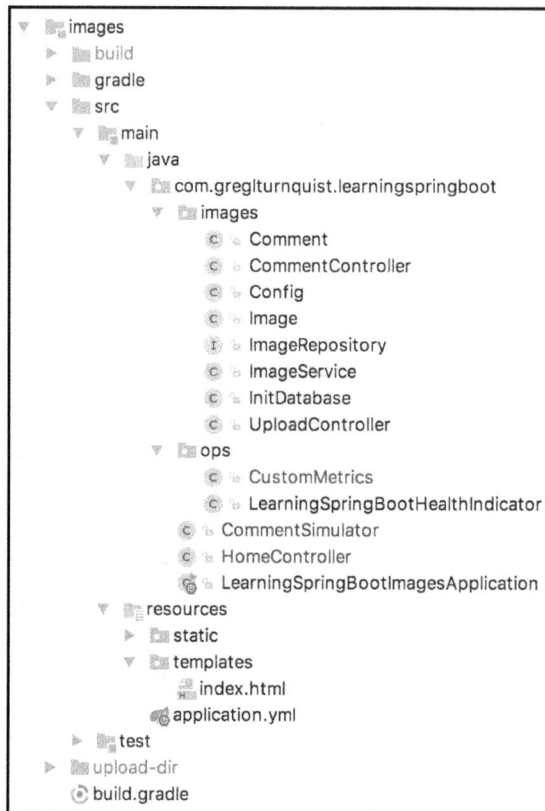

```
▼  images
  ▶  build
  ▶  gradle
  ▼  src
    ▼  main
      ▼  java
        ▼  com.gregturnquist.learningspringboot
          ▼  images
              C  Comment
              C  CommentController
              C  Config
              C  Image
              I  ImageRepository
              C  ImageService
              C  InitDatabase
              C  UploadController
          ▼  ops
              C  CustomMetrics
              C  LearningSpringBootHealthIndicator
            C  CommentSimulator
            C  HomeController
            ⬡  LearningSpringBootImagesApplication
      ▼  resources
        ▶  static
        ▼  templates
            index.html
          application.yml
    ▶  test
  ▶  upload-dir
    build.gradle
```

With that completed, we now need to tweak the launcher for our `comments` microservice like this:

```
@SpringCloudApplication
public class LearningSpringBootCommentsApplication {

  public static void main(String[] args) {
    SpringApplication.run(
        LearningSpringBootCommentsApplication.class);
  }
}
```

This last bit of code is, virtually, identical to what we have seen in previous chapters except for the following:

- `@SpringCloudApplication` replaces the previous `@SpringBootApplication`. This new annotation extends `@SpringBootApplication`, giving us the same autoconfiguration, component scanning, and property support (among other things) that we have come to love. Additionally, it adds `@EnableDiscoveryClient` to register with Eureka and `@EnableCircuitBreaker` so we can create fallback commands if a remote service is down (something we'll see explored later in this chapter).
- The name of the class has been changed to better describe its job.

> There are both `@EnableEurekaClient` and `@EnableDiscoveryClient` annotations available. `DiscoveryClient` is the abstract interface that Spring Cloud Netflix puts above `EurekaClient` in the event that future service registry tools are built. At this point in time, there is little difference in our code, except the convenient usage of a single annotation,`@SpringCloudApplication`, to turn our component into a microservice.

Having split up `images` and `comments`, we should make a similar adjustment to the top-level class for `images`:

```
@SpringCloudApplication
public class LearningSpringBootImagesApplication {

    public static void main(String[] args) {
        SpringApplication.run(
            LearningSpringBootImagesApplication.class, args);
    }
}
```

In the preceding code, we have applied the same type to the `images` microservice as we did to the `comments` microservice (`@SpringBootApplication` → `@SpringCloudApplication`).

For each of our microservices to talk to Eureka, we need to add the following code to `src/main/resources/application.yml` (in both `images` and `comments`):

```
eureka:
  client:
    serviceUrl:
      defaultZone: http://localhost:8761/eureka/
```

This single-property configuration file can be described as follows:

- `eureka.client.serviceUrl.defaultZone` instructs our `DiscoveryClient`-powered application to look for Eureka at `http://localhost:8761/eureka`.

> There are many more options for configuring Eureka and its clients. See `http://cloud.spring.io/spring-cloud-netflix/spring-cloud-netflix.html` for more details.

We can now move forward with splitting up our system.

Calling one microservice from another with client-side load balancing

Remember how we configured our Eureka Server earlier to run on a separate port? Every microservice has to run on a distinct port. If we assume the `images` service is our frontend (it has the Thymeleaf template, and is closest to consumers for serving up image data), then we can let it continue to run on Netty's default port of `8080`.

That leaves one decision: what port to run the `comments` service on? Let's add this to the `comments` service's `application.yml`:

```
server:
  port: 9000
```

This setting instructs Spring Boot to run `comments` on port `9000`. With that in place, let's go back to `images`, and make some adjustments.

For starters (Spring Boot starters), we need to add some extra things to the `images` `build.gradle` file:

```
compile('org.springframework.cloud:spring-cloud-starter-eureka')
compile('org.springframework.cloud:spring-cloud-starter-hystrix')
```

These changes include the following:

- `spring-cloud-starter-eureka` is the dependency needed to register our microservice as a Eureka client. It brings in several transitive dependencies, the most important one for this section being **Ribbon**.
- `spring-cloud-starter-hystrix` is the dependency for the circuit-breaker pattern, which we will dig into later in this chapter.

The Spring Framework has had, for a long time, the powerful `RestTemplate` utility. To make a remote call, we just do something like this:

```
List<Comment> comments = restTemplate.exchange(
  "http://localhost:9000/comments/{imageId}",
  HttpMethod.GET,
  null,
  new ParameterizedTypeReference<List<Comment>>() {},
  image.getId()).getBody();
```

There's a lot going on here, so let's take it apart:

- `restTemplate.exchange()` is the generic method for making remote calls. There are shortcuts such as `getForObject()` and `getForEntity()`, but when dealing with generics (such as `List<Comment>`), we need to switch to `exchange()`.
- The first argument is the URL to the `comments` service that we just picked. It has the port number we selected along with the route (`/comments/{imageId}`, a template) where we can serve up a list of comments based on the image's ID.
- The second argument is the HTTP verb we wish to use--`GET`.
- The third argument is for headers and any body. Since this is a `GET`, there are none.
- The fourth argument is the return type of the data. Due to limitations of Java's generics and type erasure, we have created a dedicated anonymous class to capture the type details for `List<Comment>`, which Spring can use to interact with Jackson to properly deserialize.

- The final argument is the parameter (`image.getId()`) that will be used to expand our URI template's `{imageId}` field.
- Since `exchange()` returns a Spring `ResponseEntity<T>`, we need to invoke the `body()` method to extract the response body.

There is a big limitation in this code when dealing with microservices--the URL of our target service can change.

Getting locked into a fixed location is never good. What if the `comments` service changes ports? What if we need to scale up multiple copies in the future?

Frankly, that's unacceptable.

The solution? We should tie in with Netflix's Ribbon service, a software load balancer that also integrates with Eureka. To do so, we only need some small additions to our `images` service.

First, we should create a `RestTemplate` object. To do so, let's add a `Config` class as follows:

```
@Configuration
public class Config {

  @Bean
  @LoadBalanced
  RestTemplate restTemplate() {
    return new RestTemplate();
  }
}
```

We can describe the preceding code as follows:

- `@Configuration` marks this as a configuration class containing bean definitions. Since it's located underneath `LearningSpringBootImagesApplication`, it will be automatically picked up by component scanning.
- `@Bean` marks the `restTemplate()` method as a bean definition.
- The `restTemplate()` method returns a plain old Spring `RestTemplate` instance.
- `@LoadBalanced` instructs Netflix Ribbon to wrap this `RestTemplate` bean with load balancing advice.

We can next inject our `RestTemplate` bean into the `HomeController` like this:

```
private final RestTemplate restTemplate;

public HomeController(ImageService imageService,
 RestTemplate restTemplate) {
    this.imageService = imageService;
    this.restTemplate = restTemplate;
}
```

This uses constructor injection to set the controller's final copy of `restTemplate`.

With a **load-balanced, Eureka-aware** `restTemplate`, we can now update our `index()` method to populate the `comments` model attribute like this:

```
restTemplate.exchange(
    "http://COMMENTS/comments/{imageId}",
    HttpMethod.GET,
    null,
    new ParameterizedTypeReference<List<Comment>>() {},
    image.getId()).getBody());
```

This code is almost identical to what we typed out earlier except for one difference-- the URL has been revamped into `http://COMMENTS/comments/{imageId}`. `COMMENTS` is the logical name that our `comments` microservice registered itself with in Eureka.

The logical name for a microservice used by Eureka and Ribbon is set using `spring.application.name` inside its `src/main/resources/application.yml` file:

- `comments`: spring.application.name: `comments`
- `images`: spring.application.name: `images`

> The logical name is case insensitive, so you can use either `http://COMMENTS/comments/{imageId}` or `http://comments/comments/{imageId}`. Uppercase helps make it clear that this is a logical hostname, not a physical one.

With this in place, it doesn't matter where we deploy our system nor how many instances are running. Eureka will dynamically update things, and also support multiple copies registered under the same name. Ribbon will handle routing between all instances.

That's nice except that we still need to move the `CommentReadRepository` we built in the previous chapter to the `comments` microservice!

In the previous chapter, we differentiated between reading comments with a `CommentReadRepository` and writing comments with a `CommentWriteRepository`. Since we are concentrating all MongoDB operations in one microservice, it makes sense to merge both of these into one `CommentRepository` like this:

```
public interface CommentRepository
  extends Repository<Comment, String> {

    Flux<Comment> findByImageId(String imageId);

    Flux<Comment> saveAll(Flux<Comment> newComment);

    // Required to support save()
    Mono<Comment> findById(String id);

    Mono<Void> deleteAll();
}
```

Our newly built repository can be described as follows:

- We've renamed it as `CommentRepository`
- It still extends `Repository<Comment, String>`, indicating it only has the methods we need
- The `findByImageId()`, `save()`, `findOne()`, and `deleteAll()` methods are all simply copied into this one interface

> **TIP**
>
> It's generally recommended to avoid sharing databases between microservices, or at least avoid sharing the same tables. The temptation to couple in the database is strong, and can even lead to integrating through the database. Hence, the reason to move ALL MongoDB comment operations to one place nicely isolates things.

Using this repository, we need to build a REST controller to serve up lists of comments from `/comments/{imageId}`:

```
@RestController
public class CommentController {

    private final CommentRepository repository;

    public CommentController(CommentRepository repository) {
```

```
        this.repository = repository;
    }

    @GetMapping("/comments/{imageId}")
    public Flux<Comment> comments(@PathVariable String imageId) {
        return repository.findByImageId(imageId);
    }
}
```

This previous tiny controller can be easily described as follows:

- `@RestController` indicates this is a Spring WebFlux controller where all results are written directly into the HTTP response body
- `CommentRepository` is injected into a field using constructor injection
- `@GetMapping()` configures this method to respond to GET `/comments/{imageId}` requests.
- `@PathVariable String imageId` gives us access to the `{imageId}` piece of the route
- The method returns a `Flux` of comments by invoking our repository's `findByImage()` using the `imageId`

Having coded things all the way from populating the UI with comments in our `images` service, going through Ribbon and Eureka, to our `comments` service, we are fetching comments from the system responsible for managing them.

> `RestTemplate` doesn't speak Reactive Streams. It's a bit too old for that. But there is a new remote calling library in Spring Framework 5 called `WebClient`. Why aren't we using it? Because it doesn't (yet) support Eureka logical hostname resolution. Hence, the part of our application making `RestTemplate` calls is blocking. In the future, when that becomes available, I highly recommend migrating to it, based on its fluent API and support for Reactor types.

In addition to linking two microservices together with remote calls, we have decoupled comment management from image management, allowing us to scale things for efficiency and without the two systems being bound together too tightly.

With all these changes in place, let's test things out. First of all, we must ensure our Eureka Server is running:

```
  .   ____          _            __ _ _
 /\\ / ___'_ __ _ _(_)_ __  __ _ \ \ \ \
( ( )\___ | '_ | '_| | '_ \/ _` | \ \ \ \
 \\/  ___)| |_)| | | | | || (_| |  ) ) ) )
  '  |____| .__|_| |_|_| |_\__, | / / / /
 =========|_|==============|___/=/_/_/_/
 :: Spring Boot ::         (v2.0.0.M5)
2017-08-12 09:48:47.966: Setting initial instance status as:
 STARTING
2017-08-12 09:48:47.993: Initializing Eureka in region us-east-1
2017-08-12 09:48:47.993: Client configured to neither register nor
 que...
2017-08-12 09:48:47.998: Discovery Client initialized at timestamp
 150...
2017-08-12 09:48:48.042: Initializing ...
2017-08-12 09:48:48.044: The replica size seems to be empty.
 Check the...
2017-08-12 09:48:48.051: Finished initializing remote region
 registrie...
2017-08-12 09:48:48.051: Initialized
2017-08-12 09:48:48.261: Registering application unknown with
 eureka w...
2017-08-12 09:48:48.294: Setting the eureka configuration..
2017-08-12 09:48:48.294: Eureka data center value
eureka.datacenter
 is...
2017-08-12 09:48:48.294: Eureka environment value
 eureka.environment i...
2017-08-12 09:48:48.302: isAws returned false
2017-08-12 09:48:48.303: Initialized server context
2017-08-12 09:48:48.303: Got 1 instances from neighboring DS node
2017-08-12 09:48:48.303: Renew threshold is: 1
2017-08-12 09:48:48.303: Changing status to UP
2017-08-12 09:48:48.307: Started Eureka Server
2017-08-12 09:48:48.343: Tomcat started on port(s): 8761 (http)
2017-08-12 09:48:48.343: Updating port to 8761
2017-08-12 09:48:48.347: Started
LearningSpringBootEurekaServerApplica...
```

In this preceding subset of console output, bits of Eureka can be seen as it starts up on port 8761 and switches to a state of UP. It may seem quirky to see messages about **Amazon Web Services (AWS)**, but that's not surprising given Eureka's creators (Netflix) run all their systems there. However, `isAws returned false` clearly shows the system knows it is NOT running on AWS.

> If you look closely, you can spot that the Eureka Server is running on Apache Tomcat. So far, we've run everything on Netty, right? Since Eureka is a separate process not involved in direct operations, it's okay for it not to be a Reactive Streams-based application.

Next, we can fire up the `images` service:

```
  /\ /  __'_ _ _ _(_)_ __ __ _
 ( ( )___ | '_ | '_| | '_ / _` |
  \/  ___)| |_)| | | | | || (_| |  ) ) ) )
   '  |____| .__|_| |_|_| |___, | / / / /
  ========|_|==============|___/=/_/_/_/
  :: Spring Boot ::   (v2.0.0.M5)
  ...
  2017-10-20 22:29:34.319: Registering application images with
eureka
     wi...
  2017-10-20 22:29:34.320: Saw local status change event
  StatusChangeEve...
  2017-10-20 22:29:34.321: DiscoveryClient_IMAGES/retina:images:
  registe...
  2017-10-20 22:29:34.515: DiscoveryClient_IMAGES/retina:images -
  regist...
  2017-10-20 22:29:34.522: Netty started on port(s): 8080 (http)
  2017-10-20 22:29:34.523: Updating port to 8080
  2017-10-20 22:29:34.906: Opened connection
  [connectionId{localValue:2,...
  2017-10-20 22:29:34.977: Started
  LearningSpringBootImagesApplication i...
```

This preceding subsection of console output shows it registering itself with the Eureka service through `DiscoveryClient` under the name IMAGES.

At the same time, the following tidbit is logged on the Eureka Server:

```
Registered instance IMAGES/retina:images with status UP
(replication=false)
```

We can easily see that the `images` service has registered itself with the name `IMAGES`, and it's running on `retina` (my machine name).

Finally, let's launch the `comments` microservice:

```
  .   ____
 /\ / ___'_ _ _ _(_)_ _ __ _
( ( )___ | '_ | '_| | '_ / _` |
 \/  ___)| |_)| | | | | | (_| |  ) ) ) )
  '  |____| .__|_| |_|_| |_\__, | / / / /
 ========|_|==============|___/=/_/_/_/
 :: Spring Boot ::   (v2.0.0.M5)
 ...
2016-10-20 22:37:31.477: Registering application comments with
 eureka ...
2016-10-20 22:37:31.478: Saw local status change event
 StatusChangeEve...
2016-10-20 22:37:31.480:
 DiscoveryClient_COMMENTS/retina:comments:9000...
2016-10-20 22:37:31.523:
 DiscoveryClient_COMMENTS/retina:comments:9000...
2016-10-20 22:37:32.154: Netty started on port(s): 9000 (http)
2016-10-20 22:37:32.155: Updating port to 9000
2016-10-20 22:37:32.188: Opened connection
 [connectionId{localValue:2,...
2016-10-20 22:37:32.209: Started
LearningSpringBootCommentsApplication...
```

In this last output, our comment handling microservice has registered itself with Eureka under the logical name `COMMENTS`.

And again, in the Eureka Server logs, we can see a corresponding event:

```
Registered instance COMMENTS/retina:comments:9000 with status UP
(replication=false)
```

The `COMMENTS` service can be found at `retina:9000` (author alert--that's my laptop's hostname, yours will be different), which matches the port we configured that service to run on.

To see all this from a visual perspective, let's navigate to `http://localhost:8761`, and see Eureka's webpage:

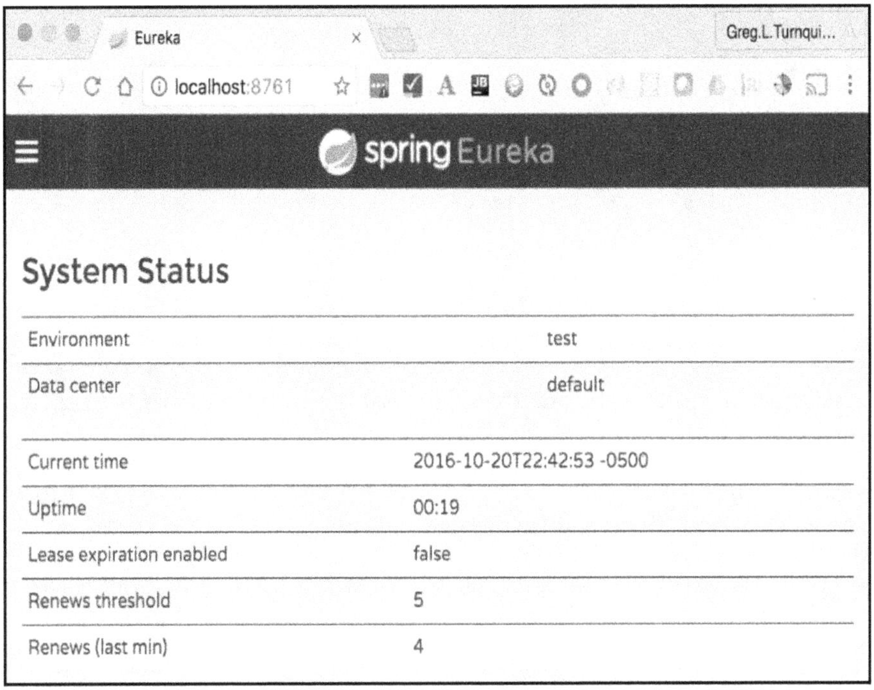

This preceding web page is not provided by Netflix Eureka, but is crafted by the Spring Cloud Netflix project (hence Spring Eureka at the top) instead. It has some basic details about the environment including uptime, refresh policies, and others.

Further down on the page is some more interesting information:

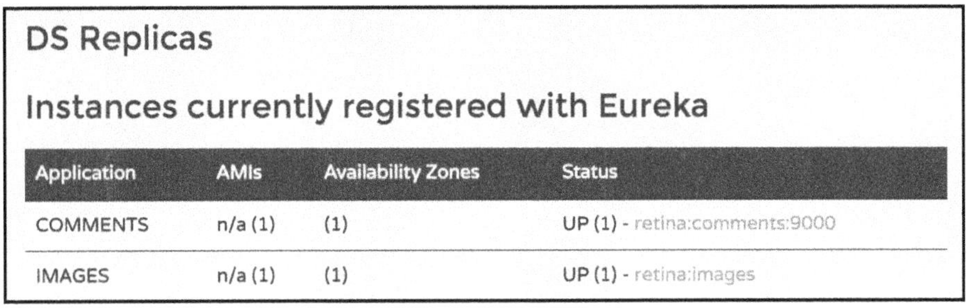

DS (Discovery Service) Replica details are listed on the web page. Specifically, we can see the logical applications on the left (COMMENTS and IMAGES), their status on the right (both UP), and hyperlinks to every instance (retina:comments:9000 and retina:images).

If we actually click on the retina:comments:9000 hyperlink, it takes us to the Spring Boot info endpoint:

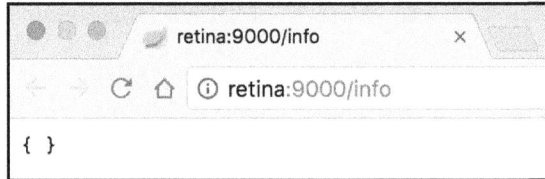

In this case, there is no custom info provided. But it also proves that the service is up and operational.

We may have verified everything is up, but let's prove that our new and improved microservice solution is in operation by visiting http://localhost:8080.

If we load up a couple of new images and submit some comments, things can now look like this:

Learning Spring Boot - 2nd Edition

Id	Name	Image			
5809914283a5d2ac3e0ea0f6	platform-spring-boot.png		Delete		Submit
5809916283a5d2ac3e0ea0f7	B05771_MockupCover_Normal.jpg		Delete	• Cool cover! • Can't wait to get my copy	Submit

Choose File   No file chosen

Upload

What's happening under the hood? If we look at the `images` microservice's console, we can see a little action:

```
2016-10-20 22:53:07.260  Flipping property:
 COMMENTS.ribbon.ActiveConn...
2016-10-20 22:53:07.286  Shutdown hook installed for:
 NFLoadBalancer-P...
2016-10-20 22:53:07.305  Client:COMMENTS instantiated a
 LoadBalancer:D...
2016-10-20 22:53:07.308  Using serverListUpdater
 PollingServerListUpda...
2016-10-20 22:53:07.325  Flipping property:
 COMMENTS.ribbon.ActiveConn...
2016-10-20 22:53:07.326  DynamicServerListLoadBalancer for client
 COMM...
    DynamicServerListLoadBalancer: {
       NFLoadBalancer:name=COMMENTS,
       current list of Servers=[retina:9000],
    }ServerList:org.springframework.cloud.netflix
    .ribbon.eureka.DomainExt...
2016-10-20 22:53:08.313  Flipping property:
 COMMENTS.ribbon.ActiveConn...
2016-10-20 22:54:33.870  Resolving eureka endpoints via
 configuration
```

There's a lot of detail in the preceding output, but we can see **Netflix Ribbon** at work handling software load balancing. We can also see `DynamicServerListLoadBalancer` with a current list of servers containing `[retina:9000]`.

So, what would happen if we launched a second copy of the `comments` service using `SERVER_PORT=9001` to ensure it didn't clash with the current one?

In the console output, we can spot the new instance registering itself with Eureka:

```
DiscoveryClient_COMMENTS/retina:comments:9001 - registration
 status: 204
```

If we go back and visit the Spring Eureka web page again at
`http://localhost:8761`, we can see this updated listing of replicas:

DS Replicas

Instances currently registered with Eureka

Application	AMIs	Availability Zones	Status
COMMENTS	n/a (2)	(2)	UP (2) - retina:comments:9001 , retina:comments:9000
IMAGES	n/a (1)	(1)	UP (1) - retina:images

If we start posting comments on the site, they will rotate, going between each
`comments` microservice.

> **TIP**
>
> Normally, when using RabbitMQ, each instance of `comments` will
> register its own queue, and hence, receive its own copy of newly
> posted comments. This would result in double posting in this
> scenario. However, Spring Cloud Stream has a solution--**consumer
> groups**. By having
> `spring.cloud.stream.bindings.input.group=comments` in
> `comments` microservice's `application.yml`, we declare that only
> one such queue should receive each individual message. This
> ensures that only one of the microservices *actually* processes a given
> event. See
> `http://docs.spring.io/spring-cloud-stream/docs/Elmhurst.M1/`
> `reference/htmlsingle/index.html#consumer-groups` for more
> details.

With microservice-to-microservice remote calls tackled (and supported for scaling
up), it's time to pursue another problem often seen in microservice-based solutions.

Implementing microservice circuit breakers

The ability to invoke a remote microservice comes with an implicit risk--there is
always a chance that the remote service is down.

Remember using @SpringCloudApplication? As a reminder, that annotation contains:

```
@SpringBootApplication
@EnableDiscoveryClient
@EnableCircuitBreaker
public @interface SpringCloudApplication {
}
```

The last annotation, @EnableCircuitBreaker, enables **Netflix Hystrix**, the circuit breaker solution (http://martinfowler.com/bliki/CircuitBreaker.html).

In short, a circuit breaker is something that, when it detects a certain threshold of failure, will open the circuit and prevent any future remote calls for a certain amount of time. The purpose is to prevent cascade failures while giving the remote service an opportunity to heal itself and come back online. Slamming a service in the middle of startup might be detrimental.

For example, if the images microservice's HomeController makes a call to comments, and the system is down, it's possible for the calling thread to get hung up waiting for the request to timeout properly. In the meantime, incoming requests are served by a slightly reduced threadpool. If the problem is bad enough, it can hamper calls coming into the frontend controller, effectively spreading the remote service outage to users.

A side effect when operating multiple instances of such a service is that it can also speed up the failover to an alternate instance of the service.

In exchange for opening the circuit on a service (and failing a call), we can provide a fallback command. For example, if Netflix's recommendation engine happens to be down when a user finishes a show, it will fallback to showing a list of newly released shows. This is definitely better than a blank screen, or, worse, a cryptic stack trace on the website or someone's TV.

In the previous section, we had this fragment of code inside HomeController.index():

```
restTemplate.exchange(
    "http://COMMENTS/comments/{imageId}",
    HttpMethod.GET,
    null,
    new ParameterizedTypeReference<List<Comment>>() {},
    image.getId()).getBody());
```

We want to wrap this remote call to the `comments` system with a circuit breaker/fallback command.

First, we need to move the code into a separate method as follows:

```
@HystrixCommand(fallbackMethod = "defaultComments")
public List<Comment> getComments(Image image) {
  return restTemplate.exchange(
    "http://COMMENTS/comments/{imageId}",
    HttpMethod.GET,
    null,
    new ParameterizedTypeReference<List<Comment>>() {},
    image.getId()).getBody();

}
```

This tiny Hystrix command can be described as follows:

- This shows the exact same `restTemplate` call we wrote using Ribbon and Eureka earlier in this chapter
- `@HystrixCommand(fallback="defaultComments")` wraps the method with an aspect that hooks into a Hystrix proxy
- In the event the remote call fails, Hystrix will call `defaultComments`

What would make a good fallback command? Since we're talking about user comments, there is nothing better than an empty list, so a separate method with the same signature would be perfect:

```
public List<Comment> defaultComments(Image image) {
  return Collections.emptyList();
}
```

In this scenario, we return an empty list. But what makes a suitable fallback situation will invariably depend on the business context.

Hystrix commands operate using Spring **AOP (Aspect Oriented Programming)**. The standard approach is through Java proxies (as opposed to AspectJ weaving, which requires extra setup). A well-known issue with proxies is that in-class invocations don't trigger the enclosing advice. Hence, the Hystrix command method must be put inside another Spring bean, and injected into our controller.

There is some classic advice to offer when talking about Hystrix's AOP **advice**--be careful about using thread locals. However, the recommendation against thread locals is even stronger when we are talking about Reactor-powered applications, the basis for this entire book. That's because Project Reactor uses **work stealing**, a well-documented concept that involves different threads pulling work down when idle. Reactor's scheduler is thread agnostic, which means that we don't know where the work is actually being carried out. So don't use thread locals when writing Reactor applications. This impacts other areas too such as Spring Security, which uses thread locals to maintain contextual security status with `SecurityContextHolder`. We'll visit this subject in `Chapter 18`, *Securing Your App with Spring Boot*.

The following shows our method pulled into a separate class:

```
@Component
public class CommentHelper {
  private final RestTemplate restTemplate;

  CommentHelper(RestTemplate restTemplate) {
    this.restTemplate = restTemplate;
  }

  // @HystrixCommand code shown earlier

  // fallback method
}
```

We've already seen the `@HystrixCommand` code as well as the fallback. The other parts we wrote include:

- The `CommentHelper` class is flagged with an `@Component` annotation, so, it's picked up and registered as a separate Spring bean
- This component is injected with the `restTemplate` we defined earlier via constructor injection

To update our `HomeController` to use this instead, we need to adjust its injection point:

```
private final CommentHelper commentHelper;

public HomeController(ImageService imageService,
  CommentHelper commentHelper) {
    this.imageService = imageService;
```

```
        this.commentHelper = commentHelper;
    }
```

The code in `HomeController` is almost the same, except that instead of injecting a `RestTemplate`, it injects `commentHelper`.

Finally, the call to populate comments in the `index()` method can be updated to use the new `commentHelper`:

```
put("comments", commentHelper.getComments(image));
```

At this point, instead of calling `restTemplate` to make a remote call, we are invoking `commentHelper`, which is wrapped with Hystrix advice to handle failures, and, potentially, open a circuit.

> Notice earlier that I said, "*In the event the remote call fails, Hystrix will call defaultComments.*", but didn't mention anything about opening the circuit? Perhaps that's confusing, since this whole section has been about the circuit breaker pattern. Hystrix tabulates every failure, and *only* opens the circuit when a certain threshold has been breached. One missed remote call isn't enough to switch to an offline state.

Monitoring circuits

Okay, we've coded up a command with a circuit breaker, and given it a fallback command in the event the remote service is down. But how can we monitor it? Simply put--how can we detect if the circuit is open or closed?

Introducing the **Hystrix Dashboard**. With just a smidgeon of code, we can have another Spring Boot application provide us with a graphical view of things. And from there, we can test out what happens if we put the system under load, and then break the system.

To build the app, we first need to visit `http://start.spring.io`, and select **Hystrix Dashboard** and `Turbine`. If we also select `Gradle` and `Spring Boot 2.0.0`, and enter in our similar artifact details, we can produce another app. (Notice how handy it is to simply let *everything* be a Spring Boot app?)

The build file is the same except for these dependency settings:

```
buildscript {
    ext {
```

```
      springBootVersion = '2.0.0.M5'
      springCloudVersion = 'Finchley.M3'
    }
    ...
  }
  ...
dependencies {
  compile('org.springframework.cloud:spring-cloud-starter-
    hystrix-dashboard')
}

dependencyManagement {
  imports {
    mavenBom "org.springframework.cloud:spring-cloud-
      dependencies:${springCloudVersion}"
  }
}
```

We can explain this preceding build file as follows:

- We pick up `spring-cloud-starter-hystrix-dashboard` to build a UI for monitoring circuits
- Again, we select Spring Cloud's **Finchley** BOM release with the `dependencyManagement` settings

To display the Hystrix dashboard, this is all we need:

```
@SpringBootApplication
@EnableHystrixDashboard
public class LearningSpringBootHystrixDashboard {

  public static void main(String[] args) {
    SpringApplication.run(
      LearningSpringBootHystrixDashboard.class);
  }
}
```

This previous tiny application can be described as such:

- `@SpringBootApplication` declares this to be a Spring Boot application. We don't need `@SpringCloudApplication`, because we don't intend to hook into Eureka, nor institute any circuit breakers.
- `@EnableHystrixDashboard` will start up a UI that we'll explore further in this section.
- The class `public static void main` is used to launch this class.

To configure this service, we need the following settings:

```
server:
  port: 7979
```

Hystrix Dashboard is usually run on port `7979`.

With this in place, let's launch the application and take a peek. To see the dashboard, we must navigate to `http://localhost:7979/hystrix`:

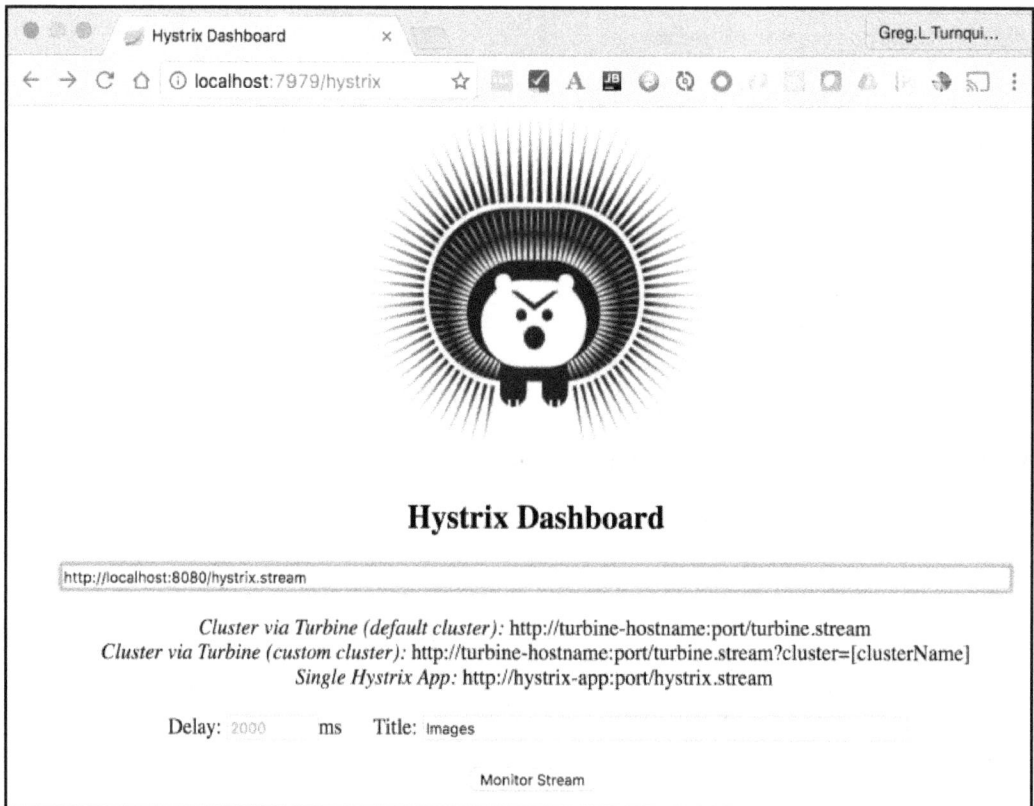

Here we have a pretty simple interface, as seen in the preceding screenshot. It tells us we have options regarding what we want to view. The simplest variant is to have the dashboard look at one microservice's collection of circuits. This preceding screenshot shows the URL for the `images` service, the one we wrote a `@HystrixCommand` for.

Since each microservice that has `@EnableCircuitBreaker` (pulled in via `@SpringCloudApplication`) has a `/hystrix.stream` endpoint outputting circuit metrics, we can enter that service's URL.

After clicking `Monitor Stream`, we can see this nice visual display of our single circuit:

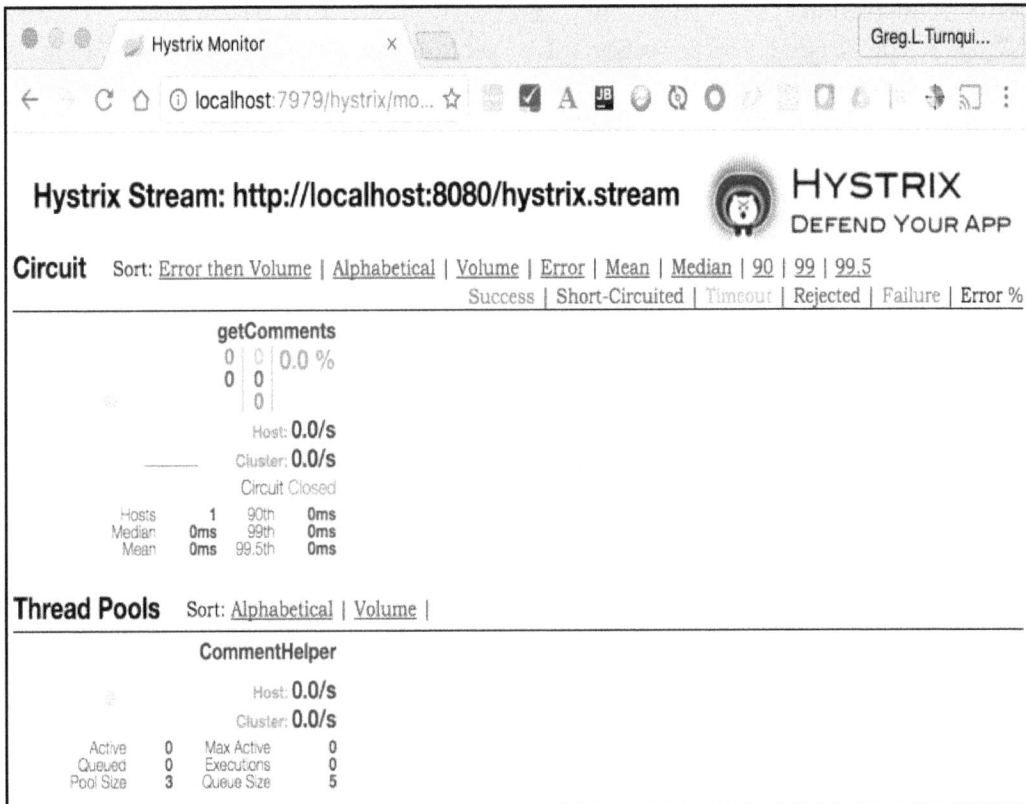

There's a lot on the preceding screen, so let's break it down:

- Across the top is the ability to sort various circuits based on different criteria. We only have one circuit, so it's not that important.
- `getComments` is shown underneath `Circuit`. The color coding of the numbers runs across the top, from `Success` to `Failure`, with everything currently showing 0.

- There is an overall failure percentage (also at 0%).
- There is a rate of activity for the host and for the cluster (also at 0/second).
- It may be hard to spot, but there's a flat horizontal line just left of Cluster. This will actually update based on traffic, showing spikes.
- Finally, it tracks the cost of making remote calls, and includes some statistics such as **Mean**, **Median**, **90** percentile, **95** percentile, and **99.5** percentile.
- The `Thread Pools` section can show how taxed the system is from a threading perspective. This can help us tune `@HystrixCommand` if we need to adjust thread-pool settings.

With circuit monitoring set up, why don't we institute a failure, and watch the whole thing go down and then recover?

To do that, we need to update our simulator that we created earlier in this book:

```
@Profile("simulator")
@Component
public class CommentSimulator {

  private final HomeController homeController;
  private final CommentController commentController;
  private final ImageRepository repository;

  private final AtomicInteger counter;

  public CommentSimulator(HomeController homeController,
    CommentController commentController,
    ImageRepository repository) {
      this.homeController = homeController;
      this.commentController = commentController;
      this.repository = repository;
      this.counter = new AtomicInteger(1);
  }

  @EventListener
  public void simulateComments(ApplicationReadyEvent event) {
    Flux
      .interval(Duration.ofMillis(1000))
      .flatMap(tick -> repository.findAll())
      .map(image -> {
        Comment comment = new Comment();
        comment.setImageId(image.getId());
        comment.setComment(
          "Comment #" + counter.getAndIncrement());
```

```
            return Mono.just(comment);
        })
        .flatMap(newComment ->
         Mono.defer(() ->
          commentController.addComment(newComment)))
          .subscribe();
    }

    @EventListener
    public void simulateUsersClicking(ApplicationReadyEvent event) {
      Flux
        .interval(Duration.ofMillis(500))
        .flatMap(tick ->
         Mono.defer(() ->
          homeController.index(new BindingAwareModelMap())))
          .subscribe();
    }
  }
```

The following are some key points to note about this preceding code:

- The @Profile annotation indicates that this component is only active when spring.profiles.active=simulator is set in the environment variables.
- By constructor injection, it gets copies of both, CommentController and HomeController.
- simulateActivity() is triggered when Spring Boot generates an ApplicationReadyEvent.
- The Flux generates a tick every 1000 ms. This tick is transformed into a request for all images, and then a new comment is created against each one, simulating user activity.
- simulateUsersClicking() is also triggered by the same ApplicationReadyEvent. It has a different Flux that simulates a user loading the home page every 500 ms.

In both of these simulation flows, the downstream activity needs to be wrapped in a Mono.defer in order to provide a target Mono for the downstream provider to subscribe to.

Finally, both of these Reactor flows must be subscribed to, or they will never run.

If we relaunch the `images` service, and watch the Hystrix Dashboard, we get a nice, rosy picture:

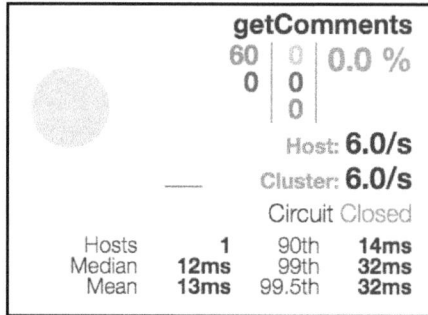

```
                          getComments
                    60    0   0.0 %
                     0    0
                          0
                         Host: 6.0/s
                   ---- Cluster: 6.0/s
                         Circuit Closed
        Hosts      1     90th    14ms
        Median   12ms    99th    32ms
        Mean     13ms   99.5th   32ms
```

The bubble on the left of the preceding screenshot is green, and the green **60** at the top indicates that the volume of traffic for its window of monitoring shows **60** successful hits. Looking at the rate (**6.0/s**), we can deduce this is a 10-second window.

> **TIP**
>
> I realize that in print, the bubble along with all the numbers are gray, but you can tell success/failure by noting that the circuit is **Closed**, meaning, traffic is flowing through it.

Let's switch over to our IDE, and kill the `comments` microservice:

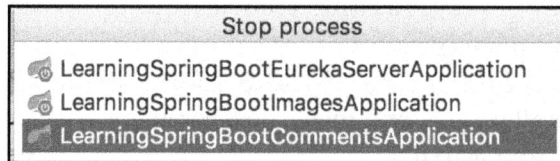

```
                        Stop process
     LearningSpringBootEurekaServerApplication
     LearningSpringBootImagesApplication
     LearningSpringBootCommentsApplication
```

> **ⓘ**
>
> This preceding screenshot shows IntelliJ IDEA. Your IDE's kill switch may appear different.

If we jump back to the dashboard, things look very different:

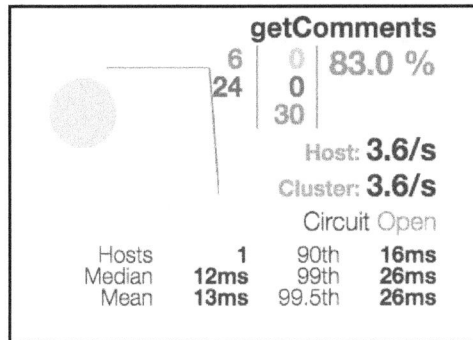

The 10 second window shows **6** successful calls, **30** failed calls, and **24** short circuited calls. The horizontal status line takes a precipitous drop, and the green bubble has now turned red. Additionally, the circuit is now **Open**.

> **TIP**
> Again, you may not be able to discern the bubble is red in print, but the circuit is now **Open**, indicating the failures are being replaced with short-circuited calls.

If we follow this outage a little longer, things migrate all the way to 100% failure:

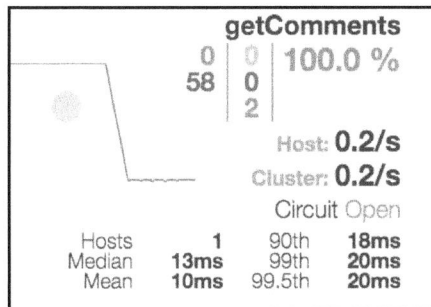

Now there are only two failures with **58** short-circuited calls. In essence, with the circuit **Open**, there is no point in trying to make remote calls and wasting resources. Instead, we use the fallback method without question. We can also see the graph has flatlined at the bottom.

We can simulate our ops team rushing in and fixing things by restarting the `comments` service:

With a little bit of time, this service will come back up and re-register with Eureka, making it available. After that, the circuit breaker must wait a minimum amount of time before a remote call will even be attempted.

Hystrix's default setting is 50% failure or higher to open the circuit. Another subtle property is that a minimum number of requests must be made to possibly open the circuit. The default is 20, meaning that 19 failures in a row would not open it. When the circuit is opened, Hystrix keeps the circuit open a minimum amount of time before looking at the rolling window (default: 5000 ms). Hystrix maintains a rolling window, by default, 10 seconds split up into 10 buckets. As a new bucket of metrics is gathered, the oldest is dropped. This collection of buckets is what is examined when deciding whether or not to open the circuit.

> **TIP**
>
> As you can see, there is a lot of sophistication to Hystrix's metrics. We'll just use the defaults here. But if you're interested in adjusting Hystrix's various settings, visit `https://github.com/Netflix/Hystrix/wiki/configuration` where all its parameters are documented.

When we make a remote call, the circuit is immediately closed:

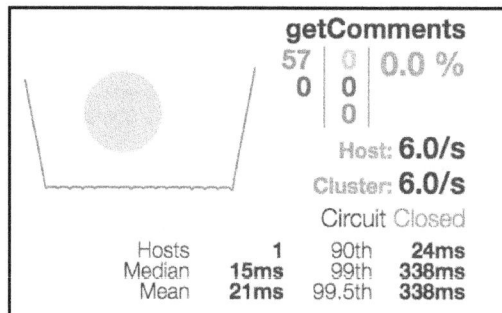

Successful calls climbs to **57**, and the number of short-circuited and failed calls clears out in a few seconds time. The graph turns around and climbs back up, showing a nice recovery.

> The circuit breaker we have in place watches REST calls from `images` to `comments`. The means the mechanism by which new `comments` are sent over the wire via RabbitMQ is, inherently, fault tolerant. While `comments` was down, the new comments pile up in RabbitMQ's exchange until the queue restored itself, and the system caught up.

This nice little scenario shows how we can keep a visual eye on microservice-to-microservice operations.

Offloading microservice settings to a configuration server

One thing that quickly adds up when building a microservice-based solution are all the properties that must be managed. It's one thing to manage a single application's `application.yml` file, and make tweaks and adjustments. But working with all these services, and having to jump to the correct file underneath each application's `src/main/resources` folder quickly becomes daunting. On top of that, when trying to make changes or adjustments, it is easy to overlook the settings of one microservice.

A key piece of the twelve-factor app (`https://12factor.net/`) is externalizing configuration. We already took a big step using Spring Boot's powerful property support. But Spring Cloud brings another key technology to the table that takes property support to the next level--**Spring Cloud Config Server**.

The **Config Server** let's us put all the properties into a centralized location, and feed them via an application to our existing microservices.

To see how, let's dive into creating one. First, go to `http://start.spring.io` and select `Config Server` (along with our other favorite settings).

When we do that, we get a familiar Gradle build file containing the following dependencies:

```
buildscript {
  ext {
    springBootVersion = '2.0.0.M5'
    springCloudVersion = 'Finchley.M3'
  }
  ...
}
...
dependencies {
  compile('org.springframework.cloud:spring-cloud-config-server')
}

dependencyManagement {
  imports {
    mavenBom "org.springframework.cloud:spring-cloud-
      dependencies:${springCloudVersion}"
  }
}
```

We can explain this preceding build file as follows:

- `spring-cloud-starter-config-server` is only needed to run a config server, not a config server client
- The `dependencyManagement` shows us the release train of Spring Cloud we are using

In a way very analogous to the Hystrix Dashboard, we will create a Config Server:

```
@SpringBootApplication
@EnableConfigServer
public class LearningSpringBootConfigServer {

  public static void main(String[] args) {
    SpringApplication.run(
      LearningSpringBootConfigServer.class, args);
  }
}
```

This preceding app isn't hard to unravel:

- `@SpringBootApplication` marks this as a Spring Boot application. Since this is the cornerstone of the rest of our microservices (including Eureka), it doesn't use Eureka.
- `@EnableConfigServer` launches an embedded Spring Cloud Config Server, full of options. We'll use the defaults as much as possible.
- It has a `public static void main` to launch itself.

With that, we just need a couple of property settings in `application.yml`:

```
server:
  port: 8888
spring:
  cloud:
    config:
      server:
        git:
          uri: https://github.com/gregturn/learning-spring-boot-
            config-repo
```

- Let's set its port to `8888`, since that is the default port for Spring Cloud Config clients
- By setting `spring.cloud.config.server.git.uri` to `https://github.com/gregturn/learning-spring-boot-config-repo`, we tell the Config Server where to get its property settings for all the other services

That's it! That's all we need to build a Config Server. We can launch it right now, but there is one thing missing--all the other properties of the application!

To configure properties for our Eureka Server, we need to add a `eureka.yml` that looks like this:

```
server:
  port: 8761

eureka:
  instance:
    hostname: localhost
  client:
    registerWithEureka: false
    fetchRegistry: false
```

```
        serviceUrl:
          defaultZone:
            http://${eureka.instance.hostname}:${server.port}/eureka/
```

If you'll notice, this is the *exact* same setting we put into the Eureka Server's `application.yml` earlier in this chapter. We are simply moving it into our config repo.

To make our Eureka Server talk to a Config Server, we need to add this to its build file:

```
        compile('org.springframework.cloud:spring-cloud-starter-config')
```

What does this single dependency do?

- `spring-cloud-starter-config` empowers the Eureka Server to talk to the Config Server for property settings

> It's important to note that `spring-cloud-starter-config` is for *clients* to the Config Server. The dependency that was added to the Config Server itself was `spring-cloud-starter-config-server`, which is only needed to create a Config Server.

There is a certain order by which Spring Boot launches things. Suffice it to say, property sources must be read early in the Spring lifecycle in order to work properly. For this reason, Spring Cloud Config clients *must* have a `bootstrap.yml` file. The one for the Eureka Server must look like this:

```
        spring:
          application:
            name: eureka
```

Not a whole lot needs to be in here, but at a minimum, `spring.application.name` needs to be set so that the Config Server knows which property file to fetch from its config repo. By default, Spring Cloud Config clients will seek `{spring.application.name}.yml`, so in this case, `eureka.yml`.

Assuming we have committed `eureka.yml` to our GitHub-based config repo and launched the config server, we can actually see what is served up:

Let's tear apart the details of this preceding screenshot:

- `http://localhost:8888/eureka/default` looks up
  `spring.application.name=eureka`, and finds the default state of things
- The name `eureka` is at the top along with information like its label and
  SHA version
- The config server entry lists the available Spring property sources
  (`eureka.yml`) along with each property found in that property source

> **TIP**
>
> It's possible to retrieve different versions of configuration settings.
> All we have to do is set `spring.cloud.config.label=foo` in
> `bootstrap.yml` to fetch an alternative label. When we use Git as
> the repository, a label can refer to either a branch or a tag.

In essence, the Spring Cloud Config Server is Yet Another Way™ to craft a property source that the Spring Framework can intrinsically consume.

Next, let's move all the properties for `images` from its `application.yml` file into the config repo's `images.yml` like this:

```
eureka:
  client:
    serviceUrl:
      defaultZone: http://localhost:8761/eureka/

spring:
  cloud:
    stream:
      bindings:
        output:
          destination: learning-spring-boot-comments
          group: comments-service
          content-type: application/json
```

With all these settings moved to the Config Server's `images.yml` file, we can replace the `application.yml` with the following `src/main/resources/bootstrap.yml` file:

```
spring:
  application:
    name: images
```

Earlier in this chapter, `spring.application.name=images`, along with all the other settings, were combined in `application.yml`. To work with Spring Cloud Config Server, we split out `spring.application.name`, and put it inside `bootstrap.yml`.

We can do the same for `comments` by moving all of its property settings into `comments.yml`. You can see it at https://github.com/gregturn/learning-spring-boot-config-repo/blob/master/comments.yml, if you wish, along with `hystrix-dashboard.yml`.

Instead, we'll give `comments` the following `src/main/resources/bootstrap.yml` file:

```
spring:
  application:
    name: comments
```

And do the same for our Hystrix Dashboard app:

```
spring:
  application:
    name: hystrix-dashboard
```

You know what's truly amazing about all this? We don't have to touch the services. At all.

> Is running *lots* of microservices inside your IDE driving you nuts? Constantly starting and stopping can get old, real fast. IntelliJ IDEA has the Multirun (`https://plugins.jetbrains.com/plugin/7248`) plugin that lets you group together several launch configurations into a single command. If you use Eclipse, the CDT (C/C++ Development Tooling) module provides a component called **Launch Groups** that lets you do the same. The following screenshot shows the IntelliJ IDEA Multirun plugin configured for our microservices.

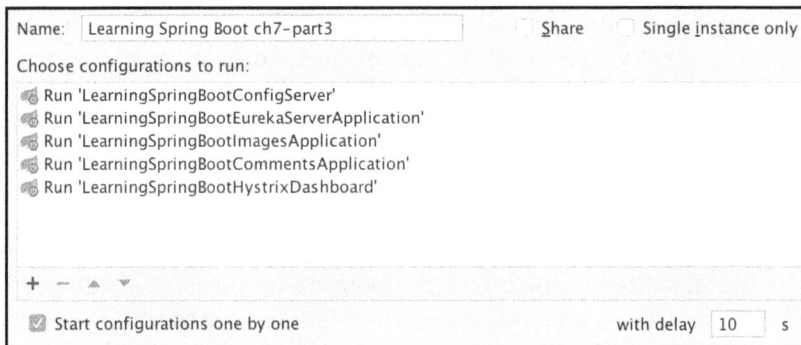

Notice the little 10 second delay in the bottom-right corner of the preceding screenshot? The Config Server needs to be up and operational before any other services start, or they'll fall on default settings.

Using the Multirun plugin, if we launch everything, we should have a nice little system up:

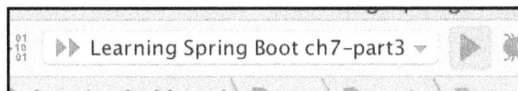

Each service, when it launches, should show something like this:

```
or : Fetching config from server at: http://localhost:8888
or : Located environment: name=comments, profiles=[default], label=master, v
on : Located property source: CompositePropertySource [name='configService',
on : No active profile set, falling back to default profiles: default
```

Without touching a line of code, and simply moving most of what we've already written into another location (or into `bootstrap.yml`), we have extracted the entire configuration of our social media site to a remote location, making configuration a snap to maintain.

So, is our little snap-a-picture social media platform ready for IPO? Heh, maybe not *yet*. But we've made a major enhancement that will make us more stable and ready for growth by breaking things up into microservices without breaking the bank.

> There are *lots* of options in the Spring Cloud Config Server. You can register it with Eureka, direct clients to fail fast if it's not up, have clients retry if its down at startup, and more. Security options include the ability to secure the Config Server so that not just anyone can access it (something we'll visit in `Chapter 18`, *Securing Your App with Spring Boot*). For more details, see
> `http://cloud.spring.io/spring-cloud-config`.
>
> Spring Cloud Config Server currently supports GitHub, GitLab, and Bitbucket out of the box. This means that you can quickly put your configuration on a publicly hosted GitHub repository, but you can also install GitLab inside your data center, and point there, instead, to reduce the risk of public repository outages.

Summary

In this chapter, we took a quick tour of building a microservice-based solution using several Spring Cloud projects combined with their Netflix OSS counterparts. This lets us make each component smaller, easier to maintain, and more scalable in the long run.

With little effort, we made it possible to run multiple copies of services, and not have other microservices be impacted by such changes. Services could call other services, we were able to introduce some resiliency, and we could offload the configuration of this system to an externalized, centralized repository.

In the next chapter, we will shift our focus back to user experience, and introduce Spring's WebSocket support to help make the UX more dynamic.

WebSockets with Spring Boot

17

Hell yeah @springboot rocks! (after winning JAX Innovation Award 2016)

– Andrew Rubalcaba @Han_Cholo

In the previous chapter, we learned how to split our application into microservices driven by bounded contexts. Yet, we still linked things together in an efficient manner using Spring Cloud.

When it comes to building a social media platform, the standard has been set very high. We all expect dynamic updates to whatever content we view. If someone comments on a topic that we are also viewing, we expect to be alerted to the update immediately. Such fluid changes are made possible through the power of WebSockets.

In this chapter, we will cover the following topics:

- Publishing saved comments to a chat service
- Broadcasting saved comments to web subscribers
- Configuring a WebSocket broker
- Consuming messages from the web asynchronously
- Introducing user chatting with channel-wide and user-specific messages

We will use Spring's reactive WebSocket API found in WebFlux while also using a little JavaScript in our template.

Publishing saved comments to a chat service

In the previous chapter, we connected our `images` service to the `comments` service via Spring Cloud Stream. This let us transmit new comments over the wire to a service dedicated to storing them in a MongoDB data store.

The following screenshot shows us entering a new comment:

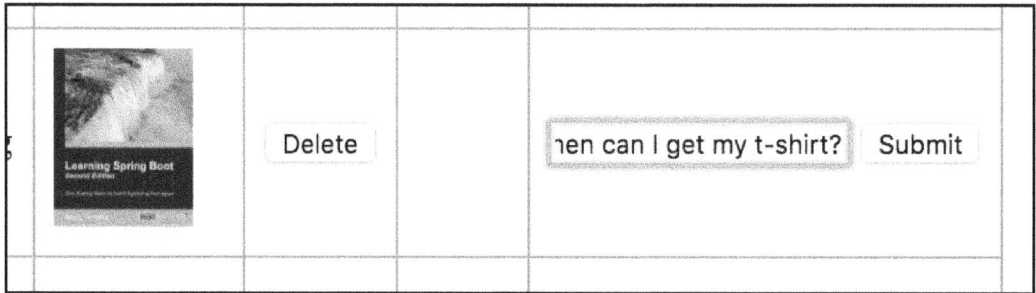

To carry on this use case to its natural conclusion, it's expected that after storing a message, we'd want to share it with everyone, right? To do so, let's pick up with the `comment` microservice's `CommentService`.

In the previous chapter, the `comments` service transformed an incoming stream of `Flux<Comment>` into a `Flux<Void>`, a stream of voids. This had the effect of, essentially, dropping the stream at this point. In this chapter, we want to take that incoming stream of comments and forward them.

This is accomplished by altering the `Comment.save()` operation as follows:

```
@StreamListener
@Output(Processor.OUTPUT)
public Flux<Comment> save(@Input(Processor.INPUT) Flux<Comment>
  newComment) {
    return repository
      .saveAll(newComment)
      .map(comment -> {
        log.info("Saving new comment " + comment);
        meterRegistry
          .counter("comments.consumed", "imageId",
comment.getImageId())
          .increment();
        return comment;
```

```
        });
    }
```

This previous code is almost identical to what we had before except for the following changes:

- The last step of the map operation now returns `comment` instead of `Mono.empty()`
- The method now has a return type of `Flux<Comment>`

With this tweak, the return results from `save()` are transmitted over the `Source.OUTPUT` channel.

> `Processor.INPUT` and `Processor.OUTPUT` are just channel names. They don't say *where* anything goes. That's why we need to configure `bindings`.

Our `comments.yml` properties file stored on the Config Server needs to be upgraded as follows:

```yaml
server:
  port: 9000

spring:
  cloud:
    stream:
      bindings:
        input:
          destination: learning-spring-boot-comments
          group: comments-service
          content-type: application/json
        output:
          destination: learning-spring-boot-chat
          group: comments-chat
          content-type: application/json
```

The preceding code is mostly the same as the previous chapter, but with the following:

- `spring.cloud.stream.bindings.input` and its properties are the same as before
- `spring.cloud.stream.bindings.output.destination` points to a different exchange to avoid colliding with the one feeding messages *into* this service

- `spring.cloud.stream.bindings.output.group` provides a logical grouping to ensure proper handling if we ever scale up to more than one instance of `comments` service
- `spring.cloud.stream.bindings.output.content-type` is marked `application/json`, indicating we don't expect the consumer to use the same domain class, but will probably deserialize into their own POJO instead

With these changes, we can expect an output as follows:

```
2017-07-05 00:00:36.769  INFO 92207 --- [ments-service-1]
c.g.l.comments.CommentService : Saving new comment Comment(id=null,
imageId=581d6669596aec65dc9e6c05, comment=Nice cover!)
```

With all these changes, our `comments` microservice is geared up to transmit saved comments to someone else able to broadcast to users. It may be tempting to send them *back* to the `images` service. But let's continue with the concept of keeping a narrow scope, and send this traffic to a different, chat-focused microservice instead. We can even call it the `chat` service!

Creating a chat service to handle WebSocket traffic

If we visit `http://start.spring.io`, select **Gradle**, **Spring Boot 2.0**, **Eureka Discovery**, **Config Client**, **Stream Rabbit**, **Lombok**, and **Reactive Web**, we'll have a nice little service ready to chat:

```
compile('org.springframework.boot:spring-boot-starter-webflux')
compile('org.projectlombok:lombok')
compile('org.springframework.cloud:spring-cloud-starter-stream-
  rabbit')
compile('org.springframework.cloud:spring-cloud-stream-reactive')
compile('org.springframework.cloud:spring-cloud-starter-eureka')
compile('org.springframework.cloud:spring-cloud-starter-config')
```

These aforementioned dependencies in our new chat service can be described as follows:

- `spring-boot-starter-webflux`: This comes with a Reactive Streams capable WebSocket API

- `lombok`: This is the library that gets us out of the business of coding getters, setters, and other boilerplate Java code
- `spring-cloud-starter-stream-rabbit`: This is the Spring Cloud Stream library that uses RabbitMQ as the underlying technology
- `spring-cloud-stream-reactive`: This layers on Reactive Streams support
- `spring-cloud-starter-eureka`: This makes the microservice capable of registering itself with our Eureka Server and of consuming other Eureka-based services
- `spring-cloud-starter-config`: This lets the microservice get its configuration details from the Config Server

There is little value in looking at the rest of the build file, since it's the same as our other microservices.

With these dependencies, the only thing needed to make this Yet Another Microservice™ is to fashion our Spring Boot `public static void main` like this:

```
@SpringCloudApplication
@EnableEurekaClient
public class LearningSpringBootChatApplication {

  public static void main(String[] args) {
    SpringApplication.run(
      LearningSpringBootChatApplication.class, args);
  }
}
```

The last code can be described quite simply:

- `@SpringCloudAppplication` is a `@SpringBootApplication` combined with a Eureka Discovery, and with circuit breaker enabled

We're close. Early in this book, we would put the needed settings in `application.yml` (or `application.properties`), but since we have adopted Spring Cloud Config Server, we, instead, need to create the following `bootstrap.yml` file:

```
spring:
  application:
    name: chat
```

This `bootstrap.yml` file now identifies our application as the `chat` microservice to Eureka, and will cause it to ask the Config Server for `chat.yml` on startup.

To support that, we need to add the following to our Config Server's Git repository:

```
server:
  port: 8200

spring:
  cloud:
    stream:
      bindings:
        input:
          destination: learning-spring-boot-chat
          group: comments-chat
          content-type: application/json
        newComments:
          destination: learning-spring-boot-chat
          group: comments-chat
          content-type: application/json
        clientToBroker:
          destination: learning-spring-boot-chat-user-messages
          group: app-chatMessages
        brokerToClient:
          destination: learning-spring-boot-chat-user-messages
          group: topic-chatMessages
```

Wow! That's a lot of settings. Let's take them apart:

- `server.port` shows this service will listen on port `8200`. (Why not?)
- `spring.cloud.stream.bindings.input` contains the *exact* same settings we saw earlier in the comments `spring.cloud.stream.bindings.output` settings. This ensures that the two are talking to each other.
- We also have `spring.cloud.stream.bindings.newComments`, `.clientToBroker`, and `.brokerToClient`. This part is a little complex, so let's discuss what happens.

> **TIP**
>
> Before we dig into moving WebSocket messages around, don't forget to commit this change, and *push* to origin!

Brokering WebSocket messages

Something that's important to understand is the flow of messages. So far, we have seen messages sent from the website into the `comments` service, stored into a MongoDB database, and then forwarded to our `chat` service.

At this point, we are trying to onramp these messages to WebSockets. But what does that mean? A WebSocket is a very lightweight, two-way channel between a web page and the server. WebSockets, on their own, don't dictate much about what travels over this thin pipe, but one thing is for certain--each web page, when connected to a server, has a separate **session**.

Spring WebFlux provides an API that lets us hook into this WebSocket-oriented session, whether to transmit or receive. But no WebSocket session is immediately linked to another WebSocket session. If we were using Spring Framework 4's WebSocket API, we would be leveraging its most sophisticated Messaging API. This API was born in Spring Integration, and is the same concept found in Spring Cloud Streams. Spring MVC comes with a built-in broker to help bridge messages between different sessions. In essence, a message that originates in one WebSocket session must be transmitted to the broker where it can then be forwarded to any *other* WebSocket session that might be interested.

With Spring WebFlux, we have no such Messaging API, no such broker, and no higher level constructs such as user-based messaging. But it's no big deal! We can fashion it ourselves--using the Spring Cloud Stream tools we are already familiar with.

Through the rest of this chapter, we will chain together these streams of messages, and it will be most elegant.

Broadcasting saved comments

To consume messages sent via Spring Cloud Stream, the `chat` application needs its own `CommentService`:

```
@Service
@EnableBinding(Sink.class)
public class CommentService implements WebSocketHandler {

  private final static Logger log =
    LoggerFactory.getLogger(CommentService.class);
    ...
}
```

The preceding code can be described as follows:

- `@Service` marks this as a Spring bean, picked up automatically when the **chat** microservice starts
- `@EnableBinding(Sink.class)` shows this to be a receiver for Spring Cloud Stream messages
- Our service implements `WebSocketHandler`, a WebFlux interface that comes with a `handle(WebSocketSession)` method (which we'll use shortly)
- An Slf4j `Logger` is used to print out traffic passing through

This service needs to consume the messages sent from Spring Cloud Stream. However, the destination for these messages is *not* another Spring Cloud Stream destination. Instead, we want to pipe them into a WebSocket session.

To do that, we need to pull messages down from a RabbitMQ-based `Flux`, and forward them to a `Flux` connected to a WebSocket session. This is where we need another one of those `FluxSink` objects:

```
private ObjectMapper mapper;
private Flux<Comment> flux;
private FluxSink<Comment> webSocketCommentSink;

CommentService(ObjectMapper mapper) {
  this.mapper = mapper;
  this.flux = Flux.<Comment>create(
    emitter -> this.webSocketCommentSink = emitter,
    FluxSink.OverflowStrategy.IGNORE)
     .publish()
     .autoConnect();
}
```

This last bit of code can easily be described as follows:

- We need a Jackson `ObjectMapper`, and will get it from Spring's container through constructor injection.
- To create a `FluxSink` that lets us put comments one by one onto a `Flux`, we use `Flux.create()`, and let it initialize our sink, `webSocketCommentSink`.

- When it comes to backpressure policy, it's wired to ignore backpressure signals for simplicity's sake. There may be other scenarios where we would select differently.
- `publish()` and `autoConnect()` kick our `Flux` into action so that it's ready to start transmitting once hooked into the WebSocket session.

The idea we are shooting for is to put events directly onto `webSocketCommentSink`, and then hitch the corresponding `flux` into the WebSocket API. Think of it like `webSocketCommentSink` as the object we can append comments to, and `flux` being the consumer pulling them off on the other end (after the consumer subscribes).

With our `webSocketCommentSink` configured, we can now hook it into our Spring Cloud Stream `Sink`, as follows:

```
@StreamListener(Sink.INPUT)
public void broadcast(Comment comment) {
  if (webSocketCommentSink != null) {
    log.info("Publishing " + comment.toString() +
    " to websocket...");
    webSocketCommentSink.next(comment);
  }
}
```

The preceding code can be described as follows:

- The `broadcast()` method is marked as a `@StreamListener` for `Sink.INPUT`. Messages get deserialized as `Comment` objects thanks to the `application/json` setting.
- The code checks if our `webSocketCommentSink` is null, indicating whether or not it's been created.
- A log message is printed.
- The `Comment` is dropped into our `webSocketSink`, which means that it will become available to our corresponding `flux` automatically.

With this service in place, we can expect to see the following in the **chat** service's logs when a new comment arrives:

```
2017-08-05 : Publishing Comment(id=581d6774596aec682ffd07be,
imageId=581d6669596aec65dc9e6c05, comment=Nice cover!) to websocket...
```

The last step is to push this `Flux` of comments out over a WebSocket session. Remember the `WebSocketHandler` interface at the top of our class? Let's implement it:

```
@Override
public Mono<Void> handle(WebSocketSession session) {
    return session.send(this.flux
        .map(comment -> {
          try {
            return mapper.writeValueAsString(comment);
          } catch (JsonProcessingException e) {
              throw new RuntimeException(e);
          }
        })
        .log("encode-as-json")
        .map(session::textMessage)
        .log("wrap-as-websocket-message"))
      .log("publish-to-websocket");
}
```

This `WebSocketHandler` can be described as follows:

- We are handed a `WebSocketSession` which has a very simple API
- The `Comment`-based `Flux` is piped into the WebSocket via its `send()` method
- This `Flux` itself is transformed from a series of `Comment` objects into a series of JSON objects courtesy of Jackson, and then, finally, into a series of `WebSocketMessage` objects

It's important to point out that in Spring Framework 4, much of this was handled by the inner working of Spring's WebSocket API as well as its Messaging API. There was no need to serialize and deserialize Java POJOs into JSON representations. That was provided out of the box by Spring's converter services.

In Spring Framework 5, in the WebFlux module, the WebSocket API is very simple. Think of it as streams of messages coming and going. So, the duty of transforming a chain of `Comment` objects into one of JSON-encoded text messages is paramount. As we've just seen, with the functional paradigm of Reactor, this is no bother.

> Getting bogged down in POJO overload? Seeing `Comment` domain objects in every microservice? Don't panic! While we *could* write some common module that was used by every microservice to hold this domain object, that may not be the best idea. By letting each microservice manage their own domain objects, we reduce coupling. For example, only the `comments` service actually marks the `id` field with Spring Data Commons's `@Id` annotation, since it's the only one talking to MongoDB. What may appear identical in code actually carries slightly semantic differences that can arise down the road.

Configuring WebSocket handlers

We've coded our `CommentService` to implement Spring's `WebSocketHandler` interface, meaning, it's *ready* to transmit traffic over a WebSocket. The next step is to hook this service into the machinery.

We can start by creating a Spring configuration class:

```
@Configuration
public class WebSocketConfig {
   ...
}
```

This Spring configuration class is devoted to configuring WebSocket support, and is marked up with the `@Configuration` annotation, indicating it's a source of Spring bean definitions.

With that in place, we now come to the core piece of registering WebSocket functionality:

```
@Bean
HandlerMapping webSocketMapping(CommentService commentService) {
  Map<String, WebSocketHandler> urlMap = new HashMap<>();
  urlMap.put("/topic/comments.new", commentService);

  Map<String, CorsConfiguration> corsConfigurationMap =
    new HashMap<>();
  CorsConfiguration corsConfiguration = new CorsConfiguration();
  corsConfiguration.addAllowedOrigin("http://localhost:8080");
  corsConfigurationMap.put(
    "/topic/comments.new", corsConfiguration);

  SimpleUrlHandlerMapping mapping = new SimpleUrlHandlerMapping();
  mapping.setOrder(10);
```

```
        mapping.setUrlMap(urlMap);
        mapping.setCorsConfigurations(corsConfigurationMap);

        return mapping;
    }
```

This preceding little chunk of code can be taken apart as follows:

- `@Bean` indicates this entire method is used to construct a Spring bean.
- It's a `HandlerMapping` bean, Spring's interface for linking routes with handler methods.
- The name of the method, `webSocketMapping`, indicates this method is about wiring routes for WebSocket message handling.
- It asks for a copy of the `CommentService` bean we defined earlier. Since Spring Boot activates component scanning, an instance of that service will be created automatically, thanks to the `@Service` annotation we put on it earlier.
- We create a Java `Map`, designed for mapping string-based routes onto `WebSocketHandler` objects, and dub it a `urlMap`.
- We load the map with `/topic/comments.new`, and link it with our `CommentService`, a class that implements the `WebSocketHandler` interface.
- There's the sticky issue of microservices, whereby, our `chat` service runs on a different port from the frontend `image` service. Any modern web browser will deny a web page calling a different port from the original port it was served. To satisfy security restrictions (for now), we must implement a custom **Cross-origin Resource Sharing** or **CORS** policy. In this case, we add an **Allowed Origin** of `http://localhost:8080`, the address where the frontend `image` service resides.
- With both the `urlMap` and the `corsConfiguration` policy, we construct `SimpleUrlHandlerMapping`. It also needs an order level of `10` to get viewed ahead of certain other route handlers provided automatically by Spring Boot.

Essentially, this bean is responsible for mapping WebSocket routes to handlers, whether that is to target client-to-server, or server-to-client messaging. The message route we've designed so far is a WebSocket message that originates on the server when a new comment is created, and is pushed out to all clients so they can be alerted to the new comment.

In Spring Framework 4, there is an annotation-based mechanism that lets us configure these routes directly on the handlers themselves. But for Spring Framework 5 (WebFlux), we must configure things by hand. CORS is also critical to handle given the way we split things up across multiple microservices.

Another critical component in the same configuration class is listed next:

```
@Bean
WebSocketHandlerAdapter handlerAdapter() {
   return new WebSocketHandlerAdapter();
}
```

This preceding, somewhat boring looking, Spring bean is critical to the infrastructure of WebSocket messaging. It connects Spring's `DispatcherHandler` to a `WebSocketHandler`, allowing URIs to be mapped onto handler methods.

> Don't confuse `DispatcherHandler`, a Reactive Spring component responsible for handling Reactor-based web requests with the venerable `DispatcherServlet`, a servlet-based component that performs an analogous function. This WebSocket handling is purely Reactive Streams-oriented.

Consuming WebSocket messages from the web page

With everything configured on the server, it's time to wire things up in the client. Because JavaScript has a WebSocket API, and we aren't using subprotocols such as **Simple** (or **Streaming**) **Text Oriented Message Protocol** (**STOMP**), we don't need any extra libraries.

So we can augment our Thymeleaf template, `index.html`. It's important to point out that our template is in the `images` microservice, not the `chat` microservice we just created. Add the following chunk of code toward the bottom of the HTML:

```
<script th:inline="javascript">
    /*<![CDATA[*/
    (function() {
        ... custom JavaScript code here...
    })();
    /*]]>*/
</script>
```

This preceding chunk of code can be explained as follows:

- The HTML `<script>` tag combined with `th:inline="javascript"` allows Thymeleaf to process it.
- To avoid HTML parsing in various browsers as well as our IDE, the entire code is wrapped with CDATA tags.
- To ensure our JavaScript code doesn't litter the global namespace, we have enclosed it in an **immediately-invoked function expression (IIFE)** `(function() { /* code */ })();`. The code inside this block *cannot* be reached from anywhere outside, and this is a Good Thing™. There is no chance we'll run into anyone else's variables without deliberate action.

To repeat this point--we write any JavaScript used to send and receive messages over the WebSocket in the `images` microservice. That's because it's where our Thymeleaf template is served from. To actually send and receive WebSocket messages, it will connect to the **chat** microservice.

To subscribe to WebSocket messages, we need to subscribe as follows:

```
var socket = new WebSocket(
  'ws://localhost:8200/topic/comments.new');
socket.onopen = function(event) {
  console.log('Connected to chat service!');
  console.log(event);
}
socket.onmessage = function(event) {
  console.log('Received ' + event.data + '!');
  var parsedMessage = JSON.parse(event.data);
  var ul = document.getElementById(
    'comments-' + parsedMessage.imageId);
  var li = document.createElement('li');
  li.appendChild(
    document.createTextNode(parsedMessage.comment));
  ul.appendChild(li);
}
```

The last code can be described as follows:

- We start by creating a WebSocket connection at `ws://localhost:8200/topic/comments.new`.
- With a JavaScript `WebSocket` object assigned to our `socket` variable, we then assign event handlers to `onopen` and `onmessage`.
- The `onopen` handler is processed when a connection is first opened on the server. In this case, it merely logs that we have connected.
- The `onmessage` handler is processed everytime a message is issued from the server. In this case, we log the event's `data`, parse it (assuming it's JSON), construct an HTML LI, and append it to the page's already existing UL based on the comment's `imageId`.

> **TIP**
>
> This code uses native JavaScript, but if you're using React.js, jQuery, or some other JavaScript toolkit, feel free to use its APIs to generate new DOM elements.

Moving to a fully asynchronous web client

Now we are geared up to receive asynchronous messages from the server as comments are created, and display them dynamically on the site. However, there is something else that warrants attention.

Remember how, in the previous chapter, we had an HTML form for the user to fill out comments? The previous chapter's controller responded to such POSTs like this:

```
@PostMapping("/comments")
public Mono<String> addComment(Mono<Comment> newComment) {

    /* stream comments to COMMENTS service */

    return Mono.just("redirect:/");
}
```

`redirect:/` is a Spring Web signal to re-render the page at `/` via an HTTP redirect. Since we are shifting into dynamically updating the page based on asynchronous WebSocket messages, this is no longer the best way.

What are the issues? A few can be listed as follows:

- If the comment hasn't been saved (yet), the redirect would re-render the page with no change at all.
- The redirect may cause an update in the midst of handling the new comment's WebSocket message. Based on the race conditions, the comment may not yet be saved, causing it to not appear, and the refresh may miss the asynchronous message, causing the entire comment to not be displayed unless the page is manually refreshed.
- Setting up a WebSocket handler with every new comment isn't efficient.

Either way, this isn't a good use of resources, and could introduce timing issues. Instead, it's best if we convert this into an AJAX call.

To do so, we need to alter the HTML like this:

```
<td>
  <input th:id="'comment-' + ${image.id}" type="text" value="" />
  <button th:id="${image.id}" class="comment">Submit</button>
</td>
```

Instead of a form with a text input and a `Submit` input, we remove the HTML form and replace it with a button:

- The `<input>` contains an `id` attribute unique to its corresponding image
- The `<button>` has a similar `id` attribute

The `<button>` also has `class="comment"`, which we'll use to find, and decorate it with an event handler to process clicks as follows:

```
// Register a handler for each button to make an AJAX call
document.querySelectorAll('button.comment')
  .forEach(function(button) {
    button.addEventListener('click', function() {
      var comment = document.getElementById(
        'comment-' + button.id);

      var xhr = new XMLHttpRequest();
      xhr.open('POST', /*[[@{'/comments'}]]*/'', true);

      var formData = new FormData();
      formData.append('comment', comment.value);
      formData.append('imageId', button.id);

      xhr.send(formData);
```

```
        comment.value = '';
    });
});
```

This last block of JavaScript, contained inside our tidy little `(function(){})()`, has the following:

- `document.querySelectorAll('button.comment')` uses a native JavaScript query selector to find all the HTML buttons that have the class `comment`.
- Iterating over each button, an event listener is added, responding to the `click` events.
- When a click is received, it fetches the corresponding comment input.
- Then it fashions an `XMLHttpRequest` object, opening a `POST` operation set for asynchronous communications.
- With Thymeleaf's JavaScript support, it will plug in the URL for `@{'/comments'}` upon rendering.

- Then it constructs a `FormData`, and loads the same fields as the previous chapter as if we had filled out an HTML form on the page.
- It transmits the form data over the wire. Since we don't depend on the results, they are ignored.
- Finally, it clears out the comment input's entry box.

> In this example, we're using JavaScript's native APIs. But if you're using Rest.js, jQuery, Restangular, lodash, or any other toolkit, feel free to assemble your AJAX call using that instead. The point is to asynchronously transmit the data instead of navigating to another page.

Handling AJAX calls on the server

To support the fact that we are now making an AJAX call, and not expecting a redirect, we need to make alterations on the server side.

For one thing, we need to change the `image` microservice's `CommentController` from being view-based to being a REST controller. Earlier in this book, it looked like this:

```
@Controller
@EnableBinding(Source.class)
public class CommentController {
   ...
}
```

`@Controller` marked it as a Spring WebFlux controller that was expected to return the HTTP redirect.

To tweak things for AJAX calls, update it to look like this:

```
@RestController
@EnableBinding(Source.class)
public class CommentController {
   ...
}
```

By replacing `@Controller` with `@RestController`, we have marked this class as a Spring WebFlux controller with results written directly into the HTTP response body.

With that in place, we can now rewrite `addComment` as shown here:

```
@PostMapping("/comments")
public Mono<ResponseEntity<?>> addComment(Mono<Comment>
newComment)
  {
    if (commentSink != null) {
      return newComment
        .map(comment -> {
          commentSink.next(MessageBuilder
           .withPayload(comment)
           .setHeader(MessageHeaders.CONTENT_TYPE,
           MediaType.APPLICATION_JSON_VALUE)
            .build());
          return comment;
        })
        .flatMap(comment -> {
          meterRegistry
           .counter("comments.produced", "imageId",
comment.getImageId())
             .increment();
          return Mono.just(ResponseEntity.noContent().build());
        });
```

```
    } else {
        return Mono.just(ResponseEntity.noContent().build());
    }
}
```

What did we change? The following:

- The return type has switched from Mono<String> to
  Mono<ResponseEntity<?>>. ResponseEntity<?> is a Spring Web
  container that holds HTTP response headers, body, and status code.
- The logic for forwarding messages to the comments service over a
  FluxSink to Spring Cloud Stream is the same as the previous chapter.
- The last line of both the if and the else clauses uses the static builder
  methods of ResponseEntity to generate an HTTP 204 (No Content)
  response. It indicates success, but no response body is included.
  Considering the client isn't interested in any content, that's good enough!

Let's check our handiwork. If we start up everything (remember to launch the Config
Server before the others), and open two separate browser tabs, we can see the effects.

In the following screenshot, one user enters a new comment (Nice cover!):

Name	Image			
B05771_MockupCover_Normal_.jpg		Delete		Nice cover! Submit
bazinga.png		Delete		Submit

Another user with their own browser is looking at the same images. When the first user clicks on **Submit**, the message automatically appears on the second user's window, as follows:

Name	Image			
B05771_MockupCover_Normal_.jpg		Delete	• Nice cover!	Submit
bazinga.png		Delete		Submit

No page reloads, and no need to refresh the data and pull it from the `comments` service.

We can also see the message activity in the second user's browser console:

```
Received {"id":"599b90cec4d95697c2bea08b","imageId":"0a84bee9-f441-48bf-9c6a-558dab29c9d2","comment":"Nice cover!"}!
```

Introducing user chatting

What social media platform doesn't provide a means for users to communicate with each other? In this section, we'll enhance our application to allow chatting between users. This is another way to use asynchronous WebSocket messaging between clients and servers.

To start, let's add a new HTML element at the bottom of our template like this:

```
<div id="chatBox">
    Greetings!
    <br/>
    <textarea id="chatDisplay" rows="10" cols="80"
        disabled="true"></textarea>
    <br/>
    <input id="chatInput" type="text" style="width: 500px"
        value="" />
    <br/>
    <button id="chatButton">Send</button>
```

```
        <br/>
    </div>
```

This preceding HTML code is placed right underneath the Upload widget for sending new pictures. It contains:

- A simple greeting.
- An HTML `textarea` for displaying messages, `80` columns wide and `10` rows tall. It is disabled to make it a read-only message output.
- A text input for entering new messages.
- A button to submit new messages.

> It's true that any and all styling should be done through CSS, but we are trying to keep things simple, and not turn this into a UX-based book.

To post new messages from the text input box, we need to add another bit of code inside our piece of JavaScript:

```
var outboundChatMessages = new
  WebSocket('ws://localhost:8200/app/chatMessage.new');
// Post new chat messages
outboundChatMessages.onopen = function(event) {
  document.getElementById('chatButton')
    .addEventListener('click', function () {
      var chatInput = document.getElementById('chatInput');
      console.log('Publishing "' + chatInput.value + '"');
      outboundChatMessages.send(chatInput.value);
      chatInput.value = '';
      chatInput.focus();
    });
}
```

This last bit of code does the following:

- It creates another WebSocket connection, this time to `ws://localhost:8200/app/chatMessage.new` (which we'll code further down).
- Registers a handler function to be invoked when the `onopen` event of the WebSocket is triggered.
- Finds the `chatButton`, and registers an event handler for the `click` events.

- When clicked, fetches the `chatInput` text input.
- Using the WebSocket variable, it sends the value of the `chatInput` text input. NOTE: This is pure text. No JSON encoding needed.
- Clears out `chatInput`, and switches focus back to it.

This will transport raw strings to the server. How these messages are received will be defined shortly, but while we're here, why not go ahead and code up the other side, that is, when these messages are transmitted from server to client?

Are you getting nervous about seeing `http://localhost:8200`? It's appeared in a couple places so far (and will again as we write more code). It's a bit arbitrary, and also doesn't lend itself to scaling in production, right? We could stuff this value into the Config Server Git repo, and then write some JavaScript to scarf it out, but that sounds a little complicated. And it still wouldn't solve the scaling issue. The truth is that there is a much simpler solution in `Chapter 18`, *Securing Your App with Spring Boot*. So we'll stick with hard-coded URLs for now.

To display chat messages as they arrive, add the following:

```
var inboundChatMessages =
  new WebSocket('ws://localhost:8200/topic/chatMessage.new');
// Listen for new chat messages
inboundChatMessages.onmessage = function (event) {
  console.log('Received ' + event.data);
  var chatDisplay = document.getElementById('chatDisplay');
  chatDisplay.value = chatDisplay.value + event.data + 'n';
};
```

The preceding code does the following:

- Creates a third WebSocket connection to `ws://localhost:8200/topic/chatMessage.new`
- On the WebSocket's `onmessage` handler, registers a function handler to be invoked with every new message
- When an event arrives, grabs hold of the `chatDisplay`
- Appends the message's `data` to the `chatDisplay`, and adds a newline character

> **TIP**
>
> Confused by the paths /app/chatMessage.new and
> /topic/chatMessage.new? The first is for sending messages from
> the client to our server-side application, while the latter is for
> sending messages from server to client. There is no requirement that
> they be prefixed by /app or /topic. It's just a convention to help
> denote where the messages are traveling.

We just defined a route to *send* user messages to the server as well as a route to *receive*
messages from the server. The next step is to register these routes in our server-side
code. We do so by updating our WebSocketConfig class's webSocketMapping like
this:

```
@Bean
HandlerMapping webSocketMapping(CommentService commentService,
    InboundChatService inboundChatService,
    OutboundChatService outboundChatService) {
    Map<String, WebSocketHandler> urlMap = new HashMap<>();
    urlMap.put("/topic/comments.new", commentService);
    urlMap.put("/app/chatMessage.new", inboundChatService);
    urlMap.put("/topic/chatMessage.new", outboundChatService);

    Map<String, CorsConfiguration> corsConfigurationMap =
      new HashMap<>();
    CorsConfiguration corsConfiguration = new CorsConfiguration();
    corsConfiguration.addAllowedOrigin("http://localhost:8080");
    corsConfigurationMap.put(
        "/topic/comments.new", corsConfiguration);
    corsConfigurationMap.put(
        "/app/chatMessage.new", corsConfiguration);
    corsConfigurationMap.put(
        "/topic/chatMessage.new", corsConfiguration);

    SimpleUrlHandlerMapping mapping = new
      SimpleUrlHandlerMapping();
    mapping.setOrder(10);
    mapping.setUrlMap(urlMap);
    mapping.setCorsConfigurations(corsConfigurationMap);

    return mapping;
}
```

This last code contains many changes, so let's take them apart one by one:

- Previously, this method only injected `CommentService`. Now we *also* inject `InboundChatService` as well as `OutboundChatService`. These are two services we must define based on the need to **broker** WebSocket messages between sessions. (Don't panic! We'll get to that real soon).
- We have two new routes added to the `urlMap`--`/app/chatMessage.new` and `/topic/chatMessage.new`--which we just saw used in the web layer.
- These same routes must also be added to our CORS policy.

> Are you a little nervous about the CORS policy? Worried about managing hard-coded ports in your code when we just showed how that's not necessary in the previous chapter? Concerned about what this means when it comes time to secure everything? Don't worry, we'll show how this can be handled in `Chapter 18`, *Securing Your App with Spring Boot*.

With this adjustment to our `chat` microservice's `WebSocketConfig`, we must now configure how incoming WebSocket messages are handled. It's important to realize that if we receive the `Flux` of messages, and turn around and broadcast them on the same `WebSocketSession`, the only person receiving the messages will be the person that sent them--an echo server if you will.

This is why we need a broker if we want to broadcast such messages. Incoming messages must be received, relayed to a broker, and then picked up on the other side by *all* clients.

Now, where can we find a broker? We already have one! We've been using Spring Cloud Stream to transport messages over RabbitMQ on our behalf. We can do the same for these messages as well.

It's important to remember that Spring Cloud Stream operates on the channel paradigm. Everything is sent and received over channels. Up until now, we've gotten by using `Source`, `Sink`, and `Processor`, three interfaces that work with `output` and `input`. To handle new comment-based messages, client-to-server user messages, and server-to-client user messages, those two channels aren't enough.

So, we need to define a new set of streams. We can do that by creating our own interface, `ChatServiceStreams` in the `chat` microservice, as shown here:

```
public interface ChatServiceStreams {

    String NEW_COMMENTS = "newComments";
    String CLIENT_TO_BROKER = "clientToBroker";
    String BROKER_TO_CLIENT = "brokerToClient";

    @Input(NEW_COMMENTS)
    SubscribableChannel newComments();

    @Output(CLIENT_TO_BROKER)
    MessageChannel clientToBroker();

    @Input(BROKER_TO_CLIENT)
    SubscribableChannel brokerToClient();
}
```

This preceding declarative cornerstone of our **chat** service can be described as follows:

- Three channel names are defined at the top--`NEW_COMMENTS`, `CLIENT_TO_BROKER`, and `BROKER_TO_CLIENT`. They each map onto a channel name of `newComments`, `clientToBroker`, and `brokerToClient`.
- `newComments()` is defined as an input linked to the `NEW_COMMENTS` channel via the `@Input` annotation, and has a return type of `SubscribableChannel`, meaning, it can be used to consume messages.
- `clientToBroker()` is defined as an output linked to the `CLIENT_TO_BROKER` channel via the `@Output` annotation, and has a return type of `MessageChannel`, which means that it can be used to transmit messages.
- `brokerToClient()` is defined as an input linked to the `BROKER_TO_CLIENT` channel via the `@Input` annotation, and also has a return type of `SubscribableChannel`, which means it, too, can be used to consume messages.

We need this interface in place so we can then dive into creating that `InboundChatService` we promised to build earlier:

```
@Service
@EnableBinding(ChatServiceStreams.class)
public class InboundChatService implements WebSocketHandler {
```

```
      private final ChatServiceStreams chatServiceStreams;

      public InboundChatService(ChatServiceStreams chatServiceStreams)
      {
        this.chatServiceStreams = chatServiceStreams;
      }

      @Override
      public Mono<Void> handle(WebSocketSession session) {
        return session
          .receive()
          .log("inbound-incoming-chat-message")
          .map(WebSocketMessage::getPayloadAsText)
          .log("inbound-convert-to-text")
          .map(s -> session.getId() + ": " + s)
          .log("inbound-mark-with-session-id")
          .flatMap(this::broadcast)
          .log("inbound-broadcast-to-broker")
          .then();
      }

      public Mono<?> broadcast(String message) {
        return Mono.fromRunnable(() -> {
          chatServiceStreams.clientToBroker().send(
            MessageBuilder
              .withPayload(message)
              .build());
        });
      }
    }
}
```

This preceding service code, registered to handle messages coming in on
/app/chatMessage.new can be described as follows:

- @Service marks it as a Spring service that should launch automatically
  thanks to Spring Boot's component scanning.
- @EnableBinding(ChatServiceStreams.class) signals Spring Cloud
  Stream to connect this component to its broker-handling machinery.
- It implements the WebSocketHandler interface--when a client connects,
  the handle(WebSocketSession) method will be invoked.
- Instead of using the @StreamListener annotation as in the previous code,
  this class injects a ChatServiceStreams bean (same as the binding
  annotation) via constructor injection.

- To handle a new `WebSocketSession`, we grab it and invoke its `receive()` method. This hands us a `Flux` of potentially endless `WebSocketMessage` objects. These would be the incoming messages sent in by the client that just connected. NOTE: Every client that connects will invoke this method independently.
- We map the `Flux<WebSocketMessage>` object's stream of payload data into a `Flux<String>` via `getPayloadAsText()`.
- From there, we transform each raw message into a formatted message with the WebSocket's session ID prefixing each message.
- Satisfied with our formatting of the message, we `flatMap` it onto our `broadcast()` message in order to broadcast it to RabbitMQ.
- To hand control to the framework, we put a `then()` on the tail of this Reactor flow so Spring can subscribe to this `Flux`.
- The `broadcast` method, invoked as every message is pulled down, marshals and transmits the message by first building a Spring Cloud Streams `Message<String>` object. It is pushed out over the `ChatServiceStreams.clientToBroker()` object's `MessageChannel` via the `send()` API. To **reactorize** it, we wrap it with `Mono.fromRunnable`.

Whew! That's a lot of code! Such is the effect of **functional reactive programming** (**FRP**). Not a lot of effort is spent on imperative constructs and intermediate results. Instead, each step is chained to the next step, forming a transforming flow, pulling data from one input (the `WebSocketSession` in this case), and steering it into a channel for the broker (`ChatServiceStreams.clientToBroker()`).

Remember earlier when we created a `chat.yml` file in our Config Server's Git repo? Here's the key fragment:

```
spring:
  cloud:
    stream:
      bindings:
        clientToBroker:
          destination: learning-spring-boot-chat-user-messages
          group: app-chatMessages
```

It contains an entry for `spring.cloud.stream.bindings.clientToBroker`, where `clientToBroker` matches the *channel name* we set in `ChatServiceStreams`. It indicates that messages transmitted over the `clientToBroker` channel will be put on RabbitMQ's `learning-spring-boot-chat-user-messages` exchange, and grouped with other messages marked `app-chatMessages`.

This sets things up to broadcast any user-based chat message to everyone. We just need to have every user listen for them!

To do so, we need to create that *other* service we promised to build earlier,
`OutboundChatService`:

```
@Service
@EnableBinding(ChatServiceStreams.class)
public class OutboundChatService implements WebSocketHandler {

    private final static Logger log =
        LoggerFactory.getLogger(CommentService.class);

    private Flux<String> flux;
    private FluxSink<String> chatMessageSink;

    public OutboundChatService() {
        this.flux = Flux.<String>create(
            emitter -> this.chatMessageSink = emitter,
            FluxSink.OverflowStrategy.IGNORE)
            .publish()
            .autoConnect();
    }

    @StreamListener(ChatServiceStreams.BROKER_TO_CLIENT)
    public void listen(String message) {
        if (chatMessageSink != null) {
            log.info("Publishing " + message +
                " to websocket...");
            chatMessageSink.next(message);
        }
    }

    @Override
    public Mono<Void> handle(WebSocketSession session) {
        return session
            .send(this.flux
            .map(session::textMessage)
            .log("outbound-wrap-as-websocket-message"))
            .log("outbound-publish-to-websocket");

    }
}
```

The code can be described as follows:

- Again, the @Service annotation marks this as an automatically wired Spring service.
- It has the same EnableBinding(ChatServicesStreams.class) as the inbound service, indicating that this, too, will participate with Spring Cloud Streams.
- The constructor call wires up another one of those FluxSink objects, this time for a Flux or strings.
- @StreamListener(ChatServiceStreams.BROKER_TO_CLIENT) indicates that this service will be listening for incoming messages on the brokerToClient channel. When it receives one, it will forward it to chatMessageSink.
- This class also implements WebSocketHandler, and each client attaches via the handle(WebSocketSession) method. It is there that we connect the flux of incoming messages to the WebSocketSession via its send() method.
- Because WebSocketSession.send() requires Flux<WebSocketMessage>, we map the Flux<String> into it using session::textMessage. Nothing to serialize.
- There is a custom log flag when the Flux finished, and another for when the entire Flux is handled.

That's it!

With InboundChatService routing individual messages from client to server to broker, we are able to take individual messages and broadcast them to ALL users. Then, with OutboundChatService pulling down copies of the message *for each WebSocket session*, each user is able to receive a copy.

Don't forget, we also added a binding to chat.yml on the Config Server to OutboundChatService as well:

```
spring:
  cloud:
    stream:
      bindings:
        brokerToClient:
          destination: learning-spring-boot-chat-user-messages
          group: topic-chatMessages
```

And remember that little bit of JavaScript we wrote to subscribe to `ws://localhost:8200/topic/chatMessage.new`? It will receive the broadcast messages.

> `Flux` and `FluxSink`--if you haven't caught on, linking async operations with pre-established `Flux` objects is easily handled by this pattern. We've seen it several times now. If both sides of an async service use a `Flux`, it's not necessary. But if something bars hooking them directly, this mechanism easily bridges the gap.

The names `InboundChatService` and `OutboundChatService` are somewhat arbitrary. The important point to note is that one is responsible for transporting WebSocket messages from the client to the broker through the server. Those are *incoming*. After crossing the broker, we describe them at this stage as being *outgoing*. The naming convention is meant to help remember what does what. Neither Spring Boot nor Spring Cloud Stream care about what these classes are named.

With this enhancement, we can fire things up and see what it looks like.

In the following screenshot of our new chat box there is a conversation involving two users:

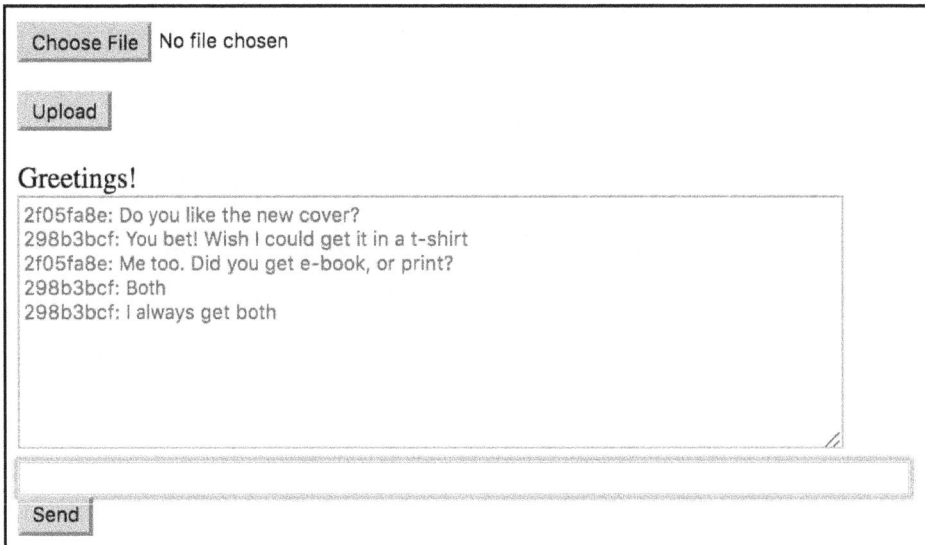

Choose File | No file chosen

Upload

Greetings!

2f05fa8e: Do you like the new cover?
298b3bcf: You bet! Wish I could get it in a t-shirt
2f05fa8e: Me too. Did you get e-book, or print?
298b3bcf: Both
298b3bcf: I always get both

Send

The prefix values (2f05fa8e and 298b3bcf) are pure WebSocket session IDs. Kind of tricky to connect with a human user, ehh? Nevertheless, this interchange is what is seen by all parties. (Since both sides see the same exchange, no need to show *both* browser tabs.)

However, if we peek inside the browser's JavaScript console, we get a new insight. The following is a screenshot from the user with 2f05fa8e as their session ID:

```
Publishing "Do you like the new cover?"
Received 2f05fa8e: Do you like the new cover?
Received 298b3bcf: You bet! Wish I could get it in a t-shirt
Publishing "Me too. Did you get e-book, or print?"
Received 2f05fa8e: Me too. Did you get e-book, or print?
Received 298b3bcf: Both
Received 298b3bcf: I always get both
>
```

We can immediately see the first message (Do you like the new cover?) being published, and received right back. Following that, the other user sends a separate message (You bet! Wish I could get a t-shirt).

If we inspect the other user's JavaScript console, we can see the other side of the conversation:

```
Received 2f05fa8e: Do you like the new cover?
Publishing "You bet! Wish I could get it in a t-shirt"
Received 298b3bcf: You bet! Wish I could get it in a t-shirt
Received 2f05fa8e: Me too. Did you get e-book, or print?
Publishing "Both"
Received 298b3bcf: Both
Publishing "I always get both"
Received 298b3bcf: I always get both
>
```

The first message was from the first user (Do you like the new cover?) followed by the second user's response (You bet!...), and so forth.

Simple. Elegant. Asynchronous. That's what WebSockets are for. And here we have a simple usage.

Sending user-specific messages

So far, we have crafted a relatively rich application using different types of broadcast messages.

For example, when a new comment is written, it's sent to every client. Only the clients actually displaying the relevant image will update anything. But the message was sent nonetheless. Also, when a user enters a new chat message, it's sent to everybody. For these use cases, this solution is fine. WebSockets make the process quite efficient.

But there are definitely scenarios when we want to send a message to just one subscriber. A perfect example we'll pursue in this section is adding the ability to "@" a user with a chat message. We only want such a message sent to that specific user. What would be even better? If we could do this without ripping up everything we've done so far.

We can start with the `ChatController` inside the `chat` microservice. We should be able to look at the incoming message, and sniff out anything starting with @. If we find it, then we should be able to extract the username, and send the message to that user and that user alone. If a message does NOT start with @, simply broadcast the message to everyone as before.

Registering users without authentication

In this chapter, we haven't yet picked up security. That will be covered in `Chapter 18`, *Securing Your App with Spring Boot*. For now, we need something to take its place.

As a workaround, we can introduce the concept of the user entering his or her own username and sending it with the HTTP-based request used to create the WebSocket.

To offer the user a place to enter their username, we can put this at the top of the Thymeleaf template:

```
<input id="username" type="text" />
<button id="connect">Connect</button>
<button id="disconnect" style="display: none">Disconnect</button>
```

There is a both a `Connect` and a `Disconnect` button to analogously log in/log out of the WebSocket session.

Now we can wire it so that clicking the `Connect` button, actually creates the WebSocket connection:

```
document.getElementById('connect')
  .addEventListener('click', function () {
    document.getElementById('connect').style.display = 'none';
    document.getElementById('disconnect').style.display = 'inline';

    var usernameInput = document.getElementById('username');

    document.getElementById('chatBox').style.display = 'inline';
```

This is what happens when `Connect` is clicked:

- The `connect` button is hidden while the `disconnect` button is shown
- We get hold of the `username` input
- The `chatBox` is switched from hidden to displayed

From here, the rest of the flow of creating a WebSocket is followed, including the extra `user` parameter supplied by the `userInput` input as we subscribe for `/topic/chatMessage.new`:

```
inboundChatMessages =
  new WebSocket(
    'ws://localhost:8200/topic/chatMessage.new?user='
    + usernameInput.value);
inboundChatMessages.onmessage = function (event) {
  console.log('Received ' + event.data);
  var chatDisplay = document.getElementById('chatDisplay');
  chatDisplay.value = chatDisplay.value + event.data + 'n';
};
```

This preceding subscription code for incoming chat messages works as follows:

- We again create a JavaScript `WebSocket`, but it has an extra query argument, `user`, populated with the `usernameInput` value
- The route we subscribe to is `/topic/chatMessage.new`, the same one that `OutboundChatService` publishes to
- The `onmessage` handler is assigned a function that updates the `chatDisplay` textarea with the new event's `data`

To wrap things up, we add the following event listener in case `Disconnect` is clicked:

```
document.getElementById('disconnect')
  .addEventListener('click', function () {
    document.getElementById('connect').style.display = 'inline';
    document.getElementById('disconnect').style.display = 'none';
    document.getElementById('chatBox').style.display = 'none';

    if (newComments != null) {
      newComments.close();
    }
    if (outboundChatMessages != null) {
      outboundChatMessages.close();
    }
    if (inboundChatMessages != null) {
      inboundChatMessages.close();
    }
});
```

This last code nicely does the following things:

- It hides the `Disconnect` button and the chat box while showing the `Connect` button
- It closes all the WebSockets

Linking a user to a session

We are still missing a critical ingredient--linking the username entered to the user's WebSocket session.

Since every one of our `WebSocketHandler` services we built may need access to this user data, we should build a **shim** called `UserParsingHandshakeHandler` to slip in like this:

```
abstract class UserParsingHandshakeHandler
  implements WebSocketHandler {

    private final Map<String, String> userMap;

    UserParsingHandshakeHandler() {
      this.userMap = new HashMap<>();
    }

    @Override
```

```
public final Mono<Void> handle(WebSocketSession session) {

    this.userMap.put(session.getId(),
      Stream.of(session.getHandshakeInfo().getUri()
        .getQuery().split("&"))
        .map(s -> s.split("="))
        .filter(strings -> strings[0].equals("user"))
        .findFirst()
        .map(strings -> strings[1])
        .orElse(""));

    return handleInternal(session);
  }

  abstract protected Mono<Void> handleInternal(
    WebSocketSession session);

  String getUser(String id) {
    return userMap.get(id);
  }
}
```

The previous code can be described as follows:

- This abstract class implements WebSocketHandler; it will be invoked when a new WebSocketSession is created
- It contains a mapping between session ID and username, called userMap, initialized in the constructor
- The implementation of handle(WebSocketSession) takes the userMap and puts a new entry keyed off the session's ID
- The value stored under that session ID is extracted from the session's handshake, granting access to the original URI
- With some Java 8 stream magic, we can extract the query string from this URI, and find the user argument
- findFirst() produces an Optional, so we can either map over the answer or fall back to an empty string (no user)
- Having loaded the userMap, we then invoke the concrete subclass through a custom abstract method, handleInternal(WebSocketMessage)
- To facilitate looking up the current username, getUser(String) is provided to look up user based on session ID

This chunk of code will handle user details, allowing each concrete `WebSocketHandler` to do its thing while also having access to the current session's username.

To use this new handshake handler, we need to update the `InboundChatService` like this:

```
@Service
@EnableBinding(ChatServiceStreams.class)
public class InboundChatService extends
UserParsingHandshakeHandler
{

    private final ChatServiceStreams chatServiceStreams;

    public InboundChatService(ChatServiceStreams
chatServiceStreams){
        this.chatServiceStreams = chatServiceStreams;
    }

    @Override
    protected Mono<Void> handleInternal(WebSocketSession session) {
        return session
          .receive()
          .log(getUser(session.getId())
             + "-inbound-incoming-chat-message")
          .map(WebSocketMessage::getPayloadAsText)
          .log(getUser(session.getId())
             + "-inbound-convert-to-text")
          .flatMap(message ->
             broadcast(message, getUser(session.getId())))
          .log(getUser(session.getId())
             + "-inbound-broadcast-to-broker")
          .then();
    }

    public Mono<?> broadcast(String message, String user) {
        return Mono.fromRunnable(() -> {
          chatServiceStreams.clientToBroker().send(
            MessageBuilder
             .withPayload(message)
             .setHeader(ChatServiceStreams.USER_HEADER, user)
             .build());
        });
    }

}
```

It's almost the same as what we coded earlier in this chapter, with a few key differences:

- It now extends `UserParsingHandshakeHandler` instead of `WebSocketHandler`.
- Instead of implementing `handle(WebSocketSession)`, we must now write `handleInternal(WebSocketSession)`. This is a classic pattern of using a parent abstract class to intercept and then delegate.
- `broadcast()` takes two arguments--`message` and `user`. The `user` field is populated using `getUser(session.getId())`.
- `broadcast()` builds a `Message` like it did earlier in this chapter, but also adds a custom header containing the user of the creator of the message.

> **TIP**
>
> Part of the power of the Message API are headers. You can use standard headers as well as make up your own to suit your needs. In this case, we mark up every message with the originator. Other useful details could include the timestamp of creation and origin address. Really, anything.

Sending user-to-user messages

The last step in implementing user-to-user messages is to apply a filter to `OutboundChatService`. Since we coded up `UserParsingHandshakeHandler`, we have to adjust the service to handle this:

```
@Service
@EnableBinding(ChatServiceStreams.class)
public class OutboundChatService
  extends UserParsingHandshakeHandler {
    ...
}
```

For starters, we need to change this class to extend `UserParsingHandshakeHandler` instead of `WebSocketHandler`.

There's no need to alter the constructor call where our `FluxSink` is configured. However, the handler itself must be adjusted as follows:

```
@Override
protected Mono<Void> handleInternal(WebSocketSession session) {
  return session
    .send(this.flux
```

```
        .filter(s -> validate(s, getUser(session.getId()))))
        .map(this::transform)
        .map(session::textMessage)
        .log(getUser(session.getId()) +
            "-outbound-wrap-as-websocket-message"))
    .log(getUser(session.getId()) +
        "-outbound-publish-to-websocket");
}
```

The details can be explained as follows:

- Just like `InboundChatService`, we must now implement `handleInternal(WebSocketSession)`.
- It has the same `session.send(Flux)` call, but that `Flux` has a couple of extra steps added, including a filter and an extra map.
- The `filter` call validates each message, deciding whether or not *this* user should get it. (We'll write that `validate()` method in a moment).
- Assuming the message is valid for this user, it uses a local `transform` method to tweak it.
- The rest of the machinery used to convert this string message into a `WebSocketMessage<String>` and pipe it over the WebSocket is the same as before.

When dealing with streams of messages, layering in a filter is no biggie. See how in the following code:

```
private boolean validate(Message<String> message, String user) {
    if (message.getPayload().startsWith("@")) {
        String targetUser = message.getPayload()
            .substring(1, message.getPayload().indexOf(" "));

        String sender = message.getHeaders()
            .get(ChatServiceStreams.USER_HEADER, String.class);

        return user.equals(sender) || user.equals(targetUser);
    } else {
        return true;
    }
}
```

This last code can be described as follows:

- `validate` accepts a `Message<String>` and the name of the current user (not the user that sent the message).
- It first checks the payload, and if it starts with @, it looks deeper. If the message does NOT start with @, it just lets it on through.
- If the message starts with @, it proceeds to extract the target user by parsing the text between @ and the first space. It also extracts the original sender of the message using the `User` header.
- If the current user is either the sender or the receiver, the message is allowed through. Otherwise, it is dropped.

A filtering function like this makes it easy to layer various options. We used it to target user-specific messages. But imagine putting things like security checks, regional messages, time-based messages, and more!

To wrap this up, we need to also code a little transformation to make the user-to-user experience top notch:

```
private String transform(Message<String> message) {
    String user = message.getHeaders()
      .get(ChatServiceStreams.USER_HEADER, String.class);
    if (message.getPayload().startsWith("@")) {
      return "(" + user + "): " + message.getPayload();
    } else {
        return "(" + user + ")(all): " + message.getPayload();
    }
}
```

This preceding nice little transformation can be described as follows:

- `transform` accepts a `Message<String>`, and converts it into a plain old string message
- It extracts the `User` header to find who wrote the message
- If the message starts with @, then it assumes the message is targeted, and prefixes it with the author wrapped in parentheses
- If the message does NOT start with @, then it prefixes it with the author wrapped in parentheses plus `(all)`, to make it clear that this is a broadcast message

With this change in place, we have coded a sophisticated user-to-user chat service, running on top of RabbitMQ, using Reactive Streams.

Checking out the final product

By hooking up a username with a WebSocket ID, let's see how all this runs. Restart everything, and visit the site.

First, we login as shown in this screenshot:

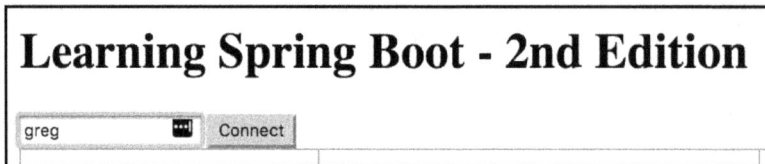

Learning Spring Boot - 2nd Edition

greg ▦ Connect

As seen in the last screenshot, the user logs in as `greg`. After that, the chat box will display itself at the bottom of the page. If we assume that `oliver` and `phil` have also logged in, we can see an exchange of messages as follows:

Greg asks how everyone likes the cover:

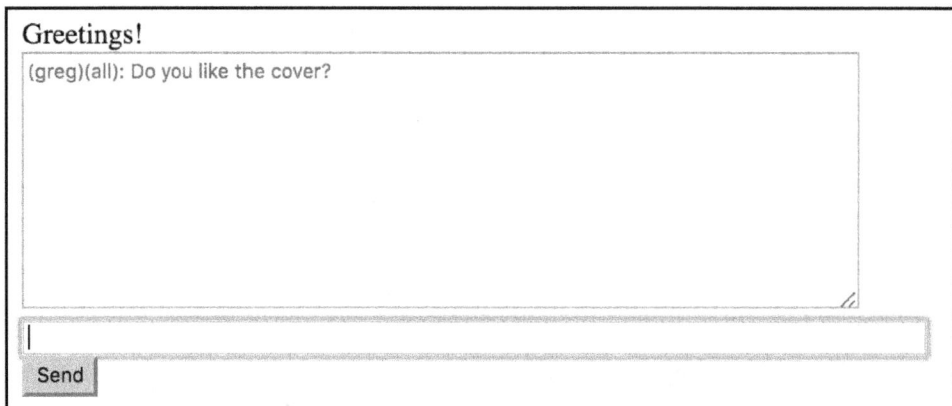

Greetings!

(greg)(all): Do you like the cover?

Send

This preceding message is seen by everyone. Again, no reason to display all three users' views, since it is identical at this stage.

Oliver gives his `$0.02`:

> **Greetings!**
>
> (greg)(all): Do you like the cover?
> (oliver)(all): I sure do
>
> [Send]

So far, the conversation is wide open, as depicted by the (`all`) tag on each message. By the way, isn't this user-based interaction easier to follow the conversation than the earlier version where we used session IDs?

Phil writes a direct question to Greg:

> **Greetings!**
>
> (greg)(all): Do you like the cover?
> (oliver)(all): I sure do
>
> @greg Are you going to offer it in a t-shirt?
> [Send]

After Phil clicks on **Send**, the following appears in Greg's browser:

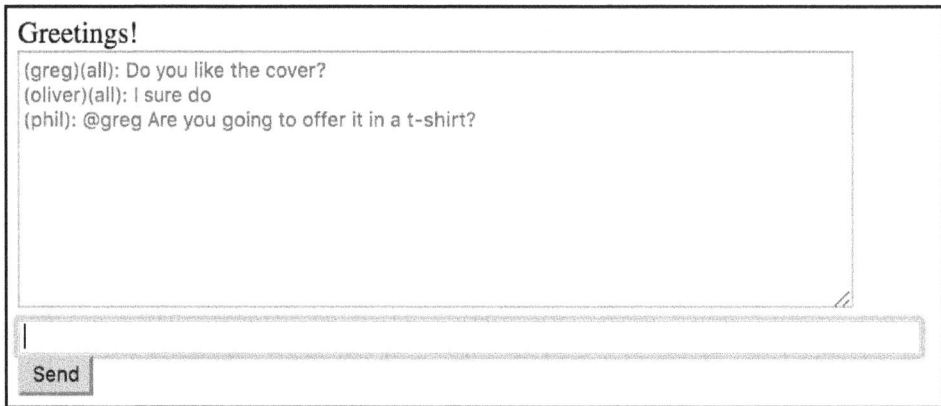

Greetings!

```
(greg)(all): Do you like the cover?
(oliver)(all): I sure do
(phil): @greg Are you going to offer it in a t-shirt?
```

| |

Send

Notice how this message does NOT have (`all`)? We know this message is direct, which is further verified by looking at Oliver's browser:

Greetings!

```
(greg)(all): Do you like the cover?
(oliver)(all): I sure do
```

| |

Send

No sign of a followup question about t-shirt availability.

And if we look at Greg's JavaScript console, we can see all of this:

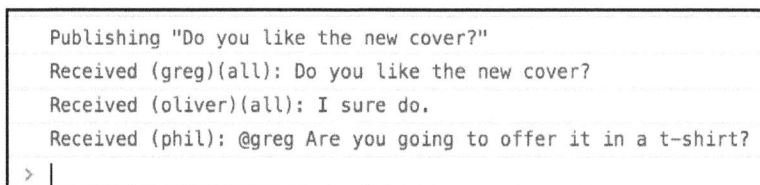

```
Publishing "Do you like the new cover?"
Received (greg)(all): Do you like the new cover?
Received (oliver)(all): I sure do.
Received (phil): @greg Are you going to offer it in a t-shirt?
> |
```

This preceding interchange shows the following:

- One message is sent from Greg's session to the server
- Two broadcast messages are received via the broker from Greg and Oliver
- One direct message is received from Phil

In conclusion, it's nice to see that by chaining together streams of messages across the system with Spring Cloud Stream, we were able to pipe exactly the messages we wanted to whom we wanted to receive them. We were able to leverage a sturdy transport broker, RabbitMQ, without getting caught up in messy details.

We took advantage of things like headers to mark up our messages, and filtered things as needed to implement business requirements. And we didn't spend all our time configuring brokers, servlet containers, or anything else. Instead, we logically defined channels and what was posted/consumed from those channels.

JSR 356 versus Spring WebFlux messaging

Perhaps, you're wondering why this chapter doesn't delve into Java's standard WebSocket API? In truth, the standard API is a good piece of technology, but due to several limitations, it doesn't suit our needs.

A big limitation of JSR 356 is that it's based on the Servlet 3.1 spec. If we were running Apache Tomcat, we'd have access to that. But being a Reactive Streams application, we are using Netty, putting it off limits.

Even if we *did* switch to Apache Tomcat, there is no support for Reactor types. This is partly due to its blocking API, despite being hitched to an asynchronous programming model.

Summary

In this chapter, we made our social media platform asynchronous, front to back, through the usage of WebSocket messages. We published new comments to all users. We introduced a way for our users to chat amongst themselves, whether that was by broadcasting to everyone, or by sending individual messages directly to each other.

In the next chapter, we will apply one of the most critical components needed for production, security.

18
Securing Your App with Spring Boot

It's not real until it's secured.

– Greg L. Turnquist @gregturn

In the previous chapter, you learned how to turn our application into a fully asynchronous, message-based app using WebSockets.

Security is hard. Even among the experts. Rob Winch, the lead for **Spring Security**, has stated in multiple forums, *"Do not implement security on your own."* A classic example is when someone wrote a utility to crack password-protected Microsoft Word documents. It had an intentional delay so that it didn't operate in subsecond time. Get it? The author of the tool didn't want to show how *easy* it was to break a Word document.

Suffice it to say, there are lots of attack vectors. Especially on the web. The fact that our applications partially run in a remote location (the browser) on someone else's machine leaves little in guarantees. In fact, whole books have been written on Spring Security. We can't cover everything, but we will cover Just Enough™ to secure our microservice-based social media platform.

In this chapter, we will cover the following topics:

- Using Spring Session to share state between services
- Creating a Gateway API
- Securing the `chat` microservice
- Securing the `images` microservice
- Authorizing methods

- Securing WebSockets
- Securing the Config Server
- Securing the Eureka Server

Securing a Spring Boot application

In this chapter, we will secure our microservice-based social media platform. This will introduce some interesting use cases, ones that Spring Security can easily handle. However, it's important to know that almost every situation is slightly different. Spring Security can handle them, but it requires understanding how it operates so that you can adapt what you learn in this chapter to our unique situation.

To kick things off, we just need one dependency added to our project:

```
compile('org.springframework.boot:spring-boot-starter-security-
    reactive')
```

In addition to adding Spring Security, we will need to define a policy, and also include authorization rules. As we move through this chapter, you'll learn what all this means.

By the way, remember the microservice-based solution we've developed in the previous chapters? What is the side effect of splitting our app into multiple services? We have to secure each and every one. This means, we have to add these dependencies to each module. Yikes! Can you imagine logging in to the **user interface** (UI), clicking on a link, and logging in again?

Yech!

Using Spring Session

Before we can dig into those nice security policies and authorization rules we just talked about, we need a solution to secure multiple microservices.

What is the exact problem? When we log in to the first piece of our social media platform, we want that status to be carried through to the other components with ease.

The solution is Spring Session (`http://projects.spring.io/spring-session/`), which supports multiple third-party data stores to offload session state including Redis, MongoDB, GemFire, Hazelcast, and others. Instead of the session data being stored in memory, it is externalized to a separate data store.

This provides multiple benefits such as the following:

- Provides scalability when running multiple instances of various services
- Avoids the need for session affinity (sticky sessions) by not requiring load balancers to route clients to the same instance
- Leverages a data store's built-in expiration options (if desired)
- Multi-user profiles

There is one other, hidden benefit that we will take immediate advantage of in this chapter--sharing session state between different microservices. Log in to the user-facing microservice, create a session with that security state, and share the session with all microservices. Bam! Automatic access.

Since we are already using MongoDB, let's use that to also store our session.

The first thing we need to do in getting Spring Session off the ground is to update each microservice with the following dependencies:

```
compile('org.springframework.boot:spring-boot-starter-security-
    reactive')
compile('org.springframework.session:spring-session-data-mongodb')
```

These preceding dependencies can be described as follows:

- `spring-boot-starter-security-reactive` brings in all the configuration support we need to define a security policy, including some critical annotations, as well as Spring WebFlux-based security components to implement our policy, including various filters
- `spring-session-data-mongodb` will bring in Spring Session MongoDB and Spring Data MongoDB, making it possible to write session data to our MongoDB service reactively

> It's important to understand that sessions and security are orthogonal concepts that nicely leverage each other. We can use one or the other for different purposes. However, when used in concert, the effect is most elegant.

To configure Spring Session to use MongoDB, we need the following added to each microservice:

```
@EnableMongoWebSession
public class SessionConfig {

}
```

This new `SessionConfig` class does the following:

- `@EnableMongoWebSession` activates Spring Session MongoDB, signaling to use MongoDB as the place to read and write any session data

This is all it takes to enable using MongoDB for session data. However, there are some lingering issues we have to sort out due to the structure of our microservice-based application that bars us from moving forward.

We used this code in the previous chapter:

```
Map<String, CorsConfiguration> corsConfigurationMap =
  new HashMap<>();
CorsConfiguration corsConfiguration = new CorsConfiguration();
corsConfiguration.addAllowedOrigin("http://localhost:8080");
corsConfigurationMap.put(
  "/topic/comments.new", corsConfiguration);
corsConfigurationMap.put(
  "/app/chatMessage.new", corsConfiguration);
corsConfigurationMap.put(
  "/topic/chatMessage.new", corsConfiguration);
```

To make our WebSocket `chat` microservice integrate with the `images`-based web page, we needed `addAllowedOrigin("http://localhost:8080")`. That way, a web request from a service on port 8080 was permitted to cross over to a service on port 8200.

When it comes to security and sessions, stitching together two different services on two different ports in the browser isn't the best way to approach things. Not only is it technically daunting, it is really a code smell--a hint that our application is leaking too much of its structure to the outside world.

The solution is to create a **Gateway API**.

Creating a Gateway API

What is a Gateway API? It's a one-stop facade where we can make all our various web requests. The facade then dispatches the requests to the proper backend service based on the configuration settings.

In our case, we don't want the browser talking to two different ports. Instead, we'd rather serve up a single, unified service with different URL paths.

In `Chapter 16`, *Microservices with Spring Boot*, we used Spring Cloud for several microservice tasks, including service discovery, circuit breaker, and load balancing. Another microservice-based tool we will make use of is **Spring Cloud Gateway**, a tool for building just such a proxy service.

Let's start by adding this to our `chat` microservice:

```
compile('org.springframework.cloud:spring-cloud-starter-gateway')
```

With Spring Cloud Gateway on the classpath, we don't have to do a single thing to activate it in our `chat` microservice. Out of the box, Spring Cloud Gateway makes the `chat` microservice our *front door* for all client calls. What does that mean?

Spring Cloud Gateway forwards various web calls based on patterns to its respective backend service. This allows us to split up the backend into various services with some simple settings, yet offer a seamless API to any client.

> Spring Cloud Gateway also allows us to pull together legacy services into one unified service. Older clients can continue talking to the old system, while newer clients adopt the new gateway. This is known as API *strangling* (http://www.kennybastani.com/2016/08/strangling-legacy-micr oservices-spring-cloud.html).

To configure which URL patterns are forwarded where, we need to add this to our `chat.yml` stored in the Config Server:

```
spring:
  cloud:
    gateway:
      routes:
      # ============================================================
      - id: imagesService
        uri: lb://IMAGES
        predicates:
        - Path=/imagesService/**
```

```
          filters:
          - RewritePath=/imagesService/(?<segment>.*), /${segment}
          - RewritePath=/imagesService, /
          - SaveSession
        - id: images
          uri: lb://IMAGES
          predicates:
          - Path=/images/**
          filters:
          - SaveSession
        - id: mainCss
          uri: lb://IMAGES
          predicates:
          - Path=/main.css
          filters:
          - SaveSession
        - id: commentsService
          uri: lb://IMAGES
          predicates:
          - Path=/comments/**
          filters:
          - SaveSession
```

Looking at the preceding code, we can discern the following:

- Each entry has an `id`, a `uri`, an optional collection of `predicates`, and an optional list of `filters`.
- Looking at the first entry, we can see that requests to `/imagesService` are routed to the load-balanced (`lb:` prefix), Eureka-registered `IMAGES` service. There are filters to strip the `imagesService` prefix.
- All requests to `/images` will also be sent to the `images` microservice. However, compared to `/imagesServices`, the full path of the request will be sent. For example, a request to `/images/abc123` will be forwarded to the `images` service as `/images/abc123`, and not as `/abc123`. We'll soon see why this is important.
- Asking for `/main.css` will get routed to `images` as well.
- All requests to `/comments` will get sent to `images`, full path intact. (Remember that `images` uses Ribbon to remotely invoke `comments`, and we don't want to change that right now).
- All of these rules include the `SaveSession` filter, a custom Spring Cloud Gateway filter we'll write shortly to ensure our session data is saved before making any remote call.

Don't forget to restart the Config Server after committing changes!

What's going on?

First and foremost, we create a Gateway API, because we want to keep image management and chatting as separate, nicely defined services. At one point in time, there was only HTTP support. WebSocket support is newly added to Spring Cloud Gateway, so we don't use it yet, but keep all of our WebSocket handling code in the gateway instead. In essence, the `chat` microservice moves to the front, and the `images` microservice moves to the back.

Additionally, with WebSocket handling kept in the gateway, we can eliminate the latency of forwarding WebSocket messages to another service. It's left as an exercise for you to move WebSocket messaging into another service, configure Spring Cloud Gateway to forward them and measure the effects.

This suggests that we should have `chat` serve up the main Thymeleaf template, but have it fetch image-specific bits of HTML from the `images` service.

To go along with this adjustment to our social media platform, let's create a Thymeleaf template at `src/main/resources/templates/index.html` in `chat` like this:

```
<!DOCTYPE html>
<html xmlns:th="http://www.thymeleaf.org">
    <head>
        <meta charset="UTF-8" />
        <title>Learning Spring Boot: Spring-a-Gram</title>
        <link rel="stylesheet" href="/main.css" />
    </head>
    <body>
        <div>
            <span th:text="${authentication.name}" />
            <span th:text="${authentication.authorities}" />
        </div>
        <hr />

        <h1>Learning Spring Boot - 2nd Edition</h1>

        <div id="images"></div>
```

```
<div id="chatBox">
    Greetings!
    <br/>
    <textarea id="chatDisplay"
            rows="10" cols="80"
            disabled="true" ></textarea>
    <br/>
    <input id="chatInput" type="text"
            style="width: 500px" value="" />
    <br/>
    <button id="chatButton">Send</button>
    <br/>
</div>

    </body>
</html>
```

This preceding template can be described as follows:

- It's the same header as we saw in the previous chapter, including the `main.css` stylesheet.
- The `<h1>` header has been pulled in from the `image` service.
- For images, we have a tiny `<div>` identified as `images`. We need to write a little code to populate that from our `images` microservice.
- Finally, we have the same chat box shown in the earlier chapter.
- By the way, we remove the connect/disconnect buttons, since we will soon leverage Spring Security's user information for WebSocket messaging!

To populate the images `<div>`, we need to write a tiny piece of JavaScript and stick it at the bottom of the page:

```
<script th:inline="javascript">
    /*<![CDATA[*/
    (function() {
        var xhr = new XMLHttpRequest();
        xhr.open('GET', /*[[@{'/imagesService'}]]*/'', true);
        xhr.onload = function(e) {
            if (xhr.readyState === 4) {
                if (xhr.status === 200) {
                    document.getElementById('images').innerHTML =
                        xhr.responseText;

                    // Register a handler for each button
                    document.querySelectorAll('button.comment')
                        .forEach(function(button) {
                            button.addEventListener('click',
```

```
                    function() {
                        e.preventDefault();
                        var comment =
                            document.getElementById(
                            'comment-' + button.id);

                        var xhr = new XMLHttpRequest();
                        xhr.open('POST',
                            /*[[@{'/comments'}]]*/'',
                            true);

                        var formData = new FormData();
                        formData.append('comment',
                                    comment.value);
                        formData.append('imageId',
                                    button.id);

                        xhr.send(formData);

                        comment.value = '';
                    });
            });

        document.querySelectorAll('button.delete')
            .forEach(function(button) {
                button.addEventListener('click',
                    function() {
                    e.preventDefault();
                    var xhr = new XMLHttpRequest();
                    xhr.open('DELETE', button.id, true);
                    xhr.withCredentials = true;
                    xhr.send(null);
                });
            });

        document.getElementById('upload')
            .addEventListener('click', function() {
                e.preventDefault();
                var xhr = new XMLHttpRequest();
                xhr.open('POST',
                        /*[[@{'/images'}]]*/'',
                        true);

                var files = document
                    .getElementById('file').files;

                var formData  = new FormData();
                formData.append('file', files[0],
```

```
                              files[0].name);

                       xhr.send(formData);
                })
            }
        }
    }
    xhr.send(null);
}) ();
/*]]>*/
</script>
```

This code can be explained as follows:

- The whole thing is an **immediately invoked function expression (IIFE)**, meaning no risk of global variable collisions.
- It creates an `XMLHttpRequest` named `xhr` to do the legwork, opening an asynchronous `GET` request to `/imagesService`.
- A callback is defined with the `onload` function. When it completes with a successful response status, the images `<div>` will have its `innerHTML` replaced by the response, ensuring that the DOM content is updated using `document.getElementById('images').innerHTML = xhr.responseText`.
- After that, it will register handlers for each of the image's comment buttons (something we've already seen). The delete buttons and one upload button will also be wired up.
- With the callback defined, the request is sent.

> Don't get confused by the fact that there are four `xhr` objects. One is used to fetch the image-based HTML content, the other three are used to handle new comments, delete images, and upload new images, when the corresponding button is clicked. They are in separate scopes and have no chance of bumping into each other.

Since we only need the image-specific bits of HTML from the `images` microservice, we should tweak that template to serve up a subset of what it did in the previous chapter, like this:

```html
<!DOCTYPE html>
<div xmlns:th="http://www.thymeleaf.org">

    <table>

        <!-- ...the rest of the image stuff we've already seen... -->
```

This last fragment of HTML can be explained as follows:

- This is no longer a complete page of HTML, hence, no `<html>`, `<head>`, and `<body>` tags. Instead, it's just a `<div>`.
- Despite being just a `<div>`, we need the Thymeleaf namespace `th` to give the IDE the right information to help us with code completion.
- From there, it goes into the table structure used to display images. The rest is commented out, since it hasn't changed.

With these changes to `chat` and `images`, along with the Spring Cloud Gateway settings, we have been able to merge what appeared as two different services into one. Now that these requests will be forwarded by Spring Cloud Gateway, there is no longer any need for CORS settings. Yeah!

This means we can slim down our WebSocket configuration as follows:

```
@Bean
HandlerMapping webSocketMapping(CommentService commentService,
  InboundChatService inboundChatService,
  OutboundChatService outboundChatService) {
    Map<String, WebSocketHandler> urlMap = new HashMap<>();
    urlMap.put("/topic/comments.new", commentService);
    urlMap.put("/app/chatMessage.new", inboundChatService);
    urlMap.put("/topic/chatMessage.new", outboundChatService);

    SimpleUrlHandlerMapping mapping = new
SimpleUrlHandlerMapping();
    mapping.setOrder(10);
    mapping.setUrlMap(urlMap);

    return mapping;
}
```

The preceding code is the same as shown earlier in this chapter, but with the CORS settings, which we briefly saw earlier, removed.

As a reminder, we are focusing on writing Java code. However, in this day and age, writing JavaScript is unavoidable when we talk about dynamic updates over WebSockets. For a full-blown social media platform with a frontend team, something like webpack (`https://webpack.github.io/`) and babel.js (`https://babeljs.io/`) would be more suitable than embedding all this JavaScript at the bottom of the page. Nevertheless, this book isn't about writing JavaScript-based apps. Let's leave it as an exercise to pull out all this JavaScript from the Thymeleaf template and move it into a suitable module-loading solution.

Securing the chat microservice

Okay, this chapter is titled *Securing Your App with Spring Boot,* yet we have spent a fair amount of time... NOT securing our app! That is about to change. Thanks to this little bit of restructuring, we can move forward with locking things down as desired.

Let's take a crack at writing some security policies, starting with the `chat` microservice:

```
@EnableWebFluxSecurity
public class SecurityConfiguration {

  @Bean
  SecurityWebFilterChain springWebFilterChain(HttpSecurity http) {
    return http
        .authorizeExchange()
            .pathMatchers("/**").authenticated()
            .and()
        .build();
  }
}
```

The preceding security policy can be defined as follows:

- `@EnableWebFluxSecurity` activates the Spring WebFlux security filters needed to secure our application
- `@Bean` marks the one method as a bean definition
- `HttpSecurity.http()` lets us define a simple set of authentication and authorization rules
- In this case, every Spring WebFlux exchange (denoted by `/**`) must be `authenticated`

> The `.pathMatchers("/**").authenticated()` rule is the first rule based upon URLs. It's also possible to put additional requirements at the method level, which we'll explore later in this chapter.

This is a nice beginning to define a security policy, but we need some way to track user data to *authenticate* against. To do so, we need a `User` domain object and a way to store such data. To minimize our effort at storing user information in a database, let's leverage Spring Data again.

First, we'll create a `User` domain object like this:

```
@Data
@AllArgsConstructor
@NoArgsConstructor
public class User {

    @Id private String id;
    private String username;
    private String password;
    private String[] roles;
}
```

This preceding `User` class can easily be described as follows:

- `@Data` uses the Lombok annotation to mark this for getters, setters, `equals`, `toString`, and `hashCode` functions
- `@AllArgsConstructor` creates a constructor call for all of the attributes
- `@NoArgsConstructor` creates an empty constructor call
- `@Id` marks this `id` field as the key in MongoDB
- `username`, `password`, and `roles` are critical fields required to properly integrate with Spring Security, as shown further in the chapter

> The names of these fields don't matter when it comes to integrating with Spring Security, as we'll soon see.

To interact with MongoDB, we need to create a Spring Data repository as follows:

```
public interface UserRepository
  extends Repository<User, String> {

    Mono<User> findByUsername(String username);
}
```

This is similar to the other repositories we have built so far in the following ways:

- It extends Spring Data Commons' `Repository`, indicating that the domain type is `User` and the ID type is `String`
- It has one finder needed for security lookups, `findByUsername`, which is returned as a reactive `Mono<User>`, signaling Spring Data MongoDB to use reactive MongoDB operations

With this handy repository defined, let's preload some user data into our system by creating an `InitUsers` class, as shown here:

```
@Configuration
public class InitUsers {

  @Bean
  CommandLineRunner initializeUsers(MongoOperations operations) {
    return args -> {
      operations.dropCollection(User.class);

      operations.insert(
        new User(
          null,
          "greg", "turnquist",
          new String[]{"ROLE_USER", "ROLE_ADMIN"}));
      operations.insert(
        new User(
          null,
          "phil", "webb",
          new String[]{"ROLE_USER"}));

      operations.findAll(User.class).forEach(user -> {
        System.out.println("Loaded " + user);
      });
    };
  }
}
```

This preceding user-loading class can be described as follows:

- `@Configuration` indicates this class contains bean definitions
- `@Bean` marks the `initializeUsers` method as a Spring bean
- `initializeUsers` requires a copy of the blocking `MongoOperations` bean defined by Spring Boot's MongoDB autoconfiguration code
- The return type is `CommandLineRunner`, which we'll supply with a lambda function
- Inside our lambda function, we drop the `User` based collection, insert two new users, and then print out the collection

Now, let's see how to put that to good use! To hook into Reactive Spring Security, we must implement its `UserDetailsRepository` interface. This interface is designed to look up a user record through any means necessary and bridge it to Spring Security as a `Mono<UserDetails>` return type. The solution can be found here:

```
@Component
public class SpringDataUserDetailsRepository implements
  UserDetailsRepository {

    private final UserRepository repository;

    public SpringDataUserDetailsRepository(UserRepository
     repository)
    {
      this.repository = repository;
    }

    @Override
    public Mono<UserDetails> findByUsername(String username) {
      return repository.findByUsername(username)
       .map(user -> new User(
         user.getUsername(),
         user.getPassword(),
         AuthorityUtils.createAuthorityList(user.getRoles())
       ));
    }
}
```

The previous code can be described as follows:

- It injects a `UserRepository` we just defined through constructor injection
- It implements the interface's one method, `findByUsername`, by invoking our repository's `findByUsername` method and then mapping it onto a Spring Security `User` object (which implements the `UserDetails` interface)
- `AuthorityUtils.createAuthorityList` is a convenient utility to translate a `String[]` of roles into a `List<GrantedAuthority>`
- If no such user exists in MongoDB, it will return a `Mono.empty()`, which is the Reactor equivalent of `null`

We map our MongoDB `User` domain object onto Spring Security's `org.springframework.security.core.userdetails.User` object to satisfy the `UserDetails` requirement. However, that doesn't mean we can't implement a custom version of this interface. Imagine we were building a medical tracking system and needed each patient record to contain a detailed profile. A custom implementation would allow us to fill in the critical fields while also adding all the other data needed to track a person.

By hooking MongoDB-stored users into Spring Security, we can now attempt to access the system.

When we try to access `localhost:8080`, we can expect a login prompt, as shown in this screenshot:

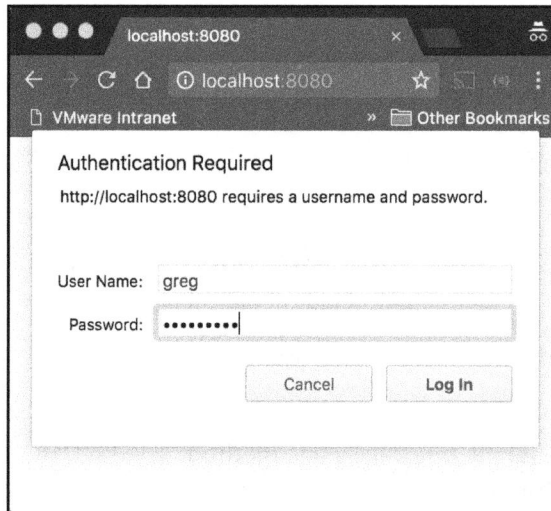

This popup (run from an incognito window to ensure there are no cookies or lingering session data) lets us nicely log in to the gateway.

Authentication versus authorization

Spring Security operates on two fundamental concepts--**authentication** and **authorization**.

These two concepts can be described as follows:

- **Authentication**: This defines who you are
- **Authorization**: This defines what you are allowed to do

The first step in any security system is to confirm the user's identify. This often involves a username and a password, but these credentialed bits can be stored in many different systems, including relational databases, directory servers, certificates, and other things. However, these are implementation details that surround verifying someone's identity. Until we know **who you are**, we can't make any determination.

HTTP Basic, HTTP FORM, and other forms of authentication are supported by Spring Security. Right now, we are using HTTP Basic on the frontend as well as the cross-service calls, given that it's the only version currently supported with Reactive Spring Security.

The second step in any security system is to decide **what the user is authorized to do**. Both a teller and a vice president at a bank can be authenticated, but they will certainly have differing permissions on what they are each allowed to do. The teller may be granted permission to open his assigned cash drawer, while the vice president may be authorized to open her customer's account.

With the `SecurityConfig` code given earlier, our `chat` microservice has instituted authentication, which is linked to the session. However, it also chose a very simple authorization strategy: anyone that is authenticated can do anything. Since the `chat` microservice does little more than communicate via a WebSocket, that is fine. In the next section, we'll see a different policy, where certain operations are restricted to a subset of users.

Sharing session details with other microservices

Something that's critical to our microservice-based social media platform is sharing the session details when putting things together. When we load the main page, it may have to pull together bits of data from multiple places. This means that after logging in to the system, the session ID that is generated has to be passed along seamlessly.

Spring Cloud Gateway can forward various requests, but Spring Session has a lazy approach to things. This means, we need to step up and save the session immediately; otherwise, the first few remote calls might fail.

To do so, we need to create a custom Spring Cloud Gateway filter as follows:

```
@Configuration
public class GatewayConfig {

  private static final Logger log =
    LoggerFactory.getLogger(GatewayConfig.class);

  /**
   * Force the current WebSession to get saved
   */
  static class SaveSessionGatewayFilterFactory
   implements GatewayFilterFactory {
     @Override
     public GatewayFilter apply(Tuple args) {
       return (exchange, chain) -> exchange.getSession()
        .map(webSession -> {
          log.debug("Session id: " + webSession.getId());
          webSession.getAttributes().entrySet()
           .forEach(entry ->
           log.debug(entry.getKey() + " => " +
           entry.getValue()));
           return webSession;
        })
        .map(WebSession::save)
        .then(chain.filter(exchange));
     }
  }

  @Bean
  SaveSessionGatewayFilterFactory
  saveSessionGatewayFilterFactory() {
     return new SaveSessionGatewayFilterFactory();
  }
}
```

This preceding filter can be described as follows:

- The @Configuration annotation indicates that this class contains beans to be picked up by Boot's component scanning
- There is an Slf4j Logger to print out debug statements

- `static class SaveSessionGatewayFilterFactory` implements the Spring Cloud Gateway's `GatewayFilterFactory` interface, allowing us to write a custom filter, which is, essentially, a function call where the inputs are transformed into a `GatewayFilter`
- To implement this functional interface, we write a lambda, accepting a WebFlux `WebServerExchange` and `GatewayFilterChain`, which gives us access to the request as well as the chain of filters to hand it off to
- We grab the exchange's `WebSession` and map over it in order to print out all its details
- Next, we map over the same `WebSession` and invoke its `save` function through a method reference
- We wrap things up with a `then()` call to invoke the filter chain on the exchange
- With `@Bean`, we define a bean in the application context that implements `SaveSessionGatewayFilterFactory`

Spring Cloud Gateway's default policy is to use the classname of the filter with `GatewayFilterFactory` removed as the name of the filter itself. Hence, `SaveSessionGatewayFilterFactory` becomes simply `SaveSession` for purposes of inserting into our configuration file, as we saw earlier.

```
spring:
  cloud:
    gateway:
      routes:
      - id: imagesService
        uri: lb://IMAGES
        predicates:
        - Path=/imagesService/**
        filters:
        - RewritePath=/imagesService/(?<segment>.*), /${segment}
        - RewritePath=/imagesService, /
        - SaveSession
        ...
```

With the preceding little filter in place, we can guarantee that all the forwarded calls made by Spring Cloud Gateway will first ensure that the current `WebSession` has been saved.

The default Spring WebFlux behavior for a web call with a `WebSession` is to issue a `Set-Cookie` directive (with the `SESSION` entry configured with the ID) back to the client in its response. Subsequent calls into WebFlux will automatically parse this cookie entry and load `WebSession` details. Spring Cloud Gateway itself forwards cookies unless explicitly configured not to. Hence, the session entry gets propagated. All that we do is ensure the security details automatically linked to the session are properly stored *before* a forwarded call is made.

Securing the images microservice

Having secured the frontend and also embedded a session ID in every gateway call to the backend, we can shift our focus to securing those backend services.

Let's start with the `images` service. First of all, we need to configure session management by creating `SessionConfig` as follows:

```
@EnableMongoWebSession
public class SessionConfig {

}
```

This preceding code can be described as follows:

- `@EnableMongoWebSession` activates the Reactor-based Spring Session MongoDB

Next, we can lock things down by creating a `SecurityConfiguration` class like this:

```
@EnableWebFluxSecurity
@EnableReactiveMethodSecurity
public class SecurityConfiguration {

  @Bean
  SecurityWebFilterChain springWebFilterChain() {
    return HttpSecurity.http()
        .securityContextRepository(
            new WebSessionSecurityContextRepository())
        .authorizeExchange()
          .anyExchange().authenticated()
          .and()
```

```
                .build();
        }
    }
```

The preceding class definition can be described as follows:

- `@EnableWebFluxSecurity` activates a collection of filters and components needed to secure Spring WebFlux endpoints.
- `@EnableReactiveMethodSecurity` adds additional support for putting annotations on methods and classes where we can plug in sophisticated security expressions (as we'll soon see).
- Next, we create a `SecurityWebFilterChain`. This is, actually, a collection of filters defined in a very specific order using Spring Security's fluent API. This API nicely lets us define what we need while leaving Spring Security to put it together in the right order.
- In this case, we want HTTP support, but with a `WebSession`-based `SecurityContextRepository`. This activates a filter that will load the exchange with a `Principal` object from our session store.
- As a minimum for authorization, all exchanges must be authenticated.

Some of this is the same as earlier, and some of it is different.

What's different? The `images` service has **method security**, meaning, it can annotate individual methods with *additional* authorization rules, which we'll see shortly. We are no longer confined to securing things based on URLs and HTTP verbs. There are also no account definitions. That's because the `images` service is not creating new sessions, but riding on the one created in the gateway by the `chat` microservice instead; (do we really want to create a separate `User` domain object in every microservice?).

Both services respond to `Authorization` headers as well as `SESSION` headers, which means that once logged in, the two can easily share information. Both, essentially, route all URLs into the same authorization rule, `.anyExchange().authenticated()`. (That's the same net effect as that of `.pathMatchers("/**").authenticated()`).

Wiring in image ownership

Spring WebFlux's `ServerWebExchange` comes prepared for security by providing a `getPrincipal()` API that returns `Mono<Principal>`. While the default version, straight out of Spring Framework, supplies `Mono.empty()`, Spring Security automatically hooks in a filter to supply a real value via `WebSessionSecurityContextRepository`.

With Spring Security and Spring Session hooked into all our web calls, we can leverage this information every time a new image is uploaded.

First of all, we can adjust our `Image` domain object as follows:

```
@Data
@AllArgsConstructor
public class Image {

  @Id private String id;
  private String name;
  private String owner;
}
```

This last code is the same POJO that we've used throughout this book with one change:

- It now has a `String owner` property. This lets us associate an image with whoever uploaded it (which we'll see shortly).

Spring Security makes it possible to inject any Spring WebFlux controller with an authentication object as follows:

```
@PostMapping(value = BASE_PATH)
public Mono<String> createFile(
  @RequestPart("file") Flux<FilePart> files,
    @AuthenticationPrincipal Principal principal) {
      return imageService.createImage(files, principal)
        .then(Mono.just("redirect:/"));
}
```

This change to our `image` service's `UploadController.createFile`, as shown in the preceding code, can be described as follows:

- Using Spring Security's `@AuthenticationPrincipal` annotation, the second parameter allows us to find out the security context of the caller.

- The actual type can be flexible, whether we want a Java `Principal`, a Spring Security subinterface `Authentication`, or a concrete instance (`UsernamePasswordAuthenticationToken` by default). This parameter can also be wrapped as a `Mono<T>` of this type.
- For simplicity, we grab it unwrapped and pass it along to `ImageService` as a new argument.

So, let's go update `ImageService.createImage()`, where `Image` objects are actually created:

```
public Mono<Void> createImage(Flux<FilePart> files,
  Principal auth) {
    return files
      .log("createImage-files")
      .flatMap(file -> {
        Mono<Image> saveDatabaseImage = imageRepository.save(
          new Image(
            UUID.randomUUID().toString(),
            file.filename(),
            auth.getName()))
            .log("createImage-save");

      ...the rest that hasn't changed...
    }
}
```

The parts that have changed in the preceding code can be described as follows:

- This method now accepts a second argument, `Principal`. This is a Java standard token.
- The code where we actually create a new `Image` is populated in the same as done earlier for the first two fields, with a random ID and the name of the file.
- The `owner` field is now populated with `auth.getName()`, supplied to us by Spring Security's context-enabling advice.

The last link in the chain of ownership is to display it on the page. To do this, we can update the model fed to that HTML fragment in `HomeController`, as follows:

```
model.addAttribute("images",
  imageService
    .findAllImages()
    .map(image -> new HashMap<String, Object>() {{
      put("id", image.getId());
      put("name", image.getName());
```

```
        put("owner", image.getOwner());
        put("comments",
          commentHelper.getComments(image,
            webSession.getId())));
    }})
);
```

This preceding fragment from `public String index()` has been updated to include the new `owner` attribute.

With that added to the template's model, we can display it by adding the following bit of HTML to our Thymeleaf template, like this:

```
<td th:text="${image.owner}" />
```

This attribute can now be seen when we log in and check things out, as seen in this screenshot:

Name	Image		Owner	O
bazinga.png		Delete	greg	
B05771_MockupCover_Normal.png		Delete	phil	

In the preceding screenshot, we see one image loaded by **greg** and one image loaded by **phil**.

Authorizing methods

For a security framework to be of value, it needs flexibility. Security rules are never confined to simple use cases. We have all dealt with customers needing very complex settings for certain operations. Spring Security makes this possible through its special dialect of **SpEL** or **Spring Expression Language**.

To get a taste of it, let's augment the `images` microservice's `ImageService.delete()` method with an authorization rule:

```
@PreAuthorize("hasRole('ADMIN') or " +
 "@imageRepository.findByName(#filename).owner " +
  "== authentication.name")
public Mono<Void> deleteImage(String filename) {

    ... rest of the method unchanged ...
}
```

This preceding code for deleting images is only different in the new annotation in the following manner:

- The method is flagged with a `@PreAuthorize` annotation, indicating that the SpEL expression must evaluate to `true` in order for the method to get called
- `hasRole('ADMIN')` indicates that a user with `ROLE_ADMIN` is allowed access
- or `@imageRepository.findByName(#filename).owner == authentication.name")` indicates that access is *also* granted if the user's name matches the image's `owner` property

> Why do we need this authorization rule again? Because without it, *any* authenticated user can delete *any* image. Probably not a good idea.

This authorization rule is just one example of the types of rules we can write. The following table lists the prebuilt rules provided by Spring Security:

SpEL function	Description
hasAuthority('ROLE_USER')	Access is granted if user has ROLE_USER
hasAnyAuthority('ROLE_USER', 'ROLE_ADMIN')	Access is granted if user has any of the listed authorities
hasRole('USER')	Shorthand for hasAuthority('ROLE_USER')
hasAnyRole('USER', 'ADMIN')	Shorthand for hasAnyAuthority('ROLE_USER', 'ROLE_ADMIN')
principal	Direct access to the Principal object representing the user

`authentication`	Direct access to the `Authentication` object obtained from the security context
`permitAll`	Evaluates to `true`
`denyAll`	Evaluates to `false`
`isAnonymous()`	Returns `true` if user is an anonymous user
`isRememberMe()`	Returns `true` if user is a remember-me user
`isAuthenticated()`	Returns `true` if user is not anonymous
`isFullyAuthenticated()`	Returns `true` if user is neither anonymous nor a remember-me user

It's possible to combine these SpEL functions with `and` and `or`.

As we saw demonstrated earlier, we can also write security checks like this:

```
@PreAuthorize("#contact.name == authentication.name")
public void doSomething(Contact contact);
```

This preceding security check will grab the method's `contact` argument and compare its `name` field against the current `authentication` object's `name` field, looking for a match.

By the way, these types of parameter-specific rules are great when we want to restrict operations to the owner of the record, a common use case. In essence, if you are logged in and operating on *your* data, then you can do something.

In addition to all these functions and comparators, we can also invoke beans (another thing shown earlier). Look at the following code, for example:

```
@PreAuthorize("@imageRepository.findByName(#filename).owner ==
  authentication.name")
```

This last security check will invoke the bean named `imageRepository` and use its `findByName` function to look up an image's owner and then compare it against the current `authentication` object.

@PreAuthorize rules can be applied to any Spring bean, but it's recommended you apply them to your **service layer methods**. In essence, any code that invokes the service layer, whether it was from a web call or somewhere else, should be secured. Wrapping higher up at the web handler can leave your service layer susceptible to unauthorized access. To guard against improper web calls, it's recommended that you use route-based rules (as shown earlier in the chat microservice's SecurityConfiguration policy).

Tailoring the UI with authorization checks

With the REST endpoints locked down, it's nice to know things are secure. However, it doesn't make sense to display options in the UI that will get cut off. Instead, it's better to simply not show them. For that, we can leverage a custom Thymeleaf security rule.

Normally, we would make use of Thymeleaf's Spring Security extension. Unfortunately, the Thymeleaf team has yet to write such support for Spring Framework 5's WebFlux module. No problem! We can craft our own and register it inside the Thymeleaf engine.

For starters, we want to define an **authorization** scoped operation that could be embedded inside a Thymeleaf th:if="${}" expression, conditionally displaying HTML elements. We can start by adding SecurityExpressionObjectFactory to the images microservice, since that fragment of HTML is where we wish to apply it:

```
public class SecurityExpressionObjectFactory
  implements IExpressionObjectFactory {

  private final
    SecurityExpressionHandler<MethodInvocation> handler;

  public SecurityExpressionObjectFactory(
    SecurityExpressionHandler<MethodInvocation> handler) {
      this.handler = handler;
  }

  @Override
  public Set<String> getAllExpressionObjectNames() {
    return Collections.unmodifiableSet(
      new HashSet<>(Arrays.asList(
        "authorization"
    )));
```

```
        }

        @Override
        public boolean isCacheable(String expressionObjectName) {
          return true;
        }

        @Override
        public Object buildObject(IExpressionContext context,
         String expressionObjectName) {
            if (expressionObjectName.equals("authorization")) {
              if (context instanceof ISpringWebFluxContext) {
                return new Authorization(
                    (ISpringWebFluxContext) context, handler);
              }
            }
            return null;
        }
    }
```

The preceding Thymeleaf expression object factory can be described as follows:

- This class implements Thymeleaf's `IExpressionObjectFactory`, the key toward writing custom expressions.
- To do its thing, this factory requires a copy of Spring Security's `SecurityExpressionHandler`, aimed at method invocations. It's injected into this factory through constructor injection.
- To advertize the expression objects provided in this class, we implement `getAllExpressionObjectNames`, which returns an unmodifiable `Set` containing `authorization`, the token of our custom expression.
- We implement the interface's `isCacheable` and point blank say that all expressions may be cached by the Thymeleaf engine.
- `buildObject` is where we create objects based on the token name. When we see **authorization**, we narrow the template's context down to a WebFlux-based context and then create an `Authorization` object with the context, Spring Security's expression handler, and a copy of the current `ServerWebExchange`, giving us all the details we need.
- Anything else, and we return `null`, indicating this factory doesn't apply.

Our expression object, `Authorization`, is defined as follows:

```
public class Authorization {

  private static final Logger log =
    LoggerFactory.getLogger(Authorization.class);

  private ISpringWebFluxContext context;
  private SecurityExpressionHandler<MethodInvocation> handler;

  public Authorization(ISpringWebFluxContext context,
    SecurityExpressionHandler<MethodInvocation> handler) {
    this.context = context;
    this.handler = handler;
  }
  ...
}
```

The code can be described as follows:

- It has an Slf4j `log` so that we can print access checks to the console, giving developers the ability to debug their authorization expressions
- Through constructor injection, we load a copy of the Thymeleaf `ISpringWebFluxContext` and the Spring Security `SecurityExpressionHandler`

With this setup, we can now code the actual function we wish to use, `authorization.expr()`, as follows:

```
public boolean expr(String accessExpression) {
  Authentication authentication =
    (Authentication) this.context.getExchange()
    .getPrincipal().block();

  log.debug("Checking if user \"{}\" meets expr \"{}\".",
   new Object[] {
     (authentication == null ?
     null : authentication.getName()),
       accessExpression});

  /*
   * In case this expression is specified as a standard
   * variable expression (${...}), clean it.
   */
  String expr =
    ((accessExpression != null
        &&
```

```
            accessExpression.startsWith("${")
            &&
            accessExpression.endsWith("}")) ?

            accessExpression.substring(2,
                accessExpression.length()-1) :
            accessExpression);

    try {
      if (ExpressionUtils.evaluateAsBoolean(
        handler.getExpressionParser().parseExpression(expr),
        handler.createEvaluationContext(authentication,
         new SimpleMethodInvocation())))  {

          log.debug("Checked "{}" for user "{}". " +
                "Access GRANTED",
             new Object[] {
                accessExpression,
                (authentication == null ?
                   null : authentication.getName())});

          return true;
        } else {
          log.debug("Checked "{}" for user "{}". " +
            "Access DENIED",
            new Object[] {
               accessExpression,
               (authentication == null ?
                null : authentication.getName())});

          return false;
        }
    } catch (ParseException e) {
       throw new TemplateProcessingException(
         "An error happened parsing "" + expr + """, e);
    }
}
```

This last Thymeleaf custom function can be described as follows:

- Our custom expr() function is named in the first line, is publicly visible, and returns a Boolean, making it suitable for th:if={} expressions.
- The first thing we need is to grab the Authentication object from the context's ServerWebExchange. Because we are inside an inherently blocking API, we must use block() and cast it to a Spring Security Authentication.

- To help developers, we log the current user's authentication details along with the authorization expression.
- In the event the whole expression is wrapped with `${}`, we need to strip that off.
- We tap into Spring Security's SpEL support by invoking `ExpressionUtils.evaluateAsBoolean()`.
- That method requires that we parse the expression via `handler.getExpressionParser().parseExpression(expr)`.
- We must also supply the SpEL evaluator with a context, including the current **authentication** as well as `SimpleMethodInvocation`, since we are focused on method-level security expressions.
- If the results are `true`, it means access has been granted. We log it and return `true`.
- If the results are `false`, it means access has been denied. We log that and return `false`.
- In the event of a badly written SpEL expression, we catch it with an exception handler and throw a Thymeleaf `TemplateProcessingException`.

The preceding code defines the `expr()` function, while the enclosing `SecurityExpressionObjectFactory` scopes the function inside `authorization`, setting us up to embed `#authorization.expr(/* my Spring Security SpEL expression*/)` inside Thymeleaf templates.

The next step in extending Thymeleaf is to define a **Dialect** with our expression object factory, as follows:

```
public class SecurityDialect extends AbstractDialect
  implements IExpressionObjectDialect {

    private final
     SecurityExpressionHandler<MethodInvocation> handler;

    public SecurityDialect(
      SecurityExpressionHandler<MethodInvocation> handler) {
        super("Security Dialect");
        this.handler = handler;
    }

    @Override
    public IExpressionObjectFactory getExpressionObjectFactory()
    {
```

```
          return new SecurityExpressionObjectFactory(handler);
  }
}
```

This previous code can be described as follows:

- `SecurityDialect` **extends** `AbstractDialect` **and implements** `IExpressionObjectDialect`
- We need a copy of Spring Security's `SecurityExpressionHandler` in order to parse Spring Security SpEL expression, and it's provided by constructor injection
- To support `IExpressionObjectDialect`, we supply a copy of our custom `SecurityExpressionObjectFactory` factory inside the `getExpressionObjectFactory()` method

With our tiny extension dialect defined, we must register it with Thymeleaf's template engine. To do so, the easiest thing is to write a custom Spring post processor, like this:

```
@Component
public class SecurityDialectPostProcessor
  implements BeanPostProcessor, ApplicationContextAware {

    private ApplicationContext applicationContext;

    @Override
    public void setApplicationContext(
      ApplicationContext applicationContext)
      throws BeansException {
        this.applicationContext = applicationContext;
    }

    @Override
    public Object postProcessBeforeInitialization(
      Object bean, String beanName) throws BeansException {
        if (bean instanceof SpringTemplateEngine) {
          SpringTemplateEngine engine =
            (SpringTemplateEngine) bean;
          SecurityExpressionHandler<MethodInvocation> handler =
            applicationContext.getBean(
              SecurityExpressionHandler.class);
          SecurityDialect dialect =
            new SecurityDialect(handler);
          engine.addDialect(dialect);
        }
        return bean;
```

```
    }

    @Override
    public Object postProcessAfterInitialization(
      Object bean, String beanName) throws BeansException {
        return bean;
    }
}
```

The preceding code can be defined as follows:

- @Component signals Spring Boot to register this class.
- By implementing the BeanPostProcessor interface, Spring will run every bean in the application context through it, giving our SecurityDialectPostProcessor the opportunity to find Thymeleaf's engine and register our custom dialect.
- Since our custom dialect needs a handle on the SecurityExpressionHandler bean, we also implement the ApplicationContextAware interface, giving it a handle on the application context.
- It all comes together in postProcessBeforeInitialization, which is invoked against every bean in the application context. When we spot one that implements Thymeleaf's SpringTemplateEngine, we grab that bean, fetch SecurityExpressionHandler from the app context, create a new SecurityDialect, and add that dialect to the engine. Every bean, modified or not, is returned back to the app context.
- Because we don't need any processing *before* initialization, postProcessAfterInitialization just passes through every bean.

With all this in place, we are ready to make some security-specific tweaks to our templates.

In the main page (chat microservice's index.html template), it would be handy to put some user-specific information. To display the username and their roles, we can update the HomeController like this:

```
@GetMapping("/")
public String index(@AuthenticationPrincipal Authentication auth,
  Model model) {
    model.addAttribute("authentication", auth);
    return "index";
}
```

This preceding adjustment to the home controller can be described as follows:

- `@AuthenticationPrincipal Authentication auth` grants us a copy of the current user's `Authentication` object
- `Model model` gives us a model object to add data to the template
- By simply sticking the `Authentication` object into the model, we can use it to display security details on the web page

Now, we can display the username and their roles, as follows:

```
<div>
  <span th:text="${authentication.name}" />
  <span th:text="${authentication.authorities}" />
</div>
<hr />
```

This little DIV element that we just defined includes the following:

- Displays the authentication's `name` property, which is the username
- Displays the authentication's `authorities` properties, which are the user's roles
- Draws a horizontal line, setting this bit of user specifics apart from the rest of the page

> Since we are using HTTP Basic security, there is no value in putting a logout button on the screen. You have to shut down the browser (or close the incognito tab) to clear out security credentials and start afresh.

We can now expect to see the following when we log in as **greg**:

We mentioned limiting things that the user can't do. The big one in our social media platform is restricted access to deleting images. To enforce this in the UI, we need to parallel the authorization rule we wrote earlier in the `images` microservice's `index.html`, as shown here:

```
<td>
  <button th:if="${#authorization.expr('hasRole(''ROLE_ADMIN'')')
  or #authorization.expr('''__${image.owner}__'' ==
  authentication.name')}"
        th:id="'/images/' + ${image.name}"
          class="delete">Delete</button>
</td>
```

This last code looks a bit more complex than the `@PreAuthorize` rule wrapping `ImageService.deleteImage()`, so let's take it apart:

- We use Thymeleaf's `th:if="..."` expression along with `${}` to construct a complex expression consisting of two `#authorization.expr()` functions chained by `or`.
- `#authorization.expr('hasRole(''ROLE_ADMIN'')')` grants access if the user has `ROLE_ADMIN`.
- `#authorization.expr('''__${image.owner}__'' == authentication.name')` grants access if the `image.owner` attribute matches the current `authentication.name`.
- By the way, the double underscore before and after `${image.owner}` is Thymeleaf's **preprocessor**. It indicates that this is done before any other part of the expression is evaluated. In essence, we need the image's owner attribute parsed first, stuffed into the authorization expression, and finally run through our custom tie-in to Spring Security's SpEL parser.

> The expressions inside `#authorization.expr()` are supposed to be wrapped in single quotes. Literal values themselves have to be wrapped in single quotes. To escape a single quote in this context requires a double single quote. Confused yet? Thymeleaf's rules for concatenation, preprocessing, and nesting expressions can, at times, be daunting. To help debug an expression, pull up the `Authorization` class coded earlier inside your IDE and set breakpoints inside the proper security expression. This will pause code execution, allowing you to see the final expression before it gets passed, hopefully making it easier to craft a suitable authorization rule.

With our nice tweaks to the UI, let's see what things look like if we have two different images uploaded, one from an admin and one from a regular user.

If **greg** is logged in, we can see the following screenshot:

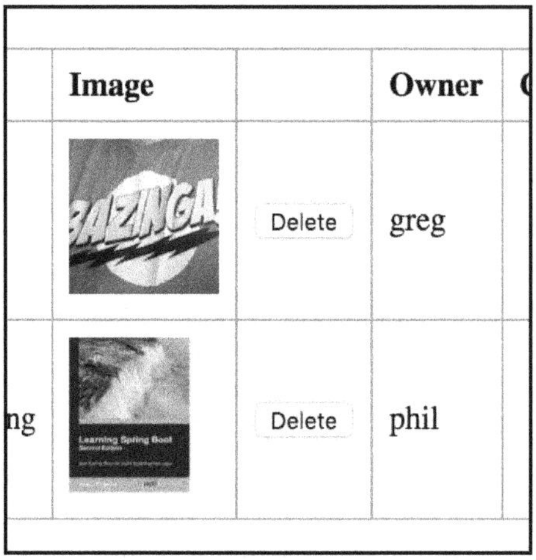

In the preceding screenshot, both images have a **Delete** button, since **greg** has `ROLE_ADMIN`.

If **phil** is logged in, we can see the following screenshot:

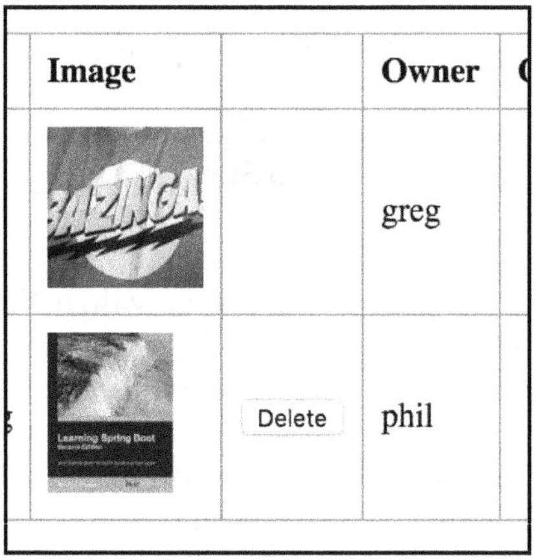

In the earlier screenshot, only the second image has the **Delete** button, since **phil** owns it.

With these nice details in place, we can easily check out the headers relayed to the backend using the browser's debug tools, as seen in this screenshot:

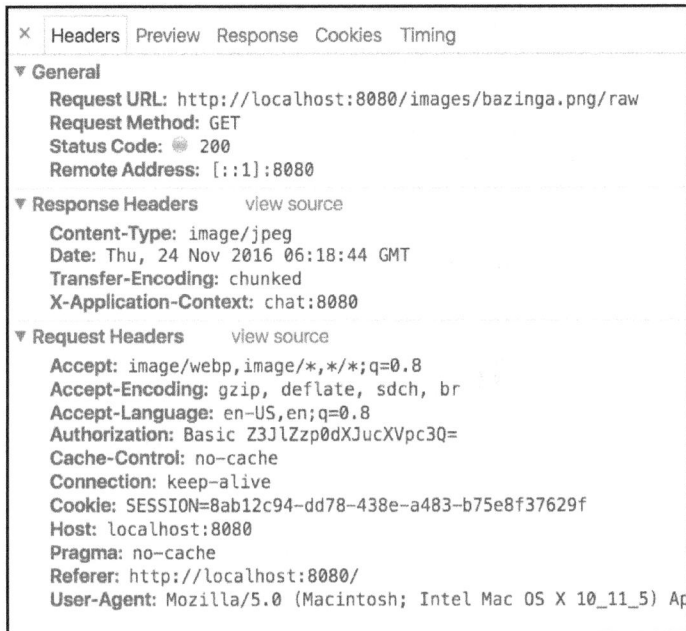

```
×   Headers  Preview  Response  Cookies  Timing

▼ General
    Request URL: http://localhost:8080/images/bazinga.png/raw
    Request Method: GET
    Status Code: ● 200
    Remote Address: [::1]:8080
▼ Response Headers        view source
    Content-Type: image/jpeg
    Date: Thu, 24 Nov 2016 06:18:44 GMT
    Transfer-Encoding: chunked
    X-Application-Context: chat:8080
▼ Request Headers         view source
    Accept: image/webp,image/*,*/*;q=0.8
    Accept-Encoding: gzip, deflate, sdch, br
    Accept-Language: en-US,en;q=0.8
    Authorization: Basic Z3JlZ3p0dXJjXVpc3Q=
    Cache-Control: no-cache
    Connection: keep-alive
    Cookie: SESSION=8ab12c94-dd78-438e-a483-b75e8f37629f
    Host: localhost:8080
    Pragma: no-cache
    Referer: http://localhost:8080/
    User-Agent: Mozilla/5.0 (Macintosh; Intel Mac OS X 10_11_5) Ap
```

This collection of request and response headers shown in the last image lets us see the following things:

- The session ID, 8ab12c94-dd78-438e-a483-b75e8f37629f, is captured in SESSION in the cookie and sent over the wire.
- There is an Authorization header that is transmitted once we have been authenticated.
- More security-based headers are used to further protect us from other attack vectors. See http://docs.spring.io/spring-security/site/docs/current/reference/html/headers.html for more details.

When we started building this social media platform early in this book, we had several operations tied into our Thymeleaf template. This type of tight interaction between controllers and views is of classic design. However, the more things shift to piecing together bits of HTML and leveraging JavaScript, the more it becomes useful to have REST-based services. Writing AJAX calls decouples the HTML from the server-side controls, which can be further leveraged if we use tools such as React.js (`https://facebook.github.io/react/`). This gets us out of the business of assembling DOM elements and lets us focus on the state of the frontend instead.

Securing WebSockets

So far, we have secured the `chat` service and the `images` service.

Or have we?

Well, we configured chat as the Gateway API for our microservices using Spring Cloud Gateway. To do that, we made it the sole source of HTTP session creation. Given that the session details were also included in forwarded web requests, our Gateway API is nicely buttoned up.

However, the `chat` microservice's critical function is brokering WebSocket messages. And we haven't lifted a finger to secure that component. Time to roll up our sleeves and get to work.

Since our WebSocket handlers are stream oriented, we merely need to slip in a parent class that authorizes things when the WebSocket session is configured, as follows:

```
abstract class AuthorizedWebSocketHandler
  implements WebSocketHandler {

  @Override
  public final Mono<Void> handle(WebSocketSession session) {
    return session.getHandshakeInfo().getPrincipal()
      .filter(this::isAuthorized)
      .then(doHandle(session));
  }

  private boolean isAuthorized(Principal principal) {
    Authentication authentication = (Authentication) principal;
    return authentication.isAuthenticated() &&
```

```
            authentication.getAuthorities().contains("ROLE_USER");
    }

    abstract protected Mono<Void> doHandle(
        WebSocketSession session);
}
```

The preceding code can be described as follows:

- This abstract class implements the `WebSocketHandler` interface with a Reactor-based `handle()` function
- The `handle` method looks up `handshakeInfo`, finding the `Principal` that will be populated by Spring Security, and filters against a custom `isAuthorized` function
- If the session is indeed authorized, an abstract `doHandle` is invoked, handing over `WebSocketSession` to the actual handlers
- The `isAuthorized` function takes the session's `Principal`, casts it to a Spring Security `Authentication`, and verifies that the user is both authenticated and also contains `ROLE_USER`

With this in place, we can update our `InboundChatService` like this:

```
@Service
@EnableBinding(ChatServiceStreams.class)
public class InboundChatService extends AuthorizedWebSocketHandler
{

    private final ChatServiceStreams chatServiceStreams;

    public InboundChatService(ChatServiceStreams
chatServiceStreams){
        this.chatServiceStreams = chatServiceStreams;
    }

    @Override
    protected Mono<Void> doHandle(WebSocketSession session) {

        ...
    }
```

The changes in the previous code can be described as follows:

- `InboundChatService` **now extends** `AuthorizedWebSocketHandler`, forcing it to accept those upstream checks
- We have replaced `handle(WebSocketSession)` with `doHandle(WebSocketSession)`
- The rest of the code is the same, so there's no reason to show it

If we apply the same changes to `OutboundChatService` and `CommentService`, we can ensure that all of our WebSocket services are locked down.

Admittedly, our policy is quite simple. However, we can easily scale based on requirements. For example, if the Admins wanted their own channel, it wouldn't be hard to add `/topic/admin/**` and require `ROLE_ADMIN`.

It's also important to recognize that this level of security is aimed at the whole channel. Adding per-message security checks could *also* be layered in by going to each concrete service, and, essentially, embedding `.filter()`, based on the details of the message.

And that's all it takes! Our WebSocket channels are now secured such that only proper incoming messages are allowed through, and only HTML served from our site will have the means to connect and send such messages.

Tracing calls

Earlier, we saw a screenshot from Chrome's debug tools, showing request and response headers. There is another tool we can use as well--Spring Boot Actuator's `trace` endpoint.

By visiting `http://localhost:8080/application/trace`, we can see all the web calls, going back in time. For example, look at this request to negotiate the WebSocket:

```
{
  "timestamp": 1480805242289,
  "info": {
    "method": "GET",
    "path": "/learning-spring-boot/160/ge00bkmu/websocket",
    "headers": {
      "request": {
        "host": "localhost:8080",
        "connection": "Upgrade",
        "pragma": "no-cache",
```

```
        "cache-control": "no-cache",
        "authorization": "Basic Z3JlZzpodXJucXVpc3Q=",
        "upgrade": "websocket",
        "origin": "http://localhost:8080",
        "sec-websocket-version": "13",
        "user-agent": "Mozilla/5.0 (Macintosh; Intel Mac OS X
          10_11_5) AppleWebKit/537.36 (KHTML, like Gecko)
          Chrome/54.0.2840.98 Safari/537.36",
        "accept-encoding": "gzip, deflate, sdch, br",
        "accept-language": "en-US,en;q=0.8",
        "cookie": "SESSION=3f0668ec-d528-43d8-a6e8-87a369571745",
        "sec-websocket-key": "L8fkEK8VtxXfxx4jBzOC9Q==",
        "sec-websocket-extensions": "permessage-deflate;
          client_max_window_bits"
      },
      "response": {
        "X-Application-Context": "chat:8080",
        "Upgrade": "websocket",
        "Connection": "upgrade",
        "Sec-WebSocket-Accept": "m8xyQSUtHR/qMEUp1xog4wwUS0E=",
        "Sec-WebSocket-Extensions": "permessage-
          deflate;client_max_window_bits=15",
        "status": "101"
      }
    }
  }
}
```

The following are some key bits that can be pointed out in the preceding code:

- The `authorization` header has a `Basic` token value, us having logged in
- The `cookie` is loaded with our `SESSION` ID
- The upgrade protocol to go from HTTP to WebSocket is evident in the response headers and the `101` status code

Let's look at one more, the request to view our `bazinga.png` image:

```
{
  "timestamp": 1480805242286,
  "info": {
    "method": "GET",
    "path": "/images/bazinga.png/raw",
    "headers": {
      "request": {
        "host": "localhost:8080",
        "connection": "keep-alive",
        "authorization": "Basic Z3JlZzpodXJucXVpc3Q=",
```

```
        "user-agent": "Mozilla/5.0 (Macintosh; Intel Mac OS X
        10_11_5) AppleWebKit/537.36 (KHTML, like Gecko)
        Chrome/54.0.2840.98 Safari/537.36",
        "accept": "image/webp,image/*,*/*;q=0.8",
        "referer": "http://localhost:8080/",
        "accept-encoding": "gzip, deflate, sdch, br",
        "accept-language": "en-US,en;q=0.8",
        "cookie": "SESSION=3f0668ec-d528-43d8-a6e8-87a369571745"
      },
      "response": {
        "X-Application-Context": "chat:8080",
        "Date": "Sat, 03 Dec 2016 22:47:21 GMT",
        "Content-Type": "image/jpeg",
        "Transfer-Encoding": "chunked",
        "status": "200"
      }
    }
  }
}
```

Some interesting fields in the last code include the following:

- The `cookie` header contains our `SESSION` ID.
- The `authorization` header includes the same token.
- The `referer` header shows the origin of the request as `http://localhost:8080/`.
- The `accept-encoding` header indicates the formats that the browser will accept, including zipped images and deflated ones.
- The `content-type` response header has JPEG, a value we hard-coded into our controller. Since all images get handled by the same part of the browser, it doesn't matter if it's not PNG.

Spring Boot Actuator's `trace` endpoint will track the last one hundred requests. It's a handy way to peek at past web calls in case you don't have the browser's development tools open at the time.

> **TIP**
>
> You can inject `TraceRepository` into your code and use `add(Map)` on any structure you want, with it getting serialized into JSON.

Securing the Config Server

So, we've locked down `chat`, `images`, and `comments`. But what about the Config Server itself? Seeing how critical it is with each microservice's configuration details, we need to insulate ourselves from a malevolent Config Server being stood up in its place.

The simplest thing to do is to add Spring Security to our Config Server. So, let's do it!

```
compile('org.springframework.boot:spring-boot-starter-security')
```

By default, Spring Security will set username to `user` and password to something random. Since we can't be updating the other services every time we restart, let's override that with a fixed password, as follows:

```
@Bean
UserDetailsService userDetailsService() {
  return new InMemoryUserDetailsManager(
    User
      .withUsername("user")
      .password("password")
      .roles("USER").build());
}
```

In Spring Boot 1.x, there was a `security.password` property to override. In the spirit of simplification, this property has been removed in Spring Boot 2.x. The new approach is to inject a `UserDetailsService` bean, as shown in the previous code fragment (which can be added to `LearningSpringBootConfigServer`). This code shows a single user, `user/password`, defined.

That's all it takes to secure our Config Server!

To signal the other services, we need to adjust their `bootstrap.yml` files. Let's start with the Eureka Server, like this:

```
spring:
  application:
    name: eureka
  cloud:
    config:
      label: session
      password: password
```

This change shown in the last code adds `spring.cloud.config.password` set to the same password we just chose.

Let's continue with `chat`:

```
spring:
  application:
    name: chat
  cloud:
    config:
      label: session
      password: password
```

In the preceding code, we have `spring.cloud.config.password` and `spring.cloud.config.label` properly set.

We can make the same changes to `images`, as follows:

```
spring:
  application:
    name: images
  cloud:
    config:
      label: session
      password: password
```

This will secure things with the exact same settings.

And finally, let's make the following changes to `comments`:

```
spring:
  application:
    name: comments
  cloud:
    config:
      label: session
      password: password
```

This will lock things down, preventing others from getting access to our settings. If someone attempted to stand up a bogus Config Server, they would have to somehow secure it with the same password on the same network address. (Not likely!).

Securing the Eureka Server

The last bastion to secure is our Eureka Server. To do so, we need to adopt similar steps to what we did with the Config Server.

First, add Spring Security to the Eureka Server, as follows:

```
compile('org.springframework.boot:spring-boot-starter-security')
```

This preceding dependency will enable Spring Security automatically. However, just like Config Server, it will generate a random password every time it launches. To pin the password, we need to add the same `UserDetailsService` bean as follows:

```
@Bean
UserDetailsService userDetailsService() {
  return new InMemoryUserDetailsManager(
    User
      .withUsername("user")
      .password("password")
      .roles("USER").build());
}
```

The recommended way to plug in the username/password settings for a Eureka client is by using the URL notation. For the `chat` service, we need to update the Config Server with this:

```
eureka:
  client:
    serviceUrl:
      defaultZone: http://user:password@localhost:8761/eureka
```

This preceding adjustment will have the `chat` microservice signing into the Eureka Server with a username, password, hostname, port, and path--all standard options with URLs.

These options can be applied to the Config Server's `images.yml` file, like this:

```
eureka:
  client:
    serviceUrl:
      defaultZone: http://user:password@localhost:8761/eureka/
```

This can also be applied to the Config Server's `comments.yml` file, as follows:

```
eureka:
  client:
    serviceUrl:
      defaultZone: http://user:password@localhost:8761/eureka/
```

> **TIP**
>
> Are you unsure that this is working? Enable security in the Eureka Server as described, but do not make these changes to the Eureka clients. When they are launched, they'll report inability to connect to Eureka. Make the changes to the Config Server, restart it, then make the changes to the clients. They will then connect. Ta dah!

We now have every component secured. We also have session state shared between the services, making it easy to expand and add new services or to refine the existing roles. Pretty much anything we can think of.

So... does it smell like too many hard-coded values? Getting nervous about this system being able to roll with the punches of the network changing underneath it? Your concern is justified. We'll soon see in Chapter 19, *Taking Your App to Production with Spring Boot*, how we can take our social media platform to the cloud, scale its components, and with minimal adjustments, overcome what *may* appear as brittle settings.

Summary

In this chapter, we applied Spring Security to each of our microservices. We then configured our `chat` service as a Gateway API using Spring Cloud Gateway. Finally, we brought on board Spring Session MongoDB and had it share session details with the other *backend* microservices.

After ensuring that `SESSION` IDs were propagated by Spring Cloud Gateway to all the backend services, we wrote authorization rules, both for REST endpoints as well as for WebSocket messages.

To wrap things up, we also secured our Config Server and our Eureka Server so that only our system can talk to them.

In the next chapter, we will take our social media platform to production. We'll deploy our microservices-based application to the cloud, and see how to scale and adjust various things. We'll also discover how Spring Boot makes adjusting things a breeze.

19
Taking Your App to Production with Spring Boot

Here is my source code

Run it on the cloud for me

I do not care how

— *Cloud Foundry haiku (Onsi Fakhouri @onsijoe)*

In the previous chapter, we learned how to secure our microservice-based social media platform.

In this chapter, we will cover the following topics:

- Configuring profile-specific beans
- Creating configuration property beans
- Overriding property settings in production
- Deploying our social media platform to the cloud

So, today is the day. We worked for weeks to build this system. And now we want to take it to production. What could happen? What could go wrong?

Answer: A lot. And...a lot.

Spring Boot comes with powerful features to make it easy to tune and adjust things in production, allowing us to minimize the code. Some of the concepts presented here are rooted in *The Twelve-Factor App* (`https://12factor.net/`) and the ability to externalize configuration settings. We've already seen parts of that through the Config Server. However, now we'll dig in and apply more as we go to production.

Profile-based sets of beans

Many cloud-based platforms use proxies wrapped around applications. This enables the platform to support many features, including caching, **content delivery networks (CDN)**, load balancing, and SSL termination. After all, why put such common infrastructure requirements on developers?

However, the side effect can break security protocols designed to protect us in the web. For example, our application may be running on a private IP address, while original requests come in on a public-facing URL. When our application sees a forwarded web request, how are we to distinguish it between a proper request versus some nefarious cross site scripting attack leveraging our service?

The first place this can affect our application is the `chat` service's WebSocket handling. It requires explicit configuration to handle such a hop. However, we only want such an adjustment in our code to apply when we are in production, not when running things in development on our workstation.

The solution is **profile-based beans**. Spring lets us configure beans to only be created if certain profiles are enabled.

In the previous chapter, we had our entire WebSocket configuration in a top-level class. We need to change that configuration class and turn it into a container class with different options based on whether or not we are in production.

The first step is to move the existing bean definitions into a new, static inner class as shown here:

```
@Configuration
public class WebSocketConfig {
  ...
  @Profile("!cloud")
```

```
@Configuration
static class LocalWebSocketConfig {
    ...
}
}
```

So far, we haven't changed a lot. What we have, can be described as follows:

- The outer class, `WebSocketConfig`, looks the same
- This new inner class, `LocalWebSocketConfig`, is annotated `@Profile("!cloud")`, meaning it only runs if there is *no* cloud profile
- The new class is called `LocalWebSocketConfig` to clarify that it only operates when we run things locally

> **TIP**
>
> What is a **cloud** profile? Spring allows settings various profiles through the `spring.profiles.active` application property. We can create all the profiles we want, even overlapping ones. However, any application deployed to **Cloud Foundry** automatically has an extra profile, that is, **cloud**, applied.

Since we plan to have both a local as well as a cloud-based configuration, it's important to distinguish what is the same and what is different. Something that will be the same are the WebSocket route mappings.

To support this, we need a single `configureUrlMappings()` method to configure this `SimpleUrlHandlerMapping`:

```
private static SimpleUrlHandlerMapping configureUrlMappings(
    CommentService commentService,
    InboundChatService inboundChatService,
    OutboundChatService outboundChatService) {
    Map<String, WebSocketHandler> urlMap = new HashMap<>();
    urlMap.put("/topic/comments.new", commentService);
    urlMap.put("/app/chatMessage.new", inboundChatService);
    urlMap.put("/topic/chatMessage.new", outboundChatService);

    SimpleUrlHandlerMapping mapping = new
      SimpleUrlHandlerMapping();
    mapping.setOrder(10);
    mapping.setUrlMap(urlMap);

    return mapping;
}
```

This is the same code we saw in the last chapter, just moved around a little:

- The three endpoints are tied to their respective services in `Map` of routes-to-`WebSocketHandlers`
- A `SimpleUrlHandlerMapping` is defined with this map of handlers
- The order is set to `10`
- The method is static since it will be placed *outside* our new `LocalWebSocketConfig` (but *inside* `WebSocketConfig`)

To tap this, we simply need to write a bean definition inside `LocalWebSocketConfig` like this:

```
@Bean HandlerMapping webSocketMapping(CommentService
  commentService, InboundChatService inboundChatService,
  OutboundChatService outboundChatService) {
    return configureUrlMappings(commentService,
        InboundChatService, outboundChatService);
}
```

This method does nothing more than invoke our WebSocket configuring method.

With the local configuration set up, we can now turn our attention towards configuring the WebSocket broker to work in the cloud. To do so, we need another inner static class inside `WebSocketConfig`, as follows:

```
@Profile("cloud")
@Configuration
@EnableConfigurationProperties(ChatConfigProperties.class)
static class CloudBasedWebSocketConfig {
```

It can be explained as follows:

- It's marked as `@Profile("cloud")`, meaning this only applies if the `cloud` profile is in force, the opposite of `LocalWebSocketConfig`
- It contains `@EnableConfigurationProperties(ChatConfigProperties.class)`, used to provide an extra set of properties
- It's named `CloudBasedWebSocketConfig` to point out its role

If you're wondering what `@EnableConfigurationProperties` means, it leads us into the next section.

Creating configuration property beans

`@EnableConfigurationProperties`, applied anywhere in our application, will cause a bean of the named type, `ChatConfigProperties`, to get added to the application context. A **configuration property bean** is meant to hold various settings that can be configured with optional defaults and can be overridden through various means.

Remember properties like `server.port` where we adjusted the default port our Netty web container listened for web requests? All the properties we've seen through this book are all configuration property beans. This annotation simply gives us the means to define our own property settings specific to our application.

In this case, `ChatConfigProperties` is aimed at configuring the WebSocket broker.

> It's not critical that the annotation be applied to this specific class. It's just convenient since it's the place where we intend to use it.

Despite enabling such property settings, we still have to inject the bean into our `CloudBasedWebSocketConfig` configuration class, as shown here:

```
private final ChatConfigProperties chatConfigProperties;

CloudBasedWebSocketConfig(ChatConfigProperties
  chatConfigProperties) {
    this.chatConfigProperties = chatConfigProperties;
}
```

Using constructor injection, we now have access to whatever property settings are provided by this configuration property bean.

> Configuration property beans are simply Spring beans with the added ability to override. It means they can be injected just like any other Spring bean.

Digging into the WebSocket broker configuration, what we need is the remote host we are willing to accept WebSocket connection requests from. Essentially, the public-facing URL of our `chat` microservice. To do that, we'll define a property called `origin` and use it as shown here:

```
@Bean HandlerMapping webSocketMapping(CommentService
  commentService, InboundChatService inboundChatService,
  OutboundChatService outboundChatService) {
    SimpleUrlHandlerMapping mapping =
      configureUrlMappings(commentService,
      InboundChatService, outboundChatService);

    Map<String, CorsConfiguration> corsConfigurationMap =
      new HashMap<>();
    CorsConfiguration corsConfiguration = new CorsConfiguration();
    corsConfiguration
      .addAllowedOrigin(chatConfigProperties.getOrigin());

    mapping.getUrlMap().keySet().forEach(route ->
      corsConfigurationMap.put(route, corsConfiguration)
    );

    mapping.setCorsConfigurations(corsConfigurationMap);

    return mapping;
}
```

This code has the same endpoints as `LocalWebSocketConfig`, thanks to the `configureUrlMappings` method. It additionally creates a CORS map, like we did in Chapter 17, *WebSockets with Spring Boot*. Only, this time, it uses the injected `getOrigin()` to plug in the public-facing URL of the `chat` service (hold tight--we'll see how shortly).

What's missing is the definition of this configuration property bean. It's shown here:

```
@Data
@ConfigurationProperties(prefix = "lsb")
public class ChatConfigProperties {

  @Value("https://${vcap.application.uris[0]}")
  private String origin;

}
```

The code can be explained as follows:

- Once again, we use Project Lombok's `@Data` annotation to avoid writing getters and setters. This is ideal for configuration property beans.
- `@ConfigurationProperty(prefix="lsb")` flags this bean as a candidate for Spring Boot's property reading rules, starting with the `lsb` prefix.
- There is a single property named `origin` that is initialized using Spring's `@Value()` annotation.
- On Cloud Foundry, `vcap.application.uris` is a property applied to every application that lists publicly visible URLs. Assuming that the first is the one we wish to use, we are applying it to our `origin` property.
- By combining the prefix (`lsb`) and the name of the property (`origin`), the full path of this property is `lsb.origin`, and it can be overridden at any time.

Overriding property settings in production

Everytime we take our application to a new environment, there are always settings that have to be adjusted. We don't want to edit code. Instead, it's easier if we could just override various properties. And we can!

This was touched on briefly in `Chapter 10`, *Quick Start with Java*, under the guise of overriding Spring Boot's property settings. However, the fact that we can write our own custom configuration property beans makes this a powerful feature for application customization.

To recap the rules listed in `Chapter 10`, *Quick Start with Java*, property settings can be overridden in the following order, highest to lowest:

1. `@TestPropertySource` annotations on test classes.
2. Command-line arguments.
3. Properties found inside `SPRING_APPLICATION_JSON` (inline JSON embedded in an env variable or system property).
4. `ServletConfig` init parameters.

5. `ServletContext` init parameters.

6. JNDI attributes from `java:comp/env`.

7. Java System properties (`System.getProperties()`).

8. OS environment variables.

9. `RandomValuePropertySource` that only has properties in `random.*`.

10. Profile-specific properties outside the packaged JAR file (`application-{profile}.properties` and YAML variants).

11. Profile-specific properties inside the packaged JAR file (`application-{profile}.properties` and YAML variants).

12. Application properties outside the package JAR file (`application.properties` and YAML variants).

13. Application properties inside the packaged JAR file (`application.properties` and YAML variants).

14. `@PropertySource` annotations on any `@Configuration` classes.

15. Default properties (specified using `SpringApplication.setDefaultProperties`).

> **TIP**
>
> By default, we can run with `vcap.application.uris[0]`. However, if we take it to another cloud solution, we can simply plug in an override to `lsb.origin` and leverage whatever environment variables the new cloud provides. This lets us escape having to alter the code again and instead focus on getting things running.

One of the most common tactics is to create an `application-{profile}.yml` file that will be automatically applied when `<profile>` is in effect. Since Cloud Foundry apps get the **cloud** profile, it would be natural to create an `application-cloud.yml` file.

However, since we adopted the Spring Cloud Config Server and specified that the `chat` service is governed by `chat.yml`, we instead merely need to add a `chat-cloud.yml` file. Then we know the following cloud-specific settings will be applied when deployed to Cloud Foundry:

```
server:
  port: 8080

eureka:
  client:
    serviceUrl:
      defaultZone: http://user:password@learning-spring-boot-
```

```
        eureka-server.cfapps.io/eureka/
instance:
  hostname: ${vcap.application.uris[0]}
  nonSecurePort: 80
```

These settings can be explained as follows:

- The `server.port` is the same as before
- The `eureka.client.serviceUrl.defaultZone` is changed to the public-facing URL for our Eureka service, so the `chat` service can find it
- Since the public-facing URL for our `chat` service is terminated by a proxy, we have to override `eureka.instance.hostname` with `${vcap.application.uris[0]}` to avoid registering an unreachable IP address with Eureka
- We must also register that we are visible (non-secure) on port 80

The following settings are identical for `comments-cloud.yml`:

```
server:
  port: 8080

eureka:
  client:
    serviceUrl:
      defaultZone: http://user:password@learning-spring-boot-
      eureka-server.cfapps.io/eureka/
    instance:
      hostname: ${vcap.application.uris[0]}
      nonSecurePort: 80
```

And the same for `images-cloud.yml`:

```
server:
  port: 8080

eureka:
  client:
    serviceUrl:
      defaultZone: http://user:password@learning-spring-boot-
      eureka-server.cfapps.io/eureka/
    instance:
      hostname: ${vcap.application.uris[0]}
      nonSecurePort: 80
```

Finally, we need to set the same instance details for the Eureka service itself via `eureka-cloud.yml`, as shown here:

```
server:
  port: 8080

eureka:
  instance:
    hostname: ${vcap.application.uris[0]}
    nonSecurePort: 80
```

If you'll notice, there is no `eureka.client.serviceUrl.defaultZone` given that this IS the Eureka service!

These additional settings added to `https://github.com/gregturn/learning-spring-boot-config-repo/tree/producti on` will ensure that our apps function smoothly in the cloud.

If we want to see our newly minted property settings, we can visit `http://learning-spring-boot.cfapps.io/configprops` and look for `ChatConfigProperties`.

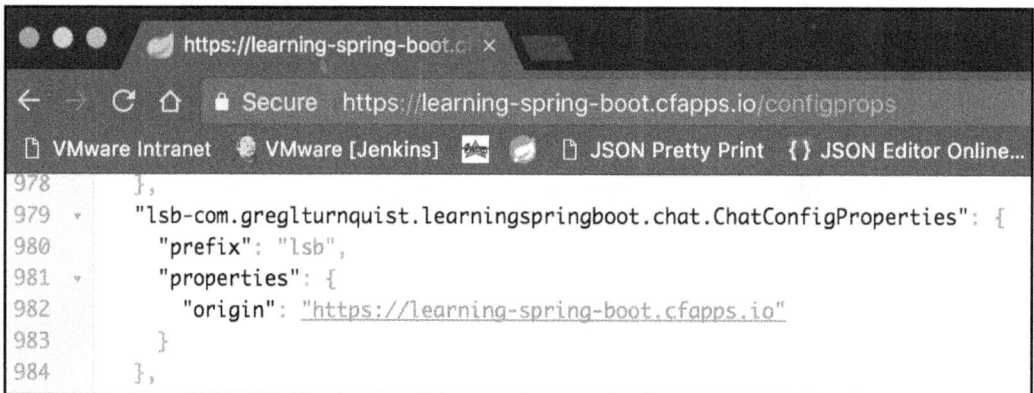

```
978        },
979   ▾    "lsb-com.greglturnquist.learningspringboot.chat.ChatConfigProperties": {
980          "prefix": "lsb",
981   ▾      "properties": {
982            "origin": "https://learning-spring-boot.cfapps.io"
983          }
984        },
```

The configuration properties can be described as follows:

- The name is captured as the prefix + the canonical path of the class
- The prefix, `lsb`, is displayed
- The `properties` lists the named properties we can tap (nesting displayed if that were the case)

From this, we can easily glean that `lsb.origin` is the property to override should we have some reason to adjust this.

@ConfigurationProperties versus @Value

In our code, we have used both strongly-type `@ConfigurationProperties` based classes as well as `@Value` labeled attributes. It's important to understand the differences before using them in your application.

`@Value` is old, preceding Spring Boot by years. It is a powerful annotation, able to inject values as well as accept default values. However, it misses several features many of us have come to rely upon when writing Boot apps, as shown in the following table:

Feature	@ConfigurationProperties	@Value
Relaxed binding	Yes	No
Meta-data support	Yes	No
SpEL evaluation	No	Yes

This matrix documents three critical features:

- **Relaxed binding**: The ability to match `server.port`, `SERVER_PORT`, and `sErVeR.pOrT` to the same attribute is quite valuable.
- **Meta-data support**: The ability to include code completion for property settings is also of incredible value, along with hover-over tips. Anything that speeds up developer effort cannot be understated in value.
- **SpEL evaluation**: The ability to write SpEL expressions to populate properties.

There is a strong suggestion to start with `@ConfigurationProperties`. When you bundle together a set of properties inside a POJO, it really is a shortcut for a fist full of `@Value` attributes. And the property binding is supercharged.

However, when you *need* SpEL expression support, as we do to get a hold of the application's URI (`${vcap.application.uris[0]}`), then it's okay to break from `@ConfigurationProperties` and switch to `@Value`.

However, if you'll notice, we continue to leverage it inside `@ConfigurationProperties`. The real hint of doing it wrong is if we try to construct a collection of properties using `@Value`. Configuration properties is a nice way to build a hierarchy of properties with little effort.

Pushing app to Cloud Foundry and adjusting the settings

Keep calm and cf push.

- Denizens of the Internet

If there's one thing critical to any smooth-running Ops center, it's the need for automation. If we do things by hand, we introduce the risk of drift among our various components in production.

The following section shows some BASH scripts for deploying our microservices-based social media platform, a first step on the path towards automated deployment.

Assuming we've built everything with Gradle, let's kick things off by deploying our Spring Boot uber JARs to Cloud Foundry:

```bash
#!/usr/bin/env bash

cf push learning-spring-boot-config-server -p config-
server/build/libs/learning-spring-boot-config-server-0.0.1-
SNAPSHOT.jar &
cf push learning-spring-boot-eureka-server -p eureka-
server/build/libs/learning-spring-boot-eureka-server-0.0.1-
SNAPSHOT.jar &
cf push learning-spring-boot -p chat/build/libs/learning-spring-boot-
chat-0.0.1-SNAPSHOT.jar &
cf push learning-spring-boot-comments -p comments/build/libs/learning-
spring-boot-comments-0.0.1-SNAPSHOT.jar &
cf push learning-spring-boot-images -p images/build/libs/learning-
spring-boot-images-0.0.1-SNAPSHOT.jar &
cf push learning-spring-boot-hystrix-dashboard -p hystrix-
dashboard/build/libs/learning-spring-boot-hystrix-dashboard-0.0.1-
SNAPSHOT.jar &
```

It can be described as follows:

- Each module is deployed using the CF CLI
  (`https://github.com/cloudfoundry/cli`), deploying with both a name
  and the JAR file
- Each command is backgrounded to speed up release

> A real microservice-based solution presumes different teams
> responsible for different modules. Hence, each team may have a
> different deployment script as well as different release schedules.

Let's get things underway and deploy! The console output shows us running our
deployment script:

```
gturnquist$ ./deploy.sh

Creating app learning-spring-boot-comments in org cosmos-refarch /
space development as gturnquist@pivotal.io...
Creating app learning-spring-boot in org cosmos-refarch / space
development as gturnquist@pivotal.io...
Creating app learning-spring-boot-config-server in org cosmos-refarch
/ space development as gturnquist@pivotal.io...
Creating app learning-spring-boot-images in org cosmos-refarch / space
development as gturnquist@pivotal.io...
Creating app learning-spring-boot-hystrix-dashboard in org cosmos-
refarch / space development as gturnquist@pivotal.io...
Creating app learning-spring-boot-eureka-server in org cosmos-refarch
/ space development as gturnquist@pivotal.io...
...
Using route learning-spring-boot-config-server.cfapps.io
Binding learning-spring-boot-config-server.cfapps.io to learning-
spring-boot-config-server...
Using route learning-spring-boot-comments.cfapps.io
Binding learning-spring-boot-comments.cfapps.io to learning-spring-
boot-comments...
Using route learning-spring-boot-eureka-server.cfapps.io
Binding learning-spring-boot-eureka-server.cfapps.io to learning-
spring-boot-eureka-server...
Using route learning-spring-boot-images.cfapps.io
Binding learning-spring-boot-images.cfapps.io to learning-spring-boot-
images...
Using route learning-spring-boot.cfapps.io
Binding learning-spring-boot.cfapps.io to learning-spring-boot...
Using route learning-spring-boot-hystrix-dashboard.cfapps.io
Binding learning-spring-boot-hystrix-dashboard.cfapps.io to learning-
```

```
spring-boot-hystrix-dashboard...
...
Uploading learning-spring-boot-config-server...
Uploading learning-spring-boot-hystrix-dashboard...
Uploading learning-spring-boot-comments...
Uploading learning-spring-boot-eureka-server...
Uploading learning-spring-boot-images...
Uploading learning-spring-boot...
...
Starting app learning-spring-boot-hystrix-dashboard in org cosmos-
refarch / space development as gturnquist@pivotal.io...
Starting app learning-spring-boot-comments in org cosmos-refarch /
space development as gturnquist@pivotal.io...
Starting app learning-spring-boot-images in org cosmos-refarch / space
development as gturnquist@pivotal.io...
Starting app learning-spring-boot-eureka-server in org cosmos-refarch
/ space development as gturnquist@pivotal.io...
Starting app learning-spring-boot in org cosmos-refarch / space
development as gturnquist@pivotal.io...
Starting app learning-spring-boot-config-server in org cosmos-refarch
/ space development as gturnquist@pivotal.io...
...
App started

(the rest ommitted for brevity)
```

All components of our social media platform are now deployed to the cloud.

Be warned! This isn't enough. There are custom settings that must be applied after the bits are uploaded.

Let's start with the section that configures our Eureka server, as shown here:

```
#!/usr/bin/env bash

cf set-env learning-spring-boot-eureka-server spring.cloud.config.uri
https://learning-spring-boot-config-server.cfapps.io
cf set-env learning-spring-boot-eureka-server
spring.cloud.config.label production
```

Eureka needs to be configured with a Config Server URI and which label to fetch from GitHub, as done using `cf set-env`.

Next, we can look at the settings for the `chat` microservice:

```
cf set-env learning-spring-boot spring.cloud.config.uri
https://learning-spring-boot-config-server.cfapps.io
cf set-env learning-spring-boot spring.cloud.config.label production
```

```
cf bind-service learning-spring-boot learning-spring-boot-mongodb
cf set-env learning-spring-boot spring.data.mongodb.uri
${vcap.services.learning-spring-boot-mongodb.credentials.uri}

cf bind-service learning-spring-boot learning-spring-boot-rabbitmq
```

The `chat` service needs a Config Server URI (with the GitHub label), a MongoDB service binding and URI setting, and a RabbitMQ service binding.

Next, we can look at the settings for the `comments` microservice, as shown here:

```
cf set-env learning-spring-boot-comments spring.cloud.config.uri
https://learning-spring-boot-config-server.cfapps.io
cf set-env learning-spring-boot-comments spring.cloud.config.label
production

cf bind-service learning-spring-boot-comments learning-spring-boot-
mongodb
cf set-env learning-spring-boot-comments spring.data.mongodb.uri
${vcap.services.learning-spring-boot-mongodb.credentials.uri}

cf bind-service learning-spring-boot-comments learning-spring-boot-
rabbitmq
```

The `comments` service needs a Config Server URI (with the GitHub label), a MongoDB service binding and URI setting, and a RabbitMQ service binding.

Next, we can look at the settings for the `images` microservice, as shown here:

```
cf set-env learning-spring-boot-images spring.cloud.config.uri
https://learning-spring-boot-config-server.cfapps.io
cf set-env learning-spring-boot-images spring.cloud.config.label
production

cf bind-service learning-spring-boot-images learning-spring-boot-
mongodb
cf set-env learning-spring-boot-images spring.data.mongodb.uri
${vcap.services.learning-spring-boot-mongodb.credentials.uri}

cf bind-service learning-spring-boot-images learning-spring-boot-
rabbitmq
```

The `images` service needs a Config Server URI (with the GitHub label), a MongoDB service binding and URI setting, and a RabbitMQ service binding.

> **TIP**
>
> While all three services are binding to the same MongoDB service, they could actually use separate MongoDB services. The code was carefully written to avoid integrating inside the database. Each service has separate collections. However, for the sake of brevity, just one service is used in this code.

With this in place, let's run the following configuration script:

```
gturnquist$ ./config.sh

Setting env variable 'spring.cloud.config.uri' to
'https://learning-spring-boot-config-server.cfapps.io' for app
learning-spring-boot-eureka-server in org cosmos-refarch / space
development as gturnquist@pivotal.io...
Setting env variable 'spring.cloud.config.label' to 'production' for
app learning-spring-boot-eureka-server in org cosmos-refarch / space
development as gturnquist@pivotal.io...
Setting env variable 'spring.cloud.config.uri' to
'https://learning-spring-boot-config-server.cfapps.io' for app
learning-spring-boot in org cosmos-refarch / space development as
gturnquist@pivotal.io...
Setting env variable 'spring.cloud.config.label' to 'production' for
app learning-spring-boot in org cosmos-refarch / space development as
gturnquist@pivotal.io...
Binding service learning-spring-boot-mongodb to app learning-spring-
boot in org cosmos-refarch / space development as
gturnquist@pivotal.io...
Setting env variable 'spring.data.mongodb.uri' to
'${vcap.services.learning-spring-boot-mongodb.credentials.uri}' for
app learning-spring-boot in org cosmos-refarch / space development as
gturnquist@pivotal.io...
Binding service learning-spring-boot-rabbitmq to app learning-spring-
boot in org cosmos-refarch / space development as
gturnquist@pivotal.io...

(the rest omitted for brevity)
```

Having applied these settings, we need to restart everything. To do so, we need the following script:

```
#!/usr/bin/env bash

cf restart learning-spring-boot-config-server

sleep 10

cf restart learning-spring-boot-eureka-server &
```

```
cf restart learning-spring-boot &
cf restart learning-spring-boot-comments &
cf restart learning-spring-boot-images &
```

Why the delay after restarting the Config Server? It's important that it's given a chance to be up and operational before the other applications. So, let's run it as follows:

```
$ ./restart.sh

Stopping app learning-spring-boot-config-server in org cosmos-refarch
/ space development as gturnquist@pivotal.io...
Starting app learning-spring-boot-config-server in org cosmos-refarch
/ space development as gturnquist@pivotal.io...

     state      since                   cpu       memory        disk
details
#0   running    2017-01-11 10:11:07 PM  207.4%    426.7M of 1G  146M
of 1G

Stopping app learning-spring-boot-images in org cosmos-refarch / space
development as gturnquist@pivotal.io...
Stopping app learning-spring-boot-eureka-server in org cosmos-refarch
/ space development as gturnquist@pivotal.io...
Stopping app learning-spring-boot in org cosmos-refarch / space
development as gturnquist@pivotal.io...
Stopping app learning-spring-boot-comments in org cosmos-refarch /
space development as gturnquist@pivotal.io...

Starting app learning-spring-boot-eureka-server in org cosmos-refarch
/ space development as gturnquist@pivotal.io...
Starting app learning-spring-boot-images in org cosmos-refarch / space
development as gturnquist@pivotal.io...
Starting app learning-spring-boot-comments in org cosmos-refarch /
space development as gturnquist@pivotal.io...
Starting app learning-spring-boot in org cosmos-refarch / space
development as gturnquist@pivotal.io...

App started

(the rest ommitted for brevity)
```

We can easily check their status like this:

```
$ cf apps

Getting apps in org cosmos-refarch / space development as
gturnquist@pivotal.io...
OK

name                                   requested state    instances
memory     disk     urls
learning-spring-boot                           started          1/1
1G         1G       learning-spring-boot.cfapps.io
learning-spring-boot-comments                  started          1/1
1G         1G       learning-spring-boot-comments.cfapps.io
learning-spring-boot-config-server             started          1/1
1G         1G       learning-spring-boot-config-server.cfapps.io
learning-spring-boot-eureka-server             started          1/1
1G         1G       learning-spring-boot-eureka-server.cfapps.io
learning-spring-boot-hystrix-dashboard  started          1/1
1G         1G       learning-spring-boot-hystrix-dashboard.cfapps.io
learning-spring-boot-images                    started          1/1
1G         1G       learning-spring-boot-images.cfapps.io
```

Let's take a peek. We can do so by visiting
`http://learning-spring-boot.cfapps.io` (in an incognito tab to ensure a fresh
session):

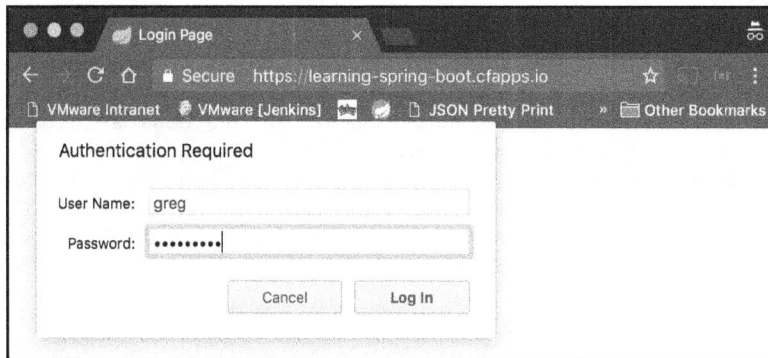

We will see the all too familiar login page.

If we log in as `greg`/`turnquist`, delete the default images and load up our favorites
from earlier, we can expect to see this:

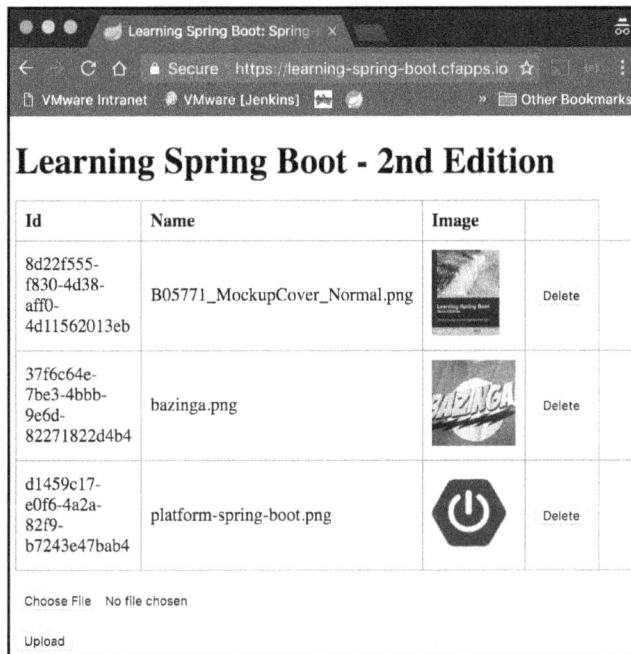

Our favorite chat channel is at the bottom of the page, as shown in the following screenshot:

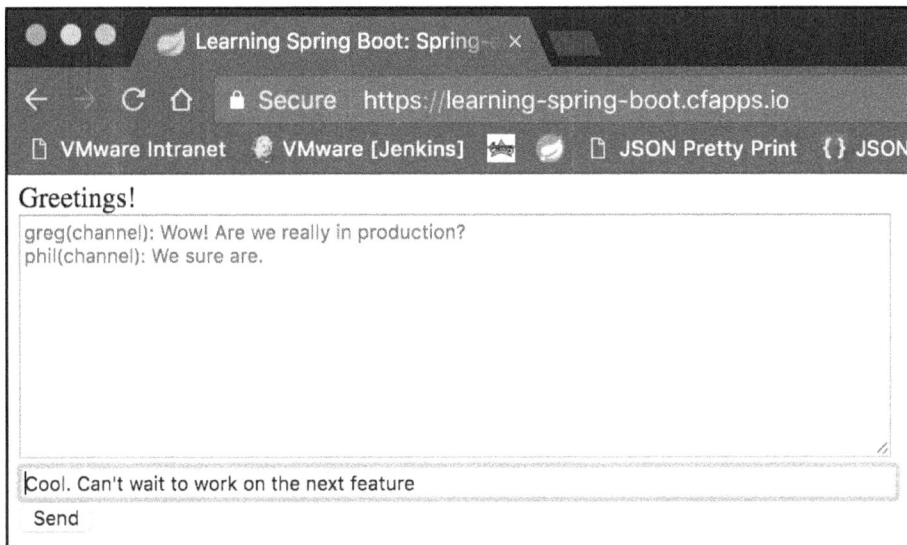

For extra maintenance, the following script can be used to delete all the apps (but not the related AMQP and MongoDB services):

```
#!/usr/bin/env bash

cf delete -f learning-spring-boot-config-server &
cf delete -f learning-spring-boot-eureka-server &
cf delete -f learning-spring-boot &
cf delete -f learning-spring-boot-comments &
cf delete -f learning-spring-boot-images &
cf delete -f learning-spring-boot-hystrix-dashboard &
```

Using the CF CLI, all the services are deleted in a background job.

> Doesn't Cloud Foundry support manifest YAML files? While it's true, manifest files have limitations that I prefer to avoid. Hence, I'd rather directly script the CF CLI operations directly, or use something ever more powerful.

Summary

In this chapter, we created profile-specific configuration settings to handle the WebSocket broker in either a local or cloud-based environment. We plugged in a custom configuration property bean and used it to grab necessary details from our cloud provider so our chat channel would work properly. We then built some BASH scripts to deploy things to the cloud, configure necessary properties, and restart/cleanup if needed.

This is just the beginning. We touched upon a lot of things in this book, including web apps, data access, testing, tools, messaging, microservices, security, and production. And we did it all *reactively*, ensuring we use resources more efficiently and effectively.

Think our social media platform is worth a billion dollars? Maybe, maybe not. However, by using the length and breadth of Spring Boot 2.0, Spring Framework 5, and its reactor-based paradigm end to end, we've learned a lot in how to build a scalable system.

Hopefully, I've whetted your appetite to go out and discover what else Spring Boot has to offer as you work on your next big project.

Please visit `https://github.com/learning-spring-boot/learning-spring-boot-2nd-edition-code` and "star" it. That way, you'll be alerted as Spring Boot 2.0 reaches GA release and this code base is upgraded to match. Also sign up for updates at `http://greglturnquist.com/books/learning-spring-boot` so you can be alerted to the latest news including code mods, contests, and more!

Spring Boot 2.0 Cookbook 3

Configure, test, extend, deploy, and monitor your Spring Boot application
both outside and inside the cloud

Getting Started with Spring Boot

20

Spring Boot has a lot of starters that are already a part of the Spring Boot family. This chapter will provide you with an overview of `http://start.spring.io/`, available starter modules, and will also show you how to make a project Bootiful, as Josh Long likes to call it.

In this chapter, we will learn about the following topics:

- Using a Spring Boot template and starter
- Creating a simple application
- Launching an application using Gradle
- Using the command-line runners
- Setting up a database connection
- Setting up a data repository service
- Scheduling executors

Introduction

In the fast-paced world of today's software development, the speed of application creation and the need for rapid prototyping are becoming more and more important. If you are developing a software using a JVM language, Spring Boot is exactly the kind of framework that will give you the power combined with the flexibility that will enable you to produce high-quality software at a rapid pace. So, let's take a look at how Spring Boot can help you to make your application Bootiful.

Using a Spring Boot template and starter

Spring Boot comes with over 40 different starter modules, which provide ready-to-use integration libraries for many different frameworks, such as database connections that are both relational and NoSQL, web services, social network integration, monitoring libraries, logging, template rendering, and the list just keeps going on. While it is not practically feasible to cover every single one of these components, we will go over the important and popular ones to get an idea of the possibilities and the ease of application development that Spring Boot provides us with.

How to do it...

We will start by creating a basic simple project skeleton, and Spring Boot will help us achieve this:

1. Head over to `http://start.spring.io`
2. Fill out a simple form with the details about our project
3. Click on **Generate Project alt +** a premade project skeleton will download; this is where we begin

How it works...

You will see the **Project Dependencies** section, where we can choose the kind of functionalities that our application will perform: Will it connect to a database? Will it have a web interface? Do we plan to integrate with any of the social networks bake in operational support? and so on. By selecting the desired technologies, the appropriate starter libraries will be added automatically to the dependency list of our pregenerated project template.

Before we proceed with the generation of our project, let's go over what exactly a Spring Boot starter is and the benefits it provides us with.

Spring Boot aims to make it easy to get started with creating an application. Spring Boot starters are bootstrap libraries that contain a collection of all the relevant transitive dependencies that are needed to start a particular functionality. Each starter has a special file, which contains the list of all the provided dependencies Spring provides. Let's take a look at the following link for a `spring-boot-starter-test` definition as an example:

`https://github.com/spring-projects/spring-boot/blob/master/spring-boot-project/spring-boot-starters/spring-boot-starter-test/src/main/resources/META-INF/spring.provides`

Here we will see the following code:

```
provides: spring-test, spring-boot, junit, mockito, hamcrest-library,
jsonassert, json-path
```

This tells us that by including `spring-boot-starter-test` in our build as a dependency, we will automatically get `spring-test`, `spring-boot`, `junit`, `mockito`, `hamcrest-library`,`jsonassert`, and `json-path`. These libraries will provide us with all the necessary things in order to start writing application tests for the software that we will develop, without needing to manually add these dependencies to the build file individually.

With more than 100 starters provided, and with the ongoing community additions increasing the list, it is very likely that unless, we find ourselves with the need to integrate with a fairly common or popular framework, there is already a starter out there that we can use.

The following table shows you the most notable ones so as to give you an idea of what is available:

Starter	Description
spring-boot-starter	This is the core Spring Boot starter that provides you with all the foundational functionalities. It is depended upon by all other starters, so no need to declare it explicitly.
spring-boot-starter-actuator	This starter provides you with a functionality to monitor, manage an application, and audit.
spring-boot-starter-jdbc	This starter provides you with a support to connect and use JDBC databases, connection pools, and so on.

`spring-boot-starter-data-jpa` `spring-boot-starter-data-*`	The JPA starter provides you with needed libraries so you can use **Java Persistence API** (**JPA**): Hibernate, and others. Various `data-* family` starters provide support for a number of datastores, such as MongoDB, Data REST, or Solr.
`spring-boot-starter-security`	This brings in all the needed dependencies for Spring Security.
`spring-boot-starter-social-*`	This allows you to integrate with Facebook, Twitter, and LinkedIn.
`spring-boot-starter-test`	This is a starter that contains the dependencies for `spring-test` and assorted testing frameworks: JUnit and Mockito, among others.
`spring-boot-starter-web`	This gives you all the needed dependencies for web application development. It can be enhanced with `spring-boot-starter-hateoas`, `spring-boot-starter-websocket`, `spring-boot-starter-mobile`, or `spring-boot-starter-ws`, and assorted template-rendering starters: `sping-boot-starter-thymeleaf` or `spring-boot-starter-mustache`.
`spring-cloud-starter-*`	Various `cloud-*` family starters providing support for a number of frameworks, such as Netflix OSS, Consul, or AWS.

Creating a simple application

Now that we have a basic idea of the starters that are available to us, let's go ahead and create our application template at `http://start.spring.io`.

How to do it...

The application that we are going to create is a book catalog management system. It will keep a record of books that were published, who the authors were, the reviewers, publishing houses, and so forth. We will name our project BookPub, and apply the following steps:

1. First let's switch to the full version by clicking the link below the **Generate Project alt +** button
2. Choose **Gradle Project** at the top
3. Use **Spring Boot** version **2.0.0(SNAPSHOT)**
4. Use the default proposed **Group** name: com.example
5. Enter bookpub for an **Artifact** field
6. Provide BookPub as a **Name** for the application
7. Specify com.example.bookpub as our **Package Name**
8. Select **Jar** as **Packaging**
9. Use **Java Version** as 8
10. Select the **H2**, **JDBC**, and **JPA** starters from the **Search for dependencies** selection so that we can get the needed artifacts in our build file to connect to an H2 database
11. Click on **Generate Project alt +** to download the project archive

How it works...

Clicking on the **Generate Project alt +** button will download the bookpub.zip archive, which we will extract from our working directory. In the newly created bookpub directory, we will see a build.gradle file that defines our build. It already comes preconfigured with the right version of a Spring Boot plugin and libraries, and even includes the extra starters, which we have chosen. The following is the code of the build.gradle file:

```
dependencies {
    compile("org.springframework.boot:spring-boot-starter-data-jpa")
    compile("org.springframework.boot:spring-boot-starter-jdbc")
    runtime("com.h2database:h2")
    testCompile("org.springframework.boot:spring-boot-starter-test")
}
```

We have selected the following starters:

- `org.springframework.boot:spring-boot-starter-data-jpa`: This starter pulls in the JPA dependency.
- `org.springframework.boot:spring-boot-starter-jdbc`: This starter pulls in the JDBC supporting libraries.
- `com.h2database`: H2 is a particular type of database implementation, namely H2.
- `org.springframework.boot:spring-boot-starter-test`: This starter pulls all the necessary dependencies for running tests. It is only being used during the test phase of the build, and it is not included during the regular application compile time and runtime.

As you can see, the `runtime("com.h2database:h2")` dependency is a runtime one. This is because we don't really need, and probably don't even want to know, the exact type of database to which we will connect at the compile time. Spring Boot will autoconfigure the needed settings and create appropriate beans once it detects the presence of the `org.h2.Driver` class in the classpath when the application is launched. We will look into the inner workings of how and where this happens later in this chapter.

The `data-jpa` and `jdbc` are Spring Boot starter artifacts. If we look in these dependency JARs once they are downloaded, or using Maven Central, we will find that they don't contain any actual classes, only the various metadata. The two containing files that are of interest are `pom.xml` and `spring.provides`. Let's first look at the `spring.provides` file in the `spring-boot-starter-jdbc` JAR artifact, as follows:

```
provides: spring-jdbc, spring-tx, tomcat-jdbc
```

This tells us that, by having this starter as our dependency, we will transitively get the `spring-jdbc`, `spring-tx`, and `tomcat-jdbc` dependency libraries in our build. The `pom.xml` file contains the proper dependency declarations that will be used by Gradle or Maven to resolve the needed dependencies during the build time. This also applies to our second starter: `spring-boot-starter-data-jpa`. This starter will transitively provide us with the `spring-orm`, `hibernate-entity-manager`, and the `spring-data-jpa` libraries.

At this point, we have enough libraries/classes in our application classpath so as to give Spring Boot an idea of what kind of application we are trying to run and what type of facilities and frameworks need to be configured automatically by Spring Boot to stitch things together.

Earlier, we mentioned that the presence of the `org.h2.Driver` class in the classpath will trigger Spring Boot to automatically configure the H2 database connection for our application. To see exactly how this will happen, let's start by looking at our newly created application template, specifically at `BookPubApplication.java`, which is located in the `src/main/java/com/example/bookpub` directory in the root of the project. We do this as follows:

```
package com.example.bookpub;

import org.springframework.boot.SpringApplication;
import org.springframework.boot.autoconfigure.
SpringBootApplication;

@SpringBootApplication
public class BookPubApplication {

  public static void main(String[] args) {
    SpringApplication.run(BookPubApplication.class, args);
  }
}
```

This is effectively our entire and fully runnable application. There's not a whole lot of code here and definitely no mention of configuration or databases anywhere. The key to making magic is the `@SpringBootApplication` meta-annotation. In this, we will find the real annotations that will direct Spring Boot to set things up automatically:

```
@SpringBootConfiguration
@EnableAutoConfiguration
@ComponentScan (excludeFilters = @Filter(type =
                                  FilterType.CUSTOM,
              classes = TypeExcludeFilter.class))
public @interface SpringBootApplication {...}
```

Let's go through the following list of annotations mentioned in the preceding code snippet:

- `@SpringBootConfiguration`: This annotation is in itself a meta-annotation; it tells Spring Boot that the annotated class contains Spring Boot configuration definitions, such as the `@Bean`, `@Component`, and `@Service` declarations, and so on. Inside, it uses the `@Configuration` annotation, which is a Spring annotation, and not just Spring Boot, as it is a Spring Framework core annotation, used to mark classes containing Spring configuration definitions.

It is important to note that using `@SpringBootConfiguration` over `@Configuration` is helpful when executing tests with Spring Boot Test framework, as this configuration will automatically be loaded by the Test framework when the test is annotated with `@SpringBootTest`. As it is noted in the Javadoc, an application should only ever include one `@SpringApplicationConfiguration`, and most idiomatic Spring Boot applications will inherit it from `@SpringBootApplication`.

- `@ComponentScan`: This annotation tells Spring that we want to scan our application packages starting from the package of our annotated class as a default package root for the other classes that may be annotated with `@Configuration`, `@Controller`, and other applicable annotations, which Spring will automatically include as part of the context configuration. The applied `TypeExcludeFilter` class provides filtering out for various classes to be excluded from `ApplicationContext`. It is mostly used by `spring-boot-test` to exclude classes that should be used only during tests; however, it is possible to add your own beans that extend from `TypeExcludeFilter` and provide filtering for other types that are deemed necessary.

- `@EnableAutoConfiguration`: This annotation is a part of the Spring Boot annotation, which is a meta-annotation on its own (you will find that Spring libraries rely very heavily on the meta-annotations so they can group and compose configurations together). It imports the `EnableAutoConfigurationImportSelector` and `AutoConfigurationPackages.Registrar` classes that effectively instruct Spring to automatically configure the conditional beans depending on the classes available in the classpath. (We will cover the inner workings of autoconfiguration in detail in Chapter 23, *Writing Custom Spring Boot Starters*.)

The `SpringApplication.run(BookPubApplication.class, args);` code line in the main method basically creates a Spring application context that reads the annotations in `BookPubApplication.class` and instantiates a context, which is similar to how it would have been done had we not used Spring Boot and stuck with just a regular Spring Framework.

Launching an application using Gradle

Typically, the very first step of creating any application is to have a basic startable skeleton. As the Spring Boot starter has created the application template for us already, all we have to do is extract the code, build, and execute it. Now let's go to the console and launch the application with Gradle.

How to do it...

Change the location of our directory to where the `bookpub.zip` archive was extracted from and execute the following command from the command line:

```
$ ./gradlew clean bootRun
```

> **TIP**
>
> If you don't have `gradlew` in the directory, then download a version of Gradle from `https://gradle.org/downloads` or install it via Homebrew by executing `brew install gradle`. After Gradle is installed, run `wrapper` in the `gradle` folder to get the Gradle `wrapper` files generated. Another way is to invoke `$gradleclean bootRun`.

The output of the preceding command will be as follows:

```
  .   ____          _            __ _ _
 / / ___'_ __ _ _(_)_ __  __ _ 
( ( )\___ | '_ | '_| | '_ \/ _` | 
 / ___)| |_)| | | | | || (_| |  ) ) ) )
  '  |____| .__|_| |_|_| |_\__, | / / / /
 =========|_|==============|___/=/_/_/_/
 :: Spring Boot ::   (v2.0.0.BUILD-SNAPSHOT)
2017-12-16 23:18:53.721 : Starting BookPubApplication on mbp with
PID 43850
2017-12-16 23:18:53.781 : Refreshing org.springframework.context.
annotation.Annotatio
2017-12-16 23:18:55.544 : Building JPA container
EntityManagerFactory for persistence
2017-12-16 23:18:55.565 : HHH000204: Processing
PersistenceUnitInfo [name: default
2017-12-16 23:18:55.624 : HHH000412: Hibernate Core
{5.2.12.Final}
2017-12-16 23:18:55.625 : HHH000206: hibernate.properties not
found
2017-12-16 23:18:55.627 : HHH000021: Bytecode provider name :
```

```
javassist
2017-12-16 23:18:55.774 : HCANN000001: Hibernate Commons
Annotations {5.0.1.Final
2017-12-16 23:18:55.850 : HHH000400: Using dialect:
org.hibernate.dialect.H2Dialect
2017-12-16 23:18:55.902 : HHH000397: Using
ASTQueryTranslatorFactory
2017-12-16 23:18:56.094 : HHH000227: Running hbm2ddl schema
export
2017-12-16 23:18:56.096 : HHH000230: Schema export complete
2017-12-16 23:18:56.337 : Registering beans for JMX exposure on
startup
2017-12-16 23:18:56.345 : Started BookPubApplication in 3.024
seconds (JVM running...
2017-12-16 23:18:56.346 : Closing
org.springframework.context.annotation.AnnotationC..
2017-12-16 23:18:56.347 : Unregistering JMX-exposed beans on
shutdown
2017-12-16 23:18:56.349 : Closing JPA EntityManagerFactory for
persistence unit 'def...
2017-12-16 23:18:56.349 : HHH000227: Running hbm2ddl schema
export
2017-12-16 23:18:56.350 : HHH000230: Schema export complete
BUILD SUCCESSFUL
Total time: 52.323 secs
```

How it works...

As we can see, the application started just fine, but as we didn't add any functionality or configure any services, it existed straight away. From the startup log, however, we do see that the autoconfiguration did take place. Let's take a look at the following lines:

```
Building JPA container EntityManagerFactory for persistence unit
'default'
HHH000412: Hibernate Core {5.2.12.Final}
HHH000400: Using dialect: org.hibernate.dialect.H2Dialect
```

This information tells us that, because we added the jdbc and data-jpa starters, the JPA container was created and will use Hibernate 5.2.12.Final to manage the persistence using H2Dialect. This was possible because we had the right classes in the classpath.

Using the command-line runners

With our basic application skeleton ready, let's add some meat to the bones by making our application do something.

Let's start by first creating a class named `StartupRunner`. This will implement the `CommandLineRunner` interface, which basically provides just one method: `public void run(String... args)` --that will get called by Spring Boot only once after the application has started.

How to do it...

1. Create the file named `StartupRunner.java` under the `src/main/java/com/example/bookpub/` directory from the root of our project with the following content:

```
package com.example.bookpub;

import com.example.bookpub.repository.BookRepository;
import org.apache.commons.logging.Log;
import org.apache.commons.logging.LogFactory;
import org.springframework.beans.factory.annotation.Autowired;
import org.springframework.boot.CommandLineRunner;
import org.springframework.scheduling.annotation.Scheduled;

public class StartupRunner implements CommandLineRunner {
    protected final Log logger =
LogFactory.getLog(getClass());
    @Override
    public void run(String... args) throws Exception {
        logger.info("Hello");
    }
}
```

2. After we have defined the class, let's proceed by defining it as `@Bean` in the `BookPubApplication.java` application configuration, which is located in the same folder as our newly created `StartupRunner.java` file as follows:

```
@Bean
public StartupRunner schedulerRunner() {
    return new StartupRunner();
}
```

How it works...

If we run our application again, by executing $ ./gradlew clean bootRun, we will get an output that is similar to the previous one. However, we will see our Hello message in the logs as well, which is as follows:

```
2017-12-16 21:57:51.048   INFO ---
com.example.bookpub.StartupRunner          : Hello
```

Even though the program will get terminated on execution, at least we made it do something!

Command-line runners are a useful functionality to execute the various types of code that only have to be run once, after startup. Some also use this as a place to start various executor threads, but Spring Boot provides a better solution for this task, which will be discussed at the end of this chapter. The command-line runner interface is used by Spring Boot to scan all of its implementations and invoke each instance's run method with the startup arguments. We can also use an @Order annotation or implement an Ordered interface so as to define the exact order in which we want Spring Boot to execute them. For example, **Spring Batch** relies on the runners to trigger the execution of the jobs.

As the command-line runners are instantiated and executed after the application has started, we can use the dependency injection to our advantage to wire in whatever dependencies we need, such as datasources, services, and other components. These can be utilized later while implementing run.

> It is important to note that if any exception is thrown in the run(String... args) method, this will cause the context to close and an application to shut down. Wrapping the risky code blocks with try/catch is recommended to prevent this from happening.

Setting up a database connection

In every application, there is a need to access some data and conduct some operations on it. Most frequently, this source of data is a datastore of some kind, namely a database. Spring Boot makes it very easy to get started in order to connect to the database and start consuming the data via the JPA, among others.

Getting ready

In our previous example, we created the basic application that will execute a command-line runner by printing a message in the logs. Let's enhance this application by adding a connection to a database.

Earlier, we already added the necessary `jdbc` and `data-jpa` starters as well as an H2 database dependency to our `build` file. Now we will configure an in-memory instance of the H2 database.

> **TIP**
>
> In the case of an embedded database, such as H2, **Hyper SQL Database** (**HSQLDB**), or Derby, no actual configuration is required besides including the dependency on one of these in the `build` file. When one of these databases is detected in the classpath and a `DataSource` bean dependency is declared in the code, Spring Boot will automatically create one for you.

To demonstrate the fact that just by including the H2 dependency in the classpath, we will automatically get a default database, let's modify our `StartupRunner.java` file to look as follows:

```
public class StartupRunner implements CommandLineRunner {
    protected final Log logger = LogFactory.getLog(getClass());
    @Autowired
    private DataSource ds;
    @Override
    public void run(String... args) throws Exception {
        logger.info("DataSource: "+ds.toString());
    }
}
```

Now, if we proceed with the running of our application, we will see the name of the datasource printed in the log, as follows:

```
2017-12-16 21:46:22.067 com.example.bookpub.StartupRunner
:DataSource: org.apache.tomcat.jdbc.pool.DataSource@4...
{...driverClassName=org.h2.Driver; ... }
```

So, under the hood, Spring Boot recognized that we've autowired a `DataSource` bean dependency and automatically created one initializing the in-memory H2 datastore. This is all well and good, but probably not all too useful beyond an early prototyping phase or for the purpose of testing. Who would want a database that goes away with all the data as soon as your application shuts down and you have to start with a clean slate every time you restart the application?

How to do it...

Let's change the defaults in order to create an embedded H2 database that will not store data in-memory, but rather use a file to persist the data among application restarts, by performing the following steps:

1. Open the file named `application.properties` under the `src/main/resources` directory from the root of our project and add the following content:

   ```
   spring.datasource.url =
   jdbc:h2:~/test;DB_CLOSE_DELAY=-1;DB_CLOSE_ON_EXIT=FALSE
   spring.datasource.username = sa
   spring.datasource.password =
   ```

2. Start the application by executing `./gradlew clean bootRun` from the command line

3. Check your home directory, and you should see the following file in there: `test.mv.db`

> The user home directory is located under `/home/<username>` on Linux and under `/Users/<username>` on macOS X.

How it works...

Even though, by default, Spring Boot makes certain assumptions about the database configuration by examining the classpath for the presence of supported database drivers, it provides you with easy configuration options to tweak the database access via a set of exposed properties grouped under `spring.datasource`.

The things that we can configure are `url`, `username`, `password`, `driver-class-name`, and so on. If you want to consume the datasource from a JNDI location, where an outside container creates it, you can configure this using the `spring.datasource.jndi-name` property. The complete set of possible properties is fairly large, so we will not go into all of them. However, we will cover more options in Chapter 24, *Application Testing*, where we will talk about mocking data for application tests using a database.

By looking at various blogs and examples, you may notice that some places use dashes in property names like `driver-class-name`, while others use camel-cased variants: `driverClassName`. In Spring Boot, these are actually two equally supported ways of naming the same property, and they get translated into the same thing internally.

If you want to connect to a regular (non-embedded) database, besides just having the appropriate driver library in the classpath, we need to specify the driver of our choice in the configuration. The following code snippet is what the configuration to connect to MySQL would resemble:

```
spring.datasource.driver-class-name: com.mysql.jdbc.Driver
spring.datasource.url:
jdbc:mysql://localhost:3306/springbootcookbook
spring.datasource.username: root
spring.datasource.password:
```

If we wanted Hibernate to create the schema automatically, based on our entity classes, we would need to add the following line to the configuration:

```
spring.jpa.hibernate.ddl-auto=create-drop
```

Don't do it in the production environment, otherwise, on startup, all the table schemas and data will be deleted! Use the update or validate values instead, where needed.

You can go even further in the abstraction layer and, instead of autowiring a `DataSource` object, you could go straight for `JdbcTemplate`. This would instruct Spring Boot to automatically create a DataSource and then create a `JdbcTemplate` wrapping the datasource, thus providing you with a more convenient way of interacting with a database in a safe way. The code for `JdbcTemplate` is as follows:

```
@Autowired
private JdbcTemplate jdbcTemplate;
```

You can also look in the `spring-boot-autoconfigure` source at an `org.springframework.boot.autoconfigure.jdbc.DataSourceAutoConfiguration` file to see the code behind the datasource creation magic.

Setting up a data repository service

Connecting to a database and then executing good old SQL, though simplistic and straightforward, is not the most convenient way to operate on the data, map it in a set of domain objects, and manipulate the relational content. This is why multiple frameworks emerged to aid you with mapping the data from tables to objects, better known as **object-relational mapping (ORM)**. The most notable example of such a framework is Hibernate.

In the previous example, we covered how to set up a connection to a database and configure the settings for the username and password, and we also discussed which driver to use, and so on. In this recipe, we will enhance our application by adding a few entity objects that define the structure of the data in the database and a `CrudRepository` interface to access the data.

As our application is a book-tracking catalogue, the obvious domain objects would be `Book`, `Author`, `Reviewers`, and `Publisher`.

How to do it...

1. Create a new package folder named `entity` under the `src/main/java/com/example/bookpub` directory from the root of our project.
2. In this newly created package, create a new class named `Book` with the following content:

```
@Entity
public class Book {
  @Id
  @GeneratedValue
  private Long id;
  private String isbn;
  private String title;
  private String description;

  @ManyToOne
  private Author author;
  @ManyToOne
  private Publisher publisher;

  @ManyToMany
  private List<Reviewers> reviewers;
```

```
    protected Book() {}

    public Book(String isbn, String title, Author author,
        Publisher publisher) {
      this.isbn = isbn;
      this.title = title;
      this.author = author;
      this.publisher = publisher;
    }
    //Skipping getters and setters to save space, but we do
need them
  }
```

3. As any book should have an author and a publisher, and ideally some reviewers, we need to create these entity objects as well. Let's start by creating an `Author` entity class, under the same directory as our `Book`, as follows:

```
@Entity
public class Author {
  @Id
  @GeneratedValue
  private Long id;
  private String firstName;
  private String lastName;
  @OneToMany(mappedBy = "author")
  private List<Book> books;

  protected Author() {}

  public Author(String firstName, String lastName) {...}
    //Skipping implementation to save space, but we do
need
       it all
}
```

4. Similarly, we will create the `Publisher` and `Reviewer` classes, as shown in the following code:

```
@Entity
public class Publisher {
  @Id
  @GeneratedValue
  private Long id;
  private String name;
  @OneToMany(mappedBy = "publisher")
  private List<Book> books;
```

```
    protected Publisher() {}

    public Publisher(String name) {...}
}

@Entity
public class Reviewer {
  @Id
  @GeneratedValue
  private Long id;
  private String firstName;
  private String lastName;

  protected Reviewer() {}

  public Reviewer(String firstName, String lastName)
      {...}
}
```

5. Now we will create our `BookRepository` interface by extending Spring's `CrudRepository` interface under the `src/main/java/com/example/bookpub/repository` package, as follows:

```
@Repository
public interface BookRepository
        extends CrudRepository<Book, Long> {
  public Book findBookByIsbn(String isbn);
}
```

6. Finally, let's modify our `StartupRunner` class in order to print the number of books in our collection, instead of some random datasource string, by autowiring a newly created `BookRepository` and printing the result of a `.count()` call to the log, as follows:

```
public class StartupRunner implements CommandLineRunner {
  @Autowired private BookRepository bookRepository;

  public void run(String... args) throws Exception {
    logger.info("Number of books: " +
      bookRepository.count());
  }
}
```

How it works...

As you have probably noticed, we didn't write a single line of SQL, or even mention anything about database connections, building queries, or things like that. The only hint about the fact that we are dealing with the database-backed data in our code is the presence of class and field annotations: `@Entity`, `@Repository`, `@Id`, `@GeneratedValue`, and `@ManyToOne`, along with `@ManyToMany` and `@OneToMany`. These annotations, which are a part of the JPA, along with the extension of the `CrudRepository` interface, are our ways of communicating with Spring about the need to map our objects to the appropriate tables and fields in the database and provide us with the programmatic ability to interact with this data.

Let's go through the following annotations:

- `@Entity` indicates that the annotated class should be mapped to a database table. The name of the table will be derived from the name of the class, but it can be configured, if needed. It is important to note that every entity class should have a default `protected` constructor, which is needed for automated instantiation and Hibernate interactions.

- `@Repository` indicates that the interface is intended to provide you with the access and manipulation of data for a database. It also serves as an indication to Spring during the component scan that this instance should be created as a bean that will be available for use and injection into other beans in the application.

- The `CrudRepository` interface defines the basic common methods to read, create, update, and delete data from a data repository. The extra methods that we will define in our `BookRepository` extension, `public Book findBookByIsbn(String isbn)`, indicate that Spring JPA should map the call to this method to a SQL query selecting a book by its ISBN field. This is a convention-named mapping that translates the method name into a SQL query. It can be a very powerful ally, allowing you to build queries, such as `findByNameIgnoringCase(String name)` and others.

- The `@Id` and `@GeneratedValue` annotations provide you with an indication that an annotated field should be mapped to a primary key column in the database and that the value for this field should be generated, instead of being explicitly entered.

- The `@ManyToOne` and `@ManyToMany` annotations define the relational field associations that refer to the data stored in the other tables. In our case, multiple books belong to one author, and many reviewers review multiple books.

- The `mappedBy` attribute in the `@OneToMay` annotation defines a reverse association mapping. It indicates to Hibernate that the mapping source of truth is defined in the `Book` class, in the `author` or `publisher` fields.

> For more information about all the vast capabilities of Spring Data, visit `http://docs.spring.io/spring-data/data-commons/docs/current /reference/html/`.

Scheduling executors

Earlier in this chapter, we discussed how the command-line runners can be used as a place to start the scheduled executor thread pools to run the worker threads in intervals. While that is certainly a possibility, Spring provides you with a more concise configuration to achieve the same goal: `@EnableScheduling`.

Getting ready

We will enhance our application so that it will print a count of books in our repository every 10 seconds. To achieve this, we will make the necessary modifications to the `BookPubApplication` and `StartupRunner` classes.

How to do it...

1. Let's add an `@EnableScheduling` annotation to the `BookPubApplication` class, as follows:

```
@SpringBootApplication
@EnableScheduling
public class BookPubApplication {...}
```

2. As a @Scheduled annotation can be placed only on methods without arguments, let's add a new run() method to the StartupRunner class and annotate it with the @Scheduled annotation, as shown in the following line:

```
@Scheduled(initialDelay = 1000, fixedRate = 10000)
public void run() {
    logger.info("Number of books: " +
        bookRepository.count());
}
```

3. Start the application by executing ./gradlew clean bootRun from the command line so as to observe the Number of books: 0 message that shows in the logs every 10 seconds.

How it works...

@EnableScheduling, as many other annotations that we have discussed and will discuss in this book, is not a Spring Boot; it is a Spring Context module annotation. Similar to the @SpringBootApplication and @EnableAutoConfiguration annotations, this is a meta-annotation and internally imports SchedulingConfiguration via the @Import(SchedulingConfiguration.class) instruction, which can be found inside ScheduledAnnotationBeanPostProcessor that will be created by the imported configuration and will scan the declared Spring beans for the presence of the @Scheduled annotations. For every annotated method without arguments, the appropriate executor thread pool will be created. It will manage the scheduled invocation of the annotated method.

Configuring Web Applications 21

In the previous chapter, we learned about how to create a starting application template, add some basic functionalities, and set up a connection to a database. In this chapter, we will continue to evolve our BookPub application and give it a web presence.

In this chapter, we will learn about the following topics:

- Creating a basic RESTful application
- Creating Spring Data REST service
- Configuring custom servlet filters
- Configuring custom interceptors
- Configuring custom HttpMessageConverters
- Configuring custom PropertyEditors
- Configuring custom type formatters

Creating a basic RESTful application

While the command-line applications do have their place and use, most of today's application development is centered around web, REST, and data services. Let's start with enhancing our `BookPub` application by providing it with a web-based API in order to get access to the book catalogs.

We will start where we left off in the previous chapter, so there should already be an application skeleton with the entity objects and a repository service defined and a connection to the database configured.

How to do it...

1. The very first thing that we will need to do is add a new dependency to `build.gradle` with the `spring-boot-starter-web` starter to get us all the necessary libraries for web-based functionality. The following code snippet is what it will look like:

```
dependencies {
  compile("org.springframework.boot:spring-boot-starter-data-
jpa")
  compile("org.springframework.boot:spring-boot-starter-jdbc")
  compile("org.springframework.boot:spring-boot-starter-web")
  runtime("com.h2database:h2")
  runtime("mysql:mysql-connector-java")
  testCompile("org.springframework.boot:spring-boot-starter-
test")
}
```

2. Next, we will need to create a Spring controller that will be used to handle the web requests for the catalog data in our application. Let's start by creating a new package structure to house our controllers so that we have our code nicely grouped by its appropriate purposes. Create a package folder called `controllers` in the `src/main/java/com/example/bookpub` directory from the root of our project.

3. As we will be exposing the book data, let's create the controller class file called `BookController` in our newly created package with the following content:

```
@RestController
@RequestMapping("/books")
public class BookController {
  @Autowired
  private BookRepository bookRepository;

  @RequestMapping(value = "", method = RequestMethod.GET)
  public Iterable<Book> getAllBooks() {
    return bookRepository.findAll();
  }
```

```
@RequestMapping(value = "/{isbn}", method =
   RequestMethod.GET)
public Book getBook(@PathVariable String isbn) {
   return bookRepository.findBookByIsbn(isbn);
   }
}
```

4. Start the application by running `./gradlew clean bootRun`.
5. After the application has started, open the browser and go to `http://localhost:8080/books` and you should see a response: `[]`.

How it works...

The key to getting the service exposed to web requests is the `@RestController` annotation. This is yet another example of a meta-annotation or a convenience annotation, as the Spring documentation refers to it at times, which we have seen in previous recipes. In `@RestController`, two annotations are defined: `@Controller` and `@ResponseBody`. So we could just as easily annotate `BookController`, as follows:

```
@Controller
@ResponseBody
@RequestMapping("/books")
public class BookController {...}
```

Let's take a look at the following annotations from the preceding code snippet:

- `@Controller`: This is a Spring stereotype annotation that is similar to `@Bean` and `@Repository` and declares the annotated class as an MVC
- `@ResponseBody`: This is a Spring MVC annotation indicating that responses from the web-request-mapped methods constitute the entire content of the HTTP response body payload, which is typical for the RESTful applications
- `@RequestMapping`: This is a Spring MVC annotation indicating that requests to `/books/*` URL will be routed to this controller.

Creating Spring Data REST service

In the previous example, we fronted our `BookRepository` interface with a REST controller in order to expose the data behind it via a web RESTful API. While this is definitely a quick and easy way to make the data accessible, it does require us to manually create a controller and define the mappings for all the desired operations. To minimize the boilerplate code, Spring provides us with a more convenient way: `spring-boot-starter-data-rest`. This allows us to simply add an annotation to the repository interface and Spring will do the rest to expose it to the web.

We will continue from where we finished in the previous recipe, and so the entity models and the `BookRepository` interface should already exist.

How to do it...

1. We will start by adding another dependency to our `build.gradle` file in order to add the `spring-boot-starter-data-rest` artifact:

```
dependencies {
  ...
  compile("org.springframework.boot:spring-boot-starter-data-
rest")
  ...
}
```

2. Now, let's create a new interface to define `AuthorRepository` in the `src/main/java/com/example/bookpub/repository` directory from the root of our project with the following content:

```
@RepositoryRestResource
public interface AuthorRepository extends
  PagingAndSortingRepository<Author, Long> {
}
```

3. While we are at it—given how little code it takes—let's create the repository interfaces for the remaining entity models, `PublisherRepository` and `ReviewerRepository` by placing the files in the same package directory as `AuthorRepository` with the following content:

```
@RepositoryRestResource
public interface PublisherRepository extends
   PagingAndSortingRepository<Publisher, Long> {
}
```

Otherwise, you can use the following code instead of the preceding code:

```
@RepositoryRestResource
public interface ReviewerRepository extends
   PagingAndSortingRepository<Reviewer, Long> {
}
```

4. Start the application by running `./gradlew clean bootRun`

5. After the application has started, open the browser and go to `http://localhost:8080/authors` and you should see the following response:

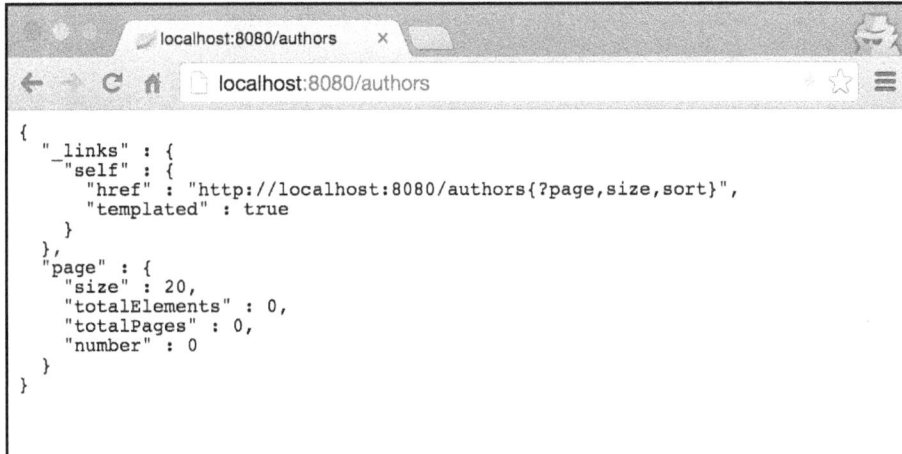

How it works...

As is evidenced from the browser view, we will get significantly more information than we got when we wrote the books controller. This is in part due to us extending not a `CrudRepository` interface, but a `PagingAndSortingRepository` one, which in turn is an extension of `CrudRepository`. The reason that we've decided to do this is to get the extra benefits provided by `PagingAndSortingRepository`. This will add the extra functionality to retrieve entities using the pagination and being able to sort them.

The `@RepositoryRestResource` annotation, while optional, provides us with the ability to have finer control over the exposure of the repository as a web data service. For example, if we wanted to change the URL `path` or `rel` value, to `writers` instead of `authors`, we could have tuned the annotation as follows:

```
@RepositoryRestResource(collectionResourceRel = "writers", path =
"writers")
```

As we included `spring-boot-starter-data-rest` in our build dependencies, we will also get the `spring-hateoas` library support, which gives us nice ALPS metadata, such as a `_links` object. This can be very helpful when building an API-driven UI, which can deduce the navigational capabilities from the metadata and present them appropriately.

Configuring custom servlet filters

In a real-world web application, we almost always find a need to add facades or wrappers to service requests, to log them, filter out bad characters for XSS, perform authentication, and so on. Out of the box, Spring Boot automatically adds `OrderedCharacterEncodingFilter` and `HiddenHttpMethodFilter`, but we can always add more. Let's see how Spring Boot helps us achieve this task.

Among the various assortments of Spring Boot, Spring Web, Spring MVC, and others, there is already a vast variety of different servlet filters that are available and all we have to do is define them as beans in the configuration. Let's say that our application will be running behind a load balancer proxy and we would like to translate the real request IP that is used by the users instead of the IP from the proxy when our application instance receives the request. Luckily, Apache Tomcat 8 already provides us with an implementation: `RemoteIpFilter`. All we will need to do is add it to our filter chain.

How to do it...

1. It is a good idea to separate and group the configurations into different classes in order to provide more clarity about what kind of things are being configured. So, let's create a separate configuration class called `WebConfiguration` in the `src/main/java/com/example/bookpub` directory from the root of our project with the following content:

```
@Configuration
public class WebConfiguration {
    @Bean
    public RemoteIpFilter remoteIpFilter() {
        return new RemoteIpFilter();
    }
}
```

2. Start the application by running `./gradlew clean bootRun`.

3. In the startup log, we should see the following line, indicating that our filter has been added:

```
...FilterRegistrationBean : Mapping filter: 'remoteIpFilter'
to: [/*]
```

How it works...

The magic behind this functionality is actually very simple. Let's start from the separate configuration class and work our way to the filter bean detection.

If we look in our main class, `BookPubApplication`, we will see that it is annotated with `@SpringBootApplication`, which in turn is a convenience meta-annotation that declares `@ComponentScan` among others. We discussed this in detail in one of our earlier recipes. The presence of `@ComponentScan` instructs Spring Boot to detect `WebConfiguration` as a `@Configuration` class and add its definitions to the context. So, anything that we will declare in `WebConfiguration` is as good as if we were to put it right in `BookPubApplication` itself.

The `@BeanpublicRemoteIpFilterremoteIpFilter() {...}` declaration simply creates a Spring bean for the `RemoteIpFilter` class. When Spring Boot detects all the beans of `javax.servlet.Filter`, it will add them to the filter chain automatically. So, all we have to do, if we want to add more filters, is to just declare them as `@Bean` configurations. For example, for a more advanced filter configuration, if we want a particular filter to apply only to specific URL patterns, we can create a `@Bean` configuration of a `FilterRegistrationBean` type and use it to configure the precise settings.

> **TIP**
>
> To make supporting this use-case easier Spring Boot provides us with configuration properties that can be used instead of manually configuring the `RemoteIpFilter` bean for occasions when Tomcat servlet container is being used. Use `server.use-forward-headers=true` to indicate to Spring Boot that it needs to automatically configure support for proxy headers, to provide proper request obfuscation. Specifically for Tomcat, one can also use `server.tomcat.remote_ip_header=x-forwarded-for` and `server.tomcat.protocol_header=x-forwarded-proto` properties to configure what specific header names should be used to retrieve the values.

Configuring custom interceptors

While servlet filters are a part of the Servlet API and have nothing to do with Spring besides being automatically added in the filter chain --Spring MVC provides us with another way of wrapping web requests: `HandlerInterceptor`. According to the documentation, `HandlerInterceptor` is just like a filter. Instead of wrapping a request in a nested chain, an interceptor gives us cutaway points at different phases, such as before the request gets handled, after the request has been processed, before the view has been rendered, and at the very end, after the request has been fully completed. It does not let us change anything about the request, but it does let us stop the execution by throwing an exception or returning false if the interceptor logic determines so.

Similar to using filters, Spring MVC comes with a number of premade `HandlerInterceptors`. The commonly used ones are `LocaleChangeInterceptor` and `ThemeChangeInterceptor`; but there are certainly others that provide great value. So let's add `LocaleChangeInterceptor` to our application in order to see how it is done.

How to do it...

Despite what you might think, after seeing the previous recipe, adding an interceptor is not as straightforward as just declaring it as a bean. We actually need to do it via `WebMvcConfigurer` or by overriding `WebMvcConfigurationSupport`. Let's take a look at the following steps:

1. Let's enhance our `WebConfiguration` class to implement `WebMvcConfigurer`:

   ```
   public class WebConfiguration implements WebMvcConfigurer
   {...}
   ```

2. Now we will add a `@Bean` declaration for `LocaleChangeInterceptor`:

   ```
   @Bean
   public LocaleChangeInterceptor localeChangeInterceptor() {
     return new LocaleChangeInterceptor();
   }
   ```

3. This will actually create the interceptor Spring bean, but will not add it to the request handling chain. For this to happen, we will need to override the `addInterceptors` method and add our interceptor to the provided registry:

   ```
   @Override
   public void addInterceptors(InterceptorRegistry registry) {
     registry.addInterceptor(localeChangeInterceptor());
   }
   ```

4. Start the application by running `./gradlew clean bootRun`
5. In the browser, go to `http://localhost:8080/books?locale=foo`
6. Now, if you look at the console logs, you will see a bunch of stack trace errors basically saying the following:

   ```
   Caused by: java.lang.UnsupportedOperationException: Cannot
   change HTTP accept header - use a different locale resolution
   strategy
   ```

> While the error is not because we entered an invalid locale, but because the default locale resolution strategy does not allow the resetting of the locale that is requested by the browser, the fact that we got an error shows that our interceptor is working.

How it works...

When it comes to configuring the Spring MVC internals, it is not as simple as just defining a bunch of beans at least not always. This is due to the need to provide a more fine-tuned mapping of the MVC components to requests. To make things easier, Spring provides us with a collection of default methods in `WebMvcConfigurer` interface that we can extend and override the settings of that we need.

In the particular case of configuring interceptors, we are overriding the `addInterceptors(InterceptorRegistry registry)` method. This is a typical callback method where we are given a registry in order to register as many additional interceptors as we need. During the MVC autoconfiguration phase, Spring Boot, just like in the case of filters, detects instances of `WebMvcConfigurer` and sequentially calls the callback methods on all of them. It means that we can have more than one implementation of the `WebMvcConfigurer` class if we want to have some logical separation.

Configuring custom HttpMessageConverters

While we were building our RESTful web data service, we defined the controllers, repositories, and put some annotations on them; but nowhere did we do any kind of object translation from the Java entity beans to the HTTP data stream output. However, behind the scenes, Spring Boot automatically configured `HttpMessageConverters` so as to translate our entity beans into a JSON representation written to HTTP response using the `Jackson` library. When multiple converters are available, the most applicable one gets selected based on the message object class and the requested content type.

The purpose of `HttpMessageConverters` is to translate various object types into their corresponding HTTP output formats. A converter can either support a range of multiple data types or multiple output formats, or a combination of both. For example, `MappingJackson2HttpMessageConverter` can translate any Java object into `application/json`, whereas `ProtobufHttpMessageConverter` can only operate on instances of `com.google.protobuf.Message` but can write them to the wire as `application/json`, `application/xml`, `text/plain`, or `application/x-protobuf`. `HttpMessageConverters` support not only writing out to the HTTP stream but also converting HTTP requests to appropriate Java objects as well.

How to do it...

There are a number of ways in which we can configure converters. It all depends on which one you prefer or how much control you want to achieve.

1. Let's add `ByteArrayHttpMessageConverter` as `@Bean` to our `WebConfiguration` class in the following manner:

```
@Bean
public
  ByteArrayHttpMessageConverter
    byteArrayHttpMessageConverter() {
  return new ByteArrayHttpMessageConverter();
}
```

2. Another way to achieve this is to override the `configureMessageConverters` method in the `WebConfiguration` class, which extends `WebMvcConfigurerAdapter`, defining such a method as follows:

```
@Override
public void configureMessageConverters
          (List<HttpMessageConverter<?>> converters) {
  converters.add(new ByteArrayHttpMessageConverter());
}
```

3. If you want to have a bit more control, we can override the
   `extendMessageConverters` method in the following way:

```
@Override
public void extendMessageConverters
            (List<HttpMessageConverter<?>> converters) {
    converters.clear();
    converters.add(new ByteArrayHttpMessageConverter());
}
```

How it works...

As you can see, Spring gives us multiple ways of achieving the same thing and it all depends on our preference or particular details of the implementation.

We covered three different ways of adding `HttpMessageConverter` to our application. So what is the difference, one might ask?

Declaring `HttpMessageConverter` as `@Bean` is the quickest and simplest way of adding a custom converter to the application. It is similar to how we added servlet filters in an earlier example. If Spring detects a bean of the `HttpMessageConverter` type, it will add it to the list automatically. If we did not have a `WebConfiguration` class that implements `WebMvcConfigurer`, it would have been the preferred approach.

When the application needs to define a more precise control over the settings, like interceptors, mappings, etc, it is best to use `WebMvcConfigurer` implementation to configure those, as it would be more consistent to override the `configureMessageConverters` method and add our converter to the list. As there can be multiple instances of `WebMvcConfigurers`, which could be either added by us or via the auto-configuration settings from various Spring Boot starters, there is no guarantee that our method can get called in any particular order.

If we need to do something even more drastic such as removing all the other converters from the list or clearing it of duplicate converters, this is where overriding `extendMessageConverters` comes into play. This method gets invoked after all the `WebMvcConfigurers` get called for `configureMessageConverters` and the list of converters is fully populated. Of course, it is entirely possible that some other instance of `WebMvcConfigurer` could override `extendMessageConverters` as well; but the chances of this are very low so you have a high degree of having the desired impact.

Configuring custom PropertyEditors

In the previous example, we learned how to configure converters for an HTTP request and response data. There are other kinds of conversions that take place, especially in regards to dynamically converting parameters to various objects, such as Strings to Date or an Integer.

When we declare a mapping method in a controller, Spring allows us to freely define the method signature with the exact object types that we require. The way in which this is achieved is via the use of the `PropertyEditor` implementations. `PropertyEditor` is a default concept defined as part of the JDK and designed to allow the transformation of a textual value to a given type. It was initially intended to be used to build Java Swing / **Abstract Window Toolkit (AWT)** GUI and later proved to be a good fit for Spring's need to convert web parameters to method argument types.

Spring MVC already provides you with a lot of `PropertyEditor` implementations for most of the common types, such as Boolean, Currency, and Class. Let's say that we want to create a proper `Isbn` class object and use this in our controller instead of a plain String.

How to do it...

1. First, we will need to remove the `extendMessageConverters` method from our `WebConfiguration` class as the `converters.clear()` call will break the rendering because we removed all of the supported type converters

2. Let's create a new package called `model` under the `src/main/java/com/example/bookpub` directory from the root of our project

3. Next we create a class named `Isbn` under our newly created package directory from the root of our project with the following content:

```
package com.example.bookpub.model;

import org.springframework.util.Assert;

public class Isbn {
    private String eanPrefix;
    private String registrationGroup;
    private String registrant;
```

```java
private String publication;
private String checkDigit;

public Isbn(String eanPrefix, String registrationGroup,
            String registrant, String publication,
            String checkDigit) {

    this.eanPrefix = eanPrefix;
    this.registrationGroup = registrationGroup;
    this.registrant = registrant;
    this.publication = publication;
    this.checkDigit = checkDigit;
}

public String getEanPrefix() {
    return eanPrefix;
}

public void setEanPrefix(String eanPrefix) {
    this.eanPrefix = eanPrefix;
}

public String getRegistrationGroup() {
    return registrationGroup;
}

public void setRegistrationGroup
            (String registrationGroup)  {
    this.registrationGroup = registrationGroup;
}

public String getRegistrant() {
    return registrant;
}

public void setRegistrant(String registrant) {
    this.registrant = registrant;
}

public String getPublication() {
    return publication;
}

public void setPublication(String publication) {
    this.publication = publication;
}

public String getCheckDigit() {
```

```
            return checkDigit;
        }

        public void setCheckDigit(String checkDigit) {
            this.checkDigit = checkDigit;
        }

        public static Isbn parseFrom(String isbn) {
            Assert.notNull(isbn);
            String[] parts = isbn.split("-");
            Assert.state(parts.length == 5);
            Assert.noNullElements(parts);
            return new Isbn(parts[0], parts[1], parts[2],
                parts[3], parts[4]);
        }

        @Override
        public String toString() {
            return eanPrefix + '-'
                + registrationGroup + '-'
                + registrant + '-'
                + publication + '-'
                + checkDigit;
        }
    }
```

4. Let's create a new package called `editors` under the `src/main/java/com/example/bookpub` directory from the root of our project

5. Let's create a class named `IsbnEditor` under our newly created package directory from the root of our project with the following content:

```
package com.example.bookpub.editors;

import org.springframework.util.StringUtils;
import com.example.bookpub.model.Isbn;

import java.beans.PropertyEditorSupport;

public class IsbnEditor extends PropertyEditorSupport {
    @Override
    public void setAsText(String text) {
        if (text == null) {
            setValue(null);
        }
        else {
            String value = text.trim();
```

```
            if (!StringUtils.isEmpty(value)) {
                setValue(Isbn.parseFrom(value));
            } else {
                setValue(null);
            }
        }
    }

    @Override
    public String getAsText() {
        Object value = getValue();
        return (value != null ? value.toString() : "");
    }
}
```

6. Next, we will add a method, `initBinder`, to `BookController` where we will configure the `IsbnEditor` method with the following content:

```
@InitBinder
public void initBinder(WebDataBinder binder) {
  binder.registerCustomEditor(Isbn.class, new
    IsbnEditor());
}
```

7. Our `getBook` method in `BookController` will also change in order to accept the `Isbn` object, in the following way:

```
@RequestMapping(value = "/{isbn}", method =
  RequestMethod.GET)
public Book getBook(@PathVariable Isbn isbn) {
    return bookRepository.findBookByIsbn(isbn.toString());
}
```

8. Start the application by running `./gradlew clean bootRun`

9. In the browser, go to
   `http://localhost:8080/books/978-1-78528-415-1`

10. While we will not observe any visible changes, `IsbnEditor` is indeed at work, creating an instance of an `Isbn` class object from the `{isbn}` parameter

How it works...

Spring automatically configures a large number of default editors; but for custom types, we have to explicitly instantiate new editors for every web request. This is done in the controller in a method that is annotated with `@InitBinder`. This annotation is scanned and all the detected methods should have a signature of accepting `WebDataBinder` as an argument. Among other things, `WebDataBinder` provides us with an ability to register as many custom editors as we require for the controller methods to be bound properly.

> It is very important to know that `PropertyEditor` is not thread-safe! For this reason, we have to create a new instance of our custom editors for every web request and register them with `WebDataBinder`.

In case a new `PropertyEditor` is needed, it is best to create one by extending `PropertyEditorSupport` and overriding the desired methods with custom implementation.

Configuring custom type formatters

Mostly because of its statefulness and lack of thread safety, since version 3, Spring has added a `Formatter` interface as a replacement for `PropertyEditor`. The formatters are intended to provide a similar functionality but in a completely thread-safe manner and focusing on a very specific task of parsing a String in an object type and converting an object to its String representation.

Let's suppose that for our application, we would like to have a formatter that would take the ISBN number of a book in a String form and convert it to a book entity object. This way, we can define the controller request methods with a `Book` argument when the request URL signature only contains an ISBN number or a database ID.

How to do it...

1. First, let's create a new package called `formatters` in the `src/main/java/com/example/bookpub` directory from the root of our project

2. Next, we will create the `Formatter` implementation called `BookFormatter` in our newly created package directory from the root of our project with the following content:

```
public class BookFormatter implements Formatter<Book> {
  private BookRepository repository;
  public BookFormatter(BookRepository repository) {
    this.repository= repository;
  }
  @Override
  public Book parse(String bookIdentifier, Locale locale)
      throws ParseException {
    Book book = repository.findBookByIsbn(bookIdentifier);
    return book != null ? book :
        repository.findById(Long.valueOf(bookIdentifier))
          .get();
  }
  @Override
  public String print(Book book, Locale locale) {
    return book.getIsbn();
  }
}
```

3. Now that we have our formatter, we will add it to the registry by overriding an `addFormatters(FormatterRegistry registry)` method in the `WebConfiguration` class:

```
@Autowired
private BookRepository bookRepository;
@Override
public void addFormatters(FormatterRegistry registry) {
  registry.addFormatter(new BookFormatter(bookRepository));
}
```

4. Finally, let's add a new request method to our `BookController` class located in the `src/main/java/com/example/bookpub/controllers` directory from the root of our project that will display the reviewers for a given ISBN of a book:

```
@RequestMapping(value = "/{isbn}/reviewers", method =
    RequestMethod.GET)
public List<Reviewer> getReviewers(@PathVariable("isbn")
    Book book) {
  return book.getReviewers();
}
```

5. Just so we can have some data to play with, let's manually (for now) populate our database with some test data by adding two more autowired repositories to the `StartupRunner` class:

```
@Autowired
private AuthorRepository authorRepository;
@Autowired
private PublisherRepository publisherRepository;
```

6. The following code snippet is destined for the `run(...)` method of `StartupRunner`:

```
Author author = new Author("Alex", "Antonov");
author = authorRepository.save(author);
Publisher publisher = new Publisher("Packt");
publisher = publisherRepository.save(publisher);
Book book = new Book("978-1-78528-415-1",
    "Spring Boot Recipes", author, publisher);
bookRepository.save(book);
```

7. Start the application by running `./gradlew clean bootRun`

8. Let's open `http://localhost:8080/books/978-1-78528-415-1/reviewers` in the browser and you should be able to see the following results:

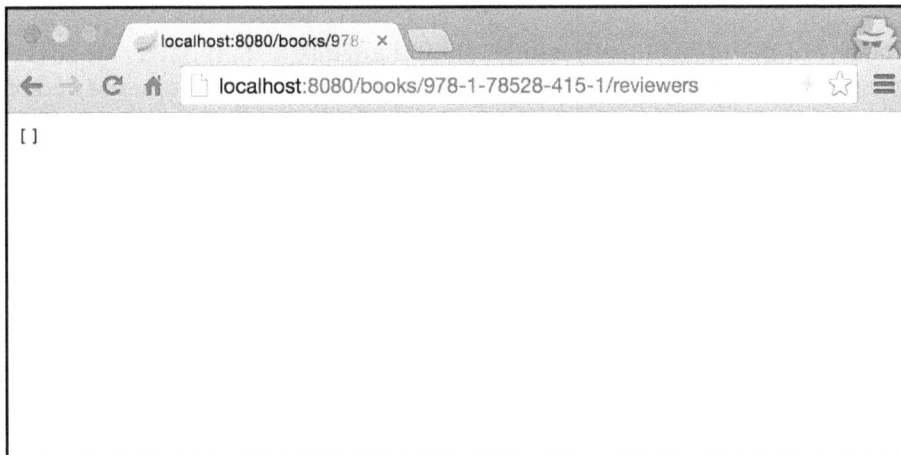

How it works...

The formatter facility is aims to provide a similar functionality to `PropertyEditors`. By registering our formatter with `FormatterRegistry` in the overridden `addFormatters` method, we are instructing Spring to use our formatter to translate a textual representation of our book into an entity object and back. As formatters are stateless, we don't need to do the registration in our controller for every call; we have to do it only once and this will ensure Spring uses it for every web request.

> It is also good to remember that if you want to define a conversion of a common type, such as String or Boolean, for example trimming text, it is best to do this via `PropertyEditors` in controller's `InitBinder` because such a change is probably not globally desired and is only needed for a particular functionality.

You have probably noticed that we also autowired `BookRepository` to a `WebConfiguration` class, as this was needed to create `BookFormatter`. This is one of the cool parts about Spring --it lets us combine the configuration classes and make them dependent on the other beans at the same time. As we indicated that in order for a `WebConfiguration` class to be created we need `BookRepository`, Spring ensured that `BookRepository` will be created first and then automatically injected as a dependency during the creation of the `WebConfiguration` class. After `WebConfiguration` is instantiated, it is processed for configuration instructions.

The rest of the added functionalities should already be familiar as we covered them in our previous recipes. We will explore how to automatically populate databases with schemas and data in Chapter 24, *Application Testing*, in detail, where we will also talk about application testing.

22

Web Framework Behavior Tuning

In this chapter, we will learn about the following topics:

- Configuring route matching patterns
- Configuring custom static path mappings
- Tuning Tomcat via ServletWebServerFactory
- Choosing embedded servlet containers
- Adding custom connectors

Introduction

In Chapter 21, *Configuring Web Applications*, we explored how to configure web applications in Spring Boot with our custom filters, interceptors, and so on. We will continue to look further into enhancing our web application by doing behavior tuning, configuring the custom routing rules and patterns, adding additional static asset paths, adding and modifying servlet container connectors, and other properties such as enabling SSL.

Configuring route matching patterns

When we build web applications, it is not always the case that a default out-of-the-box mapping configuration is applicable. At times, we want to create RESTful URLs that contain characters such as dot (.), which Spring treats as a delimiter-defining format, like path.xml; or we might not want to recognize a trailing slash, and so on. Conveniently, Spring provides us with a way to accomplish this with ease.

In Chapter 21, *Configuring Web Applications*, we introduced a WebConfiguration class, which extends from WebMvcConfigurerAdapter. This extension allows us to override methods that are geared toward adding filters, formatters, and many more. It also has methods that can be overridden in order to configure the path match, among other things.

Let's imagine that the ISBN format does allow the use of dots to separate the book number from the revision with a pattern looking like [isbn-number].[revision].

How to do it...

We will configure our application to not use the suffix pattern match of .* and to not strip the values after the dot when parsing the parameters. Let's perform the following steps:

1. Let's add the necessary configuration to our WebConfiguration class with the following content:

```
@Override
public void
  configurePathMatch(PathMatchConfigurer configurer) {
    configurer.setUseSuffixPatternMatch(false).
      setUseTrailingSlashMatch(true);
}
```

2. Start the application by running ./gradlew clean bootRun.

3. Let's open `http://localhost:8080/books/978-1-78528-415-1.1` in the browser to see the following results:

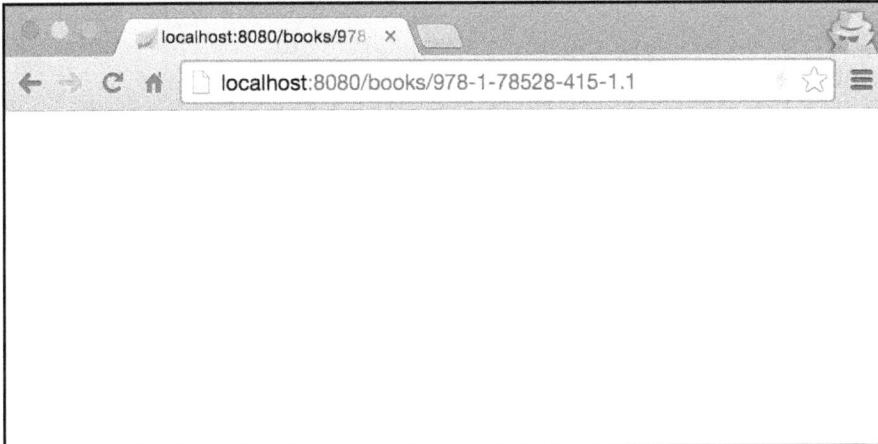

4. If we enter the correct ISBN, we will see a different result, as follows:

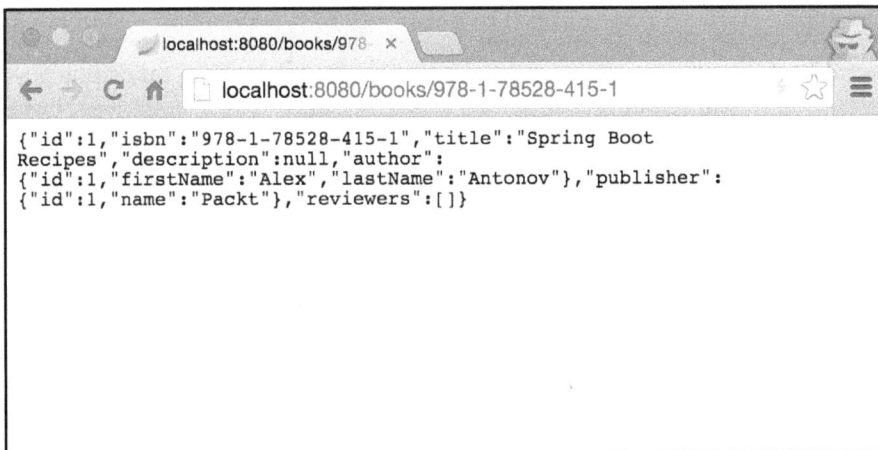

How it works...

Let's look at what we did in detail. The
`configurePathMatch(PathMatchConfigurer configurer)` method gives us the
ability to set our own behavior in how we want Spring to match the request URL path
to the controller parameters:

- `configurer.setUseSuffixPatternMatch(false)`: This method
  indicates that we don't want to use the `.*` suffix, so as to strip the trailing
  characters after the last dot. This means that Spring parses out the entire
  `978-1-78528-415-1.1` ISBN as an `{isbn}` parameter for
  `BookController`.
  So, `http://localhost:8080/books/978-1-78528-415-1.1` and
  `http://localhost:8080/books/978-1-78528-415-1` will become
  different URLs.
- `configurer.setUseTrailingSlashMatch(true)`: This method
  indicates that we want to use the trailing `/` symbol in the URL as a match as
  if it were not there. This effectively makes
  `http://localhost:8080/books/978-1-78528-415-1` the same as
  `http://localhost:8080/books/978-1-78528-415-1/`.

If you want to do further configuration of how the path matching takes place, you can
provide your own implementation of `PathMatcher` and `UrlPathHelper`, but these
would be required in the most extreme and custom-tailored situations and are not
generally recommended.

Configuring custom static path mappings

In the previous recipe, we looked at how to tune the URL path mapping for requests
and translate them into controller methods. It is also possible to control how our web
application deals with static assets and the files that exist on the filesystem or are
bundled in the deployable archive.

Let's say that we want to expose our internal `application.properties` file via the
static web URL of
`http://localhost:8080/internal/application.properties` from our
application. To get started with this, proceed with the steps in the next section.

How to do it...

1. Let's add a new method, `addResourceHandlers`, to the `WebConfiguration` class with the following content:

```
@Override
public void addResourceHandlers(ResourceHandlerRegistry
registry) {
    registry.addResourceHandler("/internal/**")
            .addResourceLocations("classpath:/");
}
```

2. Start the application by running `./gradlew clean bootRun`

3. Let's open
`http://localhost:8080/internal/application.properties` in the browser to see the following results:

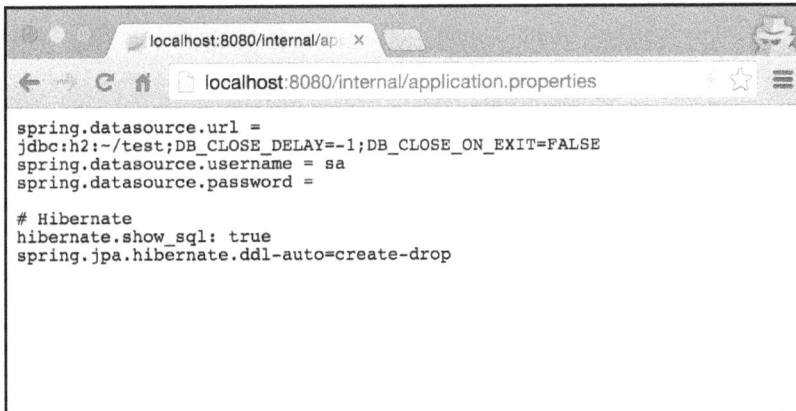

How it works...

The method that we overrode,
`addResourceHandlers(ResourceHandlerRegistry registry)`, is another
configuration method from `WebMvcConfigurer`, which gives us the ability to define
custom mappings for static resource URLs and connect them with the resources on
the filesystem or application classpath. In our case, we defined a mapping of anything
that is being accessed via the `/ internal` URL to be looked for in
the `classpath:/` path of our application (for the production environment, you
probably don't want to expose the entire classpath as a static resource!).

So let's look at what we did in detail, as follows:

- The `registry.addResourceHandler("/internal/**")` method adds a resource handler to the registry to handle our static resources, and returns `ResourceHandlerRegistration` to us, which can be used to further configure the mapping in a chained fashion. The `/internal/**` is a path pattern that will be used to match against the request URL using `PathMatcher`. We have seen how `PathMatcher` can be configured in the previous example, but by default an `AntPathMatcher` implementation is used. We can configure more than one URL pattern to be matched to a particular resource location.
- The `addResourceLocations("classpath:/")` method is called on the newly created instance of `ResourceHandlerRegistration`, and it defines the directories where the resources should be loaded from. These should be valid filesystems or classpath directories, and more than one can be entered. If multiple locations are provided, they will be checked in the order in which they were entered.

We can also configure a caching interval for the given resource using the `setCachePeriod(Integer cachePeriod)` method.

Tuning Tomcat via ServletWebServerFactory

Spring Boot exposes many of the server properties that can be used to configure things such as PORT, SSL, and others by simply setting the values in `application.properties`. However, if we need to do any more complex tuning, Spring Boot provides us with a `ServletWebServerFactory` interface to programmatically define our configuration.

Even though the session timeout can be easily configured by setting the `server.session.timeout` property in `application.properties` to our desired value in seconds, we will do it using `ServletWebServerFactory` to demonstrate how it is done.

How to do it...

1. Let's say that we want our session to be for one minute. To make this happen, we will ad a `ServletWebServerFactory` bean to our `WebConfiguration` class with the following content:

```
@Bean
public ServletWebServerFactory servletContainer() {
  TomcatServletWebServerFactory tomcat =
        new TomcatServletWebServerFactory();
  tomcat.getSession().setTimeout(Duration.ofMinutes(1));
  return tomcat;
}
```

2. Just for the purpose of demonstration, we will get the session from the request to force its creation. To do this, we will add a new request mapping to our `BookController` class with the following content:

```
@RequestMapping(value = "/session", method =
   RequestMethod.GET)
public String getSessionId(HttpServletRequest request) {
  return request.getSession().getId();
}
```

3. Start the application by running `./gradlew clean bootRun`.

4. Let's open `http://localhost:8080/books/session` in the browser to see the following results:

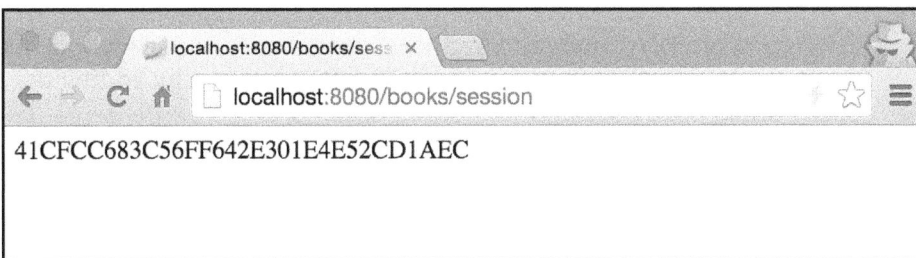

If we wait for more than a minute and then reload this page, the session ID will change to a different one.

How it works...

The ServletWebServerFactory interface defines the WebServer getWebServer(ServletContextInitializer... initializers) method. Out of the box, Spring Boot provides concrete factory implementations for the TomcatServletWebServerFactory, JettyServletWebServerFactory, and UndertowServletWebServerFactory application servers. Since we are using Tomcat in our example, we will be using the provided TomcatServletWebServerFactory class to configure the behavior of the session.

During application startup, Spring Boot autoconfiguration detects the presence of the factory and invokes the getWebServer(...) method, passing the reference to a collection of ServletContextInitializer beans. Typically, those initializers are created and managed by Spring Boot internally, but we can always create some custom ServletContextInitializer beans to add custom behavior that should be executed during the startup life cycle of the application server.

Choosing embedded servlet containers

If we decide that we want to use Jetty as our servlet container, we will need to add a Jetty starter to our build file.

How to do it...

1. As Tomcat already comes as a transitive dependency of Spring Boot, we will need to exclude it from our build dependency tree by adding the following to build.gradle:

```
configurations {
  compile.exclude module: "spring-boot-starter-tomcat"
}
```

2. We will also need to add a compile dependency to our build dependencies on Jetty:

```
compile("org.springframework.boot:spring-boot-starter-jetty")
```

3. To fix the compiler errors, we will need to remove the bean declaration of Tomcat's `RemoteIpFilter` from our `WebConfiguration` class, as the Tomcat dependency has been removed.

4. Start the application by running `./gradlew clean bootRun`

5. If we now look at the console logs, we will see that our application is running in Jetty:

```
2017-12-16 --- o.eclipse.jetty.server.AbstractConnector
  : Started ServerConnector...
2017-12-16 ---.o.s.b.web.embedded.jetty.JettyWebServer
  : Jetty started on port(s) 8080 (http/1.1)...
```

How it works...

The reason that this works is because of Spring Boot's autoconfiguration magic. We had to remove the Tomcat dependency from the `build` file in order to prevent a dependency collision between Tomcat and Jetty. Spring Boot does a conditional scan of the classes in the classpath and depending on what it detects, it determines which servlet container will be used.

If we look in the `ServletWebServerFactoryAutoConfiguration` class, we will see the following conditional code that checks this:

```
/**
 * Nested configuration if Jetty is being used.
 */
@Configuration
@ConditionalOnClass({ Servlet.class, Server.class,
Loader.class})
@ConditionalOnMissingBean(value =
ServletWebServerFactory.class,
                          search = SearchStrategy.CURRENT)
public static class EmbeddedJetty {

  @Bean
  public JettyServletWebServerFactory
      JettyServletWebServerFactory() {
          return new JettyServletWebServerFactory();
  }

}
```

The `@ConditionalOnClass` annotation tells Spring Boot to use only the `EmbeddedJetty` configuration if the classes of Jetty, namely `org.eclipse.jetty.server.Server` and `org.eclipse.jetty.util.Loader`, are present in the classpath.

Adding custom connectors

Another very common scenario in the enterprise application development and deployment is to run the application with two separate HTTP port connectors: one for HTTP and the other for HTTPS

Getting ready

We will start by going back to using Tomcat; so for this recipe, we will undo the changes that we implemented in the previous example.

In order to create an HTTPS connector, we will need a few things; but most importantly, we will need to generate the certificate keystore that is used to encrypt and decrypt the SSL communication with the browser.

If you are using Unix or macOS, you can do it by running the following command:

```
$JAVA_HOME/bin/keytool -genkey -alias tomcat -keyalg RSA
```

On Windows, this can be achieved via the following command:

```
"%JAVA_HOME%binkeytool" -genkey -alias tomcat -keyalg RSA
```

During the creation of the keystore, you should enter the information that is appropriate to you, including passwords, name, and so on. For the purpose of this book, we will use the default password: `changeit`. Once the execution is complete, a newly generated keystore file will appear in your home directory under the name: `keystore`.

> You can find more information about preparing the certificate keystore at `https://tomcat.apache.org/tomcat-8.0-doc/ssl-howto.html#Prepare_the_Certificate_Keystore`.

How to do it...

With the keystore creation complete, we will need to create a separate `properties` file in order to store our configuration for the HTTPS connectors, such as port. After that, we will create a configuration property binding object and use it to configure our new connector. Perform the following steps:

1. First, we will create a new properties file named `tomcat.https.properties` in the `src/main/resources` directory from the root of our project with the following content:

   ```
   custom.tomcat.https.port=8443
   custom.tomcat.https.secure=true
   custom.tomcat.https.scheme=https
   custom.tomcat.https.ssl=true
   custom.tomcat.https.keystore=${user.home}/.keystore
   custom.tomcat.https.keystore-password=changeit
   ```

2. Next, we will create a nested static class named `TomcatSslConnectorProperties` in our `WebConfiguration` class with the following content:

   ```
   @ConfigurationProperties(prefix = "custom.tomcat.https")
   public static class TomcatSslConnectorProperties {
     private Integer port;
     private Boolean ssl = true;
     private Boolean secure = true;
     private String scheme = "https";
     private File keystore;
     private String keystorePassword;
     //Skipping getters and setters to save space, but we do need
   them

     public void configureConnector(Connector connector) {
       if (port != null)
         connector.setPort(port);
       if (secure != null)
         connector.setSecure(secure);
       if (scheme != null)
         connector.setScheme(scheme);
       if (ssl!= null)
         connector.setProperty("SSLEnabled", ssl.toString());
       if (keystore!= null &&keystore.exists()) {
         connector.setProperty("keystoreFile",
           keystore.getAbsolutePath());
         connector.setProperty("keystorePassword",
   ```

```
                        keystorePassword);
        }
      }
    }
```

3. Now, we will need to add our newly created `tomcat.http.properties`
   file as a Spring Boot property source and enable
   `TomcatSslConnectorProperties` to be bound. This can be done by
   adding the following code right prior to the class declaration of the
   `WebConfiguration` class:

```
@Configuration
@PropertySource("classpath:/tomcat.https.properties")
@EnableConfigurationProperties(WebConfiguration.TomcatSslConne
ctorProperties.class)
public class WebConfiguration extends WebMvcConfigurerAdapter
{...}
```

4. Finally, we will need to modify a `ServletWebServerFactory` Spring
   bean, where we will add our HTTPS connector. We will do that by
   changing the following code in the `WebConfiguration` class:

```
@Bean
public ServletWebServerFactory servletContainer
            (TomcatSslConnectorProperties properties) {
    TomcatServletWebServerFactory tomcat =
        new TomcatServletWebServerFactory();
    tomcat.addAdditionalTomcatConnectors
        (createSslConnector(properties));
    tomcat.getSession().setTimeout(Duration.ofMinutes(1));
    return tomcat;
}
private Connector createSslConnector
            (TomcatSslConnectorProperties properties) {
    Connector connector = new Connector();
    properties.configureConnector(connector);
    return connector;
}
```

5. Start the application by running `./gradlew clean bootRun`.

6. Let's open
   `https://localhost:8443/internal/tomcat.https.properties` in the browser to see the following results:

```
custom.tomcat.https.port=8443
custom.tomcat.https.secure=true
custom.tomcat.https.scheme=https
custom.tomcat.https.ssl=true
custom.tomcat.https.keystore=${user.home}/.keystore
custom.tomcat.https.keystore-password=changeit
```

How it works...

In this recipe, we did a number of things; so let's break them down one change at a time.

The first change, ignoring the need to create the keystore, was the creation of the `tomcat.https.properties` and `TomcatSslConnectorProperties` objects to bind them to. Previously, we already dealt with making changes to the various settings in `application.properties` when configuring our datasource. At that time, though, we did not have to create any binding objects because Spring Boot already had them defined.

As we learned earlier, Spring Boot already exposes many properties to configure the application settings, including a whole set of settings for the `server` section. These values get bound to an internal Spring Boot class: `ServerProperties`

> A complete list of the common application properties can be found in the Spring Boot reference documentation at `http://docs.spring.io/spring-boot/docs/current/reference/html/common-application-properties.html`.

What we did with our addition was simply mimic Spring Boot and create our own configuration group with a binding object behind it. The reason that we didn't use the already existing `server.tomcat.` prefix, and instead opt for `custom.tomcat`, was mostly governed by the need to separate our config values from the default ones. Since we are adding a second connector, we want to have a clean separation between the default configuration properties and our custom ones.

The `@ConfigurationProperties(prefix = "custom.tomcat.https")` method is an important annotation for our `TomcatSslConnectorProperties` object. It tells Spring Boot to automatically bind the properties with the `custom.tomcat.https` prefix to fields that are declared in `TomcatSslConnectorProperties`. In order for the binding to take place—in addition to defining the fields in the class—it is very important to define the getters and setters as well. It is also worth mentioning that during the binding process, Spring will automatically try to convert the property values to their appropriate data types. For example, the value of `custom.tomcat.https.keystore` gets automatically bound to a private file keystore field object.

> The converters, which we learned about earlier, will also be used during the process of converting to custom-defined data types.

The next step is to tell Spring Boot to include the properties that are defined in `tomcat.https.properties` in the list of properties. This is achieved by adding `@PropertySource("classpath:/tomcat.https.properties")` next to `@Configuration` in the `WebConfiguration` class.

After the values are imported, we will need to tell Spring Boot to automatically create an instance of `TomcatSslConnectorProperties` for us to use. This is done by adding the following annotation next to `@Configuration`:

```
@EnableConfigurationProperties(WebConfiguration.TomcatSslConnectorProp
erties.class)
```

This will instruct Spring Boot to automatically create a bean of type `TomcatSslConnectorProperties` and bind it with the values from the specified `classpath:/tomcat.https.properties` file. This bean can later be used for autowiring into different places, such as when we create a `ServletWebServerFactory` bean.

After all the property support is set and done, we will proceed with the actual code to create a second connector. The creation of the `ServletWebServerFactory` bean provides Spring Boot with a factory to use in order to create `WebServer`. The convenient `configureConnector(Connector connector)` method, which we added to `TomcatSslConnectorProperties`, gives us a good place to encapsulate and consolidate all the settings that are needed to configure the newly created `Connector` instance.

23
Writing Custom Spring Boot Starters

In this chapter, we will cover the following topics:

- Understanding Spring Boot autoconfiguration
- Creating a custom Spring Boot autoconfiguration starter
- Configuring custom conditional bean instantiations
- Using custom @Enable annotations to toggle configurations

Introduction

In the previous chapters, we did a lot of configuration, and even more autoconfiguration, while developing our Spring Boot application. Now, it is time to take a look behind the scenes to find out the magic behind Spring Boot autoconfiguration and write some starters of our own as well.

This is a very useful capability to possess, especially for large software enterprises where the presence of a proprietary code is inevitable. It is very helpful to be able to create internal custom starters that would automatically add some of the configuration or functionalities to the applications. Some likely candidates would be custom configuration systems, libraries, and configurations that deal with connecting to databases, using custom connection pools, HTTP clients, servers, and more. We will go through the internals of Spring Boot autoconfiguration, take a look at how new starters are created, explore conditional initialization and wiring of beans based on various rules, and see that annotations can be a powerful tool, providing the consumers of the starters with more control over dictating what configurations should be used and where.

Understanding Spring Boot autoconfiguration

Spring Boot has a lot of power when it comes to bootstrapping an application and configuring it with exactly the things that are needed, all without much of the glue code that is required of us, the developers. The secret behind this power actually comes from Spring itself, or rather from the Java Configuration functionality that it provides. As we add more starters as dependencies, more and more classes will appear in our classpath. Spring Boot detects the presence or absence of specific classes and based on this information, makes some decisions, which are fairly complicated at times, and automatically creates and wires the necessary beans to the application context.

Sounds simple, right?

In the previous recipes, we added a number of Spring Boot starters such as `spring-boot-starter-data-jpa`, `spring-boot-starter-web`, `spring-boot-starter-data-test`, and so on. We will use the same code that we finished in the previous chapter, in order to see what actually happens during the application startup and the decisions that Spring Boot will make while wiring our application together.

How to do it...

1. Conveniently, Spring Boot provides us with an ability to get the `CONDITIONS EVALUATION REPORT` by simply starting the application with the `debug` flag. This can be passed to the application either as an environment variable, `DEBUG`, as a system property, `-Ddebug`, or as an application property, `--debug`.
2. Start the application by running `DEBUG=true ./gradlew clean bootRun`.
3. Now, if you look at the console logs, you will see a lot more information printed there that is marked with the `DEBUG` level log. At the end of the startup log sequence, we will see the `CONDITIONS EVALUATION REPORT` as follows:

```
=========================
CONDITIONS EVALUATION REPORT
=========================
Positive matches:
```

```
-------------------
...
DataSourceAutoConfiguration
      - @ConditionalOnClass classes found:
        javax.sql.DataSource,org.springframework.jdbc.
        datasource.embedded.EmbeddedDatabaseType
        (OnClassCondition)
        ...
Negative matches:
-------------------
...
GsonAutoConfiguration
      - required @ConditionalOnClass classes not found:
        com.google.gson.Gson (OnClassCondition)
        ...
```

How it works...

As you can see, the amount of information that is printed in the debug mode can be somewhat overwhelming, so I've selected only one example of positive and negative matches each.

For each line of the report, Spring Boot tells us why certain configurations have been selected to be included, what they have been positively matched on, or, for the negative matches, what was missing that prevented a particular configuration being included in the mix. Let's look at the positive match for `DataSourceAutoConfiguration`:

- The `@ConditionalOnClass` classes found tells us that Spring Boot has detected the presence of a particular class, specifically two classes in our case: `javax.sql.DataSource` and `org.springframework.jdbc.datasource.embedded.EmbeddedDatabaseType`.
- The `OnClassCondition` indicates the kind of matching that was used. This is supported by the `@ConditionalOnClass` and `@ConditionalOnMissingClass` annotations.

While `OnClassCondition` is the most common kind of detection, Spring Boot also uses many other conditions. For example, `OnBeanCondition` is used to check the presence or absence of specific bean instances, `OnPropertyCondition` is used to check the presence, absence, or specific value of a property, as well as any number of the custom conditions that can be defined using the `@Conditional` annotation and `Condition` interface implementations.

The negative matches show us a list of configurations that Spring Boot has evaluated, which means that they do exist in the classpath and were scanned by Spring Boot but didn't pass the conditions required for their inclusion. `GsonAutoConfiguration`, while available in the classpath as it is a part of the imported `spring-boot-autoconfigure` artifact, was not included because the required `com.google.gson.Gson` class was not detected as present in the classpath, thus failing the `OnClassCondition`.

The implementation of the `GsonAutoConfiguration` file looks as follows:

```
@Configuration
@ConditionalOnClass(Gson.class)
public class GsonAutoConfiguration {

  @Bean
  @ConditionalOnMissingBean
  public Gson gson() {
    return new Gson();
  }

}
```

After looking at the code, it is very easy to make the connection between the conditional annotations and report information that is provided by Spring Boot at the start time.

Creating a custom Spring Boot autoconfiguration starter

We have a high-level idea of the process by which Spring Boot decides which configurations to include in the formation of the application context. Now, let's take a stab at creating our own Spring Boot starter artifact, which we can include as an autoconfigurable dependency in our build.

In Chapter 21, *Configuring Web Applications*, you learned how to create database Repository objects. So, let's build a simple starter that will create another CommandLineRunner that will take the collection of all the Repository instances and print out the count of the total entries for each.

We will start by adding a child Gradle project to our existing project that will house the codebase for the starter artifact. We will call it db-count-starter.

How to do it...

1. We will start by creating a new directory named db-count-starter in the root of our project.
2. As our project has now become what is known as a multiproject build, we will need to create a settings.gradle configuration file in the root of our project with the following content:

```
include 'db-count-starter'
```

3. We should also create a separate build.gradle configuration file for our subproject in the db-count-starter directory in the root of our project, with the following content:

```
apply plugin: 'java'

repositories {
  mavenCentral()
  maven { url "https://repo.spring.io/snapshot" }
  maven { url "https://repo.spring.io/milestone" }

}

dependencies {
  compile("org.springframework.boot:spring-boot:2.0.0.BUILD-
SNAPSHOT")
  compile("org.springframework.data:spring-data-
commons:2.0.2.RELEASE")
}
```

4. Now we are ready to start coding. So, the first thing is to create the directory structure, src/main/java/com/example/bookpubstarter/dbcount, in the db-count-starter directory in the root of our project.

5. In the newly created directory, let's add our implementation of the `CommandLineRunner` file named `DbCountRunner.java` with the following content:

```
public class DbCountRunner implements CommandLineRunner {
    protected final Log logger =
LogFactory.getLog(getClass());

    private Collection<CrudRepository> repositories;

    public DbCountRunner(Collection<CrudRepository>
repositories) {
        this.repositories = repositories;
    }

    @Override
    public void run(String... args) throws Exception {
        repositories.forEach(crudRepository ->
            logger.info(String.format("%s has %s entries",
                getRepositoryName(crudRepository.getClass()),
                crudRepository.count())));
    }

    private static String
            getRepositoryName(Class crudRepositoryClass) {
        for(Class repositoryInterface :
                crudRepositoryClass.getInterfaces()) {
            if (repositoryInterface.getName().
startsWith("com.example.bookpub.repository")) {
                return repositoryInterface.getSimpleName();
            }
        }
        return "UnknownRepository";
    }
}
```

6. With the actual implementation of `DbCountRunner` in place, we will now need to create the configuration object that will declaratively create an instance during the configuration phase. So, let's create a new class file called `DbCountAutoConfiguration.java` with the following content:

```
@Configuration
public class DbCountAutoConfiguration {
    @Bean
    public DbCountRunner dbCountRunner
            (Collection<CrudRepository> repositories) {
```

```
            return new DbCountRunner(repositories);
      }
   }
```

7. We will also need to tell Spring Boot that our newly created JAR artifact contains the autoconfiguration classes. For this, we will need to create a `resources/META-INF` directory in the `db-count-starter/src/main` directory in the root of our project.

8. In this newly created directory, we will place the file named `spring.factories` with the following content:

```
org.springframework.boot.autoconfigure.EnableAutoConfiguration
=
com.example.bookpubstarter.dbcount.DbCountAutoConfiguration
```

9. For the purpose of our demo, we will add the dependency to our starter artifact in the main project's `build.gradle` by adding the following entry in the dependencies section:

```
compile project(':db-count-starter')
```

10. Start the application by running `./gradlew clean bootRun`.

11. Once the application is compiled and has started, we should see the following in the console logs:

```
    2017-12-16 INFO com.example.bookpub.StartupRunner         :
Welcome to the Book Catalog System!
    2017-12-16 INFO c.e.b.dbcount.DbCountRunner               :
AuthorRepository has 1 entries
    2017-12-16 INFO c.e.b.dbcount.DbCountRunner               :
PublisherRepository has 1 entries
    2017-12-16 INFO c.e.b.dbcount.DbCountRunner               :
BookRepository has 1 entries
    2017-12-16 INFO c.e.b.dbcount.DbCountRunner               :
ReviewerRepository has 0 entries
    2017-12-16 INFO com.example.bookpub.BookPubApplication    :
Started BookPubApplication in 8.528 seconds (JVM running for
9.002)
    2017-12-16 INFO com.example.bookpub.StartupRunner         :
Number of books: 1
```

How it works...

Congratulations! You have now built your very own Spring Boot autoconfiguration starter.

First, let's quickly walk through the changes that we made to our Gradle build configuration and then we will examine the starter setup in detail.

As the Spring Boot starter is a separate, independent artifact, just adding more classes to our existing project source tree would not really demonstrate much. To make this separate artifact, we have a couple of choices: making a separate Gradle configuration in our existing project, or creating a completely separate project altogether. The most ideal solution, however, was to just convert our build to Gradle Multi-Project Build by adding a nested project directory and subproject dependency to the `build.gradle` file of the root project. By doing this, Gradle actually creates a separate JAR artifact for us but we don't have to publish it anywhere, only include it as a compile `project(':db-count-starter')` dependency.

> For more information about Gradle multi-project builds, you can check out the manual at `http://gradle.org/docs/current/userguide/multi_project_buil ds.html`.

The Spring Boot Auto-Configuration starter is nothing more than a regular Spring Java Configuration class annotated with the `@Configuration` annotation and the presence of `spring.factories` in the classpath in the `META-INF` directory with the appropriate configuration entries.

During the application startup, Spring Boot uses `SpringFactoriesLoader`, which is a part of Spring Core, in order to get a list of the Spring Java Configurations that are configured for the `org.springframework.boot.autoconfigure.EnableAutoConfiguration` property key. Under the hood, this call collects all the `spring.factories` files located in the `META-INF` directory from all the jars or other entries in the classpath, and builds a composite list to be added as application context configurations. In addition to the `EnableAutoConfiguration` key, we can declare the following automatically initializable startup implementations in a similar fashion:

- `org.springframework.context.ApplicationContextInitializer`
- `org.springframework.context.ApplicationListener`
- `org.springframework.boot.autoconfigure.AutoConfigurationIm portListener`

- `org.springframework.boot.autoconfigure.AutoConfigurationImportFilter`
- `org.springframework.boot.autoconfigure.template.TemplateAvailabilityProvider`
- `org.springframework.boot.SpringBootExceptionReporter`
- `org.springframework.boot.SpringApplicationRunListener`
- `org.springframework.boot.env.PropertySourceLoader`
- `org.springframework.boot.env.EnvironmentPostProcessor`
- `org.springframework.boot.diagnostics.FailureAnalyzer`
- `org.springframework.boot.diagnostics.FailureAnalysisReporter`
- `org.springframework.test.contex.TestExecutionListener`

Ironically enough, a Spring Boot Starter does not need to depend on the Spring Boot library as its compile time dependency. If we look at the list of class imports in the `DbCountAutoConfiguration` class, we will not see anything from the `org.springframework.boot` package. The only reason that we have a dependency declared on Spring Boot is because our implementation of `DbCountRunner` implements the `org.springframework.boot.CommandLineRunner` interface.

Configuring custom conditional bean instantiations

In the previous example, you learned how to get the basic Spring Boot Starter going. On the inclusion of the jar in the application classpath, the `DbCountRunner` bean will be created automatically and added to the application context. In the very first recipe of this chapter, we have also seen that Spring Boot has an ability to do conditional configurations depending on a few conditions, such as the presence of specific classes in the classpath, existence of a bean, and others.

For this recipe, we will enhance our starter with a conditional check. This will create the instance of `DbCountRunner` only if no other bean instance of this class has already been created and added to the application context.

How to do it...

1. In the `DbCountAutoConfiguration` class, we will add an `@ConditionalOnMissingBean` annotation to the `dbCountRunner(...)` method, as follows:

```
@Bean
@ConditionalOnMissingBean
public DbCountRunner
    dbCountRunner(Collection<CrudRepository> repositories) {
    return new DbCountRunner(repositories);
}
```

2. We will also need to add a dependency on the `spring-boot-autoconfigure` artifact to the dependencies section of the `db-count-starter/build.gradle` file:

```
compile("org.springframework.boot:spring-boot-autoconfigure:2.0.0.BUILD-SNAPSHOT")
```

3. Now, let's start the application by running `./gradlew clean bootRun` in order to verify that we will still see the same output in the console logs as we did in the previous recipe

4. If we start the application with the DEBUG switch so as to see the Auto-Configuration Report, which we already learned in the first recipe of this chapter, we will see that our autoconfiguration is in the Positive Matches group, as follows:

```
DbCountAutoConfiguration#dbCountRunner
        - @ConditionalOnMissingBean (types:
com.example.bookpubstarter.dbcount.DbCountRunner;
SearchStrategy: all) found no beans (OnBeanCondition)
```

5. Let's explicitly/manually create an instance of `DbCountRunner` in our main `BookPubApplication` configuration class, and we will also override its `run(...)` method, just so we can see the difference in the logs:

```
protected final Log logger = LogFactory.getLog(getClass());
@Bean
public DbCountRunner dbCountRunner
                    (Collection<CrudRepository> repositories)
{
    return new DbCountRunner(repositories) {
        @Override
        public void run(String... args) throws Exception {
```

```
        logger.info("Manually Declared DbCountRunner");
      }
   };
 }
```

6. Start the application by running `DEBUG=true ./gradlew clean bootRun`.

7. If we look at the console logs, we will see two things: the Auto-Configuration Report will print our autoconfiguration in the Negative Matches group and, instead of the count output for each repository, we will see `Manually Declared DbCountRunner` text to appear:

```
DbCountAutoConfiguration#dbCountRunner
     - @ConditionalOnMissingBean (types:
com.example.bookpubstarter.dbcount.DbCountRunner;
SearchStrategy: all) found the following [dbCountRunner]
(OnBeanCondition)
2017-12-16 INFO com.example.bookpub.BookPubApplication$1   :
Manually Declared DbCountRunner
```

How it works...

As we learned from the previous recipe, Spring Boot will automatically process all the configuration class entries from `spring.factories` during the application context creation. Without any extra guidance, everything that is annotated with an `@Bean` annotation will be used to create a Spring Bean. This functionality is actually a part of the plain old Spring Framework Java Configuration. What Spring Boot adds on top is the ability to conditionally control the rules for when certain `@Configuration` or `@Bean` annotations should be executed and when it is best to ignore them.

In our case, we used the `@ConditionalOnMissingBean` annotation to instruct Spring Boot to create our `DbCountRunner` bean only if there was no other bean matching either the class type or bean name already declared elsewhere. As we explicitly created an `@Bean` entry for `DbCountRunner` in the `BookPubApplication` configuration, this took precedence and caused `OnBeanCondition` to detect the existence of the bean; thus instructing Spring Boot not to use `DbCountAutoConfiguration` during the application context setup.

Using custom @Enable annotations to toggle configuration

Allowing Spring Boot to automatically evaluate the classpath and detected configurations that are found there makes it very quick and easy to get a simple application going. However, there are times when we want to provide the configuration classes but require consumers of the starter library to explicitly enable such a configuration, rather than relying on Spring Boot to decide automatically if it should be included or not.

We will modify our previous recipe to make the starter be enabled via a meta-annotation rather than using the `spring.factories` route.

How to do it...

1. First, we will comment out the content of the `spring.factories` file located in `db-count-starter/src/main/resources` in the root of our project, as follows:

```
#org.springframework.boot.autoconfigure.EnableAutoConfiguratio
n=
#com.example.bookpubstarter.dbcount.DbCountAutoConfiguration
```

2. Next, we will need to create the meta-annotation. We will create a new file named `EnableDbCounting.java` in the `db-count-starter/src/main/java/com/example/bookpubstarter/dbcount` directory in the root of our project with the following content:

```
@Target(ElementType.TYPE)
@Retention(RetentionPolicy.RUNTIME)
@Import(DbCountAutoConfiguration.class)
@Documented
public @interface EnableDbCounting {
}
```

3. We will now add the `@EnableDbCounting` annotation to our `BookPubApplication` class and also remove the `dbCountRunner(...)` method from it, as shown in the following snippet:

```
@SpringBootApplication
@EnableScheduling
@EnableDbCounting
public class BookPubApplication {

    public static void main(String[] args) {
        SpringApplication.run(BookPubApplication.class, args);
    }

    @Bean
    public StartupRunner schedulerRunner() {
        return new StartupRunner();
    }
}
```

4. Start the application by running `./gradlew clean bootRun`.

How it works...

After running the application, the first thing that you might have noticed is that the printed counts all showed 0, even though `StartupRunner` had printed `Number of books: 1` to the console, as shown in the following output:

```
c.e.b.dbcount.DbCountRunner          : AuthorRepository has 0 entries
c.e.b.dbcount.DbCountRunner          : BookRepository has 0 entries
c.e.b.dbcount.DbCountRunner          : PublisherRepository has 0
entries
c.e.b.dbcount.DbCountRunner          : ReviewerRepository has 0 entries
com.example.bookpub.StartupRunner    : Welcome to the Book Catalog
System!
com.example.bookpub.StartupRunner    : Number of books: 1
```

This is because Spring Boot is randomly executing `CommandLineRunners` and, as we changed the configuration to use the `@EnableDbCounting` annotation, it gets processed before the configuration in the `BookPubApplication` class itself. As the database population is done by us in the `StartupRunner.run(...)` method and the execution of `DbCountRunner.run(...)` happens before this, the database tables have no data and so report the 0 count.

If we want to enforce the order, Spring provides us with this ability using the `@Order` annotation. Let's annotate the `StartupRunner` class with `@Order(Ordered.LOWEST_PRECEDENCE - 15)`. As `LOWEST_PRECEDENCE` is the default order that is assigned, we will ensure that `StartupRunner` will be executed after `DbCountRunner` by slightly reducing the order number. Let's run the app again and now we will see that the counts are properly displayed.

Now that this little ordering issue is behind us, let's examine what we did with the `@EnableDbCounting` annotation in a bit more detail.

Without `spring.factories` containing the configuration, Spring Boot does not really know that the `DbCountAutoConfiguration` class should be included during the application context creation. By default, the configuration component scan will look only from the `BookPubApplication` package and below. As the packages are different—`com.example.bookpub` versus `com.example.bookpubstarter.dbcount`—the scanner won't pick it up.

This is where our newly created meta-annotation comes into play. In the `@EnableDbCounting` annotation, there is a key-nested annotation, `@Import(DbCountAutoConfiguration.class)`, which makes things happen. This is an annotation that is provided by Spring, which can be used to annotate other annotations with declarations of which configuration classes should be imported in the process. By annotating our `BookPubApplication` class with `@EnableDbCounting`, we transitively tell Spring that it should include `DbCountAutoConfiguration` as a part of the application context as well.

Using the convenience meta-annotations, `spring.factories`, and conditional bean annotations, we can now create sophisticated and elaborate custom autoconfiguration Spring Boot starters in order to solve the needs of our enterprises.

24

Application Testing

In this chapter, we will cover the following topics:

- Creating tests for MVC controllers
- Configuring a database schema and populating it
- Creating tests using an in-memory database
- Creating tests using mock objects
- Creating a JPA component test
- Creating a WebMvc component test
- Writing tests using Cucumber
- Writing tests using Spock

Introduction

In the previous chapters, we did a lot of coding. We created a new Spring Boot application from scratch, added an MVC component and some database services to it, made a few tweaks to the application behavior, and even wrote our very own Spring Boot starter. It is now time to take the next step and learn what kind of tools and capabilities Spring Boot offers when it comes to testing all this code, and how well it integrates with the other popular testing frameworks.

We will see how to use Spring JUnit integration to create unit tests. Next, we will explore the options of setting up the database with test data to test against it. We will then look to the **behavior-driven development** (**BDD**) tools Cucumber and Spock and see how they integrate with Spring Boot.

Creating tests for MVC controllers

In the previous chapters, we made a lot of progress in gradually creating our application, but how do we know that it actually does what we want it to do? More importantly, how do we know for sure that after six months, or even a year from now, it will still continue to do what we expected it to do at the very beginning? This question is best answered by creating a set of tests, preferably automated, that run a suite of assertions against our code. This ensures that we constantly get the same and expected output given the specific input. Tests give us the much-needed peace of mind that our application not only elegantly is coded and looks beautiful, but that it also performs reliably and is as error-free as possible.

In Chapter 23, *Writing Custom Spring Boot Starters*, we left off with our web application fitted with a custom-written Spring Boot starter. We will now create some basic tests to test our web application and to ensure that all the controllers expose the expected RESTful URLs, which we can rely on as the service API. This type of testing is a bit beyond what is commonly known as **unit testing** as it tests the entire web application, it requires the application context to be fully initialized, and all the beans should be wired together in order to work. This kind of testing is sometimes referred to as **integration** or **service testing**.

How to do it...

1. Spring Boot gets us going by creating a placeholder test file, `BookPubApplicationTests.java`, in the `src/test/java/com/example/bookpub` directory at the root of our project with the following content:

```
@RunWith(SpringRunner.class)
@SpringApplicationConfiguration(classes =
    BookPubApplication.class)
public class BookPubApplicationTests {
  @Test
  public void contextLoads() {
  }
}
```

2. In `build.gradle`, we also get a test dependency on `spring-boot-starter-test`, as follows:

```
testCompile("org.springframework.boot:spring-boot-starter-
test")
```

3. We will go ahead and extend the basic template test to contain the following code:

```
import static org.hamcrest.Matchers.containsString;
import static org.junit.Assert.assertEquals;
import static org.junit.Assert.assertNotNull;
import static
org.springframework.test.web.servlet.setup.MockMvcBuilders.web
AppContextSetup;
import static
org.springframework.test.web.servlet.request.MockMvcRequestBui
lders.get;
import static
org.springframework.test.web.servlet.result.MockMvcResultMatch
ers.content;
import static
org.springframework.test.web.servlet.result.MockMvcResultMatch
ers.jsonPath;
import static
org.springframework.test.web.servlet.result.MockMvcResultMatch
ers.status;

@RunWith(SpringRunner.class)
@SpringBootTest(webEnvironment =
SpringBootTest.WebEnvironment.RANDOM_PORT)
public class BookPubApplicationTests {
    @Autowired
    private WebApplicationContext context;
    @Autowired
    private TestRestTemplate restTemplate;
    @Autowired
    private BookRepository repository;

    @LocalServerPort
    private int port;

    private MockMvc mockMvc;

    @Before
    public void setupMockMvc() {
        mockMvc = webAppContextSetup(context).build();
    }

    @Test
    public void contextLoads() {
        assertEquals(1, repository.count());
    }
```

```
@Test
public void webappBookIsbnApi() {
    Book book =
        restTemplate.getForObject("http://localhost:" +
            port + "/books/978-1-78528-415-1", Book.class);
    assertNotNull(book);
    assertEquals("Packt", book.getPublisher().getName());
}

@Test
public void webappPublisherApi() throws Exception {
    mockMvc.perform(get("/publishers/1")).
                andExpect(status().isOk()).andExpect(content().
                    contentType(MediaType.parseMediaType
                        ("application/hal+json;charset=UTF-8"))).
                andExpect(content().
                            string(containsString("Packt"))).
                andExpect(jsonPath("$.name").value("Packt"));
    }
}
```

4. Execute the tests by running `./gradlew clean test`.

5. By looking at the console output, we can tell that our tests have succeeded and are running, but we don't really see much information besides the following lines (truncated for brevity):

```
:compileJava
:compileTestJava
:testClasses
:test
2016-10-13 21:40:44.694  INFO 25739 --- [        Thread-4]
ationConfigEmbeddedWebApplicationContext : Closing
org.springframework.boot.context.embedded.AnnotationConfigEmbe
ddedWebApplicationContext@206f4aa6: startup date [Mon Apr 13
21:40:36 CDT 2015]; root of context hierarchy
2016-10-13 21:40:44.704  INFO 25739 --- [        Thread-4]
j.LocalContainerEntityManagerFactoryBean : Closing JPA
EntityManagerFactory for persistence unit 'default'
2016-10-13 21:40:44.705  INFO 25739 --- [        Thread-4]
org.hibernate.tool.hbm2ddl.SchemaExport  : HHH000227: Running
hbm2ddl schema export
2016-10-13 21:40:44.780  INFO 25739 --- [        Thread-4]
org.hibernate.tool.hbm2ddl.SchemaExport  : HHH000230: Schema
export complete
BUILD SUCCESSFUL
Total time: 24.635 secs
```

6. Better insight can be gathered by viewing the HTML reports that are generated by Gradle, which can be opened in the browser and reside in `build/reports/tests/index.html`, as shown in the following screenshot:

Test Summary

| 3 | 0 | 0 | 0.645s | 100% |
| tests | failures | ignored | duration | successful |

Packages   **Classes**

Class	Tests	Failures	Ignored	Duration	Success rate
org.test.bookpub.BookPubApplicationTests	3	0	0	0.645s	100%

7. Clicking on `com.example.bookpub.BookPubApplicationTests` will take us to the individual test case breakdown, which shows the status of each test and how long it took to get executed, as follows:

Class org.test.bookpub.BookPubApplicationTests

all > org.test.bookpub > BookPubApplicationTests

| 3 | 0 | 0 | 0.645s | 100% |
| tests | failures | ignored | duration | successful |

Tests   Standard output

Test	Duration	Result
contextLoads	0.007s	passed
webappBookIsbnApi	0.530s	passed
webappPublisherApi	0.108s	passed

8. The more curious minds can also click on the **Standard output** button in order to see the runtime application logs that are produced during the execution of the test.

How it works...

Now that we have created our first test, let's examine the code in detail.

We will first look at the following annotations that have been declared for the `BookPubApplicationTests` class:

- `@RunWith(SpringRunner.class)`: This is a standard JUnit annotation that we can configure so as to use the `SpringRunner`, providing functionality to bootstrap the Spring Boot framework to the standard JUnit tests.
- `@SpringBootTest(webEnvironment=SpringBootTest.WebEnvironment.RANDOM_PORT)`: This is an annotation that marks the class as a Spring Boot test. It will use the Spring Boot framework to configure the test class instance, provide appropriate configuration, autowiring, and so on. The `webEnvironment=SpringBootTest.WebEnvironment.RANDOM_PORT` attribute means that the current test is going to use a real, running service instance and will require a complete context initialization and application startup, as if it were the real deal. The `RANDOM_PORT` value is used to tell Spring Boot to start the Tomcat server on a randomly-chosen HTTP port, which we will later obtain by declaring the `@LocalServerPortprivate int port;` value field. This ability to select a random HTTP port is very handy when running tests on a Jenkins or any other CI server where, if multiple jobs are running in parallel, you could encounter port collision.

With the class annotations magic dispelled, let's look at the content of the class itself. As this is a Spring Boot test, we can declare any objects that are managed by Spring to be `@Autowired` during the execution or set to a specific environment value using a `@Value` annotation. In our test, we autowired the `WebApplicationContext` and `BookRepository` objects, as well as an instance of `TestRestTemplate`, which we will use in the execution of the standard JUnit `@Test` annotated test cases.

In the first test case, the `contextLoads()` method, we will just assert that we have the `BookRepository` connection established and that it contains one book entry.

Our second test will ensure that our web application responds to a RESTful URL for a `Book` lookup via `ISBN - "/books/{isbn}"`. For this test, we will use the instance of `TestRestTemplate` and make a RESTful call to the running instance on a randomly-selected port. Spring Boot provides the value of the `port` field.

In the `webappBookIsbnApi` test, we are using a full URL with the starting part being `"http://localhost:"` + `port`, which is technically not required if `TestRestTemplate` was autowired and injected by Spring Boot. In this case, it is possible to use a relative URL, looking like `Book book = restTemplate.getForObject("/books/978-1-78528-415-1", Book.class);`, and `TestRestTemplate` will automatically determine the port of the running test server instance.

Alternatively, we can execute the same flavor of tests by going through the `MockMvc` object. This is provided by the Spring Test Framework and allows you to perform MVC testing without actually doing client-side-based testing through `RestTemplate`, but instead doing it fully on the server side where the controller requests are executed from the same context as the tested application.

In order to use `MockMvc`, we will use the `MockMvcBuilders` utility to build an instance using `@Autowired WebApplicationContext`. We will do this in the setup method so that we don't have to do it in every test explicitly.

It is also possible to get Spring Boot to automatically create an instance of `MockMvc`, if we annotate our test using `WebEnvironment.MOCK` instead of `RANDOM_PORT`. That configuration will only make the test run in the mock context, and no real server will be started. Our example shows how to combine having a real server instance and `MockMVC` in the same test class.

`MockMvc` provides us with a very extensive set of capabilities in order to execute assertions on practically all the things that are related to a web request. It is designed to be used in a method-chained fashion, allowing us to link the various tests together and forming a nice, continuous logical chain:

- `perform(get(...))`: This method sets up the web request. In our particular case, we perform a GET request but the `MockMvcRequestBuilders` class provides us with static helper functions for all the common method calls.

- `andExpect(...)`: This method can be invoked multiple times, where each call represents an evaluation of a condition against the result of the `perform(...)` call. The argument of this call is any implementation of the `ResultMatcher` interface along with many stock ones that are provided by the `MockMvcResultMatchers` static utility class. This really opens up the possibility of having an infinite number of different checks such as verifying the response status, content type, values stored in a session, flash scope, verify redirects, contents of the rendering model or headers, and much more. We will use a third-party `json-path` add-on library (which is automatically brought as a `spring-boot-test` dependency) to test the JSON response data in order to ensure that it contains the right elements in the right tree hierarchy.
  `andExpect(jsonPath("$.name").value("Packt"))` validates that we have a name element at the root of the JSON document with a value of `Packt`.

> To learn more about the various possibilities that are available in MockMvc, you can refer to `https://github.com/spring-projects/spring-mvc-showcase/tree/master/src/test/java/org/springframework/samples/mvc`.

Configuring a database schema and populating it

Earlier in the book, in `Chapter 21`, *Configuring Web Applications*, we manually added a few entries to the database in the `StartupRunner's run(...)` method. While doing so programmatically can be a quick and easy way to get something going very quickly, in the long run, it is not really a good idea to do so, especially when you are dealing with a large amount of data. It is also good practice to separate the database preparations, changes, and other configurations from the rest of the running application code, even if it is setting up the test cases. Thankfully, Spring has provided you with the support to make this task fairly easy and straightforward.

We will continue with the state of the application as we left it in the previous recipe. Spring provides us with a couple of ways to define how both the structure and data should be populated in the database. The first way relies on using Hibernate to automatically create the table structure by inferring it from our defined `@Entity` objects and using the `import.sql` file to populate the data. The second approach is to use the plain old Spring JDBC capability, which relies on using the `schema.sql` file that contains the database table definition and a corresponding `data.sql` file that contains the data.

How to do it...

1. First, we will remove the programmatic database population which we created in `Chapter 21`, *Configuring Web Applications*. So let's comment out the following code from the `StartupRunner's run(...)` method:

```
Author author = new Author("Alex", "Antonov");
author = authorRepository.save(author);
Publisher publisher = new Publisher("Packt");
publisher = publisherRepository.save(publisher);
Book book = new Book("978-1-78528-415-1", "Spring Boot
Recipes", author, publisher);
bookRepository.save(book);
```

2. If we were to run our tests, they might fail if the `test.h2.db` file is missing because they expect the data to be in the database. We will populate the database by creating a Hibernate `import.sql` file in the `src/main/resources` directory at the root of our project with the following content:

```
INSERT INTO author (id, first_name, last_name) VALUES (1,
'Alex', 'Antonov')
INSERT INTO publisher (id, name) VALUES (1, 'Packt')
INSERT INTO book (isbn, title, author_id, publisher_id) VALUES
('978-1-78528-415-1', 'Spring Boot Recipes', 1, 1)
```

3. On running the tests again by running `./gradlew clean test`, they are magically started and get passed again.

4. Another way to do this is to use the Spring JDBC support for `schema.sql` and `data.sql`. Let's rename the newly-created `import.sql` file to `data.sql` and create a `schema.sql` file in the same directory with the following content:

```
-- Create syntax for TABLE 'author'
DROP TABLE IF EXISTS `author`;
CREATE TABLE `author` (
  `id` bigint(20) NOT NULL AUTO_INCREMENT,
  `first_name` varchar(255) DEFAULT NULL,
  `last_name` varchar(255) DEFAULT NULL,
  PRIMARY KEY (`id`)
);
-- Create syntax for TABLE 'publisher'
DROP TABLE IF EXISTS `publisher`;
CREATE TABLE `publisher` (
  `id` bigint(20) NOT NULL AUTO_INCREMENT,
  `name` varchar(255) DEFAULT NULL,
  PRIMARY KEY (`id`)
);
-- Create syntax for TABLE 'reviewer'
DROP TABLE IF EXISTS `reviewer`;
CREATE TABLE `reviewer` (
  `id` bigint(20) NOT NULL AUTO_INCREMENT,
  `first_name` varchar(255) DEFAULT NULL,
  `last_name` varchar(255) DEFAULT NULL,
  PRIMARY KEY (`id`)
);
-- Create syntax for TABLE 'book'
DROP TABLE IF EXISTS `book`;
CREATE TABLE `book` (
  `id` bigint(20) NOT NULL AUTO_INCREMENT,
  `description` varchar(255) DEFAULT NULL,
  `isbn` varchar(255) DEFAULT NULL,
  `title` varchar(255) DEFAULT NULL,
  `author_id` bigint(20) DEFAULT NULL,
  `publisher_id` bigint(20) DEFAULT NULL,
  PRIMARY KEY (`id`),
  CONSTRAINT `FK_publisher` FOREIGN KEY (`publisher_id`)
REFERENCES `publisher` (`id`),
  CONSTRAINT `FK_author` FOREIGN KEY (`author_id`) REFERENCES
`author` (`id`)
);
-- Create syntax for TABLE 'book_reviewers'
DROP TABLE IF EXISTS `book_reviewers`;
CREATE TABLE `book_reviewers` (
  `book_id` bigint(20) NOT NULL,
```

```
`reviewers_id` bigint(20) NOT NULL,
  CONSTRAINT `FK_book` FOREIGN KEY (`book_id`) REFERENCES
`book` (`id`),
  CONSTRAINT `FK_reviewer` FOREIGN KEY (`reviewers_id`)
REFERENCES `reviewer` (`id`)
  );
```

5. As we are now manually creating the database schema, we will need to tell the Hibernate mapper not to automatically derive one from the entities and populate the database with it. So, let's set the `spring.jpa.hibernate.ddl-auto=none` property in the `application.properties` file in the `src/main/resources` directory at the root of our project.

6. Execute the tests by running `./gradlew clean test` and they should get passed.

How it works...

In this recipe, we actually explored two ways of achieving the same thing, and this is quite common when you are living in the Spring ecosystem. Depending on the components that are used, whether it's a plain Spring JDBC, Spring JPA with Hibernate, or the Flyway or Liquibase migrations, the approach of populating and initializing the database differs but the end result remains pretty much the same.

Both Flyway and Liquibase are frameworks that provide incremental database migration capabilities. This comes in very handy when one wants to maintain the incremental log of the database changes in a programmatic, describable fashion with the ability to quickly put the database in a desired state for a particular version. While these frameworks differ in their approach in terms of providing such support, they are similar in their purpose. More detailed information can be obtained at their respective sites, `http://flywaydb.org` and `http://www.liquibase.org`.

In the preceding example, we explored two different ways of populating and initializing the database.

Initializing the database with Spring JPA and Hibernate

In this approach, most of the work is actually done by the `Hibernate` library and we merely set up the appropriate configurations and create conventionally expected files that are needed for Hibernate to do the work:

- The `spring.jpa.hibernate.ddl-auto=create-drop` setting instructs Hibernate to use the `@Entity` models and, based on their structure, automatically deduces the database schema. Upon starting the application, the calculated schema will be used to preinitialize the database table structure; when the application is shut down, it will all be destroyed. Even in the event that the application was forcefully terminated or it abruptly crashed, upon startup, if the existing tables are detected, they will be dropped and recreated from scratch. So it's probably not a good idea to rely on this for a production environment.

> **TIP**
>
> If the `spring.jpa.hibernate.ddl-auto` property is not explicitly configured, Spring Boot uses create-drop for embedded databases such as H2 by default, so be careful and set it appropriately.

- Hibernate expects that the `import.sql` file is residing in the root of the classpath. This is used to execute the declared SQL statements upon application startup. While any valid SQL statement can go in the file, it is recommended that you put in the data-importing statements such as `INSERT` or `UPDATE` and steer clear of table structure mutations, as the schema definition is already taken care of by Hibernate.

Initializing the database with Spring JDBC

If the application does not use JPA, or you don't want to depend on the Hibernate functionality explicitly, Spring offers you another way of getting the database set up, as long as the `spring-boot-starter-jdbc` dependency is present. So let's take a look at what we did to get it to work, as shown in the following list:

- The `spring.jpa.hibernate.ddl-auto=none` setting tells Hibernate not to do any automatic handling of the database if the Hibernate dependency also exists, as it does in our case. This setting is good practice for a production environment as you probably don't want to get all of your database tables wiped clean inadvertently. That would be one hell of a disaster, that's for sure!

- The `schema.sql` file is expected to exist in the root of the classpath. It is executed by Spring during the schema creation of the database upon every startup of the application. However, unlike Hibernate, this will not drop any of the existing tables automatically, so it might be a good idea to either use `DROP TABLE IF EXISTS` to delete an existing table before creating the new one, or use `CREATE TABLE IF NOT EXISTS` as part of the table creation SQL if you only want to create new tables when they don't already exist. This makes it a lot more flexible to declare the database structure evolution logic, thus making it safer to be used in production as well.

- The `data.sql` file is expected to exist in the root of the classpath. This is used to execute the data population SQL, so this is where all the `INSERT INTO` statements go.

Given that this is a Spring native functionality, we will also get the ability to define the schema and data files not only globally, but also as per the specific database platform. For example, we can have one set of files that we can use for Oracle, `schema-oracle.sql`, and a different one for MySQL, `schema-mysql.sql`. The same applies to the `data.sql` variants as well; however, they don't have to be defined per platform, so while you might have platform-specific schema files, there could be a shared data file. The `spring.datasource.platform` configuration value can be explicitly set if you want to override Spring Boot's automatically deduced value.

> **TIP**
> In case one wants to override the default names of `schema.sql` and `data.sql`, Spring Boot provides the configuration properties, which we can use to control `spring.datasource.schema` and `spring.datasource.data`.

Creating tests using an in-memory database

In the previous recipe, we explored how to get our databases set up with the desired tables and populated with the required data. When it comes to testing, one of the typical challenges is to get the environment set up correctly and predictably so that when the tests are executed, we can safely assert the behavior in a deterministic fashion. In an application that connects to a database, making sure that the database contains a deterministic dataset on which the assertions can be evaluated is extremely important. For an elaborate test suite, it is also necessary to be able to refresh or change that dataset based on the tests. Thankfully, Spring has some nice facilities that aid you in accomplishing this task.

We will pick up from the state of our `BookPub` application as we left it in the previous recipe. At this point, we have the `schema.sql` file defining all the tables, and we also need the database with some starting data that is defined in `data.sql`. In this recipe, we will extend our tests to use the specific data fixture files that are tailored to a particular test suite.

How to do it...

1. Our first step will be to create a `resources` directory in the `src/test` directory at the root of our project.
2. In this directory, we will start placing our fixture SQL data files. Let's create a new file named `test-data.sql` in the resources directory with the following content:

   ```
   INSERT INTO author (id, first_name, last_name) VALUES (2,
   'Greg', 'Turnquist')
   INSERT INTO book (isbn, title, author_id, publisher_id) VALUES
   ('978-1-78439-302-1', 'Learning Spring Boot', 2, 1)
   ```

3. We now need a way to load this file when our test runs. We will modify our `BookPubApplicationTests` class in the following way:

   ```
   public class BookPubApplicationTests {
       ...
       @Autowired
       private BookRepository repository;
       @Autowired
       private RestTemplate restTemplate;
   ```

```
@Autowired
private DataSource ds;
@LocalServerPort
private int port;

private MockMvc mockMvc;
private static boolean loadDataFixtures = true;

@Before
public void setupMockMvc() {
    ...
}

@Before
public void loadDataFixtures() {
    if (loadDataFixtures) {
        ResourceDatabasePopulator populator =
          new ResourceDatabasePopulator(
            context.getResource("classpath:/test-
data.sql"));
        DatabasePopulatorUtils.execute(populator, ds);
        loadDataFixtures = false;
    }
}

@Test
public void contextLoads() {
    assertEquals(2, repository.count());
}

@Test
public void webappBookIsbnApi() {
    ...
}

@Test
public void webappPublisherApi() throws Exception {
    ...
}
}
```

4. Execute the tests by running ./gradlew clean test, and they should continue to get passed despite us adding another book and its author to the database.

5. We can also use the method of populating the database that we learned in the previous recipe. As the test code has its own `resources` directory, it is possible to add another `data.sql` file to it, and Spring Boot will use both the files to populate the database. Let's go ahead and create the `data.sql` file in the `src/test/resources` directory at the root of our project with the following content:

```
INSERT INTO author (id, first_name, last_name) VALUES (3,
'William', 'Shakespeare')
INSERT INTO publisher (id, name) VALUES (2, 'Classical Books')
INSERT INTO book (isbn, title, author_id, publisher_id) VALUES
('978-1-23456-789-1', 'Romeo and Juliet', 3, 2)
```

> **TIP**
>
> As Spring Boot collects all the occurrences of the data filesfrom the classpath, it is possible to place the data files in JARs or different physical locations that all end up being at the root of the classpath. It is also important to remember that the loading order of these scripts is not deterministic, and if you rely on certain referential IDs, it is better if you use selects to get them instead of making assumptions.

6. As we added another book to the database and we now have three of them, we should fix the assertion in our `contextLoads()` test method:

```
assertEquals(3, repository.count());
```

7. Execute the tests by running `./gradlew clean test` and they should continue to get passed.

8. It would be a fair statement to say that when running unit tests, an in-memory database is probably more suitable for the role than a persistent one. Let's create a dedicated test configuration instance of the `application.properties` file in the `src/test/resources` directory at the root of our project with the following content:

```
spring.datasource.url =
jdbc:h2:mem:testdb;DB_CLOSE_DELAY=-1;DB_CLOSE_ON_EXIT=FALSE
spring.jpa.hibernate.ddl-auto=update
```

It is important to know that Spring Boot loads only one `application.properties` file from the classpath. When we created another `application.properties` in `src/test/resources`, the previous one from `src/main/resources` was no longer loaded and thus none of the properties defined in it were merged in the environment. For this reason, you should configure all of the property values that are required. In our case, we had to redefine the `spring.jpa.hibernate.dll-auto` property, even though it was already declared in the `src/main/resources/application.properties` location.

9. Execute the tests by running `./gradlew clean test` and the tests should continue to get passed.

How it works...

In this recipe, we relied on the facility that is provided by Spring to initialize and populate the database in order to get our database populated with the data required to run the tests and assert on them. However, we also wanted to be able to use some data that was only relevant to a particular test suite. For this, we turned to the `ResourceDatabasePopulator` and `DatabasePopulatorUtils` classes to insert the desired data right before the test got executed. These are exactly the same classes that are used internally by Spring in order to handle the `schema.sql` and `data.sql` files, except now, we are explicitly defining the script files that we want to execute.

So, let's break up what we did step by step, as follows:

- We created a setup method named `loadDataFixtures()`, which we annotated with a `@Before` annotation to tell JUnit to run it before every test.
- In this method, we obtained a resource handle to the `classpath:/test-data.sql` data file that resides in our application's classpath and where we store our test data and execute it against `@Autowired DataSource ds`.

- As Spring can only autowire dependencies in the instances of the class, and the `@Before` annotated setup methods get executed for every test, we had to get a little creative in order to avoid repopulating our database with the duplicate data for every test instead of once per test suite/class. To achieve this, we created a `static boolean loadDataFixtures` variable that retained its state for every instance of the `BookPubApplicationTests` class, thus ensuring that we executed `DatabasePopulatorUtils` only once. The reason that the variable has to be static is as a new instance of the test class gets created for every test method that it runs in the class; having the `boolean` flag at the instance level will not do the trick.

> Alternatively, we could have used the `@Sql` annotation instead of the `loadDataFixtures()` method and marked our `BookPubApplicationTests` class as `@Transactional` to make sure that the `test-data.sql` file got populated before every test method was run. Then we could have rolled back to the pre-execution state of the database.

This makes test setup a bit simpler and the transactional part allows for having tests that mutate the data in the database without worrying about race conditions, but this has the downside of executing the SQL population before every test, which adds a bit of extra latency.

To make this work, we need to remove the `loadDataFixtures()` method and add the following annotations to the `BookPubApplicationTests` class:

```
@Transactional
@Sql(scripts = "classpath:/test-data.sql")
```

- For the finishing touch, we decided to have a separate `application.properties` file to be used for testing purposes. We added this to our `src/test/resources` classpath with a testing configuration of the in-memory database instead of using the file-based persistent one.

- Unlike `application.properties`, where only one file can be loaded from the classpath, Spring supports a number of profile configurations which will be merged together. So, instead of declaring a completely separate `application.properties` file, we could create an `application-test.properties` file and set an active profile to test while running the tests.

Creating tests using mock objects

In the previous recipe, we used a data fixture file to populate an in-memory database in order to run our tests on predictable and static sets of data. While this makes the tests consistent and deterministic, we are still paying the price of having to create a database, populate it with data, and initialize all the JPA and connectivity components, which could be viewed as an excessive step for a test. Luckily, Spring Boot provides internal support for being able to mock beans and inject them as components in the tests for setup and further use as dependencies within an application context.

Let's examine how we can use the power of Mockito so that we don't need to rely on the database at all. We will learn how to elegantly mock the `Repository` instance objects using the Mockito framework and some `@MockBean` annotation cleverness.

How to do it...

1. First, we will create a new `MockPublisherRepositoryTests` test class in the `src/test/java/com/example/bookpub` directory at the root of our project with the following content:

```
import static org.assertj.core.api.Assertions.assertThat;
import static org.mockito.BDDMockito.given;
import static org.mockito.BDDMockito.reset;

@RunWith(SpringRunner.class)
@SpringBootTest(webEnvironment =
SpringBootTest.WebEnvironment.NONE)
public class MockPublisherRepositoryTests {
    @MockBean
    private PublisherRepository repository;

    @Before
    public void setupPublisherRepositoryMock() {
        given(repository.count()).willReturn(5L);
    }

    @Test
    public void publishersExist() {
        assertThat(repository.count()).isEqualTo(5L);
    }

    @After
```

```
        public void resetPublisherRepositoryMock() {
            reset(repository);
        }
    }
```

2. Execute the tests by running `./gradlew clean test` and the tests should get passed

How it works...

There are a few magical things happening here. Let's start with the annotations that we put into the `MockPublisherRepositoryTests` class:

- The `@SpringBootTest` annotation's `webEnvironment` attribute was replaced with `WebEnvironment.NONE`. This is to inform Spring Boot that we don't want a full application web server to be initialized for this test, since we will only be interacting with the repository object, without making calls to controllers or using any part of the WebMvc stack. We did this to save test startup time, and if one is curious to see the difference, just simply switching it back to the `WebEnvironment.RANDOM_PORT` value and rerunning the test would show that the time has almost doubled. (On my beefy MacBook Pro, it increased from 5 seconds to almost 9.)

With the application changes examined, let's now look at what we did in the `MockPublisherRepositoryTests` class itself:

- The `@MockBean` annotation instructs Spring that this dependency is not a real instance, but a `mock` object currently backed by the Mockito framework. This has an interesting effect in that it actually replaces our `PublisherRepository` bean instance in the context with the mock one, so, everywhere within the context, all dependencies for `PublisherRepository` get wired with the mocked version instead of a real, database-backed one.

Now that we know how the mocked instance of `PublisherRepository` gets injected into our tests, let's take a look at the newly-created test setup methods. The two methods of particular interest are `setupPublisherRepositoryMock()` and `resetPublisherRepositoryMock()`. They are described as follows:

- The `setupPublisherRepositoryMock()` method is annotated with `@Before`, which tells JUnit to execute this method before running every `@Test` method in the class. We will use the Mockito framework in order to configure the behavior of our mocked instance. We configure it such, that when the `repository.count()` method is called, it will return 5 as a result. The Mockito, Junit, and Hamcrest libraries provide us with many convenient DLS-like methods, which we can use to define such rules with an English-like, easy-to-read style.

- The `resetPublisherRepositoryMock()` method is annotated with `@After`, which tells JUnit to execute this method after running every `@Test` method in the class. At the end of every test, we will need to reset the mocked behavior, so we will use the `reset(...)` method call to clear out all of our settings and get the mock ready for the next test, which can be used in another test suite altogether.

> Ideally, there is no need to reset the `mock` object at the end of the test run, as each test class gets its own context spawned up, so between test classes the instance of a mock is not shared. It is considered good practice to create many smaller tests instead of a single large one. There are, however, some use cases that warrant resetting the mock when it is being managed by a container injection, so I thought it was worth mentioning. For the best practices on using `reset(...)`, see `https://github.com/mockito/mockito/wiki/FAQ#can-i-reset-a-mock`.

Creating a JPA component test

Most of our previous test examples had to start up the entire application and configure all the beans in order to execute. While that is not a big issue for our simple application, which has little code, it might prove an expensive and lengthy process for some larger, more complex enterprise-grade services. Considering that one of the key aspects of having good test coverage is a low execution time, we might want to opt out of having to bootstrap the entire application in order to test just one component, or *slice*, as Spring Boot refers to it.

In this recipe, we will try to create a similar test to our previous
`PublisherRepository` one, but without starting the entire container and initializing
all the beans. Conveniently, Spring Boot provides us with the `@DataJpaTest`
annotation, which we can put on our test class, and it will automatically configure all
the components necessary for the JPA functionality, but not the entire context. So
beans like controllers, services, and so on, will be missing. This test is very good at
quickly testing the validity of entity domain object bindings, to make sure the field
names, associations, and so on, have been configured correctly.

How to do it...

1. Let's create a new `JpaAuthorRepositoryTests` test class in the
   `src/test/java/com/example/bookpub` directory at the root of our
   project with the following content:

```java
import static org.assertj.core.api.Assertions.assertThat;

@RunWith(SpringRunner.class)
@DataJpaTest
public class JpaAuthorRepositoryTests {
    @Autowired
    private TestEntityManager mgr;

    @Autowired
    private AuthorRepository repository;

    @Test
    public void testAuthorEntityBinding() {
        Long id = mgr.persistAndGetId(createAuthor(),
                                      Long.class);

        Author author = repository.findById(id).get();
        assertThat(author.getFirstName()).
                isEqualTo("Mark");
        assertThat(author.getLastName()).
                isEqualTo("Twain");
    }

    private Author createAuthor() {
        return new Author("Mark", "Twain");
    }
}
```

2. Execute the tests by running `./gradlew clean test` and the tests should continue to pass

How it works...

The key difference from our previous test is the absence of the `@SpringBootTest` annotation, which has been replaced with the `@DataJpaTest` annotation. The apparent simplicity of the test class itself is possible thanks to the `@DataJpaTest` annotation doing the bulk of the declarations and workload to configure the test environment. If we look inside the annotation definition, we will see a myriad of different internal annotations configuring all the necessary components. The important ones are the `@AutoConfigure*` annotations, such as `@AutoConfigureDataJpa` or `@AutoConfigureTestDatabase`. Those annotations essentially instruct Spring Boot to import the necessary component configurations when bootstrapping the test. For example, in `@DataJpaTest`, only `Cache`, `DataJpa`, `TestDatabase`, and `TestEntityManager` components would be configured and made available, which significantly reduces the test footprint, both memory-wise as well as startup and execution times. The specific configuration classes are then loaded, as we've seen before, from the `META-INF/spring.factories` descriptors provided by various artifacts.

With the right components initialized, we can take advantage of some preconfigured beans, such as `TestEntityManager`, which gives us the ability to interact with the test instance of the database, pre-initialize the desired state of its content, and manipulate test data. This gives us the guarantee that after each test suite is done executing, we will get a clean slate for the next set without the need of an explicit cleanup. This makes it easier to write tests, without having to worry about the order of execution and potential over stepping of changes from test suite to test suite, avoiding the inadvertent dirty state that makes tests inconsistent.

Creating a WebMvc component test

Another one of the collection of `*Test` slices is `@WebMvcTest`, which allows us to create tests for the WebMvc part of the application, quickly testing controllers, filters, and so on, while providing ability to use `@MockBean` to configure the necessary dependencies such as services, data repositories, and so on.

This is another very useful testing slice provided by the Spring Boot Test Framework, and we will explore its use in this recipe, taking a look at how we can create an Mvc layer test for our `BookController` file, mocking the `BookRepository` service with a predefined dataset and making sure the returned JSON document is what we would expect based on that data.

How to do it...

1. First, we will create a new `WebMvcBookControllerTests` test class in the `src/test/java/com/example/bookpub` directory at the root of our project with the following content:

```
import static org.hamcrest.Matchers.containsString;
import static org.mockito.BDDMockito.given;
import static
org.springframework.test.web.servlet.request.MockMvcRequestBui
lders.get;
import static
org.springframework.test.web.servlet.result.MockMvcResultMatch
ers.content;
import static
org.springframework.test.web.servlet.result.MockMvcResultMatch
ers.jsonPath;
import static
org.springframework.test.web.servlet.result.MockMvcResultMatch
ers.status;

@RunWith(SpringRunner.class)
@WebMvcTest
public class WebMvcBookControllerTests {
    @Autowired
    private MockMvc mockMvc;

    @MockBean
    private BookRepository repository;

    // The 2 repositories below are needed to
    //successfully initialize StartupRunner
    @MockBean
    private AuthorRepository authorRepository;
    @MockBean
    private PublisherRepository publisherRepository;

    @Test
    public void webappBookApi() throws Exception {
```

```
            given(repository.findBookByIsbn("978-1-78528-415-1"))
                .willReturn(new Book("978-1-78528-415-1",
                                     "Spring Boot Recipes",
                                     new Author("Alex",
    "Antonov"),
                                     new Publisher("Packt")));

            mockMvc.perform(get("/books/978-1-78528-415-1")).
                    andExpect(status().isOk()).
                    andExpect(content().
                             contentType(MediaType.parseMediaType
    ("application/json;charset=UTF-8"))).
                    andExpect(content().
                             string(containsString("Spring Boot
    Recipes"))).
                    andExpect(jsonPath("$.isbn").
                             value("978-1-78528-415-1"));
        }
    }
```

2. Execute the tests by running `./gradlew clean test` and the tests should continue to pass

How it works...

The functionality of `@WebMvcTest` is very similar to the `@DataJpaTest` annotation we have seen in the previous recipe. The difference is really just a set of components that get initialized during the test bootstrap. Unlike `@DataJpaTest`, this time there are no database components that are provided for us, but instead we get the `WebMvc` and `MockMvc` configurations, which bring all the necessary foundations for initializing controllers, filters, interceptors, and so on. For that reason, we had to add `AuthorRepository` and `PublisherRepository` as mock beans into our test code, because otherwise the test would fail to start because Spring Boot would be unable to satisfy the bean dependency that the `StartupRunner` class has on those two repositories.

Another solution to this problem could be removing the dependency on those two repositories from the `StartupRunner` class, since we've commented out the code that uses them earlier in this chapter, in the *Configuring database schema and populating it* recipe. If that was not possible, I wanted to demonstrate how to handle the situation where you have bean dependencies in other classes, unrelated directly to the test, but causing startup failures during initialization and execution.

As one can see, unlike our previous recipe test, where we did not use any bean mocking since it was testing a lower-layer component without further dependencies, this time we need to provide a `BookRepository` mock, which is being used by our `BookController` class, the functionality of which we are testing.

We have already seen how to use the `@Before` annotation to preconfigure mock objects in the `MockPublisherRepositoryTests` class, so this time we are doing the configuration directly in the `webappBookApi` test method, similar to the style you will see when we learn about writing tests using the Spock framework.

Inside the `given(...)` call, we pre-configure the behavior of the `BookRepository` mock object, instructing it to return a specific `Book` instance when its `findBookByIsbn` method gets called with `"978-1-78528-415-1"` as an argument.

Our next call to `mockMvc.perform` with `/books/978-1-78528-415-1` triggers the invocation of the `BookController` `getBook` method, which delegates the pre-wired mocked instance of `bookRepository` and uses our pre-configured `Book` object instance to run validation logic upon.

As evident from the log, we can see that only the WebMvc layer has been bootstrapped. No database or other components have been initialized, which has resulted in significant savings in runtime, taking only 3 seconds compared to the 9 seconds it took for a complete application bootstrap test earlier.

Writing tests using Cucumber

Unit testing has been an expected part of the software development life cycle for quite some time now, and one can hardly imagine writing code without having unit tests along with it. The art of testing does not stay the same, and advances in testing philosophies have extended the concept of unit testing even further, introducing things such as service testing, integration testing, and, lastly, what is known as BDD that proposes to create the test suites describing the application behavior at large without getting down to the minute implementation details at the lower levels of the code. One such framework, which has gained a lot of popularity first in the Ruby world and later expanding to other languages including Java, is the Cucumber BDD.

For the purpose of this recipe, we will pick up on our previous example and continue enhancing the testing suite by adding the Cucumber-JVM implementation, which will provide us with the Java-based version of the original Ruby Cucumber framework, and create a few tests in order to demonstrate the capabilities and integration points with the Spring Boot application.

> This recipe is by no means intended to cover the entire set of functionalities provided by the Cucumber testing framework and is mostly focused on the integration points of Cucumber and Spring Boot. To learn more about Cucumber-JVM, you can go to `https://cukes.info/docs#cucumber-implementations` or `https://github.com/cucumber/cucumber-jvm` for details.

How to do it...

1. The first thing that we need to do is add the necessary dependencies for the Cucumber libraries to our `build.gradle` file, as follows:

```
dependencies {
    compile("org.springframework.boot:spring-boot-starter-
data-jpa")
    compile("org.springframework.boot:spring-boot-starter-
jdbc")
    compile("org.springframework.boot:spring-boot-starter-
web")
    compile("org.springframework.boot:spring-boot-starter-
data-rest")
    compile project(":db-count-starter")
    runtime("com.h2database:h2")
    runtime("mysql:mysql-connector-java")
```

```
    testCompile("org.springframework.boot:spring-boot-starter-
test")
    testCompile("info.cukes:cucumber-spring:1.2.5")
    testCompile("info.cukes:cucumber-java8:1.2.5")
    testCompile("info.cukes:cucumber-junit:1.2.5")
}
```

2. Next, we will need to create a test driver class to run Cucumber tests. Let's create a RunCukeTests.java file in the src/test/java/com/example/bookpub directory at the root of our project with the following content:

```
@RunWith(Cucumber.class)
@CucumberOptions(plugin={"pretty",
"html:build/reports/cucumber"},
                  glue = {"cucumber.api.spring",
                          "classpath:com.example.bookpub"},
                  monochrome = true)
public class RunCukeTests {
}
```

3. With the driver class created, we are ready to start writing what Cucumber refers to as Step Definitions. I will talk briefly about what these are in the *How it works...* section of this recipe. For now, let's create a RepositoryStepdefs.java file in the src/test/java/com/example/bookpub directory at the root of our project with the following content:

```
@WebAppConfiguration
@ContextConfiguration(classes = BookPubApplication.class,
                  loader = SpringBootContextLoader.class)
public class RepositoryStepdefs {
    @Autowired
    private WebApplicationContext context;
    @Autowired
    private DataSource ds;
    @Autowired
    private BookRepository bookRepository;

    private Book loadedBook;

    @Given("^([^"]*) fixture is loaded$")
    public void data_fixture_is_loaded(String fixtureName)
      throws Throwable {
        ResourceDatabasePopulator populator
          = new ResourceDatabasePopulator
                (context.getResource("classpath:/" +
```

```
        fixtureName + ".sql"));
                DatabasePopulatorUtils.execute(populator, ds);
        }

        @Given("^(d+) books available in the catalogue$")
        public void books_available_in_the_catalogue(int
bookCount)
            throws Throwable {
                assertEquals(bookCount, bookRepository.count());
        }

        @When("^searching for book by isbn ([d-]+)$")
        public void searching_for_book_by_isbn(String isbn)
            throws Throwable {
                loadedBook = bookRepository.findBookByIsbn(isbn);
                assertNotNull(loadedBook);
                assertEquals(isbn, loadedBook.getIsbn());
        }

        @Then("^book title will be ([^"]*)$")
        public void book_title_will_be(String bookTitle)
            throws Throwable {
                assertNotNull(loadedBook);
                assertEquals(bookTitle, loadedBook.getTitle());
        }
    }
```

4. Now, we will need to create a corresponding testing feature definition file named `repositories.feature` in the `src/test/resources/com/example/bookpub` directory at the root of our project with the following content:

```
@txn
Feature: Finding a book by ISBN
  Background: Preload DB Mock Data
    Given packt-books fixture is loaded

  Scenario: Load one book
    Given 3 books available in the catalogue
    When searching for book by isbn 978-1-78398-478-7
    Then book title will be Orchestrating Docker
```

5. Lastly, we will create one more data SQL file named `packt-books.sql` in the `src/test/resources` directory at the root of our project with the following content:

```
INSERT INTO author (id, first_name, last_name) VALUES (5,
'Shrikrishna', 'Holla')
INSERT INTO book (isbn, title, author_id, publisher_id) VALUES
('978-1-78398-478-7', 'Orchestrating Docker', 5, 1)
```

6. Execute the tests by running `./gradlew clean test` and the tests should get passed.

7. With the addition of Cucumber, we also get the results of the tests in both the JUnit report and Cucumber-specific report HTML files. If we open `build/reports/tests/index.html` in the browser and click on the **Classes** button, we will see our scenario in the table, as shown in the following screenshot:

Test Summary

11	0	0	2.695s	100%
tests	failures	ignored	duration	successful

Packages   **Classes**

Class	Tests	Failures	Ignored	Duration	Success rate
Scenario: Load one book	5	0	0	2.111s	100%
com.example.bookpub.BookPubApplicationTests	3	0	0	0.486s	100%
com.example.bookpub.JpaAuthorRepositoryTests	1	0	0	0.068s	100%
com.example.bookpub.MockPublisherRepositoryTests	1	0	0	0.016s	100%
com.example.bookpub.RunCukeTests	0	0	0	-	-
com.example.bookpub.WebMvcBookControllerTests	1	0	0	0.014s	100%

8. Selecting the **Scenario: Load one book** link will take us to the detailed report page, as shown in the following screenshot:

Class Scenario: Load one book

all > default-package > Scenario: Load one book

5	0	0	1.616s	100%
tests	failures	ignored	duration	successful

Tests   Standard output

Test	Duration	Result
Given 3 books available in the catalogue	0s	passed
Given packt-books fixture is loaded	0s	passed
Then book title will be Orchestrating Docker	0s	passed
When searching for book by isbn 978-1-78398-478-7	0s	passed
classMethod	1.616s	passed

9. As we can see, the descriptions are nicer than the class and method names that we saw in the original JUnit-based test cases.

10. Cucumber also generates its own report, which can be viewed by opening `build/reports/cucumber/index.html` in the browser.

11. Being a behavior-driven testing framework, the feature files allow us not only to define individual conditions, but also to declare entire scenario outlines, which make the defining of multiple assertions of similar data easier. Let's create another feature file named `restful.feature` in the `src/test/resources/com/example/bookpub` directory at the root of our project with the following content:

```
@txn
Feature: Finding a book via REST API
  Background:
    Given packt-books fixture is loaded

  Scenario Outline: Using RESTful API to lookup books by ISBN
    Given catalogue with books
    When requesting url /books/<isbn>
    Then status code will be 200
    And response content contains <title>

    Examples:
      |isbn             |title                |
      |978-1-78398-478-7|Orchestrating Docker|
      |978-1-78528-415-1|Spring Boot Recipes |
```

12. We will also create a corresponding `RestfulStepdefs.java` file in the `src/test/java/com/example/bookpub` directory at the root of our project with the following content:

```
import cucumber.api.java.Before;
import cucumber.api.java.en.Given;
import cucumber.api.java.en.Then;
import cucumber.api.java.en.When;

import static org.hamcrest.CoreMatchers.containsString;
import static org.junit.Assert.assertTrue;
import static org.junit.Assert.assertNotNull;
import static
org.springframework.test.web.servlet.request.MockMvcRequestBui
lders.get;
import static
org.springframework.test.web.servlet.result.MockMvcResultMatch
ers.status;
import static
org.springframework.test.web.servlet.result.MockMvcResultMatch
ers.content;

@WebAppConfiguration
@ContextConfiguration(classes = BookPubApplication.class,
loader = SpringBootContextLoader.class)
public class RestfulStepdefs {
  @Autowired
  private WebApplicationContext context;
  @Autowired
  private BookRepository bookRepository;

  private MockMvc mockMvc;
  private ResultActions result;

  @Before
  public void setup() throws IOException {
    mockMvc =
        MockMvcBuilders.webAppContextSetup(context).build();
  }

  @Given("^catalogue with books$")
  public void catalogue_with_books() {
    assertTrue(bookRepository.count() > 0);
  }

  @When("^requesting url ([^"]*)$")
  public void requesting_url(String url) throws Exception {
    result = mockMvc.perform(get(url));
```

```
        }

        @Then("^status code will be ([d]*)$")
        public void status_code_will_be(int code) throws
            Throwable {
          assertNotNull(result);
          result.andExpect(status().is(code));
        }

        @Then("^response content contains ([^"]*)$")
        public void response_content_contains(String content)
            throws Throwable {

          assertNotNull(result);
          result.andExpect(
            content().string(containsString(content))
          );
        }
    }
```

13. Execute the tests by running `./gradlew clean test` and the tests should continue to get passed.

How it works...

If you feel a bit lost after looking at all this code and following along without having a full understanding of what exactly is going on, here you will find a detailed breakdown of everything that we did.

Let's start with a quick overview of what **Step Definitions** are. As the Cucumber framework uses the **Gherkin** feature document files in order to describe the business rules that are to be tested, which are represented in the form of English-like sentence statements, these need to be translated into executable code. This is the job of the Step Definition classes. Every step in a defined feature scenario needs to be matched to a method in a Step Definition class that will execute it. This matching is done by declaring a regular expression in the step annotations above the methods. The regex contains the matching groups that Cucumber uses so as to extract the method arguments and pass them to the executing method.

In `RepositoryStepdefs`, we can see this in the following method:

```
        @Given("^([^"]*) fixture is loaded$")
        public void data_fixture_is_loaded(String fixtureName) {...}
```

The @Given annotation contains the regular expression that matches the Given packt-books fixture is loaded text, loaded from repositories.feature file, and extracts the packt-books text from the pattern, which is then passed as a fixtureName argument to the method. The @When and @Then annotations work on exactly the same principle. So, in effect, what the Cucumber framework does is it matches the English-like worded rules from the feature files to the matched patterns of the executing methods and extracts parts of the rules as arguments to the matched methods.

> More information on Gherkin and how to use it can be found at https://cukes.info/docs/reference#gherkin.

With the basic Cucumber overview explained, let's shift our focus to how the tests integrate with Spring Boot and are configured.

It all starts with the driver harness class, which in our case is RunCukeTests. This class itself does not contain any tests, but it has two important annotations that stitch things together, @RunWith(Cucumber.class) and @CucumberOptions:

- @RunWith(Cucumber.class): This is a JUnit annotation that indicates that JUnit runner should use the Cucumber feature files to execute the tests.

@CucumberOptions: This provides additional configuration for Cucumber:

- plugin={"pretty", "html:build/reports/cucumber"}: This tells Cucumber to generate its reports in HTML format in the build/reports/cucumber directory.
- glue = {"cucumber.api.spring", "classpath:com.example.bookpub"}: This is a very important setting, as it tells Cucumber which packages to load and from where to load them during the execution of the tests. The cucumber.api.spring package needs to be present in order to take advantage of the cucumber-spring integration library, and the com.example.bookpub package is the location of our Step Definition implementation classes.
- monochrome = true: This tells Cucumber not to print the output with the ANSI color as we integrate with JUnit, as it will not look correct in the saved console output files.

A complete list of the options can be found at `https://cukes,.info/docs/reference/jvm#list-all-options`.

Now let's look at the `RepositoryStepdefs` class. It starts with the following annotations at the class level:

- `@WebAppConfiguration` instructs Spring that this class needs `WebApplicationContext` to be initialized, and it will be used for testing purposes during the execution
- `@ContextConfiguration(classes = BookPubApplication.class` and `loader = SpringBootContextLoader.class)` instruct Spring to use the `BookPubApplication` class as a configuration for the Spring application context, as well as to use the `SpringBootContextLoader` class from Spring Boot in order to bootstrap the testing harness

It is important to note that these annotations have to match all the Step Definition classes, or only one of the classes will be annotated with the `@ContextConfiguration` annotation to wire in the Spring support for the Cucumber test.

As the `cucumber-spring` integration does not know about Spring Boot but only about Spring, we can't use the `@SpringBootTest` meta-annotation. We have to resort to using only the annotations from Spring in order to stitch things together. Thankfully, we don't have to go through many hoops, but just declare the exact annotation that `SpringBootTest` facades by passing the desired configuration classes and loader.

Once the proper annotations are in place, Spring and Spring Boot will take over and provide us with the same convenience of autowiring beans as dependencies of our Step Definition classes.

One interesting characteristic of the Cucumber tests is the instantiation of a new instance of the Step Definition class for every execution of a **Scenario**. Even though the method namespace is global—meaning that we can use the methods that are declared in the different Step Definition classes—they operate on states defined in them and are not directly shared. It is, however, possible to `@Autowire` an instance of another Step Definition in a different Step Definition instance and rely on public methods or fields to access and mutate the data.

As a new instance gets created per scenario, the definition classes are stateful and rely on internal variables to keep a state among transitions from assertion to assertion. For example, in the `@When` annotated method, a particular state gets set, and in the `@Then` annotated method, a set of assertions on that state get evaluated. In our example of the `RepositoryStepdefs` class, we will internally set the state of the `loadedBook` class variable in its `searching_for_book_by_isbn(...)` method, which later gets used to assert on so as to verify the match of the book's title in the `book_title_will_be(...)` method afterwards. Due to this, if we mix the rules from the different definition classes in our feature files, the internal states would not be accessible among the multiple classes.

When integrating with Spring, one can use the injection of the mocked objects—as we have seen in `MockPublisherRepositoryTests` from one of our previous examples—and can have the shared `@Given` annotated method be used to set up the particular behavior of the mock for the given test. Then we can use the same dependency instance and inject it into another definition class that can be used in order to evaluate the `@Then` annotated assertion methods.

Another approach is the one that we saw in the second definition class, `RestfulStepdefs`, where we injected `BookRepository`. However, in `restful.feature`, we will be using the `Given packt-books fixture is loaded` behavior declaration that translates to the invocation of `data_fixture_is_loaded` method from the `RepositoryStepdefs` class, which shares the same instance of the injected `BookRepository` object, inserting the `packt-books.sql` data into it.

If we were to have a need to access the value of the `loadedBook` field from the `RepositoryStepdefs` instance inside the `RestfulStepdefs` class, we could declare the `@Autowired RepositoryStepdefs` field inside `RestfulStepdefs` and make the `loadedBook` field `public` instead of `private` to make it accessible to the outside world.

Another neat feature of the Cucumber and Spring integration is the use of the `@txn` annotation in the feature files. This tells Spring to execute the tests in a transaction wrapper, reset the database between the test executions, and guarantee a clean database state for every test.

Due to the global method namespace among all the Step Definition classes and test behavior defining feature files, we can use the power of Spring injection to our advantage so as to reuse the testing models and have a common setup logic for all of the tests. This makes the tests behave similarly to how our application would function in a real production environment.

Writing tests using Spock

Another no-less-popular testing framework is Spock, which was written in Groovy by Peter Niederwieser. Being a Groovy-based framework, it is ideally suited to create testing suites for a majority of the JVM-based languages, especially for Java and Groovy itself. The dynamic language traits of Groovy make it well suited to write elegant, efficient, and expressive specifications in the Groovy language without the need for translations. It is done in Cucumber with the help of the Gherkin library. Being based on top of JUnit, and integrating with it through the JUnit's `@RunWith` facility, just like Cucumber does, it is an easy enhancement to the traditional unit tests and works well with all the existing tools, which have built-in support or integration with JUnit.

In this recipe, we will pick up from where the previous recipe left off and enhance our test collection with a couple of Spock-based tests. In these tests, we will see how to set up MockMVC using the Spring dependency injection and testing harnesses. These will be used by the Spock test specifications in order to validate the fact that our data repository services will return the data as expected.

How to do it...

1. In order to add the Spock tests to our application, we will need to make a few changes to our `build.gradle` file first. As Spock tests are written in Groovy, the first thing to do is add a `groovy` plugin to our `build.gradle` file, as follows:

```
apply plugin: 'java'
apply plugin: 'eclipse'
apply plugin: 'groovy'
apply plugin: 'spring-boot'
```

2. We will also need to add the necessary Spock framework dependencies to the `build.gradle` dependencies block:

```
dependencies {
  ...
  testCompile('org.spockframework:spock-core:1.1-groovy-2.4-
rc-2')
  testCompile('org.spockframework:spock-spring:1.1-groovy-2.4-
rc-2')
  ...
}
```

3. As the tests will be in Groovy, we will need to create a new source directory for the files. Let's create the `src/test/groovy/com/example/bookpub` directory in the root of our project.

4. Now we are ready to write our first test. Create a `SpockBookRepositorySpecification.groovy` file in the `src/test/groovy/com/example/bookpub` directory at the root of our project with the following content:

```
package com.example.bookpub;

import com.example.bookpub.entity.Author;
import com.example.bookpub.entity.Book
import com.example.bookpub.entity.Publisher
import com.example.bookpub.repository.BookRepository
import com.example.bookpub.repository.PublisherRepository
import org.mockito.Mockito
import org.springframework.beans.factory.annotation.Autowired
import
org.springframework.boot.test.autoconfigure.web.servlet.AutoCo
nfigureMockMvc
import org.springframework.boot.test.context.SpringBootTest
import org.springframework.boot.test.mock.mockito.MockBean
import
org.springframework.jdbc.datasource.init.DatabasePopulatorUtil
s
import
org.springframework.jdbc.datasource.init.ResourceDatabasePopul
ator
import org.springframework.test.web.servlet.MockMvc
import
org.springframework.transaction.annotation.Transactional
import
org.springframework.web.context.ConfigurableWebApplicationCont
```

```
ext
import spock.lang.Specification

import javax.sql.DataSource

import static org.hamcrest.CoreMatchers.containsString
import static
org.springframework.test.web.servlet.request.MockMvcRequestBui
lders.get
import static
org.springframework.test.web.servlet.result.MockMvcResultMatch
ers.content
import static
org.springframework.test.web.servlet.result.MockMvcResultMatch
ers.status;

@SpringBootTest
@AutoConfigureMockMvc
class SpockBookRepositorySpecification extends Specification {
  @Autowired
  private ConfigurableWebApplicationContext context

  @Autowired
  private DataSource ds;

  @Autowired
  private BookRepository repository;

  @Autowired
  private MockMvc mockMvc;

  void setup() {
    ResourceDatabasePopulator populator =
      new ResourceDatabasePopulator(
        context.getResource("classpath:/packt-books.sql"));
    DatabasePopulatorUtils.execute(populator, ds);
  }

  @Transactional
  def "Test RESTful GET"() {
    when:
      def result = mockMvc.perform(get("/books/${isbn}"));

    then:
      result.andExpect(status().isOk())
      result.andExpect(
        content().string(containsString(title))
      );
```

```
      where:
        isbn                | title
        "978-1-78398-478-7"|"Orchestrating Docker"
        "978-1-78528-415-1"|"Spring Boot Recipes"
      }

      @Transactional
      def "Insert another book"() {
        setup:
          def existingBook =
            repository.findBookByIsbn("978-1-78528-415-1")
          def newBook = new Book("978-1-12345-678-9",
            "Some Future Book", existingBook.getAuthor(),
            existingBook.getPublisher()
          )

        expect:
          repository.count() == 3

        when:
          def savedBook = repository.save(newBook)

        then:
          repository.count() == 4
          savedBook.id > -1
      }
    }
```

5. Execute the tests by running `./gradlew clean test` and the tests should get passed.

6. As Spock integrates with JUnit, we can see the execution report of the Spock tests together with the rest of our test suite. If we open `build/reports/tests/index.html` in the browser and click the **Classes** button, we will see our specification in the table, as shown in the following screenshot:

Test Summary

25	0	0	4.691s	100%
tests	failures	ignored	duration	successful

Packages **Classes**

Class	Tests	Failures	Ignored	Duration	Success rate
Scenario: Load one book	5	0	0	1.782s	100%
978-1-78398-478-7 l Orchestrating Docker l	6	0	0	0.030s	100%
978-1-78528-415-1 l Spring Boot Recipes l	6	0	0	0.018s	100%
com.example.bookpub.BookPubApplicationTests	3	0	0	0.422s	100%
com.example.bookpub.JpaAuthorRepositoryTests	1	0	0	0.051s	100%
com.example.bookpub.MockPublisherRepositoryTests	1	0	0	0.009s	100%
com.example.bookpub.RunCukeTests	0	0	0	-	-
com.example.bookpub.SpockBookRepositorySpecification	2	0	0	2.358s	100%
com.example.bookpub.WebMvcBookControllerTests	1	0	0	0.021s	100%

7. Selecting the **com.example.bookpub.SpockBookRespositorySpecification** link will take us to the detailed report page, which is as follows:

Class org.test.bookpub.SpockBookRepositorySpecification

all > org.test.bookpub > SpockBookRepositorySpecification

2	0	0	0.280s	100%
tests	failures	ignored	duration	successful

Tests   Standard output

Test	Duration	Result
Insert another book	0.061s	passed
Test RESTful GET	0.219s	passed

8. Next, we will take our tests a bit further and explore the mocking functionality of the database repositories. Let's use `PublisherRepository` as our candidate to mock, and wire it into the `BookController` class to provide a `getBooksByPublisher` functionality. Let's add the following content to the `BookController` class in the `src/main/java/com/example/bookpub/controllers` directory at the root of our project:

```
@Autowired
private PublisherRepository publisherRepository;

@RequestMapping(value = "/publisher/{id}", method =
RequestMethod.GET)
public List<Book> getBooksByPublisher(@PathVariable("id") Long
id) {
    Optional<Publisher> publisher =
        publisherRepository.findById(id);
    Assert.notNull(publisher);
    Assert.isTrue(publisher.isPresent());
    return publisher.get().getBooks();
}
```

9. Let's add the following to the `Publisher` class in the `src/main/java/com/example/bookpub/entity` directory at the root of our project:

```
@OneToMany(mappedBy = "publisher")
@JsonBackReference
private List<Book> books;
```

10. Lastly, let's add a getter and setter for the books to the `Publisher` entity class as well:

```
public List<Book> getBooks() {
    return books;
}

public void setBooks(List<Book> books) {
    this.books = books;
}
```

11. With all the code additions completed, we are ready to add another test to the `SpockBookRepositorySpecification.groovy` file in the `src/test/groovy/com/example/bookpub` directory at the root of our project with the following content:

```
...
class SpockBookRepositorySpecification extends Specification {
    ...
    @MockBean
    private PublisherRepository publisherRepository

    @Transactional
    def "Test RESTful GET books by publisher"() {
        setup:
            Publisher publisher =
                    new Publisher("Strange Books")
            publisher.setId(999)
            Book book = new Book("978-1-98765-432-1",
                "Mystery Book",
                new Author("John", "Doe"),
                publisher)
            publisher.setBooks([book])
            Mockito.when(publisherRepository.count()).
                thenReturn(1L)
            Mockito.when(publisherRepository.findById(1L)).
                thenReturn(Optional.of(publisher))

        when:
            def result =
              mockMvc.perform(get("/books/publisher/1"))

        then:
            result.andExpect(status().isOk())
            result.andExpect(content().
                string(containsString("Strange Books")))

        cleanup:
            Mockito.reset(publisherRepository)
    }
}
```

12. Execute the tests by running `./gradlew clean test` and the tests should continue to get passed.

How it works...

As you saw from this example, writing tests can be just as elaborate and sophisticated as the production code being tested itself. Let's examine the steps that we took in order to get the Spock tests integrated into our Spring Boot application.

The first thing that we did was to add a Groovy plugin in order to make our build Groovy-friendly, and we also added the required Spock library dependencies of `spock-core` and `spock-spring`, both of which are required to make Spock work with Spring's dependency injection and contexts.

The next step was to create the `SpockBookRepositorySpecification` Spock specification, which extends the Spock's specification abstract base class. Extending the `Specification` class is very important because this is how JUnit knows that our class is the test class that needs to be executed. If we look in the `Specification` source, we will see the `@RunWith(Sputnik.class)` annotation, just like the one that we used in the Cucumber recipe. In addition to the JUnit bootstrapping, the `Specification` class provides us with many helpful methods and mocking support as well.

> For more information about the detailed capabilities that are offered by Spock, you can refer to the Spock documentation that is available at `http://spockframework.github.io/spock/docs/current/index.html`.

It is also worth mentioning that we used the same annotations for the `SpockBookRepositorySpecification` class as we did for our Spring Boot-based tests, as shown in the following code:

```
@SpringBootTest
@AutoConfigureMockMvc
```

The reason that we had to add `@AutoConfigureMockMvc` in addition to `@SpringBootTest` is to add functionality to allow us to use the `@Autowire` `MockMvc` instance instead of having to create one ourselves. Regular `@SpringBootTest` does not automatically create and configure an instance of a `MockMvc` object, so we could have either created it manually, as we did in `BookPubApplicationTests`, or added the `@AutoConfigureMockMvc` annotation, which is what gets used inside `@WebMvcTest`, to let Spring handle it for us. The good news is that we can always use the same annotation compositions as used by Spring Boot, and annotate our classes directly, which is exactly what we did.

Unlike Cucumber, Spock combines all the aspects of the test in one `Specification` class, dividing it into multiple blocks, as follows:

- `setup`: This block is used to configure the specific test with variables, populating data, building mocks, and so on.
- `expect`: This block is one of the stimulus blocks, as Spock defines it, designed to contain simple expressions asserting a state or condition. Besides evaluating the conditions, we can only define variables in this block, and nothing else is allowed.
- `when`: This block is another stimulus type block, which always goes together with `then`. It can contain any arbitrary code and is designed to define the behavior that we are trying to test.
- `then`: This block is a response type block. It is similar to `expect` and can only contain conditions, exception checking, variable definition, and object interactions, such as how many times a particular method has been called and so forth.

> More information on interaction testing is available on Spock's website at `http://spockframework.github.io/spock/docs/current/interaction_based_testing.html`.

- `cleanup`: This block is used to clean the state of the environment and potentially undo whatever changes were done as part of the individual test execution. In our recipe, this is where we will reset our `PublisherRepository` mock object.

Spock provides us with the instance-based `setup()` and `cleanup()` methods as well, which can be used to define the setup and cleanup behavior that is common to all the tests in the specification.

If we look at our `setup()` method, this is where we can configure the database population with the test data. An interesting and important nuance is that the `setup()` method gets executed before every test method, not once per class. It is important to keep that in mind when doing things like populating a database to avoid re-insertion of the same data multiple times without proper rollback.

To help us with that is the `@Transactional` annotation of the test methods. Just like the `@txn` tag in the Cucumber feature files, this annotation instructs Spock to execute the annotated method and its corresponding `setup()` and `cleanup()` executions with a transaction scope, which get rolled back after the particular test method is finished. We rely on this behavior to get a clean database state for every test, so we don't end up inserting duplicate data during the execution of the `setup()` method every time each of our tests runs.

Most of you are probably wondering why we had to add the `@JsonBackReference` annotation to our `Publisher` entity class. The answer has to do with the Jackson JSON parser and how it handles circular dependency. In our model, we have a book belonging to a publisher and each publisher has multiple books. When we created our `Publisher` class with the `Books` mock and assigned a publisher instance to a book—which later got put in the publisher's book collection—we created a circular reference. During the execution of the `BookController.getBooksByPublisher(...)` method, the Jackson renderer would have thrown `StackOverflowError` while trying to write the object model to JSON. By adding this annotation to `Publisher`, we told Jackson how the objects reference each other, so instead of trying to write out the complete object tree, Jackson now handles it correctly, thus avoiding the circular reference loop situation.

The last thing that is important to keep in mind is how Spring Boot handles and processes the repository interfaces that are annotated with `@RepositoryRestResource`. Unlike the `BookRepository` interface, which we have annotated with a plain `@Repository` annotation and later explicitly declared as an autowire dependency of our `BookController` class, we did not create an explicit controller to handle RESTful requests for the rest of our repository interfaces such as `PublisherRepository` and others. These interfaces get scanned by Spring Boot and automatically wrapped with the mapped endpoints that trap the requests and delegate the calls to the backing `SimpleJpaRepository` proxy. Due to this setup, we can use only the mock object replacement approach for these objects that have been explicitly injected as bean dependencies such as with our example of `BookRepository`. The good news is that in these situations, where we don't explicitly expect beans to be wired and only use some annotations to stereotype the interfaces for Spring Boot to do its magic, we can rely on Spring Boot to do the job correctly. We know that it has tested all the functionalities behind it so that we don't have to test them. To test the actual repository and entity functionality, we can use the `@DataJpaTest` annotation to do a specific JPA slice test instead.

25

Application Packaging and Deployment

In this chapter, we will cover the following topics:

- Creating a Spring Boot executable JAR
- Creating Docker images
- Building self-executing binaries
- Spring Boot environment configuration, hierarchy, and precedence
- Adding a custom PropertySource to the environment using EnvironmentPostProcessor
- Externalizing an environmental configuration using property files
- Externalizing an environmental configuration using environment variables
- Externalizing an environmental configuration using Java system properties
- Externalizing an environmental configuration using JSON
- Setting up Consul
- Externalizing an environmental configuration using Consul and envconsul

Introduction

What good is an application unless it is being used? In today's day and age—when DevOps has become the way of doing software development, when the cloud is the king, and when building microservices is considered the thing to do—a lot of attention is being focused on how applications get packaged, distributed, and deployed in their designated environments.

The Twelve-Factor App methodology has played an instrumental role in defining how a modern **Software as a Service (SaaS)** application is supposed to be built and deployed. One of the key principles is the separation of environmental configuration definitions from the application and storage of this in the environments. The Twelve-Factor App methodology also favors the isolation and bundling of the dependencies, development versus production parity, and ease of deployment and disposability of the applications, among other things.

> The Twelve-Factor App methodology can be found at
> `http://12factor.net/`.

The DevOps model also encourages us to have complete ownership of our application, starting from writing and testing the code all the way to building and deploying it. If we are to assume this ownership, we need to ensure that the maintenance and overhead costs are not excessive and won't take away much time from our primary task of developing new features. This can be achieved by having clean, well-defined, and isolated deployable artifacts, which are self-contained, self-executed, and can be deployed in any environment without having to be rebuilt.

The following recipes will walk us through all the necessary steps to achieve the goal of low-effort deployment and maintenance while having clean and elegant code behind it.

Creating a Spring Boot executable JAR

The Spring Boot magic would not be complete without providing a nice way to package the entire application including all of its dependencies, resources, and so on in one composite, executable JAR file. After the JAR file is created, it can simply be launched by running a `java -jar <name>.jar` command.

We will continue with the application code that we built in the previous chapters and will add the necessary functionalities to package it. Let's go ahead and take a look at how to create the Spring Boot Uber JAR.

The Uber JAR is typically known as an application bundle encapsulated in a single composite JAR file that internally contains a /lib directory with all the dependent inner jars and optionally a /bin directory with the executables.

How to do it...

1. Let's go to our code directory from Chapter 24, *Application Testing*, and execute ./gradlew clean build

2. With the Uber JAR built, let's launch the application by executing java -jar build/libs/ch6-0.0.1-SNAPSHOT.jar

3. This will result in our application running in the JAR file with the following console output:

```
  .   ____          _            __ _ _
 /\\ / ___'_ __ _ _(_)_ __  __ _ \ \ \ \
( ( )\___ | '_ | '_| | '_ \/ _` | \ \ \ \
 \\/  ___)| |_)| | | | | || (_| |  ) ) ) )
  '  |____| .__|_| |_|_| |_\__, | / / / /
 =========|_|==============|___/=/_/_/_/
 :: Spring Boot ::   (v2.0.0.BUILD-SNAPSHOT)
...
(The rest is omitted for conciseness)
...
2017-12-17 INFO: Registering beans for JMX exposure on
startup
2017-12-17 INFO: Tomcat started on port(s): 8080 (http)
8443
(https)
2017-12-17 INFO: Welcome to the Book Catalog System!
2017-12-17 INFO: BookRepository has 1 entries
2017-12-17 INFO: ReviewerRepository has 0 entries
2017-12-17 INFO: PublisherRepository has 1 entries
2017-12-17 INFO: AuthorRepository has 1 entries
2017-12-17 INFO: Started BookPubApplication in 12.156
seconds (JVM
running for 12.877)
2017-12-17 INFO: Number of books: 1
```

How it works...

As you can see, getting the packaged executable JAR file is fairly straightforward. All the magic is already coded and provided to us as part of the Spring Boot Gradle plugin. The addition of the plugin adds a number of tasks, which allow us to package the Spring Boot application, run it and build the JAR, TAR, WAR files, and so on. For example, the bootRun task, which we have been using throughout this book, is provided by the Spring Boot Gradle plugin, among others. We can see a complete list of the available Gradle tasks by executing ./gradlew tasks. When we run this command, we will get the following output:

```
------------------------------------------------------------
All tasks runnable from root project
------------------------------------------------------------
Application tasks
----------------
bootRun - Run the project with support for auto-detecting main
class and reloading static resources
run - Runs this project as a JVM application
Build tasks
-----------
assemble - Assembles the outputs of this project.
bootJar - Assembles an executable jar archive containing the main
classes and their dependencies.
build - Assembles and tests this project.
buildDependents - Assembles and tests this project and all
projects
that depend on it.
buildNeeded - Assembles and tests this project and all projects it
depends on.
classes - Assembles classes 'main'.
clean - Deletes the build directory.
jar - Assembles a jar archive containing the main classes.
testClasses - Assembles classes 'test'.
Build Setup tasks
-----------------
init - Initializes a new Gradle build. [incubating]
Distribution tasks
------------------
assembleBootDist - Assembles the boot distributions
assembleDist - Assembles the main distributions
bootDistTar - Bundles the project as a distribution.
bootDistZip - Bundles the project as a distribution.
distTar - Bundles the project as a distribution.
distZip - Bundles the project as a distribution.
installBootDist - Installs the project as a distribution as-is.
```

```
installDist - Installs the project as a distribution as-is.
```

The preceding output is not complete; I've excluded the non-relevant task groups such as IDE, documentation, and so on, but you will see them on your console. In the task list, we will see tasks such as bootRun, bootJar, and others. These tasks have been added by the Spring Boot Gradle plugin and executing them gets the required Spring Boot steps added to the build pipeline. You can see the actual task dependency if you execute ./gradlew tasks --all, which will not only print the visible tasks, but also the depended, internal tasks, and the task dependencies. For example, when we were running the build task, all the following dependent tasks were executed as well:

```
build - Assembles and tests this project. [assemble, check]
assemble - Assembles the outputs of this project. [bootJar,
distTar, distZip, jar]
```

You can see that the build task will execute the assemble task, which in turn will call bootJar, where the creation of the Uber JAR is actually taking place.

The plugin also provides a number of very useful configuration options. While I am not going to go into detail about all of them, I'll mention the two that I find very useful:

```
bootJar {
    classifier = 'exec'
    baseName = 'bookpub'
}
```

This configuration allows us to specify the executable JAR file classifier, along with the JAR baseName, allowing for having the regular JAR contain just the application code and the executable JAR with the classifier in the name, bookpub-0.0.1-SNAPSHOT-exec.jar.

Another useful configuration option allows us to specify which dependency JARs require unpacking because, for some reason, they can't be included as nested inner JARs. This comes in very handy when you need something to be available in the system Classloader such as setting a custom SecurityManager via the startup system properties:

```
bootJar {
    requiresUnpack = '**/some-jar-name-*.jar'
}
```

In this example, the contents of the some-jar-name-1.0.3.jar dependency will be unpacked into a temporary folder on a filesystem when the application is launched.

Creating Docker images

Docker, Docker, Docker! I hear this phrase more and more in all the conferences and tech meetups that I have attended. The arrival of Docker has been welcomed by the community with open arms and it has instantly become a hit. The Docker ecosystem has been rapidly expanding with many other companies providing services, support, and complementing frameworks such as **Apache Mesos**, Amazon Elastic Beanstalk, ECS, and Kubernetes, just to name a few. Even Microsoft is providing Docker support in their Azure Cloud Service and is partnering with Docker to bring Docker to Windows operating system.

The reason for Docker's overwhelming popularity lies in its ability to package and deploy applications in a form of self-contained containers. The containers are more lightweight than the traditional full-blown virtual machines. Multiple numbers of them can be run on top of a single OS instance, thus increasing the number of applications that can be deployed on the same hardware compared to traditional VMs.

In this recipe, we will take a look at what it would take to package our Spring Boot application as a Docker image and how to deploy and run it.

Building a Docker image and just running it on your development machine is doable, but not as much fun as being able to share it with the world. You will need to publish it somewhere for it to be deployable, especially if you are thinking of using it with Amazon or some other cloud-like environment. Luckily, Docker provides us with not only the container solution, but also with a repository service, Docker Hub, located at `https://hub.docker.com`, where we can create repositories and publish our Docker images. So think of it like Maven Central for Docker.

How to do it...

1. The first step will be to create an account on Docker Hub so that we can publish our images. Go to `https://hub.docker.com` and create an account. You can also use your GitHub account and log in using it if you have one.
2. Once you have an account, we will need to create a repository named `springbootcookbook`.
3. With this account created, now is the time to build the image. For this, we will use one of the Gradle Docker plugins. We will start by changing `build.gradle` to modify the `buildscript` block with the following change:

```
buildscript {
  dependencies {
    classpath("org.springframework.boot:spring-boot-gradle-
      plugin:${springBootVersion}")
    classpath("se.transmode.gradle:gradle-docker:1.2")
  }
}
```

4. We will also need to apply this plugin by adding the `apply plugin:` `'docker'` directive to the `build.gradle` file.

5. We also need to explicitly add the `application` plugin to `build.gradle` as well, since it is no longer automatically included by the Spring Boot Gradle plugin.

6. Add `apply plugin: 'application'` to the list of plugins in the `build.gradle` file.

7. Lastly, we will need to add the following Docker configuration to the `build.gradle` file as well:

```
task distDocker(type: Docker,
                overwrite: true,
                dependsOn: bootDistTar) {
    group = 'docker'
    description = "Packs the project's JVM application
    as a Docker image."

    inputs.files project.bootDistTar
    def installDir = "/" + project.bootDistTar.archiveName
                        - ".${project.bootDistTar.extension}"

    doFirst {
        tag "ch6"
        push false
        exposePort 8080
        exposePort 8443
        addFile file("${System.properties['user.home']}
        /.keystore"), "/root/"
        applicationName = project.applicationName
        addFile project.bootDistTar.outputs.files.singleFile

        entryPoint =
["$installDir/bin/${project.applicationName}"]
    }
}
```

8. Assuming that you already have Docker installed on your machine, we can proceed to creating the image by executing `./gradlew clean distDocker`.

9. For Docker installation instructions, please visit the tutorial that is located at `https://docs.docker.com/installation/#installation`. If everything has worked out correctly, you should see the following output:

```
> Task :distDocker
Sending build context to Docker daemon   68.22MB
  Step 1/6 : FROM aglover/java8-pier
   ---> 3f3822d3ece5
  Step 2/6 : EXPOSE 8080
   ---> Using cache
   ---> 73717aaca6f3
  Step 3/6 : EXPOSE 8443
   ---> Using cache
   ---> 6ef3c0fc3d2a
  Step 4/6 : ADD .keystore /root/
   ---> Using cache
   ---> 6efebb5a868b
  Step 5/6 : ADD ch6-boot-0.0.1-SNAPSHOT.tar /
   ---> Using cache
   ---> 0634eace4952
  Step 6/6 : ENTRYPOINT /ch6-boot-0.0.1-SNAPSHOT/bin/ch6
   ---> Using cache
   ---> 39a853b7ddbb
Successfully built 39a853b7ddbb
Successfully tagged ch6:0.0.1-SNAPSHOT
BUILD SUCCESSFUL
Total time: 1 mins 0.009 secs.
```

10. We can also execute the following Docker images command so as to see the newly created image:

```
$ docker images
REPOSITORY              TAG              IMAGE ID
CREATED                 VIRTUAL   SIZE
ch6                     0.0.1-SNAPSHOT   39a853b7ddbb      17
minutes ago       1.04 GB
aglover/java8-pier     latest            69f4574a230e      11
months ago        1.01 GB
```

11. With the image built successfully, we are now ready to start it in Docker by executing the following command:

    ```
    docker run -d -P ch6:0.0.1-SNAPSHOT.
    ```

12. After the container has started, we can query the Docker registry for the port bindings so that we can access the HTTP endpoints for our service. This can be done via the docker ps command. If the container is running successfully, we should see the following result (names and ports will vary):

    ```
    CONTAINER ID          IMAGE              COMMAND
    CREATED               STATUS             PORTS
    NAMES
    37b37e411b9e          ch6:latest         "/ch6-boot-0.0.1-
    S..."
    10 minutes ago        Up 10 minutes      0.0.0.0:32778-
    >8080/tcp,     0.0.0.0:32779->8443/tcp    drunk_carson
    ```

13. From this output, we can tell that the port mapping for the internal port 8080 has been set up to be 32778 (your port will vary for every run). Let's open http://localhost:32778/books in the browser to see our application in action, as shown in the following screenshot:

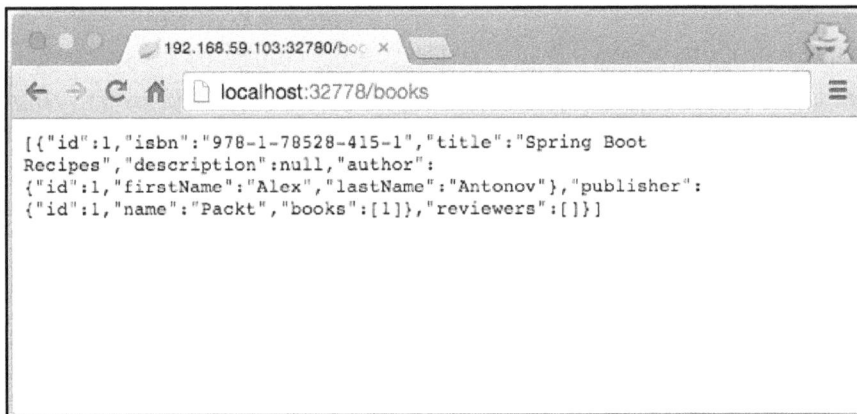

If you are using macOS X with `boot2docker`, then you won't be running the Docker container locally. In this scenario, you will be using the `boot2docker ip` instead of the local host to connect to the application. For more tips on how to make the `boot2docker` integration easier, please visit `http://viget.com/extend/how-to-use-docker-on-os-x-the-missing-guide`. One can also use a nice Docker façade, generously created by Ian Sinnott, which will automatically start boot2docker and handle the environment variables as well. To get the wrapper, go to `https://gist.github.com/iansinnott/0a0c212260386bdbfafb`.

How it works...

In the preceding example, we saw how easy it is to have our `build` package the application in a Docker container. The additional Gradle-Docker plugin does the bulk of the work of the `Dockerfile` creation, image building, and publishing; all we have to do is give it some instructions on what and how we want the image to be. Because the Spring Boot Gradle plugin uses a `boot` distribution, the Gradle-Docker plugin does not know that it needs to use a bootified TAR archive. To help with that, we override the `distDocker` task. Let's examine these instructions in detail:

- The `group` and `description` attributes merely help with displaying the task properly when the `./gradlew tasks` command is executed.
- The `inputs.files project.bootDistTar` directive is very important. This is what instructs the `distDocker` task to use the TAR archive created by the Spring Boot distribution, instead of the generic one.
- The `def installDir = "/" + project.bootDistTar.archiveName - ".${project.bootDistTar.extension}"` directive is creating a variable, containing the directory where the untarred artifacts will be placed inside the Docker container.
- The `exposePort` directive tells the plugin to add an `EXPOSE <port>` instruction to the Dockerfile so that when our container is started, it will expose these internal ports to the outside via port mapping. We saw this mapping while running the `docker ps` command.

- The `addFile` directive tells the plugin to add an `ADD <src> <dest>` instruction to the Dockerfile so that when the container is being built, we will copy the file from the source filesystem in the filesystem in the container image. In our case, we will need to copy the `.keystore` certificate file that we configured in one of our previous recipes for the HTTPS connector, which we instructed in `tomcat.https.properties` to be loaded from `${user.home}/.keystore`. Now, we need it to be in the `/root/` directory directory as, in the container, our application will be executed under the root. (This can be changed with more configurations.)

> The Gradle-Docker plugin uses the project name as a name for the image by default. The project name, in turn, is being inferred by Gradle from the project's directory name, unless an explicit property value is configured. As the code example is for `Chapter 25, Application Packaging and Deployment` the project directory is named `ch25`, thus the name of the image. The project name can be explicitly configured by adding `name='some_project_name'` in `gradle.properties`.

If you look at the resulting Dockerfile, which can be found in the `build/docker/` directory at the root of the project, you will see the following two instructions:

```
ADD ch25-boot-0.0.1-SNAPSHOT.tar /
ENTRYPOINT ["/ch6-boot-0.0.1-SNAPSHOT/bin/ch6"]
```

The `ADD` instruction adds the TAR application archive that was produced by the `bootDistTar` task and contains our application bundled up as a tarball. We can even see the contents of the produced tarball by executing `tar tvf build/distributions/ch6-boot-0.0.1-SNAPSHOT.tar`. During the building of the container, the contents of the TAR file will be extracted in the `/` directory in the container and later used to launch the application.

It is followed by the `ENTRYPOINT` instruction. This tells Docker to execute `/ch6-boot-0.0.1-SNAPSHOT/bin/ch6`, which we saw as part of the tarball content, once the container is started, thus automatically launching our application.

The first line in the Dockerfile, which is `FROM aglover/java8-pier`, is the instruction to use the `aglover/java8-pier` image, which contains the Ubuntu OS with Java 8 installed as a base image for our container, on which we will install our application. This image comes from the Docker Hub Repository and is automatically used by the plugin, but can be changed via the configuration settings, if so desired.

If you created an account on Docker Hub, we can also publish the created Docker image to the registry. As fair warning, the resulting image could be many hundreds of megabytes in size so uploading it could take some time. To publish this image, we will need to change the tag to tag "<docker hub username>/<docker hub repository name>" and add the push true setting to the distDocker task definition in build.gradle:

```
task distDocker(type: Docker,
                overwrite: true,
                dependsOn: bootDistTar) {
    ...
  doFirst {
      tag "<docker hub username>/<docker hub repository
name>"
      push true
      ...
  }
}
```

The tag property sets up the created image tag and, by default, the plugin assumes that it is residing in the Docker Hub Repository. This is where it will be publishing it if the push configuration is set to true, as it is in our case.

> For a complete list of all the Gradle-Docker plugin configuration options, take a look at the
> https://github.com/Transmode/gradle-docker GitHub project page.

When launching a Docker image, we use the -d and -P command-line arguments. Their uses are as follows:

- -d: This argument indicates the desire to run the container in a detached mode where the process starts in the background
- -P: This argument instructs Docker to publish all the internally exposed ports to the outside so that we can access them

> For a detailed explanation of all the possible command-line options, refer to https://docs.docker.com/reference/commandline/cli/.

Building self-executing binaries

As of Spring Boot version 1.3, the Gradle and Maven plugins support the option of generating true executable binaries. These look like normal JAR files, but have the content of JAR fused together with the launch script that contains the command-building logic and is capable of self-starting itself without the need to execute the `java -jar file.jar` command explicitly. This capability comes in very handy as it allows for the easy configuration of Linux autostart services such as `init.d` or `systemd`, and `launchd` on macOS X.

Getting ready

For this recipe, we will use our existing application build. We will examine how the self-starting executable JAR files get created and how to modify the default launch script to add support for the custom JVM start up arguments, such as the `-D` start up system properties, JVM memory, Garbage Collection, and other settings.

For this recipe, make sure that `build.gradle` is using Spring Boot version 2.0.0 or above. If it is not, then change the following setting in the `buildscript` configuration block:

```
ext {
    springBootVersion = '2.0.0.BUILD-SNAPSHOT'
}
```

The same upgrade of the Spring Boot version should be done in the `db-counter-starter/build.gradle` file as well.

How to do it...

1. Building a default self-executing JAR file is very easy; actually, it is done automatically once we execute the `./gradlew clean bootJar` command.
2. We can proceed to launch the created application simply by invoking `./build/libs/bookpub-0.0.1-SNAPSHOT.jar`.

3. In an enterprise environment, it is rare that we are satisfied with the default JVM launch arguments as we often need to tweak the memory settings, GC configurations, and even pass the startup system properties in order to ensure that we are using the desired version of the XML parser or a proprietary implementation of class loader or security manager. To accomplish those needs, we will modify the default `launch.script` file to add support for the JVM options. Let's start by copying the default `launch.script` file from the `https://github.com/spring-projects/spring-boot/blob/master/spring-boot-project/spring-boot-tools/spring-boot-loader-tools/src/main/resources/org/springframework/boot/loader/tools/launch.script` Spring Boot GitHub repository in the root of our project.

The `launch.script` file is supported only on Linux and OS X environments. If you are looking to make self-executing JARs for Windows, you will need to provide your own `launch.script` file that is tailored for the Windows shell command execution. The good news is that it is the only special thing that is required; all the instructions and concepts in this recipe will work just fine on Windows as well, provided that the compliant `launch.script` template is being used.

4. We will modify the copied `launch.script` file and add the following content right above the *line 142* mark (this is showing only the relevant part of the script so as to condense the space):

```
...
# Find Java
if [[ -n "$JAVA_HOME" ]] && [[ -x "$JAVA_HOME/bin/java" ]];
then
javaexe="$JAVA_HOME/bin/java"
elif type -p java 2>&1> /dev/null; then
javaexe=java
elif [[ -x "/usr/bin/java" ]]; then
javaexe="/usr/bin/java"
else
echo "Unable to find Java"
exit 1
fi
# Configure JVM Options
jvmopts="{{jvm_options:}}"
arguments=(-Dsun.misc.URLClassPath.disableJarChecking=true
$jvmopts $JAVA_OPTS -jar $jarfile $RUN_ARGS "$@")
# Action functions
start() {
...
```

5. With the custom `launch.script` file in place, we will need to add the options setting to our `build.gradle` file with the following content:

```
applicationDefaultJvmArgs = [
    "-Xms128m",
    "-Xmx256m"
]

bootJar {
    classifier = 'exec'
    baseName = 'bookpub'
    launchScript {
        script = file('launch.script')
        properties 'jvm_options' :
applicationDefaultJvmArgs.join(' ')
    }
}
```

6. We are now ready to launch our application. First, let's use the `./gradlew clean bootRun` command, and if we look at the JConsole VM Summary tab, we will see that our arguments indeed have been passed to the JVM, as follows:

Current heap size:	69,370 kbytes
Maximum heap size:	233,472 kbytes
Garbage collector:	Name = 'PS MarkSweep', Collections = 2, Total time spent = 0.136 seconds
Garbage collector:	Name = 'PS Scavenge', Collections = 34, Total time spent = 0.144 seconds
Operating System:	Mac OS X 10.10.3
Architecture:	x86_64
Number of processors:	8
Committed virtual memory:	4,299,488 kbytes
VM arguments:	-Xms128m -Xmx256m -Dfile.encoding=UTF-8 -Duser.country=US -Duser.language=en -Duser.variant

7. We can also build the self-starting executable JAR by running the `./gradlew clean bootJar` command and then executing `./build/libs/bookpub-0.0.1-SNAPSHOT-exec.jar` in order to launch our application. We should expect to see a similar result in JConsole.

8. Alternatively, we can also use the `JAVA_OPTS` environment variable to override some of the JVM arguments. Say we want to change the minimum memory heap size to 128 megabytes. We can launch our application using the `JAVA_OPTS=-Xmx128m ./build/libs/bookpub-0.0.1-SNAPSHOT-exec.jar` command and this would show us the following effect in JConsole:

Current heap size: 49,311 kbytes	**Committed memory:** 125,952 kbytes
Maximum heap size: 125,952 kbytes	**Pending finalization:** {0} objects
Garbage collector: Name = 'PS MarkSweep', Collections = 2, Total time spent = 0.207 seconds	
Garbage collector: Name = 'PS Scavenge', Collections = 81, Total time spent = 0.287 seconds	

Operating System: Mac OS X 10.10.3		**Total physical memory:** 16,777,216 kbytes
Architecture: x86_64		**Free physical memory:** 410,752 kbytes
Number of processors: 8		**Total swap space:** 5,242,880 kbytes
Committed virtual memory: 4,161,596 kbytes		**Free swap space:** 1,152,000 kbytes

VM arguments: -Xms128m -Xmx256m -Xmx128m -Dsun.misc.URLClassPath.disableJarChecking=true

How it works...

With a small customization to `launch.script`, we were able to create a self-executing deployable application, packaged as a self-contained JAR file, which on top of everything else can also be configured in order to be launched using the various OS-specific autostarting frameworks.

The Spring Boot Gradle and Maven plugins provide us with lots of options for parameter customization and even an ability to embed mustache-like template placeholders in `launch.script`, which can later be replaced with values during build time. We have leveraged this capability to inject our JVM arguments into the file using the `launchScript{properties}` configuration setting.

In our custom version of `launch.script`, we added the `jvmopts="{{jvm_options:}}"` line, which will be replaced with the value of the `jvm_options` parameter during the build and packaging time. This parameter is declared in our `build.gradle` file as a value of the `launchScript.properties` argument : `launchScript{properties 'jvm_options' : applicationDefaultJvmArgs.join(' ')}`.

The JVM arguments can be hardcoded, but it is much better to maintain consistency between how our application starts using the `bootRun` task and how it starts when launched from the self-executing JAR. To achieve this, we will use the same `applicationDefaultJvmArgs` collection of arguments that we will define for the `bootRun` execution purpose, only with all the different arguments collapsed in a single line of text separated by white spaces. Using this approach, we have to define the JVM arguments only once and use them in both modes of execution.

> It is important to notice that this reuse also applies to the application distributions that are built using the `distZip` and `distTar` tasks defined by Gradle's `application` plugin, as well as Spring Boot Gradle's `bootDistZip` and `bootDistTar`.

We can modify the build to create the Docker image by launching our self-executing JAR instead of the contents of the TAR file produced by the `distTar` task by default. To do this, we will need to change our `distDocker` configuration block using the following code:

```
task distDocker(type: Docker, overwrite: true,
                dependsOn: bootJar) {
    . . .
    inputs.files project.bootJar
    doFirst {
        . . .
        addFile file("${System.properties['user.home']}/.keystore"),
            "/root/"
        applicationName = project.applicationName
        addFile project.bootJar.outputs.files.singleFile

        def executableName = "/" +
            project.bootJar.outputs.files.singleFile.name
        entryPoint = ["$executableName"]
    }
}
```

This will make our `distDocker` task put the executable jar inside a Docker image instead of a TAR archive.

Spring Boot environment configuration, hierarchy, and precedence

In the previous few recipes, we looked at how to package our application in a variety of ways and how it can be deployed. The next logical step is the need to configure the application in order to provide some behavioral control as well as some environment-specific configuration values, which could and most likely will vary from environment to environment.

A common example of such an environmental configuration difference is the database setup. We certainly don't want to connect to a production environment database with an application running on our development machine. There are also cases where we want an application to run in different modes or use a different set of profiles, as they are referred to by Spring. An example could be running an application in live or simulator mode.

For this recipe, we will pick up from the previous state of the code base and add the support for different configuration profiles as well as examine how to use the property values as placeholders in other properties.

How to do it...

1. We will start by adding an @Profile annotation to the @Bean creation of schedulerRunner by changing the definition of the schedulerRunner(...) method in BookPubApplication.java, located in the src/main/java/org/test/bookpub directory at the root of our project, to the following content:

```
@Bean
@Profile("logger")
public StartupRunner schedulerRunner() {
    return new StartupRunner();
}
```

2. Start the application by running ./gradlew clean bootRun.

3. Once the application is running, we should no longer see the previous log output from the StartupRunner class, which looked like this:

```
2017-12-17 --- org.test.bookpub.StartupRunner : Number of
books: 1
```

4. Now, let's build the application by running `./gradlew clean bootJar` and start it by running `./build/libs/bookpub-0.0.1-SNAPSHOT-exec.jar --spring.profiles.active=logger`; we will see the log output line show up again.

5. Another functionality that is enabled by the profile selector is the ability to add profile-specific property files. Let's create an `application-inmemorydb.properties` file in the `src/main/resources` directory at the root of our project with the following content:

```
spring.datasource.url =
jdbc:h2:mem:testdb;DB_CLOSE_DELAY=-1;DB_CLOSE_ON_EXIT=FALSE
```

6. Let's build the application by running `./gradlew clean bootJar` and start it by running `./build/libs/bookpub-0.0.1-SNAPSHOT-exec.jar --spring.profiles.active=logger,inmemorydb`, which will use the `inmemorydb` profile configuration in order to use the in-memory database instead of the file-based one.

How it works...

In this recipe, we experimented with using profiles and applying additional configuration settings based on the active profiles. Profiles were first introduced in Spring Framework 3.2 and were used to conditionally configure the beans in context, depending on which profiles were active. In Spring Boot, this facility was extended even further to allow configuration separation as well.

By placing an `@Profile("logger")` annotation on our `StartupRunner@Bean` creation method, Spring will be instructed to create the bean only if the logger profile has been activated. Conventionally, this is done by passing the `--spring.profiles.active` option in the command line during the application startup. In the tests, another way that this can be done is using the `@ActiveProfiles("profile")` annotation on the `Test` class, but it is not supported for the execution of a normal application. It is also possible to negate profiles such as `@Profile("!production")`. When such an annotation is used (with ! marking the negation), the bean will be created only if no profile production is active.

During startup, Spring Boot treats all the options that get passed via the command line as application properties, and thus anything that gets passed during startup ends up as a property value that is capable of being used. This same mechanism not only works for new properties but can be used as a way of overriding the existing properties as well. Let's imagine a situation where we already have an active profile defined in our `application.properties` file that looks like this: `spring.profiles.active=basic`. By passing the `--spring.profiles.active=logger` option via the command line, we will replace the active profile from `basic` to `logger`. If we want to include some profiles regardless of the active configuration, Spring Boot gives us a `spring.profiles.include` option to configure. Any profiles that are set up this way will be added to the list of active profiles.

As these options are nothing more than regular Spring Boot application properties, they all follow the same hierarchy for override precedence. The options have been outlined as follows:

- **Command-line arguments**: These values supersede every other property source in the list, and you can always rest assured that anything passed via `--property.name=value` will take precedence over the other means.
- **JNDI attributes**: They are the next in precedence priority. If you are using an application container that provides data via a JNDI `java:comp/env` namespace, these values will override all the other settings from below.
- **Java system properties**: These values are another way to pass the properties to the application either via the `-Dproperty=name` command-line arguments or by calling `System.setProperty(...)` in the code. They provide another way to replace the existing properties. Anything coming from `System.getProperty(...)` will win over the others in the list.
- **OS environment variables**: Whether from Windows, Linux, OS X, or any other, they are a common way to specify a configuration, especially for locations and values. The most notable one is `JAVA_HOME`, which is a common way to indicate where the JVM location resides in the filesystem. If neither of the preceding settings are present, the `ENV` variables will be used for the property values instead of the ones mentioned as follows:

As the OS environment variables typically don't support dots (`.`) or dashes (`-`), Spring Boot provides an automatic remapping mechanism that replaces the underscores (`_`) with dots (`.`) during the property evaluation; it also handles the case conversion. Thus, `JAVA_HOME` becomes synonymous with `java.home`.

- `random.*`: This provides special support for the random values of primitive types that can be used as placeholders in configuration properties. For example, we can define a property named `some.number=${random.int}` where `${random.int}` will be replaced by some random integer value. The same goes for `${random.value}` for textual values and `${random.long}` for longs.

- `application-{profile}.properties`: They are the profile-specific files that get applied only if a corresponding profile gets activated.

- `application.properties`: They are the main property files that contain the base/default application configuration. Similar to the profile-specific ones, these values can be loaded from the following list of locations, with the top one taking priority over the lower entries:
  - `file:config/`: This is a `/config` directory located in the current directory:
  - `file::` This is the current directory
  - `classpath:/config`: This is a `/config` package in the classpath
  - `classpath::` This is a root of the classpath

- **@Configuration annotated classes annotated with @PropertySource**: These are any in-code property sources that have been configured using annotations. We have seen an example of such usage the *Adding custom connectors* recipe from `Chapter 22`, *Web Framework Behavior Tuning*. They are very low in the precedence chain and are only preceded by the default properties.

- **Default properties**: They are configured via the `SpringApplication.setDefaultProperties(...)` call and are seldom used, as it feels very much like hardcoding values in code instead of externalizing them in configuration files.

Adding a custom PropertySource to the environment using EnvironmentPostProcessor

In cases where the enterprise is already using a particular configuration system, custom written or off the shelf, Spring Boot provides us with a facility to integrate this into the application via the creation of a custom `PropertySource` implementation.

How to do it...

Let's imagine that we have an existing configuration setup that uses a popular Apache Commons Configuration framework and stores the configuration data in XML files:

1. To mimic our supposed pre-existing configuration system, add the following content to the dependencies section in the `build.gradle` file:

```
dependencies {
  ...
  compile project(':db-count-starter')
  compile("commons-configuration:commons-
      configuration:1.10")
  compile("commons-codec:commons-codec:1.6")
  compile("commons-jxpath:commons-jxpath:1.3")
  compile("commons-collections:commons-collections:3.2.1")
  runtime("com.h2database:h2")
  ...
}
```

2. Follow this up by creating a simple configuration file named `commons-config.xml` in the `src/main/resources` directory at the root of our project with the following content:

```
<?xml version="1.0" encoding="ISO-8859-1" ?>
<config>
  <book>
    <counter>
      <delay>1000</delay>
      <rate>${book.counter.delay}0</rate>
    </counter>
  </book>
</config>
```

3. Next, we will create the `PropertySource` implementation file named `ApacheCommonsConfigurationPropertySource.java` in the `src/main/java/org/test/bookpub` directory at the root of our project with the following content:

```
public class ApacheCommonsConfigurationPropertySource
   extends EnumerablePropertySource<XMLConfiguration> {
  private static final Log logger = LogFactory.getLog(
  ApacheCommonsConfigurationPropertySource.class);

  public static final String
     COMMONS_CONFIG_PROPERTY_SOURCE_NAME = "commonsConfig";

  public ApacheCommonsConfigurationPropertySource(
     String name, XMLConfiguration source) {
    super(name, source);
  }

  @Override
  public String[] getPropertyNames() {
    ArrayList<String> keys =
       Lists.newArrayList(this.source.getKeys());
    return keys.toArray(new String[keys.size()]);
  }

  @Override
  public Object getProperty(String name) {
    return this.source.getString(name);
  }

  public static void addToEnvironment(
     ConfigurableEnvironment environment, XMLConfiguration
       xmlConfiguration) {
    environment.getPropertySources().addAfter(
      StandardEnvironment.
        SYSTEM_ENVIRONMENT_PROPERTY_SOURCE_NAME, new
          ApacheCommonsConfigurationPropertySource(
            COMMONS_CONFIG_PROPERTY_SOURCE_NAME,
              xmlConfiguration));
    logger.trace("ApacheCommonsConfigurationPropertySource
      add to Environment");
  }
}
```

4. We will now create the `EnvironmentPostProcessor` implementation class so as to bootstrap our `PropertySource` named `ApacheCommonsConfigurationEnvironmentPostProcessor.java` in the `src/main/java/org/test/bookpub` directory at the root of our project with the following content:

```
package com.example.bookpub;

import org.apache.commons.configuration.ConfigurationException;
import org.apache.commons.configuration.XMLConfiguration;
import org.springframework.boot.SpringApplication;
import org.springframework.boot.env.EnvironmentPostProcessor;
import org.springframework.core.env.ConfigurableEnvironment;

public class ApacheCommonsConfigurationEnvironmentPostProcessor
        implements EnvironmentPostProcessor {

    @Override
    public void postProcessEnvironment(
                    ConfigurableEnvironment environment,
                    SpringApplication application) {
        try {
            ApacheCommonsConfigurationPropertySource
                .addToEnvironment(environment,
                    new XMLConfiguration("commons-
                                        config.xml"));
        } catch (ConfigurationException e) {
            throw new RuntimeException("Unable to load
commons-config.xml", e);
        }
    }
}
```

5. Finally, we will need to create a new directory named `META-INF` in the `src/main/resources` directory at the root of our project and create a file named `spring.factories` in it with the following content:

```
# Environment Post Processors
org.springframework.boot.env.EnvironmentPostProcessor=
com.example.bookpub.ApacheCommonsConfigurationEnvironmentPostP
rocessor
```

6. With the setup done, we are now ready to use our new properties in our application. Let's change the configuration of the @Scheduled annotation for our StartupRunner class located in the src/main/java/org/test/bookpub directory at the root of our project, as follows:

```
@Scheduled(initialDelayString = "${book.counter.delay}",
    fixedRateString = "${book.counter.rate}")
```

7. Let's build the application by running ./gradlew clean bootJar and start it by running ./build/libs/bookpub-0.0.1-SNAPSHOT-exec.jar --spring.profiles.active=logger in order to ensure that our StartupRunner class is still logging the book count every ten seconds, as expected.

How it works...

In this recipe, we have explored how to add our own custom PropertySource that allowed us to bridge the existing system in the Spring Boot environment. Let's look into the inner workings of how the pieces fit together.

In the previous section, we learned how the different configuration definitions stacked up and what rules were used to overlay them on top of each other. This will help us to better understand how the bridging of an Apache Commons Configuration, using a custom PropertySource implementation, works. (This should not be confused with an @PropertySource annotation!)

In Chapter 23, *Writing Custom Spring Boot Starters*, we learned about the use of spring.factories, and so we already know that this file serves to define the classes that should automatically be incorporated by Spring Boot during application startup. The only difference this time is that instead of configuring the EnableAutoConfiguration settings, we will configure the SpringApplicationRunListener ones.

We created the following two classes to support our needs:

- `ApacheCommonsConfigurationPropertySource`: This is the extension of the `EnumerablePropertySource` base class that provides you with internal functionality in order to bridge XMLConfiguration from Apache Commons Configuration to the world of Spring Boot by providing transformation to get the specific property values by name via the `getProperty(String name)` implementation, and the list of all the supported property names via the `getPropertyNames()` implementation. In situations where you are dealing with the use case when the complete list of the available property names is not known or is very expensive to compute, you can just extend the `PropertySource` abstract class instead of using `EnumerablePropertySource`.

- `ApacheCommonsConfigurationEnvironmentPostProcessor`: This is the implementation of the `EnvironmentPostProcessor` interface that gets instantiated by Spring Boot during the application startup and receives notification callback after the initial environment initialization has been completed, but before the application context startup. This class is configured in `spring.factories` and is automatically created by Spring Boot.

In our post-processor, we implement the `postProcessEnvironment(ConfigurableEnvironment environment, SpringApplication application)` method, which gives us access to the `ConfigurableEnvironment` instance. By the time this callback is invoked, we will get an environment instance that has already been populated with all of the properties from the preceding hierarchy. However, we will get the opportunity to inject our own `PropertySource` implementation anywhere in the list, which we will successfully do in the `ApacheCommonsConfigurationPropertySource.addToEnvironment(...)` method.

In our case, we will choose to insert our source right below `systemEnvironment` in the order of precedence, but if needs be, we can alter this order to whatever highest precedence we desire. Just be careful not to place it so high that your properties become impossible to override via the command-line arguments, system properties, or environment variables.

Externalizing an environmental configuration using property files

The previous recipe taught us about the application properties and how they are provisioned. As was mentioned at the beginning of this chapter, during application deployment, it is almost inevitable to have some property values that are environment dependant. They can be database configurations, service topologies, or even simple feature configurations where something might be enabled in development but not quite ready for production just yet.

In this recipe, we will learn how to use an externally residing properties file for an environment-specific configuration, which might reside in the local filesystem or out in the wild on the internet.

In this recipe, we will use the same application with all the existing configurations as we used in the previous recipe. We will use it to experiment with starting up using the external configuration properties that are living in the local filesystem and from an internet URL, such as GitHub or any other.

How to do it...

1. Let's start by adding a bit of code to log the value of our particular configuration property so that we can easily see the change in it as we do different things. Add an `@Bean` method to the `BookPubApplication` class located in the `src/main/java/org/test/bookpub` directory at the root of our project with the following content:

```
@Bean
public CommandLineRunner configValuePrinter(
    @Value("${my.config.value:}") String configValue) {
  return args -> LogFactory.getLog(getClass()).
    info("Value of my.config.value property is: " +
      configValue);
}
```

2. Let's build the application by running `./gradlew clean bootJar` and start it by running `./build/libs/bookpub-0.0.1-SNAPSHOT-exec.jar --spring.profiles.active=logger` so as to see the following log output:

```
2017-12-17 --- ication$$EnhancerBySpringCGLIB$$b123df6a :
Value of
    my.config.value property is:
```

3. The value is empty, as we expected. Next, we will create a file named `external.properties` in our home directly with the following content:

```
my.config.value=From Home Directory Config
```

4. Let's run our application by executing `./build/libs/bookpub-0.0.1-SNAPSHOT-exec.jar --spring.profiles.active=logger --spring.config.location=file:/home/<username>/external.properties` in order to see the following output in the logs:

```
2017-12-17 --- ication$$EnhancerBySpringCGLIB$$b123df6a :
Value of my.config.value property is: From Home Directory
Config
```

For macOS users, the home directories can be found in the `/Users/<username>` folder.

5. We can also load the file as an HTTP resource and not from the local filesystem. So, place a file named `external.properties` with the content of `my.config.value=From HTTP Config` somewhere on the web. It can even be checked in a GitHub or BitBucket repository, as long as it is accessible without any need for authentication.

6. Let's run our application by executing `./build/libs/bookpub-0.0.1-SNAPSHOT-exec.jar --spring.profiles.active=logger --spring.config.location=http://<your file location path>/external.properties` in order to see the following output in the logs:

```
2017-12-17 --- ication$$EnhancerBySpringCGLIB$$b123df6a :
Value of my.config.value property is: From HTTP Config
```

How it works...

Before delving into the details of an external configuration setup, let's quickly look at the code that was added in order to print the property value in the log. The element of focus is the `@Value` annotation that can be used on class fields or method arguments; it also instructs Spring to automatically inject the annotated variable with the value defined in the annotation. If the value is positioned in the wrapping curly braces prefixed with a dollar sign, (`${  }`), Spring will replace this with the value from the corresponding application property or with the default value, if it is provided, by adding the textual data after the colon (`:`).

In our case, we defined it as `@Value("${my.config.value:}")String configValue`, so unless an application property named `my.config.value` exists, the default value of an empty String will be assigned to the `configValue` method argument. This construct is quite handy and eliminates the need to explicitly wire in the instance of an environment object just to get a specific property value out of it, as well as simplifying the code during testing, with less objects to mock.

The support for being able to specify the location of the application properties configuration file is geared towards supporting a dynamic multitude of environmental topologies, especially in cloud environments. This is often the case when the compiled application gets bundled into different cloud images that are destined for different environments and are being specially assembled by deployment tools such as Packer, Vagrant, and others.

In this scenario, it is very common to drop a configuration file in the image filesystem while making the image, depending on what environment it is destined for. Spring Boot provides a very convenient ability to specify, via the command-line arguments, where the configuration properties file, which should be added to the application configuration bundle, resides.

Using the `--spring.config.location` startup option, we can specify a location of one or multiple files, which can then be separated by a comma (`,`) to be added to the default ones. The file designations can be either files from a local filesystem, a classpath, or a remote URL. The locations will be resolved either by the `DefaultResourceLoader` class or, if configured via a `SpringApplication` constructor or setter, by the implementation that is provided by the `SpringApplication` instance.

If the location contains directories, the names should end with a `/` so as to let Spring Boot know that it should look for the `application.properties` file in these directories.

If you want to change the default name of the file, Spring Boot provides you with this ability as well. Just set the `--spring.config.name` option to whatever filename that you want.

> It is important to remember that the default search paths for the configuration of `classpath:`, `classpath:/config`, `file:`, `file:config/` will always be used regardless of the presence of the `--spring.config.location` setting. This way, you can always retain your default configuration in `application.properties` and just override the ones that you need via the start up settings.

Externalizing an environmental configuration using environment variables

In the previous recipes, we have, a number of times, alluded to the fact that configuration values to a Spring Boot application can be passed and overridden by using OS environment variables. Operating systems rely on these variables to store information about various things. We probably have to set JAVA_HOME or PATH a few times, and these are examples of environment variables. OS environment variables is also a very important feature if one deploys their application using a PaaS system such as Heroku or Amazon AWS. In these environments, configuration values such as database access credentials and various API tokens are all provided over the environment variables.

Their power comes from the ability to completely externalize the configuration of simple key-value data pairs without the need to rely on placing a property or some other files in a particular location, and having this hardcoded in the application code base. These variables are also agnostic to the particular operating system and can be consumed in the Java program in the same way, System.getenv(), regardless of which OS the program is running on.

In this recipe, we will explore how this power can be leveraged to pass the configuration properties to our Spring Boot applications. We will continue to use the code base from the previous recipe and experiment with a few different ways of starting the application and using the OS environment variables in order to change the configuration values of some properties.

How to do it...

1. In the previous recipe, we added a configuration property named `my.config.value`. Let's build the application by running `./gradlew clean bootJar` and start it by running `MY_CONFIG_VALUE="From ENV Config" ./build/libs/bookpub-0.0.1-SNAPSHOT-exec.jar --spring.profiles.active=logger` so as to see the following output in the logs:

   ```
   2017-12-17 --- ication$$EnhancerBySpringCGLIB$$b123df6a :
   Value of
       my.config.value property is: From ENV Config
   ```

2. If we want to use the environment variables while running our application via the Gradle `bootRun` task, the command line will be `MY_CONFIG_VALUE="From ENV Config" ./gradlew clean bootRun` and should produce the same output as in the preceding step.

3. Conveniently enough, we can even mix and match how we set the configurations. We can use the environment variable to configure the `spring.config.location` property and use it to load other property values from the external properties file, as we did in the previous recipe. Let's try this by launching our application by executing `SPRING_CONFIG_LOCATION= file:/home/<username>/external.properties ./gradlew bootRun`. We should see the following in the logs:

   ```
   2017-12-17 --- ication$$EnhancerBySpringCGLIB$$b123df6a :
   Value of
   my.config.value property is: From Home Directory Config
   ```

   While using environment variables is very convenient, it does have maintenance overhead if the number of these variables gets to be too many. To help deal with this issue, it is good practice to use a method of delegation by setting the `SPRING_CONFIG_LOCATION` variable to configure the location of the environment-specific properties file, typically by loading them from a URL location.

How it works...

As you learned from the section on environment configuration hierarchy, Spring Boot offers multiple ways of providing the configuration properties. Each of these is managed via an appropriate `PropertySource` implementation. We looked at how to create a custom implementation of `PropertySource` when we were implementing `ApacheCommonsConfigurationPropertySource`. Spring Boot already provides a `SystemEnvironmentPropertySource` implementation for us to use out of the box. This even gets automatically registered with the default implementation of the environment interface: the `SystemEnvironment`.

As the `SystemEnvironment` implementation provides a composite façade on top of a multitude of different `PropertySource` implementations, the overriding takes place seamlessly, simply because the `SystemEnvironmentPropertySource` class sits higher up in the list than the `application.properties` file one.

An important aspect that you should notice is the use of `ALL_CAPS` with underscores (_) in order to separate the words instead of the traditional conventional `all.lower.cased` format with dots (.) separating the words used in Spring Boot to name the configuration properties. This is due to the nature of some operating systems, namely Linux and OS X, which prevent the use of dots (.) in the names and instead encourages the use of the `ALL_CAPS` underscore-separated notation.

In situations where the usage of environment variables to specify or override the configuration properties is not desired, Spring provides us with the – `Dspring.getenv.ignore` system property, which can be set to true and prevents the usage of environment variables. You might want to change this setting to true if you see errors or exceptions in the log due to the running of your code on some application servers or a particular security policy configuration that might not allow access to environment variables.

Externalizing an environmental configuration using Java system properties

While environment variables can, on rare occasions, be hit or miss, the good old Java system properties can always be trusted to be there for you. In addition to using the environment variables and command-line arguments represented by the property names prefixed with a double dash (--), Spring Boot provides you with the ability to use the plain Java system properties to set or override the configuration properties.

This can be useful in a number of situations, particularly if your application is running in a container that sets certain values during startup via the system properties that you want to get access to, or if a property value is not set via a command-line -D argument, but rather in some library via code and by calling `System.setProperty(...)`, especially if property value is being accessed from inside a static method of sorts. While arguably these cases are rare, it takes only one to make you bend over backwards in an effort to try and integrate this value into your application.

In this recipe, we will use the same application executable that was used for the previous one, with the only difference being that we are using Java system properties instead of command-line arguments or environment variables to set our configuration properties at runtime.

How to do it...

1. Let's continue our experiments by setting the `my.config.value` configuration property. Build the application by running `./gradlew clean bootJar` and start it by running `java -Dmy.config.value="From System Config" -jar ./build/libs/bookpub-0.0.1-SNAPSHOT-exec.jar` so as to see the following in the logs:

```
2017-12-17 --- ication$$EnhancerBySpringCGLIB$$b123df6a :
Value of my.config.value property is: From System Config
```

2. If we want to be able to set the Java system property while running our application using the Gradle's `bootRun` task, we will need to add this to the `applicationDefaultJvmArgs` configuration in the `build.gradle` file. Let's add `-Dmy.config.value=Gradle` to this list and start the application by running `./gradlew clean bootRun`. We should see the following in the logs:

```
2017-12-17 --- ication$$EnhancerBySpringCGLIB$$b123df6a :
Value of my.config.value property is: Gradle
```

3. As we made the `applicationDefaultJvmArgs` setting to be shared with `launch.script`, rebuilding the application by running `./gradlew clean bootJar` and starting it by running `./build/libs/bookpub-0.0.1-SNAPSHOT-exec.jar` should yield the same output in the logs as in the preceding step.

How it works...

You might have already guessed that Java system properties are consumed by a similar mechanism that is used for environment variables, and you would be correct. The only real difference is the implementation of `PropertySource`. This time, a more generic `MapPropertySource` implementation is used by `StandardEnvironment`.

What you have also probably noticed is the need to launch our application using the `java -Dmy.config.value="From System Config" -jar ./build/libs/bookpub-0.0.1-SNAPSHOT-exec.jar` command instead of just simply invoking the self-executing packaged JAR by itself. This is because, unlike the environment variables and command-line arguments, Java system properties have to be set on the Java executable ahead of everything else.

We did manage to work around this need by effectively hardcoding the values in our `build.gradle` file, which, combined with the enhancements that we made to `launch.script`, allowed us embed the `my.config.value` property in the command line in the self-executing jar, as well as use it with the Gradle's `bootRun` task.

The risk of using this approach with the configuration properties is that it will always override the values that we set in the higher layers of the configuration, such as `application.properties` and others. Unless you are explicitly constructing the Java executable command line and not using the self-launching capabilities of the packaged JAR, it is best not to use Java system properties and consider using the command-line arguments or environment variables instead.

Externalizing an environmental config using JSON

We have looked at a number of different ways to externally add or override the values of specific properties, either by using environment variables, system properties, or command-line arguments. All those options provide us with a great deal of flexibility, but with the exception of external property files, are all limited to setting one property at a time. When it comes to using property files, the syntax is not exactly the best at representing nested, hierarchical data structures, and can get a bit tricky. To avoid this situation, Spring Boot provides us with an ability to also pass, externally, JSON-encoded content containing an entire config hierarchy of settings.

In this recipe, we will use the same application executable that was used for the previous one, with the only difference being using external JSON content to set our configuration properties at runtime.

How to do it...

1. Let's continue our experiments by setting the `my.config.value` configuration property. Build the application by running `./gradlew clean bootJar` and start it by running `java -jar ./build/libs/bookpub-0.0.1-SNAPSHOT-exec.jar --spring.application.json={"my":{"config":{"value":"From external JSON"}}}` so as to see the following in the logs:

   ```
   2017-12-17 --- ication$$EnhancerBySpringCGLIB$$b123df6a :
   Value of my.config.value property is: From external JSON
   ```

2. If we want to be able to set the content using Java system properties, we can use `-Dspring.application.json` instead, assigning the same JSON content as the value.

3. Alternatively, we can also rely on the `SPRING_APPLICATION_JSON` environment variable to pass the same JSON content in the following way:

```
SPRING_APPLICATION_JSON={"my":{"config":{"value":"From
external JSON"}}} java -jar ./build/libs/bookpub-0.0.1-
SNAPSHOT-exec.jar --spring.profiles.active=logger
```

How it works...

Just like every other configuration approach we have looked at, the JSON content is consumed by a dedicated `EnvironmentPostProcessor` implementation. The only difference is the flattening of the JSON tree into a flat property map, to match the dot-separated properties naming style. In our case, the `my->config->value` nested map gets converted into a flat map with only one key, `my.config.value`, with the value of `From external JSON`.

The setting of the JSON content can come from ANY property source, available from the environment at the time of loading, which contains a key named `spring.application.json` with a value of valid JSON content, and is not only limited to being set by an Environment Variable or using the `SPRING_APPLICATION_JSON` name or Java System Property.

This capability can be very useful to provide externally-defined, environment-specific configuration in bulk. The best way is to do so via setting the `SPRING_APPLICATION_JSON` environment variable on the machine instance using machine/image provisioning tools such as Chef, Puppet, Ansible, Packer, and so on. This enables you to store an entire configuration hierarchy in one JSON file externally, and then simply provision the correct content on the specific machine during provisioning time by just setting an Environment Variable. All applications running on that machine will automatically consume it upon startup.

Setting up Consul

So far, everything that we have been doing with the configuration was connected to the local set of data. In a real, large-scale enterprise environment, this is not always the case and quite frequently there is the desire to be able to make the configuration changes at large, across hundreds or even thousands of instances or machines.

There are a number of tools that exist to help you with this task, and in this recipe, we will take a look at one that, in my opinion, stands out from the group, giving you the ability to cleanly and elegantly configure the environment variables for a starting application using a distributed data store. The tool's name is **Consul**. It is an open source product from Hashicorp and is designed to discover and configure the services in a large, distributed infrastructure.

In this recipe, we will take a look at how to install and configure Consul and experiment with some key functionalities that it provides. This will give us the necessary familiarity for our next recipe, where we will be using Consul to provide the configuration values that are needed to start our application.

How to do it...

1. Go to `https://consul.io/downloads.html` and download the appropriate archive, depending on the operating system that you are using. Consul supports Windows, OS X, and Linux, so it should work for the majority of readers.

   > If you are an OS X user, you can install Consul using Homebrew by running `brew install caskroom/cask/brew-cask` followed by `brew cask install consul`.

2. After the installation, we should be able to run `consul --version` and see the following output:

   ```
   Consul v1.0.1
   Protocol 2 spoken by default, understands 2 to 3 (agent will
   automatically use protocol >2 when speaking to compatible
   agents)
   ```

3. With Consul successfully installed, we should be able to start it by running the `consul agent -server -bootstrap-expect 1 -data-dir /tmp/consul` command and our terminal window will display the following:

   ```
   ==> WARNING: BootstrapExpect Mode is specified as 1; this is
   the same as Bootstrap mode.
   ==> WARNING: Bootstrap mode enabled! Do not enable unless
   necessary
   ==> WARNING: It is highly recommended to set GOMAXPROCS higher
   than 1
   ```

```
==> Starting Consul agent...
==> Starting Consul agent RPC...
==> Consul agent running!
         Node name: <your machine name>'
         Datacenter: 'dc1'
            Server: true (bootstrap: true)
       Client Addr: 127.0.0.1 (HTTP: 8500, HTTPS: -1, DNS:
8600, RPC: 8400)
      Cluster Addr: 192.168.1.227 (LAN: 8301, WAN: 8302)
    Gossip encrypt: false, RPC-TLS: false, TLS-Incoming: false
             Atlas: <disabled>
==> Log data will now stream in as it occurs:
    2017/12/17 20:34:43 [INFO] serf: EventMemberJoin: <your
machine name> 192.168.1.227
    2017/12/17 20:34:43 [INFO] serf: EventMemberJoin: <your
machine name>.dc1 192.168.1.227
    2017/12/17 20:34:43 [INFO] raft: Node at
192.168.1.227:8300 [Follower] entering Follower state
    2017/12/17 20:34:43 [INFO] consul: adding server <your
machine name> (Addr: 192.168.1.227:8300) (DC: dc1)
    2017/12/17 20:34:43 [INFO] consul: adding server <your
machine name>.dc1 (Addr: 192.168.1.227:8300) (DC: dc1)
    2017/12/17 20:34:43 [ERR] agent: failed to sync remote
state: No cluster leader
    2017/12/17 20:34:45 [WARN] raft: Heartbeat timeout
reached, starting election
    2017/12/17 20:34:45 [INFO] raft: Node at
192.168.1.227:8300 [Candidate] entering Candidate state
    2017/12/17 20:34:45 [INFO] raft: Election won. Tally: 1
    2017/12/17 20:34:45 [INFO] raft: Node at
192.168.1.227:8300 [Leader] entering Leader state
    2017/12/17 20:34:45 [INFO] consul: cluster leadership
acquired
    2017/12/17 20:34:45 [INFO] consul: New leader elected:
<your machine name>
    2017/12/17 20:34:45 [INFO] raft: Disabling
EnableSingleNode (bootstrap)
    2017/12/17 20:34:45 [INFO] consul: member '<your machine
name>' joined, marking health alive
    2017/12/17 20:34:47 [INFO] agent: Synced service 'consul'
```

4. With the Consul service running, we can verify that it contains one member by running the `consul members` command, and should see the following result:

```
Node                    Address           Status  Type    Build
Protocol   DC
<your_machine_name> 2.168.1.227:8301 alive  server  0.5.2      2
dc1
```

5. While Consul can also provide discovery for services, health checks, distributed locks, and more, we are going to focus on the key/value service as this is what will be used to provide the configuration in the next recipe. So, let's put the `From Consul Config` value in the key/value store by executing the `curl -X PUT -d 'From Consul Config'` `http://localhost:8500/v1/kv/bookpub/my/config/value` command.

> If you are using Windows, you can get curl from `http://curl.haxx.se/download.html`.

6. We can also retrieve the data by running the `curl` `http://localhost:8500/v1/kv/bookpub/my/config/value` command and should see the following output:

   `[{"CreateIndex":20,"ModifyIndex":20,"LockIndex":0,"Key":"bookpub/my/config/value","Flags":0,"Value":"RnJvbSBDb25zdWwgQ29uZmln"}]`

7. We can delete this value by running the `curl -X DELETE` `http://localhost:8500/v1/kv/bookpub/my/config/value` command.

8. In order to modify the existing value and change it for something else, execute the `curl -X PUT -d 'newval'` `http://localhost:8500/v1/kv/bookpub/my/config/value?cas=20` command.

How it works...

A detailed explanation about how Consul works and all the possible options for its key/value service would take a book of its own, so here we will look only at the basic pieces. It is strongly recommended that you read Consul's documentation at `https://consul.io/intro/getting-started/services.html`.

In *step 3*, we started the Consul agent in server mode. It acts as a main master node and, in real deployment, the local agents running on the individual instances will be using the server node to connect to and retrieve data from. For our test purposes, we will just use this server node as if it were a local agent.

The information displayed upon startup shows us that our node has started as a server node, establishing an HTTP service on port `8500` as well as the DNS and RPC services, if that's how one chooses to connect to it. We can also see that there is only one node in the cluster, ours, and we are the elected leader running in a healthy state.

As we will be using the convenient RESTful HTTP API via cURL, all of our requests will be using localhost on port `8500`. Being a RESTful API, it fully adheres to CRUD verb terminology, and to insert the data, we will use a `PUT` method on a `/v1/kv` endpoint in order to set the `bookpub/my/config/value` key.

Retrieving the data is even more straightforward: we just make a `GET` request to the same `/v1/kv` service using the desired key. The same goes for `DELETE`, with the only difference being the method name.

The update operation requires a bit more information in the URL, namely the `cas` parameter. The value of this parameter should be the `ModifyIndex` of the desired key, which can be obtained from the `GET` request. In our case, it has a value of 20.

Externalizing an environmental config using Consul and envconsul

In the previous recipe, we had our Consul service installed and experimented with its key/value capabilities to learn how we could manipulate the data in it in order to integrate Consul with our application and make the data extraction process seamless and non-invasive from an application standpoint.

As we don't want our application to know anything about Consul and have to explicitly connect to it, even though such a possibility exists, we will employ another utility, also created as open source by Hashicorp, called **envconsul**. It will connect to the Consul service for us, extract the specified configuration key/value tree, and expose it as the environment variables to be used while also launching our application. Pretty cool, right?

Getting ready

Before we get started with launching our application, which was created in the previous recipes, we need to install the envconsul utility.

Download the binary for your respective operating system from `https://github.com/hashicorp/envconsul/releases` and extract the executable to any directory of your choice, though it is better to put it somewhere that is in the PATH.

Once envconsul is extracted from the downloaded archive, we are ready to start using it so as to configure our application.

How to do it...

1. If you have not already added the value for the `my/config/value` key to Consul, let's add it by running `curl -X PUT -d 'From Consul Config'` `http://localhost:8500/v1/kv/bookpub/my/config/value`.

2. The first step is to make sure envconsul can connect to the Consul server and that it extracts the correct data based on our configuration key. Let's execute a simple test by running the `envconsul --once --sanitize --upcase --prefix bookpub env` command. We should see the following in the output:

```
. . .
TERM=xterm-256color
SHELL=/bin/bash
LANG=en_US.UTF-8
HOME=/Users/<your_user_name>
. . .
MY_CONFIG_VALUE=From Consul Config
```

3. After we have verified that envconsul is returning the correct data to us, we will use it to launch our `BookPub` application by running `envconsul -- once --sanitize --upcase --prefix bookpub ./gradlew clean bootRun`. Once the application has started, we should see the following output in the logs:

```
2017-12-17 --- ication$$EnhancerBySpringCGLIB$$b123df6a :
Value of my.config.value property is: From Consul Config
```

4. We can do the same thing by building the self-starting executable JAR by running `./gradlew clean bootJar`, and start it by running `envconsul --once --sanitize --upcase --prefix bookpub ./build/libs/bookpub-0.0.1-SNAPSHOT-exec.jar` to make sure we see the same output in the logs as in the preceding step. If you see `Gradle` instead of `From Consul Config`, make sure the `applicationDefaultJvmArgs` configuration in `build.gradle` does not have `-Dmy.config.value=Gradle` in it.

5. Another marvelous ability of envconsul is not only to export the configuration key values as environment variables, but also to monitor for any changes and restart the application if the values in Consul change. Let's launch our application by running `envconsul --sanitize --upcase --prefix bookpub ./build/libs/bookpub-0.0.1-SNAPSHOT-exec.jar`, and we should see the following value in the log:

```
2017-12-17 --- ication$$EnhancerBySpringCGLIB$$b123df6a :
Value of my.config.value property is: From Consul Config
```

6. We will now use the consul command to get the current `ModifyIndex` of our key and update its value to `From UpdatedConsul Config` by opening another terminal window and executing `curl http://localhost:8500/v1/kv/bookpub/my/config/value`, grabbing the `ModifyIndex` value, and using it to execute `curl -X PUT -d 'From UpdatedConsul Config' http://localhost:8500/v1/kv/bookpub/my/config/value?cas=<ModifyIndex Value>`. We should see our running application magically restart itself and our newly updated value displayed in the log at the end:

```
2017-12-17 --- ication$$EnhancerBySpringCGLIB$$b123df6a :
Value of my.config.value property is: From UpdatedConsul
Config
```

How it works...

What we just did was pretty sweet, right? Let's examine the magic going on behind the scenes in more detail. We will start by dissecting the command line and explaining what each argument control option does.

Our first execution command line was `envconsul --once --sanitize --upcase --prefix bookpub ./gradlew clean bootRun`, so let's take a look at exactly what we did, as follows:

- First, one might notice that there is no indication about which Consul node we should be connecting to. This is because there is an implicit understanding or an assumption that you already have a Consul agent running locally on `localhost:8500`. If this is not the case for whatever reason, you can always explicitly specify the Consul instance to connect via the `--consul localhost:8500` argument added to the command line.
- The `--prefix` option specifies the starting configuration key segment in which to look for the different values. When we were adding keys to Consul, we used the following key: `bookpub/my/config/value`. By specifying the `--prefix bookpub` option, we tell envconsul to strip the `bookpub` part of the key and use all the internal tree elements in `bookpub` to construct the environment variables. Thus, `my/config/value` becomes the environment variable.
- The `--sanitize` option tells envconsul to replace all the invalid characters with underscores (_). So, if we were to only use `--sanitize`, we would end up with `my_config_value` as an environment variable.
- The `--upcase` option, as you might already have guessed, changes the environment variable key to all upper case characters, so when combined with the `--sanitize` option, `my/config/value` key gets transformed into the `MY_CONFIG_VALUE` environment variable.
- The `--once` option indicates that we only want to externalize the keys as environment variables once and do not want to continuously monitor for changes in the Consul cluster. If a key in our prefix tree has changed its value, we re-externalize the keys as environment variables and restart the application.

This last option, `--once`, provides a very useful choice of functionalities. If you are interested only in the initial bootstrapping of your application via the use of a Consul-shared configuration, then the keys will be set as environment variables, the application will be launched, and envconsul will consider its job done. However, if you would like to monitor the Consul cluster for changes to keys/values and, after the change has taken place, restart your application reflecting the new change, then remove the `--once` option and envconsul will restart the application once the change has occurred.

Such behavior can be very useful and handy for things such as a near-instantaneous changes to the database connection configuration. Imagine that you need to do a quick failover from one database to another and your JDBC URL is configured via Consul. All you need to do is push a new JDBC URL value and envconsul will almost immediately detect this change and restart the application, telling it to connect to a new database node.

Currently, this functionality is implemented by sending a traditional SIGTERM signal to an application running process, telling it to terminate and, once the process is exited, restart the application. This might not always be the desired behavior, especially if it takes some time for an application to start up and be capable of taking traffic. You don't want your entire cluster of web applications to be shut down, even if it will only be for a few minutes.

To provide a better handling of this scenario, envconsul was enhanced to be able to send a number of standard signals that can be configured via a newly added `--kill-signal` option. Using this option, we can specify any of the SIGHUP, SIGTERM, SIGINT, SIGQUIT, SIGUSR1, or SIGUSR2 signals to be used instead of the default SIGTERM, to be sent to a running application process once the key/value changes have been detected.

The process signal handling in Java is not as clear and straightforward due to most of the behavior being very specific to a particular operating system and the JVM that is run atop it. Some of the signals in the list will terminate the application anyway or, in the case of SIGQUIT, the JVM will print Core Dump into the standard output. However, there are ways to configure the JVM, depending on the operating system, to let us use SIGUSR1 and SIGUSR2 instead of acting on those signals itself, but unfortunately that topic falls outside the scope of this book.

Here is a sample example of how to deal with **Signal Handlers**: `https://github.com/spotify/daemon-java`, or see the Oracle Java documentation at `https://docs.oracle.com/javase/8/docs/technotes/guides/troubleshoot/signals.html` for a detailed explanation.

26
Health Monitoring and Data Visualization

In this chapter, we will cover the following recipes:

- Writing custom health indicators
- Configuring management context
- Emitting metrics
- Monitoring Spring Boot via JMX
- Managing Spring Boot via SSHd Shell and writing custom remote Shell commands
- Integrating Micrometer metrics with Graphite
- Integrating Micrometer metrics with Dashing

Introduction

In the previous chapter, you learned a few techniques to efficiently package and get the application ready for deployment and we looked at a number of techniques to provide an environmental configuration without changing the code. With the deployment and configuration woes behind us, the last (but not least) important step remains—ensuring that we have complete visibility, monitoring, and management control of our application, as it is running in the production environment and is exposed to the harsh environment of customers' (ab)use.

Just as airline pilots don't like to fly blind, developers don't get excited if they can't see how their beloved application, that they worked hard on, performs in production. We want to know, at any given time, what the CPU utilization is like, how much memory we are consuming, whether our connection to the database is up and available, the number of customers who use the system in any given time interval, and so on. Not only do we want to know all these things, but we also want to be able to see it in pretty charts, graphs, and visual dashboards. These come in very handy to put on the big Plasma displays for monitoring as well as impressing your boss, so as to show that you are on the top of things and have it all under control.

This chapter will help you learn the necessary techniques to enhance our application in order to expose custom metrics, health statuses, and so on, as well as how to get the monitoring data out of our application and either store it in Graphite for historical reference or use this data to create real-time monitoring dashboards using the Dashing and Grafana frameworks. We will also take a look at the capability to connect to running instances and perform various management tasks using the powerful CRaSH framework integration.

Writing custom health indicators

Knowing the state of the application that is running in production, especially in a large-scale distributed system, is just as (if not more) important as having things such as automated testing and deployment. In today's fast-paced IT world, we can't really afford much downtime, so we need to have the information about the health of the application at our fingertips, ready to go at a minute's notice. If the all-so-important database connections go down, we want to see it right away and be able to quickly remedy the situation; the customers are not going to be waiting around for long before they go to another site.

We will resume working on our `BookPub` application in the state in which we left it in the previous chapter. In this recipe, we will add the necessary Spring Boot starters to enable the monitoring and instrumentation of our application and will even write our own health indicator.

How to do it...

1. The first thing that we need to do is add a dependency to the Spring Boot Actuator starter in our `build.gradle` file with the following content:

```
dependencies {
    ...
    compile("org.springframework.boot:spring-boot-starter-
    data-rest")
    // compile("org.springframework.boot:spring-boot-starter-
    jetty") //
    Need to use Jetty instead of Tomcat
    compile("org.springframework.boot:spring-boot-starter-
    actuator")
    compile project(':db-count-starter')
    ...
}
```

2. Adding this dependency alone already gives us the ability to access the Spring management `/actuator/*` endpoints, such as `/env`, `/info`, `/metrics`, and `/health`, (though they are disabled by default, unless a `management.endpoints.web.exposure.include=*` property is configured in the `application.properties` file). So, let's start our application by executing the `./gradlew clean bootRun` command line and then we can access the newly available `/health` endpoint by opening our browser and going to `http://localhost:8080/actuator/health` so as to see the new endpoint in action, as shown in the following screenshot:

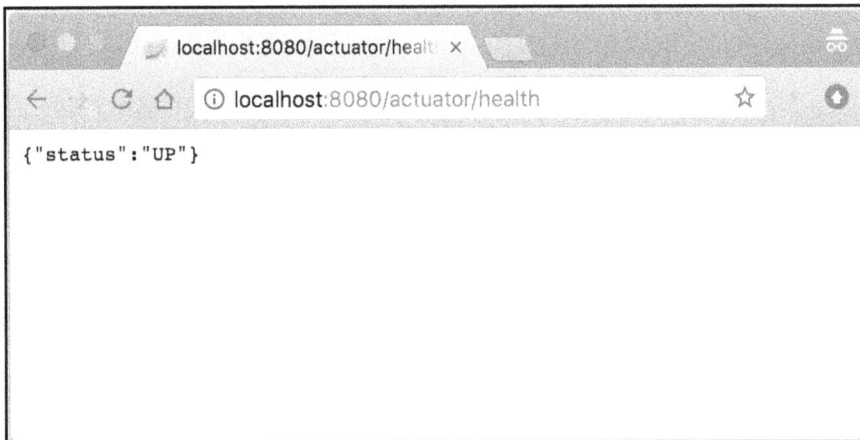

3. To get more details about the health state of our application, let's configure it to show the detailed health output by adding the `management.endpoint.health.show-details=always` property to the `application.properties` file and then restarting our application. Now, when we go to `http://localhost:8080/actuator/health` in the browser, we should see something similar to the following screenshot:

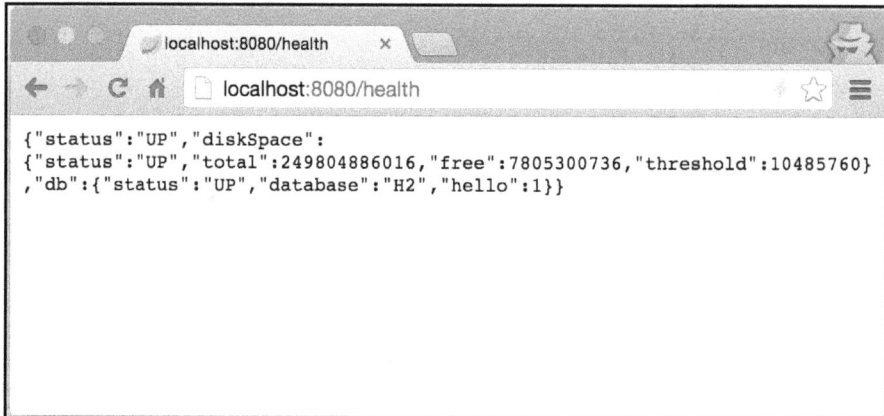

4. With the `actuator` dependency added, and detailed `/health` endpoint configured, we can now add and perform all kinds of monitoring functions on our application. Let's go ahead and populate the `/info` endpoint with some data by adding a directive to the `build.gradle` file located at the root of our project with the following content:

```
springBoot {
    buildInfo {
        properties {
            additional = [
                'description' : project.description
            ]
        }
    }
}
```

5. Next, we will create a new properties file named `gradle.properties` in the root directory of our project with the following content:

```
version=0.0.1-SNAPSHOT
description=BookPub Catalog Application
```

6. We will also add `rootProject.name='BookPub-ch7'` to the `settings.gradle` file located in the root directory of our project.

7. Now, let's start our application by executing `./gradlew clean bootRun` and then we can access the newly available `/info` endpoint by opening our browser and going to `http://localhost:8080/actuator/info` to see the new endpoint in action, as follows:

8. As we have got the hang of how things work, let's go ahead and make our custom health indicator, which will be accessible via the `/health` endpoint in order to report the count status of the entries for each of our repositories. If they are greater than or equal to zero, we are UP, otherwise we are not really sure what's going on. Obviously, if an exception has occurred, we would be reporting DOWN. Let's start by relaxing the `getRepositoryName(...)` method visibility from `private` to `protected` in the `DbCountRunner.java` file located in the `db-count-starter/src/main/java/com/example/bookpubstarter/dbcount` directory at the root of our project.

9. Next, we will add the same dependency to the `compile("org.springframework.boot:spring-boot-starter-actuator")` library in the `build.gradle` file in the `db-count-starter` directory at the root of our project.

10. Now, we will create a new file named `DbCountHealthIndicator.java` in the `db-count-starter/src/main/java/com/example/bookpubstarter/dbcount` directory at the root of our project with the following content:

```java
public class DbCountHealthIndicator implements HealthIndicator
{
    private CrudRepository repository;

    public DbCountHealthIndicator(CrudRepository repository) {
        this.repository = repository;
    }

    @Override
    public Health health() {
        try {
            long count = repository.count();
            if (count >= 0) {
                return Health.up().withDetail("count",
                count).build();
            } else {
                return Health.unknown().withDetail("count",
                count).build();
            }
        } catch (Exception e) {
            return Health.down(e).build();
        }
    }
}
```

11. Next, we will modify the `@Import` annotation in the `EnableDbCounting.java` file located in the `db-count starter/src/main/java/com/example/bookpubstarter/dbcount` directory at the root of our project with the following content:

```java
@Import({DbCountAutoConfiguration.class,
        HealthIndicatorAutoConfiguration.class})
```

12. Finally, for the automatic registration of our `HealthIndicator` class, we will enhance the `DbCountAutoConfiguration.java` file located in the `db-count-starter/src/main/java/com/example/bookpubstarter/dbcount` directory at the root of our project with the following content:

```
@Autowired
private HealthAggregator healthAggregator;
@Bean
public HealthIndicator
dbCountHealthIndicator(Collection<CrudRepository>
repositories) {
    CompositeHealthIndicator compositeHealthIndicator = new
      CompositeHealthIndicator(healthAggregator);
    for (CrudRepository repository : repositories) {
        String name = DbCountRunner.getRepositoryName
          (repository.getClass());
        compositeHealthIndicator.addHealthIndicator(name, new
          DbCountHealthIndicator(repository));
    }
    return compositeHealthIndicator;
}
```

13. So, let's start our application by executing the `./gradlew clean bootRun` command line, and then we can access the `/health` endpoint by opening our browser and going to `http://localhost:8080/actuator/health` to see our new `HealthIndicator` class in action, as follows:

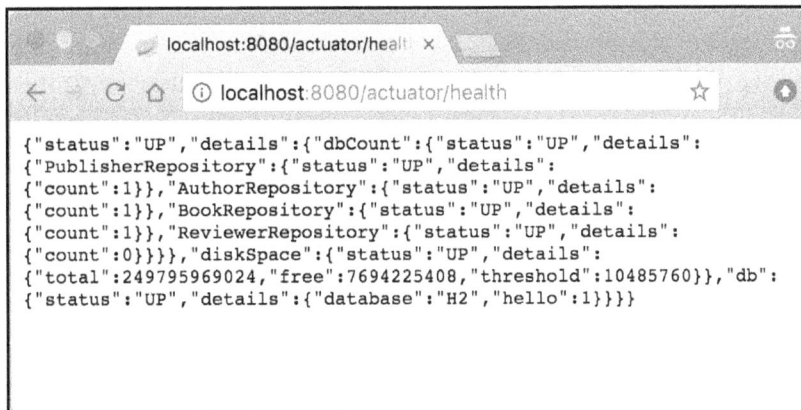

How it works...

The Spring Boot Actuator starter adds a number of important features that give insight into the runtime state of the application. The library contains a number of autoconfigurations that add and configure the various endpoints to access the runtime monitoring data and health of the application. Those endpoints all share a common context path: `/actuator`. To expose any other endpoints besides `/info` and `/health`, we need to explicitly expose them by setting the `management.endpoints.web.exposure.include=*` property. When the value is set to `*`, it will expose all of the endpoints. The following endpoints are available to aid us in getting an insight into the application runtime state and configuration:

- `/env`: This endpoint enables us to query the application about all of the environment variables that the application has access to via the environment implementation, which we have seen earlier. It is very useful when you need to debug a particular issue and want to know a value of any given configuration property. If we access the endpoint by going to `http://localhost:8080/actuator/env`, we will see a number of different configuration sections, for example, the class path resource `[tomcat.https.properties]`, `applicationConfig:` `[classpath:/application.properties]`, `commonsConfig`, `systemEnvironment`, `systemProperties`, and others. They all represent an instance of an individual `PropertySource` implementation that is available in the environment and depending on their place in the hierarchy, may or may not be used to provide the value resolution at the runtime. To find out exactly which entry is used to resolve a particular value, for example, for the `book.count.rate` property, we can query it by going to the `http://localhost:8080/actuator/env/book.counter.rate` URL. By default, we should get 10,000 as a result unless, of course, a different value was set via the system environment or command-line arguments as an override. If you really want to dig deep into the code, the `EnvironmentEndpoint` class is responsible for handling the logic behind this capability.

- `/configprops`: This endpoint provides you with an insight into the settings of the various configuration property objects, such as our `WebConfiguration.TomcatSslConnectorProperties` starter. It is slightly different from the `/env` endpoint as it provides insight into the configuration object bindings. If we open the browser to go to `http://localhost:8080/actuator/configprops` and search for `custom.tomcat.https`, we will see the entry for our configuration property object that we will use to configure `TomcatSslConnector`, which was automatically populated and bound for us by Spring Boot.

- `/conditions`: This endpoint serves as a web-based analog to the AutoConfiguration Report, which we saw in Chapter 23, *Writing Custom Spring Boot Starters*. This way, we can get the report using the browser at any time without having to start the application with the specific flags to get it printed.

- `/beans`: This endpoint is designed to list all the beans that have been created by Spring Boot and are available in application context.

- `/mappings`: This endpoint exposes a list of all the URL mappings that are supported by the application as well as a reference to the `HandlerMapping` bean implementation. This is very useful for answering the question of where would a specific URL get routed to. Try going to `http://localhost:8080/actuator/mappings` to see the list of all the routes that our application can handle.

- `/threaddump`: This endpoint allows extraction of the Thread Dump information from the running application. It is rather useful when trying to diagnose a potential thread deadlock.

- `/heapdump`: This endpoint is similar to `/dump` with the exception that it produces Heap Dump information instead.

- `/info`: This endpoint shows the basic description and application information that we added and we've seen this in action, so it should be familiar to us as of now. The nice support in the build tools gives us the ability to configure additional or replace existing values inside our `build.gradle` configuration, which would then be propagated to be consumed by the `/info` endpoint. Additionally, any properties defined in the `application.properties` file, that start with `info.` will be displayed while accessing the `/info` endpoint, so you are definitely not limited to only the `build.gradle` configuration. Configuring this specific endpoint in order to return the relevant information can be very helpful when building various automated discovery and monitoring tools as it is a great way to expose application-specific information in the form of a nice JSON RESTful API.

- `/actuator`: This endpoint gives a nice JSON-formatted list of links in a **Hypertext Application Language** (**HAL**) style for all the available actuator endpoints.

- `/health`: This endpoint provides information about the general application health status as well as a detailed breakdown and health status of the individual components.

- `/metrics`: This endpoint gives an overview of all the various data points that are emitted by the metrics subsystem. You can experiment with it by accessing it via the `http://localhost:8080/actuator/metrics` URL in the browser. We will cover this in more detail in the next recipe.

Now that we know in general what is being provided for us by Spring Boot Actuator, we can move on to take a look at the details of what we did to get our custom `HealthIndicator` class working and how the whole health monitoring subsystem in Spring Boot functions.

As you saw, getting the basic `HealthIndicator` interface to work is very easy; all we have to do is create an implementing class that will return a `Health` object upon a call to the `health()` method. All you have to do is expose the instance of the `HealthIndicator` class as `@Bean` for Spring Boot to pick it up and add it to the `/health` endpoint.

In our case, we went a step further because we had to deal with the need to create
`HealthIndicator` for each `CrudRepository` instance. To accomplish this, we
created an instance of `CompositeHealthIndicator` to which we added all the
instances of `DbHealthIndicator` for each `CrudRepository`. We then returned this
as `@Bean` and this is what was used by Spring Boot to represent the health status.
Being a composite, it preserved the inner hierarchy as is evident from the returned
JSON data representing the health status. We also added some extra data element to
provide the indication of the entry count as well as the name of each particular
repository so that we can tell them apart.

Looking at the code, you are probably wondering: what is this `HealthAggregator`
instance that we've wired in? The reason that we needed a `HealthAggregator`
instance is because `CompositeHealthIndicator` needs to know how to decide if the
inner composition of all the nested `HeathIndicators` represents good or bad health
as a whole. Imagine that all the repositories, but one, return UP but one is DOWN. What
does this mean? Is the composite indicator healthy as a whole or should it also report
DOWN because one inner repository has issues?

By default, Spring Boot already creates and uses an instance of `HealthAggregator`,
so we just autowired it and used it in our use case as well. We did have to explicitly
add the import of the `HealthIndicatorAutoConfiguration` and
`MetricsDropwizardAutoConfiguration` classes in order to satisfy the bean
dependency during slice tests for `DataJpaTest` and `WebMvcTest`, since those only
partially instantiate the context, and the actuator autoconfigurations are missing.

Even though the default implementation is an instance of
`OrderedHealthAggregator`, which just collects all the inner status responses and
chooses the lowest on the priority level out of DOWN, OUT_OF_SERVICE, UP, and
UNKNOWN, it doesn't always have to be that way. For example, if the composite
indicator consists of the indicators for redundant service connections, your combined
result could be UP as long as at least one of the connections is healthy. Creating a
custom `HealthAggregator` interface is very easy; all you have to do is either extend
`AbstractHealthAggregator` or implement a `HealthAggregator` interface itself.

Configuring management context

Spring Boot Actuator out of the box creates a set of management endpoints and the supporting beans in the main application context and those endpoints are available on the `server.port` configured HTTP port. There are, however, cases where for security or isolation reasons we would want to separate the main application context from the management one or expose the management endpoints on a different port than the main application.

Spring Boot provides us with an ability to configure a separate child application context for the management beans, which would inherit everything from the main application context, but allow for defining beans that are only available for the management functions as well. The same goes for exposing the endpoints on a different port or even using different connector security in such a way that the main application could be using SSL, but the management endpoints are accessible using plain HTTP.

How to do it...

Let's imagine that, for whatever reason, we want to change our JSON converter to output field names using `SNAKE_CASE` (all lowercase letters separating words with an underscore).

1. First, let's create a class holding our configuration for the management context named `ManagementConfiguration.java` located in the `src/main/java/com/example/bookpub` directory at the root of our project with the following content:

```
@ManagementContextConfiguration
public class ManagementConfiguration
        implements WebMvcConfigurer {
  @Override
  public void configureMessageConverters(
            List<HttpMessageConverter<?>> converters) {
    HttpMessageConverter c = new
     MappingJackson2HttpMessageConverter(
        Jackson2ObjectMapperBuilder.json().
propertyNamingStrategy(PropertyNamingStrategy.SNAKE_CAS).
        build()
        );
    converters.add(c);
  }
}
```

2. We also need to add this class to `spring.factories` located in the `src/main/resources/META-INF` directory at the root of our project with the following content:

```
org.springframework.boot.actuate.autoconfigure.web.ManagementC
ontextConfiguration=com.example.bookpub.ManagementConfiguratio
n
```

3. To avoid our configuration being detected by the component scan for the main application context, we need to exclude it by adding the following to `BookPubApplication.java` located in the `src/main/java/com/example/bookpub` directory at the root of our project:

```
@ComponentScan(excludeFilters =
    @ComponentScan.Filter(
        type = FilterType.ANNOTATION,
        classes = ManagementContextConfiguration.class
    )
)
```

4. To have a separate management context, we need to launch it using a different port, so let's amend `application.properties` located in the `src/main/resources` directory at the root of our project with the following content:

```
management.server.port=8081
management.endpoints.web.exposure.include=*
```

5. Finally, let's start our application by executing `./gradlew clean bootRun` and then we can access the `/threaddump` endpoint by opening our browser and going to `http://localhost:8081/actuator/threaddump` to see our new configuration take place. The field names of the returned JSON should all be in lowercase and words should be separated using an underscore, or in SNAKE_CASE, as it is called. Alternatively, by going to the `http://localhost:8080/books/978-1-78528-415-1` endpoint, we should continue seeing JSON field names in the LOWER_CAMEL_CASE format.

How it works...

Spring Boot recognizes that there are many reasons and it needs to be able to provide separate configuration for the way management endpoints and other actuator components work, which is different from the main application. The first level of such configurations can be achieved by setting the myriad of available properties that intuitively start with `management.*`. We have used one such property, `management.server.port`, to set the port for the management interface to be `8081`. We could also set things like the SSL configuration, security settings, or network IP interface address to bind the listener to. We also have the capability to configure each individual actuator endpoint by setting their corresponding properties, which start with `management.endpoint.<name>.*` and have a variety of settings, depending on the specific endpoint goals.

For security reasons, the data that is exposed by the various management endpoints, especially the ones from sensitive ones such as `/health`, `/env`, and others can be very lucrative for malicious people on the outside. To prevent this from happening, Spring Boot provides us with the ability to configure if we want the endpoints to be available via `management.endpoint.<name>.enabled=false`. We can specify which individual endpoints we want to disable by setting an appropriate `management.endpoint<name>.enabled=false` property as well, or using `management.endpoints.web.exposure.exclude=<name>` to tell Spring Boot if this endpoint should be enabled, but not exposed via the WEB HTTP API method of access.

Alternatively, we can set `management.server.port=-1` to disable the HTTP exposure of these endpoints or use a different port number in order to have the management endpoints and live services on different ports. If we want to enable access only via a localhost, we can achieve this by configuring `management.server.address=127.0.0.1` to prevent external access. Even the context URL path can be configured to something else, say `/admin`, via `management.server.context-path=/admin`. This way, to get access to a `/health` endpoint, we would go to `http://127.0.0.1/admin/health` instead of the default `/actuator` context path. This can be useful if you want to control and restrict access via the firewall rules, so you can just add a filter to block external access to anything, `/admin/*`, for all the applications from the outside. With the addition of Spring Security, an authentication can also be configured to require a user login to get access to the endpoints.

In situations when controlling behavior using properties is not enough, Spring Boot provides a mechanism to provide alternative application context configuration via the use of `spring.factories` and the accompanying `ManagementContextConfiguration` annotation. This enables us to tell Spring Boot which configurations should be automatically loaded when management context is being created. The intended use of this annotation is to have the configuration live in a separate, sharable dependency library, outside of the main application's code.

In our example, because we put it in the same codebase (for simplicity), we had to do an extra step and define the exclusion filter in the `BookPubApplication.java` file to exclude the `ManagementContextConfiguration` classes from component scan when setting up the main application. The reason we had to do that is simple—if we look inside the `ManagementContextConfiguration` annotation definition, we will see that it is a meta-annotation with the `@Configuration` annotation inside it. What this means is that when our main application is being configured, the component scan will automatically detect all the classes in the classpath tree of the application code that are annotated with `@Configuration`, and as such, it will put all the configurations marked with `ManagementContextConfiguration` in the main context as well. We have avoided that using the exclusion filter. Alternatively, a better way is to have those configurations in a separate library using a different package hierarchy, which would prevent the component scan picking them up, but the autoconfiguration will still works because of the `spring.factories` entry for `org.springframework.boot.actuate.autoconfigure.web.ManagementContextConfiguration` telling Spring Boot to automatically add those configurations to the management context.

In order to have the management context separate from the main application, it is necessary to configure it to run on a separate port using the `management.server.port` property. Without this setting, all of the objects will be using shared application context.

Emitting metrics

The previous recipe gave an overview of the capabilities provided by Spring Boot Actuators. We played with different management endpoints such as `/info` and `/health` and even created our own health metrics to add to the default set. However, besides the health status, there are a number of things that we, as developers and operations folks, want to be able to see and monitor on an ongoing basis, and just knowing that the uplink is functional is not good enough. We would also like to see the number of open sessions, concurrent requests to the application, latency, and so on. In this recipe, you will learn about the metric reporting facilities in Spring Boot as well as how to add our own metrics and some quick and simple ways of visualizing them.

Getting ready

To help us visualize the metrics better, we will use a great open source project, `spring-boot-admin`, located at `https://github.com/codecentric/spring-boot-admin`. It provides a simple web UI on top of the Spring Boot Actuators to give a nicer view of the various data.

We will create a simple admin application in Gradle using the instructions from `https://github.com/codecentric/spring-boot-admin#server-application` by performing the following simple steps:

1. Go to `start.spring.io` and create a new application template with the following fields:

    - **Generate a: Gradle Project**
    - **With: Java**
    - **Spring Boot: 2.0.0 (SNAPSHOT)**
    - **Group:** `org.sample.admin`
    - **Artifact:** `spring-boot-admin-web`
    - **Name:** `Spring Boot Admin Web`
    - **Description:** `Spring Boot Admin Web Application`
    - **Package Name:** `org.sample.admin`
    - **Packaging: Jar**
    - **Java Version: 8**

2. Select the **Actuator** option under **Search for dependencies**

3. Click on **Generate Project alt +** to download the application template archive

4. Extract the contents from the directory of your choice

5. In the extracted directory, execute the `gradle wrapper` command line to generate a gradlew script

6. In the `build.gradle` file, add the following dependencies to the `dependencies` block:

```
compile("de.codecentric:spring-boot-admin-server:2.0.0-
SNAPSHOT")
compile("de.codecentric:spring-boot-admin-server-ui:2.0.0-
SNAPSHOT ")
```

7. We also need to update the `repositories` block with a reference to use the `snapshots` repository (as the time of writing, the SBA is not yet released):

```
maven { url
"https://oss.sonatype.org/content/repositories/snapshots/" }
```

8. Open the `SpringBootAdminWebApplication.java` file located in the `src/main/java/spring-boot-admin-web` directory and add the following annotations to the `SpringBootAdminWebApplication` class:

```
@SpringBootApplication
@EnableAdminServer
public class SpringBootAdminWebApplication {

    public static void main(String[] args) {
        SpringApplication.run(
                        SpringBootAdminWebApplication.class,
                        args);
    }
}
```

9. Open the `application.properties` file located in the `src/main/resources` directory and add the following settings:

```
server.port: 8090
spring.application.name: Spring Boot Admin Web
spring.cloud.config.enabled: false
spring.jackson.serialization.indent_output: true
```

10. We are now ready to start our Admin Web Console by running `./gradlew bootRun` and open the browser to `http://localhost:8090` to see the following output:

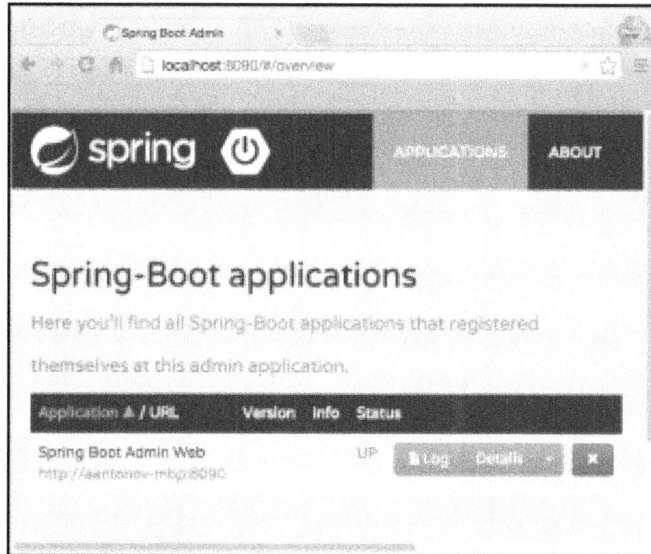

How to do it...

1. With the **Admin Web** up and running, we are now ready to start adding various metrics to our `BookPub` application. Let's expose the same information about our data repositories as we did in `HealthIndicators`, but this time, we will expose the counts data as a metric. We will continue to add code to our `db-count-starter` subproject. So, let's create a new file named `DbCountMetrics.java` in the `db-count-starter/src/main/java/com/example/bookpubstarter/dbcount` directory at the root of our project with the following content:

```
public class DbCountMetrics implements MeterBinder {
    private Collection<CrudRepository> repositories;

    public DbCountMetrics(Collection<CrudRepository>
repositories)
    {
        this.repositories = repositories;
    }
```

```
@Override
public void bindTo(MeterRegistry registry) {
    for (CrudRepository repository : repositories) {
        String name = DbCountRunner.getRepositoryName
            (repository.getClass());
        String metricName = "counter.datasource."
                            + name;
        Gauge.builder(metricName, repository,
                        CrudRepository::count)
            .tags("name", name)
            .description("The number of entries in "
                        + name + "repository")
            .register(registry);
    }
    }
}
```

2. Next, for the automatic registration of `DbCountMetrics`, we will enhance `DbCountAutoConfiguration.java` located in the `db-count-starter/src/main/java/com/example/bookpubstarter/dbcount` directory at the root of our project with the following content:

```
@Bean
public DbCountMetrics
  dbCountMetrics(Collection<CrudRepository> repositories) {
    return new DbCountMetrics(repositories);
}
```

3. In order for the Thread Dump to properly display in the Spring Boot Admin UI, we need to change our JSON converter from SNAKE_CASE to LOWER_CAMEL_CASE by changing `ManagementConfiguration.java` located in the `src/main/java/com/example/bookpub` directory at the root of our project with the following content:

```
propertyNamingStrategy(
    PropertyNamingStrategy.LOWER_CAMEL_CASE
)
```

4. So, let's start our application by executing `./gradlew clean bootRun` and then we can access the `/metrics` endpoint by opening our browser and going to `http://localhost:8081/actuator/metrics` to see our new `DbCountMetrics` class added to the existing metrics list, as follows:

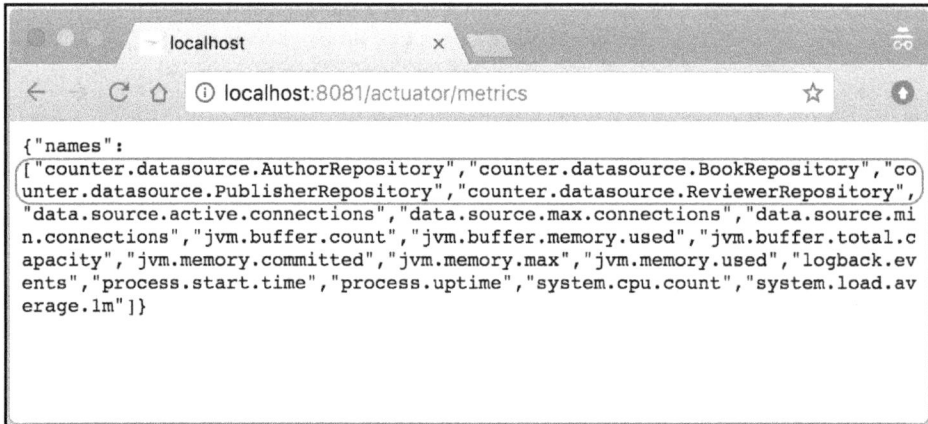

```
{"names":
["counter.datasource.AuthorRepository","counter.datasource.BookRepository","co
unter.datasource.PublisherRepository","counter.datasource.ReviewerRepository",
"data.source.active.connections","data.source.max.connections","data.source.mi
n.connections","jvm.buffer.count","jvm.buffer.memory.used","jvm.buffer.total.c
apacity","jvm.memory.committed","jvm.memory.max","jvm.memory.used","logback.ev
ents","process.start.time","process.uptime","system.cpu.count","system.load.av
erage.1m"]}
```

5. Our next step would be to get our application to appear in the Spring Boot Admin Web, which we created earlier. To make this happen, we will need to add a dependency on the `compile("de.codecentric:spring-boot-admin-starter-client:2.0.0-SNAPSHOT")` library to `build.gradle` in the directory at the root of our project.

6. Additionally, `application.properties` located in the `src/main/resources` directory in the root of our project needs to be enhanced with the following entries:

```
spring.application.name=BookPub Catalog Application
server.port=8080
spring.boot.admin.client.url=http://localhost:8090
```

7. Once again, let's start our application by executing `./gradlew clean bootRun`, and if we now go to Spring Boot Admin Web by directing our browser to `http://localhost:8090`, we should see a new entry for our application named `BookPub Catalog Application` appear in the list. If we click on the **Details** button on the right-hand side and scroll down to the **Health** section, we will see our custom health indicators along with the others reported in a form of nicer looking hierarchical entries in a table, as follows:

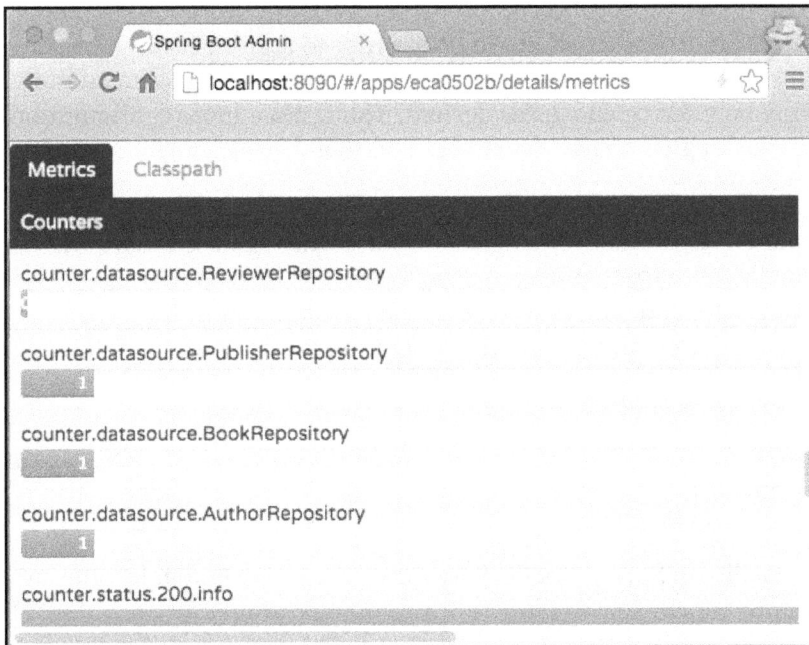

How it works...

A few words about Spring Boot Admin Web before we delve into the details of creating and emitting metrics. It is a simple web GUI that, in the backend, uses the same endpoints exposed by Spring Boot Actuator, which we learned about in the previous recipe. The data is extracted from the application as we click on the various links in Admin Web and displayed in a nice graphical way—no magic!

We only had to configure a few properties in addition to adding the client library dependency in order to get our application to connect and register with Admin Web:

- `spring.application.name=BookPub Catalog Application`: This configures the name of the application that we have chosen to use. It is also possible to take the value from the description property defined in `gradle.properties` using the resource processing task in Gradle. Admin Web uses this value when displaying the application list.
- `spring.boot.admin.client.url=http://localhost:8090`: This configures the location of the Admin Web application so that our application knows where to go in order to register itself. As we are running on port `8080`, we chose to configure Admin Web to listen on port `8090`, but any port can be chosen as desired. You can see more configuration options by visiting `https://codecentric.github.io/spring-boot-admin/current/`.

If we also want to enable the logging level control through the UI, we will need to add a Jolokia JMX library to our `compile("org.jolokia:jolokia-core:+")` build dependency as well as a `logback.xml` file in the `src/main/resources` directory in the root of the project with the following content:

```
<configuration>
  <include
resource="org/springframework/boot/logging/logback/base.xml"/>
  <jmxConfigurator/>
</configuration>
```

The metrics facility in Spring Boot is very powerful and extendable, offering a number of different approaches for emitting and consuming metrics. Starting with Spring Boot 2.0, the `Micrometer.io` library is being used under the hood to provide a very comprehensive monitoring solution. Out of the box, Spring Boot already configures a number of data metrics that monitor the system resources, such as heap memory, thread counts, system uptime, and many others as well as the database usage and HTTP session counts. The MVC endpoints are also instrumented to gauge the request latency, which is measured in milliseconds, as well as a counter for each endpoint request status.

Various metrics, such as gauges, counters, timers, and so on, are emitted via the
`MeterRegistry` implementation that is provided by Spring Boot at runtime. The
registry can be easily autowired into any Spring-managed object and be used to emit
metrics.

For example, we can easily count the number of times a particular method gets
invoked. All we need to do is to autowire an instance of `MeterRegistry` into our
object during creation, and place the following line at the beginning of the method:

```
meterRegistry.counter("objectName.methodName.invoked").increment();
```

Each time the method gets called, the particular metric count will be incremented.

This approach will give us the counts that we can increment, but if we want to
measure latency or any other arbitrary value, we will need to use `Gauge` to submit
our metrics. To measure how long it will take for our method to execute, we can use
`MeterRegistry` and at the beginning of the method, record the time:

```
long start = System.currentTimeMillis();
```

We will then place our code and before the return, capture the time again:

```
long end = System.currentTimeMillis();.
```

Then, we will emit the
metric `meterRegistry.gauge("objectName.methodName.latency", end -
start);`, which will update the last. The use of `gauge` for timing purposes is very
rudimentary and `MeterRegistry` actually provides a specialized type of
meter—Timer. The Timer meter, for example, provides the ability to wrap runnable
or callable lambdas and automatically time the execution. Another benefit of using a
Timer instead of `Gauge` is that a Timer meter keeps both the event counts as well as
the latency it took to execute each occurrence.

The `MeterRegistry` implementation covers most of the simple use cases and is very
handy when we operate in our own code and have the flexibility to add them where
we need to. However, it is not always the case, and in these cases, we will need to
resort to wrapping whatever it is we want to monitor by creating a custom
implementation of `MeterBinder`. In our case, we will use it to expose the counts for
each of the repositories in the database as we can't insert any monitoring code into the
`CrudRepository` proxy implementations.

Whenever the `MeterRegistry` implementation does not provide enough flexibility, for example, when there is a need to wrap an object in a meter like `Gauge`, most meter implementations provide fluid builders to gain more flexibility. In our example, to wrap the repository metrics, we used a `Gauge` fluid builder to construct `Gauge`:

```
Gauge.builder(metricName, repository, CrudRepository::count)
```

The main builder method takes the following three arguments:

- `metricName`: This specifies the name to use to uniquely identify this metric
- `repository`: This provides an object on which we invoke the method that should return a numeric value that `gauge` will report
- `CrudRepository::count`: This is the method that should be called on the `repository` object to get the current count of entries

This enables us to build flexible wrappers because all we have to do is provide an object that would expose the necessary numeric value and a function reference to a function that should be called on the instance to get that value during the `gauge` evaluation.

The `MeterBinder` interface, used to export the Meter, has only one method defined, `void bindTo(MeterRegistry);`, which the implementer needs to code with the definition of what exactly is being monitored. The implementation class needs to be exposed as `@Bean`, and it will automatically be picked up and processed during the application initialization. Assuming that one actually registered the created `Meter` instance with the provided `MeterRegistry` implementation, typically by terminating the fluid builder's chain by calling `.builder(...).register(registry)`, the metrics will be exposed via `MetricsEndpoint`, which will expose all the meters registered with the registry every time the `/metrics` actuator is called.

It is important to mention that we have created the `MeterBinder` and `HealthIndicator` beans inside the main application context and not in the management one. The reason being that even though the data is being exposed via the management endpoints, the endpoint beans, such as `MetricsEndpoint`, get defined in the main application context, and thus expect all the other autowired dependencies to be defined there as well.

This approach is safe because in order to get access to the information, one needs to go through the `WebMvcEndpointHandlerMapping` implementation facade, which is created in the management context and use the delegate endpoint from the main application context. Take a look at the `MetricsEndpoint` class and the corresponding `@Endpoint` annotation to see the details.

Monitoring Spring Boot via JMX

In today's day and age, the RESTful HTTP JSON services are a de facto way of accessing data, but this is not the only way to do so. Another fairly popular and common way of managing systems in real time is via JMX. The good news is that Spring Boot already comes with the same level of support to expose the management endpoints over JMX as it does over HTTP. Actually, these are exactly the same endpoints; they are just wrapped around the MBean container.

In this recipe, we will take a look at how to retrieve the same information via JMX as we did via HTTP as well as how to expose some MBeans, which are provided by third-party libraries through HTTP using the Jolokia JMX library.

Getting ready

If you haven't done so already for the previous recipe, then add the Jolokia JMX library to our `compile("org.jolokia:jolokia-core:+")` build dependency and add the `management.jolokia.enabled=true` property to `application.properties`, as we will need them to expose MBeans via HTTP.

How to do it...

1. After we add the Jolokia JMX dependency, all we need to do is build and start our application by executing `./gradlew clean bootRun` and now we can simply launch jConsole to see the the various endpoints exposed under the `org.springframework.boot` domain:

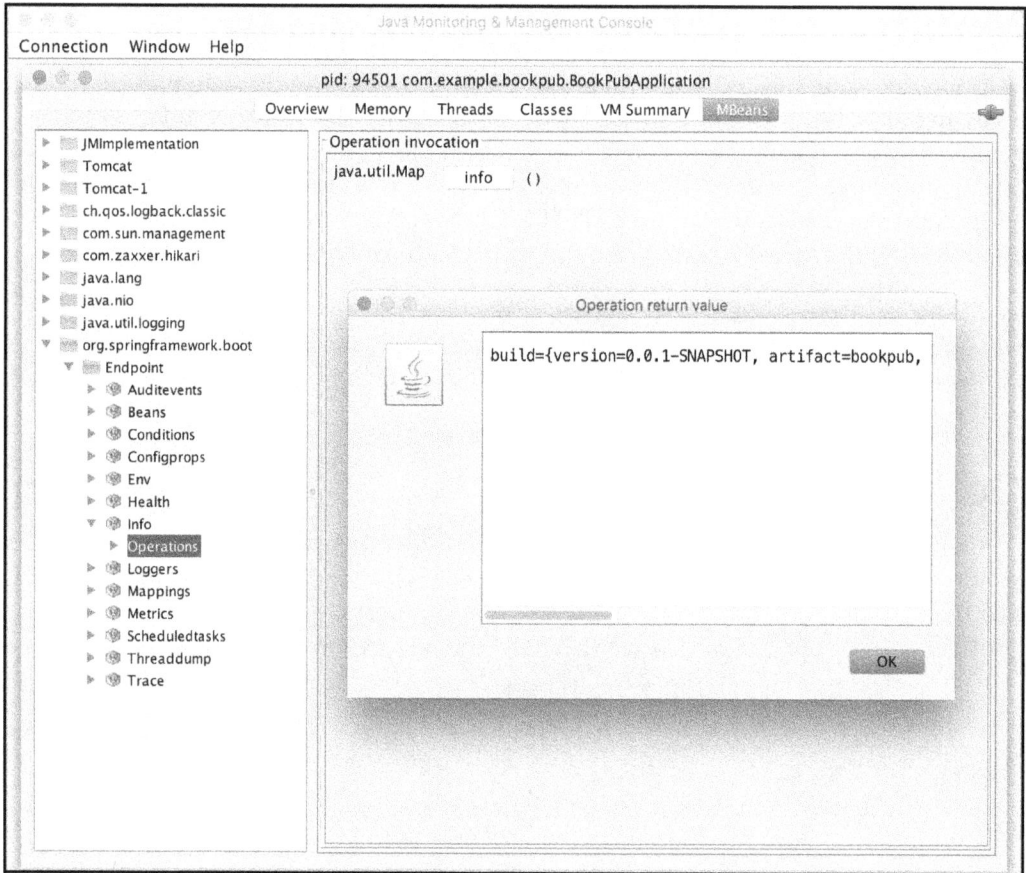

2. Having the Jolokia JMX library added to the classpath, Spring Boot also enables the accessing of all the registered MBeans via HTTP API using the `/jolokia` endpoint. To find out the `maxThreads` setting for our Tomcat HTTP port `8080` connector, we can either look it up using jConsole by selecting the `maxThreads` attribute on the `Tomcat:type=ThreadPool,name="http-nio-8080"` MBean to get the value of `200` or we can use Jolokia JMX HTTP by opening our browser and going to `http://localhost:8081/actuator/jolokia/read/Tomcat:type=ThreadPool,name=%22http-nio-8080%22/maxThreads` and we should see the following JSON response:

```
{"request":
  {"mbean":"Tomcat:name="http-nio-8080",type=ThreadPool",
   "attribute":"maxThreads",
   "type":"read"
  },
  "value":200,"timestamp":1436740537,"status":200}
```

How it works...

By default, the Spring Boot Actuator, when added to the application, comes with all the endpoints and management services enabled. This includes the JMX access as well. If, for some reason, one would like to disable the exposure of a particular endpoint via JMX, this can easily be configured by adding `management.endpoints.jmx.exclude=<id>` or in order to disable the exporting of all the Spring MBeans, we can configure the `spring.jmx.enabled=false` setting in `application.properties`.

The presence of the Jolokia library in the classpath triggers Spring Boot `JolokiaManagementContextConfiguration`, which would automatically configure `ServletRegistrationBean` accepting requests on the `/jolokia` actuator path. It is also possible to set various Jolokia-specific configuration options via the `management.endpoint.jolokia.config.*` set of properties. A complete list is available at `https://jolokia.org/reference/html/agents.html#agent-war-init-params`. In case you would like to use Jolokia, but want to manually set it up, we can tell Spring Boot to ignore its presence by configuring a `management.endpoint.jolokia.enabled=false` property setting in `application.properties`.

Managing Spring Boot via SSHd Shell and writing custom remote Shell commands

Some of you are probably reminiscing about the good old days where all the administration was done via SSH directly on the machine, where one has complete flexibility and control, or even using SSH to connect to a management port and apply whatever changes were needed directly to a running application. Even though Spring Boot has removed native integration with the CRaSH Java Shell in version 2.0, there is an open source project, `sshd-shell-spring-boot`, which brings back that ability.

For this recipe, we will use the health indicator and management endpoint, which we created earlier in this chapter. We will expose the same capabilities via the SSH console access.

How to do it...

1. The first step to getting SSHd Shell to work is to add the necessary dependency starters to our `build.gradle` file, as follows:

```
dependencies {
    ...
    compile("org.springframework.boot:spring-boot-starter-
actuator")
    compile("io.github.anand1st:sshd-shell-spring-boot-
starter:3.2.1")
    compile("de.codecentric:spring-boot-admin-starter-
client:2.0.0-SNAPSHOT")
    compile("org.jolokia:jolokia-core:+")
    ...
}
```

2. We also need to explicitly enable it by setting the following property in `application.properties`, located in the `src/main/resources` directory in the root of our project it needs to be enhanced with the following entries:

```
sshd.shell.enabled=true
management.endpoint.shutdown.enabled=true
```

3. Now, let's start our application by executing `./gradlew clean bootRun` and then connect to it via SSH by executing `ssh -p 8022 admin@localhost`.

4. We will be prompted for a password so let's find the autogenerated hash key in the application startup log, which would look as follows:

```
********** User password not set. Use following password to
login:
8f20cf10-7d67-42ac-99e4-3a4a77ca6c5f **********
```

5. If the password is entered correctly, we will be greeted by the following welcome prompt:

```
Enter 'help' for a list of supported commands
app>
```

6. Next, we will invoke our existing `/health` endpoint by typing health and we should get the following result:

```
{
  "status" : "UP",
  "details" : {
    "dbCount" : {
      "status" : "UP",
      "details" : {
        "ReviewerRepository" : {
          ...
        },
        "PublisherRepository" : {
          ...
        },
        "AuthorRepository" : {
          ...
        },
        "BookRepository" : {
          ...
        }
      }
    },
    "diskSpace" : {
      "status" : "UP",
      "details" : {
        "total" : 249795969024,
        "free" : 14219882496,
        "threshold" : 10485760
      }
    },
```

```
      "db" : {
        "status" : "UP",
        "details" : { "database" : "H2", "hello" : 1 }
      }
    }
  }
```

7. Typing `help` will show the list of all the existing commands so you can play with some of them to see what they do and then we will proceed with adding our own SSHd Shell command, which will enable us to add new publishers to the system via the command line.

8. Make a new directory named commands in `src/main/java/com/example/bookpub/command` at the root of our project.

9. Add a file named `Publishers.java` in the `src/main/java/com/example/bookpub/command` directory at the root of our project with the following content:

```java
package com.example.bookpub.command;

import com.example.bookpub.entity.Publisher;
import com.example.bookpub.repository.PublisherRepository;
import org.springframework.beans.factory.annotation.Autowired;
import org.springframework.stereotype.Component;
import
sshd.shell.springboot.autoconfiguration.SshdShellCommand;
import sshd.shell.springboot.console.ConsoleIO;

import java.util.HashMap;
import java.util.Map;

@Component
@SshdShellCommand(value = "publishers", description =
"Publisher management. Type 'publishers' for supported
subcommands")
public class PublishersCommand {
    @Autowired
    private PublisherRepository repository;

    @SshdShellCommand(value = "list", description = "List of
publishers")
    public String list(String _arg_) {
        List list = new ArrayList();

        repository.findAll().forEach(publisher ->
            list.add(publisher);
```

```
        );

        return ConsoleIO.asJson(list);
    }

    @SshdShellCommand(value = "add", description = "Add a new
publisher. Usage: publishers add <name>")
    public String add(String name) {
        Publisher publisher = new Publisher(name);
        try {
            publisher = repository.save(publisher);
            return ConsoleIO.asJson(publisher);
        } catch (Exception e) {
            return String.format("Unable to add new publisher
named %s%n%s", name, e.getMessage());
        }
    }

    @SshdShellCommand(value = "remove", description = "Remove
existing publisher. Usage: publishers remove <id>")
    public String remove(String id) {
        try {
            repository.deleteById(Long.parseLong(id));
            return ConsoleIO.asJson(String.format("Removed
publisher %s", id));
        } catch (Exception e) {
            return String.format("Unable to remove publisher
with id %s%n%s", id, e.getMessage());
        }
    }
}
```

10. With the commands built up, now let's start our application by executing `./gradlew clean bootRun` and then connect to it via SSH by executing `ssh -p 8022 admin@localhost` and log in using the generated password hash.

11. When we type publishers, we will see the list of all the possible commands, as follows:

```
app> publishers
Supported subcommand for publishers
add      Add a new publisher. Usage: publishers add <name>
list     List of publishers
remove   Remove existing publisher. Usage: publishers remove
<id>
```

12. Let's add a publisher by typing `publishers add Fictitious Books` and we should see the following message:

```
{
    "id" : 2,
    "name" : "Fictitious Books"
}
```

13. If we will now type publishers list, we will get a list of all the books:

```
[ {
    "id" : 1,
    "name" : "Packt"
}, {
    "id" : 2,
    "name" : "Fictitious Books"
} ]
```

14. Removing a publisher is a simple command `publishers remove 2` that should respond with the "`Removed publisher 2`" message.

15. Just to confirm that the publisher is really gone, execute publishers list and we should see the following output:

```
[ {
    "id" : 1,
    "name" : "Packt"
} ]
```

How it works...

The SSHd Shell integration with Spring Boot provides you with many commands out of the box. We can invoke the same management end points that were available to us over HTTP and JMX. We can get access to the JVM information, make changes to the logging configuration, and even interact with the JMX server and all the registered MBeans. The list of all the possibilities is really impressive and very rich in functionalities, so I would definitely advise you to read the reference documentation on SSHd Shell by going to `https://github.com/anand1st/sshd-shell-spring-boot`.

In Spring Boot, the expectation is that any class annotated with `@SshdShellCommand` will be automatically picked up and registered as an SSHd Shell command. The value of the annotation attribute translates into the main command name. In our case, we set the class annotation attribute value field to `publishers` and this became the top-level command name in the SSH Shell console.

If the command contains sub-commands, as in our publishers command example, then, the methods of the class that are also annotated with `@SshdShellCommand` get registered as sub-commands to the main command. If a class has only one method, it will automatically become the only command for a given class that would be executed when the command name is typed. If we want multiple sub-commands to reside in the class command, as we did with publishers, each method that translates into a command needs to be annotated with `@SshdShellCommand`.

Currently, SSHd Shell framework has a limitation of being able to pass only one attribute argument to the command, but there is work going on to expand on that capability. In the mean time, it is recommended that JSON payload is used to communicate with the commands as inputs or outputs.

The following attributes are available on the annotations:

- `value`: This attribute defines the command or sub-command name. Even though the name of the method does not need to match the name of the command, it is a good convention for keeping the two in sync to make the code more readable.
- `description`: This attribute defines the text that gets displayed when the `help` command is invoked. It is a good place to communicate with the users how the command is expected to be used, what inputs it takes, and so on. It is a good idea to provide as much description and documentation as possible as in the Shell, one would like to clearly educate the users of what needs to happen and how to call the command. The man pages are great so keep the documentation top notch.
- `roles`: This attribute enables us to define a security constraint on who is allowed to execute the given command. If Spring Security is also used, SSHd Shell provides the ability to configure a custom or specific `AuthenticationProvider` to be used for handling user authentication and role binding. For example, it would be easy to connect your application to the company's LDAP server and allow developers to use their regular credentials and also configure different role access controls, based on the needs of the particular organization.

Each command can be queried for its usage by using help, or in the case of a command containing sub-commands, by typing the name of the top-level command.

While SSHd Shell comes with many built-in commands, one can easily add custom commands, taking advantage of standard Spring / Spring Boot programming style, using the `@Autowired` and `@Component` annotations to get the necessary dependencies to be wired in and automatically configured during the application start life cycle.

SSHd Shell also provides a nice functionality enabling the use of post-processors, invoked by a pipe (`|`) symbol. The current support allows for output highlighting `| h packt`, which will highlight the word `packt` in the output, or emailing response output `| m my@email.com`, which will email the response of a command to the specified email address, given that **Spring Mail** is also configured and available.

It would be great if we could chain different commands together, like in Linux proper, so as to help process the output and filter out the necessary data when the amount of information tends to get overwhelming. Imagine that our publishers list command returns not `2`, but `2000` publishers. From this list, we want to find the ones that start with `Pa`.

Even though SSHd Shell does not provide this type of functionality out of the box, it does offer us an ability to implement our own post-processors by defining beans that extend the `BaseUserInputProcessor` class. Let's create one that would provide support for filtering JSON responses, something similar to how the `jq` command-line utility works.

To achieve this, let's create another class named `JsonPathUserInputProcessor.java` in the `src/main/java/com/example/bookpub/command` directory at the root of our project with the following content:

```
@Component
@Order(3)
public class JsonPathUserInputProcessor
            extends BaseUserInputProcessor {

    private final Pattern pattern = Pattern.compile("[wW]+s?|s?jq
(.+)");

    @Override
    public Optional<UsageInfo> getUsageInfo() {
        return Optional.of(new UsageInfo(Arrays.<UsageInfo.Row>asList(
                new UsageInfo.Row("jq <arg>", "JSON Path Query <arg>
in response output of command execution"),
                new UsageInfo.Row("", "Example usage: help | jq
$.<name>"))));
```

```
    }

    @Override
    public Pattern getPattern() {
        return pattern;
    }

    @Override
    public void processUserInput(String userInput) throws
      InterruptedException, ShellException{
        String[] part = splitAndValidateCommand(userInput, "|", 2);
        Matcher matcher = pattern.matcher(userInput);
        Assert.isTrue(matcher.find(), "Unexpected error");
        String jsonQuery = matcher.group(1).trim();
        try {
            String output = processCommands(part[0]);
            Object response = JsonPath.read(output, jsonQuery);
            ConsoleIO.writeJsonOutput(response);
        } catch (Exception e) {
            ConsoleIO.writeOutput(String.format("Unable to process
            query %s%n%s", jsonQuery, e.getMessage()));
        }
    }
}
```

Using the pipe functionality, we can easily chain the `publishers list` command with the `jq` command in the following way:

```
publishers list | jq $..[?(@.name =~ /Pa.*/i)]
```

In our example, this should return us only one record, as follows:

```
[ {
    "id" : 1,
    "name" : "Packt"
} ]
```

While it is not a full-fledged pipe functionality, the use of input processors allows for adding functionalities such as sorting, filtering, and displaying rendering, which give more flexibility to modularize and reuse common behaviors.

The SSHd Shell Spring Boot integration comes with a number of configuration options allowing us to disable the component, configure authentication settings, and specify usernames, passwords, and even key certificates. For example, if we want to use a specific username and password, we can do so by configuring the following properties:

```
sshd.shell.username=remote
sshd.shell.password=shell
```

In a real-world enterprise environment, it is more common to use the shared keys for restricted access and these can be configured using the `sshd.shell.publicKeyFile=<key path>` or `sshd.shell.hostKeyFile=<key path>` properties. Alternatively, and probably a better approach, as was already mentioned earlier, using a custom `AuthenticationProvider` implementation together with Spring Security allows the integrate of authentication mechanisms into the company's authentication system.

Integrating Micrometer metrics with Graphite

Earlier in this chapter, you learned about the monitoring capabilities that are provided by Spring Boot. We saw examples of writing custom `HealthIndicators`, creating metrics, and using `MeterRegistry` to emit data. The simple Spring Boot Admin Web framework gave us some nice graphical UI to visualize the data, but all of these metrics were in-the-moment, with no long-term retention and historical access. Not being able to observe the trends, detect the deviations from the baseline, and compare today with last week is not a very good strategy, especially for an enterprise-complex system. We all want to be able to have access to the time series data going weeks, if not months, back and set up alarms and thresholds, if something goes unplanned.

This recipe will introduce us to an amazing time series graphical tool: Graphite. Graphite is a two-part system. It provides storage for numeric time series data as well as a service to render this data in a form of on-demand graphs or expose the graph data as a JSON stream. You will learn how to integrate and configure Spring's Micrometer monitoring framework with Graphite in order to send the monitoring data from a Spring Boot application to Graphite and play a bit with Graphite to visualize the different statistics that we've gathered.

Getting ready

Graphite is an application that is written in Python and is, thus, capable of running on virtually any system supporting Python and its libraries. There are multiple ways of installing Graphite on any given system, ranging from compilation from a source, using `pip` all the way, to prebuilt RPMs for various Linux distributions.

For all the different installation strategies, take a look at the Graphite documentation at `http://graphite.readthedocs.org/en/latest/install.html`. OS X users can read a very good step-by-step guide located at `https://gist.github.com/relaxdiego/7539911`.

For the purposes of this recipe, we will use a premade Docker container containing Graphite as well as its counterpart Grafana. While there is an abundance of various prebuilt variants of Docker images containing combinations of Graphite and Grafana, we will use the one from `https://registry.hub.docker.com/u/alexmercer/graphite-grafana/` as it contains all the right configurations that will make it easy for us to get started quickly:

1. The first step will be to download the desired Docker container image. We will do this by executing `docker pull alexmercer/graphite-grafana`. The container size is about 500 MB; so the download might take a few minutes depending on your connection speed.
2. Both Graphite and Grafana store their data in the database files. We will need to create external directories, which will reside outside the container, and we will connect them to a running instance via Docker data volumes.
   - Make a directory for the Graphite data anywhere in your system, for example, in `<user_home>/data/graphite`.
   - Make a directory for the Grafana data, for example, in `<user_home>/data/grafana`.
3. In this container, the Graphite data will go to `/var/lib/graphite/storage/whisper`, while Grafana stores its data in `/usr/share/grafana/data`. So, we will use these paths as internal volume mount destinations when starting the container.

4. Run the container by executing `docker run -v`
    `<user_home>/data/graphite:/var/lib/graphite/storage/whispe`
    `r -v <user_home>/data/grafana:/usr/share/grafana/data -p`
    `2003:2003 -p 3000:3000 -p 8888:80 -d alexmercer/graphite-`
    `grafana`.

    - In Docker, the `-v` option configures a volume mount binding. In our example, we configured the external `<user_home>/data/graphite` directory to be the same as the `/var/lib/graphite/storage/whisper` directory reference in the container. The same goes for the `<user_home>/data/grafana` mapping. We can even look in the `<user_home>/data/graphite or data/grafana` directories to see them contain the subdirectories and files.
    - The `-p` option configures the port mappings similar to the directory volumes. In our example, we mapped the following three different ports to be accessible from outside the container to the internal ports to which the various services are bound: `2003:2003`: This port mapping externalizes the Graphite data stream listener known as **Carbon-Cache Line Receiver**, to which we will connect in order to send the metrics data.
    `3000:3000`: This port mapping externalizes the Grafana Web Dashboard UI, which we will use to create visual dashboards on top of the Graphite data.
    `8888:80`: This port mapping externalizes the Graphite Web UI. Though it is running on port `80` in the container, it is unlikely that on our development machine, port `80` is open; so it is better to map it to some other higher number port such as `8080` or `8888` in our case, as `8080` is already taken by our `BookPub` application.

5. If everything has gone according to the plan, Graphite and Grafana should be up and running and thus, we can access Graphite by pointing our browser to `http://localhost:8888` and we should see the following output:

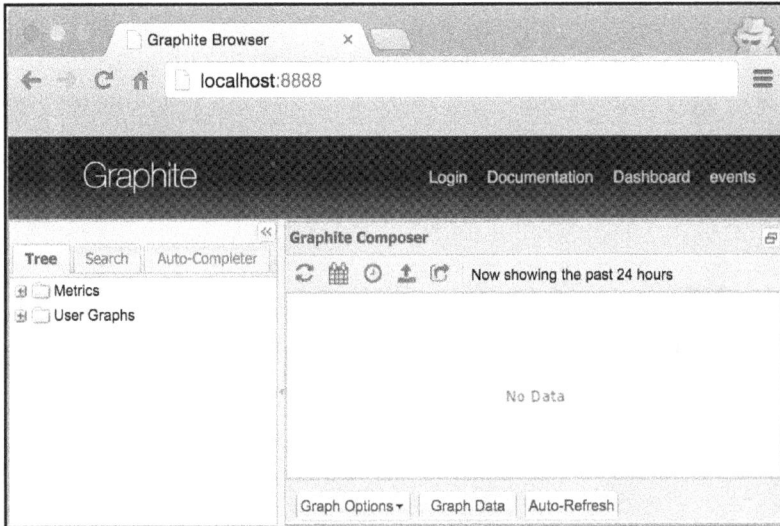

6. To see Grafana, point the browser to `http://localhost:3000` so as to see the following output:

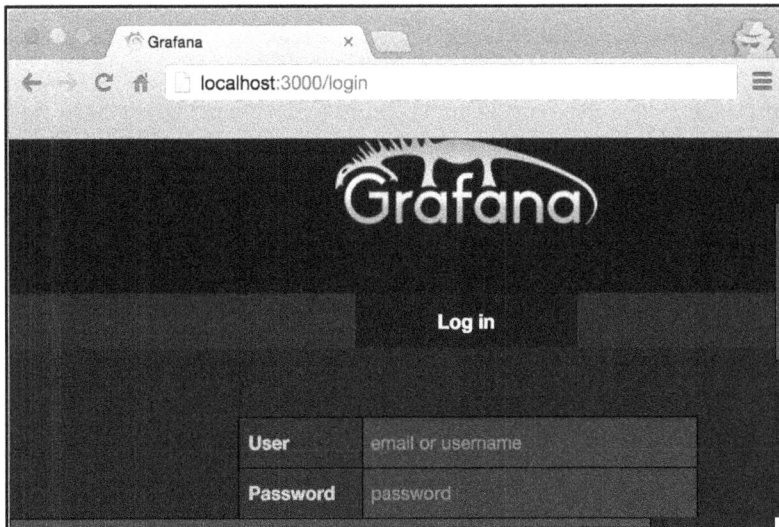

7. The default login and password for Grafana are `admin/admin` and can be changed via the Web UI Admin.

> For the OS X users who use boot2docker, the IP would not be of the `localhost`, but rather a result of the boot2docker IP call.

8. Once we are in Grafana, we will need to add our Graphite instance as `DataSource`, so click on the icon, go to **Data Sources**, and add a new source of the `Type Graphite, Url http://localhost:80, Access` proxy:

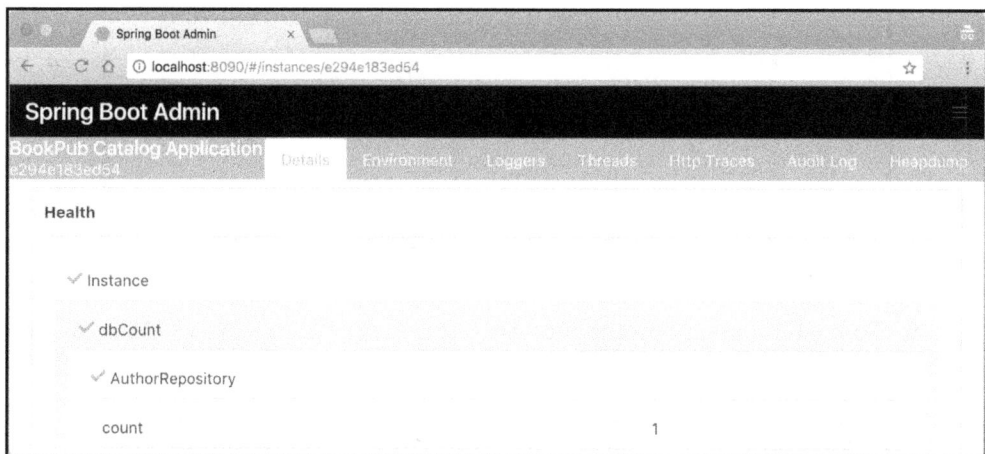

How to do it...

With Graphite and Grafana up and running, we are now ready to start configuring our application in order to send the metrics to the Graphite listener on port 2003. To do this, we will use the Codahale/Dropwizard metrics library, which is fully supported by Spring Boot and thus requires a minimum amount of configuration:

1. The first thing on our list is to add the necessary library dependencies. Extend the dependencies block in the `build.gradle` file with the following content:

```
compile("io.micrometer:micrometer-registry-
graphite:latest.release")
```

2. Create a file named `MonitoringConfiguration.java` in the `src/main/java/com/example/bookpub` directory at the root of our project with the following content:

```java
@Configuration
@ConditionalOnClass(GraphiteMeterRegistry.class)
public class MonitoringConfiguration {

    private static final Pattern blacklistedChars =
                        Pattern.compile("[{}(),=[]/]");

    @Bean
    public MeterRegistryCustomizer<GraphiteMeterRegistry>
                            meterRegistryCustomizer() {
        return registry -> {
            registry.config()
                .namingConvention(namingConvention());
        };
    }

    @Bean
    public HierarchicalNameMapper hierarchicalNameMapper(){
        return (id, convention) -> {
            String prefix = "bookpub.app.";
            String tags = "";

            if (id.getTags().iterator().hasNext()) {
                tags = "."
                        + id.getConventionTags(convention)
                        .stream()
                        .map(t -> t.getKey() + "."
                                            + t.getValue()
                        )
                        .map(nameSegment ->
                                nameSegment.replace(" ", "_")
                        )
                        .collect(Collectors.joining("."));
            }

            return prefix
                    + id.getConventionName(convention)
                    + tags;
        };
    }

    @Bean
    public NamingConvention namingConvention() {
        return new NamingConvention() {
```

```
                    @Override
                    public String name(String name,
                                         Meter.Type type,
                                         String baseUnit) {
                        return format(name);
                    }

                    @Override
                    public String tagKey(String key) {
                        return format(key);
                    }

                    @Override
                    public String tagValue(String value) {
                        return format(value);
                    }

                    private String format(String name) {
                        String sanitized =
                            Normalizer.normalize(name,
                                        Normalizer.Form.NFKD);
                        // Changes to the original
                        // GraphiteNamingConvention to use "dot"
                        // instead of "camelCase"
                        sanitized =
                            NamingConvention.dot.tagKey(sanitized);

                        return blacklistedChars
                                    .matcher(sanitized)
                                    .replaceAll("_");
                    }
                };
            }
        }
```

3. We will also need to add the configuration property settings for our
    Graphite instance to the `application.properties` file in the
    `src/main/resources` directory at the root of our project:

```
management.metrics.export.graphite.enabled=true
management.metrics.export.graphite.host=localhost
management.metrics.export.graphite.port=2003
management.metrics.export.graphite.protocol=plaintext
management.metrics.export.graphite.rate-units=seconds
management.metrics.export.graphite.duration-units=milliseconds
management.metrics.export.graphite.step=1m
```

4. Now, let's build and run our application by executing `./gradlew clean bootRun` and if we have configured everything correctly, it should start without any issues.

5. With the application up and running, we should start seeing some data that is in the Graphite and `bookpub` data nodes getting added to the tree under metrics. To add some more realism, let's open our browser and load a book URL, `http://localhost:8080/books/978-1-78528-415-1/`, a few dozen times to generate some metrics.

6. Let's go ahead and look at some of the metrics in Graphite and set the data time range to 15 minutes in order to get some close-look graphs, which will look similar to the following screenshot:

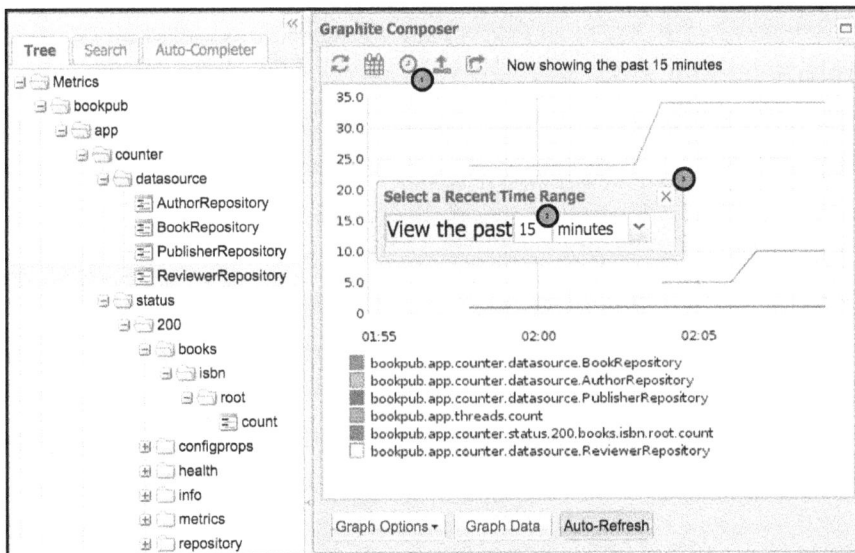

7. We can also create some fancy looking dashboards using this data in Grafana by creating a new dashboard and adding a **Graph** panel, as shown in the following screenshot:

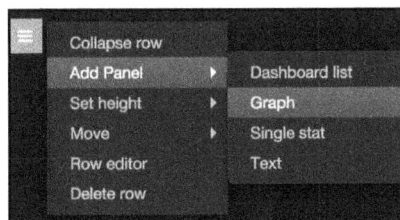

8. The newly created **Graph** panel will look like this:

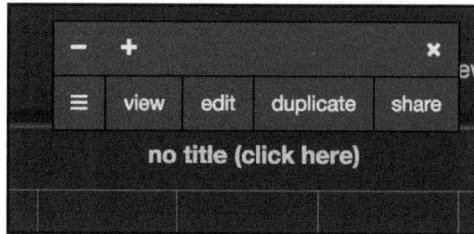

9. Click on the **no title (click here)** label, choose **edit**, and enter the metric name `bookpub.app.http.server.requests.exception.None.method.GET` `.status.200.uri._books__isbn_.count` in the text field as shown in the following screenshot:

10. Clicking on **Dashboard** will take you out of the edit mode.

For a more detailed tutorial, visit `http://docs.grafana.org/guides/` `gettingstarted/`.

How it works...

To enable exporting metrics via Graphite, we added an extra dependency on the `io.micrometer:micrometer-registry-graphite` library. Under the hood, however, it depends on the Dropwizard metrics library to provide Graphite integration, so it will add the following new dependencies to our `build` file:

- `io.dropwizard.metrics:metrics-core`: This dependency adds the basic Dropwizard functionality, `MetricsRegistry`, common API interfaces, and base classes. This is the bare minimum that is required to get Dropwizard working and integrated into Spring Boot to handle the metrics.
- `io.dropwizard.metrics:metrics-graphite`: This adds support for `GraphiteReporter` and is needed in order to configure Dropwizard to send the monitoring data that it collects to our Graphite instance.

In order to keep things clean and nicely separated, we created a separate configuration class with all the monitoring-related beans and settings: `MonitoringConfiguration`. In this class, we configured three `@Bean` instances: a custom `MeterRegistryCustomizer` implementation to customize the `GraphiteMeterRegistry` instance, `HigherarchicalNameMapper`, and `NamingConvention` to go along with it.

The reason why we had to create our own customization is twofold. We wanted to comply with the classic Graphite metric naming scheme, which uses the dot (`.`) notation to separate metric names in a hierarchy. Unfortunately, for whatever reason, Micrometer Graphite implementation has opted for using the `camelCase` collapsing notation instead, which made metric names like `counter.datasource.BookRepository` translate into the `counterDatasourceBookRepository` name to be displayed inside Graphite. Having such a long name, without hierarchical tree makes for a very difficult search and discovery inside Graphite UI, when many metrics are present. Also, all the metrics get placed under a root (`/`) tree, without creating a dedicated application folder, which also leads to poor readability and usage. We have added code to our `HigherarchicalNameMapper` instance to prepend the application prefix to all the metrics being exported to Graphite so that they all get put into `subtree`: `/bookpub/app/*.`:

```
String prefix = "bookpub.app.";
...
return prefix + id.getConventionName(convention) + tags;
```

The `NamingConvention` provides precise configuration about how to convert particular Meter names, keys, values, and tags into proper Graphite variants. Inside the `format(String name)` method, we declare that we want to use a dot (`.`) separation between elements via the `NamingConvention.dot` implementation.

The `management.metrics.export.graphite` group of properties define how to send the data to the Graphite instance. We configured it to do so every 1 minute, translate all the time duration intervals, such as the latency measurements, into milliseconds and all the variable rates, such as the number of requests per some time frame, into seconds. Most of these values have their default configuration settings for Graphite provided, but can be changed, if desired.

Notice that we've used the `@ConditionalOnClass` annotation to indicate that we only want to apply this `@Configuration` if the Micrometer Graphite provided class `GraphiteMeterRegistry.class` is present in the classpath. This is needed to not try to instantiate Graphite beans during tests, as there might not be a Graphite instance running and available in the testing environment.

As you can see from the available metrics from Graphite UI, there are many metrics that are provided out of the box. Some notable ones are about JVM and OS metrics, which expose the memory and thread metrics to Graphite in the memory and threads data nodes among other data. They can be found in `Metrics/bookpub/app/jvm`, `Metrics/bookpub/app/process`, or `Metrics/bookpub/app/system` in the Graphite tree.

Micrometer core library provides a number of meter binders for additional system metrics. If there is a need to export things like thread or executor information, or get a view into the file descriptors, one can export additional beans by simply declaring a method returning `new JvmThreadMetrics()` or `new FileDescriptorMetrics()` for example.

The running application will gather all the metrics registered with `MeterRegistry` and every configured exporter (in our case, `GraphiteMeterRegistry`) reports all these metrics at a timed interval to its destination. The proper exporter implementations run in a separate `ThreadPool`, thus outside of the main application threads and not interfering with them. However, this should be kept in mind in case the Meter implementations use some `ThreadLocal` data internally, which would not be available to exporters.

Integrating Micrometer metrics with Dashing

The previous recipe has given us a glimpse of how we can collect the various metrics from our application during its runtime. We've also seen how powerful the ability to visualize this data as a set of graphs of historical trends can be.

While Grafana and Graphite offer us the very powerful capability of manipulating the data in the form of graphs and building elaborate dashboards that are full of thresholds, applied data functions, and much more, sometimes we want something simpler, more readable, and something widgety. This is exactly the kind of dashboard experience that is provided by Dashing.

Dashing is a popular dashboard framework developed by Shopify and written in Ruby/Sinatra. It provides you with an ability to create an assortment of dashboards that are comprised of different types of widgets. We can have things such as graphs, meters, lists, numeric values, or just plain text to display the information.

In this recipe, we will install the Dashing framework, learn how to create dashboards, send and consume the data to report from an application directly as well as fetch it from Graphite, and use the Dashing API to push the data to the Dashing instance.

Getting ready

In order to get Dashing to run, we will need to have an environment that has a Ruby 1.9+ installed with RubyGems.

Typically, Ruby should be available on any common distribution of Linux and OS X. If you are running Windows, I would suggest using `http://rubyinstaller.org` in order to get the installation bundle.

Once you have such an environment available, we will install Dashing and create a new dashboard application for our use, as follows:

1. Installing Dashing is very easy; simply execute the gem install dashing command to install Dashing RubyGems on your system.
2. With the RubyGem successfully installed, we will create the new dashboard named `bookpub_dashboard` by executing the dashing new `bookpub_dashboard` command in the directory where you want the dashboard application to be created.
3. Once the dashboard application has been generated, go to the `bookpub_dashboard` directory and execute the `bundle` command to install the required dependency gems.

4. After the gems bundle has been installed, we can start the dashboard application by executing the `dashing start` command and then pointing our browser to `http://localhost:3030` to see the following result:

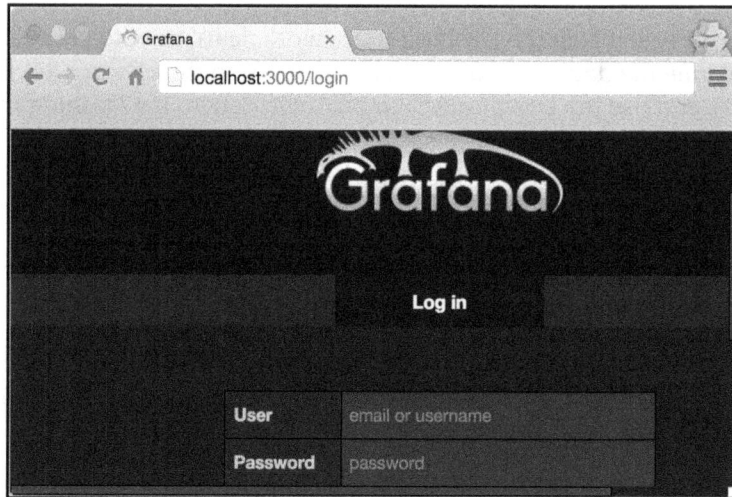

How to do it...

If you look carefully at the URL of our shiny new dashboard, you will see that it actually says `http://localhost:3030/sample` and displays a sample dashboard that was automatically generated. We will use this sample dashboard to make some changes in order to display some metrics from our application directly as well as get some raw metrics from the Graphite data API endpoint.

To demonstrate how to connect the data from the application `/actuator/metrics` endpoint so as to display it in the Dashing dashboard, we will change the `Buzzwords` widget to display the counts of our data repositories, as follows:

1. Before we start, we will need to add the `'httparty', '>= 0.13.3'` gem to the `Gemfile` file located in the `bookpub_dashboard` directory, which will enable us to use an HTTP client in order to extract the monitoring metrics from the HTTP endpoints.

2. After adding the gem, run the `bundle` command one more time to install the newly added gem.

3. Next, we will need to modify the `sample.erb` dashboard definition located in the `bookpub_dashboard/dashboards` directory, replacing `<div data-id="buzzwords" data-view="List" data-unordered="true" data-title="Buzzwords" data-moreinfo="# of times said around the office"></div>` with `<div data-id="repositories" data-view="List" data-unordered="true" data-title="Repositories Count" data-moreinfo="# of entries in data repositories"></div>`.

4. With the widget replaced, we will create a new data provisioning job file named `repo_counters.rb` in the `bookpub_dashboard/jobs` directory with the following content:

```
require 'httparty'

repos = ['AuthorRepository', 'ReviewerRepository',
'BookRepository', 'PublisherRepository']

SCHEDULER.every '10s' do
  data =
JSON.parse(HTTParty.get("http://localhost:8081/metrics").body)
  repo_counts = []

  repos.each do |repo|
    current_count = data["counter.datasource.#{repo}"]
    repo_counts << { label: repo, value: current_count }
  end

  send_event('repositories', { items: repo_counts })
end
```

5. With all the code changes in place, let's start our dashboard by executing the `dashing start` command. Go to `http://localhost:3030/sample` in the browser to see our new widget displaying the data as shown in the following icon:

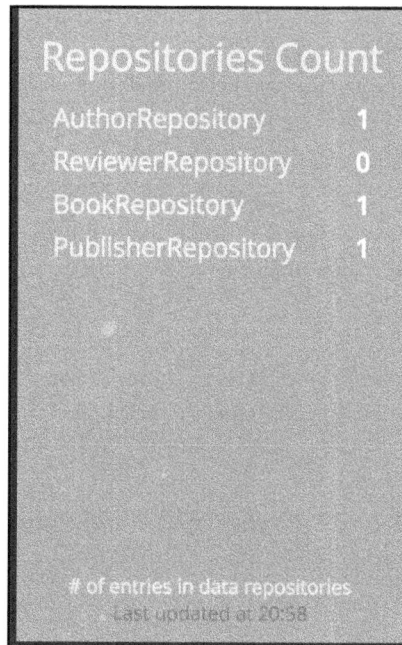

6. If we use the remote Shell to log in to the application, as we did earlier in this chapter, and add a publisher, we would see the counter on the dashboard increase.

7. Another way to push the data to the dashboard is to use their RESTful API. Let's update the text in the top left text widget by executing `curl -d '{ "auth_token": "YOUR_AUTH_TOKEN", "text": "My RESTful dashboard update!" }'` `http://localhost:3030/widgets/welcome`.

8. If everything has worked correctly, we should see the text updated to our new value, `My RESTful dashboard update!`, under the **Hello** title.

9. In an environment where multiple instances of the same application kind are running, it is probably not a good idea to directly pull the data from each node, especially if they are very dynamic and can come and go as they please. It is advised that you consume the data from a more static and well-known location, such as a Graphite instance. To get a demonstration of volatile data metrics, we will consume the memory pool data for the `Eden`, `Survivor`, and `OldGen` spaces and display them instead of the **Convergence**, **Synergy**, and **Valuation** graph dashboards. We will start by replacing the content of the `sample.rb` job file located in the `bookpub_dashboard/jobs` directory with the following content:

```
require 'httparty'
require 'date'

eden_key =
"bookpub.app.jvm.memory.used.area.heap.id.PS_Eden_Space"
survivor_key =
"bookpub.app.jvm.memory.used.area.heap.id.PS_Survivor_Space"
oldgen_key =
"bookpub.app.jvm.memory.used.area.heap.id.PS_Old_Gen"

SCHEDULER.every '60s' do
  data =
JSON.parse(HTTParty.get("http://localhost:8888/render/?from=-1
1minutes&target=#{eden_key}&target=#{survivor_key}&target=#{ol
dgen_key}&format=json&maxDataPoints=11").body)

  data.each do |metric|
    target = metric["target"]
    # Remove the last data point, which typically has empty
value
    data_points = metric["datapoints"][0...-1]
    if target == eden_key
      points = []
      data_points.each_with_index do |entry, idx|
        value = entry[0] rescue 0
        points << { x: entry[1], y: value.round(0)}
      end
      send_event('heap_eden', points: points)
    elsif target == survivor_key
      current_survivor = data_points.last[0] rescue 0
      current_survivor = current_survivor / 1048576
      send_event("heap_survivor", { value:
                 current_survivor.round(2)})
    elsif target == oldgen_key
      current_oldgen = data_points.last[0] rescue 0
```

```
                    last_oldgen = data_points[-2][0] rescue 0
                    send_event("heap_oldgen", {
                              current: current_oldgen.round(2),
                              last: last_oldgen.round(2)
                          })
            end
        end
    end
```

10. In the `sample.erb` template located in the
    `bookpub_dashboard/dashboards` directory, we will replace the **Synergy**,
    Valuation, and **Convergence** graphs with the following alternatives:

    - `<div data-id="synergy" data-view="Meter" data-title="Synergy" data-min="0" data-max="100"></div>` gets
      replaced with `<div data-id="heap_survivor" data-view="Meter" data-title="Heap: Survivor" data-min="0" data-max="100" data-moreinfo="In megabytes"></div>`

    - `<div data-id="valuation" data-view="Number" data-title="Current Valuation" data-moreinfo="In billions" data-prefix="$"></div>` gets replaced with `<div data-id="heap_oldgen" data-view="Number" data-title="Heap: OldGen" data-moreinfo="In bytes" ></div>`

    - `<div data-id="convergence" data-view="Graph" data-title="Convergence" style="background-color:#ff9618"></div>` gets replaced with `<div data-id="heap_eden" data-view="Graph" data-title="Heap: Eden" style="background-color:#ff9618" data-moreinfo="In bytes"></div>`

11. After all the changes are made, we can restart the dashboard application
    and reload our browser to `http://localhost:3030` to see the following
    result:

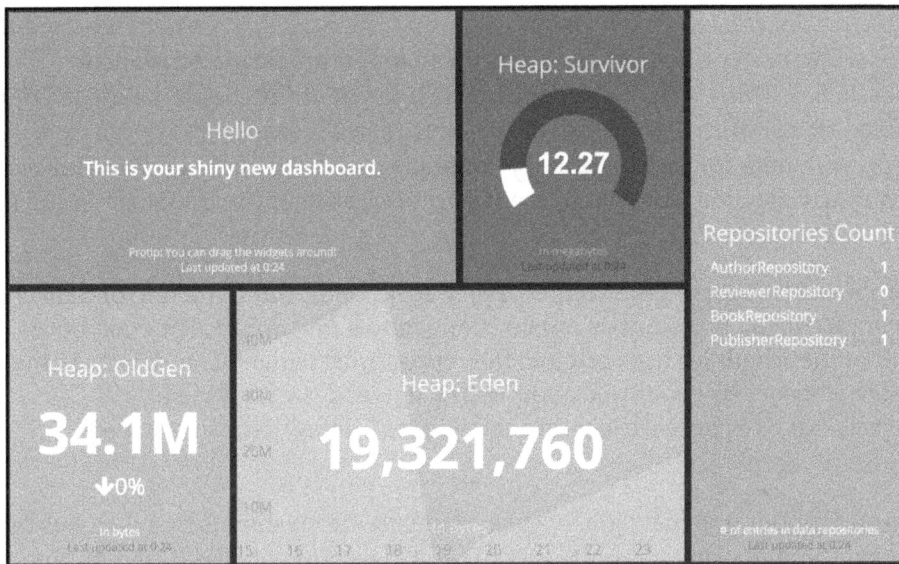

How it works...

In this recipe, we have seen how to extract the data directly from our application and via Graphite, and render it using the Dashing dashboard as well as pushing information directly to Dashing using their RESTful API. It is no secret that it is better to see something once than hear about it seven times. This is true when it comes to trying to get a holistic picture of the key metrics that represent how the systems behave at runtime and to be able to act on the data quickly.

Without going in to great detail about the internals of Dashing, it is still important to mention a few things about how data gets in to Dashing. This can happen in the following two ways:

- **Scheduled jobs**: This is used to pull data from the external sources
- **RESTful API**: This is used to push data to Dashing from outside

The scheduled jobs are defined in the jobs directory in the generated dashboard application. Each file has a piece of ruby code wrapped in the SCHEDULER.every block, which computes the data points and sends an event to an appropriate widget with the new data for an update.

In our recipe, we created a new job named `repo_counters.rb` where we used the `httparty` library in order to make a direct call to our application instance's `/actuator/metrics/#{name}` endpoint and extracted the counters for each of the predefined repositories. Looping over the metrics, we created a `repo_counts` collection with data for each repository containing a label display and a value count. The resulting collection was sent to the repositories widget for an update in the form of `event: send_event('repositories', { items: repo_counts })`.

We configured this job to get executed every 10 seconds, but if the rate of data change is not very frequent, the number can be changed to a few minutes or even hours. Every time the scheduler runs our job, the repositories widget is updated via the client-side websockets communication with the new data. Looking in dashboards/`sample.erb`, we can find the widget's definition using `data-id="repositories"`.

Besides adding our own new job, we also changed the existing `sample.rb` job to pull data from Graphite using Graphite's RESTful API to populate the different types of widgets in order to display the memory heap data. As we were not pulling data directly from the application instance, it was a good idea not to put the code in the same job because the jobs could—and in our case, do—have different time intervals. As we send data to Graphite only once every minute, it does not make sense to pull it any less frequently than this.

To get the data out of Graphite, we used the following API call:

```
/render/?from=-11minutes&target=
bookpub.app.jvm.memory.used.area.heap.id.PS_Eden_Space &target=
bookpub.app.jvm.memory.used.area.heap.id.PS_Survivor_Space &target=
bookpub.app.jvm.memory.used.area.heap.id.PS_Old_Gen
&format=json&maxDataPoints=11
```

Take a look at the following parameters mentioned in the preceding code snippet:

- `target`: This parameter is a repeated value that defines a list of all the different metrics that we want to retrieve.
- `from`: This parameter specifies the time range; in our case, we asked for data going back 11 minutes to.
- `format`: This parameter configures the desired output format. We chose JSON but many others are available. Refer to `http://graphite.readthedocs.org/en/latest/render_api.html#format`.
- `maxDataPoints`: This parameter indicates how many entries we want to get.

The reason we asked for 11 entries and not 10 is due to a frequent occurrence where the last entry of short-ranged requests, which consist of only a few minutes, sometimes get returned as empty. We just use the first 10 entries and ignore the most recent ones to avoid weird data visualization.

Iterating over the target data, we will populate the appropriate widgets such as `heap_eden`, `heap_survivor`, and `heap_oldgen`, with their designated data, as follows:

- `heap_eden`: This is a `Graph` widget, as defined in the `sample.erb` template in the form of a `data-view="Graph"` attribute, so it wants a data input in the form of the points collection containing a value for x and y. The x value represents a timestamp, which conveniently gets returned to us by Graphite and is automatically converted to the minutes display value by the Graph widget. The y value represents the memory pool utilization in bytes. As the value from Graphite is in the form of a decimal number, we will need to convert it to a whole number so as to make it look better.

- `heap_survivor`: This is a `Meter` widget, as defined in the `sample.erb` template in the form of a `data-view="Meter"` attribute, so it wants a data input as a simple value number between a template configured range. In our case, the range is set as the `data-min="0"` `data-max="100"` attribute. Even though we chose to round the number to two decimal positions, it could probably just be an integer as it is precise enough for the purpose of a dashboard display. You will also notice that inside `sample.rb`, we convert the raw value, which is in bytes, into megabytes, for better readability— `current_survivor = current_survivor / 1048576`.

- `heap_oldgen`: This is a `Number` widget, as defined in the `sample.erb` template in the form of a `data-view="Number"` attribute, so it wants a data input as a current value and optionally a last value; in this case, a percentage change with the change direction will be displayed as well. As we get the last 10 entries, we have no issues in retrieving both the current and last values so we can easily satisfy this requirement.

In this recipe, we also experimented with Dashing's RESTful API by trying to use a `curl` command to update the value of the welcome widget. This was a push operation and can be used in situations where there is no data API exposed, but you have the capability of creating some sort of a script or piece of code that could send the data to Dashing instead. To achieve this, we used the following command: `curl -d '{ "auth_token": "YOUR_AUTH_TOKEN", "text": "My RESTful dashboard update!" }' http://localhost:3030/widgets/welcome`.

The Dashing API accepts data in a JSON format, sent via a POST request that contains the following parameters needed for the widgets as well as the widget ID, which is a part of the URL path itself:

- `auth_token`: This allows for a secure data update and can be configured in the dashboard root directory in the `config.ru` file.
- `text`: This is a `widget` property that is being changed. As we are updating a Text widget, as defined in the `sample.erb` template in the form of a `data-view="Text"` attribute, we need to send it to text to update.
- `/widgets/<widget id>`: This URL path identifies the particular widget where the update is destined to. The `id` corresponds to a declaration in the `sample.erb` template. In our case, it looks like `data-id="welcome"`.

The definition of the various widgets can also be manipulated and a very rich collection of the various widgets has been created by the community, which is available at `https://github.com/Shopify/dashing/wiki/Additional-Widgets`. The widgets get installed in the widgets directory in the dashboard and can be installed by simply running `dashing install <GIST>`, where GIST is the hash of the GitHub Gist entry.

The dashboard template files, similar to our `sample.erb` template, can be modified in order to create the desired layout for each particular dashboard as well as multiple dashboard templates, which can be rotated or directly loaded manually.

Each dashboard represents a grid in which the various widgets get placed. Each widget is defined by a `<div>` entry with the appropriate configuration attributes and it should be nested in the `<li>` grid element. We can use the data element attributes to control the positioning of each widget in the grid, which is as follows:

- `data-row`: This represents the row number where the widget should be positioned
- `data-col`: This represents the column number where the widget should be positioned
- `data-sizex`: This defines the number of columns the widget will span horizontally
- `data-sizey`: This defines the number of rows the widget will span vertically

The existing widgets can be modified to change their look and feel as well as extend their functionality; so the sky is the limit for what kind of information display we can have. You should definitely check out `http://dashing.io` for more details.

Spring Boot DevTools

27

In this chapter, we will learn about the following topics:

- Adding Spring Boot DevTools to a project
- Configuring LiveReload
- Configuring dynamic application restart triggers
- Using Remote Update

Introduction

In a world of DevOps, agile software development practices, the introduction of microservices, and with more and more teams doing continuous development and deployment, it becomes even more important to be able to quickly see the code changes to an application without going through the whole process of re-compiling the entire project, rebuilding, and restarting the application.

The arrival of containerization services such as Docker has also presented a challenge in terms of access to the actual application running environment. It has changed the notion of a machine by abstracting and encapsulating the runtime environment, removing the ability to use any port to get access.

Spring Boot DevTools provides the ability to do selective class reloading and debugging applications running inside Docker containers using HTTP remote debug tunnel, in order to give developers a quick feedback loop to see their changes reflected in the running application without long rebuild and restart cycles.

Adding Spring Boot DevTools to a project

Starting with Spring Boot 1.3, we have the ability to take advantage of DevTools components in our projects to enable things like automatic application restarts upon code change, reloading the browser windows for the UI, or remotely reloading applications.

The DevTools module is available for both Maven and Gradle, and works nicely with either Eclipse or IntelliJ IDEA editors.

> In this chapter, we will cover integration with Gradle and IntelliJ IDEA, but for detailed information about using Spring Boot DevTools, take a look at the documentation at `http://docs.spring.io/spring-boot/docs/current/reference/html/using-boot-devtools.html`.

How to do it...

Continuing with our `BookPub` project, we will be adding a DevTools module to the main build configuration by performing the following steps:

1. Add the following content to the `build.gradle` file located at the root of the project:

   ```
   dependencies {
       ...
       compile("io.dropwizard.metrics:metrics-graphite:3.1.0")
       compile("org.springframework.boot:spring-boot-devtools")
       runtime("com.h2database:h2")
       ...
   }
   ```

2. Start the application by running `./gradlew clean bootRun`.

3. After application startup, you might notice in the console log an output warning about the inability to register with Spring Boot admin (unless you have one running) that looks like this: **Failed to register application as Application....** Let's make a live change to the `application.properties` file located in the `build/resources/main` directory from the root of our project and add a property entry with the following content:

   ```
   spring.boot.admin.auto-registration=false
   ```

---

[906]

4. Without doing anything else, upon saving the file, we should see the console log showing us that the application context is being restarted.

How it works...

As you have probably learned by now, when we add a `spring-boot-devtools` module as a dependency there is some autoconfiguration magic that takes place to add a number of components. A number of listeners and autoconfigurations extend the application context to handle the code changes and do appropriate restarts and reloads, both local and remote.

In our recipe, we did a quick test to make sure the restart functionality worked and everything had been configured by making a property change in the `application.properties` file. You have probably noticed that instead of making the change in `src/main/resources/application.properties`, we made the change to the compiled version located under the `build/resources/main` directory. The reason for this was because of the property placeholder replacements for the `info.` block that we used during the Gradle build phase. If we were to only make a change in the original file and use the IntelliJ compile option, it would not perform the required replacements and thus result in a restart failure.

When the DevTools are enabled, the application after being started, begins to monitor the classpath for changes to the classes that are on that classpath. When any class or a resource changes, it will serve as a trigger for DevTools to reload the application by refreshing the classloader containing the project's codebase (which is not the same classloader that holds the classes from the static dependency artifacts).

> See the detailed explanation of the inner workings at the following link:
> `http://docs.spring.io/spring-boot/docs/current/reference/`
> `html/using-boot-devtools.html#using-boot-devtools-restart`

After the reloadable classloader has completed the refresh, the application context gets restarted automatically, thus effectively causing the application restart.

Configuring LiveReload

Those who work on frontend web applications will probably agree that being able to automatically reload the page once the backend code or resource change has taken place will save a few clicks and prevent situations where a forgotten reload leads to wasteful debugging efforts and chasing an error that does not exist. Thankfully, DevTools comes to the rescue by providing a LiveReload server implementation, which can be used together with a LiveReload browser extention to automatically reload the page when the backend change occurs.

How to do it...

If the DevTools module is added to the build dependencies, the LiveReload server has been automatically started. We do, however, need to install and enable the browser extensions by performing the following steps:

1. Unless the browser already has the LiveReload extension installed, go to `http://livereload.com/extensions/` and install the appropriate extension for your browser of choice (Firefox, Safari, and Chrome are supported).

   > For Internet Explorer users, there is a third-party extension available that can be found at `https://github.com/dvdotsenko/livereload_ie_extension/downloads`.

2. After the extension is installed, it typically needs to be enabled on the page by clicking a button in the toolbar. This is what it would look like in the Chrome browser:

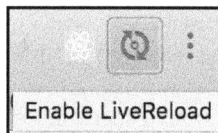

3. After enabling the extension, we can go ahead and make another change as we did in the previous recipe (or any other code or resource change), or simply execute the `touch build/resources/main/application.properties` command. We should see the application reload taking place on the backend as well as the browser page reloading after.

How it works...

With the addition of the LiveReload browser extension, and a running LiveReload server embedded into our `BookPub` application, the browser is now capable of connecting to the backend server using a web socket to monitor changes. When the Spring Boot DevTools detects a change that should trigger a reload, it will trigger the reload as well as send a notification to the browser to reload the page as well.

> **TIP**
>
> If there is ever a need to disable the LiveReload part of the DevTools functionality, it can easily be achieved by adding the `spring.devtools.livereload.enabled=false` property via any of the supported configuration options, be that a property file, environment variable, or a system property.

Configuring dynamic application restart triggers

In the previous recipes, we have looked into the basic capabilities of DevTools when it comes to restarting the application upon code or resource change and communicating to the browser to reload the page. This section will address the various configuration options that we can leverage to indicate to Spring Boot DevTools exactly what we want those events to be triggered by, and when.

How to do it...

By default, adding a DevTools module to a project will make it monitor all the classes or resources, which could become undesired behavior, especially when it comes to multi-module repositories. This becomes true when building and launching projects from within an IDE like IntelliJ or Eclipse. We need to tell DevTools to exclude the `db-count-starter` sub-module in our project from the watch list by adjusting the configuration settings:

1. Let's create a file named `spring-devtools.properties` under the `db-count-starter/src/main/resources/META-INF` directory from the root of our project with the following content:

   ```
   restart.exclude.db-count-starter=/db-count-
   starter/build/(classes|resources)/main
   ```

2. Next we need to launch our application from within an IDE by opening the `BookPubApplication` class located under the `src/main/java/com/example/bookpub` directory from the root of our project and starting the `main(String[] args)` method either in **run** or **debug** mode

3. With the `db-count-starter` module excluded, we can safely make a change to a file, for example a `spring.factories` resource located under the `db-count-starter/build/resources/main/META-INF` directory from the root of our project, only to see the application not being restarted

4. If we want to completely disable the restart capability, we can do so by adding the following property to `application.properties` located under the `src/main/resources` directory from the root of our project:

   ```
   spring.devtools.restart.enabled=false
   ```

5. After relaunching our application, even the changes to the `build/resources/main/application.properties` file, which is what's being loaded from the classpath, will not trigger the application restart

How it works...

In this recipe, we have looked at a number of different reload trigger configurations, so let's look at each of them individually to understand where best to use them:

- `spring.devtools.restart.enabled`: This property offers the simplest of controls, fully enabling or disabling the restart functionality of DevTools. With the value of `false`, no restart of the application will take place, regardless of the class or resource changes on the classpath.

- `spring.devtools.restart.exclude`: This property provides an ability to stop specific classpaths from being reloaded. This property accepts values in a comma-separated form using the Ant Path matching pattern style. The default exclude value is `"META-INF/maven/**,META-INF/resources/**,resources/**,static/**,public/**,templates/**,**/*Test.class,**/*Tests.class,git.properties,META-INF/build-info.properties"`.

- `spring.devtools.restart.additional-exclude`: This property provides the convenience of being able to add to the default excludes list without having to copy/paste the default values, but rather simply adding to them while retaining the original defaults. It takes the same comma-separated Ant Path matching pattern style of input.
- `spring.devtools.restart.additional-paths`: This property provides the ability to watch for resources that are outside of the classpath. For example, this could be a `config` directory that gets loaded at application startup, and you want to restart the application if the config entry changes. It takes a comma-separated list of absolute file paths.
- `spring.devtools.restart.poll-interval`: This property specifies how long to pause, in milliseconds, between checking for classpath changes. The default value is `1000` milliseconds, but if there is a need to save some CPU cycles, this will do the trick.
- `spring.devtools.restart.quiet-period`: This property controls how much time should pass, in milliseconds, without any changes to the classpath before the restart will take place. This is needed to ensure the restarts don't get overwhelming if there are continuous changes taking place. The default value is `400` milliseconds, but it can be changed if needed.
- `spring.devtools.restart.trigger-file`: This property provides explicit control over when a restart happens by watching a `trigger` file for change. This is useful for situations where the classpath gets continuously changed, and you don't want to get caught in a restart loop.

All the preceding property settings listed are usually shared between all the application projects that developers work on, so DevTools provides the ability to have global properties defined in this, making it convenient to share the development configurations across many projects without having to copy/paste the same values in all the different codebases.

Internally, this capability is implemented as `PropertySource`, which gets added to the top of the configuration precedence hierarchy. This means that not only the `spring.devtools` configuration family, but any property added to the global file will be applied to all applications using DevTools.

Another way to control reload triggers is with the use of `META-INF/spring-devtools.properties` with the `restart.exclude.<name>` and `restart.include.<name>` configurations inside them. By default, the restart of the application only gets triggered by changes to the actual classes or resources that are directly on the classpath and not bundled into JARs. This allows you to keep the majority of the classes in the non-reloadable base classloader, greatly limiting the number of entries that need to be monitored for changes.

In situations where developers work with multiple projects that are dependent on each other, or work in a multi-module repository, like the `BookPub` one, it might be desirable to add some JARs into a reloadable classloader and watch them for change. This would typically be applied to dependencies that point to the `build/libs` or `target` directories, where the JARs inside them are a direct result of a build task execution and typically get rebuilt frequently.

Another use case, which we explored in this recipe, is the inclusion or exclusion of `build/classes` or `target/classes` from the watch list. If a multi-module project is loaded in an IDE, it is common for the classpath to contain direct reference to the build directories of the sub-modules instead of the compiled JAR artifact, and depending on the use case, we might or might not choose to include or exclude those from triggering the reload.

The `<name>` part of the keys is not important as long as it is unique, because all the `META-INF/spring-devtools.properties` files will be loaded as composites, regardless whether if they live inside the JARs or right in the project. The suggested approach is to use a sub-module/artifact name, as it will typically ensure uniqueness. If more than one pattern applies, the name can be appended with a sequence number, for example `restart.exclude.db-count-starter-1` and `restart.exclude.db-count-starter-2`. The value of each key should contain a valid regex pattern that can be evaluated against every entry in the classpath to determine whether that particular classpath URL should go into the reloadable or base classloader.

Using Remote Update

With the growing popularity of Docker, more and more applications are being built and deployed as Docker containers. One of the great features of Docker is the isolation of the runtime environment from the host OS, but that same isolation makes it difficult to make continuous changes and test your application in a true environment. Each time there is a change to a property file or a Java class, one needs to rebuild everything, create a new Docker image, restart the container, and so on. That's a lot of work to be doing for every change.

Even though, unfortunately, as of version 2.0, Spring Boot has removed the capability of doing a remote debug, there is still the very helpful ability to remotely reload the code changes from within your IDE as you work on the code, without the need to at least rebuild the application JAR and Docker image.

The **Remote Restart** capability provides a solution for better continuous development and makes it possible to do dynamic application restarts remotely, as if it were on a local machine.

How to do it...

As you have probably guessed, Remote Restart involves an agent running locally and sending instructions to the remote client. DevTools provides an implementation of such an agent—`RemoteSpringApplication`:

1. In order to enable Remote Restart, we need to add a property to `application.properties` located under the `src/main/resources` directory from the root of our project with the following content:

   ```
   spring.devtools.remote.secret=our-secret
   ```

2. The next step would be to create a Java application launch configuration for the `RemoteSpringApplication` class in the IDE.

   It is important to make sure the program arguments field has the base URL of the application you are trying to debug together with the port. Ensure that the working directory points to the main project, and the classpath of the module is pointing to the main project module as well.

The figure on the next page shows what such a configuration would look like in IntelliJ IDEA. The Eclipse IDE would have a similar form as well.

3. After filling out all the fields, we need to start RemoteSpringApplication from within our IDE by clicking **Run**. If all has been configured correctly, we should see a similar output in the log:

```
              .   ___          -
  _ _ _
     / / __'_ _ _ _(_)_ _ _ _                  _
    ( ( )__ | '_ | '_| | '_/_` |        | _ __ _ _ __| |_ __
    /  __)| |_)| | | | | | || (_| []::::::[]  / -_) ' / _ _/ -_) )
  ) ) )
       '  |___| ._|_| |_|_| |___, |        |_|___|_|_|___/___|/ /
  / /
  =========|_|==============|___/===============================/_/_
  /_/
       :: Spring Boot Remote ::   (v2.0.0.BUILD-SNAPSHOT)
       2017-12-26 21:33:28.520   INFO
```

```
o.s.b.devtools.RemoteSpringApplication    : Starting
RemoteSpringApplication v2.0.0.BUILD-SNAPSHOT ...
    2017-12-26 21:33:28.524   INFO
o.s.b.devtools.RemoteSpringApplication    : No active profile set,
falling back to default profiles: default
    2017-12-26 21:33:28.781   INFO
s.c.a.AnnotationConfigApplicationContext : Refreshing
org.springframework.context.annotation.AnnotationConfigApplicationCont
ext@6babf3bf: startup date [Tue Dec 26 21:33:28 CST 2017]; root of
context hierarchy
    2017-12-26 21:33:29.295   WARN
o.s.b.d.r.c.RemoteClientConfiguration     : The connection to
http://127.0.0.1:8080 is insecure. You should use a URL starting with
'https://'.
    2017-12-26 21:33:29.368 DEBUG
o.s.b.devtools.restart.ChangeableUrls     : Matching URLs for reloading
: [file:/.../ch8/build/classes/main/,
file:/.../ch8/build/resources/main/]
    2017-12-26 21:33:29.401   INFO o.s.b.d.a.OptionalLiveReloadServer
: LiveReload server is running on port 35729
    2017-12-26 21:33:29.443   INFO
o.s.b.devtools.RemoteSpringApplication    : Started
RemoteSpringApplication in 1.497 seconds (JVM running for 2.248)
```

4. To simulate remoteness, we will launch the application in a separate command shell, executing the `./gradlew clean bootJar` command followed by executing `./build/libs/bookpub-0.0.1-SNAPSHOT-exec.jar`.

5. Once the application has started, take a look at one of the last lines in the log that should look something like the following:

```
INFO 50926 --- [              main]
ication$$EnhancerBySpringCGLIB$$11c0ff63 : Value of
my.config.value property is:
```

6. The property value of `my.config.value` is not being set, because we don't have one defined in our `application.properties` file, and we didn't use any environment variables or startup system property settings to set it.

7. Let's pretend we need to do a live change and modify our `application.properties` file located under the `build/resources/main` directory from the root of our project with the following content:

```
my.config.value=Remote Change
```

8. Now we should see in the console that our application has automatically restarted and, after all is done, we should see something similar to the following:

```
INFO 50926 --- [  restartedMain]
ication$$EnhancerBySpringCGLIB$$11c0ff63 : Value of
my.config.value property is: Remote Change
```

How it works...

It might look like voodoo magic, but the science behind the Remote Restart functionality is pretty straightforward. Under the hood, when a DevTools module is included, the HTTP endpoint handler for /.~~spring-boot!~/restart automatically gets added. This allows the RemoteSpringApplication process to send the code change payload via an HTTP tunnel to the remote application and back.

To make sure that no malicious outside debug connection gets to connect to our remote application, the value of the spring.devtools.remote.secret property gets sent across and verified to establish the authenticity of the request.

In *step 2* of the recipe, we launched the RemoteSpringApplication process with a program arguments value of http://127.0.0.1:8080, which is how RemoteSpringApplication knows how to communicate with our remote application. The RemoteSpringApplication class itself scans for the local file changes from an IDE by monitoring the classpath.

In *step 6* of the recipe, when we added the property to our config in the code, it is very important to note that we made the change to the application.properties file located in the running classpath of the RemoteSpringApplication class not under src/main/resources, but under the build/resources/main directory, where Gradle has placed all the compiled files—hopefully that's the same directory your IDE is using as a classpath to run RemoteSpringApplication. If that's not the path your IDE is using, you should make the change in the appropriate folder, where the IDE has compiled the classes—for IntelliJ IDEA that would be the out/production/resources directory by default.

If DevTools needs to be enabled inside an application running as a Docker container, we need to explicitly configure the `build` script to do so by adding the following to the `build.gradle` file in the main project:

```
bootJar {
    ...
    excludeDevtools = false
}
```

The reason we need to do this is because, by default, when a Spring Boot application gets re-packaged for production deployment, which is the case when building a Docker container image, the DevTools module is excluded from the classpath during build time. To prevent this from happening, we need to tell the build system to not exclude the module in order to take advantage of its capabilities, namely the Remote Restart.

28
Spring Cloud

In this chapter, we will learn about the following topics:

- Getting started with Spring Cloud
- Service discovery using Spring Cloud Consul
- Using Spring Cloud Netflix—Feign
- Service discovery using Spring Cloud Netflix—Eureka
- Using Spring Cloud Netflix—Hystrix

Introduction

Throughout this book, we have learned how to create an application, configure RESTful services, do testing, integrate metrics and other management components, and handle packaging and deployment, among other things. Now, the time has come to look at the world outside the application—the ubiquitous cloud environment.

In this chapter, we will look at how to make applications cloud-friendly, how to deal with the dynamic nature of the distributed applications running in the cloud, how to make our applications visible to the world, how to discover other service endpoints, how to call them, and how to handle various error conditions.

Getting started with Spring Cloud

The Spring Cloud family of projects provides integration extensions for Spring Boot of various frameworks, which offer functionality for distributed service discovery, configuration, routing, service invocation, and more. Through the use of uniform API, we can add these concepts to our applications and later have the flexibility to change the specific implementation if such a need arises without making deep-cutting changes to our codebase.

How to do it...

We will start by enhancing our `BookPub` project with base Spring Cloud modules by adding them to the main build configuration:

1. Add the following content to the `build.gradle` file located at the root of the project:

```
...
apply plugin: 'docker'

dependencyManagement {
    imports {
        mavenBom 'org.springframework.cloud:spring-cloud-
dependencies:Finchley.BUILD-SNAPSHOT'
    }
}

jar {
    baseName = 'bookpub'
    version = '0.0.1-SNAPSHOT'
}

...

dependencies {
    ...
    compile("org.springframework.boot:spring-boot-devtools")
    compile("org.springframework.cloud:spring-cloud-context")
    compile("org.springframework.cloud:spring-cloud-commons")
    runtime("com.h2database:h2")
    ...
}
```

2. Start the application by running `./gradlew clean bootRun`

3. After the application has been started, even though it seems like nothing new has happened, if we open our browser at `http://localhost:8081/actuator/env` (the management endpoint for environment), we will see new property sources appear:

```
{
  "name": "springCloudClientHostInfo",
  "properties": {
    "spring.cloud.client.hostname": {
      "value": "127.0.0.1"
    },
    "spring.cloud.client.ip-address": {
      "value": "127.0.0.1"
    }
  }
}
```

4. Create a `bootstrap.properties` file under the `src/main/resources` directory from the root of our project with the following content (the same properties should be commented out inside `application.properties` at this point):

```
spring.application.name=BookPub-ch9
```

5. Start the application by running `./gradlew clean bootRun`

6. After the application has been started, open our browser at `http://localhost:8081/env` and we will see new property sources appear:

```
{
  "name": "applicationConfig:
[classpath:/bootstrap.properties]",
  "properties": {
    "spring.application.name": {
      "value": "BookPub-ch9",
      "origin": "class path resource
[bootstrap.properties]:1:25"
    }
  }
}
```

How it works...

Before we dive under the hood of how things work, let's review the changes that we have made to our project. The first step was to enhance the `build.gradle` build configuration by importing a **Bill of Material** (**BOM**) declaration for a Spring Cloud release train—`mavenBom 'org.springframework.cloud:spring-cloud-dependencies:Finchley.BUILD-SNAPSHOT'`. While we could have selectively imported explicitly-defined versions of the `spring-cloud-context` and `spring-cloud-commons` libraries, by relying on a packaged BOM, we are sure that we will be using the correct versions of different artifacts that have been tested for compatibility with each other.

> Specific versions of each Spring Cloud modules that are included in a particular Release Train can be seen at `http://cloud.spring.io/`.

We start by adding dependencies on the `spring-cloud-context` and `spring-cloud-commons` libraries, to illustrate the basic common facilities Spring Cloud provides, before diving into a specific starter integration such as `spring-cloud-netflix` or `spring-cloud-consul`. Those basic libraries provide a foundation of interfaces and common functionality that is being used to build upon in all the different cloud-specific integrations. Here is what their purpose is:

- `spring-cloud-commons`: This provides a collection of shared common interfaces and base classes that define the notions of service discovery, service routing, load balancing, circuit breaking, feature capabilities, and some basic configuration. For example, this is the library that autoconfigures the environment with the `springCloudClientHostInfo` property source.
- `spring-cloud-context`: This is the base foundation that is responsible for bootstrapping and configuring the various integrations, such as a specific implementation of service discovery like Consul, or a specific implementation of circuit breaker like **Hystrix**. This is achieved by creating an isolated Bootstrap application context, which is responsible for loading and configuring all the components before the main application is started.

Bootstrap application context gets created early on in the application start cycle and it is configured by a separate file—`bootstrap.properties` (a YAML variant is also supported). Since it is very typical for an application running in the cloud to rely on many external sources of configuration, service lookup, and so on, the purpose of the

Bootstrap context is to configure those functions and obtain all of the necessary configuration from outside.

To clearly separate application configuration from Bootstrap, we put things that describe the application, or configure external configs, or other environmental variants like where to call for service discovery, into `bootstrap.properties` instead of `application.properties`. In our example, we have placed `spring.application.name` config into `bootstrap.properties`, because that information will be needed during the Bootstrap phase; it could be used to look up configuration from a remote config store.

Since Bootstrap application context is indeed a real Spring application context, there exists a parent-child relationship between the two, where Bootstrap application context becomes the parent of the Spring Boot application context. This means that all the beans and the property sources defined in the Bootstrap context become available for consumption from within the application context as well.

When Spring Cloud is added to the application, it automatically provides the integration framework for specific Spring Cloud modules, like Spring Cloud Consul, to be plugged in via the use of the by now well-known `spring.factories` configuration declarations. The annotations provided inside `spring-cloud-commons`, namely `@SpringCloudApplication`, `@EnableDiscoveryClient`, `@EnableCircuitBreaker`, and the `@BootstrapConfiguraion` and `PropertySourceLocator` interfaces provided by the `spring-cloud-context` library, are designed to define the integration points to be used to self-configure specific components such as discovery clients like Consul, circuit breakers like Hystrix, or remote configuration sources like **ZooKeeper**.

Let's examine those in detail:

- `@SpringCloudApplication`: This annotation is like `@SpringBootApplication`, meta-annotation in nature, except it also wraps the `@EnableDiscoveryClient` and `@EnableCircuitBreaker` annotations in addition to also being meta-annotated with `@SpringBootApplication`. It is a good idea to use this annotation when you want to enable both the discovery client and the circuit breaker functionality in your application.
- `@EnableDiscoveryClient`: This annotation is used to indicate that Spring Cloud should initialize the provided discovery client for service registry, depending on the included integration library, such as Consul, Eureka, ZooKeeper, and so on.

- `@EnableCircuitBreaker`: This annotation is used to indicate that Spring Cloud should initialize the circuit breaker capabilities, based on the specific dependency of the integration library, such as Hystrix.

- `PropertySourceLocator`: This is used by the integration libraries to implement specific functionality of how to extract remote configuration from the provided datastore. Each integration module, providing ability to load remote configuration, would register an implementing bean of this type that exposes an implementation of `PropertySource` that is backed by the integration.

- `@BootstrapConfiguration`: This annotation is like the `@ManagementContextConfiguration` annotation, and is (mostly) a marker annotation geared to identify the key inside the `spring.factories` descriptor to indicate which configuration classes should be loaded during the Spring Cloud Bootstrap process and be part of the Bootstrap application context. Those configurations are read by `BootstrapApplicationListener` during startup and initialize the specified configurations. Typically, this is where the configuration classes, which define and expose `PropertySourceLocator`—implementing beans, are configured.

Service discovery using Spring Cloud Consul

In a world of distributed computing, it is very common for services to become a disposable commodity. The typical life cycle of a service could be measured in days, if not in hours, and it is not unheard of for an instance to just crash for whatever reason, only to have a new one come up automatically seconds later. When the state of applications is so ephemeral, it becomes really hard to maintain a statically-connected architecture, with services knowing where exactly their dependent services are located, as the topology is always changing.

To help with this problem, the service discovery layer comes into play, maintaining a centralized and distributed state of service registrations, ready to reply on demand with the most current information. Applications register themselves upon startup, providing information about their location and possibly about their capabilities, level of service, health check status, and even more.

Earlier in the book, in `Chapter 25`, *Application Packaging and Deployment*, we were introduced to Consul, and used it for external application configuration consumption. In this recipe, we will continue to look further into the capabilities of Consul and will learn about how to use the `spring-cloud-consul` modules to automatically register our application with Consul.

How to do it...

Take a look at the following steps to set up service discovery:

1. Replace the `spring-cloud-commons` and `spring-cloud-context` modules with `spring-cloud-starter-consul-all` by modifying the `build.gradle` file located in the root of our project with the following content:

   ```
   ...

   dependencies {
       ...
       compile("io.dropwizard.metrics:metrics-graphite:3.1.0")
       compile("org.springframework.boot:spring-boot-devtools")
       //compile("org.springframework.cloud:spring-cloud-
   context")
       //compile("org.springframework.cloud:spring-cloud-
   commons")
       compile("org.springframework.cloud:spring-cloud-starter-
   consul-all")
       runtime("com.h2database:h2")
       ...
   }
   ...
   ```

2. With Consul dependencies added, we will proceed with enabling our application to automatically register with the local agent upon startup by modifying the `BookPubApplication.java` file located under the `src/main/java/com/example/bookpub` directory from the root of our project with the following content:

   ```
   ...
   @EnableScheduling
   @EnableDbCounting
   @EnableDiscoveryClient
   ```

```
public class BookPubApplication {
    ...
}
```

3. Given that Consul was successfully installed using the steps described in the *Setting up Consul* recipe in `Chapter 25`, *Application Packaging and Deployment*, we should be able to start it by running `consul agent -server -bootstrap-expect 1 -data-dir /tmp/consul` and our Terminal window should display the following output:

```
==> Starting Consul agent...
==> Starting Consul agent RPC...
==> Consul agent running!
            Version: 'v1.0.2'
    ...
```

4. After the Consul agent is up and running successfully, we will proceed by starting our application by running `./gradlew clean bootRun`

5. As we watch the startup logs scroll by, there are a couple of interesting entries that indicate the application is interacting with the agent, so watch for the following content in the logs:

```
    ...
2017-12-26 --- b.c.PropertySourceBootstrapConfiguration :
Located property source: CompositePropertySource
[name='consul', propertySources=[ConsulPropertySource
[name='config/BookPub-ch9/'], ConsulPropertySource
[name='config/application/']]]
    ...
2017-12-26 --- o.s.c.consul.discovery.ConsulLifecycle    :
Registering service with consul: NewService{id='BookPub-
ch9-8080', name='BookPub-ch9', tags=[],
address='<your_machine_name>', port=8080,
check=Check{script='null', interval=10s, ttl=null,
http=http://<your_machine_name>:8081/health, tcp=null,
timeout=null}}
2017-12-26 --- o.s.c.consul.discovery.ConsulLifecycle    :
Registering service with consul: NewService{id='BookPub-
ch9-8080-management', name='BookPub-ch9-management',
tags=[management], address='://<your_machine_name>',
port=8081, check=Check{script='null', interval=10s, ttl=null,
http=http://chic02qv045g8wn:8081/health, tcp=null,
timeout=null}}
    ...
```

6. Just to verify that our application has registered and is in communication with the local Consul agent, let's open `http://localhost:8081/actuator/consul` in the browser to see the Consul agent information, as shown in the following screenshot:

How it works...

When we added `spring-cloud-starter-consul-all` as a build dependency, it automatically pulled all the necessary components to enable Consul functionality for our application. We automatically got the `spring-cloud-consul-binder`, `spring-cloud-consul-core`, `spring-cloud-consul-config`, and `spring-cloud-consul-discovery` artifacts added to our classpath. Let's take a look at the them:

- `spring-cloud-consul-core`: This artifact provides base autoconfiguration to expose generic `ConsulProperties`, as well as the `ConsulClient` initialization and setting of the `/consul` management endpoint, if the Spring Boot Actuator functionality is enabled.

- `spring-cloud-consul-config`: This provides the `ConsulPropertySourceLocator` implementation, used during Bootstrap, to configure the `ConsulPropertySource` bean, which allows remote configuration consumption from the Consul key/value store. It also sets up a `ConfigWatch` change observer, which fires `RefreshEvent` to the application context, if a configuration key value changes in Consul key/value store while the application is running. This allows for a possible configuration properties reload without having to redeploy and restart the application.
- `spring-cloud-consul-discovery`: This provides all the functionality and implementations needed for service discovery, service registration, and service invocation.
- `spring-cloud-consul-binder`: This provides integration of Consul event functionality with Spring Cloud Stream Framework, enabling it to send and receive events from Consul and respond to them within the application. While outside of the scope of this chapter, more information can be obtained from `http://cloud.spring.io/spring-cloud-stream/`.

While addition of `spring-cloud-consul-config` to the classpath will automatically register `ConsulPropertySource`, it is not so for the `spring-cloud-consul-discovery` module. The service discovery functionality is more intrusive and thus requires an additional step of acknowledgement from the developers to indicate that it is indeed wanted. This is accomplished by adding the `@EnableDiscoveryClient` annotation to the main application class; in our case it is `BookPubApplication`.

Once the `@EnableDiscoveryClient` annotation is added, Spring Cloud (`EnableDiscoveryClientImportSelector` class from the `spring-cloud-commons` module, to be more precise) scans all `spring.factories` files for the presence of the `org.springframework.cloud.client.discovery.EnableDiscoveryClient` key, and loads all the associated configurations into the main application context. If we look inside the `spring.factories` file located in the `spring-cloud-consul-discovery` JAR under the `META-INF/` directory, we will see the following entry:

```
# Discovery Client Configuration
org.springframework.cloud.client.discovery.EnableDiscoveryClient=
org.springframework.cloud.consul.discovery.ConsulDiscoveryClientConfig
uration
```

This tells us that when the discovery client is enabled, `ConsulDiscoveryClientConfiguration` will be consumed and all of its defining beans will be added to the application context.

A similar approach can be used if a custom service discovery mechanism is being used. One will need to create a custom configuration class, exposing a custom implementation of the `DiscoveryClient` interface, and configure it in the `spring.factories` file bundled within the archive. Once that JAR gets loaded, the configuration will be automatically consumed if discovery client functionality is enabled.

> Spring Cloud Consul libraries provide very fine-grained ability to configure and pick and choose the selected functions, if not all apply for a particular use-case. For detailed information about various configuration and usage options see `http://cloud.spring.io/spring-cloud-consul/`.

Using Spring Cloud Netflix – Feign

In the previous recipe, we looked at how to enable service discovery capability for our application in order to be able to register our service with the world as well as to know what other services exist and where they are located. This recipe will help us better interact with that information and consume those services without having to explicitly code any logic to handle service discovery and all of the related concerns that come with it.

To achieve this goal, we will look at another Spring Cloud integration, provided by the Spring Cloud Netflix module family—Netflix Feign. Feign, which makes writing Java HTTP clients easier. Its purpose is to simplify the process of binding service API calls to their corresponding HTTP API counterparts. It provides automatic service mapping and discovery, ability to translate Java types to HTTP request URL paths, parameters and response payloads, as well as error handling.

For the sake of simplicity, in this recipe, we will be creating a `Client` controller, which will act as an external client of our `BookPub` application service, calling our APIs via Feign-annotated Java service interfaces, relying on Consul to provide service discovery functionality.

How to do it...

1. We will start by adding Netflix Feign module dependencies to our project. Let's modify our `build.gradle` file located in the root of our project with the following content:

```
dependencies {
    ...
    compile("org.springframework.cloud:spring-
    cloud-starter-consul-all")
    compile("org.springframework.cloud:spring-
    cloud-starter-openfeign")
    runtime("com.h2database:h2")
    ...
}
```

2. With the dependency added, our next step is to create a Java API interface describing how we want to define our interaction with the `BookPub` service. Let's create an `api` package under the `src/main/java/com/example/bookpub` directory from the root of our project.

3. Inside the newly-created `api` package, let's create our API class file named `BookPubClient.java` with the following content:

```
package com.example.bookpub.api;

import com.example.bookpub.entity.Book;
import org.springframework.cloud.netflix.feign.FeignClient;
import org.springframework.web.bind.annotation.PathVariable;
import org.springframework.web.bind.annotation.RequestMapping;
import org.springframework.web.bind.annotation.RequestMethod;

@FeignClient("http://BookPub-ch9")
public interface BookPubClient {
    @RequestMapping(value = "/books/{isbn}",
                    method = RequestMethod.GET)
    public Book findBookByIsbn(@PathVariable("isbn") String
isbn);
}
```

4. After we have defined the API, it is time to tell our application that we want to enable Feign support. We will do that by making a change to the `BookPubApplication.java` file located under the `src/main/java/com/example/bookpub` `directory` from the root of our project with the following content:

```
. . .
@EnableDiscoveryClient
@EnableFeignClients
public class BookPubApplication {...}
```

5. Finally, let's create a client controller to invoke `BookPubClient` by making a new file named `ClientController.java` under the `src/main/java/com/example/bookpub/controllers` directory from the root of our project with the following content:

```
. . .
@RestController
@RequestMapping("/client")
public class ClientController {

    @Autowired
    private BookPubClient client;

    @RequestMapping(value = "/book/{isbn}",
                method = RequestMethod.GET)
    public Book getBook(@PathVariable String isbn) {
        return client.findBookByIsbn(isbn);
    }
}
```

6. With everything set and done, let's start the application by executing the `./gradlew clean bootRun` command.

> Make sure that the Consul agent is also running in the background, otherwise service registration will fail.

7. Once the application is up and running, let's
   open `http://localhost:8080/client/book/978-1-78528-415-1` in
   the browser to see the Consul agent information, as shown in the following
   screenshot:

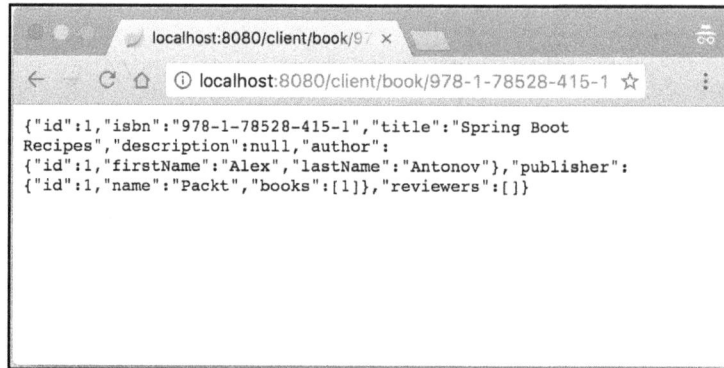

8. If we look at the application console logs, we will also see entries indicating
   that our Feign client is initialized and functioning. You should see
   something similar to this:

```
2017-12-26 --- c.n.u.concurrent.ShutdownEnabledTimer :
Shutdown hook installed for: NFLoadBalancer-PingTimer-BookPub-
ch9
2017-12-26 --- c.netflix.loadbalancer.BaseLoadBalancer :
Client:BookPub-ch9 instantiated a
LoadBalancer:DynamicServerListLoadBalancer:{NFLoadBalancer:nam
e=BookPub-ch9,current list of Servers=[],Load balancer
stats=Zone stats: {},Server stats: []}ServerList:null
2017-12-26 --- c.n.l.DynamicServerListLoadBalancer : Using
serverListUpdater PollingServerListUpdater
 2017-12-26 --- c.netflix.config.ChainedDynamicProperty :
Flipping property: BookPub-ch9.ribbon.ActiveConnectionsLimit
to use NEXT property:
niws.loadbalancer.availabilityFilteringRule.activeConnectionsL
imit = 2147483647
 2017-12-26 --- c.n.l.DynamicServerListLoadBalancer :
DynamicServerListLoadBalancer for client BookPub-ch9
initialized:
DynamicServerListLoadBalancer:{NFLoadBalancer:name=BookPub-
ch9,current list of Servers=[192.168.1.194:8080],Load balancer
stats=Zone stats: {unknown=[Zone:unknown; Instance count:1;
Active connections count: 0; Circuit breaker tripped count: 0;
Active connections per server: 0.0;]
 },Server stats: [[Server:192.168.1.194:8080; Zone:UNKNOWN;
```

```
Total Requests:0; Successive connection failure:0; Total
blackout seconds:0; Last connection made:Wed Dec 31 18:00:00
CST 1969; First connection made: Wed Dec 31 18:00:00 CST 1969;
Active Connections:0; total failure count in last (1000)
msecs:0; average resp time:0.0; 90 percentile resp time:0.0;
95 percentile resp time:0.0; min resp time:0.0; max resp
time:0.0; stddev resp time:0.0]
   ]}ServerList:ConsulServerList{serviceId='BookPub-ch9',
tag=null}
```

9. One last thing that we should do is to get our tests to work with all the newly added frameworks. Because Spring Cloud does not add itself to the test life cycle, we should explicitly disable any reliance on beans created by Spring Cloud libraries during tests. To do so let's add to our `application.properties` file located under the `src/test/resources` directory from the root of the project of the following properties:

```
spring.cloud.bus.enabled=false
spring.cloud.consul.enabled=false
spring.cloud.consul.discovery.enabled=false
eureka.client.enabled=false
autoconfigure.exclude=com.example.bookpub.
MonitoringConfiguration.class
```

10. We also need to add a Mock dependency on `BookPubClient` into the `JpaAuthorRepositoryTests.java` and `WebMvcBookControllerTests.java` files located under the `src/test/java/com/example/bookpub` directory from the root of the project with the following content:

```
@MockBean
private BookPubClient client;
```

How it works...

Similar to what we saw in the previous recipe, the use of the `@EnableFeignClients` annotation on the main application class, `BookPubApplication`, explicitly tells Spring Cloud that it should scan for all the interfaces annotated with `@FeignClient` and create service client implementations based on their definitions.
The `@EnableFeignClients` annotation is similar in nature to the `@ComponentScan` one, providing attributes to control which packages to scan for the `@FeignClient` annotated classes or explicitly list the API classes that should be used.

Out of the box, all Feign client implementations are configured using components defined in the `FeignClientsConfiguration` class, but one can provide alternative configuration classes using the `defaultConfiguration` attribute of the `@EnableFeignClients` annotation.

In a nutshell, every interface definition, annotated with `@FeignClient`, gets a service implementation consisting of a Java dynamic proxy object, which handles all the interface method calls (usually using `FeignInvocationHandler` to handle all the requests). The invocation handler is responsible for doing a few things.

Once any method is invoked, first the service instances are located using the provided discovery client (in our case it is `ConsulDiscoveryClient`) based on the `name` attribute of the `@FeignClient` annotation. In our example, we have declared the value of `name` attribute to be `http://BookPub-ch9`, so all the service instances from the registry which have their name set to `BookPub-ch9` will be returned as possible candidates. This name can be just a service name itself, or, as we did in our example, an optional protocol can be specified. This is a useful feature, as not all service discovery providers support ability to specify exactly how the service should be called, so if we want to make a secure call using HTTPS, we can explicitly specify the protocol to help Feign make the right call.

There are a number of other configuration attributes available on the annotation, for example, to tell Feign to make a direct call to a specified URL instead of doing a service lookup, there is a `url` attribute that can be configured.

> To see a complete list of possible attributes and their use-cases, go to https://cloud.spring.io/spring-cloud-netflix/single/spring-cloud-netflix.html#spring-cloud-feign.

The list of instances for a given service gets wrapped with an internal load balancer, provided by another Netflix library—Ribbon. It uses a specified algorithm to rotate between the instances of a service as well as to take the bad instances out of circulation if the discovery client says they are unhealthy.

> To see a complete list of possible configuration options for things like load balancing rules, and other settings, go to https://cloud.spring.io/spring-cloud-netflix/single/spring-cloud-netflix.html#spring-cloud-ribbon.

When a specific instance has been determined, an HTTP request gets created, using the standard Spring `HttpMessageConverter` beans to transform the method arguments into HTTP request path variables and query parameters. After all that is done, the request gets sent using a configured HTTP client and the response gets converted into a return type declared on the API interface using the same converters.

Now that we know what `@FeignClient` annotation is all about and what happens under the hood once an API-defined method gets invoked, let's take a look at how to annotate the interface methods that should be translated into remote service calls. Conveniently, and done so on purpose, we can use exactly the same annotations as we are already used to, when declaring controller mappings inside the `@Controller` annotated classes. Each method in our API interface, which we want to map to a remote service, should be annotated with the `@RequestMapping` annotation. The `path` attribute corresponds to a URL path of the remote service we want to invoke.

In our example, we want to call our `BookController.getBook(...)` method, which translates to the `/books/{isbn}` URL path. This is exactly what we put as a value for the `path` attribute, and make sure we also annotate the `isbn` argument in our `findBookByIsbn(...)` method with `@PathVariable("isbn")` to link it to a `{isbn}` placeholder in the mapping template.

As a general rule of thumb, the `@RequestMapping` annotation functions exactly the same as if it were used in a controller, except the configuration relates to an outgoing request instead of an inbound one. It might be especially confusing when configuring the `consumes` attribute of the annotation, that is, `consumes = "application/json"`, because it indicates that it is a remote side that expects JSON as a content-type of the payload.

Service discovery using Spring Cloud Netflix – Eureka

We've already seen how to do service discovery using HashiCorp Consul and integrate it with our application. This recipe will go over an alternative, and a very popular service discovery framework from Netflix-Eureka. Eureka was developed by Netflix to help solve the problem of service discovery, health checking, and load balancing for their RESTful services in AWS.

Unlike Consul, Eureka is solely focused on the task of service discovery, and does not provide many additional functionalities, such as key/value store service or event delivery. It is, however, very good at what it does and should be considered a viable candidate for a service discovery solution.

How to do it...

Before we get to the steps to add Eureka to our application, we need to get the Eureka service itself up and running. Thankfully, the Spring Cloud folks have been awesome enough to provide a sample project that makes creating an instance of Eureka server and running it a breeze. Let's take a look at the following steps:

1. To get things up and running just go to `https://github.com/spring-cloud-samples/eureka` and git clone the `git@github.com:spring-cloud-samples/eureka.git` repository to your machine.

2. After that's done, run `./gradlew clean bootRun` to start the server:

3. Once the server is up and running, we need to add the following dependencies to the `build.gradle` file located at the root of our project:

   ```
   //compile("org.springframework.cloud:spring-cloud-starter-
   consul-all")
   compile("org.springframework.cloud:spring-cloud-starter-
   feign")
   compile("org.springframework.cloud:spring-cloud-starter-
   eureka-client")
   ```

4. Ironically, that's all we had to do, at this point, we just restart our application by executing the `./gradlew clean bootRun` command.

   > Make sure the Eureka server is running in the background, otherwise, though the application will start, the `BookPubClient` calls will fail.

5. Once the application is up and running, let's open `http://localhost:8080/client/book/978-1-78528-415-1` in the browser and we should see exactly the same response as in our previous recipe.

6. Just to see that our application did indeed register with Eureka, we can open the browser at the `http://localhost:8761` URL and we should see our service listed under instances list:

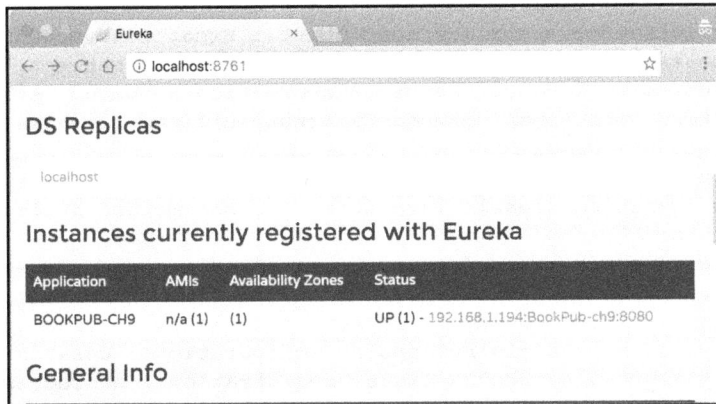

How it works...

With a seemingly effortless change, we have switched one service discovery provider, Consul, for another, Eureka. What looked like not much of a change on the outside actually did quite a bit of work under the hood. The reason we were able to do it so easily is the common set of APIs provided by the `spring-cloud-commons` and `spring-cloud-context` foundational libraries. Automated module loading support via the `spring.factores` descriptor allowed for transparent substitution in the initialization of a different service discovery provider. As long as we retained the `@EnableDiscoveryClient` annotation on our `BookPubApplication` class, Spring Cloud did the heavy lifting, taking care of loading the appropriate autoconfiguration files and setting up all the right beans to get our application working with Eureka.

We had to remove the Consul dependency from our classpath at the very first step of the recipe, and that had to be done in order to disambiguate the `DiscoveryClient` implementation. Without doing so, our application context would have ended up with two different implementations of the `DiscoveryClient` interface, which in itself would not be bad, except that Spring Cloud would have to disambiguate and choose one, and might not choose the one we want.

If we leave the `spring-cloud-starter-consul-all` dependency in our `build.gradle` file, and attempt to run the application, it will fail during startup and in the logs we will see the following entry:

```
WARN 5592 --- [  restartedMain]
ConfigServletWebServerApplicationContext : Exception encountered
during context initialization - cancelling refresh attempt:
org.springframework.beans.factory.BeanCreationException: Error
creating bean with name 'jmxMBeanExporter' defined in class path
resource
[org/springframework/boot/actuate/autoconfigure/endpoint/jmx/JmxEndpoi
ntAutoConfiguration.class]: Invocation of init method failed; nested
exception is
org.springframework.beans.factory.UnsatisfiedDependencyException:
Error creating bean with name
'org.springframework.cloud.client.serviceregistry.ServiceRegistryAutoC
onfiguration$ServiceRegistryEndpointConfiguration': Unsatisfied
dependency expressed through field 'registration'; nested exception is
org.springframework.beans.factory.NoUniqueBeanDefinitionException: No
qualifying bean of type
'org.springframework.cloud.client.serviceregistry.Registration'
available: expected single matching bean but found 2:
eurekaRegistration,consulRegistration
```

As you can see from the exception, Spring autowiring can't decide which one of the service registries should be used. This is because both Eureka and Consul automatically have created an instance of `Registration`, and the autowiring wants only one.

Since there is a hard requirement for only having one registry, it is best not to configure multiple discovery client dependency libraries to avoid errors. If, for some reason, multiple libraries have to reside in the classpath, one should use configuration properties to explicitly enable/disable a specific client implementation. For example, both Consul and Eureka provide configuration to toggle the state. We can set `spring.cloud.consul.discovery.enabled=true` and `eureka.client.enabled=false` in `application.properties` if we prefer to use Consul to provide service discovery functionality.

Using Spring Cloud Netflix – Hystrix

Throughout this chapter we have looked at all the aspects that apply to having a successful microservice application running in the cloud environment. We have learned about how to integrate better into a dynamically changing ecosystem, consuming remote configuration properties, registering service, and discovering and calling other services. In this recipe, we will take a look at another very important aspect of operating in a distributed, highly-volatile cloud environment circuit breakers.

The particular implementation of circuit breaker functionality which we are going to look at is Netflix Hystrix. It provides a very powerful and convenient way to annotate our service calls and handle things like remote service failures, queue backups, overloads, timeouts, and so on. By having circuit breakers in an application, developers can ensure overall application stability if a particular service endpoint becomes overloaded by requests, or experiences an outage of any kind.

How to do it...

1. To get started with Hystrix we need to add the `spring-cloud-starter-hystrix` library to our project. Let's modify our `build.gradle` file located in the root of our project with the following content:

```
dependencies {
    ...
    compile("org.springframework.cloud:
      spring-cloud-starter-consul-all")
    compile("org.springframework.cloud:
      spring-cloud-starter-openfeign")
    compile("org.springframework.cloud:
      spring-cloud-starter-eureka-client")
    compile("org.springframework.cloud:
      spring-cloud-starter-netflix-hystrix")
    runtime("com.h2database:h2")
    runtime("mysql:mysql-connector-java")
    ...
}
```

2. After adding the Hystrix dependency, we need to enable Hystrix for our application. Similar to how we enabled service discovery, we will do that by making a change to the `BookPubApplication.java` file located under the `src/main/java/com/example/bookpub` directory from the root of our project with the following content:

```
...
@EnableDiscoveryClient
@EnableFeignClients
@EnableCircuitBreaker
public class BookPubApplication {...}
```

3. Now, let's make a few changes to `BookController.java`, located under the `src/main/java/com/example/bookpub/controllers` directory from the root of our project, with the following content:

```
@RequestMapping(value = "", method = RequestMethod.GET)
@HystrixCommand(fallbackMethod = "getEmptyBooksList")
public Iterable<Book> getAllBooks() {
    //return bookRepository.findAll();
    throw new RuntimeException("Books Service Not Available");
}

public Iterable<Book> getEmptyBooksList() {
    return Collections.emptyList();
}
...
```

4. Due to Hystrix internal functionality, we also need to modify our entity models to have them eager-load the relational associations. In the `Author.java`, `Book.java`, and `Publisher.java` files located under the `src/main/java/com/example/bookpub/entity` directory from the root of our project, let's make the following changes:

- In `Author.java`, make the following change:

```
@OneToMany(mappedBy = "author", fetch = FetchType.EAGER)
private List<Book> books;
```

- In `Book.java`, make the following change:

```
@ManyToOne(fetch = FetchType.EAGER)
private Author author;

@ManyToOne(fetch = FetchType.EAGER)
private Publisher publisher;
```

```
@ManyToMany(fetch = FetchType.EAGER)
private List<Reviewer> reviewers;
```

- In `Publisher.java`, make the following change:

```
@OneToMany(mappedBy = "publisher", fetch = FetchType.EAGER)
private List<Book> books;
```

5. Finally, we are ready to restart our application by executing the `./gradlew clean bootRun` command.

6. When the application has started, let's open `http://localhost:8080/books` in the browser and we should see an empty JSON list as a result:

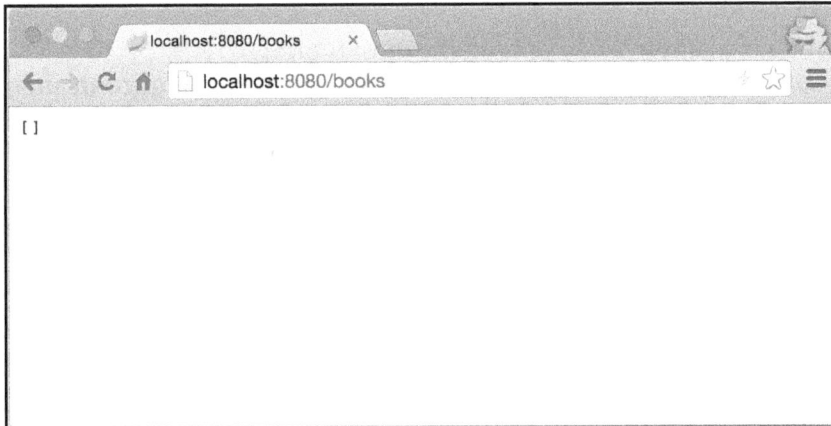

How it works...

In this recipe we have done three things after adding the Hystrix dependency library to our project. So, let's take a look at each step in detail to learn what exactly happens:

- The `@EnableCircuitBreaker` annotation, similar to `@EnableDiscoveryClient`, or `@EnableFeignClients`, which explicitly indicates that we want Spring Cloud to load appropriate configurations from `spring.factories` from all the libraries which have the `org.springframework.cloud.client.circuitbreaker.EnableCircuitBreaker` key defined.

- In the case of Hystrix, it will load `HystrixCircuitBreakerConfiguration`, which provides the necessary configuration to enable the Hystrix functionality within the application. One of the beans it creates, is the `HystrixCommandAspect` class. It's purpose is to detect all the methods which are annotated with the `@HystrixCommand` annotation and wrap them with a handler to detect errors, timeouts, and other ill-behaviors, and deal with them appropriately, based on configuration.

- This `@HystrixCommand` annotation, provided by the Hystrix library, is designed to mark methods which represent `Hystrix-guarded commands`, that is, methods which we want to protect using Hystrix against cascading failures and overloads. This annotation has a number of attributes and can be configured in a variety of different ways, depending on the desired behavior.

- In our example we have used the most typical attribute—`fallbackMethod`, which allows us to configure an alternative method, with matching signature, which can be automatically called if the real method fails the invocation for whatever reason. This is the prime use-case, and it provides the ability to specify graceful degradation of service, using sensible defaults, if possible, instead of blowing up exceptions up the stack.

- We used it to direct failed calls to the `getEmptyBooksList()` method, which returns a static empty list. This way, when the real `getAllBooks()` method fails, we gracefully degrade and return an empty collection, which renders nicely as a response JSON. In the situations when we do indeed desire a particular type of exception to be propagated up the stack, we can configure those explicitly using the `ignoreExceptions` attribute and set it to the desired exception classes.

- To configure the circuit breaker behavior of a particular command, we can set a number of different options using the `commandProperties` or `threadPoolProperties` attributes. There we can set things like execution timeouts, size of backup queues, and many others.

> For a complete list of available properties, see `https://github.com/Netflix/Hystrix/tree/master/hystrix-contrib/hystrix-javanica#configuration`.

One last thing to discuss is the modifications we made to our entity models to set the relational association annotations to use `fetch = FetchType.EAGER`. The reason we had to do so is due to the way Hibernate handles association loading. By default, those are loaded using the `FetchType.LAZY` setup, meaning that Hibernate is only going to establish the relationship, but the loading of the data will not happen until the getter methods are invoked. With Hystrix, by default, this could cause an error that looks something like this:

```
failed to lazily initialize a collection of role:
com.example.bookpub.entity.Book.reviewers, could not initialize
proxy - no Session (through reference chain:
com.example.bookpub.entity.Publisher["books"]->org.hibernate.colle
ction.internal.PersistentBag[0]->com.example.bookpub.entity.Book["
reviewers"])
```

This is due to the fact that Hystrix uses `ThreadPool` to execute method calls by default, and because the lazy-loaded data needs to access the datastore at the time of invocation, Hibernate requires an active session to be present in order to handle the request. Since Hibernate stores the session in `ThreadLocal`, it is obviously not present in the pooled executor thread that Hystrix is using during the invocation.

Once we changed the fetching to be eager, all the data is loaded during the repository interaction in the original Hibernate thread. We could, alternatively, configure our `@HystrixCommand` annotation to use the same executing thread by using the following configuration:

```
commandProperties = {
    @HystrixProperty(name="execution.isolation.strategy",
                     value="SEMAPHORE")
}
```

While Hystrix strongly recommends to use the default `THREAD` strategy, in situations when we absolutely need to be residing in the same caller thread, `SEMAPHORE` is there to help us.

Alternatively, we can set the same configuration in our `application.properties` file using `hystrix.command.default.execution.isolation.strategy=SEMAPHORE`, or, if we want to be specific to only configure particular `@HystrixCommand`, we can use the value of the `commandKey` attribute, which is the name of the annotated method by default, instead of the default section of the property name. For our specific example from the `BookController` instrumented method, the configuration key would look like `hystrix.command.getAllBooks.execution.isolation.strategy=SEMAPHORE`.

This is possible thanks to the Spring Cloud-Netflix Archaius bridge, which makes all Spring environment properties visible to the Archaius configuration manager, thus accessible by all of the Netflix components.

Spring Cloud Hystrix integration also provides a `/hystrix.stream` actuator endpoint, which can be consumed by the Hystrix dashboard for visualizing the state of all the circuit breakers in an application.

To get the dashboard running quickly, Spring Cloud provides a sample application which can be seen at `https://github.com/spring-cloud-samples/hystrix-dashboard`:

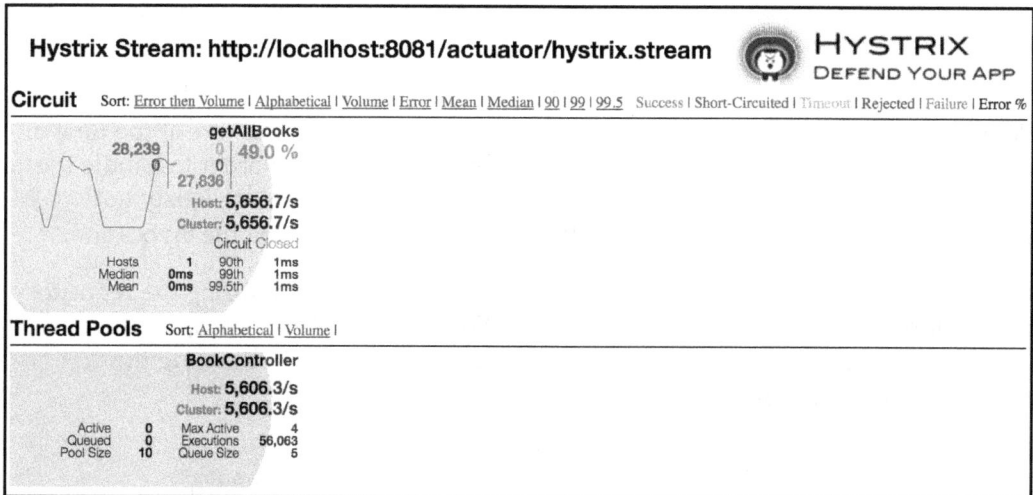

The same stream can also be fed into **Netflix Turbine Stream Aggregator**, downloadable at `https://github.com/Netflix/Turbine`, for data aggregation across multiple instances, which can later be visualized using the same dashboard.

> One can also use the `spring-cloud-starter-turbine` dependency library and the `@EnableTurbine` annotation on a basic Spring Boot application, similar to the Hystrix dashboard sample.

Bibliography

This Learning Path combines some of the best that Packt has to offer in one complete, curated package. It includes content from the following Packt products:

- *Spring 5.0 By Example*, Claudio Eduardo de Oliveira
- *Learning Spring Boot 2.0*, Greg L. Turnquist
- *Spring Boot 2.0 Cookbook*, Alex Antonov

Index

www.ingramcontent.com/pod-product-compliance
Lightning Source LLC
Chambersburg PA
CBHW081206220326
41598CB00037B/6691